AMISTAD LITERARY SERIES

TONI MORRISON

Critical Perspectives
Past and Present

Also by Henry Louis Gates, Jr.

Figures in Black: Words, Signs, and the "Racial" Self
Signifying Monkey: Toward a Theory of Afro-American Literary Criticism
Loose Canons: Notes on the Culture Wars
Black Literature and Literary Theory (editor)
The Classic Slave Narratives (editor)
Reading Black, Reading Feminist (editor)

Also by K. A. Appiah

Assertion and Conditions
For Truth in Semantics
Necessary Questions: An Introduction to Philosophy
Avenging Angel (fiction)
In My Father's House: Africa in the Philosophy of Culture
Early African-American Classics (editor)

TONI MORRISON

Critical Perspectives
Past and Present

EDITED BY

Henry Louis Gates, Jr., and K. A. Appiah

Amistad
NEW YORK, NEW YORK

Critical Perspectives Past and Present

MICHAEL C. VAZQUEZ, *Project Coordinator*

WAYNE L. APONTE
LISA GATES
SONJA OKUN

Amistad Press, Inc.
1271 Avenue of the Americas
New York, NY 10020

Distributed by:
Penguin USA
375 Hudson Street
New York, NY 10014

Designed by Stanley S. Drate, Folio Graphics Company, Inc.
Produced by March Tenth, Inc.

10 9 8 7 6 5 4 3 2 1

Library of Congress Cataloging-in-Publication Data

Toni Morrison : critical perspectives past and present / edited by
    Henry Louis Gates, Jr. and K. A. Appiah.
        p.   cm. — (Amistad literary series)
    Includes bibliographical references and index.
    ISBN 1-56743-012-0 : $24.95. — ISBN 1-56743-025-2 (pbk.) : $14.95
    1. Morrison, Toni—Criticism and interpretation.   2. Afro-American
women in literature.   I. Gates, Henry Louis.   II. Appiah, Anthony.
III. Series.
PS3563.O8749Z9   1993
813'.54—dc20   ·   92-45755
                                                          CIP

Contents

Preface

◆◆◆◆◆◆◆◆◆◆◆◆◆

Toni Morrison
(1931–   )

Toni Morrison may well be the most formally sophisticated novelist in the history of African-American literature. Indeed, her signal accomplishment as a writer is that she has managed, uncannily, to invent her own mode of literary representation. Her themes are often those expected of naturalist fiction—the burdens of history, the determining social effects of race, gender, or class—but they are also the great themes of lyrical modernism: love, death, betrayal, and the burden of the individual's responsibility for her or his own fate. Never is "history" faceless in her work, never are individuals absolved from responsibility for their own actions.

While she is clearly influenced by the magical realism of Gabriel García Márquez and his Latin American contemporaries, Morrison and Márquez meet independently at a common ancestor, William Faulkner. Grounded in Faulkner, and informed by James Baldwin's densely lyrical experiments with a fictional prose rooted in the religious vernacular (the spirituals and gospel music, King Jamesian biblical cadences and allusions, the spoken Black prophetic voice) as well as jazz, blues, and the whole range of Black secular vernacular speech rituals and discourses, Morrison has evolved a register of representation that we might think of as a magical naturalism. Her work, in this sense, spans that great divide between the lyrical modernism of Zora Neale Hurston on the one hand, and the existential naturalist experimentation of Richard Wright on the other.

Toni Morrison was born Chloe Anthony Wofford in the small town of Lorain, Ohio, the daughter of George and Ramah Willis Wofford. She earned a B.A. degree in 1953 from Howard University and an M.A. in English at Cornell University, where she completed a thesis on William Faulkner and Virginia Woolf. From 1955 to 1957 she taught English at Texas Southern University, and from 1957 to 1964 she taught at Howard. In 1965, she became a senior editor at Random House. She resumed her teaching career a decade later, serving as a visiting professor at Yale between 1976 and 1978, and then from 1984 to 1989 as the Albert Schweitzer Professor of the Humanities at the State University of New York at Albany. In 1989 she became the Robert F. Goheen Professor of the Humanities at Princeton University, where she remains a member of the program in Afro-American studies and of the creative writing department.

She has published six novels: *The Bluest Eye* (1970), *Sula* (1974), *Song of Solomon* (1977), *Tar Baby* (1981), *Beloved* (1987), and *Jazz* (1992); a volume of literary criticism, *Playing in the Dark: Whiteness and the Literary Imagination* (1992), which was based on a lecture series she delivered at Harvard University. Hers has been, deservedly, a career of accolades and acclamation. In 1977 she was awarded both the National Book Critics Circle Award and the American Academy and Institute of Arts and Letters Award for *Song of Solomon*. In 1981 she appeared on the cover of *Newsweek*, the first Black woman to be so featured on the cover of a national magazine since Zora Neale Hurston in 1943. In 1988 she was awarded the Pulitzer Prize for fiction and the Robert F. Kennedy Award for *Beloved*. Indeed, many scholars believe that Morrison will be the first African-American to receive the Nobel Prize for literature.

And yet, as critics have observed, Morrison's career is an anomaly in a crucial respect: Her writing is at once difficult and popular. A subtle craftsperson and a compelling weaver of tales, she "tells a good story," but the stories she tells are not calculated to please. Narratives of incestuous rape *(The Bluest Eye)*, of a mother's abuse of her son *(Tar Baby)* or murder of her daughter *(Beloved)*, or of a man's murder of his lover *(Jazz)*—these do not on the surface seem to be the sort of stories to attract the wide readership that Morrison commands.

It is an important feature of today's literary culture, however, that Toni Morrison, along with her contemporaries, Black woman novelists Alice Walker, Gloria Naylor, Jamaica Kincaid, and Terry McMillan, are more widely read by a broader cross section of the American reading public than any other Black writers have ever been in this country. Morrison's devoted readers are found on every continent, representing both sexes and all colors, ages, and creeds. But it is also the case that a large and cosmopolitan readership of women—including intellectuals, professionals, feminists—in addition to the more traditional, but smaller, Black reading audience, male and female, has combined to produce an audience for works by Black women larger than anyone could have imagined just two decades ago. *Song of Solomon* was the first Black Book-of-the-Month Club selection since Richard Wright's *Native Son* in 1940; *Tar Baby* was on the best-seller lists for four months.

In the fall of 1992 three Black women novelists appeared simultaneously on the *New York Times* best-seller list (McMillan, Morrison, and Walker), and Morrison appeared in *both* the fiction list (for *Jazz*) and the nonfiction list (for *Playing in the Dark*). Whereas, in the past, at most one Black writer might possibly have been expected to appeal to this sort of "crossover" readership, the current generation of Black women authors has been able to defy this dictum by effectively creating a new reading public. And Morrison's own role here has been pivotal in more than one capacity. For as an editor at Random House, Morrison resolutely published works by Black women and men from Africa, the Caribbean, and Afro-America, and did so in an often forbidding publishing climate.

Morrison's greatest capacities as a writer are her ability to create a densely lyrical narrative texture that is instantly recognizable as her own and to make the particularity of the African-American "experience" the basis for a representation of humanity *tout court*. Her novels are never "about" the Black community of Lorain, Ohio, in the thirties and forties, even when they are apparently set there. Just as James Joyce's fictional works can never be reduced to anthropological treatises about the Irish, or Wole Soyinka's drama into treatises about Yoruba, Morrison's work is always symbolic of the shared human condition, both engaging with and transcending lines of gender, race, and class. A rigorous, unsparing intellect—displayed as much in her fiction as in the sophisticated literary analysis of her *Playing in the Dark*—is surely inseparable from her considerable achievements as a narrative lyricist. The result, in all events, is to vouchsafe her unique stature in American literature—and the world's.

The selection of reviews that open this volume, drawn largely from the popular press, represent the variety of critical attention that Morrison's successive novels received immediately upon their publication.

The fifteen essays that follow map the contours of Morrison's literary achievements in greater detail. Reading Morrison's early novels as "fantastic earthy realism," Barbara Christian notes the various elements that help Morrison dramatize the sometimes destructive effects of community on young Black girls struggling toward womanhood. Keith E. Byerman, similarly attuned to the uses and abuses of community, explores the dialectic of dominant culture and folk experience in Morrison's first four novels, and the ways in which power and identity emerge from their interplay.

Roberta Rubenstein argues that Morrison's fiction dramatizes issues of boundary, attachment, separation, and division. In a psychoanalytic register, she shows how individuals and communities construct meaning and identity via contradictory processes of internalization and exclusion.

Donald B. Gibson, reading *The Bluest Eye*, maintains that Morrison's use of "countertexts" (central mythologies of the dominant culture) helps her own text dramatize the internalization of oppression. But it also enables Morrison to complicate customary notions of responsibility, Gibson suggests; even in detailing the most hurtful abuse, her interest is not in simple condemnation, but in explanation.

W. E. B. Du Bois's powerful conception of Afro-American double-consciousness guides Michael Awkward's approach to *The Bluest Eye*. Awkward, who discerns in Morrison's work a feminist revision of such precursors as Ellison and Baldwin, concludes that the condition of double-consciousness—and a distorted sense of self and place—may be an unresolvable consequence of the African encounter with the New World.

Hortense J. Spillers considers the emergence of a morally ambiguous female subjectivity in *Sula*, one at last independent of the confining dualities of patriarchal prescription. A sense of place is central to Houston A. Baker, Jr.'s meditation on *Sula*. Baker remarks on the novel's conflation of intimacy and occupancy as he examines the politics of its passions.

Marianne Hirsch finds in novels such as *Sula* and *Beloved* a contest of voices and perspectives, in which a daughterly tradition defines itself in relation to a maternal past. While white feminisms normally occlude the mother's place, Hirsch believes that Black feminism must work to restore the validity of the maternal perspective.

Valerie Smith's reading of the first three novels centers on the relation between community and ostracism, isolation and disintegration; she shows that community not only signifies empowerment for its members, but the exertion of power *over* its members. Focusing on *Tar Baby*, Marilyn Sanders Mobley descries a cultural orphan's quest for wholeness and identity and the vexing dilemma of liminality.

The themes of maternal sexuality and generational continuity among Black women are pursued further by Peter B. Erickson. He observes that Jadine's troubled rejection of norms of Black motherhood are set against the abject failure of white motherhood, of the white family as a whole.

In Susan Willis's view, Morrison's abiding concern is the preservation of Afro-American folk cultures after the dispersion of the rural, Southern, prewar Black communities—the reclamation of the neighborhood as a model of community. Surveying the first four novels, Willis identifies the conflict between the past as wellspring or resource and the dispiriting timelessness of commodity culture.

In a reading of *Beloved*, Trudier Harris points out the recurrent tropes of exchange and monetary value, underlining the sacrificial economy of slavery and its enduring consequences. She contends that the dynamics of value and subservience threaten to undermine human and familial relationships, even the mother-daughter relationship so precious to Morrison.

Valerie Smith's second essay situates *Beloved* within a larger investigation of representation and experience, discourse and slavery. If Morrison's novel is profoundly concerned with representing the Black body in pain, its paradoxical textural project, she believes, is to narrate the impossibility of speaking the unspeakable—the elusiveness of the event, the sublimity of the real.

Marilyn Sanders Mobley, in the volume's final essay, relates *Beloved* to Morrison's general project of recovering Black lived experience and argues that memory, in *Beloved*, revises the classical slave narratives by providing access to the sort of psychological interiority heretofore undocumented.

The volume concludes with a sequence of interviews that feature Morrison's own perspective on so many of the topics that have preoccupied her critics, including the power of community, the role of myth making in everyday life, and the renaissance of African-American writing.

Henry Louis Gates, Jr.

REVIEWS

THE BLUEST EYE (1970)

◆◆◆◆◆◆◆◆◆◆◆◆◆

HASKEL FRANKEL

The New York Times Book Review, November 1, 1970

Shoemakers' children go barefoot, we are told. And physicians must be reminded to heal themselves. What happens to editors who write novels? The question is not academic, as Toni Morrison is an editor with a New York publishing firm, and this is her first novel. She reveals herself, when she shucks the fuzziness born of flights of poetic imagery, as a writer of considerable power and tenderness, someone who can cast back to the living, bleeding heart of childhood and capture it on paper. But Miss Morrison has gotten lost in her construction.

The title pinpoints the focus of her book. Pecola Breedlove, in her first year of womanhood, is black, ugly and poor, living in a store front, sharing a bedroom with her brother, her crippled mother and her drunken father. Pregnant by her father, she goes to Soaphead Church, a man who believes himself possessed of holy powers. What she wants are blue eyes.

In this scene, in which a young black on the verge of madness seeks beauty and happiness in a wish for white girl's eyes, the author makes her most telling statement on the tragic effect of race prejudice on children. But the scene occurs late in the novel—far too late to achieve the impact it might have had in a different construction. For most of the way, Pecola yields center stage to Frieda and Claudia—who, aside from knowing her, and perhaps offering contrast, by themselves being black and poor (though from a happier home), serve little purpose beyond distraction.

Claudia tells the story part way into each of the four seasonal divisions of the book. From her, the narratives branch out to assorted portraits and events throughout the black community of Lorain, Ohio, with Pecola, whose story this eventually is, too often playing a secondary role until the novel zeroes in on her for the ending. Her mental breakdown, when it comes, has only the impact of reportage.

Miss Morrison never bores as she wanders around town. There are vivid scenes: Pecola's first "ministratin'"; a "pretty milk-brown lady"

3

driving Pecola from her home for the killing of a cat, by the woman's own son; the young Cholly Breedlove (later to be Pecola's father) caught during the sex act by white men and being forced to continue for their amusement. Given a scene that demands a writer's best, Miss Morrison responds with control and talent. Yet there are moments when the mind stops and questions. The novel begins: "Nuns go by as quiet as lust . . ." (How quiet is lust? Is it always?) Or: ". . . he will not unrazor his lips until spring." Does that mean he will not shave around his mouth all winter? And just what is "an ivory sleep"?

With the flaws and virtues tallied, I found myself still in favor of *The Bluest Eye*. There are many novelists willing to report the ugliness of the world as ugly. The writer who can reveal the beauty and the hope beneath the surface is a writer to seek out and to encourage.

◆◆◆◆◆◆◆◆◆◆◆◆◆

L. E. SISSMAN

The New Yorker, January 23, 1971

Toni Morrison's *The Bluest Eye* couldn't be more different. She is dealing with children, not men; she is dealing with the forties, not the present; she is dealing with the black subculture, not the military one. But the biggest difference is that she is dealing with people to whom no ultimate glory is possible. (One of her characters thinks, "There is sure to be a glory"—but that, pointedly, is in the afterlife.) She writes, affectingly and often in the freshest, simplest, and most striking prose, of young Frieda and Claudia MacTeer (Claudia is the narrator) and their friend Pecola, who is growing up with them in the steelmaking Cleveland suburb of Lorain in 1941. Pecola feels that blue eyes are a talisman of whiteness, of pride, of security, and she seeks them through prayer, through the intercession of a spoiled priest who has become a "reader and advisor," and, ultimately, through madness, when she believes blue eyes have been granted her. In carrying the reader through this short and tragic story, Miss Morrison carefully and powerfully builds up the dossiers of Pecola and the people around her: her father, Cholly Breedlove, driven to alcoholism, brutality, and incest by a life of appalling oppression and dislocation; her mother, Pauline Williams, driven back into her bitter and hard-bitten self by Cholly's rage and by the unbearable misery of her life; Soaphead Church, the "reader and advisor," who, having turned his back on life and become a quasi-hermit, finds that he has almost godlike power over the lives of others; Frieda and Claudia, whose life is only marginally less hopeless than the Breedloves'. She gives us a fresh, close look at the lives of terror and decorum of those Negroes who want to get on in a white man's world—Negroes who would now be scorned as Uncle Toms; she puts her compassionate finger on the role of crude fantasy in sustaining hope, as in the experience of Pecola's mother:

> I 'member one time I went to see Clark Gable and Jean Harlow. I fixed my hair up like I'd seen hers on a magazine. A part on the side, with one little curl on my forehead. It looked just like her. Well, almost just like. Anyway, I sat in that show with my hair done up that way and had a good time. I thought I'd see it through to the end again, and I got up to get me some candy. I was sitting back in my seat, and I taken a big bite of that candy, and it pulled a tooth right out of my mouth. I could of cried. I had good teeth, not a rotten one in my head. I don't believe I ever did get over that. There I was, five months pregnant, trying to look like Jean Harlow, and a front tooth gone. Everything went then. Look like I just didn't care no more after that. I let my hair go back, plaited it up, and settled down to just being ugly.

Here again we see, as the overriding motif of this book, the desirability of whiteness, or, as the next-best thing, the imitation of whiteness; as a corollary, blackness is perceived as ugliness, a perception that must surely have given rise in later years to the overcompensatory counter-statement "Black is beautiful."

The Bluest Eye is not flawless. Miss Morrison's touching and disturbing picture of the doomed youth of her race is marred by an occasional error of fact or judgment. She places the story in a frame of the bland white words of a conventional school "reader"—surely an unnecessary and unsubtle irony. She writes an occasional false or bombastic line: "They were through with lust and lactation, beyond tears and terror." She permits herself some inconsistencies: the real name of Soaphead Church is given as both Elihue Micah Whitcomb and Micah Elihue Whitcomb. None of this matters, though, beside her real and greatly promising achievement: to write truly (and sometimes very beautifully) of every generation of blacks—the young, their parents, their rural grandparents—in this country thirty years ago, and, I'm afraid, today.

◆◆◆◆◆◆◆◆◆◆◆◆◆◆◆◆◆◆◆◆◆◆◆◆◆◆◆◆◆◆◆◆◆◆

SULA (1974)

◆◆◆◆◆◆◆◆◆◆◆◆◆◆

SARAH BLACKBURN

The New York Times Book Review, December 30, 1973

In 1970, when Toni Morrison's first novel, *The Bluest Eye*, appeared, she reaped the benefits of a growing, middle-class women's movement that was just beginning to acknowledge the reality of its black and poor sisters. As a result, her novel probably attracted more attention than it otherwise might have in the publishing industry and was received rather uncritically by readers and reviewers: socially conscious readers—including myself—were so pleased to see a new writer of Morrison's obvious talent that we tended to celebrate the book and ignore its flaws.

The Bluest Eye was set among unforgiving provincial black people in a small Ohio town and charted the experience of two little sisters as they watched a friend first become a pariah and then sink into madness. The book's general outline—how witnessing and understanding tragedy forces the surrender of innocence and topples wide-eyed, precocious kids into unwilling maturity—is a familiar one in American, especially Southern, fiction; but its language was unique, powerful, precise and absolutely convincing, both spare and rich at once.

Now comes *Sula*, which features another pariah, spans the years 1921 to 1965, and seems to take place in the same setting: "In that place, where they tore the nightshade and blackberry patches from their roots to make room for the Medallion City Golf Course, there was once a neighborhood. . . . It is called the suburbs now, but when black people lived there it was called the Bottom. . . . They are going to raze the Time and a Half Pool Hall, where feet in long tan shoes once pointed down from chair rungs." While the setting and the characters continually convince and intrigue, the novel seems somehow frozen, stylized. A more precise yet somehow icy version of *The Bluest Eye*, it refuses to invade our present in the way we want it to and stays, instead, confined to its time and place.

The heroine, Sula, grows up in a household pulsing with larger-than-life people and activity, presided over by her powerful and probably sorcerous grandmother. Her gentle mother is devoted almost wholly to the practice and pleasures of sensuality. But her cherished friend Nel, the local goody-goody, plays perfect counterpoint to Sula's intense, life-grabbing insistence on freedom. It's this insistence that eventually gets read as recklessness, and Sula becomes a threat as her life unfolds against the rest of the black community's daily life of hardship, humiliation and scrabbling for survival:

> What was taken by outsiders to be slackness, slovenliness or even generosity was in fact a full recognition of the legitimacy of forces other than good ones. They did not believe doctors could heal—for them, none ever had done so. They did not believe death was accidental—life might be, but death was deliberate. . . . the purpose of evil was to survive it and they determined (without every knowing they had made up their minds to do it) to survive floods, white people, tuberculosis, famine and ignorance. They knew anger well but not despair, and they didn't stone sinners for the same reason they didn't commit suicide—it was beneath them.

It's out of this that Sula emerges; she leaves the Bottom and returns 10 years later, after college and city life that we never see here, to be perceived as a sinister force, sex-hungry, man-stealing, death-dealing, a figure of darkness and betrayal. Having dared to smash the taboos that are her neighbors' poor guarantees of simply surviving, she's scorned, despised, abandoned by the people she grew out of—to their immense loss.

It's possible, I guess, to talk about *Sula* as allegory—about people so paralyzed by the horrors of the past and by the demands of just staying alive that they're unable to embrace the possibilities of freedom until the moment for it has passed. But Toni Morrison's novel is too vital and rich to be confined within such limits. Her extravagantly beautiful, doomed characters are locked in a world where hope for the future is a foreign commodity, yet they are enormously, achingly alive. And this book is about them—and about how their beauty is drained back and frozen—is a howl of love and rage, playful and funny as well as hard and bitter.

When the rage gets directed at its characters as intensely as it does against the conditions that formed them, the bitterness sometimes takes over. One scene, in which the child Nel witnesses her majestic, usually holier-than-thou mother cringing before a brutal, repulsive white train conductor, is close to devastating: the mother is depicted with an unsparing irony, unforgiven.

Toni Morrison is someone who really knows how to clank a sentence, as the novelist Irving Rosenthal has put it, and her dialogue is so compressed and life-like that it sizzles. And Morrison's skill at characterization is such that, by the end, it's as if an enormous but too severely framed landscape has been unrolled and inhabited by people who seem almost mythologically strong and familiar; like the gorgeous characters of Garcia Márquez, they have a heroic quality, and it's hard to believe we haven't known them forever.

Yet the comparison can't be extended: Morrison hasn't endowed her people with life beyond their place and function in the novel, and we can't imagine their surviving outside the tiny community where they carry on their separate lives. It's this particular quality that makes "Sula" a novel whose long-range impact doesn't sustain the intensity of its first reading. Reading it, in spite of its richness and its thorough originality, one continually feels its narrowness, its refusal to brim over into the world outside its provincial setting.

As the author of frequent criticism and social commentary, Morrison has shown herself someone of considerable strength and skill in confronting current realities, and it's frustrating that the qualities which distinguish her novels are not combined with the stinging immediacy, the urgency, of her nonfiction. This last is a classically unfair carp on the part of a reviewer, but Toni Morrison is far too talented to remain only a marvelous recorder of the black side of provincial American life. If she is to maintain the large and serious audience she deserves, she is going to have to address a riskier contemporary reality than this beautiful but nevertheless distanced novel. And if she does this, it seems to me that she might easily transcend that early and unintentionally limiting classification "black woman writer" and take her place among the most serious, important and talented American novelists now working.

♦♦♦♦♦♦♦♦♦♦♦♦♦♦

JERRY H. BRYANT

The Nation, July 6, 1974

Some months ago I reviewed two books by Ed Bullins and Alice Walker, *The Reluctant Rapist* and *In Love & Trouble* (*The Nation*, November 12, 1973). I concluded that they reflected a new swing of black fiction into unexplored territory. Now that I have read Toni Morrison's second novel, *Sula*, I am more than ever convinced that something new is happening in black writing.

Sula, Ms. Morrison's protagonist, has qualities I have seen in a fictional black female only recently. When she is 11 years old, she cuts off the tip of her finger to demonstrate to a gang of threatening boys what she can do to them if she can do that to herself. She swings a child around by the wrists and half intentionally lets him slip out of her grasp into the river, where he drowns. In the shadows of her porch, she watches in an "interested" way while her mother burns to death.

Most of us have been conditioned to expect something else in black characters, especially black female characters—guiltless victims of brutal white men, yearning for a respectable life of middle-class security; whores driven to their profession by impossible conditions; housekeepers exhausted by their work for lazy white women. We do not expect to see a fierceness bordering on the demonic.

But that is what we're getting from some of the younger black writers. It is not a matter of race, or at least not simply a matter of race. A fascination with evil has crept into black fiction, an interest in the lower layers of the psyche of black characters, in their capacity to hurt and destroy. I don't see that this is as yet a "movement," or even that writers like Bullins, Walker and Morrison have by deliberate plan entered these new areas. But when Bullins shows us a cool rapist or that muderous half-rodent, half-bird that slashes to death its would-be protectors; when Walker depicts an ignorant black sharecropper cutting away his daughter's breasts and blasting her with a shotgun; and when Morrison gives us a Sula, we know we are faced wtih something different from Williams's *The Man Who Cried I Am* or Gaines's *The Autobiography of Miss Jane Pittman*—or, for that matter, Barth's *Chimera* or Pynchon's *Gravity's Rainbow*.

It is true that Morrison operates within many of the racial commonplaces. First in *The Bluest Eye* (1970), now in *Sula*, she has staked out an area of the Midwest made familiar to us by Sherwood Anderson, the small Ohio town governed by a rigid moral prudery that dampens spontaneity and twists natural appetites. She focuses on the black sections of those towns, and, to the middle-class hypocrisy attacked by Anderson, she adds the racial prejudice of the whites. But this is the weakest strain in her novels, for it is virtually impossible to do anything fresh with a vein that has been mined to exhaustion. We begin to fidget when we see her stacking the deck against such easy marks as the bourgeoisie and reaching for the heart-strings when describing the humiliation of some proud black soldiers on a Jim Crow railroad car.

Her originality and power emerge in characters like Sula, that we have seldom seen before and that do not fit the familiar black images. One-legged Eva Peace, Sula's grandmother, burns her son to death when she feels he is trying "to crawl back into my womb." Sula's mother, Hannah, entertains men without discrimination in the pantry of Eva's home. Sula's friend Nel realizes that she experienced a thrill of pleasure when she watched Sula's victim drown. Against the background of the respectability of black Medallion, Ohio, these acts and emotions appear as the thrust of some powerful new force, loosening the foundations of the old stereotypes and conventional manners.

Writers like Toni Morrison, like Ed Bullins and Alice Walker, are slowly, subtly making our old buildings unsafe. There is something ominous in the chilling detachment with which they view their characters.

It is not that their viewpoint is amoral—we are asked for judgment. It's that the characters we judge lie so far outside the guidelines by which we have always made our judgments.

For example, Morrison at first seems to combine the aims of the Black Freedom Movement and women's liberation. Sula and Nel discover when they are 11 years old "that they were neither white nor male, and that all freedom and triumph was forbidden to them." When they grow up, Nel slips on the collar of convention. She marries, has two children, becomes tied to her "nest," a slave to racism and sexism. Sula goes to the big city, gets herself an education, and returns a "liberated" woman with a strange mixture of cynicism and innocence: "She lived out her days exploring her own thoughts and emotions, giving them full rein, feeling no obligation to please anybody unless their pleasure pleased her . . . hers was an experimental life."

But the perspective Morrison gives us upon these two black women is not pure black freedom or pure women's liberation. We may wish that Nel had absorbed some of Sula's independence of mind and willingness to take risks, and had plunged so completely into the humdrum atmosphere of conventional family life, with all its sexist and racial overtones. Yet we cannot approve the freedom that licenses Sula casually to steal Nel's husband and condemn her childhood friend to a ruined life, while she just as casually abandons him. That is not freedom but selfishness, and it is immoral, however contemptuous we may be of the pitifully conventional virtues of married life, or however much we may feel that marriage oppresses women. Besides, the freedom that Sula achieves is as much a prison as it is liberation. Totally free, she becomes obsessed with herself, unable to love, uncontained by the normal rules and boundaries we have come to associate with human beings.

Morrison does not accept—nor does she expect us to accept—the unqualified tenets of either of the two current freedom movements. There is more to both society and the individual, and she subjects each of these to a merciless analysis. The result is that neither lends itself to a clear moral judgment. For all her selfishness and cruelty, Sula's presence elicits the best in people, diluting their usual meanness and small-spiritedness. Indeed, with Sula's death the "Bottom" dies, its black people rushing headlessly in a comi-tragedy of communal suicide.

The feeling I get from this, however, is not so much that of the familiar literary viewpoint of moral complexity as that of a calm sardonic irony over the impossibility of ever sorting out the good from the bad. This feeling gives *Sula* a portentousness that makes it perhaps an inadvertent prophet, whose prophecy is that all our old assumptions about morality are disintegrating before a peculiarly black assault against them. It is as if Morrison, and other young black writers with her, are saying, like Sula, "If we can do this to ourselves, you can imagine what we can do to you."

SONG OF SOLOMON (1977)

◆◆◆◆◆◆◆◆◆◆◆◆

REYNOLDS PRICE

The New York Times Book Review, September 11, 1977

Toni Morrison's first two books—*The Bluest Eye* with the purity of its terrors and *Sula* with its dense poetry and the depth of its probing into a small circle of lives—were strong novels. Yet, firm as they both were in achievement and promise, they didn't fully forecast her new book, *Song of Solomon*. Here the depths of the younger work are still evident, but now they thrust outward, into wider fields, for longer intervals, encompassing many more lives. The result is a long prose tale that surveys nearly a century of American history as it impinges upon a single family. In short, this is a full novel—rich, slow enough to impress itself upon us like a love affair or a sickness—not the two-hour penny dreadful which is again in vogue nor one of the airless cat's cradles custom-woven for the delight and job assistance of graduate students of all ages.

Song of Solomon isn't, however, cast in the basically realistic mode of most family novels. In fact, its negotiations with fantasy, fable, song, and allegory are so organic, continuous, and unpredictable as to make any summary of its plot sound absurd; but absurdity is neither Morrison's strategy nor purpose. The purpose seems to be communication of painfully discovered and powerfully held convictions about the possibility of transcendence within human life, on a time-scale of a single life. The strategies are multiple and depend upon the actions of a large cast of black Americans, most of them related by blood. But after the loving, comical and demanding polyphony of the early chapters (set in Michigan in the early 1930's), the theme begins to settle on one character and to develop around and out of him.

His name is Macon Dead, called "Milkman" because his mother nursed him well past infancy. He is the son of an upper middle-class Northern black mother and a father with obscure working-class Southern origins. These origins, which Milkman's father is intent on concealing, fuel him in a merciless drive toward money and safety—over and past the happiness of wife and daughters and son. So the son grows up into chaos and

11

genuine danger—the homicidal intentions of a woman he spurned after years of love, and an accidental involvement with a secret ring of life-long acquaintances who are sworn to avenge white violence, eye for eye.

Near the midpoint in the book—when we may begin to wonder if the spectacle of Milkman's apparently thwarted life is sufficient to hold our attention much longer—there is an abrupt shift. Through his involvement with his father's sister, the bizarre and anarchic Pilate (whose dedication to life and feeling is directly opposed to her brother's methodical acquisition of things), and with Guitar, one of the black avengers, Milkman is flung out of his private maelstrom. He is forced to discover, explore, comprehend, and accept a world more dangerous than the Blood Bank (the ghetto neighborhood of idle eccentrics, whores, bullies, and lunatics, which he visited as a boy). But this world is also rewarding, as it opens into the larger, freer sphere of time and human contingency and reveals the possibility of knowing one's origins and of realizing the potential found in the lives, failures, and victories of one's ancestors.

Although it begins as a hungry hunt for a cache of gold that his father and Pilate left in a cave in Virginia, Milkman's search is finally a search for family history. As he travels through Pennsylvania and Virginia, acquiring the jagged pieces of a story that he slowly assembles into a long pattern of courage and literal transcendence of tragedy, he is strengthened to face the mortal threat that rises from his own careless past to meet him at the end.

The end is unresolved. Does Milkman survive to use his new knowledge, or does he die at the hands of a hateful friend? The hint is that he lives—in which case Toni Morrison has her next novel ready and waiting: Milkman's real manhood, the means he invents for transmitting or squandering the legacy he has discovered.

But that very uncertainty is one more sign of the book's larger truthfulness (no big, good novel has every really ended; and none can, until it authoritatively describes the extinction from the universe of all human life); and while there are problems (occasional abortive pursuits of a character who vanishes, occasional luxuriant pauses on detail and the understandable but weakening omission of active white characters), "Song of Solomon" easily lifts above them on the wide, slow wings of human sympathy, well-informed wit, and the rare plain power to speak wisdom to other human beings. A long story, then, and better than good. Toni Morrison has earned attention and praise. Few Americans know, and can say, more than she has in this wise and spacious novel.

♦♦♦♦♦♦♦♦♦♦♦♦♦

SUSAN LARDNER

The New Yorker, November 7,1977

"**R**hapsody" comes from Greek words for "sew" and "song" and recalls a time when literature was published by recitation. Songs composed before it was discovered that words could be written down, crossed out, rewritten, and premanently engraved on paper were stitched out of memories, traditional lore, and the poet's imagination, and the singer considered himself, and was considered by his listeners, to be a mouthpiece for the muse, before it was discovered that words could be indulged in purely as a method of self-expression.

Song of Solomon (Knopf), Toni Morrison's third novel, composed and printed in the postliterate present, can be described as a domestic epic—a rhapsodic work, demonstrating the virtues of the spoken word and the abiding presence in certain corners of the world of a lively oral tradition. The spoken quality of the narration is plain on the first page of the book, where, instead of "two days earlier," or "two days beforehand," Morrison writes "two days before the event was to take place." And "the event"—an insurance agent's attempt to fly across Lake Superior using "wide blue silk wings"—becomes, in Morrison's leisurely pursuit of stray detail, the occasion for the casual introduction of all but one of the main characters, of their setting and relationship to the outside world, and of the chief clue to the genealogical mystery that gradually emerges as the story's plot. An element in the winding digression away from the winged insurance man, whose real significance is temporarily buried, is an account of the street where the attempted flight takes place. One of numerous seemingly merely quaint odds and ends, the passage is worth quoting for its own sake, as a sample of the efficiency of Morrison's descriptive dawdling, and particularly as a token of the nostalgic pleasure the book affords of almost hearing a story told:

> Town maps registered the street as Mains Avenue, but the only colored doctor in the city had lived and died on that street, and when he moved there in 1896 his patients took to calling the street, which none of them lived in or near, Doctor Street. Later, when other Negroes moved there, and when the postal service became a popular means of transferring messages among them, envelopes from Louisiana, Virginia, Alabama, and Georgia began to arrive addressed to people at house numbers on Doctor Street. The post office workers returned these envelopes or passed them on to the Dead Letter Office. Then in 1918, when colored men were being drafted, a few gave their address at the recruitment office as Doctor Street. In that way, the name acquired a quasi-official status. But not for long. Some of the city legislators, whose concern for appropriate names and the maintenance of the city's landmarks was the principal part of their political life, saw to it that "Doctor Street" was

never used in any official capacity. And since they knew that only Southside residents kept it up, they had notices posted in the stores, barbershops, and restaurants in that part of the city saying that the avenue running northerly and southerly from Shore Road fronting the lake to the junction of routes 6 and 2 leading to Pennsylvania, and also running parallel to and between Rutherford Avenue and Broadway, had always been and would always be known as Mains Avenue and not Doctor Street.

It was a genuinely clarifying public notice because it gave Southside residents a way to keep their memories alive and please the city legislators as well. They called it Not Doctor Street.

(Remember Sixth Avenue!)

The eponymous doctor is the maternal grandfather of Milkman, the book's eventual hero, but the focus of the story is on the paternal line, extending back from Milkman to his father, Macon Dead, and his aunt Pilate, to their father, a freed slave, and their Indian mother, and, finally, to Milkman's great-grandfather, name unknown, as ancestor comparable in mythical stature to the divine foremothers and fathers of ancient Greek and Roman heroes.

Song of Solomon differs from true oral composition in its relatively intricate instructure, and in its inventiveness and variety of expression. Clearly, more of the story is drawn from the author's imagination and private experience than from common tribal or racial knowledge. Still, with her constant appeal to the ear, her abounding similes and frequent catalogues, her emphasis on the ceremonial aspect of life; with her deliberate inattention to conventional notions of probability; with her reverence for the significance of names; with her artful garrulousness, Morrison counts as a genuine rhapsode, whose access to a typewriter and the presses of Knopf mainly amounts to a lucky break for readers otherwise out of earshot. As a storyteller, Morrison is worldly-wise rather than, in a technical sense, inspired. There is no summoning of the muse, just a recitation of the facts, near- and far-fetched, of the Dead family history. She moves easily in and out of the lives and thoughts of her characters, luxuriating in the diversity of circumstance and personality, and reveling in the sound of their voices and of her own, which echoes and elaborates theirs. Near the beginning, she reminisces about the association between the insurance man and his clients:

> They were always half a month or so behind, and talked endlessly to him about paying ahead—after they had a preliminary discussion about what he was doing back so soon anyway.
> "You back in here already? Look like I just got rid of you."
> "I'm tired of seeing your face. Really tired."
> "I knew it. Soon's I get two dimes back to back, here you come. More regular than the reaper. Do Hoover know about you?"

Toward the end, when Milkman pays a visit to his father's home town in Pennsylvania, the men who still live there talk to him about his grandfather:

They talked on and on, using Milkman as the ignition that gunned their memories. The good times, the hard times, things that changed, things that stayed the same—and head and shoulders above all of it was the tall, magnificent Macon Dead, whose death, it seemed to him, was the beginning of their own dying even though they were young boys at the time. Macon Dead was the farmer they wanted to be, the clever irrigator, the peach-tree grower, the hog slaughterer, the wild-turkey roaster, the man who could plow forty in no time flat and sang like an angel while he did it. He had come out of nowhere, as ignorant as a hammer and broke as a convict, with nothing but free papers, a Bible, and a pretty black-haired wife, and in one year he'd leased ten acres, the next ten more. Sixteen years later he had one of the best farms in Montour County. A farm that colored their lives like a paintbrush and spoke to them like a sermon. "You see?" the farm said them. "See? See what you can do? Never mind you can't tell one letter from another, never mind you born a slave, never mind you lose your name, never mind your daddy dead, never mind nothing."

And later, in four pages that would have to be reprinted whole for proper quotation, Morrison describes Pilate bursting into a funeral service with a shout, shifting into a whisper, then a question, then two songs, and then speaking "conversationally" to each member of the congregation, her "words tossed like stones," we are told, "into a silent canyon."

Suddenly, like an elephant who has just found his anger and lifts his trunk over the heads of the little men who want his teeth or his hide or his flesh or his amazing strength, Pilate trumpeted for the sky itself to hear, "And she was *loved!*"

Morrison doesn't always manage to avoid the natural hazards of her gift of tongues. There are patches of vacant rhetoric, at least one case of runaway imagizing involving "anaconda love" and "red corpuscle that neither knows nor understands why it is driven to spend its whole life in one pursuit," and a stretch of overweight irony featuring a white poetess. In her account of the Dead family's Packard, Morrison uses the word "careen" when she apparently means "career" ("He could see only the winged woman careening off the nose of the car"). And in the final, apocalyptic scene Milkman leaping is imagined to be "as fleet and bright as a lodestar"—an image whose vividness overwhelms the fact that "lodestar" means "polestar": bright enough to be a beacon, but not fleet.

And I have to admit having trouble figuring out the full purpose of the character named Guitar, who moves alongside the Dead family from the day Milkman is born to the end of the story. At the age of five or six, Guitar is singled out as a "cat-eyed boy," and as an adult be becomes a member of a small ascetic band of racial avengers, which systematically kills a white man, woman, or child for every unrequited murder of an equivalent black. Although he is evidently designed to carry a historical burden, and to embody an alternative to Milkman's sheltered, inert, and aimless young manhood, his conversion from Milkman's closest friend and mentor into his nemesis remains a puzzle to me. Unlike the other characters, who are firmly in Morrison's narrative grasp, Guitar is set apart by his inhuman detachment. He acts, disruptively at times, as a kind of scholiast, assuming an authority that belongs to the storyteller— for example, in his lordly remarks on love and women.

But the current of Morrison's prose is not ever seriously deflected. "At that time of day, during the middle of the week," she writes at the start, "word-of-mouth news just lumbered along." "Lumbered." Just the right word for the word-of-mouth news at eleven o'clock on a Wednesday morning. But for *Song of Solomon* never mind "lumbered": it billows.

TAR BABY (1981)

◆◆◆◆◆◆◆◆◆◆◆◆

MAUREEN HOWARD

The New Republic, March 21, 1981

Each of the characters in Toni Morrison's *Tar Baby* comes with a history, quite a complete history that is given to us in a series of stunning performances. Morrison has a dossier on every man and woman she admits to the sacred company of her fiction. It becomes apparent, as we read on from *Sula* to *Song of Solomon* to this fine new novel, that she feels it is not only her writerly duty but her great pleasure to give us the details of each life in a grand summation.

So with Valerian Street, an odd but reasonable man retired to Isle des Chevaliers in the Caribbean, we are taken back to the childhood of a rich orphan who inherits a candy company. It would have to be a candy company—the very sweetness of the enterprise works in *Tar Baby*. Valerian's town is suffused with the smell of candy, a coating of nostalgia for all who grow up there, and the business is run with an enlightened liberalism. Though that happy empire has been left behind, we must know it and all its charms as well as its structures so that we will know why this man lives in exile in a dream house of his design. The work assigned to him is done and he is free to sit in his air-conditioned green house, Bach on the stereo, a civilized outpost in an unreal world where all the choices are of his making.

There he lives, in the house called L'Arbe de la Croix, with his ditsy wife, Margaret—the Principal Beauty of Maine. And her story, well, it's equally wonderful: the poor girl with only her spectacular looks and the good fortune to be riding down the street on a float holding a polar bear's paw when Valerian passed through town. What kind of world have we entered when the Candy King chooses Miss Maine for his mate and when their house guest many years later is Jadine, an exquisite Ph.D. model, movie star, niece to the faithful black couple who attend to the Streets' every need? A world of contrivance, a playful world that we once believed in—and for the most part in *Tar Baby* Toni Morrison makes us believe in it still.

17

The very flora and fauna of the island are alive, whispering, murmuring, nodding their commentary on the stories that are being played out in the dazzling sun. I know of no other landscapes in contemporary fiction that breathe like Morrison's except perhaps the animated bush country of Patrick Whites' Australia. Such exotic settings may seem magically evoked and can lend themselves to the fabulous tale.

> Poor insulated, brokenhearted river. Poor demented stream. Now it sat in one place like a grandmother and became a swamp the Haitians called Sein de Veilles. And witch's tit is was: a shriveled fogbound oval seeping with a thick black substance that even mosquitoes could not live near.

This is both an elegant and a horrifying way for us to see the river cruelly diverted by men, but it is a risky business letting the butterflies speak and the wind pass judgment. Though it can come perilously close to Disney, the animation works most of the time in this novel to reinforce our sense of the storybook island on which the wealthy white liberals, the chic, educated black beauty, and the Uncle Toms can face each other simply. Toni Morrison gives us the children's story, and just when we are most delighted, she takes it away.

To begin with, *Tar Baby* is all so much fun: the rich in the sun; the snappy talk in the servants' quarters; the glamour of Jadine Childs, a sort of honey-colored Rosalind Russell, bored with all her success, knowing she should think seriously about herself. Then we get our hero, a big black man who's jumped ship, young, handsome—tarnished but sterling. For some days he steals chocolate candy from the kitchen to survive, then hides in Margaret Street's closet where she finds him "literally, literally a nigger in the wood pile."

The literal can be shamefully amusing. The Marx Brothers kept up laughing with it, and Ibsen takes our breath away when Hilda Wangel, "youth," comes actually knocking at the Master Builder's door. In *Tar Baby* the black fugitive is just what these feckless island people need—Jadine with her modish problem of inauthenticity, Margaret's anxious aging, Valerian's eccentric rule—someone to shock them out of the trivia of their days, their petty decisions, their witty conversations. At breakfast the Streets' repartee falls halfway between Noel Coward and Strindberg. We seem to be involved not only in a tale of wonders but in a brittle comedy of manners, a smart script (many of the scenes in *Tar Baby* play beautifully). The Streets have just argued about the possibility of their sweet, alienated son coming home for Christmas when the intruder is discovered: his name is Son. There's the added hilarity of Jadine's edge of jealousy that the gorgeous man—thief, rapist?—who cleans up so nicely is not found crouching in *her* closet.

As the black American prince, Son charms almost everyone in sight, but the tone of the novel changes. It is grown-up time. Given a son, a love, an adversary, the slick surface at L'Arbe de la Croix is scraped away. Personal history gives way to confession. The bickering games between husband and wife, servant and master, become confrontations. It is revealed that the battle for the soul of Street's son began when he was an infant and that Margaret was guilty of the most primitive torture, while Ondine, the black cook, protected the boy—her missionary work among the aborigines. But nothing is black and white (or the reverse) in *Tar Baby*, as the fable dissolves. Valerian and Margaret gain a reality: he is dazed by the guilt of his past innocence; she is shriven, competent, and tenderly ministering to her husband in his decline. Though Sidney and Ondine, the old-fashioned "live-in" couple, do not change their roles (they cannot), there is a shift in power and the black servants' final dialogues with Valerian are manacing, Pinteresque.

Meanwhile, and it is a decidedly melodramatic meanwhile, Jadine and Son have escaped to New York, there to make love grandly, to begin new lives. I don't believe in their idyll. Perhaps I am supposed to know it's too good to be true, absolutely doomed. Jadine with her worldly credentials cannot live with a poor farm boy from Florida. Here I think Morrison depends heavily on an elevated prose, an incantation that insists upon the lovers' passionate union and later upon their equally passionate parting. In one sense they are talked about too much; in another they simply talk too much. Son and Jadine come at each other like running commentaries on black men and black women, on education, debt, freedom. It is the only dull part of this serious and mostly entertaining novel.

The *longueur* of the love story is relieved by a nicely rendered interlude set in Son's hometown, Eloe. Jadine among the hicks in her cashmere sweater and Charcrel boots is a touching sight. The stifling little shacks are more foreign to her than the hotel-like splendor of L'Arbe de la Croix. The perfect couple become an unlikely pair. Of course, we cannot help but see that their problems are real and at times their invective cuts deep. Jadine says:

> It's not romantic. And it's not being free. It's dumb. You think you're above it, above money, the rat race and all that. But you're not above it, you're just without it. It's a prison, poverty is. Look at what it's absence made you do: run, hide, steal, lie.

It is true that Son romanticizes the poor and the ignorant and all the soothing sacrificial black women of his past that Jadine can never be. But he is right, too, when he rails at her: "And you? Where have you lived? Anybody ask you where you from, you give them five towns. You're not *from* anywhere. I'm from Eloe." And he is right again when he begins to taunt her, instructively, with the story of "Tar Baby."

Thematically, this novel is much tighter than Morrison's earlier works. Except for the love affair, which seems to me rhetorical and overstated, the stories do not meander or pull away from the central vision of a modern world that offers the thinness of exile and denies us the comforts of home. Valerian believes that his son was "a typical anthropologist, a cultural orphan who sought other cultures he could love without risk of pain." It is not easy to belong anywhere and we cannot be daughters and sons in the old style. Michael Street, the off-stage boy, for all the abuse done him, makes it into an independent, perhaps even a good and useful, life, but Jadine, for all her pampering, goes back to Europe with the belief that she must be as tough and hard as a soldier ant.

> Almost all of them are women and there is so much to do—the work is literally endless. . . . There is no time for dreaming. The life of their world requires organization so tight and sacrifice so complete there is little need for males and they are seldom produced.

The very end of this novel, like the finale of *Song of Solomon*, reverts to fable. In his pursuit of Jadine, Son is taken by an island woman, not to the Streets' dock, but to the dangerous shores of Isle des Chevaliers, where it is said men run naked and blind. "Choose them," the woman says—as opposed to the impossibilities of a mature life with Jadine. The land seems to receive him and Morrison writes:

> He threw out his hands to guide and steady his going. By and by he walked steadier, now steadier. The mist lifted and the trees stepped back a bit as if to make the way easier for a certain kind of man. Then he ran. Lickety-split. Lickety-split. Lickety-lickety-lickety split.

I can only presume that this storybook language means that Son is swallowed up in that childish world of magic, returned to a natural state. Sadly, the black hero perpetuates myth.

Morrison is easy in her pursuit of big themes: the mutual responsibility of parents and children, the debts we must pay in order to gain a validity and those we must walk away from in order to gain freedom. And, of course, her talent for the comic serves her well in dealing with blacks and whites, maids and masters—drawing the ironic parallels between private and cultural guilt that must haunt us all. For all the fantasy in *Tar Baby*, it is a highly realistic novel, full of the actual riddles, the unanswerable questions, of our present lives. The solutions that tie the Streets and their black servants to a crumbling dream house are hardly soothing. For Jadine and Son, there are no clear answers, only Morrison's observation of their difficult human choices.

Despite its meandering commentaries, despite some stylistic excesses, this is an admirable novel. Witty and desperate, for the most part *Tar Baby* is as carefully patterned as a well-written poem. As I unwind the thematic strands in this review, I realize that much of my pleasure has been in construing this moving and intricate plot, a pleasure I associate with the best kind of reading. *Tar Baby* is a good American novel in which we can discern a new lightness and brilliance in Toni Morrison's enchantment with language and in her curiously polyphonic stories that echo life.

JOHN IRVING

The New York Times Book Review, March 29, 1981

A novelist's vice usually resembles his virtue, for what he does best he also tends to do to excess: if he's good at being lyrical, he's too lyrical; if a cruel fate or accident seems to attend each character's childhood, that doom announces itself like a gun going off too long before the bullet's arrival. Our best and most ambitious writers indulge their vices as freely as their virtues; they are unafraid of them and think it small-minded to exercise restraint.

Thomas Hardy, for instance, much maligned for the preachy element in his prose—his instructions to mankind that intrude upon his narrative like a voice over a loudspeaker in the midst of some public crisis—chooses not to describe Tess d'Uberville's deflowering as if it affected only one victim; instead he addresses a larger injustice, which may be what many readers dislike in Hardy—especially today—but this is also what makes Hardy Hardy.

The more ambitious a novelist is, the more willing he is to elevate his characters to the level of myth—to give their births, their relationships, their deaths, even their names, the resonance of legend. Dickens conveys such an ambition in his titles (*Bleak House, Great Expectations, Hard Times*) and of course in his characters' names (Lady Dedlock, Mr. Jaggers, Gradgrind). The 19th-century novel is rich with such risk, such mischief.

Toni Morrison seems to be returning such risk and mischief to the contemporary American novel, and never more extravagantly than in *Tar Baby*, her fourth and most ambitious book. In *Song of Solomon* (1977) she gave us a hospital called Mercy Hospital, popularly called "No Mercy." That novel began with a life insurance agent leaping off the hospital roof in an attempt to fly to the other side of Lake Superior: "I will take off from Mercy and fly away on my own wings. Please forgive me. I loved you all." Toni Morrison loves them all, too—all her characters, in all her books. She mythologizes her characters almost as they're conceived, at least as soon as they're born, but she has the good novelist's sense of detail that makes these mythic people live. The boy born in the hospital on the day the life insurance gent fails to fly is Milkman; he's the first black baby born at No Mercy; his aunt is named Pilate, and she's born without a navel.

Miss Morrison has been up to this kind of dramatic exaggeration for some time. In *Sula* (1974) she managed to turn a poor black part of Ohio into a fairy tale (in a town called Medallion, the black people live in a place called the Bottom and celebrate National Suicide Day). The main character, Sula Peace, is such an upsetting heroine that her return to the town of Medallion is "accompanied by a plague of robins."

Now, in *Tar Baby*, Miss Morrison gives us a candy manufacturer named Valerian Street, a white man, who marries a woman he sees riding a winter carnival float holding the paw of a polar bear. She is Miss Maine, in fact, and is called the Principal Beauty of Maine. Valerian Street's best friend is a French dentist named Michelin. Valerian's own name was once used for a kind of candy that failed because nobody bought it but blacks in the South.

Despite this failure, Valerian Street is a wealthy man. When we meet him he is trying to live out his last years on a Caribbean island called Isle des Chevaliers. He is still attracted to Northern flowers, however, and indulges himself with a greenhouse in which he plays music to those species that don't grow in the tropics.

Miss Morrison makes greater mischief with Valerian's paradise than simply poking fun at his flowers. He lives oblivious to a story within his own family—a story too good for me to spoil for the reader (and too awful for the frail Miss Maine to cope with). The family's loyal black cook, Ondine, will reveal the tale; she and her husband, Sydney, the butler, have devoted most of their lives to serving Valerian Street. They are the white man's dream of "good Negroes," which means they love their master's child as if he were their own, they keep their place, they grow quietly and uncomplainingly old.

They also provide Miss Morrison with an opportunity to exercise her considerable gift for dialogue; this old couple's conversation is sparkling and through it the reader learns the circumstances of Valerian's retirement to the Caribbean. It is both his and his wife's sorrow that their only son won't share this paradise (the mystery of the novel, and it's a gruesome mystery, is why the son, Michael, stays away). Valerian escapes from his disappointment to his greenhouse: "When he knew for certain that Michael would always be a stranger to him, he built the greenhouse as a place of controlled ever-flowering life to greet death in."

In *Tar Baby* Toni Morrison lavishes her strongest prose on descriptions of nature: "Bees have no sting on Isle des Chevaliers, nor honey. They are fat and lazy, curious about nothing. Especially at noon. At noon parrots sleep and diamondbacks work down the trees toward the cooler undergrowth. At noon the water in the mouths of orchids left there by the breakfast rain is warm. Children stick their fingers in them and scream as though scalded."

At times this effort to see the world from nature's point of view seems precious, even cute ("Margaret was not dreaming nor was she quite asleep, although the moon looking at her face believed she was"), but the richness of the best of these passages (a description of the death of a river, for example) makes Miss Morrison's excesses tolerable.

Less tolerable, however, is her excessive use of dialogue: too much of the story is told through dialogue—and not only through the old couple's conversations. Their niece, Jadine, a super-educated, super-beautiful young woman, a Paris model who "made those white girls disappear. Just disappear right off the page," has a love affair with an escaped criminal, a poor, uneducated north Florida black. This affair is the book's erotic and dramatic center. Jadine and her lover, Son (his father was called Old Man), passionately and violently debate the best way for blacks to be independent of the white man's world. Their arguments are lengthy and become tedious, but they vividly expose the novel's racial tensions.

Jadine was educated on money given her by her aunt's and uncle's employer; her friendship with Mrs. Street is severely tested by Son's intrusion (he jumps ship and swims ashore on Isle des Chevaliers, hiding in the Street family's bedrooms for four days, sneaking food, before he is caught). Son's presence reveals the racism in both the whites and blacks in the Street household; he is—in the blacks' own words—"just a swamp nigger."

What's so powerful, and subtle, about Miss Morrison's presentation of the tension between blacks and whites is that she conveys it almost entirely through the suspicions and prejudices of her black characters. It is the white world that has created this, and in the constant warring between Sydney, Ondine, and Jadine, and between Jadine and Son, Miss Morrison uncovers all the stereotypical racial fears felt by whites and blacks alike. Like any ambitious writer, she's unafraid to employ these stereotypes—she embraces the representative quality of her characters without embarrassment, then proceeds to make them individuals too.

Jadine takes Son to New York City, but after his immersion in Caribbean life he sees black Americans with the keen perspective of a foreigner: "The black girls in New York City were crying and their men were looking neither to the right nor to the left. Not because they were heedless, or intent on what was before them, but they did not wish to see the crying, crying girls split into two parts by their tight jeans, screaming at the top of their high, high heels, straining against the pull of their braids and the fluorescent combs holding their hair."

Son then takes Jadine back to his north Florida home, where the "real" blacks live, but Jadine is bored and repulsed. In the end she returns to Paris, possibly to have a rich white man's child, while Son searches for her on Isle des Chevaliers—an almost atavistic figure returning to the swamp, losing himself in a powerfully superstitious island culture, radically different from the culture of black America.

Tar Baby is, of course, a black novel, a novel deeply perceptive of the black's desire to create a mythology of his own to replace the stereotypes and myths the white man has constructed for him. It is also a book about a woman's anger at—and her denial of—her need for an impossible man, and in this regard it is a woman's novel too. Leaving Son behind her, Jadine bravely concludes: "A grown woman did not need safety or its dreams. She *was* the safety she longed for." Yet Toni Morrison's greatest accomplishment is that she has raised her novel above the social realism that too many black novels and women's novels are trapped in. She has succeeded in writing about race and women symbolically.

This movement from realism to myth can be seen at its best, for example, in a crucial fight between Jadine and Son: "She looked at him and when he saw the sheen gone from her minky eyes and her wonderful mouth fat with disgust, he tore open his shirt, saying, 'I got a story for you.'

> "'Get out of my face.'
> "'You'll like it. It's short and to the point.'
> "'Don't touch me. Don't you touch me.'
> "'Once upon a time there was a farmer—a white farmer . . .'
> "'Quit! Leave me *alone*.'
> "'And he had this . . . farm. And a rabbit. A rabbit came along and ate a couple of his . . . ow . . . cabbages.'
> "'You better kill me. Because if you don't, when you're through, I'm going to kill you.'
> "'Just a few cabbages, you know what I mean?'
> "'I am going to kill you. *Kill* you.'
> "'So he got this great idea about how to get him. How to, to trap . . . this rabbit. And you know what he did? He made him a tar baby. He made it, you hear me? He made it!'
> "'As sure as I live,' she said, 'I'm going to kill you.'
> "But she didn't. After he banged the bedroom door, she lay in wrinkled sheets, slippery, gutted, not thinking of killing him."

Alongside the ferocity of this battle, Valerian Street's greenhouse and the problems besetting his wife (the "Bride of the Polar Bear") seem trivial in the extreme, but Miss Morrison never withholds her sympathy from her minor characters. If the excesses of the book's dialogue and lyricism are acceptable vices of ambition, the precision of Miss Morrison's minor characters and scenes reveals her craftsmanship. When she abandons that precision, it doesn't seem a lapse in her artistry so much as a way of announcing her more visceral intentions.

Some readers will find the overlapping narrative structure an irritation; this is one of the problems with Miss Morrison's dependence on dialogue to advance and fill in the story. Some readers may resist the movement toward myth in the book's deliberately symbolic ending—and some complaints, some wish to know more concretely what happens, may be justified. Will Son ever connect with Jadine again? Will Jadine allow herself to be bought by the safe, white world of Paris? And will Sydney and Ondine, despite the indignities they have been forced to suffer, continue to serve the Streets, who—at the novel's end—are devastated by the revelation of their family's inner violence?

But Toni Morrison is less interested in the final details of her characters' lives than she is interested in demonstrating the vast discrepancies between the places black people end up and the places they seek. Son chooses to lose himself in the rain forest, "where the champion daisy trees still grow," rather than give himself up to a black world that has been corrupted by whites. Son invents his own life from scratch; his almost fatal love for Jadine has only momentarily distracted him from this goal.

Thomas Hardy would have appreciated Miss Morrison's old-fashioned authorial intrusions, her wise counsel to her readers. It is an earned moment when Miss Morrison gives Valerian Street the following revelation or benediction:

> At some point in life the world's beauty becomes enough. You don't need to photograph, paint or even remember it. It is enough. No record of it needs to be kept and you don't need someone to share it with or tell it to. When that happens—that letting go—you let go because you can. The world will always be there—when you wake it will be there as well. So you can sleep and there is reason to wake. A dead hydrangea is as intricate and lovely as one in bloom. Bleak sky is as seductive as sunshine, miniature orange trees without blossom or fruit are not defective; they are that. So the windows of the greenhouse can be opened and the weather let in. The latch on the door can be left unhooked, the muslin removed, for the soldier ants are beautiful too and whatever they do will be part of it.

Although Valerian has been largely innocent of the crimes in this novel visited upon blacks and whites, Miss Morrison concludes: "An innocent man is a sin before God. Inhuman and therefore unworthy. No man should live without absorbing the sins of his kind, the foul air of his innocence, even if it did wilt rows of angel trumpets and cause them to fall from their vines."

This judgment is as sympathetic as it is severe. Thomas Hardy, full of his own instructions to damaged mankind, would have loved this book.

BELOVED (1987)

◆◆◆◆◆◆◆◆◆◆◆◆◆

ANN SNITOW*

The Village Voice Literary Supplement, September 1987

The subject of Toni Morrison's new novel, *Beloved*, is slavery, and the book staggers under the terror of its material—as so much holocaust writing does and must. Morrison's other novels teem with people, but in *Beloved* half the important characters are dead in the novel's present, 1873. Though they appear in memory, they have no future. Slavery, says one character, "ain't a battle; it's a rout"—with hardly any of what one could confidently call survivors. The mood is woe, depression, horror, a sense of unbearable loss. Still, those who remain must exorcise the deadly past from their hearts or die themselves; *Beloved* is the tale of such an exorcism.

In complex narrative loops, *Beloved* circles around and hints at the different fates of a group of slaves who once lived on a plantation in Kentucky, "Sweet Home"—of course neither "sweet" nor "home": an old woman called Baby Suggs, her son Halle, Paul A., Paul D., Paul F., Sixo, and the one young woman among them, Sethe. (Here as everywhere in the novel names raise baleful questions. Slaves have a tragically tenuous hold on names, and it is only in their final destinies that the three Pauls are allowed separate lives.)

Halle strikes a bargain with his master to sell his few free hours and use the money to buy his mother's freedom. Baby Suggs wonders why he bothers. What can a crippled old woman do with freedom? But when she stands on the northern side of the Ohio River and walks through the streets of Cincinnati, "she could not believe that Halle knew what she didn't; that Halle, who had never drawn one free breath, knew that there was nothing like it in the world."

Back at Sweet Home the decent master dies. (In slavery, a good

---

* I would like to briefly note a few second thoughts, prompted by some subsequent criticism of *Beloved*. Barbara Christian has celebrated—and named differently—the very trait that I criticized in 1987, the vacuum, the absence, at the novel's core. She calls this absence a taboo, which arises from the trauma of slavery, a gap in history, a blank in consciousness. I criticized Morrison for writing a clunky ghost, but maybe the one taking that ghost too literally was myself. The ghost is a figment with the power to stop the action and contaminate the air. She is a projection of grief. We never get half a chance to love Beloved, and her name becomes a pure and bitter irony, an irony which tempers every bit of Morrison's romanticism.

—Ann Snitow, March 1993.

master is merely a chance episode, any feeling of autonomy is merely a fool's illusion.) The new boss, "Schoolteacher," beats his slaves and measures them with rulers, keeping pseudo-scholarly lists of their "human and animal characteristics." He demonstrates that any time the whites want to, they can knock you into the middle of next week, or back into the dependency of childhood. But Sethe now has three babies by the generous-spirited Halle, and the idea that she might never see them grow (like Baby Suggs's, who saw seven of her children sold), or that they will grow only into Schoolteacher's eternal children, strengthens her resolve to join the Sweet Home slaves who plan to run, taking a "train" north. Paul F. is long gone—sold, who knows where. During the escape, Paul A. gets caught and hanged. Sixo gets caught and burned alive. Paul D. gets caught and sold in chains with a bit in his mouth. Sethe manages to get her three children on the train, but is caught herself, assaulted, beaten. Halle fails to appear at their rendezvous— lost, mysteriously lost, and never to be found again. Sethe runs anyway, because she can't forget that hungry baby who's gone on ahead, and because a new one is waiting to be born.

Half dead, and saved only by the help of a young white girl, trash almost as exiled as herself, Sethe gives birth to her baby girl, Denver, on the banks of the Ohio and manages to get them both across and truly home, to Baby Suggs's door.

Told flat, the plot of *Beloved* is the stuff of melodrama, recalling *Uncle Tom's Cabin*. But Morrison doesn't really *tell* these incidents. Bits and pieces of them leak out between the closed eyelids of her characters, or between their clenched fingers. She twists and tortures and fractures events until they are little slivers that cut. She moves the lurid material of melodrama into the middle of her people, where it gets sifted and sorted, lived and relived, until it acquires the enlarging outlines of myth and trauma, dream and obsession.

In fact, the intense past hardly manages to emerge at all. It is repressed, just as the facts of slavery are. Instead, in the foreground of the novel, Morrison places a few lonely minds in torment: Sethe, Denver, Paul D. All the drama of past desire and escape has fled to the margins of their consciousness, while Morrison's survivors are living in one extended moment of grief. Slowly, painfully, we learn that in order to keep Schoolteacher from recapturing her children, Sethe tried to kill them all, succeeding with the third, a baby girl Morrison leaves nameless. The act lies at the center of the book: incontrovertible, enormous. Sethe explains that she killed the baby because "if I hadn't killed her she would have died." Morrison makes us believe the logic down to the ground.

By 1873, eighteen years after Sethe's fatal act of resistance, slavery is technically over, whether or not the former slaves feel finished with it. Sethe's eldest two boys have run off, perhaps overfull of the mother love that almost killed them as children. Baby Suggs's house has become the entire world to Sethe and Denver—now eighteen. They live there ostracized, proud and alone—except for the active ghost of the murdered two-year-old.

This awkward spirit shakes the furniture, puts tiny handprints on the cakes, shatters mirrors, while Sethe and Denver live stolidly in the chaos, emotionally frozen. Into this landscape of regret walks Paul D., one of the dear lost comrades from Sweet Home. He has been tramping for these eighteen years, and now comes to rest on Sethe's front porch. Innocent of the secret of the baby's death, he seems to exorcise her ghost with nothing much more than his warm presence. As it turns out, she is not that easy to dismiss. The bulk of the novel dwells on the ghost's desperate return as a grown woman who calls herself "Beloved," the one word she has found on her tombstone.

At first, Beloved seems benign in her new avatar, and Sethe is ecstatic to have her daughter back. But gradually, the strange visitor in elegant clothes and mysteriously unscuffed shoes turns into a fearsome figure, seducing Paul D. in order to drag him into wrong and send him packing, eating all the best food until Sethe and Denver begin to starve, ruling the demented household. The whole center of the novel is a projection of Sethe's longing; Beloved is a snare to catch her anguished, hungry mother's heart and keep her in the prison of guilt forever. She is also memory, the return of the dreadful past. In her, the breathtaking horror of the breakup of Sweet Home lives, sucking up all the air.

And so Toni Morrison has written a novel that's airless. How could this happen to a writer this skillful, working with material this full and important? In the reading, the novel's accomplishments seem driven to the periphery by Morrison's key decision to be literal about her metaphor, to make the dead baby a character whose flesh-and-bone existence takes up a great deal of narrative space. Even Sethe and Denver complain at times about the irritating presence of their ghost. And when she returns as a woman, she is a zombie, animated by abstract ideas. Later those who loved her "realized they couldn't remember or repeat a single thing she said, and began to believe that, other than what they themselves were thinking, she hadn't said anything at all."

Symbolic thinking is one thing, magical thinking quite another. Morrison blurs the distinction in *Beloved*, stripping the real magic of its potency and the symbols of their poetry. Her undigested insistence on the magical keeps bringing this often beautiful novel to the earth. Morrison's last two strange and original books, *Song of Solomon* and *Tar Baby*, had some of this unconvincing reliance on the supernatural, too. By contrast, *The Bluest Eye*, her first, was bitten and dry-eyed; the little girl in that novel who thinks she can get blue eyes by magic sinks into the psychosis of wishing. Morrison's best magic was in *Sula*, the novel where it is most elusive, making no more solid a claim for the

Unseen than the human spiritual power to move mountains.

This isn't to say ghosts can't or shouldn't be the stuff of fiction. The present generation of South American gothicists often convince us of the living power of ghosts in the worlds they describe. And the literature of disaster is haunted by the noisy dead, clamoring to be remembered as active presences, not cut off from a continuing story. Morrison is working in these traditions when she tries to animate the resistant weight of the slave experience by pouring on magic, lurid visions, fantasies of reconciliation. And why not? In one way, she comes by her magic honestly: It is the lore of the folk she loves, a visionary inheritance that makes her people superior to those—black or white—who don't have any talent for noticing the unseen. She wants to show how the slave lives on, raising havoc, and to give Sethe, her treasured heroine, a chance to fight it out with the demon of grief. If Beloved is a drag on the narrative, a soul mixed with a great deal of dross, well so be it, Morrison seems to say. When strong, loving women would rather kill their babies than see them hauled back to slavery, the damage to every black who inherits that moment is a literal damage and no metaphor. The novel is meant to give grief body, to make it palpable.

But I suspect Morrison knows she's in some trouble here, since she harps so on the presence of Beloved, sometimes neglecting the mental life of her other characters. Their vitality is sacrificed to the inert ghost until the very end—a structure that makes thematic sense but leaves the novel hollow in the middle. Beloved is, of course, what's heavy in their hearts, but can the ghost of a tragically murdered two-year-old bear this weight of meaning? No matter how she kicks and screams, the ghost is too light to symbolize the static fact of her own death. She is a distraction from those in the flesh, who must bear the pain of a dead child's absence. She is dead, which is the only arresting thing about her, and Morrison's prose goes dead when it concerns her.

If Beloved fails in its ambitions, it is still a novel by Toni Morrison, still therefore full of beautiful prose, dialogue as rhythmically satisfying as music, delicious chracters with names like Grandma Baby and Stamp Paid, and the scenes so clearly etched they're like hallucinations. Morrison is one of the great, serious writers we have. Who else tries to do what Dickens did: create wild, flamboyant, abstractly symbolic characters who are at the same time not grotesque but sweetly alive, full of deep feeling? Usually in contemporary fiction, the grotesque is mixed with irony or zaniness, not with passion and romance. Morrison rejects irony, a choice that immediately sets her apart. Like Alice Walker (there are several small, friendly allusions to The Color Purple in Beloved), she wants to tend the imagination, search for an expansion of the possible, nurture a spiritual richness in the black tradition even after three hundred years in the white desert.

From book to book, Morrison's larger project grows clear. First, she insists that every character bear the weight of responsibility for his or her own life. After she's measured out each one's private pain, she adds on to that the shared burden of what the whites did. Then, at last, she tries to find the place where her stories can lighten her readers' load, lift them up from their own and others' guilt, carry them to glory.

In her greatest novel so far, *Sula*, she succeeded amazingly at making this crucial shift in atmosphere. Here characters suffer—from their own limitations and the world's—but their inner life miraculously expands beyond the narrow law of cause and effect. In *Sula*, Morrison found a way to offer her people an insight and sense of recovered self so dignified and glowing that no worldly pain could dull the final light. The novel ends with a song which soars over the top of its own last word, "sorrow":

> And the loss pressed down on her chest and came up into her throat. "We was girls together," she said as though explaining something. "O Lord, Sula," she cried, "girl, girl, girl, girl, girl."
>
> It was a fine cry—loud and long—but it had no bottom and it had no top, just circles and circles of sorrow.

Song of Solomon and *Tar Baby*, and now *Beloved*, have writings as beautiful as this, but they are less in control of that delicate turn from fact to wish.

Even at her best, Morrison's techniques are risky, and sometimes, in *Beloved*, she loses her gamble. Slavery resists her impulse toward the grand summation of romance. The novel revolves and searches, searches and revolves, never getting any closer to these people numbed by their overwhelming grief. *Why* could they not save those they loved? Nothing moves here; everything is static and in pieces. The fragmentary, the unresolvable are in order in a story about slavery. When Morrison embraces this hideous fact, the book is dire and powerful: Halle is never found. Baby Suggs never reassembles her scattered children, whose names and faces are now those of strangers. Sethe has collapsed inside, unable to bear what has happened to them all.

Still, for Morrison, it is the romance and not the fractured narrative of modernism that is the vehicle of her greatest feeling for her people. Though in their sorrow they resist her, she keeps inviting them to rise up on wings. She can't bear for them to be lost, finished, routed. The romantic in her longs to fuse what is broken, to give us something framed, at least one polychromatic image from above. When this works, it's glorious. And even when it doesn't, it's a magnificent intention. But there are moments in Morrison's recent novels when the brilliant, rich, and evocative image seems a stylistic tic, a shortcut to intensity. Romance can be a temptation. At the end of *Beloved* Morrison joins Sethe and Paul D. together for good. This happy union is a device laid on them from without by a solicitous author. It *should* be possible—why should pain breed only more pain?—but Morrison doesn't manage to maintain a necessary tension between what she knows and what she desires. She wishes too hard. Something in the novel goes slack.

Because Morrison is always a tiger storyteller, she struggles against her novel's tendency to be at war with itself. She keeps writing gorgeous scenes, inventing characters so compelling and clear they carry us with them, back into a novel that seems determined to expel us. The ending in particular pushes *Beloved* beyond where it seemed capable of going:

> Everybody knew what she was called, but nobody anywhere knew her name. Disremembered and unaccounted for, she cannot be lost because no one is looking for her, and even if they were, how can they call her if they don't know her name? Although she has claim, she is not claimed. In the place where the long grass opens, the girl who waited to be loved and cry shame erupts into her separate parts, to make it easy for the chewing laughter to swallow all her away.
>
> It was not a story to pass on . . .
>
> By and by all trace is gone. . . . The rest is weather. Not the breath of the disremembered and unaccounted for, but wind in the eaves, or spring ice thawing too quickly. Just weather. Certainly no clamor for a kiss.
>
> Beloved.

"Disremembered and unaccounted for." The dead may roar, but they are impotent. It is a brave and radical project to center a novel on a dead child ignored by history, cruelly forgotten along with so much else that happened to black people in slavery. A slave baby murdered by its own mother is "not a story to pass on." Even the slave who knows Sethe's reasons finds them hard to accept. Paul D. is so horrified when he finally learns about her crime that he leaves her for a time, telling her she has two legs not four. It is beastly to kill a baby, and yet Sethe asks, who was the beast? To keep Beloved out of the hands of an owner who would see her only as an animal, Sethe would rather be wild herself, do her own subduing of the human spirit, if killed it must be. As always in the last pages of her novels, Morrison gathers herself together and sings here of those who didn't even leave their names, who died before they had the chance to become the sort of people about whom you could tell real stories.

There are the novelists who try something new in each book (Doris Lessing, say, or Joanna Russ, Kurt Vonnegut, Alice Walker) and the novelists who keep on worrying the same material (Saul Bellow, Robert Stone, Philip Roth, and Morrison herself). The first group has all the advantage of surprise, offering the thrill of new territory. Some of these trips come out better than others, but the overall effect is of travel. The second group has a different task, to find the same small door into the same necessary world, to wander the same maze trying to find the way home. Each novel in this group says to its readers, here I am again; do you feel what I always feel—as fully as I want you to? Well, not this time. But Morrison is great even in pieces, and worth waiting for, however long it takes.

novel deserves to be read as much for what it cannot say as for
can. It is a book of revelations about slavery, and its seriousness
insures that it is just a matter of time before Morrison shakes that brilliant kaleidoscope of hers again and the story of pain, endurance, poetry
and power she is born to tell comes out right.

◆◆◆◆◆◆◆◆◆◆◆◆◆

MARGARET ATWOOD

The New York Times Book Review, September 13, 1987

Beloved is Toni Morrison's fifth novel and another triumph. Indeed, Ms.
Morrison's versatility and technical and emotional range appear to know
no bounds. If there were any doubts about her stature as a pre-eminent
American novelist, of her own or any other generation, *Beloved* will
put them to rest. In three words or less, it's a hair-raiser.

In *Beloved*, Ms. Morrison turns away from the contemporary scene
that has been her concern of late. This new novel is set after the end of
the Civil War, during the period of so-called Reconstruction, when a
great deal of random violence was let loose upon blacks, both the slaves
freed by Emancipation and others who had been given or had bought
their freedom earlier. But there are flashbacks to a more distant period,
when slavery was still a going concern in the South and the seeds for
the bizarre and calamitous events of the novel were sown. The setting
is similarly divided: the countryside near Cincinnati, where the central
characters have ended up, and a slave-holding plantation in Kentucky,
ironically named Sweet Home, from which they fled eighteen years before the novel opens.

There are many stories and voices in this novel, but the central one
belongs to Sethe, a woman in her mid-thirties, who is living in an Ohio
farmhouse with her daughter, Denver, and her mother-in-law Baby
Suggs. *Beloved* is such a unified novel that it's difficult to discuss it
without giving away the plot, but it must be said at the outset that it is,
among other things, a ghost story; for the farmhouse is also home to a
sad, malicious and angry ghost, the spirit of Sethe's baby daughter, who
had her throat cut under appalling circumstances eighteen years before,
when she was two. We never know this child's full name, but we—and
Sethe—think of her as Beloved, because that is what is on her tombstone.
Sethe wanted "Dearly Beloved," from the funeral service, but had only
enough strength to pay for one word. Payment was ten minutes of sex
with the tombstone engraver. This act, which is recounted early in the
novel, is a keynote for the whole book in the world of slavery and pov-

erty, where human beings are merchandise, everything has its price, and price is tyrannical.

"Who would have thought that a little old baby could harbor so much rage?" Sethe thinks, but it does, breaking mirrors, making tiny hand-prints in cake icing, smashing dishes and manifesting itself in pools of blood red light. As the novel opens, the ghost is in full possession of the house, having driven away Sethe's two young sons. Old Baby Suggs, after a lifetime of slavery and a brief respite of freedom—purchased for her by the Sunday labor of her son Halle, Sethe's husband—has given up and died. Sethe lives with her memories, almost all of them bad. Denver, her teen-age daughter, courts the baby ghost because, since her family has been ostracized by the neighbors, she doesn't have anyone else to play with.

The supernatural element is treated, not in an *Amityville Horror*, watch-me-make-your-flesh-creep mode, but with magnificent practical-ity, like the ghost of Catherine Earnshaw in *Wuthering Heights*. All the main characters in the book believe in ghosts, so it's merely natural for this one to be there. As Baby Suggs says, "Not a house in the country ain't packed to its rafters with some dead Negro's grief. We lucky this ghost is a baby. My husband's spirit was to come back in here? or yours? Don't talk to me. You lucky." In fact, Sethe would rather have the ghost there than not there. It is, after all, her adored child, and any sign of it is better, for her, than nothing.

This grotesque domestic equilibrium is disturbed by the arrival of Paul D., one of the "Sweet Home men" from Sethe's past. The Sweet Home men were the male slaves of the establishment. Their owner, Mr. Garner, is no Simon Legree; instead he'a a best-case slave-holder, treat-ing his "property" well, trusting them, allowing them choice in the run-ning of his small plantation, and calling them "men" in defiance of the neighbors, who want all male blacks to be called "boys." But Mr. Garner dies, and weak, sickly Mrs. Garner brings in her handiest male relative, who is known as "the school teacher." This Goebbels-like paragon com-bines viciousness with intellectual pretensions; he's a sort of master race proponent who measures the heads of the slaves and tabulates the results to demonstrate that they are more like animals than people. Accom-panying him are his two sadistic and repulsive nephews. From there it's all down hill at Sweet Home, as the slaves try to escape, go crazy or are murdered. Sethe, in a trek that makes the ice floe scene in *Uncle Tom's Cabin* look like a stroll around the block, gets out, just barely; her husband, Halle, doesn't. Paul D. does, but has some very unpleasant adventures along the way, including a literally nauseating sojourn in a 19th-century Georgia chain gang.

Through the different voices and memories of the book, including that of Sethe's mother, a survivor of the infamous slave-ship crossing, we experience American slavery as it was lived by those who were its objects of exchange, both at its best—which wasn't very good—and at its worst, which was as bad as can be imagined. Above all, it is seen as one of the most viciously anti-family institutions human beings have ever devised. The slaves are motherless, fatherless, deprived of their mates, their children, their kin. It is a world in which people suddenly vanish and are never seen again, not through accident or covert operation or terrorism, but as a matter of everyday legal policy.

Slavery is also presented to us as a paradigm of how most people behave when they are given absolute power over other people. The first effect, of course, is that they start believing in their own superiority and justifying their actions by it. The second effect is that they make a cult of the inferiority of those they subjugate. It's no coincidence that the first of the deadly sins, from which all the others were supposed to stem, is Pride, a sin of which Sethe is, incidentally, also accused.

In a novel that abounds in black bodies—headless, hanging from trees, frying to a crisp, locked in woodsheds for purposes of rape, or floating down stream drowned—it isn't surprising that the "whitepeople," especially the men, don't come off too well. Horrified black children see whites as men "without skin." Sethe thinks of them as having "mossy teeth" and is ready, if necessary, to bite off their faces, and worse, to avoid further mossy-toothed outrages. There are a few whites who behave with something approaching decency. There's Amy, the young runaway indentured servant who helps Sethe in childbirth during her flight to freedom, and incidentally reminds the reader that the nineteenth century, with its child labor, wage slavery and widespread and accepted domestic violence, wasn't tough only for blacks, but for all but the most privileged whites as well. There are also the abolitionists who help Baby Suggs find a house and a job after she is freed. But even the decency of these "good" whitepeople has a grudging side to it, and even they have trouble seeing the people they are helping as full-fledged people, though to show them as totally free of their xenophobia and sense of superiority might well have been anachronistic.

Toni Morrison is careful not to make all the whites awful and all the blacks wonderful. Sethe's black neighbors, for instance, have their own envy and scapegoating tendencies to answer for, and Paul D., though much kinder than, for instance, the woman-bashers of Alice Walker's novel *The Color Purple*, has his own limitations and flaws. But then, considering what he's been through, it's a wonder he isn't a mass murderer. If anything, he's a little too huggable, under the circumstances.

Back in the present tense, in chapter one, Paul D. and Sethe make an attempt to establish a "real" family, whereupon the baby ghost, feeling excluded, goes berserk, but is driven out by Paul D.'s stronger will. So it appears. But then, along comes a strange, beautiful, real flesh-and-blood young woman, about twenty years old, who can't seem to remember where she comes from, who talks like a young child, who has an odd, raspy voice and no lines on her hands, who takes an intense, devouring interest in Sethe, and who says her name is Beloved.

Students of the supernatural will admire the way this twist is handled. Ms. Morrison blends a knowledge of folklore—for instance, in many traditions, the dead cannot return from the grave unless called, and it's the passions of the living that keep them alive—with a highly original treatment. The reader is kept guessing, there's a lot more to Beloved than any one character can see, and she manages to be many things to several people. She is a catalyst for revelations as well as self-revelations; through her we come to know not only how, but why, the original child Beloved was killed. And through her also Sethe achieves, finally, her own form of self-exorcism, her own self-accepting peace.

Beloved is written in an antiminimalist prose that is by turns rich, graceful, eccentric, rough, lyrical, sinuous, colloquial and very much to the point. Here, for instance, is Sethe remembering Sweet Home:

> . . . suddenly there was Sweet Home rolling, rolling, rolling out before her eyes, and although there was not a leaf on that farm that did not want to make her scream, it rolled itself out before her in shameless beauty. It never looked as terrible as it was and it made her wonder if hell was a pretty place too. Fire and brimstone all right, but hidden in lacy groves. Boys hanging from the most beautiful sycamores in the world. It shamed her—remembering the wonderful soughing trees rather than the boys. Try as she might to make it otherwise, the sycamores beat out the children every time and she could not forgive her memory for that.

In this book, the other world exists and magic works, and the prose is up to it. If you can believe page one—and Ms. Morrison's verbal authority compels belief—you're hooked on the rest of the book.

The epigraph to *Beloved* is from the Bible, Romans 9:25: "I will call them my people, which were not my people; and her beloved, which was not beloved." Taken by itself, this might seem to favor doubt about, for instance, the extent to which Beloved was really loved, or the extent to which Sethe herself was rejected by her own community. But there is more to it than that. The passage is from a chapter in which the Apostle Paul ponders, Job-like, the ways of God toward humanity, in particular the evils and inequities visible everywhere on the earth. Paul goes on to talk about the fact that the Gentiles, hitherto despised and outcast, have now been redefined as acceptable. The passage proclaims, not rejection, but reconciliation and hope. It continues: "And it shall come to pass, that in the place where it was said unto them, Ye are not my people; there shall they be called the children of the living God."

Toni Morrison is too smart, and too much of a writer, not to have intended this context. Here, if anywhere, is her own comment on the goings-on in her novel, her final response to the measuring and dividing and excluding the Schoolteachers of this world. An epigraph to a book is like a key signature in music, and *Beloved* is written in B major.

JAZZ (1992)

◆◆◆◆◆◆◆◆◆◆◆◆◆

JOHN LEONARD

The Nation, May 25, 1992

From a newspaper clipping about a fugitive slave in Ohio who killed her own infant rather than see her returned to bondage in the South—"Now she would never know what a woman suffers as a slave . . . I will go singing to the gallows"—Toni Morrison made *Beloved*. From a photograph in James Van der Zee's *Harlem Book of the Dead* of the body of a young girl, shot at a party by a jealous boyfriend, who died refusing to identify her assailant ("I'll tell you tomorrow"), Toni Morrison has made *Jazz*. All you need is radiance and genius.

In Harlem, in 1926, a 50-year-old sample-case beauty products salesman falls in "deepdown spooky love" with a high school girl for whom "everything was like a picture show . . . and she was the one on the railroad track, or the one trapped in the sheik's tent when it caught on fire." She goes dancing without him, so he shoots her. And then his crazy wife, who irons hair, will crash the funeral and try with a knife to disfigure the dead girl's face. To find out why any of this happened, all of it on the first page of *Jazz*, you'll have to listen to the end of Morrison's song—as if Sidney Bechet had met the Archduke Trio; as if Ellington had gone Baroque.

You will get the City, designed for tall dreams, electric danger and getting away with it; for desire instead of love; for smelling good and "looking raunchy." You will get the music of colored men who float down from the sky blowing saxophones; rooftop clarinets and drums for the dead, and a flourish of fingered horns in the barrel hooch, juke joint and tonk house; the six-stringed blues guitar and a brass cut so fine "you would have thought everything had been forgiven." You'll hear about newspapers like *The Messenger* and *The Crisis*, unions like the Pullman Porters, political parties like the Readjustors, race riots like East St. Louis's; about polishing shoes, rolling tobacco and selling #2 Nut Brown door to door, along with a vanishing cream. You will have to swim back from this risky city, against the migratory tide, South again to Virginia, the sugarcane and hibiscus; the mules and possums and walnut trees; a butter press, a broken plow, a rainbow and a fox; a blade of blackbirds and a portent of redwings and a tree on a river called Treason whose roots grow backward, climbing toward leaves and wind and light; a cave where one mother is a wild thing, and a well where another mother drowns.

Jazz is a book of dispossession and of haunting. Novel by novel, Toni Morrison reimagines the lost history of her people, their love and work and nightmare passage and redemptive music. It's a brilliant project, a ghostly chorale, a constellation of humming spheres with its own gravity and now this brand-new star, which is even trickier than usual. If jazz is a music the performer composes himself, then this novel she calls *Jazz* is a book that composes itself: "I have watched your face for a long time now, and missed your eyes when you went away from me." It also *surprises* itself. But I'll get to that modernist wickedness in a minute.

> If anything I do, in the way of writing novels (or whatever I write), isn't about the village or the community or about you, then it is not about anything. I am not interested in indulging myself in some private, closed exercise of my imagination that fulfills only the obligation of my personal dreams—which is to say yes, the work must be political. . . . It seems to be that the best art is political and you ought to be able to make it unquestionably political and irrevocably beautiful at the same time.

Beautiful, certainly. I find that I want to roll around in Morrison's books, not a reviewer but an epicure, even a voluptuary. Give me, instead of overviews, her banquet of buttercakes and babies' ghosts, conjuring and "graveyard loves," Chicken Little and cooked flesh, a spittle-web of spiders and the breath of snakes, laws of hospitality and "men with the long-distance eyes"—after which, I want to fall into that Shadrack sleep "deeper than the hospital drugs; deeper than the pits of plums, steadier than the condor's wing; more tranquil than the curve of eggs." This, of course, isn't criticism; it's gourmandizing. But don't you already know as much as you want to about African oral traditions, Uncle Remus, sermons, slave songs and the blues?

Morrison has said that their music no longer belongs exclusively to her people, so novels are going to have to sing those origin myths and archetypes. I suppose that is what happened to Zora Neale Hurston once she grew out of Franz Boas: *Mules and Men* for the space age; *Their Eyes Were Watching God.* She presumes Phillis Wheatley, Lucy Terry and Harriet E. Wilson; Jessie Fauset, Georgia Douglass Jackson and Alice Childress; Paule Marshall and Gwendolyn Brooks; plus Harriet Tubman, Sojourner Truth, Rosa Parks and Fannie Lou Hamer. She also presumes Richard Wright, James Baldwin, Ralph Ellison and their brilliant literature of grievance. She presumes, as well, the Bible and Shakespeare. She ate Faulkner for a snack.

In what way, though, is she political? She never bothers to explain to her readers the epidemiology and the ecosystems of racist oppression;

they already know that stuff. But eavesdrop on this art—"You don't listen to people," Circe dissed Milkman; "your ear is on your head, but it's not connected to your brain"—and you hear about an Other America bearing no resemblance to such salacious confabulations as a "culture of poverty" and an affectless "underclass." She's not some Sojourner Dante, touring the limbos of welfare motherhood, circling a crackhead hell. Her people aren't *victims*, at least not pathologies; they have choices and resources, styles and survival skills, and their own business to get on with, inside the white whale that swallowed them. Except in *Tar Baby* and *Beloved*, Morrison's white folks are outside the main action of her characters. "We" are their bad weather and bad luck. Just as her sex and violence are mystified (become pity, howling, rainbows, waste), so the dominant culture is oddly, almost mischievously, abstracted—like probability theory (or maybe Neoplatonism). Such overt political action as occurs (a protest march in *Sula*, assassins in *Song of Solomon*, the mournful drums in *Jazz*) seems always peripheral to some other drama of baffled hopes, family wounds, confused paternity, broken connection or historical amnesia, in a separate republic of dreams. But inside this republic, what goes on is identity-making. And if we don't understand that identity is political, we don't understand anything at all.

How does it feel to a white reader to be bad luck, like chemicals in a lake? As if we're not, every minute of the day, so important? As if maybe there were complicated reasons for a Malcolm X, as there are for a Louis Farrakhan; and as if, for equally complicated reasons, Josephine Baker has more resonance than Madonna? When Sula makes fun of poor black Jude, the rest of us (that's everybody male and pale who's ever appeared in a suit, a tie and a Beltway blisterpack on Ted Koppel's *Nightline*) are merely incidental. "I mean," says Sula,

> I don't know what the fuss is about. I mean, everything in the world loves you. White men love you. They spend so much time worrying about your penis they forget their own. The only thing they want to do is cut off a nigger's privates. And if that ain't love and respect I don't know what is. And white women? They chase you all to every corner of the earth, feel for you under every bed. . . . Now ain't that love? They think rape soon's they see you, and if they don't get the rape they looking for, they scream it anyway just so the search won't be in vain. Colored women worry themselves into bad health just trying to hang on to your cuffs. Even little children—white and black, boys and girls—spend all their childhood eating their hearts out 'cause they think you don't love them. And if that ain't enough, you love yourselves. Nothing in this world loves a black man more than another black man. You hear of solitary white men, but niggers? Can't stay away from one another a whole day. So. It looks to me like you the envy of the world.

Worse, what could be more political than the fact that Morrison—with her wit, poetry and passion, breadth of sympathy, depth of feeling, range of interest, grasp of detail, powers of imaginative transformation, command of time, character, scruple, generosity and radiance, and magical mastery of the Mother Tongue—turns out to be the best writer working in America?

We should have known she was something special from virtually the first sentences of her first novel, *The Bluest Eye* (1970): "Quiet as it's kept, there were no marigolds in the fall of 1941. We thought, at the time, that it was because Pecola was having her father's baby that the marigolds did not grow." The surprise now, after the celebrity that scars and seals, is that back in 1970 she'd wanted to call herself by her *given* name, Chloe Anthony Wofford, but failed to persuade her publisher in time. Considering how crucial names always are in her fiction—Breedlove, Peace and Soaphead Church; Ajax and Jade; Baby Suggs and Stamp Paid—this looks stranger as the years go by. Naming, after all, is one of the great orchestral themes of *Song of Solomon:* If not for a Pilate and a Guitar, Macon (Milkman) Dead would not have learned to fly.

But the becoming was there to begin with, in this End-of-Childhood novel: the community and the scapegoat; caste and class; rootedness and the supernatural; prose you can sing as well as read; dreams of flight and transfiguration. Pecola imagines that if only she had blue eyes, she'd be as lovable as Shirley Temple was to Bojangles. She ends up crazy, "beating the air, a winged but grounded bird . . . picking and plucking her way between the tire rims and the sunflowers, between Coke bottles and milkweed, among all the waste and beauty of the world."

Who will mother poor Pecola, when her own mother cares more about the little white girl in the house she cleans? Not Claudia, a faithless friend. Not the sugar-brown hollyhocks girls from Meridian and Mobile who straighten their hair with Dixie peach and wash with Lifebuoy to rid themselves of "the dreadful funkiness of passion." Nor even those avatars of Black Motherhood who once upon a time felled trees, cut umbilical cords, loaded bales, rocked babies, plowed all day and came home nights "to nestle like plums under the limbs of their men." These avatars have declared themselves unavailable, past "lust and lactation, beyond tears and terror." Something's missing in this Lorain, Ohio, of kerosene lamps and dandelion soup and whores with names like Poland and China. Everybody seems to want Pecola's baby dead—"in a dark, wet place, its head covered with great O's of wool, the black face holding, like nickels, two clean black eyes, the flared nose, kissing-thick lips, and the living, breathing silk of black skin."

What's missing, as we will discover later on in Morrison's novels, is some figure like the Ancestor, that elder—down South, back in Africa—who connects her questing characters to the wisdom and solace of the textured past; the logic of lions. If Cholly Breedlove, *even* Cholly Breedlove, on his Georgia passage to find his father, had discovered such an Ancestor, he might never have raped his daughter. Cholly, instead, seems to be predicting *Jazz:*

> The pieces of Cholly's life could become coherent only in the head of a musician. Only those who talk their talk through the gold of curved metal, or in the touch of black-and-white rectangles and taut skins and strings echoing from wooden corridors, could give true form to his life. Only they would know how to connect the heart of a red watermelon to the asafetida bag to the muscadine to the flashlight . . . and come up with what all of that meant in joy, in pain, in anger, in love, and give it its final and pervading ache of freedom. Only a musician would sense, know, without even knowing that he knew, that Cholly was free. Dangerously free.

Sula flew away to big cities like Nashville and New York and came back, a plague of robins. "In that place, where they tore the nightshade and blackberry patches from their roots to make room for the Medallion City Golf Course, there was once a neighborhood." In *Sula* (1973), this neighborhood, a Bottom in the hills above an Ohio rivertown, is the narrator, a kind of chorus. It has its ways of dealing with crazies like Shadrack, witches like Sula, and white folk like us:

> They did not believe doctors could heal—for them, none had ever done so. They did not believe death was accidental—life might be, but death was deliberate. They did not believe Nature was ever askew—only inconvenient. Plague and drought were as "natural" as spring-time. If milk could curdle, God knows robins could fall. The purpose of evil was to survive it and they determined (without ever knowing they had made up their minds to do it) to survive floods, white people, tuberculosis, famine and ignorance. They knew anger well but not despair, and they didn't stone sinners for the same reason they didn't commit suicide—it was beneath them.

Which isn't to say that these stoical communities are invariably wise. There's something self-serving about their forbearance. ("As Reverend Deal moved into his sermon, the hands of the women unfolded like pairs of raven's wings and flew high above their hats in the air. . . . And they saw the Lamb's eye and the truly innocent victim: themselves.") They've a taste for scapegoats and pariahs. Lorain, after all, failed Pecola. Medallion feels better about itself with Sula around to behave so badly. Sula, who caused an innocent child to drown; Sula, who stole her best friend's husband; Sula, who watched her mother burn to death; Sula, with the flowering birthmark that seems to Nel a rose, to Jude a snake, to Shadrack a fish—this Sula, laughing at their God, is "the most magnificent hatred" the Bottom has ever known. They lay broomsticks across their doors at night, sprinkle salt on porch steps. But no more than failed crops, sick children, rednecks, social workers or plague, will this strange young woman "keep them from their God."

Some God. No wonder the rain freezes, silvering Medallion. And Nel cries "a fine cry—loud and long—but it had no bottom and it had no top, just circles and circles of sorrow."

But Sula *isn't* evil: "Had she paints or clay, or knew the discipline of the dance, or strings; had she anything to engage her tremendous curiosity and her gift for metaphor, she might have exchanged the restlessness and preoccupation with whim for an activity that provided her with all she yearned for. And like any artist with no art form, she became dangerous." Whatever she found *elsewhere*, even South, it wasn't sufficient; it wasn't Ancestral. Only the Bottom will take her back in, and even Nel lets her down. Still, Morrison needs this return of the prodigal daughter as much as Nel, "like getting the use of an eye back." Who else can love as Sula loves Ajax?

> If I take a chamois and rub real hard on the bone, right on the ledge of your cheek bone, some of the black will disappear. It will flake away into the chamois and underneath there will be gold leaf. I can see it shining through the black. I know it is there. . . .
>
> And if I take a nail file or even Eva's old paring knife—that will do—and scrape away at the gold, it will fall away and there will be alabaster. The alabaster is what gives your face its planes, its curves. That is why your mouth smiling does not reach your eyes. Alabaster is giving it a gravity that resists a total smile. . . .
>
> Then I can take a chisel and small tap hammer and tap away at the alabaster. It will crack then like ice under the pick, and through the breaks I will see the loam, fertile, free of pebbles and twigs. For it is the loam that is giving you that smell.

Already with this black, gold and alabaster, three Deweys and one-legged Eva in her wagon, a plague of robins and a ghostly ball of fur, hair and muddy strings floating in the light, we have moved out of Faulkner and into García Márquez, where the mindscapes are miraculous.

For instance, blue silk wings and red velvet rose petals and a bag of human bones; a horse named President Lincoln, a cow named Grant and a hog named General Lee; peacocks and bobcats and a spice-sweet ginger smell at night "that made you think of the East and striped tents and the *sha-sha-sha* of leg bracelets . . . the way freedom smelled, or justice, or luxury, or vengeance." If her other novels circle, and they do, *Song of Solomon* (1977) soars—from Not Doctor Street and No Mercy Hospital on Detroit's Southside, "where even love found its way with an ice pick"; to a ruined plantation, a cave of the dead and a witch named Circe, on the Susquehanna; to Shalimar, on nobody's map of Virginia, where everybody's name is Solomon and the children sing a riddle-song that proves on its decoding to be all about how you can ride the very air to Africa.

To be sure, we hear about Macon Dead Jr.'s moneymaking from his rent-houses and the lakeshore vacation cabins he builds for the black bourgeoisie. And we go with his son into bars and barbershops, to talk about Kennedy and Elijah and meet those Seven Days assassins who revenge themselves for Emmett Till and Birmingham. ("Hitler's the most natural white man in the world," says Guitar: "He killed Jews and Gypsies because he didn't have us.") We're vouchsafed details on life insurance, raffle tickets, policy slips, bootlegging, Playtex garterbelts and pink-veined marble, Dairy Queens and Belgian silk brocade, White Castles and domestic dread.

But *Song of Solomon* is really about naming, especially the ghosts. Macon Dead III is called "Milkman" because his mother nursed him a lot longer than, decently, she should have. But his father is Macon Dead Jr. and his grandfather was Macon Dead period, because of a drunken Union soldier on the journey north in a wagonload of ex-slaves. His aunt is called Pilate, his sisters Magdalene and First Corinthians, and his cousins Reba and Hagar because that's where the finger pointed in the family Bible. Circe asks Milkman, "Where'd you get a name like yours? White people name Negroes like race horses." Guitar says, "Niggers get their names the way they get everything else—the best way they can." Milkman thinks of the names black men got "from yearning, gestures, flaws, events, mistakes, weaknesses. Names that bore witness." His father dreams of an ancestor with onyx skin and "a name that was real. A name given to him at birth with love and seriousness. A name that was not a joke nor a disguise, nor a brand name."

This is the name Milkman discovers, where Charlemagne turns into Shalimar, and Sugarman to Solomon, and the ghost who cries out "Sing!" is actually naming his Indian wife. Like a sort of bodhisattva-wannabe out of *Dream of the Red Chamber*, Milkman escapes his Northern matriarchy into this lush South of peaches and turkeys and Calvins and Luthers, where he finds in folk memory and child-song not only a black Daedalus but his own lost grandfather, who came to freedom "out of nowhere, as ignorant as a hammer and broke as a convict," and tamed the wilderness, and so, of course, "they shot the top of his head off."

Never mind that Guitar waits with a gun. Or whether we can altogether admire a Daedalus who flies, no frills, to Africa, leaving behind his wife and kids. What's compelling here is that, while Milkman never meets Solomon/Daedalus or his ghostly grandfather Jake, he does at last recognize his own Aunt Pilate. Pilate got him to go South, into American history and racial memory. Pilate born without a navel ("a stomach as bald as a knee"); wearing her own name on a scrap of paper in the brass snuffbox earring; keeper of the eggs and bones; having hoed, fished, plowed and planted, grown vegetables, picked fruit, raised cattle, sold tobacco, made whiskey and talked to the dead—Pilate is the Ancestor, the Identity-Maker, an agency of levitation.

I fell off the truck with *Tar Baby* (1981). It still seems overly didactic, somehow brittle, her only novel you can't sing, the least operative. Maybe if it had been more about Thérèse and Gideon and less about Jade, the model who has been to Paris, or Son, the dreadlocked drifter who wants only to go home again, I might have had more patience with her Caribbean island and its fearful fish, puzzled clouds, stingless bees, rain forests full of angel women and ghosts of blind slaves; the various royalties (Catherine the Great, Valerian, Maria Theresa) and so many sugar metaphors; all that anthropology and Caliban; Will Shakespeare meets Uncle Remus.

But Jade looks into the eyes of the wife-killer with the "Mau Mau, Attica, chain-gang hair" and sees "spaces, mountains, savannas." And Son looks into the eyes of this arty young woman who thinks "Picasso *is* better than an Itumba mask" and sees "gold, cloisonné and honey-colored silk." He won't like imperial New York, she'll *hate* down-home Eloe, and the rest is soldier ants.

Not quite, of course. There are wonderful arias in *Tar Baby* (about stolen labor, insupportable innocence and, warming up for *Jazz*, black women in the big city); and some licorice-stick lyricism ("the fruit of the banana trees puffed up and stiff like the fingers of gouty kings"); and Valerian may be right when he says that the typical anthropologist is "a purveyor of exotics . . . a cultural orphan who sought other cultures he could love without risk or pain."

Must, however, a white woman torture her baby while a white man listens to the Goldberg Variations in a greenhouse? When Jade gets stuck in tar, couldn't we have gotten along without those tree-women with "their sacred properties," their "pace of glaciers" and their smug faith "that they alone could hold together the stones of pyramids"? Just the news; hold the Gaia. Would Toni Morrison, after all she's done, want to live in Eloe any more than Jade does? I am sorry that for Son there'll never be lions or a mating dance; that he's stuck with dice instead of tusks, a job instead of a journey. But those are the breaks. I'd like to have been Druid myself.

About Son and Jade, we're read this lesson: "One had a past, the other a future and each one bore the culture to save the race in his hands. Mama-spoiled black man, will you mature with me? Culture-bearing black woman, whose culture are you bearing?" While it's a lesson sufficient to float most modern novels, it seems thin for a Toni Morrison. She lets Son off too easily; and she denies, to Jade, all that leftover Sula.

But now we get a masterwork. *Beloved* (1988) imagines what's left out of the slave narratives. Morrison even went to Brazil to look at choke-collars and leg-irons you won't find in any of *our* museums, and then she wrote a ghost story about history. At its center is an act as awful as anything reported by the Hebrews, the Greeks or the Elizabethans. Inside *Beloved*'s circle of space/time—spellbound, dream-dazed—the living and the dead talk to and lay hands upon each other. Madness and memory cohabit. From this history, like a collective unconscious, the dead, like the repressed, return.

Though the novel begins in 1873, it has more than twenty years of explaining to do before we understand how Sethe, her 19-year-old daughter Denver and a ghost happen to be hiding from the neighbors and the past at 124 Bluestone Road in Cincinnati. We must go back to Sweet Home, Kentucky, in the early 1850s. Sethe, a teenage mother then, pregnant with her fourth child, remembers Sweet Home so: two white boys "with mossy teeth, one sucking my breast, the other holding me down, their bookreading teacher watching and writing it up." And the cowhide that left a scar-tree on her back that flowered red roses. And black boys "hanging from the most beautiful sycamore trees in the world." The flight as if from Egypt; Denver's birth in a boat, "under four summer stars" on the river passage to the free state of Ohio; and "one whole moon" of "unslaved life" before Schoolteacher on horseback arrived and Sethe like a black Medea raised her handsaw and Denver swallowed her sister's blood "right along with my mother's milk."

And this is what Paul D, "last of the Sweet Home men," recalls of Schoolteacher, Georgia prisons, the Civil War and his years on the road till Sethe; Sethe's husband, with his crazed head in the butter churn, "greased and flat-eyed as a fish"; Sixo, who had stopped speaking English "because there was no future in it," set on fire; a three-spoke neck collar and an iron mouth-bit; the rockpile and the chain gang; sleeping in coffins, hiding in caves and fighting for food with owls and pigs; bad whiskey, hissing grass, "song-murders," "laughing dead men" and "a witless colored woman jailed and hanged for stealing ducks she believed were her babies."

Paul D wants to put his story, of "sucking iron," right next to Sethe's story, of stolen milk and river passage, and imagine a future for them. But first he must chase the ghost out of the house. The ghost—a spiteful "pool of red and undulating light" that tips tables and leaves palmprints on the butter—is, of course, Sethe's murdered baby. Once chased, she'll be replaced by a huge young woman, risen from the water with "midnight skin," sugar-devouring, diamond-hungry, exactly the age Sethe's baby, grown up, would be: Beloved. And Beloved chases Paul D.

What chance have Paul D and Sethe? From his travels Paul knows it's best to love everything "just a little bit, so when they broke its back, or shoved it in a croaker sack, well, maybe you'll have a little love left over for the next one." Sethe misbelieves that "the future was a matter of keeping the past at bay"; her love is "too thick." Even the land isn't theirs. Sethe can't forgive herself for recalling the sycamores before she recalls the black boys hanging from them: "It made her wonder if hell was a pretty place too."

Morrison does a thousand splendid things in her circling. She introduces us for instance to Baby Suggs, Sethe's mother-in-law, the Ancestor, who used to preach of grace before she became ashamed of God and retired "to ponder colors" on her quilt, deciding, "There is no bad luck in the world but white folks." And to Amy, a barefoot white girl on her way to Boston to look for velvet, stopping just long enough to put spider webs on the bloody tree on Sethe's back and deliver Denver. And also to Stamp Paid: watchman, soldier, spy, busybody, tormented by the song and sadness of "the people of the broken necks, of fire-cooked blood and black girls who had lost their ribbons."

She acquaints us too with the unendingness of women's work, even out of slavery: at home, wringing out sheets "so tight the rinse water ran back up their arms," shoveling snow from the path to the outhouse, breaking ice from the rain barrel, scouring and boiling last summer's canning jars, packing mud in the hen house cracks and warming chicks with their skirts. Away from home, besides the cradling of white babies, there's laundry at the orphanage or asylum; corn shucking at the mill; fish to clean, offal to rinse, stores to sweep, lard to press, sausage to case-pack and tavern kitchens to hide in so white folks "didn't have to see them handle their food."

In fact, instead, these women gather in front of 124 (a way station, after all, for fugitive slaves, a place where history stopped), and their voices search "for the right combination," the code that breaks the back of words. When they find it there's "a wave of sound wide enough to sound deep water and knock the pods off chestnut trees. It broke over Sethe and she trembled like the baptized in its wash." Beloved, "a naked woman with fish for hair," "thunder black and glistening," runs from the house to the woods and the river and is gone. Exorcised. For now.

Amazing how all these little words of one, two or three syllables, strung together beadlike, turn into a necklace or a whip. (Shakespeare did it, too.) Put them together with the Baby Suggs "appetite for color" and helpful Cherokee Indians. Add Paul's longing "to get to a place where you could love anything you chose—not to need permission for desire." And find a woman like Sixo's: "a friend of my mind. . . . She gather me, man. The pieces I am, she gather them and give them back to me in all the right order. It's good, you know, when you got a woman who is a friend of your mind." But not in this history, which is out of happy endings.

Ghost story, history lesson, mother-epic, incantation, folk and fairy tale—of lost children and men on horseback; a handsaw, an icepick and a wishing well; Denver's "emerald light" and Amy's velvet; spiders and roosters and the madness of hummingbirds with needle beaks as dead babies are offered up to a shameful God; a devouring past of everything that is unforgiven and denied; a hunger to eat all the love in the world— Beloved belongs on the highest shelf of our literature even if half a dozen canonized Wonder Bread Boys have to be elbowed off. I can't now picture our literature without it, between Whitman and Twain, the Other in Faulkner, an African Flannery O'Connor, and who knows what other cultures she's looked into, which masks she's put on like a shaman, her secret antihistamines. Where was this book that we've always needed? Without Beloved, our imagination of America had a heart-sized hole in it big enough to die from. It didn't win every prize it deserved, and the word was that some of the critics didn't believe in ghosts. Like Shakespeare's clowns and Freud's dreams, Morrison's ghosts always tell the truth. If I had voted against *Beloved*, I'd find it convenient, too, not to believe in ghosts.

"Watch out for her; she can give you dreams." (Denver to Beloved, about their mother.)

Back to *Jazz:* Joe Trace, besides cosmetics, sells trust: "I make things easy." He has a sad eye "that let you look inside him, and a clear one that looks inside you." In his opinion, his wife, Violet, "takes better care of her parrot than she does me. Rest of the time, she's cooking pork I can't eat, or pressing hair I can't stand the smell of." He wishes he could remember their young love, coming north from Virginia, but has a tough time "trying to catch what it felt like." He tries to dismiss "the evil in my thoughts" because he isn't sure "the sooty music the blind twins were playing wasn't the cause. It can do that to you, a certain kind of guitar playing. Not like the clarinets, but close." What Joe wants at age 50 is to be free, not "to break loaves or feed the world on a fish. Nor to raise the war dead, but free to do something wild." In this, the City conspires.

Names again: Joe's name is "Trace" because when he was abandoned down South as a baby, his parents "left without a trace." He is that Trace.

Violet had her spells even before Joe met Dorcas: falling down in the street through "dark fissures in the globe light of the day"; conversations in her head with a corpse; "tears coming so fast she needs two hands to catch them." Once, she even stole a baby. But, mostly, till she went to Dorcas's funeral, she ironed hair and took care of her birds, who got to look at themselves in mirrors she arranged, including a parrot who said "Love you!" When she learns of Joe and Dorcas, she loses the birds and finds a knife. Later, she'll laugh at herself, "trying to do something bluesy, something hep, fumbling the knife, too late anyway." But the abandoned parrot keeps on crying at the window pane, in the snow: "Love you!" And the mirrors have nothing to look at.

"The children of suicides," we are told, "are hard to please and quick to believe no one loves them because they are not really here."

Dorcas, exactly like Josephine Baker, is a child of the East St. Louis race riots, which consumed her clothespin dolls and her parents. She's taken in by her Aunt Alice, who makes clothes (and do) while hating the City and the "complicated anger" and the "appetite" of its "dirty, get-on-down music." But this music, that "bends, falls to its knees to embrace them all, encourage them all . . . why don't you? since this is the it you've been looking for," is all Dorcas cares about besides movies and looking good, with her pencil-thin eyebrows and green shoes, despite "hoof marks" on her cheeks from acne. Is Dorcas the child Violet miscarried, or the one she tried to steal, or maybe Violet herself, equally motherless, archetypal orphan? Mothers and ghosts!

In *Jazz*, they are all trying to change the way they look, or in business to change the way somebody else looks, even with a knife.

So, too, is the City. Morrison has lived in New York City ever since she stopped teaching English to Stokely Carmichael and Claude Brown, down at Howard, in the nation's capital. But the only time she ever wrote of it till now was, briefly, in *Tar Baby*, where Son was bewildered and Jade transcendent: "New York oiled her joints and she moved as though they were oiled. Her legs were longer here, her neck really connected her body to her head." *Jazz*, though, sings the City like a Whitman—"thriftless, warm, scary and full of amiable strangers"; the razor-slant of daylight and night skies gone so purple with an orange heart that "the clothes of the people on the streets glow like dance-hall costumes"; "bright steel rocking above the shade below" and blocks, lots and side streets where what goes on is "anything the strong can think of and the weak will admire"; where there's a breath each morning that brightens the eye, the talk and the expectations like laughing gas; where "in halls and offices people are sitting around thinking future thoughts about projects and bridges and fast-clicking trains underneath," because "History is over, you all, and everything's ahead at last." To this city black people came, from "want and violence," and stayed, "to look at their number, hear themselves in an audience, feel themselves moving down the street among hundreds of others who moved the way they did, and who, when they spoke, regardless of the accent, treated language like the same intricate, malleable toy designed for their play."

Joe and Violet rode north in 1906 in the colored section of the Southern Sky:

> When the train trembled approaching the water surrounding the City, they thought it was like them: nervous at having gotten there at last, but terrified of what was on the other side. . . . The quick darkness in the carriage cars when they shot through a tunnel made them wonder if maybe there was a wall ahead to crash into or a cliff hanging over nothing. The train shivered with them at the thought . . . and the trembling became the dancing under their feet. Joe stood up, his fingers clutching the baggage rack above his head. He felt the dancing better that way.

And so the young country couple "laughing and tapping back at the tracks," danced into the City, which is itself a kind of jazz improvising its days and nights and blues, its dangerous freedom. And here they are—after the railroad flat in the Tenderloin, working domestic service and white folks' shoe leather, the cleaning of fish at night and of toilets in the daytime, the riots of 1917—in a Harlem in 1926 where there are mailboxes but no high schools, bootleggers but no banks. And suddenly, a Dorcas. When Joe went looking for the little tramp with a gun, who was he really missing? When Violet went with a knife to the funeral, who was she really cutting up?

If you know Toni Morrison at all by now, you know she'll go South again; if need be, all the way back to antebellum, not only for the servitude, the foreclosures, the lynchings and the mutilations but for those ghostly waters and that bag of ancestral bones. For that phantom father who came home at last from his politicking with his gold ingots, reed whistles, dollars bills and a tin of Frieda's Egyptian Hair Pomade, too late to save Violet's mother, Rose Dear, from throwing herself down a well "so narrow, so dark it was pure, breathing relief to see her stretched in a wooden box." For the trail of ruined honeycombs, bits and leavings of stolen victuals, the blue-black birds with the bolt of red on their wings and the gopher-freezing music of running water and high-tree wind, in search of Wild, *Joe's* mother, and her secret cave and her circle of stones and buttons of bone. This is the South of their own minds: why Joe has eyes of different colors and Violet falls through cracks, and what the music's all about—"I could hear," we are told by the Voice that narrates *Jazz*, "the men playing out their maple-sugar hearts, tapping it from four-hundred-year-old trees and letting it run down the trunk, wasting it because they didn't have a bucket to hold it and didn't want one either"—and why, when she bleeds to death, even Dorcas, while seeing the bright oranges, also hears something: "Listen. I don't know who is that woman singing but I know the words by heart." It is also, of course, the ultimate South of Sula: past black and gold and alabaster, down to the fertile loam and a song of reconciliation.

I haven't even mentioned Malvonne, who lives alone with "other people's stories printed in small books," or her nephew Sweetness, who steals uncanceled letters from the Post Office. Nor Neola, partly paralyzed since her fiancé abandoned her, "as though she held the broken pieces of her heart together in the crook of a frozen arm." Nor True Belle and Vera Lee and Golden Gray, whose own father comes as such a shock. Nor Hunter, nor Acton, and not even Felice, who is everything that Dorcas wasn't, and whose father is happy working on the Pullman. No matter what our narrator tells us is going to happen after Felice enters the novel, "with an Okeh record under her arms and carrying some stewmeat wrapped in butcher paper, another girl with four marcelled waves on either side of her head," nobody *this* time is going to shoot *anybody*.

You will have to think about who's telling you this story, and I might as well admit I got too clever doing so. Picking up on the epigraph to *Jazz*—from "Thunder, Perfect Mind" in *The Nag Hammadi*—and knowing that Morrison now spends part of every week at Princeton with Elaine Pagels, who wrote the book on *The Gnostic Gospels*, I said, alas, "Aha!" "Thunder, Perfect Mind" is the revelation of a *feminine* power: "I am the whore, and the holy one. I am the wife and the virgin. I am [the mother] and the daughter . . ." And so on. All this missed the obvious point.

This Voice, with a "sweettooth" for pain, complains that she hasn't any muscles so can't defend herself; has lived too long in her own mind, really ought to get out more, but is tired of having been "left standing" while her partner falls asleep; accuses herself of carelessness when things go wrong; wants to "dream a nice dream" for the reader and "be the language that wishes him well, speaks his name, wakes him when his eyes need to be open"; feels predictable and even a bit false—"What would I be without a few brilliant spots of blood to ponder?"—and apostrophizes:

> I love the way you hold me, how close you let me be to you. I like your fingers on and on, lifting, turning. I have watched your face for a long time now, and missed your eyes when you went away from me.

It finally occurred to me that I wasn't being talked to by a goddess, or a clarinet: "If I were able I'd say it. Say make me, remake me. You are free to do it and I am free to let you because look, look. Look where your hands are. Now." Where my hands were *then* was holding on to my copy of *Jazz*. And, of course, the Voice is the book itself, this physical object, our metatext . . . a whimsy and a wickedness worthy of a Nabokov. And out of this Pandora's box comes not only "something rogue, something else you have to figure in before you can figure it out" but all the love in the world—the love that Beloved was so hungry for, and Pecola never got from anybody, and Joe Trace thought he couldn't remember, and Sula knew would come to her only after "Lindbergh sleeps with Bessie Smith and Norma Shearer makes it with Stepin Fetchit"; even Hagar's "graveyard love" for Milkman, the kind that made "women pull their dresses over their heads and howl like dogs" and sat men down in doorways "with pennies in their mouths"; but most of all, with a wink and all that radiance, Toni Morrison's surpassing love for her people and her readers.

Jazz, yes; but also Mozart.

EDNA O'BRIEN

The New York Times Book Review, April 5, 1992

We are with Joe, Violet and Dorcas, the temptress whose melting shadow stalks the pages of Toni Morrison's latest novel, "Jazz." We are with youth versus age, sterility versus sex, the swamps versus the gaudy hubbub of "city."

At night in their musty apartment in Harlem, Joe and Violet, the husband and wife, get up intermittently to study the photograph of the dead girl and respond with mutterings of love, jealousy and bile. Violet, the wronged wife, is a many-faceted creature and, like Hermann Hesse's Steppenwolf, admits to many selves within herself, occasionally stumbling into a psychotic limbo. There is also Felice, Dorcas's friend, looking in on this triangular stew and on love itself, which she craves because "that's the kick." The effect is of a prism being held up before us in order to glimpse its shifting multifarious worlds.

Joe, purveyor of illusion, sells Cleopatra Cosmetics, and thus finds Dorcas and beds her clandestinely in an apartment not far from the bedroom where he and Violet had their youthful nighttime fiestas. In a fit of passion Joe shoots Dorcas, but because nobody sees him do it, Alice, her aunt and guardian, decides not "to throw money to helpless lawyers or laughing cops." Come the fateful day Violet takes a butcher's knife to Dorcas's face in the funeral parlor, is intercepted and later lets loose her pet birds into the snow, rather in the manner of the eccentric Miss Flite in Dickens's *Bleak House*.

This however, is not Victorian England, but Harlem in the 1920's, Harlem still relatively innocent, when crimes at least were crimes of passion and pity in some currency, Harlem permeated with the thrum of music, Harlem to which those black people who had run from want and violence came to find their stronger, riskier selves. In Ms. Morrison's robust language we see the sidewalks, the curbstones, Egyptian beads, Kansas fried chicken, doors ajar to speakeasies, an invitation to the low-down hellfire induction of music and sex.

In this and many audacious asides the author conjures up worlds with complete authority. She captures and makes no secret of her anger at the injustices dealt to black women who were mothers, serving women and corpse dressers, women who found refuge only in an angry church and an angry God and for whom pregnancy was worse than death. But young Violet and young Joe caught in their youthful heat had no wish for babies, so that "those miscarriages—two in the field, only one in her bed—were more inconvenience than loss."

But loss bites in strange ways. Years later, when doing the rounds with her pins and her curling tongs as a home hairdresser, Violet is kept waiting on a step and on impulse resolves to filch a baby from a pram. Her plan is thwarted but the longing remains, and the absence of a baby—or should I say the presence of an absent baby?—forms the undertow of this book. Joe in his errant way is also seeking youth, drawn as he is to a girl who, from the earliest age and perhaps in some blind premonition, cultivated the dynamics beneath her skirts.

After the murder and the outburst in the funeral parlor, Violet luxuriates in the thralldom of jealousy, picturing them in the Indigo, "the

heifer" at the round table, the stem of the glass in one hand and her other hand drumming out the rhythms "on the inside of his thigh, his thigh, his thigh, thigh, thigh." In time, her jealousy abating, Violet insinuates herself into the aunt's house to draw her out in descriptions of the girl—her skin, her hair, her wiles, her come-hither. She finds herself becoming less irate, even deeming that she might like her. Of course that does not obliterate the hate and the gnawing recognition that she is old (she is over 50) and no man will want her again; all that is left is the talking.

In sharp compassionate vignettes, plucked from different episodes of their lives, the author portrays people who are together simply because they were put down together, people tricked for a while into believing that life would serve them, powerless to change their fate—Joe with a faithless wild woman for a mother, a woman he seeks in caves and rock faces, a woman he calls to and asks if she is she—"Just say it, say anything"; Violet unable to repress the seams of erotic memory, remembering the bed with one leg propped on a dictionary: and Dorcas, foxy, provocative, believing sex to be her trump card, which for a few months it was. These are people enthralled then deceived by "the music the world makes."

Do I miss something? Yes, I miss the emotional nexus, the moment shorn of all artifice that brings us headlong into the deepest recesses of feeling, moments such as in Faulkner's "Light in August," when the fugitive Joe Christmas takes to the road knowing that it will run on forever "between the savage and spurious board fronts of oil towns," or when Leopold Bloom, in the throes of a tender letter to his mistress, pauses to address his dead son with: "Love. Hate. These are words Rudy. Soon I am old," or when poor crazed Anna Karenina, observing the bolts and irons of the oncoming train, asks God to forgive her.

I say this because at one point in the novel when Violet and Alice are ruminating, Alice muses on her own woes, on the treachery done to her by another woman, on the blood punishment she meted out on the husband long since in his grave and, putting the pressing iron down, says, "You don't know what loss is." I have a sense of being told this, I do not feel it; my pity is withheld.

It is as if Ms. Morrison, bedazzled by her own virtuosity—a virtuosity that serves her and us and contemporary fiction very well—hesitates to bring us to the last frontier, to a predicament that is both physical and metaphysical, and which in certain fictions, by an eerie transmission, becomes our very own experience. Such alchemy does not occur here.

What remains are the bold arresting strokes of a poster and not the cold astonishment of a painting.

♦♦♦♦♦♦♦♦♦♦♦♦♦♦

HENRY LOUIS GATES, JR.

They lean over me and say:
"Who deathed you who,
who, who, who, who. . . .
I whisper: "Tell you presently . . .
Shortly . . . this evening . . .
Tomorrow . . ."
Tomorrow is here
And you out there safe.
I'm safe in here, Tootsie
                    —Owen Dodson

Music and literature, rivals of the arts, have not coexisted without intruding on each other's terrain. Since what we think of as "literature" had its origins as an oral, or chanted, art, the dance of language that is writing has coveted the status of its sister art, music: music, where form and content, image and idea, are one, indissolubly linked at creation. From classical ritual and its offspring, tragedy, all the way to opera and musicals, the boundary between music and literature has proven a dynamic site of interplay, and one that has engaged many of the greatest writers of this century, from Thomas Mann and Marcel Proust to James Joyce and Wole Soyinka.

All art, so Walter Pater averred, aspires to the condition of music; and nowhere is this maxim truer than in the African-American tradition, whose music is often thought of as its greatest achievement. Few musical traditions in this country have had more modern masters than has the African-American tradition, from the blues to rhythm-and-blues, from soul to rap, from ragtime to jazz. It is a commonplace that the achievement of black literature, as considerable as it is, does not rival the range and depth of its musical counterpart. And while many black writers have used musicians and music as theme and metaphor for their writing, none have attempted to draw upon jazz as the structuring principle for an entire novel. None, that is, until Toni Morrison's new novel, *Jazz*, a novel set in Harlem in 1926, so near to—yet so far away from—the black literary movement known as the New Negro, or Harlem Renaissance.

1926: In 1926, a renaissance in the arts created by a group of writers calling themselves "New Negroes" and centered in and about Harlem, was at its zenith. Wealthy white patrons and mainstream New York publishers were sponsoring young black writers as never before. Civil rights and political leaders had come to believe that it would be through the arts that full social, political, and—eventually—economic liberation for the black elite would come. As the *New York Herald Tribune* argued

in 1925, "We are on the edge, if not already in the midst, of what might not improperly be called a Negro Renaissance . . . and it would be one of fate's quaint but by no means impossible revenges if the Negro's real contribution to American life should be in the field of art." Centuries of the degrading oppression of slavery, the thought went, would be overturned in a decade through the most sublime achievements of the arts.

And it *was* a special time: for the first time, black writers were feted as literary lions. In 1926 alone, Langston Hughes published his jazz and blues poems in a volume entitled *The Weary Blues*, as well as his manifesto of black criticism, "The Negro Artist and the Racial Mountain." Hughes, the poet Countee Cullen, and the novelist Zora Neale Hurston launched their boldly experimental magazine, *Fire!!;* photographer and critic Carl Van Vechten published his controversial novel, *Nigger Heaven;* Paul Green's *In Abraham's Bosom* won a Pulitzer Prize; Duke Ellington [composer of "I'm Gonna Hang Around My Sugar," "Jig Walk," and "(You've Got Those) Wanna Go Back Again Blues"] spent the summer touring Massachusetts mill towns and New Hampshire resort hotels, in nightly "Battle of the Bands" competitions in which he discovered how to create his classic blues compositions, "Creole Love Call" or "Black and Tan Fantasy." And Paris was still reeling from Josephine Baker's debut the year before in *Revue Nègre.*

The year 1926 is also that in which *Jazz* is set, the year in which Joe Trace a fifty-year-old door-to-door salesman of beauty products murdered his eighteen-year-old lover, Dorcas, who refused to name her assassin as she lay dying. The year his wife, Violet, a hairdresser, attempted to disfigure the corpse at her funeral.

Just as Morrison's *Beloved* was sparked by an actual historical event, so too is *Jazz.* Morrison first came across the story of the star-crossed lovers when she read Camille Billops' manuscript, *The Harlem Book of the Dead,* which contains photographs and commentary by the great African-American photographer James Van Der Zee and poems by Owen Dodson. Van Der Zee described to Camille Billops the curious origins of his photograph of a young woman's corpse in this manner:

> She was the one I think was shot by her sweetheart at a party with a noiseless gun. She complained of being sick at the party and friends said, "Well, why don't you lay down?" and they taken her in the room and laid her down. After they undressed her and loosened her clothes, they saw the blood on her dress. They asked her about it and she said, "I'll tell you tomorrow, yes, I'll tell you tomorrow." She was just trying to give him a chance to get away.

As she lay dying, the young woman refused to identify the person who shot her. What manner of love was this? Morrison protected the seedling of this story line, nurturing it for over a decade, until it assumed the shape it has here, in *Jazz.*

But what is compelling here is not only the novel's plot, but how the story is *told.* A disembodied narrator slips easily and guilelessly from

third-person all-knowingness to first-person lyricism, without ever re-
laxing its grip upon our imagination. It is a sensitive, poetic narrator, in
love with the language of fiction, enraptured with the finest and rarest
of arts, the art of telling a good tale, reflecting, as it goes along, upon
its responsibilities as a composer, and its obligation to the individual
characters whose sole destiny is to make this composition come alive, to
sing.

The lyrical composer of this strangest of tales, however, is at once
generous with the voices of its characters and jealous of their right to
speak, to be *heard*, in their own melodic voices. Like Faulkner's *As I
Lay Dying*, *Jazz* has several narrators, or points of view, whose arias or
speaking consciousness bring both harmony and contrapuntal texture:
Violet, the aggrieved wife of Joe, whose four-page-long first-person reflections burst out of the novel in a single paragraph; Joe and Felice,
Dorcas's friend who had lent her an opal ring on the fateful night of her
killing, only to lose it forever to the grave. Both Joe's and Felice's control
of the narrative are marked by quotations, markers that the narrator
has *allowed* them to speak, in their own voices; in the same way, Duke
Ellington's jazz compositions were the first that were constructed, or
scored, for his individual musicians and their peculiar timbres, their particular *sounds*.

As the music critic Martin Williams describes this effect, "Ellington
was so attuned to the sounds of his men that the very originality of his
textures and the daring of his harmonic language were determined not
in the abstract but in his inquisitiveness about, let us say, how his reed
player's low A-flat might sound when juxtaposed with the brassman's
cup-muted G." And no matter how long his musicians performed their
improvisations, no matter how bold or inventive or virtuosic their flights
of harmony might be, they always performed within the certain logic of
their composer's frame—they always, in other words, were performing
with quotation marks around their improvisations and solos. It is this
same effect that Toni Morrison has achieved in *Jazz*, a luminously literary rendering of an art of composition that Duke Ellington perfected
sometime in the summer of 1926.

A final word about Morrison's narrator: despite its revelation of a full
and lyrical consciousness, despite its extensive ruminations about its
character's consciousnesses, it remains indeterminate: it is neither male
nor female; neither young nor old; neither rich nor poor. It is *both* and
neither. But it is *alive*, alive with feelings and emotions, regard and
scorn, blindnesses and insights about the human actors that conspire to
produce this curious tale of love, betrayal, departure, reconciliation, and
union: the murdered victim, after all, emerges as a conspirator in her
own death. We will not weep for Dorcas; rather, we are left spellbound
by the narrator's final aria, a *tour de force* of longing, of longing for a
love that endures even its cruelest betrayal.

Like William Faulkner, whose work was the subject of Toni Morrison's master's thesis at Cornell and whose finest work comes to mind again and again as we read through *Jazz*, Morrison's new novel serves to redefine the very possibilities of narrative point of view. Like Duke Ellington, Morrison has found a way, paradoxically, to create an ensemble of *improvised* sound out of a *composed* music. Riffing on these two great geniuses of American literature and music, Toni Morrison has established herself as one of the truly original novelists at work in the world today.

ESSAYS

◆◆◆◆◆◆◆◆◆◆◆◆◆

The Contemporary Fables of Toni Morrison

BARBARA CHRISTIAN

Toni Morrison's works are fantastic earthy realism. Deeply rooted in history and mythology, her work resonates with mixtures of pleasure and pain, wonder and horror. Primal in their essence, her characters come at you with the force and beauty of gushing water, seemingly fantastic but as basic as the earth they stand on. They erupt, out of the world, sometimes gently, often with force and terror. Her work is sensuality combined with an intrigue that only a piercing intellect could create.

Two of her three novels: *The Bluest Eye* (1970) and *Sula* (1974) reveal a conistency of vision, for they illustrate the growth of a theme as it goes through many transformations in much the same way as a good jazz musician finds the hidden melodies within a musical phrase. Both novels chronicle the search for beauty amidst the retrictions of life, both from within and without. In both novels, the black woman, as girl and grown woman, is the turning character, and the friendship between two women or girls serves as the yardstick by which the overwhelming contradictions of life are measured. Double-faced, her focal characters look outward and search inward, trying to find some continuity between the seasons, the earth, other people, the cycles of life, and their own particular lives. Often they find that there is conflict between their own nature and the society that man has made, to the extent that one seems to be an inversion of the other. Her novels are rich then, not only in human characterizations but also in the signs, symbols, omens, sent by nature. Wind and fire, robins as a plague in the spring, marigolds that won't sprout, are as much characterizations in her novels as the human beings who people them.

PART I
The Bluest Eye: **Truth in Timbre**

> It had occurred to Pecola sometime ago that if her eyes that held the pictures, and knew the sights—if those eyes of hers were different that is to say beautiful, she herself would be different. Her teeth were good, and at least her nose was not big and flat like some of those who were thought so cute. If she looked different and Mrs. Breedlove, too. Maybe—they'd say, "Why look at pretty-eyed Pecola. We mustn't do bad things in front of those pretty eyes."

> Pretty eyes, Pretty eyes, Pretty blue eyes, Big blue pretty eyes. Run, Jip, run. Jip runs. Alice runs. They run with their blue eyes. Four blue eyes. Four pretty blue eyes Blue-jay eyes, blue-like Mrs. Forrest's blue blouse eyes. Morning glory-blue eyes. Alice-and-Jerry blue-story book-eyes.

Each night, without fail, she prayed for blue eyes.[1]

Toni Morrison's *The Bluest Eye* presents a simple theme: the story of a black girl who wants blue eyes as a symbol of beauty and therefore of goodness and happiness. This statement of the theme, though, undercuts the tragic complexity of such a desire, and complexity is precisely what Morrison is somehow able to impress us with in her first novel. Yes, we know that blue eyes, blond hair, fair skin, are the symbols of beauty valued in the West, as proclaimed by romantic novels, movies, billboards, dolls, and the reactions of people to golden objects. But do we really understand the core of that myth and the value connotations it embodies? Perhaps one of the most difficult artistic tasks to achieve is to take the known, what everyone thinks they understand, and really press its complexity and contours against the psyche. This simple theme, the desire of a black girl for blue eyes, is a real and symbolic statement about the conflict between the good and the beautiful of two cultures and how it affects the psyche of the people within those cultures. The theme is at the base of the conflict of artistic and societal values between the Anglo-American and Afro-American cultures, complicated by the psychopolitical dominance of one culture over another. As such, this novel is a book about mythic, political, and cultural mutilation as much as it is a book about race and sex hatred.

How Pecola comes to want blue eyes demands more than just telling Pecola's story. That is, Pecola's desire is more than the result of her own personal story. It encompasses three hundred years of unsuccessful interface between black and white culture. Morrison's dilemma as a writer, though is that she cannot retell three hundred years; she must make Pecola's story relevant to that history and yet be her own story. She must create both a sense of intimacy with her characters, yet enough distance to give the theme its expansive substance, if she is to communicate the tragic complexity of such a "simple" theme. Perhaps even more than the usual novel, the way in which this theme is presented is crucial to the theme itself. Morrison's construction of the book is perhaps what gives the book its essential truth more than the particular events within it.

The Bluest Eye begins with prose familiar to a few generations of Americans, black and white:

> Here is the house. It is green and white. It has a red door. It is very pretty. Here is the family. Mother, Father, Dick and Jane live in the green and white house. They are very happy.[2]

Yes—the prose of our very first primer as we sat at our very first desk in our very first school and had our very first lesson in reading. There are pictures of Dick, Jane, Father, Mother, the cat, and the dog, accompanied by simple, punctuated sentences that are drilled into the mind as we first learn to read. Words have power. Pictures have power. Five-

year-old children heard these words, saw these pictures across the landscape of America and even in the Virgin Islands where I was born,
perhaps more than any other single word-picture image. Morrison plays
the prose back at us again, somewhat accelerated, and then plays it again
at high speed as if we were listening to a runaway tape recorder set up
for programming. The speed, the frequency with which the words are
said, run together, set the tone modalities for the structure of this story
about Pecola Breedlove and her mother and father; about Claudia and
Frieda MacTeer and their mother and father; about Junior and his
mother, Geraldine, and his father; about Maureen Peal and her mother
and father; about Mr. Henry; about the whores; about Soaphead Church;
and of course about the white family for whom Mrs. Breedlove works.

We are asked to meditate on these lines familiar to us from our
childhoods, and to make sure that we do indeed continue to contemplate
them, Morrison begins the objective part of each chapter of this book
with a run-together fragment from the Dick and Jane primer, a fragment appropriate to the subject of that particular section. By removing the punctuation from these fragments, she heightens the lack
of internal integrity essential to their simplistic order. For example
"Autumn," the chapter about the house Pecola Breedlove lives in,
begins with "HEREISTHEHOUSEITISGREENITHASAREDDOOR
ITISVERYPRETTY." These undifferentiated words are juxtaposed
to Morrison's integral description of Pecola's house.

> There is an abandoned store on the southeast corner of Broadway and 35th
> Street in Lorain, Ohio. It doesn't recede into its background of leaven sky,
> nor harmonize with the gray frame houses and black telephone poles around
> it. Rather it foists itself on the eye of the passerby in a manner that is both
> irritating and melancholy. Visitors who drive to this tiny town wonder why
> it has not been torn down, while pedestrians, who are residents of the neigh-
> borhood, simply look away when they pass it.[3]

A voice intrudes, as the Dick and Jane prose recedes, a voice that
will recur throughout the book. It is the voice of Claudia MacTeer as she
speaks for herself and her sister when they were children. Her voice
speaking to us gives the reader a personal feeling for this story, for
Claudia takes us into her memories, personal experiences, girlish desires
and fears, as she and her sister try to make sense of the often confusing
world around them. In using the pronoun we, as she often does, she
seems to be reliving our own sense of our parents, the fears about menstruation, the fascination with where babies come from—the intensely
female and human mysteries into which all women, in some way, are
initiated. In her introductory statement, and in the section that begins
each chapter, she establishes the time, place, image, and structure of the
novel as well as introduces the major characters of the book. She then
becomes our central narrator.

Importantly, Claudia tells us in her introduction that this story takes place in the year 1940–41, from fall to fall, in the year when the baby Pecola had by her own father is born dead, in the year when the marigolds did not sprout. This nature image is the major structural element of the novel, for the book is divided into the seasons of the year, reflecting, sometimes ironically, on the tragedy of Pecola Breedlove. Appropriately, the year does not begin in January or in the spring, but in the fall when school starts according to the rhythm of a child's life. Autumn, too, begins the book because Pecola's story will not be the usual mythic one of birth, death, and rebirth, from planting to harvest to planting. Hers will proceed from pathos to tragedy and finally to madness, as the earth will not accept her seeds.

But isn't this story primarily Pecola's? Why is Claudia needed at all? The use of Claudia as the child narrator of Pecola's descent into madness seems to be one of Morrison's most brilliant strokes. Obviously Pecola does not have the necessary distance, space, or time to know what is happening to her. She cannot look at her own story in hindsight, for she goes mad. Claudia is telling Pecola's story after it has happened and after she has made some sense of it, a particular characteristic of hers throughout the book. But even more dramatically, this story is also Claudia's story. She does not experience the gravest effects of the myth of beauty as Pecola does. She is not seen as the ugliest of the ugly, but she does know that blue eyes and blond hair are admired by all and that she does not possess them. The dolls she receives at Christmas, the Shirley Temple mug, and so on are measures of her own lack of desirability. But Claudia fights back, resents the dolls, tries to make sense out of the contradictions she finds around her about love and beauty. She becomes the girl-woman in the book with whom we can identify, for most of us are not the extreme, as Pecola is, and do not overtly go mad. Claudia, then, becomes a way of giving voice to the graveness of Pecola's situation even as she herself is confronted with the same problems, although less intensely.

The main body of *The Bluest Eye* is divided into four chapters named for the seasons, a schema we are prepared for by Claudia's introductory statement in which she relates the failure of the marigolds to sprout with the death of Pecola's baby. "The seeds shriveled and died, her baby too." Nature images are constant throughout the book and help to organize its structure. At the center of this nature construct are the physical and psychological events that lead to the rape of Pecola and to her ill-fated pregnancy. The divisions into seasons beginning with autumn chart that development of events. These events, in fact, form the plot of this novel.

But the seasons are not only surface movement in the novel; they are ironic and brutal comments of Pecola's descent into madness. In spring, for example, lovers flow into each other and fertility rites are cyclically reenacted, as nature comes back to life; yet it is in that season that Pecola is raped by her father, the only love she is to know. Her rape in the spring is preceded by a "false spring" in the winter, personified by Maureen Peal, the green-eyed, blond black who befriends her with her talk of babies and daddies and follows that wooing with the rejection, "I am cute! And you ugly! Black and ugly Black e mos." The images of the seasons erupt every way in this book as nature itself remains constant, seemingly aloof, although embodying the essence of memory:

> I have only to break into the tightness of a strawberry, and I see summer— its dust and lowering skies. It remains for me a season of storms. The parched days and sticky nights are undistinguished in my mind, but the storms, the violent summer storms, both frightened and quenched. But my memory is uncertain; I recall a summer storm in the town where we lived and imagine a summer my mother knew in 1929. There was a tornado that year, she said, that blew away half of South Lorain. I mix up her summer with my own. Biting the strawberry, thinking of storms, I see her. A slim young girl in a pink crepe dress. One hand is on the hip; the other lolls about her thigh waiting. The wind swoops her up, high above the houses but she is still standing, hand on hip. Smiling. The anticipation and promise in her lolling hand are not altered by the holocaust. In the summer tornado of 1929, my mother's hand is unextinguished. She is strong, smiling and relaxed while the world falls down about her. So much for memory. Public fact becomes private reality, and the seasons for a Midwestern town became the *Moirai* of our small lives.[4]

The seasons, the natural process of growth, will not wait for marigolds to be planted, will not alter their pattern because someone is crying, but will inflict cold, tornadoes, and beatings upon humanity. Morrison's view of nature is uncompromising. Nature is itself a whole system in which "natural" and "social" spheres do not compete. Since it is cyclical rather than linear, there is no point of completion. It is like life; it is life, mean though precious.

These three elements—the Dick and Jane primer backdrop, the modulated voice of Claudia, and the constant continuum between the mean, precious seasons and the growth of young black girls—are the fuse from which this story of a mutilated life bursts into sparks. The character of each of these elements tells us something specific about Morrison's intent in this book.

The Dick and Jane primer reminds us of the pervasiveness of the happy family, middle-American, romantic beauty myth so we are not tempted to see its effects on Pecola's life as unique or idiosyncratic. The primer confronts the grossness of standardized bland concepts projected as desirable, the norm. Where do Dick and Jane exist? Probably only on the pages of that primer. But young children are led to believe that others are happy because they are white and perhaps because they are pretty, are not too noisy, or are living an orderly life, whatever line of demarcation or difference they can perceive as marking their own existence. The more confusing, different, poverty-ridden or depressed that a child's life is, the more she will yearn for the norm the dominant society says provides beauty and happiness. Reality is compared to the visual-word picture. Morrison contrasts her own values with examples of houses varying according to the societal norm of order and beauty. So she shows us how Geraldine's house with its prissy orderliness reflects her lack of vitality, her frigidity. However, when Pecola sees it, she thinks it is a beautiful house. We can feel her belief that this house must be full of happiness and love—hence the impact of rejection, exclusion from these desires, when Geraldine so harshly throws her out, or when we view that spacious kitchen belonging to the rich white family that Mrs. Breedlove works for: "her skin glows like taffeta in the reflection of white porcelain, white woodwork, polished cabinets and brilliant copperware." Pecola is destined to mar that kitchen and be harshly expelled by her own mother. These dwellings are contrasted to the ugly storefront that Pecola lives in, where the only living things are the coal stove, and where everyone feels ugly and fights with each other.

While the ever-present mimicking Dick and Jane words are used to give the book expansiveness, Claudia's voice brings us close to the characters as she and Frieda tell us Pecola's story, their own siftings against the backdrop of grownups who touch golden dolls with awe. So her voice guides us through the real happenings of life for her—the moment when Pecola begins to "ministrate," and their wondering if she is going to die—or her sensing the beauty and sorrow of her mother's voice as she sings the blues. The solidity of the MacTeer family is the image, the real image, of a struggling family from a young girl's point of view in contrast to the empty Dick and Jane ideal. The intimacy of growing up with a love that surrounds her, a love that is so firm in its manifestations that it might not be fully appreciated until she is much older, explodes the myth of the Dick and Jane family-beauty type.

Dick and Jane has its societal implications in our particular cultural context and Claudia's voice individualizes that context. The seasons reinforce the mythic quality of life embodied in every live particle, as they ebb and flow, are beautiful in their terribleness or gentleness. At the core of this mystery are sensuality and sexuality, exciting and problematic, but constant and real as instinctively perceived by young girls struggling from childhood into womanhood. Their experiences at this turning point quiver with possibilities: rape perhaps; the yearnings of old men like Soaphead and Mr. Henry who tenderly try to recapture their own youth or purpose in life by touching them; the girls' own excitement over the mysteries of their bodies; and of course their wonderings about love and beauty. Love, as sensual and spiritual, is what these young girls want; love, they intuit, is possible for anyone. In contrast, the societal concept of beauty sets up a hierarchy of desirability that proclaims that love is deserved only by a few. Perhaps, because grownups are distorted by the pain of their lives, they deny their own capacity for love by tearing that capacity in others apart. Pummeled by the complexity of a mean precious nature, they fear the funk of love that is necessary for the spirit to grow. In their intense yearning for, yet deep fear of, love, they distort it by giving it unattainable romantic characteristics. Beauty precedes love, the grownups seem to say, and only a few possess beauty. But the seasons go on—beyond beauty—in their many transformations. So there are marigolds and dandelions, winters that are a hateful knot, springs that are warmer but whose twigs deliver stings that last long after the whipping is over, and summers that are like tight strawberries.

As structural motifs, these three elements form the building blocks of the book. Externally the first section in each chapter begins with Claudia's voice as she reminisces about that particular season, its meaning in her life and in Pecola's. Then this section is followed by seemingly objective sections headed by Dick and Jane fragments and told by an omniscient narrator who can go backward and forward in time and space, can escape the limitations of a specific human consciousness. In these sections we learn the backgrounds of our major characters: Mr. and Mrs. Breedlove, Geraldine, Soaphead Church, all of the characters who in the immediate present help to cause Pecola's downfall. We see them as they are seen and as they see themselves, so we can understand how they got to be as they are.

Intrinsically, each chapter is unified by a particular idea that permeates the atmosphere in which Pecola is drifting, an idea that is also related to that season of the year. The chapter "Spring" illustrates how the fabric of interrelatedness between structure and theme is central to this book's character.

"Spring" begins with:

> The first twigs are thin, green and supple. They bend into a complete circle but will not break. Their delicate showy hopefulness shooting from forsythia and lilac bushes meant only a change in whipping style.[5]

It is Claudia speaking, and she goes on to tell us that Mr. Henry touched Frieda on her breasts and her Daddy beat him up and cast him outside. Frieda is afraid that she is ruined and will get fat. She and her sister decide that the whores are ruined but don't get fat because they drink whiskey. Marvelous logic! So they go searching for Pecola since her father drinks whiskey. Directed by the whores (Pecola's only grownup friends), they find her, we are told, at Mrs. Breedlove's employers' home, but only after we hear about the change in landscape from the ugliness of their part of town to the city park "laid out with rosebuds, fountains, bowling greens, picnic tables, sweetly expectant of clean white well-behaved children and parents." Pecola is waiting outside to take the wash to her house. As Mrs. Breedlove goes to get it, the three black girls, nervous in this beautiful, white kitchen, see a little girl who looks like the dolls they get at Christmas. She is looking for Polly, obviously Mrs. Breedlove. When Pecola touches the berry cobbler her mother has made for this girl-doll, she drops it, burning herself and marring the floor, the perfect kitchen, with blueberry juice. Mrs. Breedlove slaps Pecola and comforts the little girl-doll while she banishes the three black girls from Paradise.

Claudia's section, along with two other events, Cholly Breedlove's rape of his daughter and Soaphead Church's gift of blue eyes to Pecola Breedlove, are the only events that take place in the spring of 1941. These events are the plot of the chapter. But Morrison is not so much interested in communicating what happened as how it happened. The first twigs of spring bend into a complete circle but will not break. So this chapter, "Spring," is circular rather than linear. Accustomed as we are to the order of linear structures, the reverberations of "Spring" must, at first, have a dizzying effect on the reader—as dizzying as the effects of spring 1941 on the characters in this book. Morrison is not interested in the march of words epitomized by the Dick and Jane prose; that formation does not communicate the essence of her characters' spring or their thought processes as they try to graft one set of cultural values onto another. The organization of this chapter is that of the sounding of motifs and the exploration of their reverberations. The chapter is a jazz composition rather than a sonata. Chords are sounded and then transformed and resounded as they are affected by other chords. Morrison's composition would lose its essence, its force, if reduced to linear structures. Cyclical as nature, circular as spring's first twigs, this chapter defies linear analysis.

Claudia's section sounds the thematic chords of this chapter: the inverted figure of Daddy, the older man who molests girl-woman, and the inverted figure of Mother, the woman who denies her children for other children. Mr. Henry's misdemeanor, which reminds us that old men yearn for love, for touching, is but a subtle preparation for Cholly's rape of his daughter and for Soaphead Church's attraction to young girls in their respective sections of this chapter. Mrs. Breedlove's rejection of Pecola for the daughter of her employer is as much an act of love-hate as Cholly's tragic action is. By exploring the sound reverberations in the lives of Pauline Breedlove, Cholly Breedlove, and Soaphead Church, each in a distinct section of this chapter, Morrison creates an atonal composition.

The cadence of Pauline Breedlove's section begins with an ironic note: "SEEMOTHERMOTHERISVERYNICEMOTHERWILLYOUPLAY WITHJANEMOTHERLAUGHSLAUGHMOTHERLAUGH." Two voices, as in a duet, tell her story: the voice of the all knowing narrator and the distinctive voice of Pauline Breedlove herself. It is important that we hear her story in her own sound patterns and images, for her manner of perceiving the world, primarily in rural tones and images of color, is a key to her wasted life. But her sense of herself is too limited, so we also need the more expansive sounds of the narrator to explore fully the dissonance in Mrs. Breedlove's life.

Possessing a slight limp from her second year, Pauline Breedlove learned early to be separate and unworthy. "Restricted as a child, to the cocoon of her family's spinning she cultivated quiet and private pleasure, she liked, most of all to arrange things. . . . To line things up in rows. . . . She missed without knowing what she missed—paints and crayons." Her own narration emphasizes this quality. She speaks always in terms of colors. For example, when she first meets Cholly she describes it this way:

> "When I first seed Cholly, I want you to know it was like all the bits of color from that time down home when all us children went berry picking after a funeral and I put some in the pocket of my Sunday dress, and they mashed up and stained my hips. My whole dress was messed with purple, and it never did wash out. Not the dress nor me. I could feel that purple deep inside me. And that lemonade Mama used to make when Papa came in out the fields. It be cool and yellowish, with seeds floating near the bottom. And that streak of green them june bugs made on the trees the night we left from down home. All of them colors was in me. Just sitting there. So when Cholly came up and tickled my foot, it was like them berries, that lemonade, them streaks of green the june bugs all come together. Cholly was thin then, with real light eyes. He used to whistle and when I heard him, shivers come on my skin."[6]

Pauline Breedlove has the eye of an artist, a fascination with color and arrangement. Her life, though, with its move to the city where she is seen as "country," her growing dependence on Cholly, her need for quiet and private pleasures contrasted with her husband's extroverted nature, result more and more in privation, disappointment, and sorrow. She gets pregnant and, oppressed by the loneliness in her two-room apartment, begins going to the movies.

> There in the dark her memory was refreshed, and she succumbed to her earlier dreams. Along with the idea of romantic love, she was introduced to another—physical beauty. Probably the most destructive ideas in the history of human thought. Both originated in envy, thrived in insecurity, and ended in disillusion. In equating physical beauty with virtue, she stripped her mind, bound it and collected self-contempt by the heap.

> . . . She was never able after her education in the movies, to look at a face and not assign it some category in the scale of absolute beauty, and the scale was one she absorbed in full from the silver screen.[7]

When she has Pecola, her comment is, "Eyes all soft and wet. A cross between a puppy and a dying man. But I knowed she was ugly. Head full of pretty hair, but Lord she was ugly." The die is cast. Pecola, her own child, is assigned a bottom category in the scale of absolute beauty and the possession of beauty is equated with self-worth. Pecola, too, will learn to be separate and unworthy.

Having had children, Mrs. Breedlove takes on the role of the bread-winner and returns to the church. These two dominant chords in her life interact. The church allows her to bear the ugly Cholly like "a crown of thorns" and her ugly children "like a cross." Her job at the home of a well-to-do family allows her her fill of color and line and satisfies her need to arrange things. Here she finds "beauty, order, cleanliness and praise," a private world that she never introduces to her own family. What holds her to Cholly, then? It is the funk of love (a theme throughout the book), the bits of color floating up in her when he makes love to her. "When he does I feel a power. I be strong. I be pretty, I be young."

The dissonances in Pauline Breedlove's section lead us irrevocably to the third part of this composition, to an exploration of her husband's life. Beginning with "SEEFATHERHEISBIGANDSTRONGFATHER WILLYOUPLAYWITHJANEFATHERISSMILINGSMILEFATHER SMILESMILE," Morrison immediately introduces the dominant chord progression in her exploration of Cholly Breedlove's essence. The reverberations of the mystery of birth and rebirth through sex and parenting give unity to his section. This father has no mother or father, his mother having abandoned him when he was four days old and his father having disappeared almost immediately after his birth. Cholly's only knowledge of his father is his name, Samson Fuller, Morrison's ironic comment on the stereotype. Cholly is, in fact, raised by his old Aunt Jimmy and more distantly by a nice old man, Blue Jack, who used to tell him stories about his adventures with women. When Aunt Jimmy dies one chilly spring, in typical Morrison style, of peach cobbler, the chord patterns of Cholly's life are transformed. Morrison uses Aunt Jimmy's illness and funeral as both a ritualistic enactment of a vividly female culture that strengthens the sinews of black Rural America and as Cholly's initiation into manhood.

As the old woman dies, her friends come to wait with her, hugging their memories of illness to their bosoms. In a hauntingly lyrical crush of words, Morrison tells us the story of those old black women reared in the South and in so doing relates their lives to that of Pauline Breedlove:

> Then they had grown. Edging into life from the back door. Becoming. Everybody in the world was in a position to give them orders. White women said, "Do this." White children said, "Give me that." White men said, "Come here." Black men said, "Lay down." The only people they need not take orders from were black children and each other. But they took all of that and recreated it in their own image. They ran the houses of white people, and knew it. When white men beat their men, they cleaned up the blood and went home to receive abuse from the victim. They beat their children with one hand and stole for them with the other. The hands that felled trees also cut umbilical cords; the hands that wrung the necks of chickens and butched hogs also nudged African violets into bloom; the arms that loaded sheaves, bales and sacks rocked babies into sleep. They patted biscuits into flaky ovals of innocence—and shrouded the dead. They plowed all day and came home to nestle like plums under the limbs of their men. The legs that straddled a mule's back were the same ones that straddled their men's hips. And the difference was all the difference there was.[8]

As Cholly listens to them talking and dreams that his penis is changed into a long hickory stick caressed by one of the old women, we are subtly prepared for his initiation into manhood, for his first sexual encounter with a woman—a woman who will probably follow the pattern of her granny. At the funeral, a celebration of life and death, Cholly and a young girl, Darlene, go to pick berries just as Pauline does in her own youth, so far away and yet so near. In this orgiastic atmosphere led on by the instinctive cues of the female, his maleness asserts itself. But this mythic scene, complete with grape-stained lips and feasting, complete with the compelling images of the transformation into life, is distorted by the intrusion of two white men who turn Cholly's first sexual experience into a public pleasure show. "Get on wid it nigger," they squeak, "make it good." Cholly can do no more than make believe and, in a most logical movement of the human mind, hates not the white men who humiliated him but the black woman who "had created the situation, the one who bore witness to his failure, his impotence." He is at once initiated into the rituals of potency and impotency, and the woman is testament to both.

Wildly thinking that Darlene might be pregnant, he runs away, retracing his father's footsteps even as he goes looking for him in Macon. His personal cycle is completed as he finds his father there and is rejected by him. Cholly then becomes free. "Abandoned by his mother in a junkheap, rejected for a crap game by his father, there was nothing to lose. He was alone with his own perceptions and appetites and they alone interested him. It was in this godlike state that he met Pauline Williams." What we grasp about Cholly's life is that once having tasted the freedom of narcissism permitted only to the gods, he could not abide the dullness of married life.

Having explored the dominant chords of Pauline and Cholly Breedlove's lives, Morrison executes a marvelous leap of time from past years into the spring of 1941. For in the patterns that continue, as if they were circles, to dominate these parents' lives, lies the logic inherent in the rape of Pecola. All of the chord progressions are sounded simultaneously as, drunk one day, Cholly Breedlove watches his daughter washing dishes and senses her love for him. Confronted by his own unworthiness, his own lack of godliness, he hates her until she shifts her weight and repeats the same pitiful gesture that drew him to her mother. The circle of love-hatred seems to be completed in this chapter as he tries to fuck her tenderly, to somehow reconcile the love-hate within, toward Pecola, his wife, and himself.

But spring does not end there; the perversity of natural sensuality Cholly experienced in that spring of Aunt Jimmy's death, the sheer weight of the sameness of married life, his own sense of his own unworthiness, is not yet resolved even by the love-hate Cholly gives his daughter, for Pecola is left in the spring with the burden of it, with the experience of love-hate at the essence of the act itself. She must now find her way through this vortex of opposite strivings and it is to a spiritual source, to Soaphead Church, that she goes for reconciliation, for salvation, for rebirth.

Soaphead's section completes this circle of the chapter. As a fuller exploration of the chord sounded by Mr. Henry, Soaphead loves little girls whose bodies seem to him the least offensive of all human beings. Like Mr. Henry, he is a clean old man. But unlike Mr. Henry, this philosopher's attraction for little girls is rooted in his intense dislike for human beings in general, who in their physical and cultural forms are imperfect, in a continual state of decay. In short, he is a misanthrope. Morrison appropriately begins his section with "SEETHEDOGBOWWOWGOESTHEDOGDO YOUWANTTOPLAYWITHJANESEETHEDOG" for Soaphead clearly identifies with an old mangy dog who sleeps in front of his entrance and whose decrepitness creates great revulsion in him.

Soaphead's articulation of a philosophy of misanthropy is a culmination of the many chord progressions sounded by the main characters in this chapter. His distorted view of life flows from the same causes that transform Mrs. Breedlove into a cruel martyr of a mother, the same causes that impress upon Cholly Breedlove his own unworthiness, his own ugliness, the same causes that will inspire Pecola Breedlove to ask this clean old man to give her blue eyes. But he goes beyond their seemingly impetuous actions by intellectualizing and conceptualizing their common condition. Through the character of Soaphead, Morrison expands the theme of spring from that of thwarted rebirth in the lives of individuals to a statement about the tragedy of cultural mutilation.

As his former self, Elihue Micah Whitcomb, Soaphead had come from a mulatto West Indian family dedicated to preserving and heightening its British blood, not only in terms of color and shade but in the culture it represents. His family was:

> . . . industrious, orderly and energetic, hoping to prove beyond a doubt De Govineau's hypothesis that "all civilizations derive from the white race, that none can exist without its help, and that a society is great and brilliant only so far as it preserves the blood of the noble group that created it."[9]

More directly, Elihue's schoolmaster father developed his own legacy of Anglophilia into a narrow intellectual statement of the unworthiness of man, undoubtedly only slightly concealing his own distaste for himself and his son. Elihue inherits this view of man, for as he grows up he sees the sterile ugliness of the need to be British, this need to erase color, all vitality, all funk, out of life. Elihue is the tragic mulatto who is both bred to, yet aware of, the waste in the urge to acculturize. He knows the nonlife at the center of his father's narrow view of life. Morrison describes this disease so well in her description of Elihue's marriage with Velma, a lovely, laughing, big-legged girl.

She was to have been the answer to his unstated, unacknowledged question—where was the life to counter the encroaching non-life? Velma was to rescue him from the non-life he had learned on the flat side of his father's belt. But he resisted her with such skill that she was finally driven out to escape the inevitable boredom produced by such a dainty life.[10]

Leaving the island, he tries the usual professions open to one of his class and finally sinks into "a rapidly fraying gentility." When he comes to Ohio, the folk with their usual sagacity zero in on his essence. They find his English awe-inspiring, his lack of funkiness amazing, and declare him supernatural, a perception that results in his decision to become a Reader, Advisor and Interpreter of Dreams. When Pecola comes to him with her fantastic but logical request for blue eyes, he immediately understands her need: "Here was an ugly little black girl asking for beauty." Her request makes total sense to him, for he, more than any other character in the book, intellectualizes the pain, the self-mutilation, inherent in that request, so much so that he writes an arrogant and ironic letter to God, "TO HE WHO GREATLY ENNOBLED HUMAN NATURE BY CREATING IT." God had obviously done a poor job of creation, which Soaphead, by granting Pecola's request, is trying to correct. But not before he uses Pecola to get rid of the mangy dog he hates so much; not before he pays tribute to his own belief in her ugliness as he "gives" her in a godlike manner blue eyes.

"Spring" ends with Soaphead slipping into an "ivory sleep" as the old dog Bog is found dead. In contemplating its circular structure, its ironically rhythmical patterns, its theme of inversion in which old men are inverted Daddies struggling for a meaning in life by touching the first twigs of spring, in hearing its melody of thwarted sexuality (atonal though sweet) in which the intrusion of another culture into the characters' lives waylays their instinctive desire for life, we are stunned by the terrors of nature to which human beings are prone. In arranging such a pattern of sound, Morrison has wrested out of the March winds, out of the reawakening of nature, her characters' desire to be reborn, even if tragic forms are their own fruit. "Spring" is a fertility rite inverted.

Each chapter, like "Spring," has a unifying sound idea, recurrent images, translucent connectives, as each section explores in depth a variation of the theme played throughout. But not only is the structure of the book circular, it is also elliptical, for not only is each chapter of the book itself coherent, it is also linked to every other. Morrison's transitions are in the form of her characters. The focal character may be Pecola, but all of the other characters in varying degrees suffer from the insanity that will manifest itself in her madness. The story moves, connects piece by piece, through the presentation of one character after another who shows us some aspect of that insanity. In "Winter," Maureen Peal, the "high yellow dream child with long brown hair braided in two lynch ropes," has got what Geraldine (who also appears in this chapter) will struggle all of her life to get next to. Geraldine, not as singular as Maureen Peal, in this pyramid of beauty and funklessness and shade, belongs to a distinctive group of women who:

> . . . go to land-grant colleges, normal schools, and learn how to do the white man's work with refinement: home economics to prepare his food; teacher education to instruct black children in obedience; music to soothe the weary master and entertain his blunted soul. Here they learn the rest of the lessons begun in those soft houses with porch swings and pots of bleeding heart: how to behave. The careful development of thrift, patience, high morals, and good manners. In short, how to get rid of the funkiness. The dreadful funkiness of passion, the funkiness of nature, the funkiness of the wide range of human emotions.[11]

Geraldine will brush her son's hair forever in abortive attempts to wipe out the subtle and telltale signs of niggerism. She, in her prissy asexual cleanliness, is identified with cats, as Soaphead Church in his mangy cleanliness is identified with an old dog. She breeds Soapheads, the only end to which her generation could come, for as her son Junior already grasps, there is a dainty, cold self-hatred at her core. So Maureen Peal is connected to Geraldine who is connected to Soaphead who in turn is connected to Mr. Henry and so on. All of them are connected to Pecola who dramatically manifests their insanity by revealing the disease for what it is.

Pecola is the passive center of the novel, the one to whom things happen and whose only action, her prayer for and receipt of blue eyes, renders her tragic. Her tragic flaw is her particular vulnerability and her generic ill-luck to be born black and female, to be born into the chasm between two cultures. She falls into that chasm's bottomlessness while others hang on by their toenails or seem to straddle it with one foot on either side, sometimes with an amazing lack of balance. The section in the book that belongs to her, the section in which the part of her with blue eyes converges with the part of her without them is not only a terror-filled dialogue but is conclusive in its judgment of where all of the other characters really reside. Harrowed by an unfulfilled need for love, she finds a friend in the other part of herself, the part that can admire her newly acquired eyes. Morrison heads his section "LOOK LOOKHERECOMESAFRIENDTHEFRIENDWILLPLAYWITH JANETHEYWILLPLAYAGOODGAMEPLAYJANEPLAY." The friend will play with her only if she has the bluest eyes of all. Who is the fairest of us all?

In a sense, everyone in the town understands what has happened to Pecola, that the natural order has been inverted by the unnaturalness of human actions. They cannot look at her, because, as Claudia says, "All of us—all who knew her—felt so wholesome after we cleaned ourselves on her." They had all raped her. Claudia knows this, that Pecola's madness was not only caused by the fatal love of her father, but was the "fault of the earth, the land of their town." We come to know this not only through the terrifyingly connected structure of this novel but also through Morrison's style, which moves both toward and beyond her characters at the same time.

Because Morrison is always both telling Pecola's story and relating it to a wider circumference, her intense use of piled-up similes and metaphors is especially effective. You can hardly read a paragraph without being whirled into a circulating throb of asymmetrical likenesses. Listen to her description of Frieda and Claudia's response to the conversation of the grownup women. The comparisons move toward the characters while they take on an eternal vibration:

> Their conversation is like a gently wicked dance: sound meets sound, curtsies, shimmies and retires. Another sound enters but is upstaged by still another: the two circle each other and stop. Sometimes their words move in lofty spirals; other times they take strident leaps, and all of it is punctuated with warm-pulsed laughter—like the throb of a heart made of jelly. The edge, the curl of the thrust of their emotions is always clear to Frieda and me. We do not, cannot, know the meanings of all their words, for we are nine and ten years old. So we watch their faces, their hands, their feet, and listen for truth in timbre.[12]

The novel is sound, truth in timbre, as Claudia, Frieda, Pecola, all of us, learn our truths not in what is said but from the pitch, the timbre, of our society's sound. Language as tonality and as dance, African linguistic characteristics, are at the center of this book's truth as Morrison refuses to compose her characters' world in linear order, for that is not the pattern of its sound. Rather it is her metaphors in motion, her continual and overlapping improvisation on the theme, her delving into the infinite possibilities of the insides of language chords, rather than the mere sounding of the chord that moves us into the lives of her characters and beyond them into the life of life itself, into the sound of the sound itself.

> The pieces of Cholly's life could become coherent only in the head of a musician. Only those who talk their talk through the gold of curved metal, or in the touch of black and white rectangles and taut skins and strings echoing from wooden corridors, could give true form to his life. Only they would know how to connect the heart of a red watermelon to the asfetida bag to the muscadine to the flashlight on his behind to the fists of money to the lemonade in a Mason jar to a man called Blue and come up with what all of that meant in joy, in pain, in anger, in love, and give it its final and pervading ache of freedom.[13]

As if she were a musician, Morrison connects Pecola Breedlove's desire for the bluest eyes to Mrs. Breedlove's restricted spirit and Cholly Breedlove's sense of unworthiness, to Geraldine's fear of funk and Soaphead Church's sterility, to Maureen's fate as an eternal dream child and Claudia's ache to be whole. By exploring the devastating effects that the Western ideas of beauty and romantic love have on a vulnerable black girl, this novelist also demonstrates how these ideas can invert the natural order of an entire culture. The vortex, at which two conflicting orders meet, Pecola becomes the scapegoat for that part in all of us that needs to see our own fears of unworthiness embodied in some form. As black and female, Morrison concludes, the Pecolas of America are an accessible dumping ground.

PART II
Sula: The Pattern of a Fable

> Sula was a heavy brown with large quiet eyes, one of which featured a birth-mark that spread from the middle of the lid toward the eyebrow, shaped something like a stemmed rose. It gave her otherwise plain face a broken excitement and blue-blade threat like the keloid scar of the razored man who sometimes played checkers with her grandmother. The birthmark was to grow darker, as the years passed, but now it was the same shade as her gold-flecked eyes, which to the end were as steady and clean as rain.[14]

Toni Morrison's first novel, *The Bluest Eye*, reveals the inversions of an order that result in a black girl's belief that she possesses the greatest treasure, the bluest eyes imaginable. As such, it is a patterned fabric in which the warp is the myth of beauty and desirability in our society itself, while the weft, the part that shows, is the personal history of Pecola Breedlove. In *Sula*, her second novel, Morrison again takes on an apparently simple theme, the friendship of two black girls. One, Nel Wright, follows the pattern of life society has laid out for her, and the other, Sula Peace, tries to create her own pattern, to achieve her own self. Again, as in *The Bluest Eye*, the theme is but a sign of all that the novel explores, for the search for self is continually thwarted by the society from which Sula Peace comes. So the novel is not only about Nel Wright and Sula Peace, it is most emphatically about the culture that spawns them. In *The Bluest Eye*, Pecola's destiny is ultimately deter-mined by the myth of beauty and goodness one culture has foisted on another. In *Sula*, the patterns of both cultures are distinct, yet share common factors. Sula's destiny is charted by the mythology of Evil and Nature her hometown ascribes to and by the view the Bottom as well as the larger society hold of woman, her span and space. In exploring this community's system of beliefs, Morrison weaves a fable about the rela-tionship between conformity and experiment, survival and creativity. This mythological system is continually discerned in the novel's fabric through death, so ordinary in its eternal presence that it might otherwise be missed, through the drama of time as a significant event, and through the pervasive use of nature as both a creative and destructive force. As in *The Bluest Eye*, the novel's patterns help to transform a seemingly obvious theme.

Overtly, the novel is divided into an introduction, two parts—one devoted to years in the twenties, to Sula and Nel's growing up, and the other to years in the late thirties and early forties, to these women, now grown—and finally, as if an epilogue, there is 1965, a year of remembrance and understanding for Nel Greene. But Morrison immediately signals her reader that this tale about the friendship between Nel Wright and Sula Peace is integrally related to the survival of their community. The novel begins not with the presentation of these characters but with the death of their hometown. In *Sula*, as in *The Bluest Eye*, Morrison uses the motif of inversion, of derangement, as the natural order is turned upside down as a result of human society.

The introduction announces the pervasive presence of Death, as the Bottom is being torn down to make room for a golf course. We begin with the end, the death of a community of black folk, which is being deleted by the onward march of "progress," a community in which pain was so much a part of the pleasure of living that the Bottom's mores might be misleading. Then we leap from end to beginning, a beginning that was a joke, a nigger joke, because the laughter is so much a way of dealing with the pain. The Bottom, the Negro neighborhood of the town Medallion, was a white man's gift of land to a slave who had performed some heavy duties for him. Although the Bottom was really hill land where planting was backbreaking and the weather harsh, the master had persuaded the slave that this land was more desirable than valley land, that it was called the Bottom because it was the bottom of Heaven— "best land there is." Inverted, the truth is inverted, and so the Bottom on the top came to be.

This little nigger joke of how the Bottom came to be is juxtaposed in the novel to the origins of National Suicide Day, the Bottom's unique holiday. The beginning is the end, so to speak. National Suicide Day had been initiated by Shadrack, a shell-shocked soldier "who was not so much afraid of death or dying as the unexpectedness of both. It was a way of controlling the fear of death." In the essence of ritual, he initiated a day devoted to that fear, "so that everyone could get it out of the way."

What does National Suicide Day have to do with what follows—the story of Nel and her family, the story of Sula and her family, the story of their friendship? Their story, the story of the Bottom, is punctuated by death. Death occurs in each chapter and is the beginning of, or climax of, the experience in that particular section of the novel. Death becomes a way of focusing experience. As each year gives way to another, so each death gives way to a new view of life, a new discovery, a new feeling for truth.

Death is the haunt, personified by Shadrack, that moves the story; the tale of the Wright and Peace families and particularly of Nel and Sula, is the matter with which we are preoccupied. So the chapters proceed as if we are being shown the history of these families and finally the intertwining of two lives, Sula and Nel's, as they affect the Bottom, that nigger joke. The distinctive characteristics of these families from the Bottom, then, alert us to the specific belief system of their community, and the introduction of the novel, the juxtaposition of its end and its beginning, and the origins of National Suicide Day are indications that this story is a lesson in the nature of survival and continuity.

As the beginning is in the end, the end is in the beginning. Time becomes important only as it marks an event, for the people of the Bottom do not see its reckoning as an autonomous terminology. So each chapter in *Sula* is headed by a year, a time that allows us to focus on the climax of that section. The delineation of a particular year is a focus, not a limitation, as Morrison uses with great craftsmanship, this cultural characteristic of the Bottom. In adapting this quality to the novel, she heightens the magic of the written word—the flexibility to move from time to time, from one setting to another, without the need for changing props or signaling a new drift of images. So each chapter is not about the particular year for which it is named—rather some crucial event happens in that year which demands background, its whys and hows, the reasons for the event's significance. As the author, she is beyond time, collapsing the past, present, and future into the now so we might understand and feel the significance. The structure, then, so apparently neatly defined by the march of time, by a chronological pattern, is always transforming itself, for in fact we do not move forward in a straight line. Rather a particular point in time is but the focus of intertwining circles of other times and events. It is as if we were hearing an old African folktale—mythological in tone—in which content revitalizes an empty terminological system. The then is in the now; the now in the then; and the teller spins ever-intricate webs of connectiveness, until the web is completed or broken.

The mythological tone of this tale is heightened further by Morrison's pervasive use of nature images. Throughout *Sula*, images of fire, water, wind and earth are closely linked to the eternal presence of death and the Bottom's concept of time. As a result, the novel projects an integral world view, for the qualities of creativity and destructiveness are continually transforming the images of nature.

Morrison's use of nature images is not arbitrary. As in *The Bluest Eye*, the way in which the characters perceive nature is crucial to an understanding of their universe:

> In spite of their fear, they reacted to an oppressive oddity, or what they called evil days, with an acceptance that bordered on welcome. Such evil must be avoided, they felt, and precautions must naturally be taken to protect themselves from it. But they let it run its course, fulfill itself, and never invented ways either to alter it, to annihilate it or to prevent its happening again. So also were they with people.

> What was taken by outsiders to be slackness, slovenliness or even generosity was in fact a full recognition of the legitimacy of forces other than good ones. They did not believe death was accidental—life might be, but death was delib-

erate. They did not believe that Nature was ever askew—only inconvenient. Plague and drought were as "natural" as springtime. If milk could curdle, God knows robins could fall. The purpose of evil was to survive it and they determined (without ever knowing they had made up their minds to do it) to survive floods, white people, tuberculosis, famine and ignorance. They knew anger well but not despair, and they didn't stone sinners for the same reason that they didn't commit suicide—it was beneath them.[15]

Because the author probes the philosophical system compressed in these few paragraphs, this novel becomes not only an intense tale of two women's friendship but also a forceful drama of contending mythic beliefs. Her characters' philosophy of life contains no idyllic view of nature, no sympathy with the natural as an ideal, except to survive it. Theirs is a philosophy grounded in a history of struggling continually to survive, a philosophy that exhibits a cynicism about the limits of living. Nature's signs, although they are seldom controlled by the actions of men, must, in this view, relate to the course of human events. Rain falls alike on good men and bad; all are subject to the plague of robins. But the plague must mean something. As Eva greets Sula when she unexpectedly shows up in the Bottom after ten years' absence: "I might have knowed them birds meant something." Nature *is* a sign that can be read, and usually its message relates to the lives of the folk.

While the structural elements of Death, Time, and Nature unify the novel, the story of the Wright women and the Peace women specify the community's perception of itself, for its view of women is inexorably connected to its concept of survival. Part I of this patterned tale emphasizes the myriad forms of woman's behavior that the community incorporates, even as it dramatizes the beginnings of Nel and Sula's friendship. In using these two very different families, the author dramatizes not only the levels of this community's tolerance in relation to women but also its spiritual richness and poverty.

Nel's mother had been born in the Sundown House in New Orleans. The rest of her life was about getting as far away from the wild blood that brothel represents as she could. A high-toned lady, she fashioned her own daughter to be obedient, to be bland: "she drove her daughter's imagination underground," for fear that it might revert. Our introduction to Helene Wright and to Nel in the chapter "1920" comes, as it often does in this novel, through death. Helene's grandmother, who had taken her away from the Sundown House and raised her under "the dolesome eyes of a multicolored Virgin Mary," has died. Her funeral means that Helene has to do what she most fears—come close, too close, to the Sundown House. She will have to acknowledge her own mother, the whore who smells like gardenias and darkens her eyebrows with burnt matches. The trip South is significant, hence the marking of the year, for it is the first and last time Nel will leave Medallion. It is an opportunity for her to see her own mother, so adored by her father and so held in awe by the Bottom, reduced to "custard" by a white conductor. It is during this trip that she learns she is herself: "I'm me," Nel whispers. "Each time she said the word 'me,' there was a gathering in her like power, like joy, like fear." It was her new sense of me-ness that allowed her to cultivate a friend, Sula Peace, of whom her mother initially disapproves.

Sula's ancestry is counterpoint to Nel's. The tone of their respective houses emphasizes the contrast:

> Nel, who regarded the oppressive neatness of her home with dread, felt comfortable in it with Sula, who loved it and would sit on the red velvet sofa for 10 to 20 minutes at a time—still as dawn. As for Nel, she preferred Sula's woolly house where a pot of something was always cooking on the stove; where the mother, Hannah, never scolded or gave directions; where all sorts of people dropped in; where newspapers were stacked in the hallway, and dirty dishes left for hours at a time in the sink, and where a one-legged grandmother named Eva handed you goobers from deep inside her pockets or read you a dream.[16]

As Helene Wright, the light-skinned lady, has a most dubious background, so the Peace women are convoluted, marvelous folk. As portrayals of black women, they are as complex and nonstereotypical as any you will find in literature. Only such ancestral vitality and complexity could have produced Sula, as undefinable as she is black, as unique as she is a woman. When we are first introduced to Eva, her grandmother, and Hannah, her mother, we might at first mistake them for the banal stereotypes of black women in literature and film. Eva, as the mammy, is willing to save her children at all costs, even to the point of sticking her leg under a train to sell it. Hannah, as the loose, comely black woman, will "fuck practically anything." But even as we meet them, any comparisons with the "mammy" or the "loose woman" image is immediately put to rest.

Far from being the big-breasted, kind, religious, forever coping, asexual, loving-white-folks mammy, Eva is arrogant, independent, decidedly a man lover who loves and hates intensely. She is strong by virtue of her will, wit, and idiosyncrasies rather than because of her physique. That strength is nurtured and sustained by her hatred for Big Boy, the unfaithful father of her three children, a hatred that she says keeps her alive and happy. Her utterances throughout the book fall on the mean side of sharpness, refined by a rich imagination and a colorful folk wit. She answers what she considers to be foolish questions with nippy answers. So when her daughter Hannah asks her mother if she ever coddled her children, Eva's answer is richly to the point:

> "Play? Wasn't nobody playing in 1895. . . . What would I look like leapin' round that room playin' with youngins with three beets to my name? . . . No time, there wasn't no time. Not none. Soon as I get one day done here comes a night. With you coughin' and me watchin' so TB wouldn't take you off and if you sleepin' quiet I thought, O lord they dead and put my hand over your

mouth to feel if the breath was comin'. What you talkin' 'bout did I love you girl. I stayed alive for you can't you get that through your thick head or what is that between your ears, heifer?"[17]

She loved her children enough to stay alive and keep them alive; she needn't be physically endearing to them. Thus she retreats to her upstairs bedroom where she spends most of her time, but from which she directs the lives of her children, friends, strays, and a constant stream of boarders.

If Eva has got any of the traditional mammy qualities, it is that she is domineering, without any reason to feel that she should be otherwise. She does as she pleases. As a mother she had given life, and so when her son Plum returns from the war and attempts to "crawl back into her womb," she acts in her usual decisive manner; she burns him to death. Her explanation to Hannah for her actions reverberate with the hidden power inherent in the act of creativity, the power to destroy:

> "After all that carryin' on, just gettin' him out and keepin' him alive, he wanted to crawl back in my womb and well. . . . I ain't got the room no more even if he could do it. . . . He was a man, girl, a big old growed-up man. I didn't have that much room. I kept on dreaming it. Dreaming it and I knowed it was true. One night it wouldn't be no dream. It'd be true and I would have done it, would have let him if I'd've had the room but a big man can't be a baby all wrapped up inside his mammy no more; he suffocate. I done everything I could to make him leave me and go on and live and be a man but he wouldn't and I had to keep him out so I just thought of a way he could die like a man not all scrunched up and inside my womb, but like a man."[18]

Like the primeval Earth Mother Goddess, feared and worshipped by man, like the goddess of antiquity, older even than the biblical Eve, Eva both gives life and takes it away. She performs a ritual killing inspired by love—a ritual of sacrifice by fire.

In conjuring up this ritual, Morrison dramatically fuses her major structural elements, for she uses Time as the significant event and fire as a destructive element in describing an act that is the most unnatural death of all, a mother's killing of her own son. Eva's burning of Plum takes place in the year 1921 and is the climactic event ending that chapter. The motif of death is resounded here as it was in the chapter "1920," but this time it is not death as a result of old age, but a killing. Although Plum's death ends "1921," Eva's explanation of her actions does not occur until two years later, in 1923, the year she will witness Hannah's accidental death by fire. Between these two chapters, "1921" and "1923," the chapter "1922" focuses on an accidental death by water. Like water, fire has always been a sign of creativity and destructiveness in the human imagination. Morrison uses this forceful symbol in her brilliant treatment of a taboo subject, a mother's murder of her son. But she does not stop there. In weaving her fable, the author connects Eva's destruction of her creation, Plum, to Nature's accidental burning of the beautiful Hannah.

Hannah, Eva's second daughter, is a lovely character. Widowed young and left with her daughter Sula, she returns to her mother's house, evidently intent on never marrying again, perhaps because she has inherited from her mother the love of maleness for its own sake. "What she wanted, after Rekus [her husband] died and what she succeeded in having more often than not, was some touching everyday." But far from being the seductress traditionally dressed in red, who manipulates men to her own ends, Hannah is funky elegance, making no special effort to be alluring other than her natural sensuality, setting no demands on the men she knows. She remains independent in her self, for although she would make love to practically any man, she is extremely careful about whom she sleeps with, for "sleeping with someone implied for her a measure of trust and a definite commitment." So she becomes, as Morrison puts it, "a daylight lover," sex being a part of the ordinary and pleasant things she does every day, rather than a hidden activity at night. Hannah's personality, though, is not wound around sex; she emerges as the practical actor in the bustling house she lives in— the manager, so to speak. Now and then we get glimpses of her questionings, her wonderings, as in her fatal question to Eva about Plum's death. She is honest, as Eva is, but not in her mother's flamboyant fashion. Her succinct appraisal of her feelings for Sula, whom she says she loves but doesn't like, is spoken in anything but dramatic tones.

Just as Plum's murder is enmeshed in the recurring dream of incest that Eva cannot dispel, Hannah's terrible death is foreshadowed by dreams, strange human actions, and omens from nature. In her manner of writing around the point of focus, of playing variations on top of variations, Morrison tells us the second strange thing that happens first. Hannah asks her mother a pointed question, "Mamma, did you ever love us?" in her effort to understand why her mother killed her only son. In true Hannah fashion, it had taken her two years to broach the question, a question that must be answered before she dies, even if it means tangling with her ornery mother. The urgency with which Hannah approaches her mother is, of course, in the realm of human choice; the first strange omen, though, was beyond human control. There had been an unusual wind the night before Hannah's questionings, wind without rain that brought more heat rather than a cooling rain to the Bottom. Then there had been Sula's unusual craziness the day before as if she didn't know what hit her, coupled with Hannah's dream of a wedding in the red dress. Those familiar with dream books, as Eva was, know that a wedding signifies death. But the signs were flying so hot and heavy, Eva scarcely had time to notice any of them. Thoroughly thrown off by the weirdness of the day, Eva cannot find her comb, her favorite object, in her room where no one ever moved anything. As she is looking for it, she sees Hannah burning.

What Morrison does in creating this tragedy of Hannah's burning, reminiscent of the burning of witches, is to pile up sign upon sign, some caused by human beings themselves, others beyond their control, that in hindsight can be read as indications of an imminent tragedy. What a concentration of images, as the earthly and the supernatural, the seemingly trivial and the substantial mesh, it would seem, in a "perfection of judgment" upon Eva, who burns her only son only to see her daughter steamed to death because of a shift in the wind. The author has, in the classic sense, distilled the folk's sense of time by compressing the unseen with the known, the seemingly indifferent and idiosyncratic forces of nature with the order of events willed by human beings. Whatever goes around comes around. As if continuing that never-ending spiral, Eva insists that she was sure she saw Sula watch her mother burning, not with terror but interest. Eva's presumptuous act of burning her own son has triggered a series of effects that will haunt her many years hence when Sula will do battle with her. Her entire family is scorched by her act. In breaking a taboo, Eva provokes not only human repercussions but nature's wrath as well.

By dramatizing significant events in the lives of diverse characters such as Helene Wright and Eva and Hannah Peace, the novel outlines the precise perimeters of the Bottom's tolerance in relation to a woman's behavior. This community absorbs many styles—Helene's ladylike and hypocritical demeanor, Hannah's elegant sensuality, even Eva's arrogant murder of her son—as long as they remain within its definition of woman as wife, mother, or man lover. The Bottom's apparent toleration of these many styles is as restrictive as it is generous. Morrison focuses on this cultural characteristic in her presentation of the development of Nel and Sula's friendship. In addition, by placing the beginnings of their friendship between chapter "1921," when Eva burns Plum to death, and chapter "1923," the time of the accidental burning of Hannah, Morrison reminds us of the impact their female relatives are having on these impressionable twelve-year-old girls.

Out of their awareness that their lives, as black females, are restricted by their community and by the outer society, Nel and Sula are drawn to each other. As only-girl children, each takes the other as sister, sharing each other's dreams of freedom and excitement:

> So when they met, first in those chocolate halls and next through the ropes of the swing, they felt the ease and comfort of old friends. Because each had discovered years before that they were neither white nor male, and that all freedom and triumph was forbidden to them, they had set about creating something else to be. Their meeting was fortunate, for it let them use each other to grow on. Daughters of distant mothers and incomprehensible fathers (Sula's because he was dead; Nel's because he wasn't), they found in each other's eyes the intimacy they were looking for.[19]

Nel and Sula's friendship is sustained not only by their recognition of each other's restrictions but also by their anticipation of sexuality and by an ultimate bond, the responsibility for unintentionally causing the death of another. However, although the two girls share these strong bonds, they are different, for Sula, who is the adventurer, often allows "her emotions to dictate her behavior," and Nel is more cautious, more consistent. As a result, in this chapter, Sula appears to be the more focal actor of the two.

The chapter "1922" is deceptive in its flow, for it is so innocent in its springtime visions, so bittersweet in its images of budding twelve-year-old girls, that the drama of Chicken Little's drowning catches us off guard. But a note of pain, ever so slightly touched on, begins a shift in tone when Sula overhears her mother's comment that she may love her, but she does not like her. The pain of her mother's assertion is mingled with the beginning of sexual stirrings that she and Nel feel as they play by the river. Overflowing with the energy of repressed pain and pleasure, the emotional Sula swings the little boy, Chicken Little, until he falls into the river, never to be seen again.

Because of the feelings that led to it, this accidental death by water is Sula's baptism into her seach for some continuity between the natural world and the social world, between the precariousness of life and the inevitability of death. The author emphasizes the impact this death has on Sula by having Shadrack, as well as Nel, witness it. A veteran of the witnessing of horrific death, Shadrack attempts to give Sula some sense of its meaning. As the originator of National Suicide Day, he assures her of her own permanency, that she need not have fear of death. Because of his own singular concern with this fear, his one utterance in the book, the word *always*, takes on mythic proportions. Although Shadrack does not intend the meaning Sula attributes to this word, he is in a sense right, for Chicken Little's death and the emotions that surround it will always be with her, not the drowning itself so much as the feeling that she cannot rely either on herself or on others. Perhaps the old women at Chicken Little's funeral are right when

> they danced and screamed, not to protest God's will but to acknowledge it and confirm once more their conviction that the only way to avoid the Hand of God is to get in it.[20]

Morrison concludes Part I by reiterating her major structural elements, for Part I ends not with the death of someone but with a wedding, the wedding of Nel and Jude in the year 1927. Their marriage becomes *the* event in the Bottom, bringing together the community in a moment of feasting, revelry, and renewal. But as Eva has already told us, and as Hannah's death clearly illustrates, the dream of a wedding means death. This wedding seems to mean death, not only for Nel and Sula's girl friendship but for Jude and Nel's previous sense of themselves.

The delineation of Nel and Sula's personalities and the particular roads they take are finely drawn in this chapter, particularly in relation to the mores of the Bottom. Just as Sula was more focal in the chapter about these young girls' personal explorations of life and death, so Nel is the major actor in this chapter about the community's initiation of young adults into its fold. Jude chooses Nel because she has no desire to make herself and delights in caring about someone else. Like so many young men in his community, he begins thinking of marriage because he needs desperately to accomplish something of significance, this something being a job at helping to build the new River Road:

> It was while he was full of such dreams his body already feeling the rough work clothes, his hands already curved to the pick handle, that he spoke to Nel about getting married. She seemed receptive but hardly anxious. It was after he stood in lines for six days running and saw the gang boss pick out thin-armed white boys from the Virginia hills and the bull-necked Greeks and Italians and heard over and over, "Nothing else today. Come back tomorrow," that he got the message. So it was rage and the determination to take on a man's role anyhow that made him press Nel about settling down. He needed some of his appetites filled, some posture of adulthood recognized, but mostly he wanted someone to care about his hurt, to care very deeply.[21]

Jude's reasons for pressing Nel into marriage reinforce our sense of the Bottom's definition of woman. As his helpmate, Nel is a buffer between his desire for his own autonomy and the restrictions the outside world places on him. Her marriage to him will replace the need he so intensely feels to have some impact on the world and thus enable him to accept his state.

As the Bottom dances and eats, as Nel responds to Jude's kiss, Sula takes another road distinct and apart from the community. We are left to contemplate Nel and Sula's childhood as reflected in the structural lines of Morrison's tale. Nel Wright's sense of her own identity had begun with her trip to her great-grandmother's funeral and the beginning of her friendship with Sula Peace. Our first insight into Sula's ancestry begins with our hesitant comprehension of Eva's fire murder of her only son to save his manhood. Sula's personality is gravely affected by the events that surround the watery death of Chicken Little. Her mother, Hannah, as if a witch, is seared to death in so tragic and senseless a way that supernatural omens are needed to justify it. As their childhood ends, all of these events reach their logical conclusion. Nel, the daughter of the proper Helene Wright, marries Jude, losing the sense of her own identity she had gotten a glimpse of in her friendship with Sula, and Sula, daughter of the distinctive Peace women, leaves the Bottom. The patterned story of Nel and Sula's friendship, woven as it is with threads of their community's culture and their families' histories, is rhythmically embroidered with knots of death and stunningly colored by the elemental forces of Nature.

Part I explored the many styles of women's behavior that the Bottom is willing to absorb, while it traces the friendship of Nel and Sula as young girls. In contrast, Part II emphasizes the forms that this community will not tolerate, while it examines the friendship and estrangement of Nel and Sula as adult women. Foremost to Part II is the Bottom's concept of evil, for that is the way in which they characterize intolerable behavior. Although there is a progression in theme, however, the structural elements of this fable remain the same. The author immediately reiterates her framework by beginning Part II with an uncommon freak of nature, a plague of robins. Like the marigolds that would not sprout in *The Bluest Eye*, this oddity of nature holds sway in the imagination, conjuring images of dread or at least of the unknown.

In Part II, as in Part I, Nature's signs are intertwined with the persistent recurrence of death, and the time when a particular death is focused upon is the core around which each chapter is built. However, although the deaths in Part I are primarily physical, the deaths in Part II are emotional and spiritual as well. In the chapter "1937," Nel and Sula's friendship is presumably killed because Sula sleeps with Jude, Nel's husband. In the chapter "1939," Sula and Ajax's relationship is killed by Sula's attempt to possess Ajax. In 1940 Sula dies physically, but we feel to some extent that her death is due to spiritual malnutrition as much as any physical cause. In 1941 a significant number of folk in the Bottom are killed in their attempt to destroy the tunnel that they were not allowed to build. In effect they bring about their own deaths because they have been spiritually as well as physically drained by poverty, harsh weather, and starvation—a powerlessness. Death is not just a physical occurrence. Its presence is related to the folk's spiritual needs left unfulfilled by Nature and society.

Related to death, in Part II, is the figure of Sula and the images of nature that accompany her. Interestingly, the elements of air and earth are as pervasive as the elements of fire and water in the previous section. So in the chapter "1937," Sula's return is heralded by a plague of robins and by "the peculiar quality of that May," a quality that Nel alone notices. More than anything, Sula's lover, Ajax, wants to fly a plane. Sula thinks of Ajax's body in images of gold, alabaster, and loam, which she waters, and of sex with him as "the high silence of orgasm." As Sula dies in chapter "1940," she remembers the word *always* that Shadrack had uttered on the day of Chicken Little's drowning and feels her death to be "a sleep of water always." In keeping with that image of water, her funeral is concluded by a shower of rain. The collapse of the tunnel in chapter "1941" is preceded not only by Sula's death but by the sudden change from extreme cold to intense heat, which causes the earth to shift and the river to overflow. On that climactic January, Shadrack watches his ritual, National Suicide Day, come to life before his very eyes as water, earth, wind, and fire combine to create a holocaust. Part II then begins with an oddity of nature and ends with a natural disaster, one seeming to announce the return of Sula to the Bottom, the other seeming to underscore her death.

In addition to the elements of Death and Nature, Time, in Part II, continues to be crucial to Morrison's patterning of her fable. The way in which the events are arranged is not so much chronology as it is the juxtaposition of two views about the nature of living. By using Nel and Sula, two parts of an intense friendship, as the embodiment of these views, Morrison personalizes the philosophical content of her tale. But these points of view would not assume mythic proportions as they do in this novel if they were merely idiosyncratic, if they were not set within the context of a culture. This novel is a fable because it presents a culture's philosophy about life and death, good and evil.

The community sees Sula as the embodiment of evil. All of their ills and sufferings take visual form in her being. From the year 1937, when Sula returns to the Bottom, to the year 1940, when she dies, a presence charges the Bottom with an energy, the fuse of which is to defeat her by surviving her. What is it about Sula Peace that turns this community into a buttressed fort against her? The reasons are not so much explanation as intersecting circles of fear, the greatest one being the fear of difference.

Ironically, Sula is both the sum of her ancestors and greater than each part. Like Eva, she is tough, onery, and nippy. Her first action upon her return to the Bottom, in fact, is to do battle with her grandmother and to banish her to an old folks home, contrary to the mores of the Bottom. But Sula's expulsion of Eva is not her mortal sin. She and her grandmother clash on the issue that will emphasize her difference in a community that believes it needs consistency to survive: Sula wants to make herself rather than others. In a scorching dialogue between Sula and her grandmother, the perfection of judgment upon Eva comes full circle. Eva assaults Sula with the question:

> "When you gone to get married? You need to have some babies. It'll settle you."
> "I don't want to make somebody else. I want to make myself."
> "Selfish. Ain't no woman got no business floatin' around without no man."
> "You did."
> "Not by choice."
> "Mama did."
> "Not by choice, I said it ain't right for you to want to stay off by yourself. You need . . . I'm a tell you what you need."
> Sula sat up. "I need you to shut your mouth."

When Eva replies that God will strike her down, Sula retorts:

> "Which God? The one who watched you burn Plum? . . . Maybe one night when you dozing in that wagon flicking flies and swallowing spit, maybe I'll just tip on up here with some kerosene and—who knows—you may make the brightest flame of them all.[22]

As if she had carefully studied her grandmother, Sula introduces the one threat that would drive fear into Eva's heart. In so doing she dethrones the haughty mistress of the house. What is most interesting, though, is Eva's resistance to Sula's need to make herself, a concept totally alien to one who loves maleness for its own sake. Yet Sula has inherited this need for independence, this arrogance, this orneriness, at least partially from the Eva who had the gall to destroy her only son to save his maleness.

Like Hannah, Sula sleeps with the husbands of her neighbors indiscriminately. But although Hannah made the men feel complete and seemed to compliment the women by wanting their husbands, Sula sleeps with them once and discards them. Unlike her mother, Sula does not experience sex as a pleasant pastime. Orgasm becomes the moment for her when she feels her full strength and power at the same time that she experiences complete aloneness. Orgasm, for Sula, "was not eternity but the death of time and a loneliness so profound the word itself had no meaning." In sex she knows not her partner but herself.

Because of her drive for self-knowledge, and because of the imagination she brings to the memories of her ancestors and to her own experiences, Sula emerges as a unique woman. In two beautifully terse analyses, Morrison illumines her character:

> Sula was distinctly different. Eva's arrogance and Hannah's self indulgence merged in her and, with a twist that was all her own imagination, she lived out her days exploring her own thoughts and emotions giving them full reign, feeling no obligation to please anybody unless their pleasure pleased her. As willing to feel pain as to give pain, to feel pleasure as to give pleasure, hers was an experimental life—ever since her mother's remarks sent her flying up those stairs, ever since her one major feeling of responsibility had been exorcised on the bank of a river with a closed place in the middle. The first experience taught her that there was no other that you could count on; the second that there was no self to count on either. She had no center, no speck around which to grow.[23]

> She had been looking along for a friend, and it took her a while to discover that a lover was not a comrade and could never be—for a woman. And that no one would ever be that version of herself which she sought to reach out to and touch with an ungloved hand. There was only her own mood and whim, and if that was all there was, she decided to turn the naked hand toward it, discover it and let others become as intimate with their own selves as she was.
>
> In a way, her strangeness, her naïveté, her craving for the other half of her equation was the consequence of an idle imagination. Had she paints, or clay, or knew the discipline of the dance, or strings; had she anything to engage her tremendous curiosity and her gift for metaphor, she might have exchanged the restlessness and preoccupation with whim for an activity that provided her with all she yearned for. And like any artist with no art form, she became dangerous.[24]

Sula has the distinction of being herself in a community that believes that self-hood can only be selfishness. Her view of life is different from others, as if the birthmark above one of her eyes has either distorted or enlarged her vision. It is with maddening recognition that we grasp Sula's tragedy—she is too full, and yet too static, to grow. She has stared into that abyss where nothing in life can be relied on—where nothing really matters. Like Cholly Breedlove in *The Bluest Eye*, she has developed the freedom of narcissism allowed only to the gods. Such freedom is not allowed to mere mortals as the oldest stories of all cultures testify. Sula is unique, though, even in the company of mortals who try to live life as if they are divine, for she is a woman. Her life, according to the customs of all traditions, is not hers to experiment with, to create or destroy. Her life is meant to result in other lives. So like Pauline Breedlove in *The Bluest Eye*, she is an artist without an art form. When Sula stares into the abyss that sex so clearly evokes for her, she is not looking for another entity but for another version of herself, for a total union possible only when each perceives the other as possibly being his or her self. Since woman is not usually perceived by man in that total sense, Sula abandons any attempt at union and seeks only herself. Since she cannot have everything, she will at least, or at most, have herself. Marked at birth, she will pursue her own uniqueness.

But such total absorption leads to destructiveness, for the world, used to compromise, will not accept, cannot understand, such concentration—perhaps it must not, to maintain even a slim semblance of order. Using the inexplicable fact that Shadrack is civil to Sula while he shuns everyone else, convinced that she is committing the unforgettable sin—sleeping with white men—and buttressed by her disregard for their God-ordained ways, the town turns Sula into a witch, conjuring spells against her power and acting righteously to prove themselves better than the ignoble she-devil. This lone woman's effect on her community recalls the always perplexing mystery of humanity's need for an evil one, for a devil:

> Their conviction of Sula's evil changed them in accountable yet mysterious ways. Once the source of their personal misfortune was identified, they had leave to protect and love one another. They began to cherish their husbands and wives, protect their children, repair their homes and in general band together against the devil in their midst.[25]

All things have their use and even Sula's evil nature is used by her community to validate and enrich its own existence. As pariah, she gives them a focus through which they achieve some unity, at least temporarily, just as Pecola's madness in *The Bluest Eye* is used by the townsfolk as evidence of their own sanity, their own strength, their own beauty. The need human beings continually exhibit for a scapegoat, so they can justify themselves, is one of the mysteries of human existence that Morrison consistently probes in her works. Why is it that human beings need an enemy, or a martyr, to come together, to feel their own worth, or merely to survive? Why is it that human beings are fascinated with "evil," creating images in its likeness, as children create monsters? It is significant, too, the emphasis the author places on women as accessible scapegoat figures for communities, for any obviously conscious disregard of cultural mores on their part seems to represent not only a threat to the community but to the whole species as well—hence the preponderance of witches, pariahs, and insane women in the history of humanity.

Most importantly, through Morrison's characterization of Eva, Hannah, and Sula, we see that it is not merely social deviance that makes one a pariah. That cursed label is given only to one whose behavior seems so different from, so *at odds with*, the prevailing norm that it cannot be absorbed into the unconscious of the community. In this case, from her birth, the community's unconscious had already been prepared to accept Sula as distinct. It is significant that Sula's birthmark is perceived in different ways, depending on the perspective of the beholder. When Morrison first describes it, "it is something like a stemmed rose" that adds excitement to an otherwise plain face. To Shadrack, who reveres fish, it is the mark of a tadpole, identifying Sula as a friend. To Jude, the mark resembles a rattlesnake, the sting of which is taken way by Sula's smile. To the folk, the mark is Evil, the mark of Hannah's ashes, identifying Sula from her very beginning as a devil. So Sula, not Eva or Hannah, is a pariah because she is distinctly different, because she is consciously seeking to make herself rather than others, and she is totally unconcerned about what others think; in other words, she does not care.

Although Sula does not care about what the community thinks, she does care about Nel, the friend to whom she returns in the Bottom, and she comes to care about Ajax, her lover, for a time. Morrison weaves in a specific pattern the strands of the community's belief system together with the estrangement of Nel and Sula and the love affair of Ajax and Sula so we might better understand the complexity of both points of view. First, the author tells us about the community's view of Nature and Evil, after which we experience the estrangement of Nel and Sula and the community's designation of Sula as a witch. Finally, the story of Sula's and Ajax's relationship is followed by Sula's death and the death of the folk in that tunnel. In carefully charting her pattern, Morrison asks us to contemplate the meaning of her design.

The story of the apparent dissolution of the strong friendship between Nel and Sula occurs within the context of the Bottom's need to band against Sula and as such is the embodied formulation of the gap between Sula and the community from which she comes. Unlike the other folk in the Bottom, Nel is elated when Sula returns. Her joy is expressed, as their fear is, in terms of nature. She

> . . . noticed the peculiar quality of the May that followed the leaving of the
> birds. It had a sheen, a glimmering as of green, rain-soaked Saturday nights

(lit by the excitement of newly installed street lights; of lemon yellow after-noons bright with iced drinks and splashes of daffodils).[26]

For Nel, the world again becomes magical and interesting because of Sula's presence. She emphasizes their unity, how talking to Sula was like talking to herself. Yet Sula's gift of magic becomes a spiritual death for Nel because these two women are no longer one. They have taken different roads in life and have formed the meaning-ness of their lives into different patterns. Nel's life, in essence, revolves around Jude, her husband, and their three children, while Sula's life revolves around her own exploratory imagination. When Sula sleeps with Jude, obviously not so much as an act of passion, but more as an exploratory act, or even, we suspect, as a means to more intimacy with Nel, she breaks the one taboo that could shatter their girlhood friendship. Their respective reactions to this act counterpoint one another, revealing their different value systems.

In her soliloquy, Nel stares into that abyss that Sula experienced so sharply when she overheard Hannah admit that she did not like her. That is, Nel learns that one can never wholly rely on anyone. She remembers Sula's words, "The real hell of Hell is that it is forever," and counters "Sula was wrong. Hell ain't things lasting forever, Hell is change." Unable to get away from her self, which is pain, and the pain, which is her self, she learns, too, as Sula had, that there is no self to rely on. Her pain and her fear of it become in her mind a dirty ball of fur and string signifying nothing. What Sula does for Nel, as she has always done in their friendship, is to share her experimental knowledge with her. By so doing Sula underscores the illusion on which Nel's life is based. From a practical point of view, Nel has been prepared solely for the role of being a handmaiden to Jude or to someone like him. By sleeping with Jude, Sula strips Nel of her illusion, leaving her with nothing she can rely on. In contrast to Sula, who turns this jarring knowledge into a reason for exploration, Nel *knows* that "her thighs are forever empty," that her life is finished, and that she nonetheless longs for those who had crushed her:

> That was too much. To lose Jude and not have Sula to talk to about it because it was Sula that he had left her for.[27]

In one stroke, Nel loses the bases of her emotional life, her husband, Jude, and her only friend, Sula. What else is there for her to do but die—slowly.

Between Nel's soliloquy about her pain and Sula's reactions to their broken friendship, Morrison inserts the community's judgment of Sula as a witch and Sula's acceptance of that judgment. The folk's judgment of Sula is partly based on Sula's infidelity to her friend Nel; in part, Sula's acceptance of their judgment is her realization that her only true friend has become one of *them*. Sula had thought of Nel as being one with her and finds out, at least from her point of view, that Nel is just like all the women she has known who hold onto their men "because they were only afraid of losing their jobs." Nel becomes like the others, the people she visualizes as spiders, afraid of experiment, afraid of living. So their friendship freezes to death, Sula surmises, because Nel becomes dead like the rest of the town.

These are Nel and Sula's perceptions about what has happened, perceptions on opposite sides of the spectrum. But Morrison's unrelenting probing assails us with a complicated truth that lies somewhere between the pain and emptiness of Nel, husbandless with three children, left to live without any hope of really living, and Sula's pure view of people who are afraid to live because they are possessive, because they do not want to experience pain and therefore never experience pleasure. As Sula explores her feelings about her estrangement from Nel, she characterizes the women of the Bottom in this way:

> The narrower their lives, the wider their hips. Those with husbands had folded themselves into starched coffins, their sides bursting with other people's skinned dreams and bony regrets. Those without men were like sour-tipped needles featuring one constant empty eye. Those with men had had the sweetness sucked from their breath by ovens and steam kettles. Their children were like distant but exposed wounds whose aches were not less intimate because separate from their flesh. They had looked at the world and back at their children, back at the world and back again at their children, and Sula knew that one clear young eye was all that kept the knife away from the throat's curve.[28]

But Sula, too, is not immune from the need for permanence and consistency. Morrison juxtaposes Sula's caustic analysis of the women in the Bottom with her relationship with Ajax, a relationship in which Sula discovers the desire to be possessive.

Sula and Ajax's love relationship emerges as the fullest communication between a man and woman in Morrison's works. As persons, they are well suited to each other. Ajax, beautifully male and heroic (as his name implies), had been the object of Nel and Sula's adolescent dreams of anticipated sexuality. His two loves, his conjure-woman mother and airplanes, tell us that he expects women to be mentally as well as physically interesting, and that he wants more than anything to fly, far above the limits set for him. Like Sula, he resists limitations and ties. But unlike her, he has found an object other than himself on which to focus his imagination, although it is interesting that he, too, will never to able to fulfill his dream, will never be able to fly a plane. They love each other; in that they find another version of themselves in each other, at least for a while. He is attracted to Sula, suspecting that "this was perhaps the only other woman other than his mother he knew whose life was her own, who could deal with life efficiently and who was not interested in nailing him." Their relationship solidifies because they have genuine conversations, the real pleasure that Sula is seeking. But having discovered this pleasure, Sula wants to keep it, possess it, always have it when she wants it. So in the manner of age-old seduction, she adorns herself, cleans the house, and whispers to him, "Lean on me," words that epitomize the relationship between Nel and Jude, words that thrust the concept of dependence and therefore of possessiveness into their relationship. Knowing the signs, Ajax rushes off to watch the planes that he will never be allowed to fly.

Now, Sula experiences the pain of absence she had unwittingly inflicted on her friend Nel. Perhaps women feel wronged when men leave them, not only, or sometimes not at all, because they will lose their jobs, but because of the pain of absence. Sula experiences:

> An absence so decorative, so ornate, it was difficult for her to understand how she had ever endured, without falling dead or being consumed, his magnificent presence.[29]

Yet she knows that the relationship would have ended eventually, for had he not left, her insatiable curiosity would have compelled her to dig deeper and deeper into his psyche until she hurt him. Realizing the essential loneliness of her stance in life, she sings, "There aren't any more new songs, and I have sung all the ones there are." What else is there left for her to do but die?

Although Nel and Sula have taken opposite paths, they are both dying. But Nel is dying, as Sula says, "like a stump," while Sula feels that she is "going down like one of those redwoods." Death brings them together again when Nel comes to see Sula on her deathbed. Both thirty, the evil Sula is dying physically, the Bottom feels, as retribution for her sins, while the virtuous Nel's "hot brown eyes had turned to agate, and her skin had taken on the sheen of maple struck down, split and sanded at the height of its green." Sula had lived gloriously before she was struck down; Nel, on the other hand, endures physically, but only at the price of never having fulfilled herself. Their conversation, an echo of Eva's conversation with Sula, concerns how much one is allowed to live:

> "You can't have it all, Sula."
> "Why? I can do it all, why can't I have it all?"
> "You *can't* do it all. You a woman and a colored woman at that. You can't act like a man. You can't be walking around all independent-like, doing whatever you like, taking what you want, leaving what you don't."

Their exchange illuminates the difference between their philosophies. Sula exclaims:

> 'You think I don't know what your life is like just because I ain't living it? I know what every colored woman in this country is doing."
> "What's that?"

"Dying. Just like me. But the difference is they dying like a stump. Me, I going down like one of those redwoods. I sure did live in this world."

"Really? What have you got to show for it?"

"Show? To who? Girl, I got my mind. And what goes on in it. Which is to say, I got me."

"Lonely, ain't it?"

"Yes. But my lonely is *mine*. Now your lonely is somebody else's. Made by somebody else and handed to you. Ain't that something? A second-hand lonely."

As Nel leaves her, Sula crystallizes the difference.

"How you know?" Sula asked.

"Know what?" Nel wouldn't look at her.

"About who was *good*. How you know it was you?"

"What you mean?"

"I mean maybe it wasn't you. Maybe it was me."

In her final speech in this novel, Sula questions the community's insistence on its own goodness and its designation of anything that falls outside its ken as evil. She does this most specifically in relation to their view of woman, which she proclaims is entirely to the community's use without any concern for the women who must live it. In spite of the community's judgments, however, and despite their estrangement, Nel and Sula still relate to each other as they had in childhood. Although the Bottom has labeled the behavior of one of them as evil and the other as good, they continue to complement one another. As the exploratory half in their relationship, Sula had always been the one to share with Nel what it was to experience this or that. So Sula had been Nel's source of liberation from stern parents or from a rigid community that sought to destroy any imagination she had. Nel had been Sula's source of stability when crises occurred, as in the death of Chicken Little. When Nel experiences the pain of Jude's absence, it is to Sula that she wants to talk, an impossibility since Sula is the reason for his leaving. When Sula is dying, her last thought is to share with Nel this most personal of experiences. "Well, I'll be damned," she thought, "it didn't even hurt. Wait'll I tell Nel." We later learn that when Sula is dead, Nel is the one in the Bottom who makes the arrangements for her funeral and is the only one who formally attends it. The practical element in their relationship, Nel always performs well in a crisis.

In the pursuit of complex truth, Morrison has juxtaposed the world of Nel next to the world of Sula, the world in which practicality and survival are foremost to the world in which exploration and imagination make life worth living. Which world view holds the answer to life? Does either? Nel does as she is told; any sparkle she has is rubbed down to a dull glow so she can become a sensible, comforting wife, so she can do those things, however tedious, necessary for survival. But her world is dependent on another, the world of her husband or her children. Since these worlds collapse, she is left without a context. Sula pursues herself, exploring her emotions and imagination. Her world is hers, but left without a focus for her imagination, she becomes destructive, and because her stance seems contrary to the survival of her community, she is left alone, estranged from others. Finally, she turns in on herself, but the self, as her experience with Chicken Little or as her relationship with Ajax proves, cannot be totally relied on either.

Although Sula dies, Morrison does not want us to conclude that the philosophy of the Bottom is superior. The folk's major premise is that the way to conquer evil is to survive it, to outlast it. So when Sula dies, the folk feel they have won, that a brighter day is dawning, that there will be work for black men in building the tunnel, which has been planned, abandoned, and replanned. The chapter "1941" makes it plain that the evil they need to conquer cannot merely be outlasted, and that Sula's presence in the Bottom has little to do with brighter days. If anything, her absence makes things worse, for without a pariah, the folk revert to not caring about each other. What becomes clear is that Nature will always inflict disasters on them, that the evil of racism will result in jobless man and women, and that death will be always with them. With or without a pariah, evil days continue, and although the philosophy of survival may be useful in combatting them, it is a limited method. As if reminding the Bottom that it is still vulnerable to catastrophe, regardless of Sula's death, the natural fall of the year is replaced by an early frost, destroying the crops, resulting in sickness of the body and in a spiritless, stingy Thanksgiving. Then the frost is followed by the false hope of a summer January, a heat that will cause the earth to shift in the tunnel they all yearn to build. In fact, if anything, Sula's death, coupled with the natural and social ills that affect them, bring mass death to the Bottom.

Consistent in the novel, Shadrack appears as the figure who stands for the fear of death. Ironically, this shell-shocked soldier realizes through the death of Sula that his National Suicide Day ritual does not ward off death. He had reassured Sula, his only visitor in all those years, that she would *always* be. Yet she, too, had died and would never come again. On January third, on National Suicide Day, he pays no attention to the details of his ritual for he no longer believes in its efficacy, and, ironically, on this particular day, national suicide happens not in ritual but in fact. Looking at death in the sunshine and being unafraid, laughing folk follow Shadrack:

> As the initial group of about twenty people passed more houses, they called to the people standing in doors and leaning out of windows to join them; to help them open further this slit in the veil, this respite from an anxiety from dignity, from gravity, from the weight of that very adult pain that had undergirded them all those years before. Called to them to come out and play in the sunshine—as though the sunshine would last, as though there really

was hope. The same hope that kept them picking beans for other farmers, kept them from finally leaving as they talked of doing; kept them knee-deep in other people's dirt; kept them excited about other people's wars; kept them solicitous of white people's children; kept them convinced that some magic "government" was going to lift them up, out and away from the dirt, those beans, those wars.[33]

Revitalized by false hope, they dance to the site of promise—the tunnel— and in an act of defiance try to kill the tunnel they were forbidden to build. The heat, the false hope, cause the earth to shift and the water to break. Many are suffocated, drowned, or crushed to death as Shadrack rings his bell, proclaiming the unexpectedness of death. Too long insistent on outlasting evil, worn down by natural and social forces, the folk's one defiant gesture is built on a false hope that keeps them in shackles.

Morrison's fable emphasizes the paradox inherent in the philosophy of survival. True, when one is not able to destroy evil, one must try to outlast it. But human beings have to demand more from life than mere survival, or they may not survive at all. To really live life, there must be some imagination, some exploration, so there can be some creative action.

The last chapter of the novel, "1965," hammers this point home, for although some of the folk have survived and there has been some progress, the Bottom and its distinctiveness have disappeared. Ironically, black folk had moved from the Bottom only to realize too late that hill land had become valuable. In terms of monetary value, it had become, in fact, what the white farmer had told his slave a hundred years before, "the bottom of Heaven."

Structurally, this chapter acts as the Bottom's eulogy, weaving all the novel's threads together into a completed fabric. Nel is, as she must be, our point of view character, for through Sula, she has participated in another world view, distinct from her own. She alone can recognize the pattern that was being woven all those years. In talking with Eva, the mother who has outlasted her progeny, Nel is confronted with the waste and arrogance inherent in living solely to make others. Confronted by Eva's meanness, Nel recognizes the Bottom's narrowness, finally its undoing, even as she can still appreciate its marvelous distinctiveness. Nel's conversation with Eva also reminds us of the futile deaths that pervade this book: the death of Plum, Chicken Little, Hannah, and finally Sula. In confusing Nel with Sula, Eva reminds Nel of the unity of feeling she once had with this cursed woman. As if to heighten our awareness of the death of the Bottom, Nel goes to the cemetery, the only remaining monument of this community. On her way she passes Shadrack, the symbol of the fear of death throughout this novel. It is fitting that these two should be our final witnesses to this fable for they represent throughout the novel the personal embodiment of the community's concept of survival that is rooted not in the wish to live but in the fear of dying.

As a result of her confrontation with the pattern of her life, Nel realizes the emptiness she had felt all of these years was not the pain of Jude's absence but that of Sula's. It is with Sula that she had experienced the excitement of being human and had had the opportunity to go beyond the Bottom's narrow principle of surrival. Through Sula, she could have transformed her own life just as the Bottom might have. If she and it had sought to understand what Sula meant, if she and it had explored the possibilities of life, perhaps Sula might have survived, Nel might have lived, and the Bottom might still be. As it is, the tale of Sula, the marked woman, and her community, the Bottom, remains the stuff out of which legends are made.

PART III
The Vision and Craft of Toni Morrison

Toni Morrison's first two novels reveal a consistency in vision and craft. In creating fables, she weaves together the quest of young black girls for womanhood with the cultural values of their communities. She structures her tales by showing how the mythologial system of their communities, specifically their concepts of time, nature, and death, relate to their definition of woman. By so doing, she dramatizes the effects this definition has on her girl-women.

Although Morrison's major characters all struggle toward womanhood, their sense of what it means is drastically different. For Pecola, womanhood means being loved; for Nel, it is a straight narrow line; and for Sula, to be a woman means self-fulfillment. Morrison's first novel, The Bluest Eye, explores the reasons why it is so difficult for black women to achieve the definition of womanhood ascribed to by American society and still remain true to their racial identity. The second novel, Sula, penetrates further beyond the norms of any community, black or white, although through them, to a deeper analysis of selfhood as woman. Realizing that the dominant norms are both impossible or undesirable, Sula pushes beyond them. So there is a development in the concept of womanhood and selfhood from one book to the next.

The pursuit of womanhood, as it affects their wholeness, begins in earnest at that vulnerable age when Pecola and Sula are caught between the physical stages of girlhood and womanhood. It is at this quivering point that Pecola is raped and begins her search for blue eyes, and that Sula discovers the hard emotional fact that no one, not even her mother, or even herself, can be totally relied on. The approach of adolescence marks the growth of their body sexuality and the emergence of their mind consciousness. Along with sexuality comes the desire for knowledge, the knowledge of self. In both Pecola and Sula's quest for wholeness and self-knowledge, sexuality becomes the vehicle. Pecola's rape by her father is the culmination of the lie her community and family have been trapped by. "It was the only love she was to know," in her search for love, for womanness. The act itself embodies the love-hate lacerating not only her father's life but the life of her community. At age twelve, Pecola experiences sex as an act of love-terror, so she goes mad. Sula's sexuality is not fully explored in the novel until she is twenty-seven years old, but again her knowledge of herself as woman is determined largely by her attitude toward sex. She uses the act itself as a means to self-knowledge rather than intimacy with another, for she doubts the possibility of true communication with men, who would be her lovers but not her friends. Sex verifies for her the awesome powerfulness and loneliness of her self.

The community's final rejection of both Sula and Pecola relates to these women's experience of sex. The rape of Pecola and her subsequent madness completely alienates her from her community; the folk's insistence that Sula sleeps with white men becomes the damning reason for labeling her a devil. Because a particular society's definition of womanhood and therefore of the female self often incorporates that group's view of sexuality and of nature, both novels are explorations of cultural and mythic beliefs. In both novels, these beliefs are the bases for the behavior of the families and the communities from which Pecola and Sula evolve.

In *The Bluest Eye*, the emphasis is placed on the inversion of truth caused by one culture's attempt to impose its value system inappropriately on another culture. So the effect, even if it seems successful as in Geraldine's case, is grotesque. Pecola cannot and should not want to be a blue-eyed, straight-haired lady. But since that image is imposed on her as the means to wealth, love, and happiness, she is defeated by her own culture's inability to separate image from substance. Since she is *the* vulnerable character in the book, she is awake to the contradictions in the very air she breathes. Pecola's family has already been defeated by society's racism and callousness; the community of women around her, as well as her mother, Pauline, have fastened onto the prevailing concept of beauty as the reason why they cannot become all they want to be. How, then, can Pecola become a woman, how then can she be loved, since she does not have the physical characteristics necessary for happiness? Since Pecola, sensitive and poor, is frightened by life, she does not question the norm, does not fight the images that attack her essence. But then neither do any of the other black women in the book. They are all attempting to straddle the gulf between image and substance, at the price of self-hatred. Only Claudia and Frieda, girl-children as they are, rebel against the norm, but they have yet to be assailed by the beautiful terror of adolescent fantasizing. This test, the need to be seen as all things beautiful and good in the eyes of another, still lies ahead of them. Pecola's end is tragic because she, unlike her elders, cannot lie to herself; in totally believing the efficacy of the image, she reveals its absurdity.

Her doom underscores the hidden tragedy, the waste in the lives of all the black women in the novel.

Sula, in contrast, rejects her own culture's definition of woman, as a being meant to make someone else, whether that someone be man or child. She seeks herself. But the community's norms, nonetheless, are crucial to her survival and development. Because she rejects them, she becomes isolated even unto death. Her presence challenges the value system at the core of the community's existence so they reject her desire to recreate the definition of a woman to suit her own sensibility. Both Pecola and Sula's communities, then, are hindrances to them in their quest for womanhood, although Pecola differs from Sula in that she accepts the norm; it is just that she cannot achieve it.

The conflict between Pecola and Sula's vision and the visions of their communities is heightened by the ever-present image of *eyes*. Pecola wants the impossible blue eyes, a desire transmitted to her by her community and a desire that distorts her and their abilities to perceive reality. One of Sula's eyes is indelibly marked at birth, proclaiming her distinctive vision. She is as she is. Although Pecola seeks to elevate herself to the level of a desirable human being by possessing those blue eyes, Sula pursues her own divinity, refusing to restrict her essence to the limits set by the human beings around her. Thus her attempt to be more than human flies not only in the face of the prevailing definition of woman, but even the concept of what man should try to do. But the community reacts to these two women in much the same way, turning Pecola into a dumping ground for their own feelings of helplessness, inverting Sula's godlike narcissism into witchcraft. Pecola's madness makes everyone feel sane; Sula's evilness heightens everyone's goodness, thus uniting their communities. Both characters, although one seeks to confirm and the other to reject the communities' norms, are rendered tragic, as the community uses them to aggrandize itself.

Illuminating the theme of distinctive vision, Morrison weaves the threads of the outlandish, the extraordinary, into the normal fabric of her characters' worlds. Both books begin with an inversion of the truth: in *The Bluest Eyes*, the inversion about the beautiful and the true is introduced as the failure of the marigolds to sprout. In *Sula*, the origins of the Bottom is itself an inversion. Even dramatic acts at the center of these complex tales are consequences of the waste and horror of inversion. Pecola is raped in spring, the season of love, as the lie at the center of her father's vision of himself overwhelms him, and Eva, preferring infanticide to potential spiritual incest, burns her junkie soldier son to death in an attempt to save his maleness. Her fiery act haunts her generations as she witnesses her daughter's fiery accidental death and is herself threatened with a fire death by her granddaughter Sula. The family is torn asunder, its members' roles inverted, as father rapes daughter, mother kills son, and granddaughter threatens grandmother.

Such disorder can only end in death of the body or spirit. Death, a most natural occurrence in life, is too often summoned before its time as the only resolution to disharmony in these inverted worlds. Counterpointing the natural flow of birth, death, and rebirth, the seasons shift abnormally or have abnormal effects. In *The Bluest Eye*, the natural surge of blood lust in the spring results in rape; in *Sula*, the unnaturally cold fall followed by a warm winter causes the earth to shift, killing many folk of the Bottom. As if responding to the disharmony caused by humankind, Nature goes awry.

The theme of inversion, as well as the structuring of the novel, in fact, is most often reiterated by the seasons. Nature's timing. In *The Bluest Eye*, the novel's structure is defined in terms of the seasons, a natural phenomenon that will not yield to the sentimentality of humankind. Morrison's winters are harsh compositions, her springs inverted melodies of love. In *Sula*, the years as enumerated by man—1921, 1922, and so on—are significant as they signal an event of consequence and as they juxtapose the view of Sula and the view of her community. Here, too, Nature presents signs, omens that can be read or distorted by the folk, as when the plague of robins in the spring seems to announce Sula's return to the Bottom. Thus each year defines a section of the novel, but only as poised entry or climactic ending to the illumination of the characters' collective actions.

Because Morrison's probings are so relentless, her sounds so authentic, and her appreciation of complexity so profound, we are able to recognize, as do Claudia and Nel, the patterning of beauty and waste in the history of Pecola and Sula and their communities. As a result, *The Bluest Eye* and *Sula* teach us a lesson about the integral relationship between the destructive limits imposed on the black woman and the inversions of truth in this society.

Notes

1. Toni Morrison, *The Bluest Eye* (New York: Holt, Rinehart and Winston, 1970), p. 40.
2. Ibid., p. 30.
3. Ibid.
4. Ibid., p. 146.
5. Ibid., p. 78.
6. Ibid., p. 92.
7. Ibid., p. 97.
8. Ibid., pp. 109–10.
9. Ibid., p. 133.
10. Ibid., p. 134.
11. Ibid., p. 68.
12. Ibid., p. 16.
13. Ibid., p. 125.
14. Toni Morrison, *Sula* (New York: Knopf, 1974), pp. 52–53.

15. Ibid., pp. 89–90.
16. Ibid., p. 29.
17. Ibid., p. 68.
18. Ibid., pp. 71–72.
19. Ibid., p. 52.
20. Ibid., p. 66.
21. Ibid., p. 82.
22. Ibid., pp. 92–94.
23. Ibid., pp. 118–19.
24. Ibid., p. 121.
25. Ibid., p. 117.
26. Ibid., p. 94.
27. Ibid., p. 110.
28. Ibid., pp. 121–22.
29. Ibid., p. 134.
30. Ibid., p. 142.
31. Ibid., p. 143.
32. Ibid., p. 146.
33. Ibid., p. 160.

◆◆◆◆◆◆◆◆◆◆◆◆◆◆

Beyond Realism

KEITH E. BYERMAN

In contrast to the anguished narrative consciousnesses of Gayl Jones's fiction, Toni Morrison creates conventionally stable central characters. Moreover, she adds even greater reliability by using primarily omniscient narrations; even when there is a first-person narrator, as in *The Bluest Eye*, that voice is complemented by an omniscient perspective. Thus, it would seem that Morrison's fiction is much closer to that of the traditionalists. But in fact, she uses the narrative to present disordered, violent, perverse worlds less overt but no less troubling than those of Jones. These novels present us with murder, incest, necrophilia, child abuse, insanity, terrifying family secrets, and a general sense of life teetering on the edge of dissolution. Such material presented through reliable narration creates a tension that intensifies the emotional impact of the fiction.

The rational telling of extreme events forces a radical reconsideration of commonly held assumptions about black life and black-white relationships. Through its extremism, it defamiliarizes the reader by pointing to the violent effects of such ordinary phenomena as popular culture, bourgeois ideas about property, love, sexual initiation and sex roles, family, and the past. Perhaps more than any other writer under consideration in this study, Morrison shows the exploitative nature of logocentric orders.[1] She dramatizes the destructive power implicit in the control of various symbolic systems. In her fiction that power creates grotesque victims, often including those who seem to be in positions of domination. Her novels are quest tales in which key characters search for the hidden sign capable of giving them strength and/or identity. In a significant twist, those who find what they seek become the most thoroughly victimized, while those who are turned in their searches toward some other goal (which is usually an absence rather than the originally desired presence) are most often triumphant. The changed pursuit is in the direction of some black folk value, such as true community, true family name, or authentic black history. The revision of goals makes possible a loosening of the control of logocentrism so as to achieve a black selfhood that negates that control.

In *The Bluest Eye* (1970) the destructiveness of control rather than the creativity of negation predominates. Pecola Breedlove, a black girl thought by everyone to be ugly, finds herself enthralled by the blue eyes of Shirley Temple. Everywhere in her world, white skin and blue eyes are taken as signs of beauty. The image manifests itself in movies, billboards, children's drinking cups, Mary Jane candies, other characters, and in the excerpts from a primary-school reader that constitute both epigraph and chapter titles in the novel. Conversely, the lack of such traits in Pecola leads her and virtually everyone else in the book to consider her worthless. Black children deflect their self-hatred by verbally assaulting her; lighter-skinned blacks, children and adults, proclaim their superiority by alternately patronizing and attacking her; and her own mother makes clear her preferences when she slaps Pecola aside in order to comfort a white child.[2]

In response to this psychological violence, Pecola takes up a quest for blue eyes. Initially, she limits herself to drinking white milk from a cup with a Shirley Temple decal and to buying and eating Mary Jane candies. Through this popular-culture Eucharist, she hopes to be transubstantiated from common black clay into spiritual whiteness. At this stage, she achieves only the momentary happiness of seeing the white faces and wishing to have one. Later on, after the trauma of being raped by her father, she loses all sense of reality, visits a self-styled conjure man, and believes that she has actually undergone the change in eye color that she so strongly and pathetically desired. Claudia, part-time narrator and childhood companion, points out the moral of Pecola's story:

> All of us—all who knew her—felt so wholesome after we cleaned ourselves on her. We were so beautiful when we stood astride her ugliness. Her simplicity decorated us, her guilt sanctified us, her pain made us glow with health, her awkwardness made us think we had a sense of humor. Her inarticulateness made us believe we were eloquent. Her poverty kept us generous. Even her waking dreams we used—to silence our own nightmares. And she let us, and thereby deserved our contempt. We honed our egos on her, padded our characters with her frailty; and yawned in the fantasy of our strength.[3]

Perhaps more significant than the catalogue of forms of victimization in the above quotation is the "we" that makes Pecola the victim. More than the melancholy story of a little girl driven mad by the world's hostility, *The Bluest Eye* tells the story of the community and society that persecutes her. Pecola may be the central character, but she is far from the only victim of the blue eyes. "We" individually and collectively are both victimizer and victim; and, while the roles vary with each character, it is also the case that the role of victimizer results from that character's own victimization by a larger society. Each person fantasizes that he has real self-determining power. But Claudia, at the end, knows better: "We substituted good grammar for intellect; we switched habits to simulate maturity; we rearranged lies and called it truth, seeing in the new pattern of an old idea the Revelation and the Word."

This pursuit of the Word entraps the characters. Pauline Breedlove differs from her daughter Pecola only in the sense that the image she believes in comes from the movie screen rather than the milk cup. Whiteness is goodness, and she feels more at home in the white kitchen where she works than in the rundown house she shares with her family. In the chapter giving her history, we learn that she has compensated for her lameness and putative ugliness by creating order wherever possible. In most cases the order is a trivial arrangement of objects, but she learns from the movies that a white home is the paragon of order. Her work in such homes makes possible a control in her life that is impossible in her own existence as a poor black woman with a family suffering under the manipulations of that very white world she loves.

She only overcomes the self-hatred implied by such values through the self-righteousness of her religion. To reinforce this goodness she needs the evil of her husband Cholly: "She was an active church woman, did not drink, smoke, or carouse, defended herself mightily against Cholly, rose above him in every way, and felt she was fulfilling a mother's role conscientiously when she pointed out their father's faults to keep them away from having them, or punished them when they showed any slovenliness, no matter how slight, when she worked twelve to sixteen hours a day to support them. And the world agreed with her."

Cholly inverts Pauline's values. He deals with self-hatred and oppression by becoming as evil as possible, even to the point of raping his daughter and burning his own house. Behind this "bad-nigger" persona lies a history of distortions of the principal relationships and rituals of life. He is abandoned in a junkyard by his mother, who was never certain of the identity of the father. His first sexual encounter is interrupted by white men whose derisive comments render him impotent. His search for the man he believes to be his father ends at a dark alley dice game when the man chases him away, believing he has come only for money. Such events make him both anti- and asocial. He hates the girl of his sexual humiliation rather than the white men because she was a witness to his powerlessness; he has no sense of socially acceptable behavior because he has been denied primary socialization; and he is incapable of appropriate fatherly behavior because he has had no parents.

The most perverse act of his life, the rape of Pecola, is a product of his confusion of violence and love.

> She was washing dishes. Her small back hunched over the sink. Cholly saw her dimly and could not tell what he saw or what he felt. Then he became aware that he was uncomfortable; next he felt the discomfort dissolve into pleasure. The sequence of his emotions was revulsion, guilt, pity, then love. His revulsion was a reaction to her young, helpless, hopeless presence. Her back hunched that way; her head to one side as though crouching from a permanent and unrelieved blow. Why did she have to look so whipped? She was a child—unburdened—why wasn't she happy? The clear statement of her misery was an accusation. He wanted to break her neck—but tenderly. Guilt and impotence rose in a bilious duet. What could he do for her—ever? What give her? What say to her? What could a burned-out black man say to the hunched back of his eleven-year-old daughter? If he looked into her face, he would see those haunted, loving eyes. The hauntedness would irritate him— the love would move him to fury. How dare she love him? Hadn't she any

sense at all? What was he supposed to do about that? Return it? How? What could his calloused hands produce to make her smile? What of his knowledge of the world and of life could be useful to her? What could his heavy arms and befuddled brain accomplish that would earn him his own respect, that would in turn allow him to accept her love? His hatred of her slimed in his stomach and threatened to become vomit. But just before the puke moved from anticipation to sensation, she shifted her weight and stood on one foot scratching the back of her calf with her toe. . . . The timid, tucked-in look of the scratching toe—that was what Pauline was doing the first time he saw her in Kentucky. Leaning over a fence staring at nothing in particular. The creamy toe of her bare foot scratching a velvet leg. It was such a small and simple gesture, but it filled him then with a wondering softness. Not the usual lust to part tight legs with his own, but a tenderness, a protectiveness. A desire to cover her foot with his hand and gently nibble away the itch from the calf with his teeth. He did it then. . . . He did it now. . . . The confused mixture of his memories of Pauline and the doing of a wild and forbidden thing excited him. . . . Surrounding all of this lust was a border of politeness. He wanted to fuck her—tenderly. But the tenderness would not hold.

The various ways in which society has conditioned Cholly so as to control him have had the effect of denying him a socially acceptable means of expressing an authentic human emotion. Having learned that he is nothing but an object of disgust, he, like Pauline, can do nothing other than objectify Pecola. Each of them exploits her because his own exploitation makes it impossible to do otherwise.

In the larger community, objectification is also common. White storekeepers, light-skinned children, and black middle-class adults all see this black child as a piece of filth repugnant yet necessary to their own senses of cleanliness.

Alternatives to this pattern of victimization can be found in two sets of characters, the whores and the McTeer family. Though diametrically opposed in both values and ambitions, both groups offer ways of coping with the pain of experience. The whores accomplish this by being what they are:

Three merry gargoyles. Three merry harridans. Amused by a long-ago time of ignorance. They did not belong to those generations of prostitutes created in novels, with great and generous hearts, dedicated, because of the horror of circumstance, to ameliorating the luckless, barren life of men, taking money incidentally and humbly for their "understanding." Nor were they from that sensitive breed of young girl, gone wrong at the hands of fate, forced to cultivate an outward brittleness in order to protect her springtime from further shock, but knowing full well she was cut out for better things, and could make the right man happy. Neither were they the sloppy, inadequate whores who, unable to make a living at it alone, turn to drug consumption and traffic or pimps to help complete their scheme of self-destruction, avoiding suicide only to punish the memory of some absent father or to sustain the misery of some silent mother.

They are women who do their work without illusion, self-hatred, or guilt. They have no use for their customers or for those dishonest women who pretend virtue but are in fact unfaithful. They respect only the innocents, like Pecola, and truly religious women who they see as having the same honesty and integrity as themselves.

They are also the primary folk figures in the novel. Even their names—Poland, China, Maginot Line—suggest larger-than-life characters. Maginot Line entertains Pecola with outlandish stories of past loves and adventures. She keeps alive the idea of love in her recollections of Dewey Prince, the only man she did not sell herself to. China is adept at verbal dueling, constantly drawing Maginot Line back from the edge of sentimentality with sarcasm. Poland is "forever ironing, forever singing." Her songs are blues, which serve less to express personal problems than to entertain through reminders of the nature of the world in which they live. These folk arts enable them to transcend the private obsessions of other characters. The world may well be a place of misery and doom, but folk wisdom dictates that one adapts to circumstances rather than resignedly move toward evasion or self-destruction. Blues and folk tales imply that trouble is *both* personal and communal and that life is a matter of adaptation and survival rather than resignation and death. The whores treat themselves and Pecola with consideration because they neither despair nor hope.

Ironically, the McTeer family, although hostile to the behavior and attitude of the whores, make a decent life for themselves by working from the same principles. One of the functions of the family in the novel is to serve as a counterpoint for the Breedloves. Pauline slaps Pecola and protects a little white girl, whereas Mrs. McTeer takes in the black girl, even though it is a strain on her family's resources. Cholly rapes his own daughter, whereas Mr. McTeer nearly kills a boarder who fondles his daughter. The Breedloves are so absorbed in variations of self-hatred that they see each other only as objects, whereas the McTeers make themselves into a family despite all the economic, psychological, and social forces opposing them.

This is not to suggest that the McTeers are sentimentalized into the Dick-and-Jane family of the school reader. Morrison insists that it is in fact those who refuse such sentimentality who are the most heroic. The McTeers live without illusion as much as possible. The parents whip their children, complain about the burdens of life, and struggle only semisuccessfully to acquire the necessities for survival. The children must face embarrassment because of their cheap clothing and lack of money and must deal with the same assaults on their race as Pecola. But unlike the Breedloves and the light-skinned Geraldine and Maureen, they do not measure their human worth by the symbols of the dominant white culture. Although the Shirley Temple cup belongs to the McTeers and although Frieda, Claudia's sister, loves the child actress's movies, no one in the family defines himself or herself by a lack of whiteness. They accept their difference from whites as a given of their existence, not as a deprivation to be evaded or mourned.

Claudia, the narrator, is the most emphatic in asserting this difference. She serves for a while as a rebel figure, similar to the young Jane Pittman in Ernest Gaines's novel. She plots insults and attacks on Maureen Peel, who glories in her lack of melanin. More important, she almost ritualistically destroys the white doll she receives for Christmas:

> The other dolls, which were supposed to bring me great pleasure, succeeded in doing quite the opposite. When I took it to bed, its hard unyielding limbs resisted my flesh—the tapered fingertips on those dimpled hands scratched. If, in sleep, I turned, the bone-cold head collided with my own. It was a most uncomfortable, patently aggressive sleeping companion. To hold it was no more rewarding. The starched gauze or lace on the cotton dress irritated any embrace. I had only one desire: to dismember it. To see of what it was made, to discover the dearness, to find the beauty, the desirability that had escaped me, but apparently only me. Adults, older girls, shops, magazines, newspapers, window signs—all the world had agreed that a blue-eyed yellow-haired, pink-skinned doll was what every girl child treasured. . . . I could not love it. But I could examine it to see what it was that all the world said was lovable. Break off the tiny fingers, bend the flat fleet, loosen the hair, twist the head around, and the thing made one sound—a sound they said was the sweet and plaintive cry "Mama," but which sounded to me like the bleat of a dying lamb, or, more precisely, our icebox door opening on rusty hinges in July. Remove the cold and stupid eyeball, it would bleat still. "Ahhhha," take off the head, shake out the sawdust, crack the back against the brass bed rail, it would bleat still. The gauze back would split, and I could see the disk with six holes, the secret of the sound. A mere metal roundness.

The doll is an emblem of a manipulative, inverted order. Adults and children are encouraged to believe that this combination of wood, cloth, and metal is an idealization of girlhood and that the noise it makes is a human cry. Claudia herself confuses illusion and reality when she does violence to real white girls who seem to her imitations of the doll. Claudia's instinct to penetrate to the secret of the doll's voice and demystify it is appropriate, but her identification of objects and human beings is a measure of her acceptance of the culture's dehumanization. Even if the white girls take their identity from the doll, as its deliberate design and mechanism implies that they should, even if, in other words, they take the object as more real than themselves, their voices nonetheless remain human voices and their pain human pain. Claudia ultimately fails, not because of her confusion, which she overcomes, but because she refuses to live in her demystified knowledge:

> When I learned how repulsive this disinterested violence [against white girls] was, that it was repulsive because it was disinterested, my shame floundered about for refuge. The best hiding place was love. Thus the conversion from pristine sadism to fabricated hatred, to fraudulent love. It was a small step to Shirley Temple. I learned much later to worship her, just as I learned to delight in cleanliness, knowing, even as I learned, that the change was adjustment without improvement.

The state of rebellion cannot be sustained because it requires a perpetual opposition and negation without hope of victory. *The Bluest Eye*, then, is about the difficulty of achieving individuality and full humanity in an objectifying and manipulative society. To refuse that state of tension and negation is to accept self-hatred, illusion, and even madness. In this novel, the best that can be accomplished is an intimation of what a fully human condition might be.

Sula (1974) probes even more deeply for the origins of oppression, victimization, and social order. In the process, it also explores the possibilities for negating such control. Consistent with the dialectics of language, Morrison finds both control and its negation in naming. When a place, person, thing, or event is labeled, the namer assumes it to be fixed, present, and under his or her dominion. By such a practice, experience can be organized and even reified. But in *Sula* the process of designation creates possibilities not intended by the namer, possibilities that can be realized in human history, though frequently only with great suffering. The effort to escape this dialectic, as Sula does, is doomed, as she is. She cannot avoid being part of the social order, since even rebellion is named and used in the community.

The uses of naming are developed in the book long before the title character appears. The novel opens with a "nigger joke" associated with the origin of the black community. According to the legend, a white man promised freedom and land to his slave if a particularly difficult task were performed. When the work was done, the freedom was given without a second thought, but the land was a different matter. The white man convinced the black one that the rocky hill country was bottom land, since it was the "bottom of heaven." Thus, the black community of Bottom was created above the white town of Medallion. Here, as elsewhere, Morrison suggests the economic underpinnings of racism, as well as the function of language in establishing and maintaining social control. The white man manipulates the ambiguity of language to his advantage and thus determines the economic condition of blacks for generations.

But this control is not necessarily absolute: "Still, it was lovely up in the Bottom. After the town grew and the farm land turned into a village and the village into a town and the streets of Medallion were hot and dusty with progress, those heavy trees that sheltered the shacks up in the Bottom were wonderful to see. And the hunters who went there sometimes wondered in private if maybe the white farmer was right after all. Maybe it was the bottom of Heaven."[4] Thus the attempt to control through language is always subject to negation by the very nature of language itself. Compulsion can cause suffering and sorrow, as it does in the exploitation that creates and maintains the Bottom, but it cannot be totalitarian. Traces of meaning exist that make for other possibilities. Black refusal to be dehumanized by the "nigger joke" creates the ironic realization of the joke's language.

The second instance of control through naming comes in the form of National Suicide Day, created by Shadrack, a psychologically damaged veteran who walked through the fires of World War I. He suffered shell shock when, during battle, "he turned his head a little to the right and saw the face of a soldier near him fly off. Before he could register shock, the rest of the soldier's head disappeared under the inverted soup bowl of his helmet. But stubbornly, taking no direction from the brain, the body of the headless soldier ran on, with energy and grace; ignoring altogether the drip and slide of brain tissue down its back." The surprise and the messiness together render Shadrack nearly insane.

The bullet dissolves not merely the soldier's head but also Shadrack's sense of reality and identity. The world ceases to have any inherent order, and he has no name. After he leaves the hospital, "a haven of more than a year, only eight days of which he fully recollected," he is on his own, "with no past, no language, no tribe, no source, no address book, no bomb, no pencil, no clock, no pocket handkerchief, no rug, no bed, no can opener, no faded postcard, no soap, no key, no tobacco pouch, no soiled underwear and nothing nothing nothing to do." He is deprived of all the markers of an identity, which are also the markers of a social existence. Without such possessions and the social and economic orders implied by them, he cannot be a human being.

Only when he finds by accident someone who knows him, a town to live in, a job to do, and a language (that of obscenity) to speak can he begin to function. But this order cannot counteract the primal chaos of death. To live with this obsession, he must create an order for it, which he does in National Suicide Day: "In sorting it all out, he hit on the notion that if one day a year were devoted to it [death], everybody could get it out of the way and the rest of the year would be safe and free."

Significantly, this private neurosis becomes part of the social order: "As time went along, the people took less notice of these January thirds, rather they thought they did, thought they had no attitudes or feelings one way or another about Shadrack's annual solitary parade. In fact they had simply stopped remarking on the holiday because they had absorbed it into their thoughts, into their language, into their lives." Though the designation lacks for the community the traumatic significance that it holds for Shadrack, nonetheless its incorporation into the group's language holds *in potentia* meaning that will later be catastrophically realized. The mad rituals of a madman seem to be naturalized and thus neutralized by the community, but that very folk process makes the actualization of the name, through repetition, in fact feasible.

An entirely different kind of order, one that appears to be no order at all, is created by Eva, Sula's grandmother. Eva begins as the victim of a white- and male-dominated society. When she and her children are abandoned by her husband, she is left with little food and no money in the middle of the winter. She saves the life of her baby by using the last of her lard to remove fecal stones from his bowels. Realizing the hopelessness of the situation, she leaves her children with a neighbor and disappears for eighteen months. When she returns, she is missing a leg but has a substantial income. The mystery of her quest becomes the material of folk legend, and she becomes a symbol of the will to survive. With the money she builds a ramshackle house and takes in boarders and various kinds of stray beings. She establishes herself as a queen, sitting on an ersatz throne constructed from a rocking chair and a children's wagon. From this position, she entertains the men of the community.

A key element in the order Eva maintains is this relationship with men. While Morrison suggests that both Eva and her daughter Hannah are enthralled by "manlove," the men themselves seem very much mere play things. While Hannah expresses the idea by having intercourse with an willing man, Eva is more derogatory. Her former husband is nicknamed Boyboy, while her son is called Plum, and an apparently white tenant Tar baby. In the most bizarre naming, three boys she adopts are designated "the deweys," though they have neither appearance nor background in common. As a manifestation of Eva's power of naming, the boys become identical in mentality and sensibility; in fact, they become virtually a separate species.

In some sense, Eva sees herself as a god figure. She held the power of life and death over her children, she created the race of deweys, she names and manipulates men as she sees fit. When Plum returns from the war addicted to heroin, she chooses to destroy the remnants of his being by setting fire to him. Later on, she is punished for this hubris by having to watch helplessly as Hannah becomes accidentally engulfed in flame and then seared where neighbors throw water on her to put out the fire. Moreover, it is Eva's lack of the leg she apparently chose to sacrifice for money that makes it impossible to reach and save her daughter. Thus, the very sign of Eva's power comes to be the negation of that power.

The underlying order of which Shadrack and Eva are extreme metaphor is that of the community. It establishes the forms of male-female, parent-child, individual-society, and good-evil relationships. It creates rituals recognizing the mysteries of birth, sex, and death; it codifies acceptable attitudes toward power, whether personal, sexual, or racial. In other words it makes the conventions that define life in the Bottom.

Morrison is at her best perhaps when showing how such rites and conventions operate in ordinary experience. At the funeral of a child, the women participate in a mourning ceremony:

> As Reverend Deal moved into his sermon, the hands of the women unfolded like pairs of raven's wings and flew high above their hats in the air. They did not hear all of what he said; they heard the one word, or phrase, or inflection that was for them the connection between the event and themselves. For

some time it was the term "Sweet Jesus." And they saw the Lamb's eye and the truly innocent victims: themselves. . . . Then they left their pews. For with some emotions one has to stand. They spoke, for they were full and needed to say. They swayed, for the rivulets of grief or of ecstasy must be rocked. And when they thought of all that life and death locked into that little closed coffin they danced and screamed, not to protest God's will, but to acknowledge it and confirm once more their conviction that the only way to avoid the Hand of God is to get in it.

The need here is to express, not to explain. The funeral is not the cause but the occasion to reaffirm a position as both victim and elect. The ritual transforms an absence into a presence, makes a private, physical loss into a communal, spiritual gain. The language of the passage, which modulates into a litany, reinforces the pattern by suggesting the recurrence and thus permanence of structures.

But the treatment and attitude toward Sula most overtly reveal the patterns of the community. National Suicide Day could be naturalized by the people, as could Eva's arrogance. Each in some way recapitulates the need for an order, a name. But Sula refuses ordering and naming, so for the community she becomes the embodiment of evil. By ignoring or deliberately violating the conventions, she threatens the assumptions by which life in the Bottom is organized and made meaningful. By naming her evil, they seek to bring her within the framework of their worldview, but, as we shall see, this effort is itself inherently ambiguous.

Morrison establishes early on the events that make Sula's identity an essentially negative one. Sula overhears a conversation between her mother and other women during which Hannah remarks: "You love her, like I love Sula. I just don't like her." Later the same day, a little boy drowns when he slips from her hands while they are playing. "The first experience taught her there was no other that you could count on; the second that there was no self to count on either. She had no center, no speck around which to grow." For a time she has an epicenter of sorts in Nel, her girlhood friend. Some of the best passages are devoted to the rites of passage they go through together. Their experiences of emerging womanhood, of personal bonds, of death and guilt are very effectively rendered.

Ultimately, however, a break must come, for Nel eventually defines herself by community conventions, while Sula exists outside such structures. Nel's wedding, which marks the end of part 1, is the occasion of the break. It marks the moment at which Nel actualizes her underlying desire for order by making an identity through a man rather than through herself: "The two of them together would make one Jude." From this point on, Nel becomes one of the voices of the community: the last half of the novel is built around her position as one who has some understanding of Sula, yet who cannot see the world in the same way. She serves, then, as a character in the middle, between the polarities of Sula and the community.

Nel's ambivalent position becomes clear early in part 2, when Sula returns after a ten-year absence. The marriage to Jude has been frustrating in large part because of his inability to find rewarding work in a white-dominated economic system. These frustrations become self-pity which Nel is expected to nurse, in both senses of healing and feeding. Sula, however, cannot take such an attitude seriously: "I mean, I don't know what the fuss is about. I mean, everything in the world loves you. White men love you. They spend so much time worrying about your penis they forget their own. The only thing they want to do is cut off a nigger's privates. And if that ain't love and respect I don't know what is." She goes on to talk in the same vein about white women, black women, children of both races, and other black men. She does not permit an identity created by oppression or self-hatred. By this method she restores laughter and perspective to both Nel and Jude.

The same disregard for social convention leads to the dissolution of both the marriage and the friendship. Because she finds Jude interesting, Sula entices him into sexual play that is discovered by Nel. Having no sense of possessiveness or conventionalized identity, Sula feels no responsibility either to her friend's marriage or to Jude's need for love. Truly amoral, she can understand neither Nel's humiliation and outrage nor the husband's desire to leave.

For this crucial part of the story, Morrison shifts to Nel's perspective. This point of view makes it possible to see another character's experience of absence as an experience much different from that of Sula:

> Now her thighs were really empty. And it was then that what those women said about never looking at another man made some sense to her, for the real point, the heart of what they said, was the word *looked*. Not to promise never to make love to another man, not to refuse to marry another man, but to promise and know that she could never afford to look again. . . . never to look, for now she could not risk looking—and anyway, so what? For now her thighs were truly empty and dead too, and it was Sula who had taken the life from them and Jude who smashed her heart and the both of them who left her with no thighs and no heart just her brain raveling away.

The loss of Jude is the loss of identity and the loss of life. More specifically, it is the loss of what filled her thighs that has deprived her of identity. Jude's penis was her life, both personally and socially. Whatever the conditions of the marriage, having his name and his body gave her an acceptable place in the community. The absence of the phallus means a loss of status in the social order. She now becomes a "woman without a man" and unable to raise her eyes. For this change she blames Sula who, without a sense of ownership, cannot conceive of Jude as an object to be taken.

Nel's private experience is a metaphor for the community's treatment of alien behavior. Sula's refusal of positive identity cannot be tolerated, so she is explained as a demon. A folklore is created that includes both tales of her evil actions and interpretations of "signs" associated with her. Like her mother, she has sexual intercourse indiscriminately with the men of the Bottom. But unlike Hannah, her behavior is seen as arrogant rather than complimentary. Without evidence, she is accused of having had liaisons with white men, which is considered the essence of degradation. Her decision to put Eva into a nursing home is attacked, with everyone ignoring the old woman's previous behavior.

The "signs" are the means of objectifying the general feeling of distaste. They become the evidence necessary to fit Sula negatively into the social order. The "plague" of robins that accompanies her return is taken as an omen. Accidents are said to be caused by certain dark practices in which she engages. The most important of the signs is the birthmark over her eye. Each observer reads it in such a way as to validate his or her own interpretation of Sula's identity. When she is a child, it is seen as a rose bud. Jude, believing her both threatening and enticing, sees it as a snake. Shadrack, who fishes for a living and who thinks of her as a kindred alien spirit, sees it as a tadpole. The community reads it as ashes, symbolizing both her presumed indifference to her mother's fiery death and her association with hellish forces. The assignment of meaning to an accident of pigmentation makes it possible to bring Sula within a structure set up by the interpreter. Bringing her in, even as evil, brings her under control: "There was no creature so ungodly as to make them destroy it. They could kill easily if provoked to anger, but not by design, which explained why they could not 'mob kill' anyone. To do so was not only unnatural, it was undignified. The presence of evil was something to be first recognized, then dealt with, survived, outwitted, triumphed over."

To make her *their* evil was to limit and explain the damage she could do. To recognize her as truly different and alien would be to accept discontinuity, disorder, and absence. She must be named so as to render her power manageable. She came to serve an important function in the community as a scapegoat. She took on for them the evil they had previously done to each other. They became righteous as a way of defining themselves as different from her. Mothers previously indifferent to their children became fearful and then protective as stories of Sula's evil power spread. Wives threatened by her promiscuity became more attentive to their husbands. The group banded together for good now that it had identified evil. A fantasy of power is thus created that enables them to evade consciousness of the true oppressors: death and white society.

Nel, though conventional enough to blame Sula for robbing her of her marriage and thereby both her happiness and her identity, does not engage so directly in the social fantasy. Instead, she creates a new identity that equates her suffering with goodness. Thus, when she learns that Sula is dying, she goes to her out of Christian charity, but not out of friendship. What she learns at the bedside again disturbs the center around which she has organized her life. Sula shows not gratitude or remorse, but a candor that is disorienting. When Nel demands an explanation for the affair with Jude, she is told that it was merely a passing fancy. And when she attempts a moral definition of friendship, the response is even more troubling:

> "What did you take him for if you didn't love him and why didn't you think about me?" And then, "I was good to you, Sula, why don't that matter?"
> Sula turned her head away from the boarded window. Her voice was quiet and the stemmed rose over her eye was very dark. "It matters, Nel, but only to you. Not to anybody else. Being good to somebody is just like being mean to somebody. Risky. You don't get nothing for it."

Finally, Sula even asserts that perhaps she, not Nel, was the one who was good.

For years, Nel manages to evade the implications of this confrontation. She escapes her own responsibility for self-creation and action by believing that she has been a mere victim. Like the community, she achieves a false innocence by constructing a moral hierarchy with herself at the top and Sula at the bottom. To use the language of *The Bluest Eye*, both she and the Bottom clean themselves on Sula. But such a stance cannot be maintained in the realities of the concrete historical world. The death of Sula, taken to be a sign of better times, brings trouble for the community. Unable to use the strength of the evil one, the people fall back into their selfish, antagonistic ways. The condition is exacerbated when jobs promised by the whites in power do not materialize. On Suicide Day, frustrated citizens join Shadrack's parade, which ends at the construction site. Here their anger is vented in destruction of the tunnel, with the attendant deaths of dozens of people.

For Nel, the impact is delayed and results in insight rather than cataclysm. As an expression of her goodness, she visits the women in the nursing homes. Twenty-five years after Sula's death and the mass death at the tunnel, she goes to see Eva. Though the old woman is senile, she still makes disturbing observations, such as identifying Nel with Sula, and accusing her of participation in Chicken Little's drowning. Though Nel denies complicity, the accusation has an effect because she was there and did nothing to prevent the death. Thus, Eva, like her namesake, forces on another the knowledge of good and evil and thereby brings Nel out of her self-created innocence into the world of history, experience, and responsibility. The mark of this fortunate fall is her embrace of the spirit of Sula:

> "All that time, all that time, I thought I was missing Jude." And the loss pressed down on her chest and came up into her throat. "We was girls together," she said as though explaining something. "O Lord, Sula," she cried, "girl, girl, girlgirlgirl."
> It was a fine cry—loud and long—but it had no bottom and it had no top, just circles and circles of sorrow.

The cry is "fine" because it is not self-protective or dehumanizing. It expresses sorrow for what had not merely been lost but thrust away through a desire to control and order one's experience. Its lack of conventional structure—no bottom and no top—makes possible the natural and human order of circles, which accepts absence as absence, irreducible yet infinitely meaningful. Nel achieves her true humanity by giving her emptiness its rightful name. This right name makes possible insight but not manipulation; as nearly pure blues expression, it offers not domination but a working through to the truth of experience.

In *Song of Solomon* (1977) the quest is explicitly rather than implicitly for a name. Milkman Dead, a central character with very conventional values, comes to a point at which he feels the need to find out his family's true name. The discovery of this name carries with it a sense of his own humanity and also certain magical qualities connected with black folklore. Naming here has associations with African cultures in which the name is the expression of the soul; because of this, the choosing and keeping of the name is a major ritual.[5] To lose the name or, in Afro-American terms, to be "called out of one's name" is an offense against the spirit.

Consistent with these folk beliefs, the Dead family, whose name was given to them accidentally after the Civil War by a drunken white soldier, act out the designation. The father, Macon Dead, has perverted his own father's efforts to acquire and work the land by becoming an exploitative landlord and real estate speculator. He defines himself and others by accumulation of alienated property. Milkman's mother, Ruth, rejects the present by literally embracing only the past and the future. Macon tells the story of seeing her lying naked on the bed with her father's corpse. And Milkman acquired his nickname by being discovered still nursing at his mother's breast when he was four years old. Ruth, as the daughter of the town's first black doctor, displays the values of the old black bourgeoisie by assuming an attitude of hauteur toward her nouveau riche husband. Their daughters, Magdalene and First Corinthians (whose names were selected by the family tradition of choosing names at random from the Bible), despite their names, are adult virgins who have never been permitted to experience love, either because all men in the community were socially beneath them or because these men lacked sufficient property. Milkman's friend Guitar becomes associated with the Seven Days, a secret society of black men dedicated to exacting retribution for the deaths of blacks killed by whites. The murder of a black child must be avenged by the similar death of a white one on the same day of the week.

Milkman, then, is born and reared in a family that is life-denying. As a sign of this, his birth is simultaneous with the suicide of a man who leaps from the roof of the hospital. As he grows up, he acquires the attitudes of his family and friends. He becomes narcissistic and selfish and treats the members of his family with disdain.

The dialectical movement necessary to move him away from this deathhouse begins with his discovery of the home of his Aunt Pilate, a woman his father hates for some yet-to-be-determined reason. Pilate has a history and a true name, which she literally carries with her in a small brass box fashioned into an earring. Inside is the piece of paper on which her illiterate father painstakingly copied the word Pilate, the name he insisted she have despite the objections of relatives. Her mother died while giving her birth, and she and her brother later saw their father killed by whites who wanted his land. Having given birth to herself, Pilate creates a family of women much like that of Eva Peace. She herself makes money by selling illegal liquor, and the attendant disrepute is accompanied by a certain folk status since she has no navel and thus is thought to be a child of the devil. Her daughter Reba (whose proper name is the biblical Rebekkah) is marked by her luck; she wins every contest she enters and even those she accidentally happens into. Hagar is the spoiled child of her mother and grandmother, who spend their money to satisfy all of her whims.

Milkman is initially fascinated with this matriarchal household because of its difference from his patriarchal one. Here stories are told, food is tasty and plentiful, and none of the rigidity of his own home is present. Moreover, here he has his sexual initiation with Hagar.

But fascination breeds not understanding but exploitation, which takes two forms. The first is the treatment of Hagar, whom he considers a sexual object to be used at his convenience, but never to be part of his life with his family's and his own respectable friends. Finally, he decides at Christmas to break off the affair, but he chooses to do so in a letter that is the emotional equivalent of his father's eviction notices: "He went back to his father's office, got some cash out of the safe, and wrote Hagar a nice letter which ended: "Also, I want to thank you. Thank you for all you have meant to me for making me happy all these years. I am signing this letter with love, of course, but more than that, with gratitude.'"[6]

This male domination through words has the effect of driving Hagar crazy. She sets out to kill him but repeatedly cannot do so. While this insane quest goes on, Morrison introduces other stories of the suppressed humanity and creativity of women. The effect is to provide a sense of a folkloric and historical tradition of oppression. In the barber shop a recent killing is said to be the work of Winnie Ruth Judd, a white woman who kills and dismembers her victims and periodically escapes from the state hospital. For these black men, she serves as a sign of the lunacy of whites who can kill for no good reason; her private torment and motivation is irrelevant to her symbolic usefulness. More pertinent to Milkman is his dream about his mother, which he is not at all certain is in fact a dream. In it, Ruth plants tulip bulbs which immediately emerge as plants and flowers; Milkman expects her to be frightened, but her response is very different: "She leaned back from them, even hit out at them, but playfully, mischieviously. The flowers grew and grew, until he could see only her shoulders above them and her flailing arms high above those bobbing, snapping heads. They were smothering her, taking away her breath with their jagged lips. And she merely smiled and fought them off as though they were harmless butterflies." The chaos of creation, which the male fears, is embraced by the female. His mother, who is passive and serious, has a secret garden where she generates and plays with life.

It is in this context that Milkman receives a revisionist version of family history, one that reveals the importance of female creativity to his own life. He follows his mother one night on a long journey to the cemetery where her father was buried. Upon her exit, he confronts her with her monumentalizing tendency, including the incident of necrophilia told him by his father. She responds by expressing the feeling that the doctor was the only one who ever loved her and that she had reacted to his death by kneeling to kiss his hand, not by any perverse sexual gesture. More important, she explains to her son that she was the one who saved his own life. Her husband desired no more children, and insisted that she abort him. She appealed to Pilate, who helped her to defeat Macon's attempts. Thus, Milkman owes his existence to the life-affirming efforts of the two women.

He responds to her story by seeking a way to escape the entire family. In this second act of exploitation, he conspires with his father to steal a green sack from Pilate, a sack which they believe contains gold. Macon tells his son about hiding out with his sister after their father's murder, in a cave where they find buried treasure. They are discovered by a white man whom Macon kills. They flee, but the brother believes that Pilate later returned and took the gold, which is now in the green sack. Milkman and Guitar, who needs money to carry out an assassination, steal the sack, only to discover that it contains human bones.

Still obsessed with the idea of getting money and thereby power, Milkman sets out to find the cave near the old family property. He is at this point also evading both the knowledge that the women have offered and the responsibility that accompanies that knowledge. Just as his father distorted the values of the first Macon Dead by emphasizing possession over creation, so Milkman distorts his father's values by taking on his greed without any sense of responsibility and seriousness. And when he arrives in the family hometown, the folk recollections reinforce this idea. His grandfather and father are remembered but he hears in the memories a respect for material possession and manipulative energy that validates his self-image.

Only when he encounters the incredibly old woman Circe does he begin to question the object of his quest. Circe was the servant of a white family, the head of which was responsible for the murder of Milkman's grandfather. She recalls the relationship of his ancestors and the real name of his grandfather. She is also the voice of a larger history, for she tells him of the injustices committed by whites throughout the past and implicitly questions his identification with white middle-class values. She also shows him one way to act; she lives in the house of the white family with an ever-increasing pack of dogs, which she intentionally keeps inside so that they will destroy all of the objects that were purchased through the exploitation of black labor. She has willfully outlasted the whites so as to destroy everything they found precious. But she knows the price of revenge; she fully expects the dogs to eat her when she is no longer strong enough to feed them. She has reached the time envisioned by the Invisible Man's grandfather in his admonition to "agree 'em to death and destruction,"[7] but she also accepts full responsibility for her action. Her vengeance contrasts with that of Guitar in that hers is embedded in a concrete history and not an abstract, dehumanizing concept of justice.

Milkman leaves in search of the original home of his grandfather, but his quest is now ambivalent. On the one hand he wants the gold, which he still believes Pilate has hidden; on the other, he wants to know the story of his family. He has worked through concentric relational circles from himself to his parents to his grandparents. At each level the more he has probed the more he has found difference rather than the expected identity. In Shalimar he will move through one more circle, but in the process he will find a new definition of himself.

In the village he for the first time is the alien, for here his city clothes, city talk, and city values are not privileged. He is taken not as one returning to his roots, but as a threatening "white-hearted" presence. To succeed in his quest, he must undergo rituals that wil strip him of his false culture and prepare him for authentic knowledge. He hears the children reciting ancient rhymes that are vaguely meaningful to him. But in order to decode them, he must become a member of the community. This happens first with a fight that demonstrates his alien status but also tests his courage, then through the opportunity to participate in a hunt. This serves as the male initiation rite that Milkman has never had and thus his possibility of moving out of his perversely extended, narcissistic childhood. He is stripped of all the symbols of the dominant culture, much as Ike McCaslin is in Faulkner's "The Bear." Though inept, he survives the test, including an unexpected murder attempt by Guitar, who feels he has been betrayed in the pursuit of the gold. Milkman discovers that he wants to live and thus is not truly Dead. He endures and thereby receives the symbols of his success: the throbbing heart of the bobcat killed in the hunt and a woman he can truly enjoy without dominating.

Most important, he begins to decipher the children's song and finds in it the narrative of his family. It is the folktale of the flying African, Solomon, who one day discovers his magical power and uses it to fly from slavery back to his African home. He left behind a wife Ryna and twenty-one children, including Jake, Milkman's grandfather. Ryna, like Hagar, goes crazy over the loss of her man, and her children are cared for by Heddy, an Indian. The random elements of the past become a coherent family story. The men (Solomon, Jake, Macon, Milkman) seek power, either magical or material; the women (Ryna, Sing, Ruth, Hagar) must suffer for this pursuit; the children are abandoned because of it, but they are saved by a surrogate mother (Heddy, Circe, Pilate) who keeps alive the history for whoever might later need it. It is also preserved as a functional part of the community, in children's songs. Thus the narrative of power and suffering and love dialectically becomes play.

He also learns the relation of the story to identity:

> Under the recorded names were other names, just as "Macon Dead," recorded for all time in some dusty file, hid from view the real names of people, places and things. Names that had meaning. No wonder Pilate put hers in her ear. When you know your name, you should hang on to it, for unless it is noted down, it will die when you do. . . . He closed his eyes and thought of the black men in Shalimar, Roanoke, Petersburg, Newport News, Danville, in the Blood Bank, on Darling Street, in the pool halls, the barbershops. Their names. Names they got from yearnings, gestures, flaws, events, mistakes, weaknesses.

Names have a concrete history; they keep alive the complex, painful, disorderly, creative reality of human experience that dominant, logocentric structures seek to suppress. They register the hidden expressions of life in defiance of the controlling Word. They are also liberating and magical. They free Milkman from his death-wish and thus make it possible for him to die if necessary. And he frees Pilate, knowing as he now does that the sack of bones belongs not to the white man Macon murdered but to her own father. Aunt and nephew return them to the cave for proper burial. As part of the ritual of purification, Pilate rips off the earring containing her name; it is unnecessary in the presence of the body of the man who gave it to her and who now himself has his right name. At this moment, she is killed by Guitar, who, like the white man who murdered her father, values possession over human life.

With the elimination of these two generations, Milkman can achieve identity with Solomon/Shalimar the flying African:

> He could just make out Guitar's head and shoulders in the dark. "You want my life?" Milkman was not shouting now. "You need it? Here." Without wiping away the tears, taking a deep breath, or even bending his knees—he leaped. As fleet and bright as a lodestar he wheeled toward Guitar and it did not matter which one of them would give up his ghost in the killing arms of his brother. For now he knew what Shalimar knew: If you surrendered to the air, you could *ride* it.

This act of identification is simultaneously an act of differentiation, for unlike Solomon, Milkman flies into history and responsibility rather than out of it. And in the process he creates the meaning for his own name. From being the one who sucks nourishment and life from others, he becomes the provider, giving Jake his name and home, Pilate freedom from guilt, and Guitar the life he needs to take. His riding the air implies both play and control, or perhaps control through play, and is thus life-affirming even in the moment of death. The magic word, the true name, conquers for a moment of history, the Word.

While *The Bluest Eye* shows us the victimization that comes in a black community without a sustaining folklore and *Sula* shows us the oppressive nature of a community that uses its folk material as a means of control and evasion, *Song of Solomon* reveals the power that can be achieved through the embrace of a folk history. Claudia tells us of her own failure to overcome oppressive forces in the process of telling of Pecola's madness; Nel achieves an insight that makes true sorrow possible; and Milkman acquired the magical power that can hold joy and sorrow together. In *Tar Baby* (1981), Morrison makes use of the same dialectic of dominant culture and folk experience, but does so in a more complex fashion. Unlike her other works, this novel personifies the dominant culture in the two characters of Valerian and Margaret Street. One purpose seems to be to dramatize the sexually differential effects of the culture on those who wield its power. Another difference is the division of the middle character into two parts: Son and Jadine. In this way it is possible to have both success and failure in achieving insight. Finally, the setting is not the American Midwest and South, but an isolated Caribbean island, Isle des Chevaliers. Though all the major characters are American, the setting is useful in clarifying the effects of the dominant order on personality. Separated from the context of American society, the Americanness of the characters, especially in regard to race, can be more directly observed. The inclusion of native black characters serves not merely as counterpoint but also to suggest a broader sense of Afro-American folk experience.

Isle des Chevaliers is a perverse Eden. Valerian Street, a wealthy American candy manufacturer, purchased it years earlier and gradually built it into a clean, sterile paradise for himself and the few white families to whom he sold some of the land. He has created a carefully controlled environment, but primeval nature constantly threatens to reassert its authority, as is suggested by repeated personifications of butterflies, trees, flowers, and the land itself. Valerian, who has retired from his inherited business, has brought with him to the island his wife, a former beauty queen; two black servants. Sydney and Ondine; and Jadine, the niece of the blacks. Also present are two native workers, known as Yardman and Mary because no one has bothered to learn their real names.

Two elements trouble this paradise. One, an absence, is Michael, the son that Margaret perpetually believes will return but who never in fact makes an appearance. Valerian, who considers her an obsessively protective mother, can rather easily handle the absence until he learns the horrifying history of the mother-child relationship.

The other disruption is an intrusive presence in the form of Son, a black seaman who has jumped ship. Though Valerian tries to naturalize this alien influence by in effect making Son a surrogate for Michael, he is ultimately devastatingly unsuccessful. Son is a traditional figure in black history and lore, the fugitive from an unfair system; but he has reversed the journey of runaway slaves by escaping south to the plantation and its white patriarchy, loyal blacks, and tragic mulatto. He has many identities, but he very quickly learns the true names and relationships of everyone else, including the natives.

The responses to his intrusion reveal the natures and insecurities of the residents. Margaret, in whose closet he is found, has the southern white woman's rape fantasy (even though she is from Maine); she believes that a strange black man would be in a white woman's room only because he intends to sexually assault her. Sydney and Ondine, being proper "Philadelphia Negroes," see in Son a threat to the racial respectability they have achieved. Though they are servants, they have taken on middle-class values and being black, they feel contaminated by anyone of their race who does not uphold the image they have created. Valerian, considering himself in total control, experiences no fear; he invites Son into the group, confident that his patronizing liberailsm will neutralize any threat.

The response of Jadine is the most complex, for she blends together elements of the others. A sensual woman, she is both terrified and fascinated with the sexual energy of Son: she both fears and invites rape. Having an even more refined aura of respectability than her relatives, she is repulsed by his unkempt appearance, uncouth behavior, and lack of education. And yet, like her benefactor, she wants to be in control of situations and people; Son provides an opportunity to test her manipulative skills.

These conditions and personalities set up the double quest that structures the book. Jadine's is epitomized by an African woman she has seen in Paris:

> Under her long canary yellow dress Jadine knew there was too much hip, too much bust. The agency would laugh her out of the lobby, so why was she and everyone else in the store transfixed? The height? The skin like tar against the canary yellow dress? The woman walked down the aisle as though her many-colored sandals were pressing gold tracks on the floor. Two upside-down V's were scored into each of her cheeks, her hair was wrapped in a gelee as yellow as her dress. The people in the aisles watched her without embarrassment, with full glances instead of sly ones.[8]

Later, when the woman leaves the grocery, she pauses outside the door and spits on the sidewalk. In this image is all that Jadine wants: racial pride, arrogance, power in the white world yet disdain for it. In her present world, power and race are divided into the characters of Valerian and Son, and she seeks what each has. But the quests are as separate as the men, and her struggle is to unite them.

On the other hand, Son wants beauty and blackness, which are characterized for him by Jadine and the native woman Therese. In Jade he sees pulchritude, intelligence, and sophistication, all things not previously available to him. In Therese, he discovers the powerful though subterranean forces of his race.

Jade and Son serve as tarbabies for each other. Their contact with each other and the attachment of each to what the other represents denies them the freedom to pursue the goal which is truest for each of them. Ultimately, Morrison establishes a hierarchy of values that sees Son's freedom as success and Jadine's as failure. The hierarchy is based on what is earned by each character, in the sense that the struggle with the tarbaby either does or does not force the character to confront and work through the truth of the self and history. The hierarchy, which is an inversion of surface realities, can be seen in the personifications of the opposed goals Jade and Son free themselves for.

Valerian, the model of Jadine's pursuit of power, was named for an emperor and had a candy bar named after him. The bar, a pink and white confection, was successful only in black neighborhoods, while white boys thought its name and color vaguely homosexual. The family provided Valerian with everything, including a good wife when the time came. Deciding that he would not have the same obsession with the company that his relatives had, he used some of its income to purchase Isle des Chevaliers as a place of retirement and escape. When his first marriage did not work out he discovered Margaret, Miss Maine, whom he loved in large part because her complexion reminded him of his candy bar. When Jadine was orphaned, Valerian financed her education and early modeling career as a favor to Sydney and Ondine. He created, in effect, a perfect patriarchal system, with everyone created in his own image. Despite flaws in the order, such as Michael's absence and Margaret's mental aberrations, Valerian considered himself a successful deity.

But like his candy bar, his world was an insubstantial confection. One of his eccentric schemes, to have the servants join the family for Christmas dinner, backfires when Ondine, in a moment of stress, reveals Margaret's compulsion as a young mother to abuse Michael with sharp pins and lighted cigarettes. This history destroys Valerian, not because of its horror, but because it exposes his arrogant innocence and impotence. Because he refused to see Margaret and Michael as other than his creations, he could not see the depth of human frustration and suffering implied by such behavior. What he has always taken as his wife's stupidity was in fact the expression of her guilt, a guilt that makes her totally other and thus beyond his control. His power has been an unearned one, and is therefore destroyed by concrete reality. At the end of the novel, he sits in a chair mumbling, while Sydney feeds him and Margaret runs the house.

In Therese we find a very different blindness, one that is both literal and magical. Repeatedly, she and other characters refer to her failing eyesight, but this is compensated for by her ability to see what others cannot. For example, she knows of Son's presence days before Margaret finds him. She names him the chocolate-eater and thus predicts his ultimate commitment to his color rather than Valerian's. She sees the past as well as the present and future: she is said to be one of the blind race, for whom the Isle des Chevaliers is named:

> Son asked who were the blind race so Gideon told him a story about a race of blind people descended from some slaves who went blind the minute they saw Dominique. . . . Their ship foundered and sank with Frenchmen, horses and slaves aboard. The blinded slaves could not see how or where to swim so they were at the mercy of the current and the tide. They floated and trod water and ended up on that island along with the horses that had swum ashore. Some of them were only partially blinded and were rescued later by the French, and returned to Queen of France and indenture. The others, totally blind, hid. The ones who came back had children who, as they got on into middle age, went blind too. What they saw, they saw with the eye of the mind, and that, of course, was not to be trusted. Therese, he said, was one such. . . . "They ride those horses all over the hills. They learned to ride through the rainforest avoiding all sorts of trees and things. They race each other, and for sport they sleep with the swamp women in Sein de Veilles."

Therese believes Son to be one of the race; what she does not see is that he must be enslaved before he can become one of the blind and free.

Valerian and Therese are the polarities between which Jade and Son will move. And they are interacting polarities even though they have no contact with each other. Therese defines herself in part over against the white world, both that of the Valerian Streets who dominate Caribbean life and the white slave masters who originally brought her race to the islands. And Valerian carves his empire out of and against the world of the black natives; he judges his power in part by his ability to keep natural growth out of his palace and his intellectual superiority by his ability to dismiss such folk history as the blind horsemen.

Morrison does not arrange parallel movements between these poles for Sun and Jadine. Rather, she has each move between a pole and that in the other which resembles the opposite pole. Thus Son literally and figuratively alternates between Therese and those sophisticated qualities in Jade that she shares with Valerian.

Jadine stands at a crossroads; she has received her advanced degree in art history and has achieved substantial success as a model in Europe. As a consequence of the latter, a wealthy European has asked to marry her. She comes to the islands to make a choice without interference. Her choices, however, are all within the realm of white society, consistent with the values taught her by Ondine and Sydney and the opportunities provided her by Valerian.

The costs of such values are indicated in her childhood memory of Baltimore after her first encounter with Son. She remembers female dogs being in heat and willing to be mounted by males in the middle of the street. A neighbor tries to get rid of them:

> Every goddam dog in town'll be over here and he went back inside to get a mop handle to run the males off and crack the bitch over the back and send her home, she who had done nothing but be "in heat" which she couldn't help but which was her fault just the same as it was she who was beaten and cracked over the head and spine with the mop handle and made to run away and I felt sorry for her and went looking for her to see if she was hurt and when I found her she was behind the gas station standing very quietly while another dog sniffed her ass embarrassing me in the sunlight.
>
> All around her it was like that: a fast crack on the head if you let the hunger show so she decided then and there at the age of twelve in Baltimore never to be broken in the hands of any man. . . . When her mother died and she went to Philadelphia and then away to school, she was quick to learn, but no touchee, teacher, and no. I do not smile, because Never. It smoothed out a little as she grew older. The pugnacious lips because a seductive pout—eyes more heated than scary. But beneath the easy manners was a claw always ready to rein in the dogs, because Never.

She has ordered and defined her life by a firm control of sexual desire. She has equated sexuality with animality and desire with exploitation and has chosen to make herself into a gemstone rather than a woman. But Son disturbs her order: "He did not know that all the time he tinkled the [piano] keys she was holding tight to the reins of dark dogs with silver feet." Eventually, his sheer physical beauty, obvious desire for her, and "savannahs in his eyes," which suggest an African nobility, compel her to loosen the reins.

After the Christmas revelations make the Street house unbearable, the two of them go to New York, which in its modernity and sophistication is her natural territory. Here the influence of Valerian becomes clear as she seeks to remake Son into her image of the African prince, which is ultimately the only way she can accept him. Mutual affection for a time disguises this manipulative impulse, and becuse he loves her, he does not resist the education, the parties, and the pretensions. Finally, after a visit to his home, a Florida village she finds unbearably provincial, she realizes that he will always be a native Son, never an African prince, and she leaves him to return to her European suitor.

She rejects not merely him but her own Afro-American heritage and her blackness, the first represented by Florida and the latter by the Caribbean islands. She chooses the fixed life of white values, which are repeatedly associated with death, to the uncertainties of her race, which Morrison consistently associates with life and nature. Moreover, she chooses in effect to be a creation rather than a creator, an art historian rather than artist, a model rather than designer, a wife rather than woman. Thus, the very choice to have a clearly defined identity denies her access to origins and thus negates the very thing she seeks.

For Son, the struggle is much harder because he works from absence toward and then finally away from presence. His values are not dominant, his identity is not fixed, his origin is ambiguous. He lacks conventional identity:

> He was dwelling on his solitude, rocking in the wind, adrift. A man without human rites: unbaptized, uncircumcised, minus puberty rites or the formal rites of manhood. Unmarried and undivorced. He had attended no funeral, married in no church, raised no child. Propertyless, homeless, sought for but not after. . . . In those eight homeless years he had joined that great underclass of undocumented men. And although there were more of his kind in the world than students or soldiers, unlike students and soldiers they were not counted. They were an international legion of day laborers and musclemen, gamblers, sidewalk merchants, migrants, unlicensed crewmen on ships with volatile cargo, part-time mercenaries, full-time gigolos, or curbside musicians. What distinguished them from other men (aside from their terror of Social Security cards and *cedula de identidad*) was their refusal to equate work with life and an inability to stay anywhere for long.

What marks Son and others like them is their refusal to participate in those social orders which categorize and systematize; they create identities by deliberately evading the conventional markers of identity—family, job, education, religion, politics—and they equate this evasion with life. In Son's case, the absence of positive identity literally keeps him from imprisonment since he was responsible for the death of his wife.

Jade tempts him from this world of uncertainty and anonymity by offering visible signs of success: education, money, herself as physical presence and as the actual picture of elegance: in their first encounter, Son is enthralled by photographs of her printed in a Paris fashion magazine. Just as she sees in him a primitive energy to be channeled into civilization, so he sees in her sophisticated beauty in need of passion. In New York he realizes his ambition as long as she is willing to center her existence on him. But once she moves out into her world and tries to take him with her, he begins again to feel the impingement of the documented world.

He tries to overcome this by taking her to Florida, back to his origins, where the name Son has meaning because his father is called Old Man. But the language of this world is one she refuses to understand, seeing it as an alien culture unworthy of her interest. Blackness, so appealing when mediated by Son's beauty, is unattractive in its ordinary folk form of uneducated people, sexual circumspection, and the clothes of working people rather than fashion models. Most disturbing is Son's at-homeness in this world and his ability to love it and her simultaneously. This capacity for inclusion is one she lacks precisely because she, like Sydney and

Ondine and Valerian before her, has created her visible and positive identity by excluding such blackness, by making this reality an invisibility and negation. But that very act renders it an ever-present, intolerable part of her existence. Son, who loves both beauty and blackness, and in fact sees them as a totality, cannot understand her need to escape this black village.

Back in New York, the conflict reaches a climax, as each of them assumes the role of savior:

> She thought she was rescuing him from the night women who wanted him for themselves, wanted him feeling superior in a cradle, deferring to him; wanted her to settle for wifely competence when she could be almighty, to settle for fertility rather than originality, nurturing instead of building. He thought he was rescuing her from Valerian, meaning *them*, the aliens, the people who in a mere three hundred years had killed a world millions of years old. . . . Each was pulling the other away from the maw of hell—its very ridge top. Each knew the world as it was meant or ought to be. One had a past, the other a future and each one bore the culture to save the race in his hands.

The inability to achieve resolution is fundamentally an insistence by both on an origin that can be made present. Each in effect denies history: Son by believing in the possibility of returning to a prewhite black purity and Jadine by assuming that blackness was merely an aberration from the truth of Eurocentric Progress.

But Morrison makes it clear that Jadine's is the greater flaw. She must turn Son into an abstraction; her love is totalitarian and cannot incorporate the differences that are part of his concrete being. When he will not submit, she goes to the island, then to Paris to her wealthy European. He comes, on the other hand, to realize that his love must assume difference; because of this, he leaves, returns, and then pursues her back to the Caribbean.

This very gesture makes possible his rite of passage, for it beings his experience into the realm of folk experience in the sense that he cannot have that which he most needs to live, yet must go on living nonetheless. He goes to Therese, thinking she will help get back Jadine, but she knows better the meaning of his return. She deceives him by letting him believe he is going to Valerian's house, but in fact lets him off on the part of the island inhabited by the blind horsemen: "'The men. The men are waiting for you.' She was pulling the oars now, moving out. 'You can choose now. You can get free of her. They are waiting in the hills for you'." Fearful and unable to see, he stumbles over the rocks at first. "By and by he walked steadier, now steadier. The mist lifted and the trees stepped back a bit as if to make the way easier for a certain kind of man. Then he ran. Lickety-split. Lickety-split. Looking neither to the left nor to the right. Lickety-split. Lickety-split. Lickety-lickety-lickety-split."

Tar Baby marks the final step of immersion into the black folk world. Son achieves his truest nature by becoming one, not with the tellers of tales, as in Ellison, Gaines, and Walker, but with the tales themselves. Like the horsemen, he has been blinded by the prospect of enslavement, but also like them, this very handicap gives him freedom and power. He does not go back to the womb, as Jadine thought, but into the domain of the true black man.

Significantly, such a conclusion is only possible in a magical fictional world, one which in some ways mirrors the submerged Afro-American world of voodoo, conjure, and tricksters. Morrison takes as ordinary experience what more realistic black writers assume to be fantastic. She differs from Jones in taking for granted that what is considered irrational is in fact only a perversion of the natural order by a mechanistic, oppressive social system, whereas Jones is concerned to show that that system generates madness. Thus, for the author of *Tar Baby*, the sight of the blind, the magical power of the impotent, and the spiritual vitality of nonhuman nature makes greater sense than the insanities, grotesqueries, and ironies of the realm of "normality" and order. The particular dialectical structure of her work serves to develop the interrelated irrationalities of white and black culture.

Notes

1. Here *logocentric* is used to suggest the assumption of a fixed relationship between signifier and signified that does not allow for the ambiguity of language. See Derrida, *Of Grammatology*, 3–5; and Christopher Norris, *Deconstruction*, 29–31.
2. As her own marker of such characters, Morrison consistently gives them names with the diminutive suffix *-ene:* Maureen, Geraldine, Pauline *(The Bluest Eye);* Helene *(Sula);* Magadalena *(Song of Solomon);* and Ondine and Jadine *(Tar Baby).*
3. Toni Morrison, *The Bluest Eye*, 159.
4. Toni Morrison, *Sula*, 5–6.
5. See Jahn, *Muntu*, 125.
6. Toni Morrison, *Song of Solomon*, 99.
7. Ellison, *Invisible Man*, 13.
8. Toni Morrison, *Tar Baby*, 45.

◆◆◆◆◆◆◆◆◆◆◆◆◆

Pariahs and Community

ROBERTA RUBENSTEIN

Toni Morrison's fiction, like that of Penelope Mortimer and Margaret Atwood, demonstrates a central interest in the issues of boundary, attachment, and separation, though these concerns are dramatized in considerably different ways. Morrison's characters experience themselves as wounded or imprisoned, not only by virtue of their gender, but additionally by racial and economic divisions within American culture. The boundaries that circumscribe black people of both genders are not only the prejudices and restrictions that bar their entry into the mainstream but the psychological ones they internalize as they develop in a social structure that historically has excluded them.

If woman is the Other within patriarchal culture,[1] then women of ethnic minority groups, as defined by the values of white patriarchy, face a sense of double diminishment. As Pauline Breedlove of *The Bluest Eye* (1970) phrases it, "'Everybody in the world was in a position to give [black women] orders.'"[2] Or, as Margaret Wright expresses it, "Black women have been doubly oppressed. On the job, we're low women on the totem pole. White women have their problems. They're interviewed for secretarial instead of the executive thing. But we're interviewed for mopping floors and stuff like that. Sometimes we have to take what's left over in Miss Ann's refrigerator. This is all exploitation. And when we get home from work, the old man is wondering why his greens aren't cooked on time."[3]

Yet despite this doubled oppression, black women writers have celebrated and written eloquently of their sustaining values. Toni Morrison draws from a rich store of black oral tradition as well as from her own imaginative angle of vision to illuminate the potentialities for both annihilation and transcendence within black experience. In representing such extremes of possibility, she articulates, while not always resolving, some of the cultural contradictions of black women's—and men's—problematic position in white patriarchal American culture.

Morrison's fiction dramatizes both psychological and cultural dimensions of boundary through a number of recurring images and motifs. Concern with the psychological processes of identity formation is expressed through parent-child and peer relationships, often exaggerated in the form of emotionally blurred or distorted ego and body boundaries, as in symbiotic and even incestuous attachments. Another central cluster of images expresses figurative and literal maiming or mutilation. In turn, each of these images has a communal dimension, implying the divisions and splits within individuals that mirror their cultural situation. Thus, constriction of the growth of the self is implicitly linked to restrictive or oppressive cultural circumstances.

Traditionally, black communities have functioned as structures that sustain and preserve the individual, particularly in adversity. Morrison's narratives address the nature and forms of this connection between self and other, individual and group, that may ambiguously both shape people's values and impede their capacity to express them within the community's norms. Morrison also explores the false images and stereotypes that may contribute to this process. Fittingly, another central motif that appears throughout the author's canon is the diverse implications of appearances and perceptions. The way people regard themselves, and the way they are regarded, permeates every relationship and suggests the intangible boundaries that arise between individuals as well as groups.

Speaking of the visual emphasis in her fiction, Morrison has implicitly drawn a connection between perception and invisible but powerful intercultural divisions: "The interest in vision, in seeing, is a fact of black life. As slaves and ex-slaves, black people were manageable and findable, as no other slave society would be, because they were black. So there is an enormous impact from the simple division of color—more than sex, age, or anything else. The complaint is not being seen for what one is."[4]

In *The Bluest Eye*, this "complaint" functions on many levels. The Breedlove family's sense of utter hopelessness and helplessness is externalized in their appearance: both literal and spiritual poverty manifest themselves as ugliness in a world in which beauty is equated with success: poverty is ugly. Morrison deliberately invokes cultural stereotypes as a way of calling attention to errors of perception. "Cholly" and "Polly" Breedlove are virtually—as their rhyming nicknames suggest—caricatures: destitute, living in squalor, derelict, "ugly," amoral.[5] In *Tar Baby* (1981), the mysterious Son emerges as if a demon from the white unconscious: the anonymous black rapist who creeps menacingly out of the darkness, the proverbial "nigger in the woodpile."[6]

Other stereotypes originating in white culture produce equally false and damaging images. In *The Bluest Eye*, the portrait of family life described in the "Dick and Jane" frame is a childish oversimplification, not only of language but of reality:

Here is the house. It is green and white. It has a red door. It is very pretty. Here is the family. Mother, Father, Dick, and Jane live in the green-and-white house. They are very happy. See Jane. She has a red dress. She wants to play. Who will play with Jane? See the cat. It goes meow-meow. Come and play. Come play with Jane. The kitten will not play. See Mother. Mother is very nice. Mother, will you play with Jane? Mother laughs. Laugh, Mother, laugh. See Father. He is big and strong. Father, will you play with Jane? Father is smiling. Smile, Father, smile. See the dog. Bowwow goes the dog. Do you want to play with Jane? See the dog run. Run, dog, run. Look, look.

Here comes a friend. The friend will play with Jane. They will play a good game. Play, Jane, play.

As in several of Penelope Mortimer's novels, the traditional associations with the idea of home become, in *The Bluest Eye*, ironic comments on both the inaccuracy and the insufficiency of the stereotype. The image of the happy (white) family at home is inverted in the radical homelessness of Pecola Breedlove and her destitute family. Even the images of the cat and dog reappear in inverted forms, as Pecola is exploited by male members of her own community in the torment or death of other people's pets: for "Junior," his mother's adored (blue-eyed) cat; for Soaphead Church, his landlady's aged dog.

Moreover, the passage is scarcely an accurate reflection of the segment of American society that it purportedly characterizes.[7] Still less is it possible for a young black girl to recognize herself in it, for the imagination supplies the implicitly white middle-class cast of characters in the roles identified in the sketch. Through what is understood by omission, the invisible boundaries between cultures are eventually defined.

In a world in which many of the qualities deemed desirable are generated by white male fantasies, the Claudia MacTeers and Pecola Breedloves are doubly excluded; both their gender and the color of their skin mark them as outsiders. Beneath the tangible reminders of differentness or exclusion are the intangible but even more powerful expectations and assumptions of the dominant culture. What makes growing up black, female, and poor particularly problematic is that the white definitions of "reality" often do not correspond with either black or female experience. Claudia MacTeer sees that "[b]eing a minority in both caste and class, we moved about . . . on the hem of life, struggling to consolidate our weaknesses and hang on, or to creep singly up into the major folds of the garment." Or, as Sula Peace of Morrison's second novel, *Sula*, (1973) discovers, the fact that she and her friend Nel Wright are "neither white nor male" means that "all freedom and triumph was forbidden to them."[8]

As an indicator of the subtle seepage of white values into black culture, variations in skin color are evaluated with reference to whiteness. Mary Helen Washington has observed that "the intimidation of color" and the subject of female beauty are recurrent features of the oppressive experience of black women in white culture and are frequently reproduced in narratives by black women writers.[9] *The Bluest Eye*, Maureen Peal is envied less for her family's greater affluence than for her light skin, whereas to the same peers Pecola's absolute blackness confirms the other delimiting characteristics of her position at the bottom of the social scale; black boys project their "contempt for their own blackness" onto her. Those who, on the basis of such arbitrary but powerful distinctions, occupy a "higher" position on this spectrum of pigmentation are nonetheless insecure, because "[t]he line between colored and nigger was not always clear; subtle and telltale signs threatened to erode it, and the watch had to be constant."

Measured against white standards of skin color and physical beauty, the black female's options, as depicted in Morrison's first novel, are accommodation, misery, or degradation, if not all three. Unless they are, like Claudia MacTeer, endowed with enough inner strength to believe in themselves in the face of negation, they mature into a condition of inauthenticity, denying or distrusting their own experience. Living out someone else's version of reality, they cannot create themselves.

Such are the "good colored girls" who repress their anger, practice submission, attend college at land-grant institutions, and "learn how to do the white man's work with refinement." Conforming to white culture's expectations of them, they become dismembered like Claudia's decapitated white dolls, asexual and stripped of selfhood. Females like Pecola Breedlove, who fall outside the boundaries of even such marginal and self-denying acceptability, are thus radically threatening to "proper" black girls.

Morrison explores the subtle equation between perception and economic status, as if poverty and ugliness were two sides of the same false coin. Families like the ironically named Breedloves survive at the very fringe of society, where the "hem" begins to unravel. Their economic destitution and psychic abjection undermine the very bonds that attach family members to one another and form the basis for community. Barely existing as a social unit, they function even less as an emotional unit, for they lack even the "power of the weak" that characterizes oppressed groups.[10] Pauline Breedlove, disillusioned by her family life, retreats into a dream world purveyed by cinematic imagemakers of white cultural fantasies. Thus she is enslaved, not in the literal sense, but symbolically, by what are to Morrison "probably the most destructive ideas in the history of human thought": romantic love and physical beauty.

Seduced by appearances, Pauline damns her only daughter at birth. During labor she overhears white doctors commenting on the ease of childbirth for black women: "'They deliver right away and with no pain. Just like horses.'" Pauline projects onto her undeserving newborn daughter her outrage at such facile and prejudicial judgments. Baby Pecola arrives with a "head full of pretty hair, but Lord she was ugly." The emotional crippling shared by Cholly and Pauline is indeed bred into the next generation.

D. W. Winnicott has proposed that the core of what eventually forms as the individual's self-concept begins with the mirroring that occurs between mother and baby. Typically, what the baby sees when it looks into the mother's face is "himself or herself. In other words the mother is looking at the baby and *what she looks like is related to what she sees there.*"[11] In this sense, then, Pecola's first perception is her mother's reflection of her ugliness. From the seed of that initial negation grows her subsequent "fear of growing up, fear of other people, fear of life."

In a poignant sense the message Pecola reads first in her mother's eyes and eventually in everyone else's is quite accurate: the people of her community view her as the negation of what they are. Her defenseless condition threatens them with the "static and dread" that they repress within themselves. She is the dark shadow, the Other, that undermines both white and black fantasies of female goodness, beauty, and upward mobility. Her position at the bottom of the bottom symbolizes the regrettable need to pronounce someone inferior in order to defend a fragile sense of self-worth.

When the child Pecola hears her parents fighting on the other side of the partition in their makeshift "home," she virtually wishes herself into invisibility: "'Please, God. . . . Please make me disappear.' She squeezed her eyes shut. Little parts of her body faded away" until "[o]nly her tight, tight eyes were left. They were always left." Her attempt at psychological suicide ironically recalls the Cheshire Cat of Carroll's *Alice in Wonderland*, whose smile remains after the rest of its form has vanished; for Pecola it is the eyes that remain no matter how hard she wills their disappearance.

Pecola's desire to be *perceived* as a human being in order to exist at all is concentrated in her sad fantasy of obtaining blue eyes. Through them, she might see and be seen as a real person and thus acquire the self-determination denied her by her circumstances as well as by her race and gender. Never able to achieve existence in her own eyes—her own "I"—she exists only in the image reflected by others—by other eyes/I's. Existentially, she is an object, never a subject.[12]

Others of Morrison's characters are also, though more subtly, enslaved by appearances or by false images of selfhood. In *Tar Baby*, both Jadine Childs and Margaret Street are hostage to male idolatry of female beauty. Margaret was, twenty-five years earlier, the "Principal Beauty of Maine," a distinction that led Valerian Street to notice and eventually marry her. Some of the emotional warping of her personality comes from the self-image she was encouraged as a child to cultivate and to which she became enslaved. Initially, Valerian's appreciative attentions had given Margaret the feeling of "consequence under the beauty, back down beneath it where her Margaret-hood lay . . . faceless, silent, and trying like hell to please." Years later, she is still caught in the same submissive stasis, though its insufficiency has slowly warped her affections altogether.

Jadine Childs is another dubious benefactor of male worship of female beauty. A "stunning" model who trades on her looks, she lives in the conviction that she has succeeded on her own talent and a bit of luck, when in fact her European education and the opportunities to which it has given her access were subsidized by Valerian.

The trope of vision is adapted to different ends in *Sula*. Nel Wright and Sula Peace initially find "in each other's eyes the intimacy they were looking for." Each virtually creates the other as she sees who she is through the other girl's eyes. Nel later recalls that as girls they were "two throats and one eye," an image echoed in the detail of "one-eyed chickens," which in turn suggests the ill-fated Chicken Little. Sula thinks of women without men as "sour-tipped needles featuring one constant empty eye."

The recurring image of the single or shared eye reinforces the sense of shared boundaries and incidentally recalls the "communal eye" of the mythological Graie sisters, described by Nina Auerbach: "[T]hey have a single eye between them, which is passed unfailingly from sister to sister. They spend their lives endowing each other with vision."[13] After Sula and Nel separate, each suffers from limited vision. When Sula returns to the Bottom after a ten-year absence, Nel likens her reappearance to "getting the use of an eye back, having a cataract removed. . . . [Sula] made her see old things with new eyes."

Later, Sula becomes figuratively "one-eyed" and dis-membered, lacking a basic sense of connection to others and to the community. While people *see* themselves more clearly through her, she cannot *see* herself. She is radically free in the sense that Cholly Breedlove is: she has nothing to lose. Moreover, Sula herself is deceived by appearances. When she learns that the one man she can care for is not "Ajax" but "A. Jacks," her illusions are destroyed: if he is not what she has thought him to be, then she cannot trust her own perceptions.

Psychological and cultural eventualities may in a sense overdetermine an individual's limiting and limited circumstances. Pecola Breedlove's radical alienation begins with her mother's rejection of her at birth, to which are added the accumulated insults of poverty and ignorance. The mother is the figure who is, for each infant in most cultures, both the primary object of emotional attachment that enables the self to develop and the transmitter of cultural attitudes and values.[14] In *The Bluest Eye*, Pecola is literally a stranger to her mother, addressing her as "Mrs. Breedlove." When she goes to the house where her mother is a domestic and nanny for a white female child, Pauline denies even knowing who Pecola is. The cruelty of the scene repeats Pauline's initial rejection of Pecola at birth and accentuates the circular negation of selfhood: the mother becomes a fearful child before the greater power of her young white "mistress"; her own daughter experiences that fear as her mother's preference for her white "daughter," who is privileged to call Mrs.

Breedlove by the familiar name, Polly, in marked contrast to Pecola's formal address.

Sula Peace inherits another kind of legacy from her mother: Hannah is literally an easy "piece," thriving on sexual satisfaction because it is the most potent affirmation of her being. From Hannah's casual enjoyment of men, Sula learns that "sex was pleasant and frequent, but otherwise unremarkable." Other people in the community simply accept that "It was manlove that Eva bequeathed to her daughters. . . . The Peace women simply loved maleness for its own sake."

When Hannah suffers a horrible death by fire, Sula is mesmerized by the sight of her mother "dancing" in the flames and watches rather than running to her aid. Her recollection of that moment is a haunting revelation of her emotional paralysis. As she phrases it years later, "I didn't mean anything. I never meant anything. I stood there watching her burn and was thrilled." Her inappropriate emotional response at the time suggests her distance from the ordinary feelings that bind family members in affection and loyalty. Her words also suggest another meaning: having misunderstood Hannah's overheard comment about loving but "not liking" her daughter, Sula has since believed that she never *meant* anything to her own mother.

Through such misunderstandings Sula becomes a kind of emotional orphan. Like Pecola Breedlove in *The Bluest Eye*, who lives out the meaning of her mother's rejection, Sula enacts her own interpretation of her mother's words, becoming a center of negative energy, withheld emotion, and absence of guilt. In psychological terms, she has no ego: "no center, no speck around which to grow." At the core of her personality, where the patterns of self-confirmation and ethical sense should develop, is a void that has existed "ever since her one major feeling of responsibility had been exorcised on the bank of a river with a closed place in the middle. The first experience taught her there was no other that you could count on; the second that there was no self to count on either." While men are tempted by Sula's enigmatic charm, women become more attentive to their spouses and children in defense against her charismatic power. She catalyzes the anxieties of those whose paths she crosses because (in others' eyes) she lives out the amoral potentialities that most people repress.

As a result of quite different circumstances, Jadine Childs of *Tar Baby* is a cultural orphan (as well as a literal orphan: her father died when she was two, her mother ten years later) who lacks a clear model for either her female sexuality or her cultural history. As an adult woman she is confronted with the consequences of such inner confusion. When she visits her lover Son's hometown, she stays in his Aunt Rosa's house, where she feels claustrophobically enclosed in a dark, windowless, almost airless box of a room. Looking out to "the blackest nothing she had ever seen"—and, figuratively, into her own naked soul—she feels overwhelmed and defenseless. "Maybe if she stood there long enough light would come from somewhere, and she could see shadows, the outline of something, a bush, a tree, a line between earth and sky, a heavier darkness to show where this very house stopped and space began." As the language suggests, Jade experiences herself in an unbounded space that threatens the carefully defined limits of her complacent daytime self: "No man had made her feel that naked, that unclothed . . . none of them had made her feel exposed. . . . Obscene."

When later Jadine and Son make love, she is inhibited by a group of female demons whom only she can see: her own dead mother; her Aunt Ondine; Son's dead wife, whose sexual charisma is legendary; and a woman in yellow (the image of Jadine's alter ego). All the women except the last expose their breasts to her; the woman in yellow shows her the three big eggs she carries. Jade feels that she must turn her back on these succubi, who remind her of female servitude, whether economic or sexual. Yet her rejection of "breasts" and "eggs" has resulted in her narcissistic self-absorption. Fearing to live out the conventional destiny of her gender (as the night women suggest), Jadine fails to see that her current life is as much a prostitution of her womanhood as the role of Son's wife might be. As the shorter form of her name hints, she is already compromised, from Valerian's financial subsidy of her education to her career as a model who rents out her beauty.

Moreover, Ondine criticizes her niece's self-centeredness, observing that if a girl "'never learns how to be a daughter, she can't never know how to be a woman. . . . You don't need your own natural mother to be a daughter. All you need is to feel a certain . . . careful way about people older than you are. . . . A daughter is a woman that cares about where she comes from and takes care of them that took care of her.'"

Jadine's "failure" as a daughter stems in part from anger she still feels toward her dead mother: "'You left me you died you didn't care enough about me to stay alive.'" Though one wishes that the thread of Jadine's "motherlessness" were further developed in the narrative, one can speculate that the loss of her mother on the brink of her adolescence is one source of anxiety about her female identity and sexuality.[15] Ondine's self-sacrifice on Jadine's behalf has also distorted their relationship; Ondine has regarded Jadine as "a 'child' whom she could enjoy, indulge, protect and, since this 'child' was a niece[,] it was without the stress of a mother-daughter relationship."

Thus, all of the mother figures in Jadine's life—her own mother, Ondine, Margaret, and the collective night women—are in some way threatening to her. Parentless, she lacks a model of either positive mothering or "daughtering"; cultureless, she lacks a clear sense of how to achieve authenticity in either black or white worlds.

* * *

In Morrison's narratives, the ambiguous thrall of the parents, or the equally powerful effect of their absence, is an emotional reality that many of her characters, both male and female, confront. In the absence of close bonds with one or both parents, a child seeks some other person who will satisfy the need for a deep, abiding emotional attachment. A central representation of the problems of boundary and attachment that originate in the parent-child bond is that of symbiosis: the mutually dependent emotional connection that ultimately may either facilitate or impede growth of the self.

In *Sula*, three minor characters—homeless boys who come to live in the Peace household—are each called the same name, Dewey, by Eva. For the rest of their lives, they are an inseparable triad. Even their own mothers are unable to distinguish among them for, like figurative Siamese triplets whose physical boundaries are partially shared, each is joined "with the other two to become a trinity with a plural name . . . inseparable, loving nothing and no one but themselves." Fused by Eva's naming of them, "They spoke with one voice, thought with one mind."

Like the "three deweys" (the capital letter is eventually dropped), Sula Peace and Nel Wright, the only children of "distant mothers and incomprehensible [or absent] fathers," approach a kind of psychological symbiosis. In Morrison's narrative of a unique female friendship,[16] Sula and Nel initially discover their own essences and begin to grow through their reciprocal connection; each girl seems to have, both materially and metaphysically, what the other lacks. While Sula needs Nel as "the closest thing to both another and a self," Nel needs Sula to act out the denied dark forces in her own being. Sula, very much her mother's daughter, is sexually free, mercurial, amoral, and as bored by convention as Nel is wedded to it.

Nel is also her mother's daughter; when she marries Jude Greene at eighteen, she acts as an extension of her mother's desires. Her marriage is "the culmination of all [Helene] had been, thought or done in this world." Moreover, in matrimony she becomes a mirror for her husband, who sees himself "taking shape in her eyes" and who regards her as an extension of himself: "The two of them together would make one Jude." Nel's transfer of her symbiotic attachment from Sula to Jude severs the bond between the two girls that had supported both of them. From that point on, they are both partial people, each lacking emotionally what the other originally supplied. Nel participates in the orthodox rites of female maturation: marriage, maternity, childbirth, and—in the pattern typical of the relationships between men and women in the Bottom—abandonment by her husband, in this instance to the thrall of her best friend, Sula.

Sula never finds the other half of her equation again, although for a time she thinks that "Ajax" might occupy that role. Just before her death, she imagines curling into the "heavy softness" of water that might "envelop her, carry her, and wash her tired flesh always." The "sleep of water" for which she longs is an image of merging into the embracing womb, the mother from whom she has felt radically separated. The image is also linked with preceding events, including Chicken Little's drowning at Sula's hands and the death of Plum, who wanted to crawl back into his mother's womb.

In the same novel, the symbolic return to the womb is expressed on the communal level in the tragic ending to the parade on the Bottom's last National Suicide Day. The people of the community, led to the river's edge by Shadrack, release their rage and anger at the unfinished tunnel—in the construction of which they were barred from employment— by destroying the bricks and timbers at the excavation site. Entering the tunnel, a number of them find themselves instead in a suffocating "chamber of water" created by the multiplied effect of their assault on the unstable structure in the warm mud. Like Chicken Little, they are swallowed by the river. Thus, Shadrack's vision of collective suicide is literally and tragically enacted.

The event illustrates one of Morrison's recurrent themes, that of energy and passion released self-destructively when there is no positive outlet for its expression. In *Song of Solomon* (1977) Ruth Dead, starved for a closeness and affection that she cannot find in the tyrannical and sexually unavailable Macon, nurses her youngest and only male child well past infancy. The mark of their unusually prolonged symbiotic attachment and merged psychological boundaries is preserved in his name, Milkman. During his childhood, Ruth's son "had never been . . . a separate real person. He had always been a passion."[17] Similarly, Milkman has never regarded his mother as "a person, a separate individual, with a life apart from allowing or interfering with his own." As further evidence of the boundary-blurring among the members of the Dead family, Milkman can scarcely distinguish his much older "baby doll" sisters from his mother.

Moreover, Milkman's distorted view of women, derived from his autocratic father's attitude as well as from his clinging mother's and jealous sisters' behavior, warps his later attachments to women and his expectations of the world in general. In early adolescence, he is attracted to his second cousin, Pilate Dead's granddaughter, who is several years his senior. Pilate introduces Milkman to Hagar as her "brother"; Hagar's eventual parasitic attachment to him thus figuratively replaces the symbiotic bond originating in Milkman's early attachment to his possessive mother.

Both emotionally dependent women, starved for a sense of their own being, need Milkman to validate their existence; yet for both, love is a prison because it is unreciprocated. Hagar claims that Milkman is her "'home in this world'"; Ruth Dead counters, "'And I am his.'" Pilate chides them both, "'He ain't a house, he's a man'.'" When Milkman leaves Hagar after more than a dozen years and she realizes that she can neither win him back nor successfully kill him, she dies of grief. Her actual death merely confirms the psychological void within her.

By contrast, Hagar's grandmother and Milkman's aunt, Pilate Dead, is dependently attached to no one. Born to her mother posthumously, she lacks a navel, the mark of each child's original symbiosis with its mother. Though the missing navel initially sets Pilate apart as a freak of nature, its absence represents her unique freedom from the emotional dependencies that characterize the other Dead women. It also makes people believe that Pilate has supernatural, perhaps even demonic, powers. In fact, her arcane knowledge of midwifery, her natural healing powers, her ability to distill wine from plants, her anomalous physical sign, her reputed capacity to "step out of her skin," and her ability to fly "without ever leaving the ground" suggest that she is a kind of benign witch.[18] Yet, although Pilate is Milkman's spiritual midwife, her own daughter and granddaughter are less clearly the beneficiaries of her nurturance; Hagar is fatally crippled by her need for a man to affirm her selfhood.

The metaphorical counterpart to symbiosis and merged boundaries is division, the imagery of which resonates on a number of levels in Morrison's fiction. As in the narratives of Margaret Atwood, "splitness" is a symptom of emotional or spiritual injury. Thus, Pecola Breedlove's division into two "selves" at the end of *The Bluest Eye* represents her inability to see herself as a whole person or, in fact, as a person at all. Soaphead Church's deception (a product of his own self-deception) destroys her last connection to being. Her desire for the most basic confirmation of self in the eyes of others drives her mad, as she splits into the girl with blue eyes and the one "friend" who can corroborate the miracle.

In several instances, division and splitness are dramatized as opposing values or capacities either within a single character or through characters who complement each other. In *Sula*, Sula Peace and Nel Wright are each half of a figurative whole self. Morrison has acknowledged that there is "a little bit of both in each of those two women, and . . . if they have been one person, I suppose they would have been a rather marvelous person. But each lacked something that the other one had."[19]

The girls' respective domiciles are analogues of both boundary and complementarity. While Nel and her mother reside in a compulsively orderly house with "real lace curtains at the window," Sula lives in a cluttered, "woolly" house of many rooms and stairways: "[T]here were three sets [of stairs] to the second floor—more rooms, doors and stoops. There were rooms that had three doors, others that opened out on the porch only and were inaccessible from any other part of the house; others that you could get to only by going through somebody's bedroom." Sula loves the tidiness and material extravagance of Nel's house; Nel covets the disheveled atmosphere of Sula's, where there is more room for the unexpected. While Nel represents the orderly rationality of consciousness and repression, Sula embodies the darker, more mysterious and incongruous dimension of dreams and the unconscious.

When the two girls are separated by Nel's marriage to Jude, Sula ultimately becomes split off from her own feelings. Her moral torpor sets her apart, not only from other people's codes, but also from meaningful connection to them, except through her body. Spiritual lassitude takes the form of promiscuity, for like her mother, Sula's only means of self-verification is her sexuality. During lovemaking, she "needed to find the cutting edge. . . . [T]here was utmost irony and outrage in lying under someone, in a position of surrender, feeling her own abiding strength and limitless power. But the cluster did break, fall apart, and in her panic to hold it together she leaped from the edge into soundlessness and went down howling, howling in a stinging awareness of the endings of things: an eye of sorrow in the midst of all the hurricane rage of joy."

Her condition goes beyond loneliness, which assumes "the absence of other people," for "the solitude she found in that desperate terrain had never admitted the possibility of other people." Instead, pursuing temporary physical escapes from her inner void, she flirts carelessly and without premeditation with Nel's man, Jude. Unconsciously, her act is a kind of punishment of Nel for betraying the bond that joined the two of them as girls. The single encounter between Sula and Jude eventually destroys Nel's marriage because it introduces dissatisfaction and forbidden desire where satisfaction and complacency had previously reigned.

Heir to the sexual promiscuity of her mother and the indifference to social convention of her grandmother, Sula Peace is radically isolated, even though the community of the Bottom uneasily tolerates her presence. She is drawn to return to the Bottom after ten years because her community is the crucible of her identity. The "freedom" of radical separateness has become an even more oppressive prison; the void ultimately collapses inwardly upon itself. Split off from her feelings, Sula witnesses her death—as she has witnessed much of her life—as a curious but uncommitted observer. It surprises and amuses her that "'it didn't even hurt.'" In the serene detachment of her dying, Sula finds the only real peace of her life.

Through Sula's death, however, her "other self" achieves a kernel of knowledge. Almost twenty-five years later, Eva Peace makes Nel recognize her deeper resemblance to Sula. The doughty matriarch has always believed that the two girls were "'just alike. . . . Never was no difference between you.'" Nel initially rejects this identification, for, ever since she chose marriage to Jude and conventional life, she has regarded herself as different from the wayward, amoral Sula. Eva's words force her to acknowledge that her passivity and silence when Chicken Little drowned were in fact complicity in the event—no different from Sula's detachment as her mother burned.

The interwoven stories of Sula and Nel, of the Peace and Sabat matriarchies with their mixture of wild blood and tamed spirits, suggest that the limiting boundaries of race, class, and gender preclude all but a few narrow avenues to selfhood. In this narrative, the nascent self is represented as split: either suffocated into a repressive virtuousness (like Nel Wright) or drawn to pursue unconventional values (in the community's terms) and sensations that mimic real feeling but lead instead to literal immolation (Plum, Hannah) or emotional isolation (Sula). Nel's wail at the end of the narrative, a howl that has stuck in her throat since she lost both husband and friend years before, wordlessly expresses the sadness of the community of the Bottom and the inequities of the world itself. It is, appropriately, boundless, with "no bottom and . . . no top, just circles and circles of sorrow."

In Morrison's fiction, the larger divisions within a community are frequently represented through relationships between generations and contrasts between families. In *The Bluest Eye*, the economically and emotionally bankrupt Breedloves are figuratively set against the intact MacTeer family; Mrs. MacTeer's grudging love for her daughters exposes the absence of such affection in Pauline Breedlove's attitude toward Pecola. The Peace and Sabat matriarchies in *Sula* are developed through deliberate contrast; their different values shape Sula's and Nel's very different expectations for themselves.

The complementary families in *Song of Solomon* are both Deads: the self-negating family of Macon Dead and the life-affirming family of his own sister. Pilate Dead, born posthumously to her mother and orphaned in early childhood (her father was shot by whites greedy for his Virginia property), feels "cut off" from other people by her circumstances. Yet, unlike Pecola Breedlove or Sula Peace, her very separateness has led her to acquire a strong sense of her own self; she is set apart in a different sense. "[H]er alien's compassion for troubled people ripened her and— the consequence of the knowledge she had made up or acquired—kept her just barely within the boundaries of the elaborately socialized world of black people."

In contrast to the passive Ruth Dead, Milkman's biological mother, Pilate is Milkman's spiritual mother, who is responsible for his very existence: when "only a miracle" could have produced pregnancy in Ruth, Pilate had given her sister-in-law a concoction that had made her briefly both fertile and sexually irresistible to her cold husband, thus presiding over Milkman's very conception. She prevented Macon from killing the baby before it was born and aided Ruth during the delivery. As his spiritual midwife, Pilate enlarges the boundaries of Milkman's suffocating world by introducing him to the sky, "so that from then on when he looked at it, it . . . was intimate, familiar, like a room that he lived in, a place where he belonged." Eventually Milkman discovers the true family history through this woman who, though she lives in the present, is vitally in touch with the past. Milkman, by contrast, has virtually no understanding of the past but is obsessed with it, as indicated by his characteristic concentration on "things behind him. Almost as though there were no future to be had." Pilate's tutelage ultimately results in his liberation through knowledge of his real past, which frees him from his narcissism.

Milkman is aided in the discovery of both his manhood and his family history by another midwife, suggestively named Circe. Years before, this wise old crone, who seems to exist outside time and whose appearance suggests a witch out of Milkman's childhood nightmares, had presided at Pilate's birth from her dead mother. Like Pilate, Circe is also a natural healer who gives Milkman knowledge that is crucial to his discovery of his cultural heritage. Her instructions lead Milkman to the entrance into his ancestry: that most suggestive of female symbols, a cave—the very one in which his father and aunt had once huddled as children and the source of the fabled treasure. Milkman is on a treasure hunt, but the boon he finds is not the one for which he searches.

In *Tar Baby*, divisions operate simultaneously between families and generations. Jadine Childs is anomalously "split" between two pairs of figurative parents, one white and the other black. A quasi-member of both the Street and Childs families, she moves comfortably between black and white worlds and between America and Europe; she is more respectful of and socially at ease with the Streets, her financial benefactors, than with the aunt and uncle who reared and loved her. Through Jadine's brief but intense relationship with Son—a man from an economic and social strata that Jadine initially regards as beneath her—Morrison explores the implications of such psychological and cultural boundary-straddling.

Despite Jadine's apparent savoir faire, one image pointedly suggests her inner division and the vulnerability of her apparently supreme self-confidence. One day at a grocery store in Paris, Jadine had seen a tall "tar-black" woman with scarified cheeks, wearing a long canary-yellow dress. (In Morrison's novels, the most seductive, sexually free women, like Nel Wright's whore-grandmother, Rochelle, and Sula Peace's mother, Hannah, wear yellow dresses.) Jadine, struck as if in a vision, had watched this "woman's woman—that mother/sister/she" as she left the market with three eggs balanced in her hand and had followed her with her eyes "all the way to the edge of the world." From that location the woman had, inscrutably, spat upon the pavement.

In her incongruity, the woman is a manifestation of Jadine's alter ego: beneath Jade's regal elegance lie a fear of her ancestral African roots and contempt for her social inferiors, as well as anxiety about her female role and her sexuality. The woman in yellow had made Jade feel "lonely and inauthentic." Morrison has explained the figure of the woman in yellow as "the original self—the self that we betray when we lie, the one that is always there. . . . [O]ne measures one's other self against it."[20] Ironically, it is the crude, small-town Son who reaches through Jadine's affectations and, for a time, brings out the authentic self restrained beneath her cool hauteur. Yet one of Jade's first reactions to Son—in response to a sexual insult—is to spit at him, in unconscious imitation of the mysterious tar-black woman in yellow.

The splits within and constrictions of the personality as the indirect but terrible result of racism and cultural oppression are dramatized throughout Morrison's fiction. Frequently, her male characters are depicted as infantilized by their position on the fringes of white culture, which dictates their exclusion from all but the most menial forms of employment and self-respect. In *The Bluest Eye*, the first of Cholly Breedlove's "emasculations" occurs when, during his initiatory sexual experience, he and the girl are discovered by white men who force the pair to continue at gunpoint for the latters' amusement. From that humiliation, his attitude toward female sexuality is tainted with a mixture of furtiveness, shame, and anger. In the same novel, Soaphead Church is a pedophile; little girls are the only sexual objects who do not threaten his fragile and sterile masculinity.

Additionally infantilized by their often marginal position in a strongly female world, most of the male characters in the novels remain "Sons" or boys, with indicative names like Tar Baby (in *Sula*), a man who can't give up the bottle—in this case, alcohol; and Boy Boy, Eva Peace's husband, who abandons her and their three small children for another woman. Even the little boy whom Sula inadvertently drowns has the diminuitive name of Chicken Little.

The men who actually couple with women are either ineffectual shadows, womanizers, or deserters: from the MacTeers' roomer in *The Bluest Eye*—Mr. Henry, who fraternizes with prostitutes and tries to fondle Frieda MacTeer—to the men of *Sula*—Helene Wright's husband, who vanishes, and Hannah's, who dies three years after siring Sula. The one man whom Sula loves, Ajax, seems to diverge from this pattern; however, as soon as Ajax feels the tug toward permanence, he flees, afraid of relinquishing his maternally cushioned boyhood. Son, the central male character of *Tar Baby*, is an emotionally strong man. Yet his anomalous position is underscored by his status as a man on the lam—his wife's infidelity drove him to accidental homicide—who, finally, has no place to flee except into a legendary past.

The young Milkman Dead of *Song of Solomon* is, for much of his childhood and youth, infantilized by his mother and indulged to the point of satiety by women who adore him and prostrate themselves on his behalf. Accustomed to receiving without giving, he is, like many of the males in Morrison's fiction, allowed to stretch his "carefree boyhood out for thirty-one years." At the same time he is belittled by his cold father and patronized or deeply resented by his elder female siblings, who loathe his privileged maleness. His father, who eventually grudgingly gives Milkman a role in his exploitative business dealings, regards his son as an extension of his own needs, just as the Dead women do.

Morrison implies that if the enveloping white world does not emasculate or infantilize black men, it turns them into Macon Deads, imitators of the most deadening values of white patriarchal society: greed, acquisitiveness, and dominion. Milkman Dead, surrounded by a self-absorbed father and self-effacing or rejecting females, grows up in an exaggerated patriarchal microcosm. However, *Song of Solomon* ultimately provides a distinct contrast to the situation of male characters in the earlier novels, for Morrison makes the infantilized male not only the protagonist but the eventual bearer of knowledge for his community.

Several of Morrison's characters are not only emotionally maimed, as these infantilized male figures suggest, but also literally stunted. The recurrent imagery of deformity and mutilation visually represents the injurious effects of oppression and marginalization, whether resulting from gender, ethnic minority identity, economic circumstance, or their cumulative consequences. Such images or episodes also signal the distortion, violation, or confusion of boundaries of the self or body, as perceived by either the individuals or those who interact with them. Pecola Breedlove's madness in *The Bluest Eye* is the most pronounced manifestation of the difficulty of achieving autonomy in conditions that mitigate absolutely against it. In *Sula*, Shadrack, who walks through Medallion with his genitals exposed, acts out the corresponding psychological emasculation and impotence of his male peers.

The young Claudia MacTeer of *The Bluest Eye* registers the knowledge of exclusion through contempt for the alien objects of her childhood: Shirley Temple milk mugs and white baby dolls for Christmas. Through these emblems, she slowly becomes aware of herself as an outsider. Sensitive to the insult in the presumption that what every girl child desired was "a blue-eyed, yellow-haired, pink-skinned doll," she mutilates her dolls and feels—with horror—the same impulse toward little white girls.

In fact, the figurative mutilation functions in the other direction. As Claudia inevitably accommodates herself to "reality," she learns to do as little black girls (and, more broadly, as most members of oppressed groups who recognize the terms of their survival) traditionally have done: to suppress indignation and affect "fraudulent love." Her recognition that such gestures are adjustments "without improvement" spares her from total acquiescence to oppression.

In the same novel, each member of the Breedlove family, though alienated from the others, is symbolically linked to the others by various signs of literal or spiritual injury. Pecola's father, Cholly, born a bastard, was left to die by a crazy mother; a more compassionate great-aunt rescued him from abandonment and raised him until, when he was four-teen, she died. He later locates the man he believes is his biological father and is stunned when his putative relative disavows any tie. Bereft of all emotional connection, Cholly wanders about the country as a "free" man, free only in the sense that he is at the bottom, where there is nothing left to lose. In his world, even God is a "nice old white man" with blue eyes.

Radically disconnected from family or community, Cholly is another of Morrison's cultural orphans. He drifts through life until he meets Pauline, a woman with a physical deformity that parallels his emotional one. Because of her crippled foot, Pauline fears that no man will ever be able to love her; she blames her "general feeling of separateness and unworthiness" on her deformity. Appearance becomes the false measure of inner worth. Not surprisingly, the two soul-crushed people find solace and even grateful regard in one another.

Their daughter Pecola's inner crippling, begun at her birth with Pau-line's declaration of her ugliness, is reinforced as she approaches puberty. When her first menstrual period begins, she believes she is dying; she learns from the MacTeer girls that "ministratin'" means that she can generate life. While Claudia and Frieda regard their guest's acquisition of womanhood with envy and awe, the blood Pecola sheds is more accu-rately a foreshadowing of her spiritual wounding. Her poignant response to the explanation of how babies are created is to wonder, "'[H]ow do you get somebody to love you?'" During that same year she is sexually violated and impregnated by her own father, whose unpremeditated but shocking act is depicted as a misdirected expression of his love for her.

Pecola's wounding is advanced by another morally deformed member of the community. Soaphead Church, a man of mixed blood, is a fraudu-lent "spiritual advisor" to troubled souls. Though he prides himself on his sexual restraint, in his own way he is more destructive than the weak but essentially amoral Cholly Breedlove. Manipulating Pecola's faith in miracles and pressing her to commit a debased act on his behalf by poi-soning his landlady's aged dog, he violates her spiritual innocence as surely as her father abuses her physical innocence. By the age that most girls reach sexual maturity, Pecola is already a lost soul, imprisoned in a madness from which she can never flee.

In *Song of Solomon*, most members of the central family are, as their surname hints, spiritually maimed if not dead. Macon Dead, whose entire name is a pun, is a merciless, materialistic slum landlord who reigns over his family as he does his tenants, as an unfeeling autocrat. The members of his family limp through life, each in some crucial way incomplete. The youngest Dead and only son, Milkman, has an actual limp caused by one slightly shorter leg. However, the narrator informs us, "The deformity was mostly in his mind." Macon's two daughters are pathetic, emotionally stunted women. Like fairy-tale sisters awaiting the prince who might free them from the prison of their father's house, they occupy themselves by making fake rose petals out of velvet. Late in her life, the daughter named Corinthians finally is rescued by a man whose affection allows her to replace her false vanity with authentic self-esteem.

In fact, nearly all the females in *Song of Solomon*, except for the indomitable Pilate Dead, are clinging, self-effacing women who are easily humiliated or exploited by men. Ruth Foster Dead, daughter of the town's most successful black doctor and wife of one of its most successful businessmen, lived as a child in "a great big house that pressed [her] into a small package." As an adult woman still occupying that same house, Ruth resembles the domestically confined women of Penelope Mortimer's narratives, finding the patriarchal mansion "more prison than palace," as do her daughters.

Maiming and injury become self-inflicted in *Sula*, as the hint of self-mutilation and dismemberment resonates through the Peace family. Eva Peace, the enigmatic matriarch, is an ambiguous agent of both good and evil who destroys or outlives all three of her children as well as her sole grandchild, Sula. Possessed of only one leg—but a "magnificent" one—she is a grotesque but charismatic woman, around whom circle various tales concerning the loss, or perhaps the sale, of the missing limb. Sula's impulsive slashing off of a finger tip with a kitchen knife, to show her confidence when challenged by young white boys, is another manifestation of self-mutilation, as is her mother Hannah's bizarre death by fire.

In *Tar Baby*, the lonely and emotionally stunted Margaret Street had, years before, sadistically abused her infant son, Michael. As Ondine Childs describes it, she had "'cut him up. You cut your baby up. Made him bleed for you. For fun you did it. Made him scream, you, you freak. . . .' Ondine addressed the others, still shouting. 'She stuck pins in his behind. Burned him with cigarettes. Yes, she did, I saw her; I saw his little behind. She burned him!'" Ondine has kept this monstrous knowledge to herself for fear that she and Sydney would be "let go" if the truth were exposed.

When people are dehumanized by poverty, prejudice, or restricted opportunity for growth of the self, the capacity for relationship may be radically perverted. In Morrison's fiction, a central and recurring representation of emotional injury as well as violation of the boundaries of selfhood is the distortion of the bonds of affection between people. When such emotional disruption occurs between members of the same family— in several instances involving the abuse of a child by the parent (or another adult) of the opposite sex—the attachment is particularly destructive. Generally the abuse is symptomatic of disturbed family relationships as well as of a parent's excessive dependence upon a child for emotional release from intolerable circumstances.

In each of Morrison's novels to date, that perversion of the affections is dramatized through the family crime of incest. In most of the instances of incestuous attachment or possession, it is the parent's own restricted possibility for growth that precipitates the sexual or physical violation of a child of the opposite sex. The parent oversteps the very psychological boundaries that the child has formed in the process of separation from her or him.

Morrison has claimed that "love or its absence" is one of her central themes: under the name of love, "[P]eople do all sorts of things. . . . The violence is a distortion of what, perhaps, we want to do."[21] In this sense, *The Bluest Eye* is a narrative of both violence and violation—not only of the female body but of potentiality and growth of the self as well as the affections and attachments between human beings. Incest and rape become metaphors for both black and white nightmares of inverted love and suffocation of selfhood.

In that novel, father-daughter incest occurs through Cholly Breedlove's unpremeditated sexual violation of his daughter, Pecola. Even in the MacTeers' emotionally intact household, Claudia and Frieda see their father naked one night and feel "the shame brought on by the absence of shame." Mr. Henry, their debonair boarder, fondles Frieda; Soaphead Church's pedophilic fondness for little girls is another expression of the inversion or misplacement of desire, affection, and sexuality itself.

In *Sula*, Eva's only son, Plum, is literally consumed by the power of sexuality that lacks an appropriate outlet. When he returns from the war, mentally broken like Shadrack, to live a mindless, lethargic existence in his mother's house, Eva takes things into her own hands. Finding him one night in his room in his customary drugged, babylike state, she cradles him gently, then douses him with kerosene and sets him afire.

Plum's infantile state externalizes the condition of many of the men of the Bottom who can never be more than "boys" in their world circumscribed by white culture. Eva later explains to her daughter Hannah that Plum had wanted to "crawl back into [her] womb." As she continues,

> I ain't got the room no more even if he could do it. . . . I had room enough in
> my heart, but not in my womb. . . . I couldn't birth him twice. I'd be laying

here at night and he'd be downstairs in that room, but when I closed my eyes I'd see him . . . and he'd be creepin' to the bed trying to spread my legs trying to get back up in my womb. . . . I kept on dreaming it. . . . One night it wouldn't be no dream. It'd be true and I would have done it, would have let him if I'd've had the room. . . . I had to keep him out so I just thought of a way he could die like a man not all scrunched up inside my womb, but like a man.

Eva is so eloquent in her own defense that the reader is almost persuaded that the incest wish is Plum's. However, taken in context with her other actions, it is clearly Eva's own unacceptable desire—her fear that one night she "would have let him"—that corroborates Plum's infantilized state and fuels his destruction. The shocking infanticide is neither the first nor the last of her almost Godlike manipulations of others' lives.[22]

The incest theme in *Song of Solomon* is expressed through the lonely Ruth Dead, whose attachments to both her father and her son reflect an exaggerated intensity. Though her father had felt her ecstasy at his kisses as excessive, he had delivered both her daughters at their births, to her husband's repugnance. According to Macon Dead, Ruth had lain naked next to the body of her father after he expired. Ruth later gives Milkman a less sensational interpretation of this event. Yet even after her father's death, she expresses feelings toward him more characteristic of a romantic lover; still defining herself as her "daddy's daughter," she worships at his grave several times a year. Ruth's son, Milkman, only belatedly overcomes the exaggerated maternal attachment encoded in his name.

In *Tar Baby*, the incest wish is implied in the relationship between Margaret Street and her son. Margaret lives, like Ruth Dead, in a patriarchal mansion, feeling "drowned . . . in the spaciousness of that house." Also like Ruth, Margaret is caught in a loveless marriage and seeks in her son the intimacy she is unable to find with her husband. She unconsciously desires as a lover the son she had abused during his infancy, while priding herself on what she believes is an unpossessive maternal attitude: "[Of] all the people she knew in the world, [Michael] seemed to her the best. . . . She liked his company, to talk to him, to be around him. Not because he is my son, she told herself . . . but because he is interesting and he thinks I am interesting too. I am special to him. Not as a mother, but as a person. Just as he is to me." The incestuous quality of her affection is further implied by her desire to live near, or even with, her son rather than her husband.

Margaret's self-justifying response to the disclosure of her earlier abuses of her child reveals her terrible loneliness and emotional insufficiency. As a baby, Michael had imposed his devouring infant needs upon a mother incapable of meeting her own needs for affection. The infant's "implicit and explicit demand for her best and constant self" could never be appeased. "She could not describe her loathing of its prodigious appetite for security. . . . [W]hen she felt hostage to that massive insolence, that stupid trust, she could not help piercing it." The ambiguous pronoun "it" indicates the extent to which the baby Michael had been an object, not a person, to Margaret: seen as a part of herself, he was the object upon whom she had projected her self-hatred and self-estrangement.

Though Valerian Street (whose very name indicates his narcotized existence) cannot admit that his own emotional sterility has contributed to Margaret's loneliness and the perversion of her affections, at least he acknowledges that there was "something in the crime of innocence so revolting it paralyzed him. . . . What an awful thing she had done. And how much more awful not to have known it. . . . He was guilty, therefore, of innocence" Implicitly, it is this same false innocence that masks Valerian's patronizing attitude toward his dependent black retainers with the pointed surname, Childs.

The representation of boundary is amplified on the collective level in Morrison's characterization of the terms within and against which a black community defines itself. In each of her narratives, a community functions as a moral arbiter, the source of both individual and group norms. Her characters are defined in part through their acceptance of or challenge to certain collective presumptions. Conversely, as a kind of collective conscience, the community either includes or excludes its members on the basis of their accordance with its implicit—though frequently contradictory—values. Thus, separation and division are not only psychological processes but often also social ones, as the figure of the pariah is set apart from the community.

In *The Bluest Eye*, the community is the backdrop to the lives of Claudia and Frieda MacTeer and the Breedlove family, asserting itself primarily in its moral castigation of the Breedloves' misfortunes. Thus, at the end of the retrospective chronicle of Pecola Breedlove's—and the narrator's own—loss of innocence, Claudia MacTeer describes Pecola picking her way "among all the waste and beauty of the world—which is what she herself was. All of our waste which we dumped on her and which she absorbed. And all of our beauty, which was hers first and which she gave to us. . . . Even her waking dreams we used—to silence our own nightmares. And she let us, and thereby deserved our contempt. We honed our egos on her, padded our characters with her frailty, and yawned in the fantasy of our strength." This is collective anger at the restriction of possibility within a community projected onto its weakest member.

Claudia's words also suggest the way in which the community regards Pecola and her family as tainted—the moral equivalent of "ugly." During the course of the narrative, both Pecola and her father literally soil themselves: the young Cholly's bowels release when his putative father denies his connection; Pecola stains her dress with the blood of her first menstruation. In traditional societies, such body discharges are associated with pollution and are thus both dangerous and magical.[23] Julia Kristeva's observations on their symbolic aspects may be pertinently applied to images in Morrison's text:

> Excrement and its equivalents (decay, infection, disease, corpse, etc.) stand for the danger to identity that comes from without: the ego threatened by the non-ego, society threatened by its outside, life by death. Menstrual blood, on the contrary, stands for the danger issuing from within the identity (social or sexual); it threatens the relationship between the sexes within a social aggregate and, through internalization, the identity of each sex in the face of sexual difference.[24]

In Morrison's novel, both Cholly and Pecola transgress the social and sexual boundary between allowed and forbidden behavior; however, it is Pecola, the victim, who is punished. Her almost ritual function as the community's scapegoat is prefigured early in the narrative, when her male peers dance "a macabre ballet around the victim [Pecola], whom, for their own sake, they were prepared to sacrifice to the flaming pit." Like the sacrificial figures of myth and legend, Pecola is nullified as a condition of the community's purgation of anxiety and guilt generated by the threat of female sexuality, the violation of blood relationship, and the failure of sympathy. People hate and fear her as a symbol of what they might become themselves and therefore cannot dare to pity.

Claudia and her sister, in tribute to their inarticulate awareness that Pecola is the scapegoat for her community's deepest fears and anxieties about both blackness and sexuality, offer up their own magical sacrifice to nature: "'And when [the marigold seeds] come up, we'll know everything is all right.'" But of course the seeds, like Pecola and her baby, fail to thrive. Claudia compares Pecola with the moribund seeds: a stunted, deprived potentiality of nature, suffocated before she could blossom. Indeed, nature itself seems poised against those at the very bottom of the social order, buried so deeply that they cannot thrive. As the adult Claudia muses, "This soil is bad for certain kinds of flowers. Certain seeds it will not nurture, certain fruit it will not bear, and when the land kills of its own volition, we acquiesce and say the victim has no right to live. We are wrong, of course. . . ."

Pecola Breedlove is cut off from community in several senses. Even before she is sexually violated, her father consigns his family to a life "outside"; in a typical drunken rage, he almost burns their shelter down, thus forfeiting all responsibility for its occupants. Pecola's homelessness in the world becomes not only a spiritual but a literal state. Claudia MacTeer, whose family takes Pecola in for a few days, recognizes the horror of the other girl's situation: "Outdoors was the end of something, an irrevocable, physical fact, defining and complementing our metaphysical condition." Kathryn Allen Rabuzzi, in her analysis of the symbolism of "home," suggests that "so far beyond the pale of acceptability is homelessness to most people that those who lack homes are perceived as severely threatening to those who have them."[25] Though Morrison's Pecola fatefully returns to her own family (such as it is), who live in an abandoned store, she remains essentially "outdoors"—outside the boundaries of community—for the remainder of her tragic life.

In this latter sense, the Deads of *Song of Solomon* are, although not physically homeless, psychically dislocated from "home"; it is not entirely clear how the family got from Virginia to Michigan. Instructively, Morrison describes their geographical location in terms that mirror their inner boundary confusions and psychological enclosure. They share the experience of people living in the Great Lakes region who are "confused by their place on the country's edge—an edge that is border but not coast. They seem to be able to live a long time believing, as coastal people do, that they are at the frontier where final exit and fatal escape are the only journeys left."

Only Pilate Dead, who had a strong interest in geography, possesses a positive sense of her self in relation to place. As she reminisces, "'Everyplace I went I got me a rock.'" This orientation to the earth and its geography is an important stimulus for Milkman's quest for a place in the world. Pilate is his "pilot"; his journey ultimately leads him back to the South and to his historical community—the land from which Pilate's rocks originate.

In *Sula*, the community of the Bottom, in a northern Ohio town called Medallion, is not only a place but a presence—a kind of collective conscience that arbitrates the social and moral norms of its members. Functioning as a life-sustaining structure for its members, it tolerates certain kinds of eccentricity, believing that magic, dreams, and inexplicable forces operate in unpredictable ways. Yet it is also punitive to those who step absolutely outside the boundaries of the communally acceptable. As Morrison has remarked, "It seems to me there were more excesses in women and men [in the past], and people accepted them as they don't now. In the black community where I grew up, there were eccentricity and freedom, less conformity in individual habits—but close conformity in terms of the survival of the village, of the tribe."[26]

Thus, in *Sula* such eccentrics as the crazy Shadrack, a victim of both physical and mental wounds from his service in the First World War, is tolerated by the community in his performance of his bizarre annual rite, "National Suicide Day." While the ritual functions for him as a way to "order and focus" his own inner chaos, it incidentally offers a visible reminder for the community of its own aggressive and self-destructive urges. "Once the people understood the boundaries and nature of [Shadrack's] madness, they could fit him, so to speak, into the scheme of things."

It is the community of Medallion as much as Sula who is the central "character" of *Sula*. As Morrison has elaborated elsewhere, "[W]hen I wrote *Sula* I was interested in making the town, the community, the neighborhood, as strong a character as I could."[27] The perspective on events is that of the Bottom; when Sula disappears for ten years, no details of her life are confirmed. When she returns, the inhabitants of the community are convinced that she is a source of evil, for she sleeps not only with the women's husbands but, it is rumored, with white men. She is perceived as far more dangerous than someone like Shadrack because she actively threatens the defenses against moral and social transgression that lie hidden in the souls of most people.

No one realizes that Sula's apparent invulnerability masks an acute loneliness and emotional aridity. Dissociated from the values of "neighborhood" or community, she becomes dissociated from herself. Like Pecola Breedlove, Sula provides a negative energy against which members of the community test their own values, a screen upon which they project their needs and fears. As Nel ironically describes Sula's magic (before her friend's betrayal), "Sula never competed; she simply helped others define themselves." Also like Pecola, Sula is the community's pariah, one who lives out (and dies for) the restriction of possibility of an entire group. As the narrator phrases it, "Had [Sula] anything to engage her tremendous curiosity and her gift for metaphor, she might have exchanged the restlessness and preoccupation with whim for an activity that provided her with all she yearned for. And like any artist with no art form, she became dangerous."

Both *The Bluest Eye* and *Sula* are narratives of female education and concomitant loss of innocence. The metamorphoses in the lives of the several young girls of the two novels reverberate through the entire communities of which they are a part. In each novel, one female becomes an outcast against whom the group reasserts its values: each is viewed as "evil" because she transgresses, whether willingly or not, the social and sexual mores of her community. *Song of Solomon* and *Tar Baby* extend Morrison's exploration of the vital relationship between the individual and the group. However, in these latter narratives the conflict is dramatized through characters who bear their communities' moral and cultural contradictions more overtly within themselves.

A central manifestation of these contradictions is encoded in names. During the slave era when black families were inhumanly separated, retaining one's true name became a crucial means of keeping track, not simply of identity, but also of place of origin and family bloodline. In this context, Morrison has remarked, "If you come from Africa, your name is gone. It is particularly problematic because it is not just *your* name but your family, your tribe. When you die, how can you connect with your ancestors if you have lost your name? That's a huge psychological scar."[28]

In *Song of Solomon,* Pilate Dead wears her name, in her father's handwriting, as tangible proof of "where she came from": a literal possession connected to her flesh by an earring made out of a box. Milkman's eventual discovery of his grandparents' real names and their ancestry is central to his own self-discovery and achievement of manhood. In fact, his is the most problematic name in the novel. "Dead" suggests the spiritual torpor Milkman must overcome in order to live as an independent man; it also connects him through his father's line to patriarchy itself, with its valuation not of affiliation but of "owning, building, acquiring." Additionally, it is a reminder of the white world's control over black people, for the first Macon Dead's (Milkman's grandfather's) name is the result of a white man's error. The nickname "Milkman" encodes a relationship with his mother of both sustenance and suffocation. Neither is his "true" name; one signifies surfeit and indulgence, the other nonbeing. Milkman's task is the reconciliation of his two names and the discovery of his true identity behind them.

Names are important, not only as ironic comments on the characters who bear them, but as emblems of the black community's resistance to the white culture's negation of its world. In *Song of Solomon,* locations like Not Doctor Street and No Mercy Hospital (where, until Ruth Dead's son was born, black people were denied admittance) are forms of counternegation of the white world that delimits the black one. It is a measure of women's marginal place within that world that their names are picked by their parents at random from the Bible, whereas many of the men have names that signify function, trades, place, or objects—all indications of a public identity.

Milkman's escape from Deadness begins with a literal flight, as he traverses the invisible boundary between North and South in an airplane. In tidewater Virginia, his family's ancestral land, Milkman gradually assembles the diverse pieces of the puzzle of his ancestry, using the names, both true and false, of people in his family as a key. As he restores the corrupted version of a rhythmic childhood chant around the mythical flight of Solomon, he also restores his link to his cultural community by recovering its history.

The collective memory Milkman eventually reconstructs concerns his great-grandfather Solomon/Shalimar, the fabled patriarch of the family, who "flew" back to Africa, leaving his devastated wife and twenty-one children behind. Such stories are part of black American folklore, preserving the dream of rising above the brutal conditions of slavery by escape to Africa, of transcending the literal boundaries of servitude.[29]

Flight suggests liberation, whether literal or spiritual; thus, death is one kind of escape or flight and the Dead family name preserves this meaning, though in a corrupted sense.

Morrison's latter two novels both conclude with the equivocal image of flight. Through that image, both narratives explore the conflict between the need for personal autonomy and the temptation of escape from moral responsibility to others, though they implicitly reach different resolutions. In *Song of Solomon*, Milkman's ancestor escaped from slavery by flying away. Yet for those left behind, his flight created further suffering. In a sense, his miraculous escape was irresponsible in the same way that Milkman's treatment of Hagar was; in the pursuit of his own desires, each left a legacy of misery. In recognizing this correspondence, Milkman realizes how his self-preoccupation and lack of empathy have caused others harm. As he learns through Pilate, acts have consequences for which one must take responsibility; her death is the price he must pay in return for that very knowledge. In fact, two women die in order for Milkman to overcome "Deadness": to come alive as a free—and responsible—agent in his own destiny and to affirm the reciprocal values of the community.

Milkman has inherited his father's and his mother's versions of the Deads' lives; each version contradicts the other, and Pilate's contradicts both. Only as he synthesizes these stories of his family and his past can he construct his own version of the "real." The "Song of Solomon" that he reconstructs commemorates his ancestor's refusal to be owned. However, the true measure of Milkman's own liberation is his recognition that such passion for freedom must be tempered with concern for its effect on others.

He thus unites the complementary strands of moral orientation that, as Carol Gilligan has illuminatingly proposed, have characteristically been gender-defined: the male emphasis on rights and the female emphasis on responsibility to others.[30] Though feminist readers have expressed disappointment with Morrison for making her hero male rather than female,[31] it is equally noteworthy that the author portrays a hero who achieves manhood by assimilating a traditionally female moral perspective into his previously limited vision. Milkman Dead ultimately combines in himself the truths of both patriarchal and matriarchal sides of his heritage: the history of "names" leads him to discover his own identity; the sacrifices on his behalf by Pilate and others generate his new sense of himself as part of a community to which he belongs by virtue of reciprocal responsibility.

Owning his soul, Milkman frees himself to test the possibility that "[i]f you surrendered to the air, you could *ride* it." In accomplishing "flight," he surrenders his destructive need to be either infantilized or worshipped by women; he heals the rift in himself and, by extension, his community, by fusing the separate truths of male and female moral knowledge. Morrison's story thus articulates a history of separations and re-connections: black culture's radical and involuntary separation from its roots and the hero's personal odyssey of reengagement. "Boundary," in the sense of both geographical and psychological orientation in the world, is recovered when the hero affirms the genealogy and meaning of his true name.

Song of Solomon is Morrison's most positive depiction of the values of community as a crucial balance between individual liberation and recipro- cal obligation, as well as her most artistically accomplished narrative. In *Tar Baby*, the theme of cultural displacement assumes another, some- what less aesthetically satisfying, expression. Jadine Childs and Son Green regard themselves as cultural orphans, outsiders, neither defined nor limited by the boundaries of black American life. Both try to locate themselves within an ethnic tradition that is multiple and varied; each is forced to confront the meaning of the past and the possibilities of the future; each considers the values of a complex heritage that simultane- ously coexists with and opposes the dominant power structure.

Son is characterized as an anomaly, a raw, "natural" man, unpolished but also unscarred by limits, conventions, and compromises. Because of a crime he committed as a result of circumstances that many would regard as almost justifiable provocation, he is a fugitive; he is pointedly "without human rites: unbaptised, uncircumcised, minus puberty rites or the formal rites of manhood. Unmarried and undivorced. He had at- tended no funeral, married in no church, raised no child. Propertyless, homeless, sought for but not after." In his elemental form (symbolically, he emerges from out of the sea or the darkness, or appears as a shadowy reflection in a mirror), he becomes Jadine's tutor, presiding over her temporary immersion in the black culture from which she is estranged.

Like the "good colored girls" of *The Bluest Eye*, who mask their funkiness in order to edge up into the white world's greater opportuni- ties, Jadine initially wants nothing to do with a man who reminds her of what she is grateful to have left behind. Son's elemental rawness alarms her, threatens her sense of civilized restraint. She sees him through the eyes of both sets of her "parents," fearing his aggressive eroticism much as Margaret Street does and loathing his unkempt, animal-like appear- ance as Ondine and Sydney do. Yet his crudity not only repels but at- tracts her.

Son is as disgusted with Jade's smug sophistication as she is with his uncut-diamond image. He even calls her a "white girl" because she has sold herself to white values and attitudes toward beauty, sexuality, and money. However, the sheer attraction of opposites temporarily overrides these intellectual resistances. On a picnic they take together, Jade, wear- ing her "Easter white cotton [dress]—all temptation and dare," falls into a pit of tar pitch. In this almost too obviously symbolic scene, Jade's "whiteness" is literally immersed in blackness. Predictably, not long afterwards Jade falls in love with Son.

Like medieval courtly lovers, the two become exclusively absorbed in each other. Jade is nurtured by Son's devotion and care, and comes to feel herself "unorphaned" but also emotionally vulnerable. Their courtship is that of the city mouse and the country mouse. The true gap between them is suggested by the geographical distance each must travel to live in the other's world: Jade introduces Son to New York and Son takes Jade to Eloe, Florida, the small, conservative community that he fondly calls home.

To Jade, Son's community is suffocatingly provincial and his friends are uneducated inferiors, "a pack of Neanderthals who think sex is dirty or strange." Yet Jadine associates sexuality with animality and is equally concerned to keep her own eroticism "rein[ed] in." Son's peers regard Jade as his prize woman, as if "she was a Cadillac he had won, or stolen, or even bought for all they knew." Though this view offends Jade, it is no different an image than the one she consciously cultivates in her life as a model.

In resisting Eloe, Jade believes that what she is rejecting is the women who haunt her dreams, a "coven" of women who have "nothing to show but breasts." The real nature of her conflict is both personal and cultural: the struggle within herself for who and what she is, and a contest of wills between her and Son to claim "authentic" black values; each lover implicitly questions whether the other is "really a member of the tribe."[32] Each attempts to pull the other "away from the maw of hell. . . . One had a past, the other a future[,] and each one bore the culture to save the race in his hands. Mama-spoiled black man, will you mature with me? Culture-bearing black woman, whose culture are you bearing?"

The lovers' ecstatic but doomed connection symbolizes a kind of radical division between the educated and the uneducated; between power and powerlessness; and between urbanity, material well-being, rationality, and privilege on the one hand and emotional intensity, provincial values, and spiritual well-being on the other. Both protagonist and antagonist struggle to identify themselves within and against these competing claims. In the rather too programmatic clash of wills and beliefs,[33] Morrison examines the gap between outsiders and insiders, education and cultural rootedness, and competing definitions of authenticity within black experience.

Though the relationship between Jade and Son suggests a dialectical tension between opposites, a synthesis is never achieved. In fact, such diametrically opposing values are rarely reconciled except in the symbolic terms of myth and legend, and it is through those that Morrison equivocatingly concludes her narrative. In the folk tale of Tar Baby,

Bre'r Rabbit is enmeshed in the deceptive lure but uses his wits to extricate himself and regain his freedom.[34] In Morrison's novel, Son cites the story to illustrate his contention that women like Jadine are tar babies—ensnarers of black men. Convinced of the necessity for preserving the traditional culture, he regards the tar baby as the white world's corrupting lure for upwardly mobile black people. Once they are caught by the lure of affluence, they become psychologically and materially enslaved. For Jade, spoiled by the worldly pleasures that beauty, education, privilege, and money can buy, the tar baby is the "coven" of women who would ensnare her in domestic, sexual, and procreative functions—much as, earlier in the narrative, she is mired in the swampy tar pit.

To a certain extent, the conflict symbolized in the image of the tar baby transcends its ethnic sources. The tar baby is that which would ensnare and overwhelm one, threaten one's ego boundaries and one's efforts at separation from the forces, whether external or internal, that might engulf the self. It is that shadowy aspect of the Other that must be confronted as a prelude to authenticity and autonomy.

The symbolism of the tar baby is not clarified by the novel's end. Morrison has remarked elsewhere that "the tar baby came to mean the black woman who can hold things together."[35] Yet the novel does not entirely fulfill this sense and thus fails to resolve the set of tensions the author has dramatized. One questions whether Jade's encounter with Son so changes her that she relinquishes her narcissistic self-worship to become a hard-working "queen ant" struggling for the survival of her people. Instead, her flight from Son and both sets of her "parents" seems an ironic inversion of Milkman Dead's flight into authenticity and a return to her self-indulgent life.

In giving the narrative's final scene to Son, Morrison brackets Jadine's flight and comments on it with his. In one of two narrative "parentheses" that enclose the numbered chapters,[36] Son returns to Dominique, hoping to regain Jadine, even at the expense of Eloe and what it signifies. But his willing sacrifice never takes place; Jadine has already departed, and another kind of sacrifice is intended for him. He enters the darkness from which he emerged at the beginning, to be symbolically absorbed into the legend of the mythical horsemen descended from African slaves: elemental, inhuman powers of the universe. Like the Son of God, whose image is suggested in his generic name and in his appearance at the pointedly named L'Arbe de la Croix, he eventually becomes the scapegoat for the internal contradictions of a cultural group.

The figure of the pariah is clearly central to Morrison's vision, as the emblem of different levels and forms of exclusion. In her fiction, the community is understood as both a specific social structure—the vehicle through which behavior is expressed and reinforced—and a set of values (frequently contradictory) operating within that structure. As the author has remarked in this context, "The black community is a pariah community. Black people are pariahs. The civilization of black people that lives apart from but in juxtaposition to other civilizations is a pariah relationship. . . . But a community contains pariahs within it that are very useful for the conscience of that community."[37] From a variety of perspectives, Morrison's fiction expresses the complex dynamics of experience through which individuals are formed, or deformed, by the often conflicting values of their respective communities. The emotional reality of Morrison's characters may thus be understood as both a response to and a reflection of the benign or destructive boundaries of community.

Notes

1. Simone de Beauvoir, *The Second Sex*, trans. H. M. Parshley (New York: Alfred A. Knopf, 1971), pp. 139, 141, and passim.
2. Toni Morrison, *The Bluest Eye* (1970, rpt. New York: Washington Square Press, 1972), p. 109.
3. Margaret White, "I want the right to be black and me," in *Black Women in White America: A Documentary History,* ed. Gerda Lerner (New York: Pantheon, 1972), p. 607.
4. "'The Language Must Not Sweat': A Conversation with Toni Morrison, Conducted by Thomas LeClair," *The New Republic,* March 21, 1981, p. 29.
5. Cholly Breedlove's sexual violation of his daughter, Pecola, echoes Jim Trueblood's similar act in Ralph Ellison's *Invisible Man.*
6. *Tar Baby* (New York: Alfred A. Knopf, 1981), p. 83.
7. Morrison has explained that the Dick and Jane story is "a frame acknowledging the outer civilization. The primer with white children was the way life was presented to the black people. As the novel proceeded I wanted that primer version broken up and confused, which explains the typographical running together of the words." "'The Language Must Not Sweat,'" p. 29. For an analysis of the relationship between these primer sections and the characters, see Phyllis R. Klotman, "Dick-and-Jane and the Shirley Temple Sensibility in *The Bluest Eye,*" *Black American Literature Forum* (Winter 1979), pp. 123–25.
8. Toni Morrison, *Sula* (1973, rpt. New York: Bantam, 1975).
9. "The subject of the black woman's physical beauty occurs with such frequency in the writing of black women that it indicates they have been deeply affected by the discrimination against the shade of their skin and the texture of their hair. In almost every novel or autobiography written by a black woman, there is at least one incident in which the dark-skinned girl wishes to be either white or light-skinned with 'good' hair." See Mary Helen Washington, "Teaching *Black-Eyed Susans:* An Approach to the Study of Black Women Writers," in *All the Women Are White, All the Blacks Are Men, But Some of Us Are Brave: Black Women's Studies,* ed. Gloria T. Hull, Patricia Bell Scott, and Barbara Smith (Old Westbury, N.Y.: The Feminist Press, 1982), p. 210.

10. See Elizabeth Janeway, *Powers of the Weak* (New York: Morrow, 1981), esp. pp. 3–48.

11. D. W. Winnicott, *Playing and Reality* (New York: Basic Books, 1971), p. 112, emphasis in original.

12. C. O. Ogunyemi observes that the novel's title is also a pun: "'the bluest I,' the gloomy ego, the black man [sic] feeling very blue from the psychological bombardment he is exposed to from early life to late." "Order and Disorder in Toni Morrison's *The Bluest Eye*," *Critique*, Vol. 19, No. 1 (1977), p. 114. Cynthia Davis discusses Morrison's fiction from an existentialist perspective, noting that "[w]omanhood, like blackness, is Other in this society, and the dilemma of woman in a patriarchal society is parallel to that of blacks in a racist one: they are made to feel most real when *seen*." "Self, Society, and Myth in Toni Morrison's Fiction," *Contemporary Literature* (Summer 1982), p. 329, emphasis is original.

13. Nina Auerbach, *Communities of Women: An Idea in Fiction* (Cambridge: Harvard University Press, 1978), p. 3.

14. Nancy Chodorow, *The Reproduction of Mothering: Psychoanalysis and the Sociology of Gender* (Berkeley: University of California Press, 1978). See Introduction to this study, pp. 5–7.

15. John Bowlby's psychoanalytic studies emphasize the critical role that attachment between the child and its parents plays in the development of personality. The child's separation from the parents, particularly the mother, and particularly the traumatic separation of death, may have profound effects upon the individual's subsequent capacity to form and maintain positive emotional attachments. See John Bowlby, *Attachment and Loss*, Vol. 2: *Separation, Anxiety, and Loss* (New York: Basic Books, 1973).

16. Morrison emphasizes that friendship between women is a rare subject in fiction; it is "special, different, and has never been depicted as the major focus of a novel before *Sula*. Nobody ever talked about friendship between women unless it was homosexual, and there is no homosexuality in *Sula*." In *Black Women Writers at Work*, ed. Claudia Tate (New York: Continuum, 1983), p. 118. As Elizabeth Abel observes in her illuminating reading of *Sula* in this context, "Friendship in *Sula* is both the vehicle and product of self-knowledge, the uniquely valuable and rigorous relationship. By combining the adolescent need for identification with the adult need for independence, Morrison presents an ideal of female friendship dependent not on love, obligation, or compassion, but on an almost impossible conjunction of sameness and autonomy, attainable only with another version of oneself." See "(E)Merging Identities: The Dynamics of Female Friendship in Contemporary Fiction by Women," *Signs* (Spring 1981), pp. 413–35, esp. p. 429.

17. Toni Morrison, *Song of Solomon* (1977, rpt. New York: New American Library, 1978), p. 131.

18. In medieval lore, there were many associations between the umbilical cord and midwives. Furthermore, witches were often healers and were frequently associated with "flying," a central motif in Morrison's novel. One source on witchcraft describes a "flying ointment" which, smeared on the naked body, enabled magical flight. See Thomas Rogers Forbes, *The Midwife and the Witch* (New Haven: Yale University Press, 1966), p. 118.

19. Morrison, in "Intimate Things in Place: A Conversation with Toni Morrison," conducted by Robert Stepto, in *The Third Woman: Minority Women Writers of the United States*, ed. Dexter Fisher (Boston: Houghton Mifflin, 1980), p. 170.

20. "An Interview with Toni Morrison" conducted by Nellie McKay, *Contemporary Literature* (Winter 1983), p. 422.

21. "'The Seams Can't Show': An Interview with Toni Morrison" by Jane Bakerman, *Black American Literature Forum*, p. 60.
22. In an important essay examining the use of language by women writers, Margaret Homans suggests that Eva "claims God's power of life and death" in her destruction of Plum; however, "the monological power of God can be appropriated by a black woman only at the exorbitant cost of self-mutilation." "'Her Very Own Howl': The Ambiguities of Representation in Recent Women's Fiction," *Signs* (Winter 1983), p. 191.
23. See Mary Douglas, *Purity and Danger: An Analysis of Concepts of Pollution and Taboo* (New York: Routledge and Kegan Paul, 1966).
24. Julia Kristeva, *Powers of Horror: An Essay on Abjection*, trans. Leon S. Roudiez (New York: Columbia University Press, 1982), p. 71.
25. Kathryn Allen Rabuzzi, *The Sacred and the Feminine: Toward a Theology of Housework* (New York: Seabury, 1982), p. 73.
26. Morrison, in "'The Language Must Not Sweat,'" p. 28.
27. Morrison, in "Intimate Things in Place," p. 168.
28. Morrison, in "'The Language Must Not Sweat,'" p. 28. The author's earlier name was Chloe Anthony Wofford. See Tate, *Black Women Writers at Work*, p. 117.
29. For example, "People Who Could Fly," in *Black Folktales*, retold by Julius Lester (New York: Richard W. Baron, 1969), pp. 147–51, and "Flying Africans," in *A Treasury of Afro-American Folklore*, collected by Harold Courlander (New York: Crown, 1976), pp. 285–86.
30. See Carol Gilligan, *In a Different Voice: Psychological Theory and Women's Development* (Cambridge: Harvard University Press, 1982), esp. pp. 24–63.
31. Cynthia Davis criticizes Morrison for failing to alter the stereotypical gender roles of myth, in which males are heroes and females are supporting figures in a male story. All of Milkman's models are male; even Pilate, though she "embodies Morrison's values . . . is not the complete hero that Milkman is, for she lacks his recognition of meaning." Furthermore, "Until women like Pilate recover their heroic female line, they cannot replace false images with true ones, and they will be left in a world, as Morrison shows, where mothers and daughters reject one another, female friendships are difficult to sustain, the dominating models of female selfhood are baby dolls and pinups, and even heroic women like Pilate cannot pass on their values to their children and grandchildren." "Self, Society, and Myth in Toni Morrison's Fiction," pp. 339, 340–41.

   Morrison counters such objections by remarking, "I could write a book in which all the women were brave and wonderful, but it would bore me to death, and I think it would bore everybody else to death. Some women are weak and frail and hopeless, and some women are not. I write about both kinds, so one should not be more disturbing than the other. In the development of characters, there is value in the different effects." Later she adds, "I chose the man to make that journey [in *Song of Solomon*] because I thought he had more to learn than a woman would have." "An Interview with Toni Morrison," McKay, pp. 419, 428.
32. Ibid, p. 422.
33. As Maureen Howard observes, "Son and Jadine come at each other like running commentaries on black men and black women, on education, debt, freedom." "A Novel of Exile and Home," Review of *Tar Baby*, *The New Republic*, March 21, 1981, p. 30.
34. "Tar Baby," *The Book of Negro Folklore*, ed. Langston Hughes and Arna Bontemps (New York: Dodd, Mead, and Co., 1958), pp. 1–2.
35. Morrison, in "'The Language Must Not Sweat,'" p. 27.

36. Morrison's own phrase in McKay, "An Interview with Toni Morrison," p. 425.
37. Morrison, in Tate, *Black Women Writers at Work*, p. 129.

◆◆◆◆◆◆◆◆◆◆◆◆◆◆

Text and Countertext in *The Bluest Eye*

DONALD B. GIBSON

I . . . have no hesitation in regarding the white race as superior to all others in beauty. . . . Human groups are unequal in beauty; and this inequality is rational, logical, permanent, and indestructible.

> —Count Joseph Arthur de Gobineau,
> *Essay on the Inequality of
> the Human Races*

Along with the idea of romantic love, she [Pauline] was introduced to another—physical beauty. Probably the most destructive ideas in the history of human thought. Both originated in envy, thrived in insecurity, and ended in disillusion.

> —Toni Morrison, *The Bluest Eye*

Count Joseph Arthur de Gobineau, French diplomat, ethnologist, fiction writer, bearer of the infamous reputation of "father of racism," and a correspondent for sixteen years of Alexis de Tocqueville, wrote these words in the early 1850s. Tocqueville, as might be expected, disagreed strongly with Gobineau's authoritarian, anti-democratic stance and argued against the whole of such racist and reactionary thinking.[1] We might imagine further that his counterarguments fell upon deaf ears because Gobineau's arguments stem from very basic beliefs about human nature, the nature of the universe, and ideas about social organization stemming from those beliefs. Gobineau's words contain implicitly the philosophical assumptions that beauty exists in and of itself, independent of human nature or character; and it forms some part of a larger structure of the universe. Gobineau's whole system of thought seems reactive against the tide of ideas that by his time had unseated the rationalism of the Enlightenment, ushered in the American and French revolutions, and paved the way for Darwin and other thinkers who believed the world to be in process rather than fixed within established, unchangeable limits. Toni Morrison did not need to have read Gobineau to react to him, for his legacy is not only in his text but in Western civilization's air. Her novel calls into question the mode of his thought and the whole authoritarian, politically reactionary system of beliefs about the nature of reality on which his and like thought is based.

Morrison's 1970 novel, for all its eloquence and beauty of expression, engages in sustained argument with modes of thought and belief explicitly stated in Gobineau's assertion above, but likewise, and perhaps more vividly presented in cultural icons portraying physical beauty: movies, billboards, magazines, books, newspapers, window signs, dolls, and drinking cups.[2] Morrison's novel deals with the most subtle implications of the general society's definition of beauty, and the novel shows us the depth and complexity of those implications. But unlike most novels that take issue with society, the novel argues with itself, clarifying rather than simplifying, uncovering and grappling with the most problematical facets of the subject, and undercutting easily held values in order to reveal complication. The novel's text is inscribed with a countertext, an oppositional discourse so intricately intertwined with text as to render it finally incapable of independent existence, transforming each by turn into the counter of the other. While text and countertext contend for dominance, the one melds into the opposite, and at midpoint between the exchange neither is independently discernible though both are present, like an optical illusion which may alternately assume one form then another, then perhaps varying degrees of both and neither depending upon the disposition of the observer's eye and mind.[3]

The countertextual dynamic of the novel begins with the quotation from the Dick and Jane primer, an introductory gesture, which is in fact and by implication not unlike the prefatory essay to Richard Wright's *Uncle Tom's Children*, "The Ethics of Living Jim Crow" (1938) in that it introduces what is to follow, offers evidence to comment upon and support the thematic implications of the main text, and at the same time informs the main text at each point along its course, its implications engraved within every aspect of plot, character, and description. Morrison's self-consciously epigraphical introduction, the primer text, exists as text and countertext: text in that it has no apparent relation to the major text but lies in the background, the mere genesis of the problem exemplified by Pecola's wanting blue eyes and exemplary, by indirection, of the causes underlying the problematical nature of the lives of the characters in its world; countertext, by turns, in that the epigraphical introduction implies one of the primary and most insidious ways that the dominant culture exercises its hegemony, through the educational system.[4] It reveals the role of education in both oppressing the victim— and more to the point—teaching the victim how to oppress her own black self by internalizing the values that dictate standards of beauty. "Don't give the girl a fishing pole," the prefatory material tells us, "teach her how to fish," teach her how to enact self-oppression while ostensibly learning to read a simple, unproblematic text. To put this in another way the act of learning to read and write means exposure to the values of the culture from which the reading material emanates. If one wants to read or write, then one must pay for the privilege. The cost of learning to read and write carries with it the necessity to submit to values beyond and other than literacy *per se*, for words do not exist independent of value. One cannot simply learn to read without being subjected to the values engraved in the text.[5]

The introduction to *The Bluest Eye* is also an enabling act, setting up, defining, and effectively writing or reinscribing the nature of what is to be written against. It is the obverse of what in the slave narrative was the act of authentication. Here the author seizes the authority of the authenticator by appropriating and subverting the role of authenticator. That is, the authenticator's role is an authoritative role deriving its authority from socially derived power. The superiority assumed by Charles Sumner and Wendell Phillips as authenticators of Frederick Douglass's *Narrative*, for example, is assumed by Morrison herself in her text. Douglass's text is authenticated by Sumner and Phillips in the *Narrative* (though he struggles mightily both literarily and historically before wresting away their implied authority). Wright authenticates his own text in "Ethnics"; Morrison authenticates her text in the enabling act of her introduction. This is the less complicated aspect of Morrison's discourse in *The Bluest Eye*.[6]

The complications arise when we see that Morrison's sense of the meaning of "bluest eye" is not confined to the meaning we immediately ascribe. The text of the Dick and Jane primer, the epigraphical introduction to Morrison's narrative, is rendered by Morrison in three versions (1–3), each printed in such a way as to appear to grow less comprehensible.[7] The second version omits punctuation, decreasing the space between the lines and running the sentences together; the third omits spaces between words entirely and arbitrarily breaks words at the end of a line, even words of one syllable. The inference to be drawn is that the final version is incomprehensible. But that is not true. It is, arguably, perfectly comprehensible.[8] The difference between the first and third versions is that the third forces us to participate in the reading in a more active way by demanding that we identify individual words and supply from our own past experience of reading the first version the proper punctuation. The reader is once again, in the very act of reading, taught to read. The meaning is not, as it appears, drained away from first to final draft, but simply concentrated. The implication is that just as Pecola—and all black children—are subjected to the value scheme implied in the primer, so they have imposed upon them whole schemes of value, political, religious, moral, aesthetic, that have little or nothing to do with their actual lives. They are measured using standards they cannot possibly meet—because of genetics and economics—and are found wanting. Yet a paradox arises when we consider that Morrison organizes her text around the primer passage. The sections focusing on Pecola and her family are headed by a line or two from the primer text, the text standing in countertextual relation to the actuality of Pecola's and her family's lives. The final chapter of the novel opens with the primer lines

"Look, look. Here comes a friend," and we of course recall that Pecola's friend is hallucinated, the product of her madness. But she does, after all, as the countertext has it, have her blue eyes.

The implication of the novel's structure is that our lives are contained within the framework of the values of the dominant culture and subjected to those values. We have all (there is reason to believe the author does not exclude herself nor anyone else) internalized those values, and to the extent that we have, we are instruments of our own oppression.[9] The text says we are oppressed by the values of the ruling class; the countertext says we participate in our own oppression usually to the extent of being literally the very hand or arm of that oppression.

Such a conclusion is born out by Claudia's (the sometime narrator's) relating to her response as a young child to dolls. The reader will recall her literal deconstruction of a white, blue-eyed, yellow-haired doll, an act intended as a means of discovery, and performed on the childish assumption that whatever caused the doll to appear to everyone except herself an object of great value lay within the thing itself, a reasonable assumption since she has concluded that the difference between her and the white doll is an essential, intrinsic difference, not a superficial, extrinsic one. To discover the doll's reality by taking it apart is not to demystify it—it has not yet become mystified for her—but rather to wreak vengeance on it and to discover that the difference between her and the doll lies elsewhere than in the doll's innards.

The countertext has Claudia subsequently join those who approve of little white girls and disapprove of her.

> Adults, older girls, shops, magazines, newspapers, window signs—all the world had agreed that a blue-eyed, yellow-haired, pink-skinned doll was what every child treasured.

These adults are not only white but black as well.

> What made people look at them and say "Awwwww," but not for me? The eye slide of black women as they approached them on the street, and the possessive gentleness of their touch as they handled them.

Her antipathy toward white dolls and little white girls does not, as noted, last forever.[10] Claudia's admission of the fact, however, turns out to be a low-keyed indictment, but devastating in its implications, of the whole scheme of sociopolitical values held by the ruling classes and informing their ideology. She fantasizes about doing the same violence to little white girls that she does to her dolls, the closest she can come to revolt against a vicious value scheme that threatens her very being.

> If I pinched them, their eyes—unlike the crazed glint of the baby doll's eyes—would fold in pain, and their cry would not be the sound of an icebox door, but a fascinating cry of pain. When I learned how repulsive this disinterested violence was, that it was repulsive because it was disinterested, my shame floundered about for refuge. The best hiding place was love. Thus the conver-

sion from pristine sadism to fabricated hatred, to fraudulent love. It was a small step to Shirley Temple. I learned much later to worship her, just as I learned to delight in cleanliness, knowing, even as I learned, that the change was adjustment without improvement.

Claudia expresses here her understanding, a retrospective understanding and not one achieved in childhood, that social values are arbitrary, socially derived, and not existent in nature. It is not natural to have or want blue eyes, but a society may hold such a standard and through its power—its control of images through control of the means of the presentation of imagery, control of "magazines, newspapers, window signs," of current iconography—impress the reality of its values on those not having the wherewithal to resist, not having the facilities to counter the assault.

But herein lies the power of Toni Morrison's argument, for she undercuts the validity of the proposition of the dominant culture that blue eyes and cleanliness are inherently valuable by historicizing social value. Claudia "learned" to worship Shirley Temple just as she "learned" to delight in cleanliness. The text, it is implied, is that blue eyes and cleanliness are valuable because in this society such values are imposed upon its members. The countertext reads that such values are not so much relative as arbitrary. They have no reality in and of themselves. The image of Shirley Temple as representing a standard of beauty comes about not because of anything inherent within Shirley Temple but because she exists as icon in movies and on, of all things, a common drinking cup, a trivial commercial item, that for Pecola becomes something entirely other, a chalice, a grail whose milk-white content will allow her to take in the blood of the goddess, a white blood of milk—not a red blood of wine. The milk is the blood of the goddess because it is contained within the cup. Pecola gorges herself on the blood of the goddess; she indulges an insatiable appetite. If she drinks enough white milk from the chalice, she may become like the stuff she imbibes and as well become like the image adorning the container itself. One ingests the blood of the goddess in order to become her. Pecola performs a kind of masturbatory communion, an self-administered version of the ritual in which she is both priestess and communicant.[11]

This initial ritualistic act of communion prefigures a later one, later in the sequence of the book's episodes though in fact earlier in time than the communion of graham crackers and milk, bread and wine. By the time Pecola comes to live briefly with Claudia and Frieda, she has already learned to indulge the rituals, the third of which (her interaction with Soaphead Church) will lead to her transformation into the creature of her desire. She devours the candy, little yellow caramels called Mary Janes, a conflation, given the immediate context of their description in the novel and the more general context of the novel's primer frame, of Christ (Mr. Jacobowski says to Pecola, "Christ. Kantcha talk?"), of the

Jane of the primer, and of the Virgin Mary.[12] Pecola is an inverted Virgin Mary, however, a Virgin Mary demystified: not mysteriously and spiritually impregnated by God the father but brutally impregnated by Cholly Breedlove, the father, on the dirty floor of the kitchen of her storefront home. The offspring of this union is the Christ child, the stillborn Christ child, who is incapable of saving the world because incapable of saving himself.

The ritualistic significance of the eating of the Mary Janes and the relation to Shirley Temple, milk, communion, and sexuality are born out in Morrison's description of Pecola's experience with the candy.

> Each pale yellow wrapper has a picture on it. A picture of Mary Jane, for whom the candy is named. Smiling white face. Blond hair in gentle disarray, blue eyes looking at her out of a world of clean comfort. [Compare the primer Jane.] The eyes are petulant, mischievous. To Pecola they are simply pretty. She eats the candy, and its sweetness is good. To eat the candy is somehow to eat the eyes, eat Mary Jane. Love Mary Jane. Be Mary Jane.
>
> Three pennies had bought her nine lovely orgasms with Mary Jane. Lovely Mary Jane, for whom a candy is named.

The text is what we read of Pecola's experience; the countertext is the central mythology of the dominant culture, a mythology demystified and therefore disempowered by Morrison's analysis of the relation of the experience of specific individuals to the myth. Transubstantiation has occurred; the candy has been transformed into the body and blood of Mary Jane (Shirley Temple).[13] Lest we missed the implications of the ritual signification of Pecola's consumption of her Mary Janes, the reference to communion, to Christian mythology, and to the demystification of Christian ritual, Morrison reiterates the subtextual meaning of the Christian symbology by reference to the trinity: Pecola has three pennies; Mr. Jacobowski "scoots three Mary Janes toward her" (which mysteriously multiply into nine orgasms), "orgasms," not the spiritual transformation and renewal traditionally affected by ingestion of the host, but a suitable equivalent in the world Pecola inhabits.[14]

Morrison comments upon the episode through the first line of the next episode immediately following. One sentence after "Three pennies bought her nine lovely orgasms," we read, "Three whores lived in the apartment above the Breedloves' storefront."[15] Here the text comments upon, analyzes itself. Text and countertext produce a stark indictment of the prevailing values of the dominant society. The "three whores" are named "China," "Poland," and 'The Maginot Line," a commentary of its own in that the distance between the trinity (father, son and the Holy Ghost) and the naturalistic fact of Pecola's purchase of penny candy is analogous to the distance between the seemingly insignificant lives of three whores in a small midwestern town and the large-scale geopolitical and geographical dimensions of China, Poland, and The Maginot Line. The root of the analogy is Morrison's awareness in the world of this novel that no human conception, knowledge or understanding has its source outside of individual experience. The most basic myths and the broadest geopolitical conceptions have their origins in the experience of people.

The association in the text of milk and blood and the consequent evocation of the broad range of actual and mythological meanings are clearly demonstrable in the text and are not brought to it by the over-imaginative analyst. In the very midst of Mrs. McTeer's unremitting tirade against Pecola's consumption of prodigious quantities of milk, Pecola begins to menstruate—as though she is putting back into the world that which she has been accused of unjustly and unreasonably taking away. The association of menstruation and lactation, of bleeding and feeding, is unavoidable and explicit. Mrs. MacTeer speaks.

> "Anybody need three quarts of milk to *live* need to get out of here. They in the wrong place. What is this? Some kind of *dairy* farm?"
>
> Suddenly Pecola bolted straight up, her eyes wide with terror. A whinnying sound came out of her mouth.
>
> "What's the matter with *you?*" Frieda stood up too.
>
> Then we both looked where Pecola was staring. Blood was running down her legs. Some drops were on the steps. I leaped up. "Hey. You cut yourself? Look. It's all over your dress."

Mrs. MacTeer's assault, motherly assault that it is, brings about, however unintentionally, the onset of Pecola's menses. It is not, Claudia tells us, the child that the parent attacks but the condition that allows or causes the child to appear to be a problem. It is not Pecola with whom she is angry but the conditions that require her to be concerned about how much milk she drinks. Pecola responds in a way Francis Bacon has seen as a response reflective of human nature.

> Whosoever hath anything fixed in this person that doth induce contempt hath also a perpetual spur in himself to rescue and deliver himself from scorn.

Pecola rescues and delivers herself from scorn by giving back the world what she has taken away. She has consumed a natural body fluid, milk; she gives back a natural body fluid, blood. In so doing she appeases Mrs. MacTeer, turning her wrath not into mere tolerance but into a rarely expressed and articulated acceptance, approval, and support.

The reality of the situation is such, however, that initiation and the potential of deliverance (in an entirely secular sense) are available for Pecola.[16] It in any case seems so. The water has as its purpose not to drown but to cleanse; not to inundate but to initiate. Pecola is initiated, baptized into biological female adulthood; Frieda and Claudia are detraumatized, brought into a normalized relation to ordinary biological process.

> We could hear the water running into the bathtub.
>
> "You think she's going to drown her?"
>
> "Oh, Claudia. You so dumb. She's just going to wash her clothes and all."

> "Should we beat up Rosemary?" [Should we react as our mother reacted when she thought we were "playing nasty"? Does the fact of Pecola's menstruation require the drawing of blood? Does this situation require aggression on our parts?]
>
> "No. [Let us emulate mother.] Leave her alone."
>
> The water gushed, and over its gushing we could hear the music of my mother's laughter.

The meaning of the text at this moment lies in its playing off, one against the other, the total childish ignorance of Claudia and Pecola, the childish half ignorance of Frieda, and the mature, woman's knowledge of Mrs. MacTeer. From the antagonism, anger, misunderstanding, and conflict of the events leading up to this point arises a new understanding and vision, a celebratory confluence of discordant modes. This section of the novel, you will recall, begins with Mrs. MacTeer berating Pecola.

> "Three quarts of milk. That's what was *in* that icebox yesterday. Three whole quarts. Now they ain't none. Not a drop. I don't mind folks coming in and getting what they want, but three quarts of milk! What the devil does *any*-body need with *three* quarts of milk?" (Morrison's emphasis)

It ends with "the music of my mother's laughing" as she bestows on Pecola the care and comfort which may be available to the female child entering this new stage from the female parent figure. Embedded within the text, existing at various levels and a form of countertext, are three perspectives. One is the perspective of the child Claudia, the nine-year-old who at first hand witnesses many of the events of the novel. The second is the perspective of the significantly more mature retrospective narrator who understands and interprets those events, events which the younger Claudia could not possibly have understood. We see the disparity between the adult and the child perspectives when Claudia asks whether their mother is going to drown Pecola. Because the meaning of the section is obviously shaped, the question could only emanate from a consciousness that knows that the question is a childish one. Hence the question betrays a consciousness that has conceived the mind conceiving the question.[17]

The third perspective, whose existence is inferred from the existence of the total text, the novel itself, is the author's perspective—the perspective that knows of the relation between this scene (ending with the "music" of Mrs. MacTeer's laughter) and the final episodes of the novel, sexual intercourse visited upon the virgin Pecola by her father, the issue of that (her stillborn child), and Pecola's ensuing madness. In other words there lies submerged beneath "the music of my mother's laughter" a countertext, a text whose meaning we can only know retrospectively, after having read the novel. Then we know that the apparent blessing, the apparent confluence of positive meaning, value, and feeling, is only "apparent." This positive moment, one of two such moments in the novel, when Pecola relates intensely to another human being, when she is loved and accepted in a way significantly poignant to her, is mirrored on the floor of the Breedlove kitchen when Cholly, as does Mrs. MacTeer here, likewise expresses an adult, parental, sense of relatèdness, concern for, and involvement with Pecola.[18] His is *another* initiation involving fluids: not clean, gushing, fresh water, but "cold, greasy dishwater."

Text and countertext are juxtaposed at the moment Pecola responds to the onset of menses, and her response is determined by the fact that she does not know what is happening to her: "her eyes [are] wide with terror." Claudia feels that something negative is occurring; that Pecola has been somehow injured: "You cut yourself?" Frieda normalizes and brings the situation under control by indicating knowledge of what is occurring, naming it: "That's ministratin'."[19] Against Frieda's attempt to wrest the experience from out the chaos of ignorance, to banish fear through knowledge, Pecola pits her own specifically individualized response: "Am I going to die?"

Frieda's response to Pecola's question once again juxtaposes text and countertext, winding up the plot of the novel as though it were the mainspring of a clock whose steady and controlled release of tension will result in the ticking out of the plot. In a very significant sense the center of the novel, insofar as that center is based upon a text-countertext opposition, rests in this moment, this moment of moments, in Frieda's response to Pecola's question, a response less naive than ironic in its implications regarding Pecola's fate: "Noooo. You won't die. It just means you can have a baby!" The implication is that the ability to have a baby is a good thing. The fact is that for Pecola the countertext has it that her ability to have a baby is a curse, a curse not on women in general but on her. The implications of the interaction between Frieda and Pecola at this textual moment are teased out at the chapter's end when the question of the meaning of Pecola's potential to have a baby arises, are further explored by the three girls, however perfunctorily.

> That night, in bed, the three of us lay still. We were full of awe and respect for Pecola. Lying next to a real person who was really ministratin' was somehow sacred. She was different from us now—grown-up-like. She, herself, felt the distance, but refused to lord it over us.
> After a long while she spoke very softly. "It it true that I can have a baby now?"
> "Sure," said Frieda drowsily. "Sure you can."
> "But . . . how?" Her voice was hollow with wonder.
> "Oh," said Frieda, "somebody has to love you."
> "Oh."

This section of the novel, especially in the two passages quoted above, is the germ from which the remainder of the novel proceeds. Nearly everything that happens in Pecola's life demonstrates to the reader and to herself that nobody loves her and then finally somebody does love her and she does indeed have a baby,[20] though through a process that she neither seeks nor even could imagine. All of that is implicit in the conversation above. All unfolds, from this point on, leading inexorably to the kitchen floor of the Breedlove place and ultimately to the premature birth and the death of Pecola's child. Her insanity stands in countertextual relation to the underlying tone of these two passages. The transformation from girl to biologically mature female which seems happy and hopeful, as reflected in Claudia's and Freda's barely concealed envy, turns horrific, "appalling," in the root sense of that word.[21] The meanings implicit in Claudia's feelings as the three lie abed that "Lying next to a real person who was really ministratin' was somehow *sacred*" (my emphasis) are themselves aborted.

The chief word in the novel's text after this section is "Breedlove," Pecola's family name. "Breed" and "love" clearly exist oppositionally, in countertextual relation: "breed" is the biological phenomenon, a physiological occurrence having no affective source or consequence; "love" is a social, religious, or spiritual phenomenon, implying meaning beyond the simply phenomenal. The two definitions of relatedness are intertwined in the name. The fact of the tension brought about by the disparate meanings of the two words comprising the name, yet their having been yoked together to produce one name, replicates the character of the text itself. It is a text which ultimately does not allow us clearly to distinguish (nor does it invite awareness of the possible distinctions to be made) between the historical meanings of the words "breed" and "love." The novel at once maintains and breaks down the distinctions: the distinction between breeding and loving is a linguistic, moralistic distinction and not a distinction to be sustained by reference to any appeal to what is, to actuality. That is to say, Morrison suggests that the concepts are easily enough distinguished, but experience is not identical with our abstractions about it. Felt experience, Morrison insists, is far too complex and different in character from idea to correspond to our concepts regarding it. Specifically, our lexicon distinguishes "breed" and "love," but "love" in actuality, as experienced, may not be distinguishable from animalistic "breed," and the element of "breed" may lie inextricably buried within the experience of love.

The implications of the meaning of the family name, a name which comes to the family through Cholly ("*Charles* Breedlove," a good Anglo-Saxon name, is entombed within his full name as well as a host of other meanings), conflate in the narrative's climax, the sexual abuse of Pecola on a Saturday afternoon on the kitchen floor of the storefront the Breedloves occupy. All thematic and plot lines, the text-countertextual movement of the novel as well, converge at that particular juncture in time and space.

Cholly, during this scene, is allowed by Morrison to appropriate narrative authority insofar as he is permitted the privilege of having what occurs told from his vantage point. He does not usurp narrative authority, for his control stems entirely from the author's self-imposed limitation: she restricts herself at this point to the third person limited narration. Whatever authority Cholly possesses accrues not because it comes to him by nature, or because he is male, but because Morrison chooses to give it to him. She grants this black male a voice, and in allowing him voice, she again expresses countertextuality. There is some degree of distance between the perspective of Cholly and that of Morrison. Whereas Morrison is not Cholly, Cholly is likewise not Morrison. Yet, Morrison allows Cholly to be something other than simply evil. We know in the abstract that there are *no* circumstances under which a father may justifiably, knowingly have sexual intercourse with his daughter. Morrison does not tell us that what Cholly does to Pecola is all right; rather she says that what happens is very complicated, and that though Cholly is not without blame for what happens to Pecola, he is no less a victim than she.[22]

The factors motivating him on that Saturday afternoon in the Breedlove kitchen stem from the whole of his past experience, his experience as a poor, black youth, victimized by white and black oppression.[23] It is not clear where oppression begins or ends: his mother abandons him on a garbage heap, but his grandmother rescues him. Abandonment is text; rescue is countertext. The first act of oppression against him is counteracted by his grandmother. Is his abandonment an act of racial oppression? Yes, it is—however indirectly. But it is also personal oppression. There cannot be any such abstraction as "oppression" if it does not find expression through the actions of specific humans. (The first act of oppression committed directly against him is his mother's abandonment.)

The entirety of his sexual life is colored by his first experience of sexual intercourse, an experience utterly intertwined with, entirely inseparable from, race. He is thoroughly humiliated by the two white hunters who threaten him with bodily harm if he does not continue sexual intercourse with Darlene. They look on bemused and contemptuous. The hatred and hostility that would be directed at the hunters under normal circumstances is displaced onto Darlene because Cholly is unable to disobey the two white men.[24] The relation between that early experience with Darlene and the later sexual encounter with Pecola is clear enough. We learn that during the episode involving Darlene and the white hunters that he "hated her" and wished he could hurt her. He hated Pecola too and wished "to break her neck." On both occasions the same "biliousness" arises within him.

As the text reads, Cholly's voice tells the unremitting, unvarnished truth of his knowledge, understanding of, and feeling about what happens in that kitchen on that Saturday afternoon. As we have it, what we see is not clearly a rape because of the circumstances surrounding it. We know exactly why Cholly responds to Pecola as he does and that fact along with others gives rise to a countertext. Had he simply felt anger toward Pecola, then the case would be more easily judged. As it is, however, he feels hostility and love, both at the same time. He does want "to break her neck," but he wants to do it "tenderly." Nothing in the tone of the text suggests that these contrary feelings are not utterly genuine. The worst is yet to come: "He wanted to fuck her—tenderly."

In his drunken stupor he confuses Pecola not only with Darlene, whom he hated, but with Pauline, Pecola's mother, whom he loved. The encounter is in fact a reenactment, a reliving of his first meeting with Pauline but tinged with the experience with Darlene. The text makes that abundantly clear. The text also indicates that Morrison does not allow us as readers to get off as easily as we might if it were as clearly sexual abuse as his second attack on her is. We know what to think of fathers who fuck their daughters; perhaps we do not know so easily what to think when we learn of Cholly's thoughts at the time: "Not the usual lust to part tight legs with his own but a tenderness, a protectiveness. A desire to cover the foot with his hand and gently nibble away the itch from the calf with his teeth. He did it then, and started Pauline into laughter. He did it now."

It would be on the whole easier to judge Cholly if we knew less about him and if we could isolate the kitchen floor episode from the social context in which it occurs and from Cholly's past. But we cannot; we are neither invited to nor allowed. It is especially evident that this is the case as the episode moves toward termination. We need especially distinguish between what Morrison, as a function of the particular technical point of view at this juncture, tells us and does not tell us. Consider such a passage as this: "Following the disintegration—the falling away—of sexual desire, he was conscious of her wet, soapy hands on his wrists, the fingers clenching, but whether her grip was from a hopeless but stubborn struggle to be free, or from some other emotion, he could not tell." The countertext arises from the possibilities of interpretation provoked by the technical point of view. What, in fact, *was* Pecola feeling at this point? Morrison allows myriad possibilities, among them that Pecola has now been loved, is, during the course of the act, being loved, setting out the text and countertext as in the existing shady grammatical and lexical distinction between "being loved" and "being made love to." Of course the opposite is implied as well, for her father's expression of love is by all received standards anything but that.[25] The problematic is intensified when Pecola's other self, the voice arising within her psyche when she becomes psychotic, an alter ego, questions her response to her father's two assaults, introducing the possibility that she wanted and needed them. The text, whereas it does not imply anything like seduction on Pecola's part, at the same time allows the possibility that she is participant and not simply victim, victim and at the same moment participant.

Text-countertextual and counter-countertextual juxtaposition inform the novel throughout.[26] The portion of the primer book text beginning the scene just discussed reads: "SEEFATHERHEISBIGANDSTRONG FATHERWILLYOUPLAYWITHJANEFATHERISSMILINGSMILE FATHERSMILE." Of course the father about to "play with" Jane is not the inane, sterile, stereotypical stick figure of the primer text but a blood and bone human out of a different world than that of Dick and Jane, a world in fact, and in some sense unhappily, more real than theirs.

One final example of countertextuality exists in the complexity of attitude demonstrated in the novel's dialogue. Consider the array of attitudes reflected in the response of the ticket agent at the bus terminal when Cholly at fourteen seeks to buy a ticket at the rate for children twelve or younger. Cholly pretends to be twelve and though the agent hardly believes him, still he sells him the reduced rate ticket.

> "I reckon I knows a lying nigger when I sees one, but just in case you ain't, jest in case one of them mammies is really dyin' and wants to see her little old smoke before she meets her maker, I gone do it."

How are we to react to this? The agent's response to Cholly is to the reader ambiguous, though not to the agent. Rattling around inside the empty shell of this racist rhetoric is a decent human impulse. But how can we separate the decency from its container? How can we not respond to the humor of the passage and how do we regard the humor in relation to the other, not humorous elements of the response? I don't think we can react simply, and I think this is Morrison's point, a point brilliantly made in a tiny corner of her edifice.

Every element of Morrison's text has its countertext. The notion of "the bluest eye," for example, suggests that her primary concern is with the culture's standard of beauty. That, as a matter of fact, is the way that this novel has been generally understood. But if this is so, what are we to do with Claudia's observations and conclusions at the novel's end?

> All of us—all who knew her—felt so wholesome after we cleaned ourselves on her. We were so beautiful when we stood astride her ugliness. [What does the word "astride" suggest here? A species of masculine dominance? Cholly's rape?] Her simplicity decorated us, her guilt sanctified us, her pain made us glow with health.

The indictment of the society stands, but it is conceived far more realistically than the conception allows that erroneously contends that the racial issue involves simply black and white.[27] The novel has, as countertext, its class ramifications too. Claudia conceives of the world in terms of race alone when she deconstructs white dolls. Eventually she learns to have the regard for those dolls that her parents have. She understands the limitations of her perspective. That is, she recognizes that she is, because of her economic status, subject to the same social forces molding others. Her experience demonstrates that in a land where the bluest eye holds hegemony none of the dispossessed escapes its gaze.

Notes

1. Though Tocqueville's attitudes toward black people and slavery are somewhat problematical, he opposed slavery on moral and economic grounds. He also felt that whatever limitations slaves might possess came about because of lack of exposure to culture and not genetic causes. In a letter to Gobineau written in November 1853 after Tocqueville had read Gobineau's *Essay*, noted above, Tocqueville comments: "Thus I confess that having read your book I remain, as before, extremely opposed to these doctrines. I believe that they are probably false; I know that they are most certainly pernicious."
2. Morrison has herself commented on the dialectics of her fiction: "I am not interested in indulging myself in some private, closed exercise of my imagination that fulfills only the obligation of my personal dreams—which is to say yes, the work must be political. It must have that as its thrust. That's a perjorative term in critical circles now: if a work of art has any political influence in it, somehow it's tainted. My feeling is just the opposite: if it has none, it is tainted."
3. Smith in her most insightful discussion of Morrison refers to the phenomenon I describe here as Morrison's tendency to leave certain questions unresolved. I see what is apparently "unresolvability" as "countertextuality."
4. Jones sees the primary relation between the primer frame and the text as an ironic relation. Dorothy H. Lee identifies the relation between primer text and text as "counterpoint": "For each segment of the idealized picture of secure family life, Morrison offers in counterpoint the bleak specifics of Pecola's existence."
5. This point is made by several critics, among them Ogunyemi 113, Klotman 124.
6. Michael Awkward first suggested a relation between the Dick and Jane epigraph and the authentication, usually by whites, of slave narratives. My interpretation, though similar to his, is markedly different.
7. Smith believes these passages to be rendered through Claudia; I think they are presented by an omniscient narrator.
8. Most critics disagree. Smith sees the final version as "virtually unintelligible." Klotman, and Ogunyemi essentially agree.
9. Other critics have made this same observation in various ways. Byerman comments that "All the blacks in the book feel insecure and even inferior because of skin tone." Barbara Lounsberry and Grace Ann Hovet put it thusly: "In *The Bluest Eye* and the other novels, Morrison is unwilling to blame black failure entirely on outside forces or upon the hazards of minority existence."
10. This point is overlooked by a number of good critics of the novel who do not take into account the fact that Claudia's deconstruction of the white dolls is

but a phase of her development, that later she succumbs to those very values governing Pecola's judgment of herself. Byerman believes that the McTeers escape the culture's judgment: "Unlike the Breedloves and the light-skinned Geraldine and Maureen, they [the McTeers] do not measure their human worth by symbols of the dominant white culture." De Weever agrees: "Her [Claudia's] revulsion protects her from the deadly seduction which claims Pecola at the end of the novel." House asserts the same: "Rejecting material gains which are components of success dreams, she [Claudia] dislikes artificially pretty white dolls which black children receive for Christmas."

11. Byerman calls attention to the ritualistic nature of Pecola's imbibing.
12. Byerman comments on Pecola's "Christ-like" nature as seen by Claudia, seeing Pecola as a "grotesque messiah."
13. "Shirley Temple *is* Jane, the perfect daughter, only brought to life on the movie screen."
14. De Weever interprets the eating of the candy somewhat differently: "This symbolic cannibalism is a sign of Pecola's latent instability."
15. The meaning of the three prostitutes has been variously rendered. Jones identifies the three as witches of fairy tales. Ogunyemi says that "The three symbolize the helplessness of human beings in life, be it on a national, racial, or individual level. Their names evoke the helplessness of France, China, and Poland in the face of rape by more powerful forces in World War II; they evoke the helplessness of the black race raped, as it were, by the whites."
16. Bakerman sees Pecola's initiation as a "failed initiation."
17. Klotman's understanding of the narrative point of view differs somewhat. She feels that "Everything is told from the innocent viewpoint of childhood— Claudia as a nine-year-old. The narrative voice shifts, however, when the author wants us to have a more mature and objective view of the characters and their situations to an older Claudia, the author's persona."
18. Klotman seems to differ: "The only tenderness she receives is from her father, in the drunken and perverse moment before he rapes her."
19. Rosenberg sees this episode as demonstrating Frieda's competence in handling the "terror and mystery of that initial bleeding." I believe it to be far more complicated than that.
20. Pecola's linking of the act of sexual intercourse and love is initiated through the conversation of the three girls quoted above. That the notion becomes a part of her belief system is born out in the conversation with her fantasized companion toward the narrative's conclusion: "If she [Mrs. Breedlove] didn't love him [Cholly], she sure let him do it to her a lot." Whether, as Turner says, she "welcomes his second advance as an unaccustomed demonstration of his love" seems arguable.
21. Latin *pallere*, "to grow pale."
22. Morrison herself expresses the concept of countertextuality when she says of Sethe's murder of her child in *Beloved*, "She did the right thing, but she had no right to do it." Interview.
23. Byerman in an article preceding his treatment of Cholly in *Jagged Grain* sees Cholly in much the same way that I am suggesting that the whole of Morrison's novel be read: "Because we have been introduced to his way of thinking and suffering, we verge on understanding his action and sharing his confusion. Both of these responses, repulsion against the action and attraction to the actor are mutually necessary for the grotesque to work in this scene." "Intense Behavior."
24. Davis says regarding this scene that in Cholly "the humiliated black male

allies himself with the [other] by making the black woman the object of his displaced fury. . . . All he can do to restore his selfhood is to deny hers further."

25. I would insist on the countertextual reading here as opposed to all other readings that see the depiction of the interaction between Cholly and Pecola as simply rape. An example of many such readings is Jones's: "The most bitingly satirical example of the hatred bred by Cholly Breedlove is his violating the body of his own twelve-year-old daughter, Pecola, and impregnating her. All of the fiendishness of his being is epitomized in this diabolical act."

26. Byerman identifies another text-countertextual opposition: "Pecola leaves us with an ambiguous feeling. We are sorry for her victimization, but we know that she has entered a realm where her suffering will seldom enter her consciousness." "Intense Behavior."

27. Byerman concurs with this judgment: "Pecola may be the central character, but she is far from the only victim of blue eyes. 'We' individually and collectively are both victimizer and victim; and, while the roles vary with each character, it is also the case that the role of victimizer results from that character's own victimization by a larger society."

◆◆◆◆◆◆◆◆◆◆◆◆◆◆

"The Evil of Fulfillment": Scapegoating and Narration in *The Bluest Eye*

MICHAEL AWKWARD

I had found my tongue.

—Toni Morrison
The Bluest Eye

. . . all the voice in answer he could wake
Was but the mocking echo of his own.
      *   ***   ***   ***
He would cry out on life, that what it wants
Is not its own love back in copy speech,
But counter-love, original response.
And nothing ever came of what he cried . . .

—Robert Frost
"The Most of It"

. . . just as the male artist's struggle against his precursor takes the form of
what [Harold] Bloom calls revisionary swerves, flights, misreadings, so the
female writer's battle for self-creation involves her in a revisionary process.
Her battle, however, is not against her (male) precursor's reading of the world
but against the reading of her.

—Sandra Gilbert and Susan Gubar,
The Madwoman in the Attic

In the previous chapter I attempted to chart Zora Neale Hurston's successful *denigration* of the novel. *Their Eyes Were Watching God* provides particularly compelling evidence in support of Hurston's claim that "everything that [the Afro-American] touches is re-interpreted for his own use." Such reinterpretation of expressive forms requires, as I have argued, not only a sensitive exploration of the lives of black characters, but also an energetic revision of the Western forms themselves. Hurston's placement of her novel in the Afro-American expressive cultural tradition in general, and in the Afro-American literary tradition in particular, is signalled by that novel's employment (and successful resolution) of the Du Boisian concept of double consciousness in both its content and its narrative strategies.

In the present chapter, I shall focus on Toni Morrison's *The Bluest Eye*. Morrison's narrative stands as her initial attempt at generic *denigration*, as her first effort to create what she has elsewhere called "A genuine Black . . . Book."[1] But while, as in the case of Hurston's text, it is possible to read in Morrison's novel clear signs of a merging of narrative voices, the narrative events of *The Bluest Eye*—and particularly Pecola's schizophrenic double voicedness exhibited when she believes she has been granted the "bluest eyes in the whole world"[2]—portray double consciousness as a constant and, for Pecola at least, a permanently debilitating state.

The following discussion will attempt to account for the reasons *The Bluest Eye* can present merged Afro-American consciousness only in its strategies of narration. Before such accounting is possible, however, it is necessary first to discuss the specifics of Morrison's placement of herself within the Afro-American literary tradition. This placement, I will argue, evidences a self-conscious rejection of the models of such preeminent figures as James Baldwin and Ralph Ellison, and a clear exploration of the types of thematic and formal concerns found in Hurston.

I

In "Rootedness: The Ancestor as Foundation" Morrison insists that ancestors play an essential role in individual works in the Afro-American canon. She states:

> [I]t seems to me interesting to evaluate Black literature on what the writer does with the presence of the ancestor. Which is to say a grandfather as in Ralph Ellison, or a grandmother as in Toni Cade Bambara, or a healer as in Bambara or Henry Dumas. There is always an elder there. And these ancestors are not just parents, they are sort of timeless people whose relationships to the characters are benevolent, instructive and protective, and they provide a certain kind of wisdom.[3]

Despite the apparent optimistic assurance of this statement, Morrison is well aware that "the presence of the ancestor" is not always viewed by the Afro-American writer as "benevolent, instructive and protective." Indeed, she argues—just a few sentences following the above declaration—that the works of Richard Wright and James Baldwin exhibit particularly identifiable problems with the ancestor. For Morrison, Wright's corpus suggests that he "had great difficulty with that ancestor," and Baldwin's that he was confounded and disturbed by the presence or absence of an ancestor." (Although Morrison does not specify which texts she has in mind, one assumes that she is referring to Wright's *Native Son* and *Black Boy* and to Baldwin's *Go Tell It on the Mountain* and "Notes on a Native Son.")[4]

Morrison's singling out of Wright and Baldwin as figures in whose work ancestors represent troubling presences (or absences) is not, it seems to me, a random act. For in addition to both writers' *intra*textual struggles with ancestors, the Wright-Baldwin personal and literary relationship represents the most fabled *inter*textual association in Afro-American letters. Baldwin's attacks on his acknowledged precursor Wright offer intriguing Afro-American examples of what Harold Bloom has termed "the anxiety of influence."[5] In "Alas, Poor Richard," for example—an unconscionably vicious final assault on the recently deceased precursor—Baldwin asserts that the harsh criticism of *Native Son* that occupies the final pages of his essay "Everybody's Protest Novel" represented his attempt to create canonical space for his own perceptions of Afro-American life. He states: "I had used [Wright's] work as a kind of spring-board into my own. His work was a roadblock in my road, the sphinx, really, whose riddles I had to answer before I could become myself."[6]

Though it is certainly far from a sympathetic postmortem, "Alas, Poor Richard" does exhibit a great deal of sensitivity to the complex system of violent verbal revision that characterizes the Western (male) literary tradition. For Baldwin discusses not only his own problematic relationship to his precursor Wright, but also his view that he will himself inevitably represent for a younger writer an ancestral roadblock which that younger writer will need to clear away in order to create canonical space for himself or herself. He admits to not looking forward to being himself thrust into the role of villainous ancestor that he fashioned so successfully for Wright: "I do not know how I will take it when my time [to be attacked as ancestral roadblock] comes."

With the publication in 1970 of *The Bluest Eye*, it becomes evident that Baldwin's "time" had indeed come, perhaps much more quickly than he had imagined. Morrison, of course, makes no overt attack on ancestral figures of the sort that occurs in Baldwin's "Many Thousands Gone" or, for that matter, Ralph Ellison's "The World and the Jug." But her first novel does contain clear evidence of her (sometimes subtle) refigurations of key elements of Baldwin's and Ellison's corpuses. Specifically, Morrison refigures Baldwin's discussion of Wright in "Many Thousands Gone" and the Trueblood episode of Ellison's *Invisible Man*. Only by understanding the nature of Morrison's disagreements with and formal revisions of Ellison and Baldwin can we fully comprehend her rejection of these "strong"[7] male figures as literary ancestors.

II

The thrice-repeated primer that serves, in its varying degrees of decipherability, as part of *The Bluest Eye*'s prefatory material assumes a central position in the critical discourse surrounding Morrison's novel. In "Dick-and-Jane and the Shirley Temple Sensibility in *The Bluest Eye*," for example, Phyllis Klotman argues that the various versions of the

primer "are symbolic of the lifestyles that the author explores in the
novel either directly or by implication."[8] Klotman goes on to suggest her
view of the specific referents of each version of the primer:

> The first [version] is clearly that of the alien white world. . . . The second is
> the lifestyle of the two black MacTeer children, Claudia and Frieda, shaped
> by poor but loving parents trying desperately to survive. . . . The Breedloves'
> lives . . . are like the third—the distorted run-on—version of "Dick and Jane."

Another reading that suggests that the primer offers an interpretive
key to Morrison's text, Raymond Hedin's "The Structuring of Emotion
in Black American Fiction," astutely discusses Morrison's manipulation
of the contents of the primer. Hedin says:

> Morrison arranges the novel so that each of its sections provides a bitter gloss
> on key phrases from the novel's preface, a condensed version of the Dick and
> Jane reader. These phrases . . . describe the [American] culture ideal of the
> healthy, supportive, well-to-do family. The seven central elements of Jane's
> world—house, family, cat, Mother, father, dog, and friend—become, in turn,
> plot elements, but only after they are inverted to fit the realities of Pecola's
> world.[9]

Hedin is correct in his suggestion that the body of *The Bluest Eye*
represents an intentional inversion of the primer. Morrison's further
manipulations of the primer are, indeed, even more striking. She employs the primer not only as prefatory material to the text proper, but
also to introduce the chapters of *The Bluest Eye* that are recounted by
the novel's omniscient narrative voice. The seven epigraphic sections
are, as Hedin implies, thematically tied to the chapters which they directly precede. For example, the chapter which introduces the Breedlove
family to the reader is prefaced by the primer's reference to Jane's "very
happy" family: HEREISTHEFAMILYMOTHERFATHERDICKAND
JANETHEYLIVEINTHEGREENANDWHITEHOUSETHEYARE
VERYH

But the family presented in the subsequent pages of the novel is the
very antithesis of the standardized, ideal (white) American family of the
primer. The reader is informed, in fact, of the Breedloves' overwhelming
unhappiness and self-hatred. The chapter discusses, among other things:
the "calculated, uninspired, and deadly" fights of the Breedlove parents;
the father Cholly's alcoholism and the mother Polly's perversely self-
serving Christianity; the son Sammy's intense hatred of his father and
the fact that he frequently runs away from home; and the daughter
Pecola's tragic desire for blue eyes. The reader learns, in short, of the
Breedloves' psychological and physical "unattractiveness," of the family's
utter failure to conform to the standards by which the beauty and happiness of the primer family (and, by extension, American families in general) are measured.

But it is possible to make further claims for Morrison's employment
of the primer as epigraph. In her systematic analysis of an inversive

relationship between pretext (the primer) and text (her delineation of Afro-American life), the author dissects, *deconstructs*, if you will, the bourgeois myths of ideal family life. Through her deconstruction, she exposes each individual element of the myth as not only deceptively inaccurate in general, but also wholly inapplicable to Afro-American life. The emotional estrangement of the primer family members (an estrangement suggested by that family's inability to respond to the daughter Jane's desire for play) implies that theirs is solely a surface contentment. For despite Hedin's suggestion that this family is represented as "healthy" and "supportive," it appears to be made up of rigid, emotionless figures incapable of deep feeling.

Afro-American attempts to live in accord with these ultimately unhealthy standards occasion, as my subsequent discussion will demonstrate, not only an emotional barrenness similar to that of the primer family, but also intense feelings of failure and worthlessness such as those experienced by the Breedloves. By exhibiting that such negative feelings are direct functions of Afro-American adoptions of these myths, Morrison attempts to break the spell of the hypnotic propaganda of an overly materialistic America. She seeks, by means of her deconstruction, to mitigate the power of (American propagandistic) words and to make possible an emotion-privileging Afro-American environment. In her attempt to alter the reader's perception of what should be viewed as normative and healthy, Morrison's perspective is similar to that of her character Claudia when she discusses what would be for her an ideal Christmas. Claudia states:

> nobody ever asked me what I wanted for Christmas. . . . *I did not want to have anything to own, or to possess any object.* I wanted rather to *feel* something on Christmas day. The real question would have been, "Dear Claudia, *what experience would you like* on Christmas?" I could have spoken up, "I want to sit on the low stool in Big Mama's kitchen with my lap full of lilacs and listen to Big Papa play his violin for me alone." The lowness of the stool made for my body, the security and warmth of Big Mama's kitchen, the smell of the lilacs, the sound of the music, and, since it would be good to have all of my senses engaged, the taste of a peach, perhaps, afterwards. (my emphasis)

In privileging feelings and experience over ownership of objects, Claudia—and Morrison—rejects bourgeois standards of happiness. The false security of the "pretty," "green and white house" of the primer and its materialism are repudiated in favor of "experience"—the smell of lilacs, Big Papa's music, the genuine emotional security of Big Mama's kitchen.

Morrison's deconstruction of the primer and her exposure of an inversive relationship between pretext and text suggest that the author uses the primer consciously to trope certain conventions prominently found in eithteenth-, nineteenth-, and early-twentieth-century Afro-American texts. The convention that Morrison revises here is that of the authenticating document, usually written by whites to confirm a genuine Black authorship of the subsequent text. The white voice of authority—a William Lloyd Garrison in the case of Frederick Douglass' *Narrative*, a William Dean Howells in the case of Paul Laurence Dunbar's *Lyrics of Lowly Life*—has traditionally authenticated the black voice in Afro-American literature.

Robert Stepto has suggested that such white pretextual authorization of the black voice has had a significant influence in shaping the Afro-American literary enterprise. Indeed, his study *From Behind the Veil*[10] examines the various functions of strategies of authentication in selected (male-authored) Afro-American texts predicated on conscious revisions and refigurations of precursor texts. The increasing level of artistic sophistication Stepto observes in these narratives are, for him, a function of the Afro-American writers' increasing ability to manipulate strategies and documents of authentication.

The Afro-American narrative moves, according to Stepto, from white authentication of blackness to, with the examples of Ralph Ellison and Richard Wright, black self-authentication. Morrison's manipulation of the pretextual material in *The Bluest Eye*'s prefatory primer signals, it seems to me, another step in the development of the Afro-American narrative as conceived by Stepto. Morrison returns to an earlier practice—of the white voice introducing the black text—to demonstrate, as I have suggested, her refusal to allow white standards to arbitrate the success or failure of the Afro-American experience. Her manipulation of the primer is meant to suggest, finally, the inappropriateness of the white voice's attempt to authorize or authenticate the Afro-American text or to dictate the contours of Afro-American art.

Morrison's attitudes about Afro-American expressive art differ significantly from those of Ralph Ellison. For unlike Ellison, Morrison appears to have little interest in comparisons of her work to that of white authors, and views such comparisons as "offensive" and "irrelevant." In Claudia Tate's *Black Women Writers at Work*, Morrison says: "I find such criticism dishonest because it never goes into the work on its own terms. . . . [Such criticism] is merely trying to place the [Afro-American] book into an already established [read: white] literary tradition."[11] In "Rootedness" Morrison offers, in direct contrast to Ellison (and Baldwin), what are the terms by which she believes her work should be judged:

> I don't like to find my books condemned as bad or praised as good, when that condemnation or that praise is based on criteria from other paradigms. I would much prefer that they were dismissed or embraced based on the success of their accomplishment within the culture out of which I write.

Morrison demands that her work be judged according to Afro-American expressive criteria.

Such comments from Morrison stand in direct contrast to statements by Ellison. In "The World and the Jug"—an essay whose expressed goal is a delineation of the fundamental difference of his fiction from that of Wright—Ellison refutes Irving Howe's claim that Wright is his literary ancestor. He states:

> . . . perhaps you will understand when I say he did not influence me if I point out that while one can do nothing about choosing one's "relatives," one can, as artist, choose one's "ancestors." Wright was, in this sense, a "relative"; Hemingway an "ancestor." Langston Hughes, whose work I knew in grade school and whom I knew before I knew Wright, was a "relative"; Eliot, whom I was to meet only many years later, and Malraux and Dostoievsky and Faulkner, were "ancestors" . . .[12]

Ellison denies an Afro-American literary family represented by Wright and Hughes in favor of a (white) Western ancestry characterized by Hemingway and Faulkner and predicated on what he considers to be the greater quality of their achievements as artists. He insists, then, that a common (Afro-American) culture background is not determinative of literary lineage.

Unlike Ellison, Morrison rejects a (white) Western ancestry in favor of an (exclusively) Afro-American one. She strives to create not American or Western, but an identifiably Afro-American (or Black) Art, works which are identifiable as such because she "incorporate[s] into my fiction [elements] that are directly and deliberately related to what I regard as the major characteristics of Black art." Just as she refuses to voice assent to critical assessments of her work that judge it by (white) Western standards or compare it to that of white authors, so, too, does Morrison refuse to allow the white voice and perception of the primer to authorize or authenticate the supremely self-conscious example of Black Art that is *The Bluest Eye*.

Such a rejection of white criteria of judgment of Afro-American art and life is, unfortunately, not possible for the blacks who populate the pages of Morrison's first novel. The differences between her views of Afro-American art and those of Ellison (and Baldwin) are evident not only in statements such as those cited above, but also in her depiction in *The Bluest Eye* of the dangers inherent in Afro-American acceptance of white standards.

III

The black characters of *The Bluest Eye* appear to accept Western standards of beauty, morality, and success despite (for the most part) being unable themselves to achieve these standards. The first such apparent failure chronicled in the text involves the MacTeer home's state of physical and seeming emotional disrepair. In direct contrast to the primer house which is "green and white," "has a red door" and is "very pretty" is the "old, cold, and green" MacTeer house. The structure's physical disrepair is symbolized in its inability to protect its inhabitants from cold (and cold germ-bearing) winds. Its apparent emotional impoverishment is exemplified for the novels' first-person narrator by her mother's apparently insensitive reaction to her daughter's contraction of a cold and her resultant vomiting. Claudia says:

> My mother's voice drones on. She is not talking to me. She is talking to the puke, but she is calling it my name; Claudia. She wipes it up as best she can and puts a scratchy towel over the large wet place. I lie down again. The rags have fallen from the window crack, and the air is cold. I dare not call her back and am reluctant to leave my warmth. My mother's anger humiliates me; her words chafe my cheeks, and I am crying. . . . By and by I will not get sick; I will refuse to. But for now I am crying. I know I am making more snot, but I can't stop.

With a sufficient distance from this painful childhood experience, Claudia is able to see the inappropriateness of the images of cold and misery by which she characterizes her youth. As an adult she is able to see that her mother "is not angry at me, but at my sickness." Further, she is able to observe that in the anguish of her former pain was:

> a productive and fructifying pain. Love, thick and dark as Alaga syrup, eased up into that cracked window. I could smell it—taste it—sweet, musty, with an edge of wintergreen in its base—everywhere in that house. It stuck, along with my tongue, to the frosted windowpanes. It coated my chest, along with the salve, and when the flannel came undone in my sleep, the clear, sharp curves of air outlined its presence on my mouth. And in the night, when my coughing was dry and tough, feet padded into the room, hands repinned the flannel, readjusted the quilt, and rested a moment on my forehead. So when I think of autumn, I think of somebody with hands who does not want me to die.

This passage suggests Claudia's rejection of white evaluative standards vis-à-vis Afro-American life. Thus, her childhood, formerly conceived in a vocabulary of pain—her mother's droning voice, the scratchy wet towel, the coldness of the air—has been reconceptualized as filled with protective, "sweet," "thick and dark" love of a mother "who does not want me to die." The passage recalls Nikki Giovanni's discussion in the poem "Nikki-Rosa" of "Black love" and the inability of white criteria to sense its contours:

> childhood experiences are always a drag
> if you're Black
> you always remembering things like living in Woodlawn
> with no inside toilet
> and if you become famous or something
> they never talk about how happy you were to have

your mother
all to yourself and
how good the water felt when you got your bath
from one of those
big tubs that folk in chicago barbecue in . . .

       *   *   *   *

And though you're poor it isn't poverty that concerns you
and though they fought a lot
it isn't your father's drinking that makes any difference
but only that everybody is together and you
and your sister have happy birthdays and very good
Christmases
and I really hope no white person ever has cause
to write about me
because they never understand
Black love is Black wealth and they'll
probably talk about my hard childhood
and never understand that
all the while I was quite happy.[13]

Like Giovanni's persona, Claudia discovers that despite the difficulties of poverty in an opulent America, "all the while I was quite happy."

Such a rereading of her life evidences Claudia's ultimate achievements of an informed black perspective. But her achievement is not unproblematic, to be sure. Perhaps the most poignant (and certainly most "charged" in an intertextual sense) of the incidents that result in Claudia's ability to reread her own life is her attempt to understand the rationale for standards that insist on white physical superiority.

Claudia's efforts can profitably be viewed as tentative first steps toward initiation into the larger American society. Her search to comprehend the myth of white physical superiority while attempting, at the same time, to hold onto her views of her own people's beauty and cultural worth, exposes hers as a situation "betwixt and between" that the anthropologist Victor Turner has labeled liminality or marginality. In *Dramas, Fields, and Metaphors*, Turner discusses marginality in ways that help explain Afro-American double consciousness. Marginals, according to Turner:

> are simultaneous members (by ascription, optation, self-definition, or achievement) of two or more groups whose social definitions and cultural norms are distinct from, and often even opposed to, one another. . . . What is interesting about such marginals is that they often look to their group of origin the so-called inferior group, for communitas, and to the more prestigious group in which they mainly live and in which they aspire to higher status as their structural reference group.[14]

Certainly one way to conceive of the Afro-American's attempt to resolve double consciousness is as a struggle to be initiated into the larger American society. Such a struggle does not necessarily conclude in acceptance by that society (what Turner terms "aggregation"), to be sure. In other words, Afro-American double consciousness is not always resolved. As Turner insists, marginals—people situated betwixt and between antithetical, often antagonistic cultures—"have no cultural assurance of a final resolution of their ambiguity."

Social marginality (or double consciousness) can, then, be a permanent condition. To begin to resolve such ambiguity, Turner argues, it is necessary to seek both the origin and an understanding of the often self-aggrandizing myths of the "more prestigious group." The questing marginal must seek to understand the origins of myths, "how things came to be what they are." Consequently, adults' gifts of white dolls to Claudia are not, for the young girl and future narrator, pleasure-inducing toys but, rather, signs (in a semiotic sense) that she must learn to interpret correctly. Such interpretation requires mining the dolls' surfaces (pink skins, blue eyes, blond hair)—a literal search for source(s):

> I had only one desire: to dismember [the doll]. To see of what it was made, to discover the dearness, to find the beauty, the desirability that had escaped me, but apparently only me. Adults, older girls, shops, magazines, newspapers, window signs—all the world had agreed that a blue-eyed, yellow-haired, pink-skinned doll was what every girl child treasured. "Here," they said, "this is beautiful, and if you are on this day 'worthy' you may have it". . . . I could not love it. But I could examine it to see what it was that all the world said was lovable. Break off the tiny fingers, bend the flat feet, loosen the hair, twist the head around, and the thing made one sound—a sound they said was the sweet and plaintive cry "Mama," but which sounded to me like the bleat of a dying lamb, or, more precisely, our icebox door opening on rusty hinges in July.

One of this passage's dominant images—that of ritualistic sacrifice—foreshadows Pecola's employment as scapegoat by *The Bluest Eye*'s black community. This passage also offers material which enables us to contrast Claudia's and Pecola's encounters with the myth of white superiority. Gifts of white dolls arouse in Claudia not affection—which would suggest acceptance of the myth—but, rather, a sadistic curiosity: she dissects white dolls and, later, transfers this urge to little white girls, in confrontation with images of beauty that imply that her own almost antithetical appearance is exceedingly unattractive.

Pecola, on the other hand, also faced with the pervasiveness of Western culture standards of beauty, accepts unquestioningly the myth's validity. Her family's perception of its physical appearance is represented by the omniscient narrator as significantly different than that of other blacks who appear to accept Caucasian features as the norm:

> No one could have convinced them [the Breedloves] that they were not relentlessly and aggressively ugly. . . . You looked at them and wondered why they were so ugly; you looked closely and could not find the source. Then you realized that it was from conviction, their conviction. It was as though some

mysterious all-knowing master had given each one a cloak of ugliness to wear, and they each accepted it without question. The master had said, "You are ugly people." They had looked about themselves and saw nothing to contradict the statement; saw, in fact, support for it leaning at them from every billboard, every movie, every glance. "Yes," they had said. "You are right." And they took their ugliness in their hands, threw it as a mantle over them, and went about the world with it.

Jacqueline DeWeever has argued that *The Bluest Eye*'s obvious preoccupation with the often devastating effects of the pervasive Western standards of beauty on black Americans represents a foregrounding of a relatively minor scene in Ellison's *Invisible Man*.[15] In the scene in question, Ellison's protagonist encounters a sign in a Harlem store window with the following inscription: "You too can be truly beautiful. Win greater happiness with whiter complexion. Be outstanding in your social set."[16] It is certainly the case that *The Bluest Eye* manifests Morrison's revision of several aspects of Ellison's text—in particular, as I will later discuss in detail, the Trueblood episode in which the effects of incest are explored. But it seems to me most fruitful to observe this thematic concern with comparisons of black and white physical appearance in terms of the novel's female precursorial text, *Their Eyes Were Watching God*.

Morrison's discussion of an all-knowing master's decree that the Breedlove clan is ugly recalls most specifically not the invisible man's Harlem window shopping, but the infatuation of Hurston's Mrs. Turner with Caucasian features. Hurston says of the muck storekeeper:

Mrs. Turner, like all other believers has built an altar to the unattainable—Caucasian characteristics for all. Her god would smite her, would hurl her from pinnacles and lose her in deserts. But she would not forsake his altars. . . . [She held] a belief that somehow she and others through worship could attain her paradise—a heaven of straight-haired, thin-lipped, high-nose boned white seraphs. The physical impossibilities in no way injured faith. That was the mystery and mysteries are the chores of gods.[17]

Certainly Pecola's and Mrs. Turner's wishes are not exactly parallel, but they are unquestionably similar. Both believe that through energetic prayer their desires for the obliteration of the Negroid—in Pecola's case, her black eyes, in Mrs. Turner's, the Afro-American race altogether—can be achieved. Mrs. Turner, already possessing (she believes) the beauty that accompanies Caucasian features, prays that the rest of the blacks—whose pigmentation, immorality and lack of civility offend her—be whitened in a miraculous act of God. But Pecola, whose features—her "high cheek bones," "shapely lips," "insolent nostrils," and dark complexion—are undeniably black, desires from her god a seemingly much smaller miracle: to be given the bluest eyes in the world.

Just as fervently as Mrs. Turner prays for a wholesale black metamorphosis, so, too, does Pecola ask to be blessed with a symbol of beauty. Having been taught by school primers and Madison Avenue advertisers that beauty and happiness are possible only for whites, Pecola believes that the possession of the blue eyes of a white girl would significantly alter her desperately painful familial situation:

> It had occurred to Pecola some time ago that if her eyes, those eyes that held the pictures, and knew the sights—if those eyes of hers were different, that is to say, beautiful, she would be different. . . . If she looked different, beautiful, maybe Cholly would be different, and Mrs. Breedlove too. Maybe they'd say, "Why, look at pretty-eyed Pecola. We mustn't do bad things in front of those pretty eyes" . . .
>
> Each night, without fail, she prayed for blue eyes. Fervently, for a year she had prayed. Although somewhat discouraged, she was not without hope. To have something as wonderful as that happen would take a long, long time.

Like Mrs. Turner, Pecola realizes that patience is required if her dreams are to be realized.

In "Eruptions of Funk: Historicizing Toni Morrison," Susan Willis suggests that "[t]he problem at the center of Morrison's writing is how to maintain an Afro-American cultural heritage once the relationship to the black rural south has been stretched thin over distance and generations"[18] If Willis is correct about the primary focus of Morrison's work, then surely Pecola's reaction seems to be the result of her spatial and psychological distance from Black cultural survival mechanisms that have served to preserve Afro-American racial pride. But Pecola's difficulties notwithstanding, *The Bluest Eye* does suggest that this legacy—however perverse its manifestations—is alive in other members of Pecola's community. For despite the apparent compliance signalled by its reaction to white standards, this community's reactions do evidence a (silent) rejection of white myths.

The survival of Afro-American mechanisms of self-preservation can be noted, for example, in Claudia's description of the outcome of her search for the source of white beauty. She says that the impulse to dismember white dolls gives way to "The truly horrifying thing":

> . . . the transference of the same impulses to little white girls. The indifference with which I could have axed them was shaken only by my desire to do so. To discover what eluded me: the secret of the magic they weaved on others. What made people look at them and say, "Awwww," but not for me? . . .
>
> If I pinched them [little white girls], their eyes—unlike the crazed glint of the baby doll's eyes—would fold in pain, and their cry would not be the sound of an icebox door, but a fascinating cry of pain.

Claudia's somewhat sadistic dismemberment of white dolls and her subsequent torture of white girls is meant to recall, it seems to me, Bigger Thomas' axed mutilation of the dead body of Mary Dalton (presented by Richard Wright as a symbol of young white female beauty) in *Native Son*.[19] Morrison's refiguration of Wright's scene, as we shall see, is her means of adding her voice to the discourse surrounding Bigger's murder, the most renowned of which belongs to James Baldwin.

Claudia's impulses lend nominal weight to Baldwin's claim in "Many Thousands Gone" that "no Negro living in America . . . has not . . . wanted . . . to break the bodies of all white people and bring them low."[20] But while Baldwin suggests that such violent impulses are "urges of the cruelest vengeance" and motivated by "unanswerable hatred," Claudia's acts, while they are, in part, sadistic in nature (she apparently enjoys "the fascinating cry of pain" of her victims), are motivated in the main by a need to locate the source of a white physical superiority that is not immediately apparent to her. Baldwin believes that, in general, the Afro-American refusal to give in to such urges and "smash any white face he may encounter in a day" results from a noble embrace of humanity. He states:

> the adjustment [from desiring to attack whites physically to attempting peaceful coexistence with them] must be made—rather, it must be attempted, the tension perpetually suspended—for without this he [the Afro-American] has surrendered his birthright as a man no less than his birthright as a black man. The entire universe is then peopled only with his enemies, who are not only white men armed with rope and rifle, but his own far-flung and contemptible kinsmen. Their blackness is his degradation and it is their stupid and passive endurance which makes his end inevitable.

For Baldwin, such "adjustment" allows the Afro-American to claim (or reclaim) his humanity, a humanity which is, in Baldwin's words, "his birthright." This adjustment not only permits the Afro-American to demystify and de-villainize whites, but also to love his or her own people (a love of which, according to Baldwin, Bigger Thomas is incapable).

Claudia's "adjustment," however, has significantly different causes and consequences:

> When I learned how repulsive this disinterested violence [directed toward white girls] was, that it was repulsive because it was disinterested, my shame floundered about for refuge. The best hiding place was love. Thus the conversion from pristine sadism, to fabricated hatred, to fraudulent love. It was a small step to Shirley Temple. I learned much later to worship her . . . , knowing, even as I learned, that the change was *adjustment without improvement*. (my emphasis)

Claudia's "conversion" is motivated not by an embrace of humanity but, rather, by "shame." Apparently, the white-controlled societal forces that promote a single standard of beauty for which Claudia is attempting to find a rationale provide no sufficient answers to the questing marginal's quandaries about the origins of this standard. She learns only to feel ashamed of the curiosity that led to her "disinterested violence," and that her failure to accept without question the standards of white America is considered "repulsive."

Claudia terminates her search for the source of white myths and replaces the violent urges she had previously directed at whites with "fraudulent love." But the suppression of violent urges by Afro-Americans has significantly different implications for Morrison than for Baldwin. For Morrison, the Afro-American's humanity is not what is at stake, and "fraudulent love" of whites, the ultimate result of this rejection of violence, is not better or more authentically human. It is only different, only "adjustment" (an intentional repetition of Baldwin's terminology, it would appear) "without improvement."

The one feature that distinguishes Pecola (and her family) from the other Afro-Americans in the novel is the authenticity of her adoption of Western standards. The deeds of other characters—the adults' gifts of white dolls to black girls, "The eye slide of black women as [white girls] approached them on the street and the possessive gentleness of their touch as they handled them"—would appear to suggest an authentic love of whites and acceptance of white standards. But like Claudia's "fraudulent love," this apparent love is not real; rather, it is simply the response to "The Thing" that makes blacks feel guilt and shame about overt expression of Afro-American pride. In her provocative refiguration of Baldwin, Morrison implies that there is a wholesale Afro-American adoption of a self-protective mask. She suggests this further in her description of a group of boys who encircle Pecola and shout at her, "Black e mo. Black e mo. Yadaddsleepsnekked":

> They had extemporized a verse made up of two insults about matters over which the victim had no control: the color of her skin and speculations on the sleeping habits of an adult, wildly fitting in its incoherence. That they themselves were black, or that their own fathers had similarly relaxed habits was irrelevant. It was their contempt for their own blackness that gave the first insult its teeth. They seemed to have taken all of their *smoothly cultivated ignorance*, their *exquisitely learned self-hatred*, their *elaborately designed hopelessness* and sucked it all up into a fiery cone of scorn that had burned for ages in the hollows of their minds—cooled—and spilled over lips of outrage, consuming whatever was in its path. They danced a macabre ballet around the victim, whom, for their own sake, they were prepared to sacrifice to the flaming pit. (my emphasis)

This passage vividly suggests the pattern of mask wearing that permeates the Afro-American community depicted in *The Bluest Eye*. The existence of such masking helps the reader to comprehend the devastating effects on Pecola of the community's employment of her as scapegoat.

In her own view, as well as in that of the omniscient narrator, Pecola's appearance is not what distinguishes her from her black peers. Rather, she is held up as a figure of supreme ridicule strictly because, in her detachment from her cultural heritage, she exists unprotected from the disastrous effects of standards that she cannot achieve. She has not properly learned the rules of black (urban) life, or, rather, she has learned them too well. While other blacks pay *nominal* homage to the gods who created the standards by which America measures beauty and worth, and appear[,] as a consequence, to have "collected self-hatred by the heap," they actually maintain strong feelings of self-worth. They hide these feelings from gods who are interested only in surface—and not spiritual—devotion.

These people, in other words, represent a community that maintains, as does Janie in the face of Joe Starks' very similar tyranny in *Their Eyes Were Watching God*, the Afro-American survival technique of self-division. The community's worship at the altar of white beauty is only gesture, only acts "smoothly cultivated" to fool the master, to appease the gods. Because Pecola never learns of the potential benefits of masking and self-division in a white-dominated America, she represents a perfect target of scorn for the blacks who are armed with this knowledge. These Afro-Americans, in fact, use Pecola as ritual object in their ceremonies designed to exhibit to the master their "rejection" of blackness.

The Bluest Eye, then, can be said to concentrate on the factors which provoke Pecola's victimization in her own community. As we move through the seasonally cyclical, inverted world that is represented in Morrison's text, we see Pecola travel through various socioeconomic sectors of the community and be abused by each in turn. Only by understanding the specific provocations for the sacrifice of Pecola Breedlove can we comprehend the role of masking and double consciousness in the tragedy of the novel. Such an understanding will enable us to grasp the reasons that Morrison presents the (divided) Afro-American psyche as unhealed in the text's narrative events.

IV

The passage that depicts the apparent self-hatred of the boys who surround and taunt Pecola precisely suggests her role as scapegoat, a role that several critics have discussed in explications of *The Bluest Eye*. The study most devoted to such a reading of Morrison's text is Chikwenye Ogunyemi's "Order and Disorder in Toni Morrison's *The Bluest Eye*." While it is laced with inanities and facile misreadings of the text,[21] Ogunyemi's essay offers a sound analysis of the system of scapegoating operative in the novel. He states: "Running through the novel is the theme of the scapegoat: Geraldine's cat, Bob the dog, and Pecola are the scapegoats supposed to cleanse American society through their involvement in some violent rituals."[22] He goes on to insist that the abuse heaped upon Pecola—from the circle of taunting boys to her father's molestation of her—can be characterized, in each instance, as a ritual of purgation. Such purgation, or cleansing of the spiritual self, is evident in Claudia's eloquent conclusion of the text:

> All of our waste . . . we dumped on her and . . . she absorbed. And all of our
> beauty, which was hers first and which she gave to us. All of us—all who

knew her—felt so wholesome after we cleaned ourselves on her. We were so beautiful when we stood astride her ugliness. Her simplicity decorated us, her guilt sanctified us, her pain made us glow with health, her awkwardness made us think we had a sense of humor. . . . We honed our egos on her, padded our characters with her frailty, and yawned in the fantasy of our strength.

For my purposes here, a most helpful general discussion of the phenomenon of scapegoating which aids in the illumination of the motivations for such purgative abuse of Pecola is offered by Erich Neumann in *Depth Psychology and a New Ethic*. According to Neumann, scapegoating results from the necessity for the self and/or the community to rid itself of the "guilt-feeling" inherent in any individual or group failure to attain the "acknowledged values" of that group. This guilt feeling, or "shadow" as Neumann terms it, is discharged from the individual or communal self by means of:

the phenomenon of the projection of the shadow which cannot be accepted as a negative part of one's own psyche and is therefore . . . transferred to the outside world and is experienced as an outside object. It is combated, punished, and exterminated as "the alien out there" instead of being dealt with as "one's own inner problem."[23]

In combating the shadow that has been externalized and can, thus, be perceived as Other, the group is able to rid itself ceremonially of the evil that exists within both the individual member and the community at large. To be fully successful, such exorcism requires a visibly imperfect, shadow-consumed scapegoat:

evil can only be made conscious by being solemnly paraded before the eyes of the populace and then ceremoniously destroyed. The effect of purification is achieved by the process of making evil conscious through making it visible and by liberating the unconscious from this content through projection. On this level, therefore, evil, though not recognised by the individual as his own, is nevertheless recognised as evil. To put it more accurately, evil is recognised as belonging to the collective structure of one's own tribe and is eliminated in a collective manner . . .

Neumann's observations apply to "mass" or general man who, in his estimation, "cannot . . . acknowledge . . . 'his own evil' at all, since consciousness is still too weakly developed to be able to deal with the resulting conflict. It is for this reason," according to Neumann, "that evil is invariably experienced by mass man as something alien, and the victims of shadow projection are therefore, always and everywhere, the aliens."

Neumann goes on to suggest that minorities and aliens typically provide the objects for "the projection of the shadow." This projection is, for Neumann, "symptomatic of a split in the structure of the collective psyche." The self is split, in other words, into the good, desirable, unshadowed ideal self and the evil, undesirable, shadowed black self. Neumann argues that this division is motivated by:

unconscious feelings of guilt which arise, as a splitting phenomenon, from the formation of the shadow. It is our subliminal awareness that we are actually not good enough for the ideal values which have been set before us that results in the formation of the shadow; at the same time, however, it also leads to an unconscious feeling of guilt and to inner insecurity, since the shadow confutes the ego's pipedream that is identical with the ideal values.

Neumann's formulations of the scapegoat are richly suggestive in an analysis of both black-white relations and the difficulties inherent in an Afro-American sensibility that Du Bois characterizes as divided. For the Afro-American to split herself into shadow (evil, "black") and unshadowed (ideal, "American") selves, in a country which has traditionally viewed her as the (shadowed) personification of evil, is to invite such Afro-American self-contempt as is evident in *The Bluest Eye*. In circumstances where evil—which, for our purposes here, can be defined as a pronounced failure to achieve the ideal values and standards that have been set up by the tribe as exclusively desirable—must be eradicated from the community, that evil is often conceptualized both in the Euro-American psyche and in the divided Afro-American sensibility as the specifically and culturally black.

This eradication of black evil by whites is observable in such extreme instances as the lynching and mutilation of the genitals of black men under the guise of protecting white Southern womanhood. A milder (or, at least, less physically violent) intraracial form reveals itself in the passing for white of light-skinned blacks as depicted, for example, in James Weldon Johnson's *The Autobiography of an Ex-Coloured Man* and in Nella Larsen's *Passing*.[24] In both cases blackness, as a valuable human condition, is denied and destroyed. *The Bluest Eye* offers less extreme (perhaps), but nonetheless cogent examples of this hopelessly futile effort on the part of Afro-Americans to exorcize what the divided psyche often holds as the evil of blackness. Morrison's novel also vividly suggests the resultant scapegoating that occurs as a function of what Neumann terms "the projection of the shadow."

In Pecola's victimization at the hands of a circle of young black males, we see clear evidence of a projection of the shadow evil upon her. These boys' insults are described as a function of their ability to disregard their similarity to their victim; the verse they compose to belittle her ("Black e mo. . . . Yadaddsleepsnekked") reflects their own skin color and, quite possibly, familial situations. Claudia tells the reader of the boys' "smoothly cultivated ignorance": "That they themselves were black, or that their own father had similarly relaxed habits was irrelevant." This ignorance renders them incapable of recognizing the irony implicit in their castigation of Pecola by means of a verse that, because it chronicles the allegedly depraved conditions of their own lives, is also self-discrediting. This irony is lost to the boys because of the success of their projection of the shadow of blackness onto Pecola.

This manner of projection is also observable in Pecola's encounter with Geraldine and her son Junior. Morrison tells the reader that the most treasured bit of education that Geraldine has received has been:

> how to behave. The careful development of thrift, patience, high morals, and good manners. In short, *how to get rid of the funkiness*. The dreaded funkiness of passion, the funkiness of the wide range of human emotions.
>
> Whenever it erupts, this Funk, they [black women like Geraldine] wipe it away; where it crusts, they dissolve it; wherever it drips, flowers, or clings, they find it and fight it until it dies. They fight this battle all the way to the grave. The laugh that is a little bit too loud; the enunciation a little too round; the gesture a little too generous. They hold their behind in for fear of a sway too free; when they wear lipstick, they never cover the entire mouth for fear of lips too thick, and they worry, worry, worry about the edges of their hair. (my emphasis)

As I have mentioned earlier, Susan Willis argues that alienation—both in terms of "an individual's separation from his or her cultural center" as well as in the form of a frowning upon the natural Afro-American characteristics of kinky hair and thick lips—typifies the lives of Morrison's characters. For example, Willis says of Pecola's mother, Polly Breedlove:

> As a housemaid in a prosperous lakeshore home, Polly Breedlove lives a form of schizophrenia, where her marginality is constantly confronted with a world of Hollywood movies, white sheets and tender blond children. When at work or at the movies, she separates herself from her own kinky hair and decayed tooth. The tragedy of a woman's alienation is its effect on her role as mother. Her emotions split, she showers tenderness and love on her employer's child, and rains violence and disdain on her own.

Polly's self-division—characterized by Willis as "a form of schizophrenia" and as a "separat[ion from] herself"—is nowhere more poignantly exhibited than in the scene to which the critic alludes in which Pecola accidently spills a blueberry pie that her mother had made onto the newly cleaned floor of Polly's employer's kitchen. In the process, she frightens the young daughter of Polly's employer. Her mother's reaction indicates some of the consequences of her schizophrenia:

> Most of the [pie] juice splashed on Pecola's legs, and the burn must have been painful, for she cried out and began hopping about just as Mrs. Breedlove entered with a tightly packed laundry bag. In one gallop she was on Pecola, and with the back of her hand knocked her to the floor. Pecola slid in the pie juice, one leg folded under her. Mrs. Breedlove yanked her up by the arm, slapped her again, and in a voice thin with anger, abused Pecola. . . .
>
> "Crazy fool . . . my floor, mess . . . look what you . . . work . . . get on out . . . now that . . crazy . . . my floor, my floor." Her words were hotter and darker than the smoking berries.

Polly's reactions evidence no interest whatsoever in her own child's welfare, not a bit of concern about the berry burns that caused her to cry out in pain. Instead, she strikes Pecola, and displays infinitely more anxiety about the condition of "my floor" than about her daughter.

Further, her subsequent gentle soothing of her employer's crying child and attention to her soiled dress contrast—painfully—to her further besoiling of Pecola's dress and refusal to offer her daughter any parental—or even human—compassion. Most telling of all the occurrences in this scene is the interchange between Mrs. Breedlove and the white girl after Pecola (and the MacTeer sisters) depart:

> "Who were they, Polly?"
> "Don't worry none, baby."
> "You gonna make another pie?"
> "'Course, I will."
> "Who were they, Polly?"
> "Hush. Don't worry none," she whispered, and the honey in her words complemented the sundown spilling on the lake.

In addition to the clear contrast between Polly's reaction to the white girl and her daughter—"the honey in her words" to the employer's daughter as opposed to the smoking berry heat of her abuse of Pecola— this scene presents the maid's refusal to share with the white girl Pecola's identity because of her shame at being identified with the clumsy, pathetic girl who knocks the blueberry pie onto the floor.

The projection of the shadow, and its resultant scapegoating, then, can lead to the sacrifice of the black offspring, to parental detachment from the child, and to complete adoption of white standards as suggested by the "whispered . . . honey in [the] words" of Polly to the Fisher girl. Such projection can also inspire, as in the example of Geraldine, a futile effort to erase the black self entirely.

Geraldine desires to repress and deny "the funk," to exhibit no characteristically or stereotypically Afro-American qualities such as thick lips, nappy edges, and "rounded enunciation." To get rid of funkiness is, for Geraldine, to get rid of blackness and, in an America where blackness is equated with evil, to embrace the ideal national virtues of "thrift, patience, high morals, and good manners." To turn again to Neumann's discussion of scapegoating, we can conceptualize Geraldine's efforts as an attempt to exorcise the shadow of her own blackness. This energetic attempt to eliminate the funk does not allow her the pleasure of loving either her husband, whose sexual advances are unsatisfying inconveniences, or her son, whose emotional needs she meets with an affectionless efficiency.

So when she encounters Pecola in her house—this girl who represents for the entire community the literal embodiment of the shadow of blackness—and sees that the object of all her affection—her cat—is dead, Geraldine's reaction is one of a self-protective anger and horror. The text tells us:

> She looked at Pecola. Saw the dirty torn dress, the plaits sticking out on her head, hair matted where the plaits had come undone, the muddy shoes with the wad of gum peeping out from between the cheap soles, the soiled socks, one of which had been walked down into the heel of the shoe. . . . She had seen this little girl all of her life. . . . They [girls like Pecola] had stared at her with great uncomprehending eyes. Eyes that questioned nothing and asked everything. Unblinking and unabashed, they stared at her. The end of the world lay in their eyes, and the beginning, and all the waste in between. . . . Grass wouldn't grow where they lived. Flowers died. Shades fell down. . . . Like flies they hovered; like flies they settled. And this one had settled in her house.

For Geraldine, Pecola represents the repulsiveness of poverty, the vileness of blackness, the veritable eruption of funk. She equates Pecola with germ-infested pests, with flies that invade and soil carefully disinfected houses and elaborately prepared picnics. Pecola is everything that Geraldine is fighting to suppress. She is, for Geraldine, "funk," shadow, the blackness of blackness. When Geraldine tells Pecola to leave her house—"'Get out,' she said, her voice quiet. 'You nasty little black bitch. Get out of my house.'"—she is also, in effect, attempting to rid herself of her fears of her own evil, of her own unworthiness, of her own shadow of blackness.

Geraldine's efforts constitute, it seems to me, a splitting of herself into a good, moral, funkless self which she works diligently to maintain, and an evil, immoral, nappy-edged black self that she suppresses and attempts to expel. That this suppression and attempted exorcism of blackness render her incapable of enjoying life or of loving her family— or herself—seems to her a small price to pay for the warding off of the ignominy of an association with evil. Thus we see in Geraldine's characterization an example of defensive self-division similar to Janie's during her marriage to Joe Starks in *Their Eyes Were Watching God*. But while Janie, as I argued in the previous chapter, divided herself into inside and outside in order to hold on to the natural and to the culturally black, Geraldine's self-division is caused by her attempt to expel her natural "funkiness" or blackness.

With the examples of Geraldine and Polly, it becomes clear that, as is the case with Hurston's novel, an exploration of Du Boisian double consciousness is at the center of the narrative events depicted in *The Bluest Eye*. But, as in Hurston's text, Morrison's exploration of the Du Boisian formulation does not reflect an uncategorical acceptance of the older writer's views of the Afro-American psyche. According to Du Bois, the Afro-American seeks to ease the pain of participation in antithetical cultures by means of conflation of blackness and Americanness. He speaks, as I have noted, of an Afro-American

> longing . . . to merge his double self into a better and truer self. In this merging he wishes neither of the older selves to be lost. He would not Africanize America. . . . He would not bleach his Negro soul in a flood of white Americanism.[25]

Morrison presents evidence which disputes Du Bois' claims. Her characters' projections of the shadow of blackness, their unquestioning acceptance of American standards of beauty and morality, suggest that they have, indeed, bleached their black souls "in a flood of white Americanism." Theirs are not merged, but hopelessly divided selves, selves which attempt an erasure of blackness. In her exploration of divided and funk-rejected characters, Morrison both revises Du Bois and seems to refigure instances from Hurston's *Their Eyes Were Watching God*.

But while Geraldine's and Polly's shadow projections reflect suggestively the pattern of scapegoating in *The Bluest Eye*, they fail to attain the myriad symbolic implications of what must be considered the most deplorable and permanently damaging instance of scapegoating in the novel: Cholly's rape of his daughter Pecola. It is certainly possible to analyze Cholly Breedlove's incestuous act in ways that are similar to the above discussion of Geraldine and Polly: namely, as his attempt to relieve the persistent pain of the ignominy of his own sexual initiation by involving his daughter in an even more ignominious sexual act.[26] But such an analysis, while it might prove useful to a further elaboration of scapegoating in *The Bluest Eye*, would fail to address what seems to me to be the intertextually charged nature of Morrison's depiction of incest. In particular, I believe that Morrison is consciously (and *critically*) revising the Ellisonian depiction of incest in the Trueblood episode of *Invisible Man*. Her revision of Ellison, as the following discussion will attempt to demonstrate, provides particularly compelling evidence to support feminist claims about the power of feminist literary and critical texts to alter substantively our readings of male canonical works.

V

The Breedlove family in Morrison's text possesses a parodic relation to Ellison's incestuous clan. The relation is initially suggested in the names of the respective families. Ellison's designation suggests that the sharecropper and his family are the true (genuine) "bloods" (an Afro-American vernacular term for culturally immersed blacks). The Breedloves' name, however, is bestowed with bitter irony; theirs is a self-hating family in which no love is bred. In both texts, the economically destitute families are forced to sleep in dangerously close(d) quarters. In *Invisible Man* cold winters—and a lack of money with which to buy fuel—force the nubile Matty Lou into bed between her still-procreative parents. In the case of *The Bluest Eye*, Pecola sleeps in the same room as her parents, a proximity which necessitates her hearing the "Choking sounds and silence" of their lovemaking.

Further, there are stark similarities between mother and daughter in both texts which contribute to the incestuous act. In Ellison's novel, as Houston Baker argues in "To Move Without Moving: Creativity and Commerce in Ralph Ellison's Trueblood Episode" (about which I will have more to say below), the daughter Matty Lou is her mother "Kate's double—a woman who looks just like her mother and who is fully grown and sexually mature."[27] (On a night which Trueblood describes as "dark, plum black" such similarities would seem to have been a principle factor in the sharecropper's incestuous act.) And Cholly Breedlove's lust is awakened by Pecola's scratching of her leg in a manner that mirrored "what Pauline was doing the first time he saw her in Kentucky."

It is possible, with the above evidence in place, to begin to suggest the specifics of what seems to me to be Morrison's purposefully feminist revision. Read intertextually, *The Bluest Eye* provides—as I shall demonstrate below—an example par excellence of what the feminist critic Annette Kolodny has called "revisionary reading [that] open[s] new avenues for comprehending male texts."[28] The Ellisonian conceptualization of incest differse markedly from what, through the example of Morrison's text, it seems to represent for the female imagination. The gender-determined differences between the presentations of incest can, I believe, be successfully accounted for if we turn briefly at this point to contemporary feminist discussions of female reading of male canonical works.

One of the contemporary feminist criticism's initial goals was the analysis of the implications for women readers of the overwhelmingly male authored and oriented Western literary and critical canons. Among the best early examples of feminist readings of male literary works is Judith Fetterley's landmark study, *The Resisting Reader.* In her introduction to this study, Fetterley asserts her belief that women have historically been taught to read like men. Prior to the recent burgeoning of feminist criticism, the reading of the canon's decidedly phallocentric works such as (to cite examples which Fetterley uses) Ernest Hemingway's *A Farewell to Arms* and F. Scott Fitzgerald's *The Great Gatsby* encourages women's agreement with the inscribed antifemale slant of the works. Having been taught to accept the phallocentric as indisputably universal, the woman reader unconsciously internalizes the often-misogynistic messages of male texts. She loses, as a result, any faith in the validity of her own perceptions of life and, according to Fetterley, accepts male (mis)representation of women without protest. In short, she learns to read like a man: "In such [male] fictions the female reader is co-opted into participation in an experience from which she is explicitly excluded; she is asked to identify with a selfhood that defines itself in opposition to her; she is required to identify against herself."[29]

In the face of such derogative and self-negating instruction, a female must, in order to successfully participate as a woman in the reading experience, "become a resisting rather than an assenting reader and, by this refusal to assent, . . . begin the process of exorcizing the male mind that has been implanted" in women. The removal of the male implant results, for Fetterley, in "the capacity for what Adrienne Rich describes as re-vision—'the act of looking back, of seeing with fresh eyes, of entering an old text from a new critical direction.'" Feminist re-vision, according to Fetterley, offers the terms of a radically altered critical enterprise and the liberation of the critic: "books will . . . lose their power to bind us unknowingly to their designs."

Houston Baker's "To Move Without Moving" represents an excellent example in support of Fetterley's view of the (sometimes dangerously) persuasive powers of texts. For in this essay, the critical canon's most elaborate explication of the Trueblood episode of *Invisible Man*, we can observe the power of texts quite literally to bind even the most intellectually nimble readers/critics to their designs. Baker's unquestionably provocative recent study *Blues, Ideology, and Afro-American Literature* (in which the analysis of the Trueblood section appears) exhibits, particularly in a stunning reading of the economics of female slavery and the figuration of a community of female slaves in Linda Brent's *Incidents in the Life of a Slave Girl*,[30] his awareness of the ways in which feminist theory can help illuminate literary texts. This sensitivity to feminist concerns is, unfortunately, missing from his readings of Ellison. Instead, Baker's essay mirrors the strategies by which Trueblood (and Trueblood's creator) validates male perceptions of incest while, at the same time, silencing the female voice or relegating it to the evaluative periphery.

Baker's begins his reading by citing Ellison's discussion in the essay "Richard Wright's Blues" of "The function, the psychology, of artistic selection."[31] This function, according to the novelist, "is to eliminate from art form all those elements of experience which contain *no compelling significance*."[32] While Baker cites this statement by Ellison, for undoubtedly significant reasons—to suggest, ultimately, an essential parallel between Ellison and his folk artist creation Trueblood—his choice provides a means to discuss the shortcomings of his own and Ellison's treatments of the subject of incest.

If it is accurate to perceive of the artistic process as an act of omission of insignificant life experiences, then it is equally true that the critical process consists, in part, of elimination from consideration those elements of the literary text that are without significant ideological or symbolic import. While I wish to avoid straying too far into issues of relativism that have been masterfully debated by others, Ellison's statements, situated as they are in Baker's essay, lead (I think necessarily) to an inquiry as to why neither Ellison's text nor Baker's critique of it treat the female perspective on and reaction to incest as containing any "compelling significance."

In the case of the novel, Trueblood's incestuous act is judged almost exclusively by men. This male judgment is offered by a cast which includes the black school administrators who wish to remove the sharecropper from the community and Trueblood's white protectors who pressure the administrators to allow the sharecropper to remain in his home and who "wanted to hear about the gal [Matty Lou] lots of times." They form, as it were, an exclusively male evaluative circle which views Trueblood's act as either shamefully repugnant (as in the case of the black college administrators and the black preacher) or meritoriously salacious (as in the case of the white protectors who provide Trueblood and his family with material goods).

Except for the mother Kate's memorably violent reaction to seeing her husband atop their daughter, the female perspective on Trueblood's act is effectively silenced and relegated to the periphery in the sharecropper's recounting of the story. Just as the Trueblood women run to the back of the cabin upon the approach of the car bearing Mr. Norton and the unnamed protagonist of *Invisible Man*, so, too do Matty Lou's and the town's doubtlessly unified female community's emotional responses to the incestuous act remain (conveniently, it would seem) out of the reader's sight. Never in Trueblood's rendering of the story are Matty Lou's feelings foregrounded or even actually shared with the reader. Further, Trueblood is well aware of the silent scorn that the women who help Kate attend to the unconscious Matty Lou bear for him. When he returns home after an exile precipitated, in his view, by the inability of others to distinguish between "blood-sin" and "dream-sin," he orders the scornful community of women that has formed in response to his "dirty lowdown wicked dog" act off of his property: "There's a heap of women here with Kate and I runs 'em out." Having effectively run out the openly critical female community and silenced, by means of his abominable act, his wife and daughter, Trueblood is able to interpret his act in an extremely self-serving way, untroubled by the radically incompatible perspectives of women. He can assert, for example, that the reason "Matty Lou won't look at me and won't speak a word to nobody" is that she is ashamed to be pregnant. And he can, despite his belief that he is a good family man, fail to see the bitter irony in his assessment of his family situation: "Except that my wife an' daughter won't speak to me, I'm better off than I ever been before."

From a feminist perspective, Baker's reading of the Trueblood episode proves as problematic as the sharecropper's because he, too, relegates the woman's voice to the evaluative periphery and sketches his own circle of male to justify and validate the sharecropper's act. Through an imaginative employment of male voices of authority from Freud to Victor Turner and Clifford Geertz, Baker asserts that one of the dominant themes of *Invisible Man* is "black male sexuality." He speaks salutarily of the (re)productive energy of the black male phallus in

Trueblood's tale: "The black phallus—in its creative, ambulant, generative power, even under conditions of castration—is like the cosmos itself, a self-sustaining and self-renewing source of life." It is in terms of Trueblood's phallic "generative power" that Baker discusses the symbolic import of the sharecropper's incestuous act:

> The cosmic force of the phallus thus becomes, in the ritual action of the Trueblood episode, symbolic of a type of royal paternity, an aristocratic procreativity turned inward to ensure the royalty (the "truth," "legitimacy" or "authenticity") of an enduring black line of descent. In his outgoing phallic energy, therefore, the sharecropper is . . . indeed, a "hard worker" who takes care of "his family needs." . . . His family may, in a very real sense, be construed as the entire clan or "tribe" that comprises Afro-America.

Baker invokes an almost exclusively male chorus to support his reading of the Trueblood episode. He cites, for example, Geertz's discussion of the Balinese conception of "self-operating penises, ambulant genitals with a life of their own"[33] in order to corroborate the sharecropper's statements which indicate the "natural unpredictability" of male arousal. He also cites Freud's speculations about incest which argue that prehistorical man "established a taboo on sexual intercourse with the women of their own clan" in order to "prevent discord among themselves and to ensure their newly achieved form of social organization." While statements from Geertz and Freud help Baker to substantiate points about the uncontrollability of phallic energy and about Trueblood's dream signalling a historical regression (points which support the sharecropper's claim that he cannot be blamed for his "dream-sin"), they fail, because they invoke worlds in which women are indisputably at the mercy of the phallic and legislative powers of men, to allow the critic to consider the response of the victim to her father's act.

And though Baker makes a valiant effort to endow the hastily considered Matty Lou with positive qualities, viewing her—along with her mother—as one of the "bearers of new black life," she remains in the critic's interpretation of the episode—as she does in the sharecropper's narrative—simply an absence. While Baker's essay adds immeasurably to our understanding of Ellison's art and of the sharecropper as vernacular artist, it fails, unfortunately, to consider the subsequently silenced victim of Trueblood's unrestrained phallus. Only by failing to grapple seriously with the implications of Trueblood's representation of Matty Lou's state following the incestuous act—"Matty Lou won't look at me and won't speak a word to nobody"—can Baker conceive at the consequences of the taboo-breaking act as generally beneficial.

Unlike Baker's reading of the Trueblood episode of *Invisible Man* in which incest is conceptualized as material and tribal gain, Morrison's revision depicts it as painfully devastating loss. Actually, her reading of Ellison's text must be remarkably similar to Baker's, for in refiguring

Trueblood in the character of Cholly Breedlove, she surrounds her creation with images consistent with the critic's conception of the Ellisonian
character as majestic Afro-American vernacular artist free from social
restraints. Morrison says of her character:

> Only a musician would sense, know, without even knowing that he knew, that
> Cholly was free. Dangerously free. Free to feel whatever he felt—fear, guilt,
> shame, love, grief, pity. Free to be tender or violent, to whistle or weep. . . .
> He was free to live his fantasies, and free even to die, the how and the when
> of which held no interest for him . . .
> It was in this godlike state that he met Pauline Williams.

Only an Afro-American artist with the blues sensibility that Baker argues for Trueblood can organize and transform into meaningfully unified
expression the utter chaos of Cholly's life. But Morrison—the remarkably skilled novelist who does transform Cholly's life into art—provides
the blues song that is *The Bluest Eye* with a decidedly feminist slant.
For while Ellison furnished his depiction of incest with a vocabulary of
naturalism and historical regression that permit it to be read in relation
to undeniably phallocentric sociocultural interpretations of human history, Morrison's representation is rendered in what are, for a writer
with Morrison's lyrical gift, startlingly blunt terms.

Trueblood's presence inside his sexually inexperienced daughter's vagina is described in ways that suggest a significant symbolic import. The
sharecropper's dream of sexual contact with a white woman while in the
home of an affluent white man necessarily brings to mind images of
lynching and castration of Afro-American males by white men because
of the threat of black male sexuality. Consequently, Trueblood's actual
presence inside his daughter assumes less importance in the text than
his dream encounter with an unnamed white woman. Morrison, however,
provides her depiction of incest with no such historically symbolic significance:

> [Cholly's] mouth trembled at the firm sweetness of the flesh. He closed his
> eyes, letting his fingers dig into her waist. The rigidness of her shocked body,
> the silence of her stunned throat, was better than Pauline's easy laughter had
> been. The confused mixture of his memories of Pauline and the doing of a
> wild and forbidden thing excited him, and a bolt of desire ran down his geni-
> tals, giving it length, and softening the lips of his anus. Surrounding all of
> this lust was a border of politeness. He wanted to fuck her—tenderly. But
> the tenderness would not hold. The tightness of her vagina was more than he
> could bear. His soul seemed to slip down to his guts and fly out into her, and
> the gigantic thrust he made into her then provoked the only sound she made—
> a hollow suck of air in the back of her throat.

Cholly is far from the majestic figure that Baker argues for Trueblood
during his efforts to "move without movin'" in his daughter's vagina.
And though Morrison does endow the incestuous male figure with the
capacity for sympathy—citing, for example, the "border of politeness"

that accompanies his lust—Cholly's "wild," "confused" act lacks the in-scribed symbolic weight of Trueblood's transgression. While the share-cropper's inability to withdraw from his daughter's vagina represents, according to Baker, Trueblood's "say[ing] a resounding 'no' to castrat-ingly tight spots of his existence as a poor farmer in the undemocratic south," the tight sexual space represents for Cholly the forbidden area that must be forcibly entered and exited. The text of *The Bluest Eye* informs us: "Removing himself from her was so painful to him he cut it short and snatched his genitals out of the dry harbor of her vagina."

Morrison, finally, seems to be taking Ellison to task for the phallocen-tric nature of his representation of incest which marginalizes and renders as irrelevant the consequences of the act for the female victim. *The Bluest Eye* serves as a revisionary reading of the Trueblood episode of *Invisible Man*. Morrison writes her way into the Afro-American literary tradition by foregrounding the effects of incest for female victims in direct response to Ellison's refusal to consider them seriously. And so while the victims of incest in both novels ultimately occupy similarly silent, asocial positions in their respective communities, Morrison explic-itly details Pecola's tragic and painful journey, while Ellison, in confining Matty Lou to the periphery, suggests that her perspective contains for him "no compelling significance."

Unlike Ellison, Zora Neale Hurston is immensely interested in exposing patriarchy's inherent oppressiveness. In the following discus-sion, I will offer an intertextual reading of *The Bluest Eye* and *Their Eyes Were Watching God* in order to suggest the ways in which Hurston's text can be seen as a direct, "benevolent" precursor to Morrison's first novel. Material for such a claim can be most clearly observed in a further analysis of Pecola and of the text's narrative straegies.

VI

One way to begin to analyze the intertextual relationship between Hurs-ton's and Morrison's texts is to compare the titles of the novels. Henry Louis Gates, Jr. has suggested in "The Blackness of Blackness" that such an interpretive strategy leads to a full understanding of Ellison's signifying, in *Invisible Man*, on his precursor Wright. He asserts:

> [Ellison's] signifying . . . starts with the titles: Wright's *Native Son* and *Black Boy*, titles connoting race, self and presence, Ellison tropes with *Invisible Man*, invisibility an ironic response, of absence, to the would-be presence of "blacks" and "natives," while "man" suggests a more mature and stronger status than either "son" or "boy."[34]

It is similarly possible to chart a relationship between *The Bluest Eye* and *Their Eyes Were Watching God* by analyzing their respective titles.

"Their eyes were watching God" connotes a communal observation of the wondrously curious acts of a god who is undeniably present in the world; "the bluest eye" implies loneliness (the single "eye"/I), blueness in the Afro-American vernacular sense, and implicitly suggests that solitude—distance from the tribe—is a function of aspirations for the non-black, for blue eyes. In other words, Pecola's (and, I would argue, Geraldine's and Polly's) status as "The bluest I" results from her adoption of white standards of perception. Hurston's title and text, then, suggest a common, culturally based method of (non-Western) perception of the world. Morrison's, on the other hand, imply solitude, distance from the group and, consequently, a means of viewing the world that is at odds with the Afro-American cultural heritage.

Morrison's apparent refigurations of Hurston's text are further observable in her various uses of nature in *The Bluest Eye*. Janie's fate is intricately bound to nature: the pear tree image dominates Hurston's novel. What is arguably the most important scene in the first half of the novel is Janie's education under the tutelage of a voice-capable nature which teaches her about natural marriage. Her improving self-image and defensive self-division are possible only when she rediscovers nature. Janie's remarkable harmony with nature stands in direct contrast to Pecola's natural discord. While the sexual awakening of Hurston's heroine occurs in the spring and corresponds with natural reproductive cycles, Pecola's sexual maturation, signaled by the commencement of her menstruation, occurs in the fall during a brief stay in the MacTeer household. The beginnings of both protagonists' physical maturity occasion inquiries about love and marriage. Janie's questions are answered by an instructive nature:

> She saw a dust-bearing bee sink into the sanctum of a bloom; the thousand sister-calyxes arch to meet the love embrace and the ecstatic shiver of the tree from root to tiniest branch creaming in every blossom and frothing with delight. So this was a marriage! She had been summoned to behold a revelation.

Pecola, on the other hand, finds no answers in a family where love is not bred or in a northern city where she has little or no access to nature or to the wisdom of her culture. Just as Nanny reads signs of Janie's maturation into her kiss by Johnny Taylor, so too, do Frieda and Claudia view the menstruating Pecola as "grown-up-like." But this physical maturity is not accompanied by a fuller knowledge of the workings of her own body or of love and marriage, as Pecola's questions to her temporary bedmates suggest:

> After a long while [Pecola] spoke very softly. "Is it true that I can have a baby now?"
> "Sure," said Frieda drowsily. "Sure you can."
> "But . . . how?" Her voice was hollow with wonder.
> "Oh," said Frieda, "somebody has to love you."

"Oh."

There was a long pause in which Pecola and I thought this over. It would involve, I supposed, "my man," who, before leaving me, would love me. But there weren't any babies in the songs my mother sang. Maybe that's why the women were sad: the men left before they could make a baby.

Then Pecola asked a question that had never entered my mind. "How do you do that? I mean, how do you get somebody to love you?" But Frieda was asleep. And I didn't know.

Answers to Pecola's quandries are unavailable. Having never felt the love of anyone, she has no idea how to "get somebody to love" her. When she ponders how romantic adult love might be manifested, the only example available is that of her bickering parents. She wonders if their relationship represents the norm:

What did love feel like? she wondered. How do grown-ups act when they love each other? . . . Into her eyes came the picture of Cholly and Mrs. Breedlove in bed. He making sounds as though he were in pain, as though something had him by the throat and wouldn't let go. Terrible as his noises were, they were not nearly as bad as the no noise at all from her mother. It was as though she was not even there. Maybe that was love. Choking sounds and silence.

In contrast to Janie's instruction where she is able to observe the "love embrace" of elements of nature, Pecola has as her only example the "Choking sounds and silence" of her parents' sexual intercourse. Thus, while Janie gains valuable information about marriage during the period of sexual awakening, Pecola acquires only misinformation: that love must necessarily be characterized solely by pain and absence. It is possible, then, to perceive of Pecola's fate—at least with respect to her sexual awakening—as directly contrasting that of Janie. Such contrast is further observable in a more elaborate discussion of the authors' presentation of nature in their respective texts.

Phyllis Klotman argues that "nature serves as the unifying element in the novel."[35] It is true that, in terms of its strategies of narration, Morrison's text employs nature's seasons to provide *The Bluest Eye* with a sense of unity and wholeness. But nature here is represented as being at best indifferent to man. Claudia's first words in the novel suggest nature's apathy where humanity is concerned:

Quiet as it's kept, there were no marigolds in the fall of 1941. We thought, at the time, that it was because Pecola was having her father's baby that the marigolds did not grow. A little examination and much less melancholy would have proved to us that our seeds were not the only ones that did not sprout; nobody's did. Not even the gardens fronting the lake showed marigolds that year. But so deeply concerned were we with the health and safe delivery of Pecola's baby we could think of nothing but our own magic: if we planted the seeds, and said the right words over them, they would blossom, and everything would be all right. . . . For years I thought my sister was right: it was my fault. I had planted them too far down in the earth. It never occurred to

> either of us that the earth itself might have been unyielding. . . . What is
> clear now is that of all of that hope, fear, lust, love, and grief, nothing remains
> but Pecola and the unyielding earth.

Claudia's prefatory remarks imply an affinity between Pecola and the
"unyielding earth," but it is one based on their common unpreparedness
for reproduction. Nothing, not even the MacTeer girls' amateurish acts
of conjuring, can encourage the barren earth to stimulate the growth of
marigold seeds. The barren earth of Lorain, Ohio, directly contrasts with
the actively reproductive nature of the young Janie's backyard in which
the protagonist of *Their Eyes Were Watching God* observes the potential
of "ecstatic shiver[s]" in natural marriage.

Another contrast between the two novels is observable in Morrison's
apparent revision of the optimism inherent in Tea Cake's final gift to
Janie. After she kills him in self-defense, Janie finds among her third
husband's belongings a package of seeds. She plans to plant these seeds
outside her Eatonville home:

> The seeds reminded Janie of Tea Cake more than anything else because he
> was always planting things. She had noticed them on the kitchen shelf when
> she came home from the funeral and had put them in her breast pocket. Now
> that she was home, she meant to plant them for remembrance.

By planting the seeds, Janie will ensure that her memory of Tea Cake—
whose given name, Verigible Woods, indicates his intense affinity with
nature—will never die. In *Their Eyes Were Watching God*, the planting
of seeds serves as a means of preserving life. Hurston's text ends with
the suggestion that such preservation is indeed possible: "Tea Cake came
prancing around her where she was and the song of the sigh flew out of
the window and lit on the top of the pine trees. . . . Of course he wasn't
dead. He could never be dead until she herself had finished feeling and
thinking."

Morrison's text appears to revise Hurston's use of seeds, insisting
that the natural world of the North has no ability (or desire) to save or
preserve human life. The planting of seeds in *The Bluest Eye* serves to
demonstrate not nature's harmony with humanity and the possibility of
preserving (at least the memory of) life, but, rather, a barren earth's
indifference to humanity's needs.

Nevertheless, as I have shown, Pecola is continually associated with
domesticated animals who are themselves employed by members of *The
Bluest Eye*'s black community as scapegoats. But, just as she is associated with nonhuman entities such as dogs, cats, and "the unyielding
earth," she is also connected metaphorically to birds. For example, after
her encirclement by the boys and Maureen Peal's unexpected attack,
Claudia says of Pecola: "She seemed to fold into herself, like a pleated
wing." This bird-like response to abuse recalls Nanny's explanation to
Janie of the diligence of her efforts to move from the white Washburn
family's property and purchase her own home:

Ah raked and scraped and bought dis lil piece uh land so you woudn't have to stay in de white folks' yard and *tuck yo' head* befo' other chillun at school. . . . *Ah don't want yo' feathers always crumpled by folks throwin' up things in yo' face.* (my emphasis)

Nanny's loving sacrifice is an effort to keep her granddaughter from suffering the ignominy of being perceived by the black community as a white folks' nigger, as an Afro-American who is influenced and controlled by a white perception of reality.

Pecola's tragic plight, on the other hand, stems primarily from her inability to achieve a positive reading of blackness in an urban setting dominated by pervasive white standards. Stuck in "de white folks' yard" of self-promotional propaganda, and unable to liberate herself from the oppressive influence of white American standards, Pecola cannot, unlike Milkman Dead in Morrison's *Song of Solomon*, "give up the shit that weighs [her] down" and "surrender . . . to the air."[36] This pervasive whiteness, coupled with her victimization at the hands of self-protective Afro-Americans who view her as the shadow of blackness, causes her almost literally to transform into the type of victimized bird that Nanny's efforts save her granddaughter from becoming. As the narrative continues, Pecola is represented as a grotesque, flightless bird:

> The damage done [by the community's abuse] was total. She spent her days, her tendril, sap-green days, walking up and down, up and down, her head jerking to the beat of a drummer so distant only she could hear. Elbows bent, hands on shoulders, she flailed her arms like a bird in an eternal, grotesquely futile effort to fly. Beating the air, a winged but grounded bird, intent on the blue void it could not reach—could not even see—but which filled the valleys of the mind.

She remains tragically tied to white standards of beauty and is, even in her insanity, striving for "the blue void . . . [she] could not reach."

VII

The result of Pecola's victmization by her own community is a tragic schizophrenia, a psychotic double voicedness. This double voicedness results from her belief that she has been granted the beauty that she believes accompanies blue eyes. After her rape by her father and her encounter with the misanthropic Soaphead Church (which she believes concludes with her achievement of blue eyes), Pecola manufactures a friend in order to validate her newfound beauty.

Perhaps the greatest significance of Pecola's self-division to a discussion of the relation of Morrison's text to the Afro-American literary tradition is as a revision of Du Bois' conceptualization of the Afro-American psyche. For Pecola clearly loses the battle—as Du Bois conceives of it—to conflate in her person blackness and Americanness. Her loss is reflected in her schizophrenic confirmation of the beauty of (unachieved) blue eyes and in her total rejection of blackness. And so while Janie's divided consciousness healed at the conclusion of *Their Eyes Were Watching God* to the point that she is able to "pull . . . in her horizon . . . from around the waist of the world and drape . . . it over her shoulder" as a symbol of her self-unity and unity with the natural world, Pecola, burdened as she is with a permanently and debilitatingly dissociated sensibility, is depicted as involved in a futile effort to achieve the unreachable, imperceptible "blue void."

Pecola's splitting into two voices corresponds directly to the two-voiced narration of *The Bluest Eye*. The text of Morrison's novel has been narrated by two distinct voices: by Claudia and by an omniscient presence. For the greater part of the novel, these voices are in their focus and levels of emotional involvement in the matters they relate unquestionably distinct from one another. Claudia, who narrates the first chapter in each section of the novel, relates matters about her own life and that of her family, as well as information concerning Pecola about which she knows firsthand: her own dismemberment of white dolls; Mr. Henry's fondling of her sister; Mrs. Breedlove's abuse of her daughter in the Fischer home; and her sister's and her own attempts to save Pecola's baby. On the other hand, the omniscient narrator, whose voice controls the chapters that Claudia does not narrate, conveys pertinent information about the histories of characters much older than Claudia, as well as information about Pecola of which Claudia could not possibly be aware: Cholly's reaction to the white hunters who discover him and Darlene in the woods; Polly's fascination with movies; Geraldine's attempts to suppress the funkiness of passion; Cholly's motivation for raping his daughter; and Pecola's schizophrenic discussion with herself.

But after the onset of Pecola's schizophrenic double voicedness, the distinctive narrative voices of *The Bluest Eye* apparently merge into a single voice. Suddenly Claudia is privy to information which she clearly could have learned only from the omniscient narrator. She plainly comprehends, for example, the complex ritual of scapegoating in which the entire community has involved Pecola:

> All of us . . . felt so wholesome after we cleaned ourselves on her. . . . Her inarticulateness made us believe we were eloquent. Her poverty kept us generous. Even her waking dreams we used—to silence our own nightmares. And she let us, and thereby deserved our contempt. We honed our eyes on her, padded our characters with her frailty, and yawned in the fantasy of our strength.

She is informed, further, of Pecola's desire for blue eyes—information that Pecola has shared only with God and with her imaginary friend— and of the Maginot Line's love for the abused protagonist. Claudia also knows the specifics of Cholly's incestuous act, and speaks of its motivation in the same terms as the omniscient narrator: as a function of his freedom.

> Cholly loved her [Pecola]. I'm sure he did. He, at any rate, was the only one who loved her enough to touch her, envelop her, give something of himself to her. But his touch was fatal, and the something he gave her filled the matrix of her agony with death. Love is never any better than the lover. Wicked people love wickedly, violent people love violently, weak people love weakly, stupid people love stupidly, but the love of a free man is never safe. There is no gift for the beloved. The lover alone possesses his gift of love.

Not only, then, does Claudia's voice occupy the position previously reserved for the omniscient narrator, it also evidences a scope and breadth of knowledge that had heretofore belonged only to that omniscient voice.

This merging of narrative voices recalls Janie's memorable phrase when she assigns to Phoeby the role of narrator of her story to the Eatonville community: "mah tongue is in mah friend's mouf." It does indeed appear that the scope of the omniscient narrator's knowledge has, in the concluding pages of *The Bluest Eye*, been imparted to Claudia, that the last paragraphs of the novel evidence the conflation of their voices, of their "tongues." But the situation of such a conflation of narrative voices suggests that this healing of double voicedness occurs as a direct function of Pecola's own schizophrenia. Just as the improved self-image of the community depicted in Morrison's text results from its sacrifice and projection of the shadow of blackness onto Pecola, so, too, it seems, can a healed narrative double voicedness be achieved only through the sacrifice of the female protagonist in the novel's narrative events. The sacrifice of Pecola—a young girl who measures her own worth in terms of idealized white standards of beauty and morality, and goes mad as a result—is, it would appear, necessary for the achievement of the Afro-American expressive ideal of merged consciousness, of unified voice.

Despite its undoubtedly tragic conclusion, *The Bluest Eye* can be said to serve as another illustration of the Afro-American enterprise devoted to the *denigration* of the genre of the novel. Morrison's successful *denigration* of the form is accomplished not simply in her employment of dual narrative voices, but, especially, in the ultimate merging of these voices in the conclusion of her text. And so while she can depict healed consciousness as a possibility for any of the characters of *The Bluest Eye* only through the example of Claudia (whose subsequent achieved black consciousness enables her to serve as a narrator of the novel), Morrison has, through her manipulation of the white voice of the primer, through her apparent revisions of precursor texts, and through her depiction of narrative voices as ultimately conjoined, added to the Afro-American literary canon another supreme example of a Genuine Black Book.

Notes

1. Toni Morrison, "Behind the Making of *The Black Book*," *Black World*, February 1974, p. 89.
2. Toni Morrison, *The Bluest Eye* (New York: Washington Square Press, 1970), p. 157.
3. Toni Morrison, "Rootedness: The Ancestor as Foundation," *Black Women Writers (1950–1980)*, Mari Evans, ed. (New York: Doubleday, 1984), p. 343.
4. See Wright's *Native Son* (New York: Harper and Row, 1940) and *Black Boy* (New York: Harper and Row, 1945), and Baldwin's *Go Tell It on the Mountain* (New York: Dell, 1953) and the title essay of *Notes of a Native Son* (New York: Bantam, 1955), pp. 71–95.
5. See the famous essays "Everybody's Protest Novel" and "Many Thousands Gone" in *Notes of a Native Son*, pp. 9–17 and 18–36 respectively.
6. James Baldwin, "Alas, Poor Richard," *Nobody Knows My Name* (New York: Dial, 1961), p. 197.
7. "Strong" is Harold Bloom's term for discursively and tropologically competitive poets whose strength suggests itself in a willingness to battle influential precursors. See Bloom's extremely "influential" study *The Anxiety of Influence* (New York: Oxford University Press, 1973) for the critic's initial definitions of poetic strength.
8. Phyllis Klotman, "Dick-and-Jane and the Shirley Temple Sensibility in *The Bluest Eye*," *Black American Literature Forum* (1979), 13(4):123.
9. Raymond Hedin, "The Structuring of Emotion in Black American Fiction," *Novel* (1982), 161(1):123.
10. Robert Stepto, *From Behind the Veil* (Urbana: University of Illinois Press, 1979).
11. *Black Women Writers at Work*, Claudia Tate, ed. (New York: Continuum, 1983), p. 122.
12. Ralph Ellison, "The World and the Jug," *Shadow and Act* (New York: Vintage, 1964), p. 140.
13. Nikki Giovanni, "Nikka-Rosa," *Black Feelings, Black Talk, Black Judgment* (New York: William Morrow, 1970), pp. 58–59.
14. Victor Turner, *Dramas, Fields, and Metaphors* (Ithaca: Cornell University Press, 1974), p. 233.
15. See Jacqueline De Weever, "The Inverted World of Toni Morrison's *The Bluest Eye* and *Sula*," *College Language Association Journal* (1979), 22(4):402.
16. Ralph Ellison, *Invisible Man* (New York: Vintage, 1952).
17. Zora Neale Hurston, *Their Eyes Were Watching God*, 1937 (Urbana: University of Illinois Press, 1978), p. 216.
18. Susan Willis, "Eruptions of Funk: Historicizing Toni Morrison," *Black Literature and Literary Theory*, Henry Louis Gates, Jr., ed. (New York: Methuen, 1984), p. 264.
19. See *Native Son*, pp. 89–91.
20. James Baldwin, "Many Thousands Gone," p. 30.
21. Most significant of the flaws in Ogunyemi's essay is the critic's suggestion that Morrison "has fictionalized those sociological factors discussed in [Calvin] Hernton's *Sex and Racism in America* without first distancing herself enough from that work." In "Order and Disorder in Toni Morrison's *The Bluest Eye*," *Critique* (1977), 19(1):118. This comment implies that Mor-

rison—like the African critic—needs Hernton's text to explain to her the nature of sexism and racism in America. Also see his discussions of Mrs. MacTeer's "hyprocrisy" vis-à-vis her permitting Pecola to live in the Mac-Teer household temporarily, and his view that the family "merely tolerated her."

22. Chikwenye Ogunyemi, "Order and Disorder in Toni Morrison's *The Bluest Eye*," *Critique*, p. 116.
23. Erich Neumann, *Depth Psychology and a New Ethic*, 1949 (New York: Putnam, 1969), p. 50.
24. See James Weldon Johnson, *The Autobiography of an Ex-Colored Man, 1912 (New York: Hill and Wang, 1960)* and Nella Larsen, *Passing*, in *Quicksand and Passing*, Deborah McDowell, ed. 1929 (New Brunswick, N.J.: Rutgers University Press, 1986).
25. W. E. B. Du Bois, *The Souls of Black Folk*, 1903 (New York: Signet, 1969), p. 45.
26. See the description of Cholly's interrupted sexual initiation, *The Bluest Eye*, pp. 114–21.
27. Houston A. Baker, Jr., *Blues, Ideology, and Afro-American Literature* (Chicago: University of Chicago Press, 1984), p. 185.
28. Annette Kolodny, "The Map of Rereading," *The New Feminist Criticism*, Elaine Showalter, ed. (New York: Pantheon, 1985), p. 59.
29. Judith Fetterley, *The Resisting Reader* (Bloomington: Indiana University Press, 1978), p. xii.
30. *See Blues, Ideology, and Afro-American Literature*, pp. 50–56.
31. Ralph Ellison, "Richard Wright's Blues," *Shadow and Act*, p. 94.
32. "Richard Wright's Blues," p. 94, my emphasis.
33. Clifford Geertz, *The Interpretation of Cultures* (New York: Basic Books, 1973), p. 417.
34. Henry Louis Gates, Jr., "The Blackness of Blackness: A Critique of the Sign and the Signifying Monkey," *Black Literature and Literary Theory*, p. 293.
35. Phyllis Klotman, "Dick-and-Jane and the Shirley Temple Sensibility in *The Bluest Eye*," p. 125.
36. Toni Morrison, *Song of Solomon* (New York: Signet, 1977), pp. 169, 341.

◆◆◆◆◆◆◆◆◆◆◆◆◆◆

A Hateful Passion, a Lost Love

HORTENSE J. SPILLERS

> When I think of how essentially alone black women have been—alone
> because of our bodies, over which we have had so little control; alone because
> the damage done to our men has prevented their closeness and protection;
> and alone because we have had no one to tell us stories about ourselves; I
> realize that black women writers are an important and comforting presence
> in my life. Only they know my story. It is absolutely necessary that they be
> permitted to discover and interpret the entire range and spectrum of the
> experience of black women and not be stymied by preconceived conclusions.
> Because of these writers, there are more models of how it is possible for us
> to live, there are more choices for black women to make, and there is a larger
> space in the universe for us.[1]

Toni Morrison's *Sula* is a rebel idea, both for her creator[2] and for Morrison's audience. To read *Sula* is to encounter a sentimental education so sharply discontinuous from the dominant traditions of Afro-American literature in the way that it compels and/or deadlocks the responses that the novel, for all its brevity and quiet intrusion on the landscape of American fiction, is, to my mind, the single most important irruption of black women's writing in our era. I am not claiming for this novel any more than its due; *Sula* (1973) is not a stylistic innovation. But in bringing to light dark impulses no longer contraband in the black American female's cultural address, the novel inscribes a new dimension of being, moving at last in contradistinction to the tide of virtue and pathos which tends to overwhelm black female characterization in a monolith of terms and possibilities. I regard Sula the character as a literal and figurative *breakthrough* toward the assertion of what we may call, in relation to her literary "relatives," new female being.

Without predecessors in the recent past of Afro-American literature, Sula is anticipated by a figure four decades removed from Morrison's symbol smasher: Janie Starks in Zora Neale Hurston's *Their Eyes Were Watching God* (1937). By intruding still a third figure—Vyry Ware of Margaret Walker's *Jubilee* (1966)—we lay hold of a pattern of contrast among three African-American female writers, who pose not only differences of character in their perception of female possibilities, but also a widely divergent vocabulary of feeling. This article traces the changes in black female characterization from *Sula* back toward the literary past, beginning with Margaret Walker's Vyry and Zora Neale Hurston's Janie, forward again to *Sula* and Morrison. It argues that the agents which these novels project are strikingly different, and that the differences take shape primarily around questions of moral and social value. And it explores the mediations through which all three writers translate socio-moral constructs into literary modes of discourse.

Margaret Walker's Vyry Ware belongs to, embodies, a corporate ideal. The black woman in her characterization exists for the race, in its behalf, and in maternal relationship to its profoundest needs and wishes. Sula, on the other hand, lives for Sula and has no wish to "mother" anyone, let alone the black race in some symbolic concession to a collective need. If Vyry is woman-for-the-other, then Sula is woman-for-self. Janie Starks represents a dialectical point between the antitheses, and the primary puzzle of *Their Eyes Were Watching God* is the contradiction of motives through which Janie Starks has her being; in other words, Janie might have been Sula, but the latter only through a resolution of negative impulses. These three characters, then, describe peak points in a cultural and historical configuration of literary issues. In Sula's case, the old love of the collective, for the collective, is lost, and passions are turned antagonistic, since, as the myth of the black woman goes, the latter is loving only insofar as she protects her children and forgives her man. The title of this article is a kind of shorthand for these longhanded notations.

The scheme of these observations, as I have already implied, is not strictly chronological. Hurston's affinities are much closer to Morrison's than Walker's, even though Hurston's *Their Eyes Were Watching God* was written nearly fifty years ago. The critical scheme I offer here is not precisely linear, because the literary movement I perceive, which theoretically might take in more women writers than my representative selections, does not progress neatly from year to year in an orderly advance of literary issues and strategies. My method aims at a dialectics of process, with these affinities and emphases tending to move in cycles rather than straight lines. I see no myth of descent operating here as in Harold Bloom's "anxiety of influence," exerted, in an oedipal-like formation, by great writers on their successors.[3] The idea-form which I trace here, articulated in three individual writers' metaphors and patterns of theme and structure, does not emerge within this community of writers in strict sequential order. Ironically, it is exactly the right *not* to accede to the simplifications and mystifications of a strictly historiographical time line that now promises the greatest freedom of discourse to black people, to black women, as critics, teachers, writers, and thinkers.

As the opening exercise in the cultural and literary perspective that this article wishes to consider, then, we turn immediately to Morrison's *Sula*, the "youngest" of three heroines. Few of the time-honored motifs of female behavioral description will suit her: not "seduction and betrayal," applied to a network of English and American fictions; not the category of "holy fool," as exemplified in various Baldwinian configurations of female character; not the patient long-suffering female, nor the female authenticated by male imagination. Compared with past heroines of black American fiction, Sula exists foremost in her own consciousness. To that extent, *Sula* and *Their Eyes Were Watching God* are studies in contrast to Walker and share the same fabric of values. The problem that Morrison poses in *Sula* is the degree to which her heroine (or antiheroine, depending on one's reading of the character) is self-betrayed. The audience does not have an easy time in responding to the agent, because the usual sentiments about black women have been excised, and what we confront instead is the entanglement of our own conflicting desires, our own contradictory motivations concerning issues of individual woman-freedom. Sula is both loved and hated by the reader, embraced and rejected simultaneously because her audience is forced to accept the corruption of absolutes and what has been left in their place—the complex, alienated, transitory gestures of a personality who has no framework of moral reference beyond or other than herself.

Insofar as Sula is not a loving human being, extending few of the traditional loyalties to those around her, she reverses the customary trend of "moral growth" and embodies, contrarily, a figure of genuine moral ambiguity about whom few comforting conclusions may be drawn. Through Sula's unalterable "badness," black and female are now made to appear as a *single* subject in its own right, fully aware of a plenitude of predicative possibilities, for good and ill.

In Sula's case, virtue is not the sole alternative to powerlessness, or even the primary one, or perhaps even an alternative at all. In the interest of complexity, Sula is Morrison's deliberate hypothesis. A conditional subjunctive replaces an indicative certainty: "In a way her strangeness, her naiveté, her craving for the other half of her equation was the consequence of an idle imagination. Had she paints, or clay, or knew the discipline of the dance, or strings; had she anything to engage her tremendous curiosity and her gift for metaphor, she might have exchanged the restlessness and preoccupation with whim for an activity that provided her with all she yearned for. And like any *artist with no art form* she became dangerous."[4]

In careful, exquisite terms Sula has been endowed with dimensions of other possibility. How they are frustrated occupies us for most of the novel, but what strikes me keenly about the passage is that Morrison imagines a character whose destiny is not coterminous with naturalistic or mystical boundaries. Indeed the possibility of art, of intellectual vocation for black female character, has been offered as a style of defense against the naked brutality of conditions. The efficacy of art cannot be isolated from its social and political means, but Sula is specifically circumscribed by the lack of an explicit tradition of imagination or aesthetic work, and not by the evil force of "white" society, or the absence of a man, or even the presence of a mean one.

Morrison, then, imagines a character whose failings are directly traceable to the absence of a discursive/imaginative project—some *thing* to do, some object-subject relationship which establishes the identity in time and space. We do not see Sula in relationship to an "oppressor," a "whitey," a male, a dominant and dominating being outside the self. No Manichean analysis demanding a polarity of interest—black/white, male/female, good/bad—will work here. Instead, Sula emerges as an embodiment of a metaphysical chaos in pursuit of an activity both proper and sufficient to herself. Whatever Sula has become, whatever she is, is a matter of her own choices, often ill-formed and ill-informed. Even her loneliness, she says to her best friend Nel is her own—"My own lonely," she claims in typical Sula-bravado, as she lies dying. Despite our misgivings at Sula's insistence and at the very degree of alienation Morrison accords her, we are prepared to accept her negative, naysaying freedom as a necessary declaration of independence by the black female writer in her pursuit of a vocabulary of gesture—both verbal and motor—that leads us as well as the author away from the limited repertoire of powerless virtue and sentimental pathos. Sula is neither tragic nor pathetic; she does not amuse or accommodate. For black audiences, she is not consciousness of the black race personified, nor "tragic mulatto," nor, for white ones, is she "mammie," "Negress," "coon," or "maid." She is herself, and Morrison, quite rightly, seems little concerned if any of us, at this late date of Sula's appearance in the "house of fiction," minds her heroine or not.

We view Morrison's decision with interest because it departs dramatically from both the iconography of virtue and endurance and from the ideology of the infamous Ogre/Bitch complex, alternately poised as the dominant traits of black female personality when the black female personality exists at all in the vocabulary of public symbols.[5] Sula demands, I believe, that we not only see anew, but also *speak* anew in laying to rest the several manifestations of apartheid in its actual practice and in the formulation of the critical postulates that govern our various epistemologies.

That writers like Morrison, Toni Cade Bambara, and Paule Marshall among them, participate in a tradition of black women writing in their own behalf, close to its moment of inception, lends their work thorough complexity. With the exception of a handful of autobiographical narratives from the nineteenth century, the black woman's realities are virtually suppressed until the period of the Harlem Renaissance and later. Essentially, the black woman as artist, as intellectual spokesperson for her own cultural apprenticeship, has not existed before, for anyone. At the source of her own symbol-making task, this community of writers confronts, therefore, a tradition of work that is quite recent, its continuities broken and sporadic.

It is not at all an exaggeration to say that the black woman's presence as character and movement in the American world has been *ascribed* a status of impoverishment or pathology, or, at best, an essence that droops down in the midst of things, as de Beauvoir describes female mystery in *The Second Sex*. Against this social knowledge, black women writers likely agree on a single point: whatever the portrayal of female character yields, it will be rendered from the point of view of one whose eyes are not alien to the humanity in front of them. What we can safely assume, then, is that black women write as partisans to a particular historical order—their own, the black and female one, with its hideous strictures against literacy and its subtle activities of censorship even now against words and deeds that would deny or defy the black woman myth. What we can assume with less confidence is that their partisanship, as in the rebellion of Sula, will yield a synonymity of conclusions.

The contrast between Sula and Margaret Walker's Vyry Ware is the difference between captive woman and free woman, but the distinction between them has as much to do with aspects of agency and characterization as it does with the kind of sensibility or sympathy that a writer requires in building one kind of character and not another. In other words, *what* we think of Sula and Vyry, for instance, has something to do with *how* we are taught *to see* and *value* them. In the terms of fiction which they each propose, *Jubilee, Their Eyes Were Watching God*, and *Sula* all represent varying degrees of plausibility, but the critial question is not whether the events they portray are plausible, or whether they confirm what we already believe, or think we do, but, rather, how each writer deploys a concept of character. Of the three, Toni Morrison looks forward to an era of dissensions: Sula's passions are hateful, as we have observed, and though we are not certain that the loss of conventional love brings her down, we are sure that she overthrows received moralities in a heedless quest for her own irreducible self. This radical intrusion of waywardness lends a different thematic emphasis to the woman's tale of generation, receding in Sula's awareness, and the result is a novel whose formal strategies are ambiguous and even discomforting in their uncertainties. Once we have examined an analogy of the archetype from which Sula deviates by turning to Margaret Walker's *Jubilee* and have explored Hurston's novel as a structural advance of the literary issues, we will return to *Sula* in a consideration of myth/countermyth as a discourse ordained by history.

In radical opposition to notions of discontinuity, confronting us as a fictional world of consecrated time and space, *Jubilee* worries one of the traditional notions of realism—the stirring to life of the common people[6]—to a modified definition. Walker completed her big novel in the mid sixties at the University of Iowa Creative Writers' Workshop. She tells the story of the novel, twenty years in the making, in *How I Wrote Jubilee*.[7] This novel of historical content has no immediate precedent in Afro-American literary tradition. To that extent, it bears little structural resemblance to Hurston's work before it, although both Hurston and

Walker implement a search for roots, or to Morrison's work after it. *Jubilee*, therefore, assumes a special place in the canon.

From Walker's own point of view, the novel is historical, taking its models from the Russian writers of historical fiction, particularly Tolstoy. In its panoramic display, its massive configurations of characters and implied presences, its movement from a dense point of American history—the era of the Civil War—toward an inevitable, irreversible outcome—the emancipation of 10 million African Americans—*Jubilee* is certainly historical. Even though it is a tale whose end is written on the brain, in the heart, so that there is not even a chance that we will be mistaken about closure, the novel unfolds as if the issues were new. We are sufficiently excited to keep turning the page of a twice-told tale accurately reiterating what we have come to believe is the truth about the "Peculiar Institution." But the high credibility of the text in this case leads us to wonder, eventually, what else is embedded in it that compels us to read our fate by its lights. My own interpretation of the novel is that it is not only historical, but also, and primarily, Historical. In other words, "Historical," in this sense, is a metaphor for the unfolding of the Divine Will. This angle on reality is defined by Paul Tillich as a theonomy. Human history is shot through with Divine Presence so that its being and time are consistent with a plan than elaborates and completes the will of God.[8] In this view of things, human doings are only illusions of a counterfeit autonomy; in Walker's novel agents (or characters) are moving and are moved under the aegis of a Higher and Hidden Authority.

For Vyry Ware, the heroine of *Jubilee* and her family, honor, courage, endurance—in short, the heroic as transparent prophetic utterance— become the privileged center of human response. If Walker's characters are ultimately seen as one-dimensional, either good or bad, speaking in a public rhetoric that assumes the heroic or its opposite, then such portrayal is apt to a fiction whose value is subsumed in a theonomous frame of moral reference. From this angle of advocacy and preservation the writer does not penetrate the core of experience, but encircles it. The heroic intention has no interest in fluctuations or transformations or palpitations of conscience—these will pass away—but monumentality, or fixedness, becomes its striving. Destiny is disclosed to the hero or the heroine as an already-fixed and named event, and this steady reference point is the secret of permanence.

Set on a Georgia plantation before the Civil War, the novel is divided into three parts. The first recalls the infancy and youth of Vyry Ware, the central figure of the novel, and rehearses various modes of the domestic South in slavery. The second part recapitulates the war and its impact on the intimate life of families and individuals. One of the significant threads of the Peculiar Institution in objective time is closely imitated here—how the exigencies of war lead to the destruction of plantation hierarchy. In this vacuum of order a landscape of deracinated women and men dominates the countryside, and Walker's intensity of detail involves the reader in a scene of universal mobility—everything is moving, animate and inanimate, away from the centers of war toward peace, always imminent, in the shadows of Sherman's torch. Vyry and her first love Randall Ware are numbered among the casualties. They are separated as the years of war unhinge all former reality.

The third and final segment of the novel marks Vyry's maturity and the rebirth of a semblance of order in the South. The future is promising for the emancipated, and Vyry takes a new lover, Innis Brown, before the return of Randall Ware. This tying up the various threads of the narrative is undercut by a bitterly ironical perspective. The former enslaved will struggle as she or he has before now, with this difference: free by law, each remains a victim of arbitrary force, but such recognition is the reader's alone. This edge of perception reads into the novel an element of pathos so keenly defined that Vyry's fate verges on the tragic.

Variously encoded by signs associated with a magical/superstitious world order, echoes of maxims and common speech, *Jubilee* is immersed in the material. We are made to feel, in other words, the brutal pull of necessity—the captive's harsh relationship to this earth and its unrelenting requirements of labor—as they impel the captive consciousness toward a terrible knowledge of the tenuousness between life and death. The novel conjoins natural setting and social necessity in a dance of temporal unfolding; in fact, the institution of slavery described here is an elaboration of immanence of decisive in its hold on the human scene imposed upon it that Walker's humanity is actually "ventriloquized" through the medium of a third-person narrator. The narrative technique (with its overlay of mystical piety) is negotiated between omniscient and concealed narrators. Whatever the characters think, however they move and feel about their being, all is rendered through the eyes of another consciousness, not their own. We might say that the characters embody, then, historical symbols—a captive class and their captors—which have been encoded or transliterated as actors in a fiction. Walker's agents are types or valences, and the masks through which they speak might be assumed as well by any other name.

In attributing to Walker a theonomous view of human reality, I am also saying that her characters are larger than life; that they are overdrawn, that, in fact, their compelling agency and motivation are ahistorical, despite the novel's solid historical grounding. Walker's *lexis* operates under quite complicated laws, complicated because such vocabulary is no longer accessible, or even acceptable, to various mythoi of contemporary fiction. Walker is posing a subterranean structure of God terms, articulated in the novel through what we can identify as the *peripeteia*—that point of radical change in the direction that the forces of the novel are moving; in historical and secular terms this change is called emancipation. Historiographic method in accounting for the "long-range" and "immediate" causes of the Civil War and its aftermath does not name "God" as a factor in the liberation of black Americans,[9] and neither does Walker in any explicit way. But it seems clear to me that "God" is precisely what she means in all the grandeur and challenge of the Nominative, clear that the agency of Omnipresence—even more reverberative in its imprecise and ubiquitous *thereness*—is for Walker the source of one of the most decisive abruptions in our history.

Walker adopts a syntax and semantics whose meanings are recognizable in an explanation of affairs in human time. But these delegated efficacies register at a deeper level of import so that "nature," for instance, is nature and something more, and character itself acts in accordance with the same kind of mystical or "unrealistic" tendencies.

Walker's backdrop of natural representation has such forcefulness in the work that dialogue itself is undercut by its dominance, but her still life is counterposed by human doings which elaborate the malignancies of nature, that is, torture, beatings, mental cruelty, the ugly effects of nature embodied in the formal and institutional. The slaveholder and his class, in the abrogation of sympathy, lose their human form. The captors' descent into nature is seen as pernicious self-indulgence, ratified by institutional sanction, but it also violates a deeper structural motive which Walker manipulates in the development of character. Though natural and social events run parallel, they are conjoined by special arrangement, and then there is a name for it—the act of magic or invocation that the enslaved opposes to the arbitrary willfulness of authority.

The evocation of a magical program defines the preeminent formalistic features of the opening segments of the novel. Prayers for the sick and dying and the special atmosphere that surrounds the deathwatch are treated from the outset with particular thematic prominence. In several instances mood is conveyed more by conventional notation—the number thirteen, boiling black pot, full moon, squinch owl, black crone—than any decisive nuance of thought or detail; or more precisely, fear is disembodied from internal agitations of feeling and becomes an attribute of things. "Midnight came and thirteen people waited for death. The black pot boiled, and the full moon rode the clouds high in the heavens and straight up over their heads. . . . It was not a night for people to sleep easy. Every now and then the squinch owl hollered and the crackling fire would glare and the black pot boil. . . ."[10]

The suspense that gathers about this scene is brought on by the active interaction of forces that move beyond and above the characters. An outburst would surprise. Sis. Hetta's death is expected here, and nothing more. The odd and insistent contiguity that Walker establishes among a variety of natural and cultural-material signs—"black pot boiled"; "full moon rode"—identifies the kind of magical/mystical grammar of terms to which I have referred.

"Black pot" and "full moon" may be recognized as elements that properly belong to the terrain of witchcraft, but we must understand that magic and witchcraft—two semiological "stops" usually associated with African-American rebellion and revolutionary fervor throughout the New World under the whip of slavery—are ritual terms of a shorthand which authors adopt to describe a system of beliefs and practices not entirely accessible to us now. In other words, Walker is pointing toward a larger spiritual and religious context through these notations, so that ordinary diurnal events in the novel are invested with extraordinary meaning. My own terms—theonomous meaning—would relate this extraordinary attribution to the Unseen, for which Protestant theology offers other clusters of anomalous phenomena, including "enthusiasm," "ecstasy," or the equivalent of Emile Durkheim's demon of oratorical power.[11] In specific instances of the novel, we see only pointers toward, or markers of, an entirely compelling structure of feelings and beliefs, of which "black pot," for instance, is a single sign. The risk I am taking here is to urge a synonymity between "God" and, for want of a better term, "magic." At least I am suggesting that Walker's vocabulary of God terms includes magic and the magical and the enslaved person's special relationship to natural forces.

Walker achieves this "extra" reading by creating a parallelism between natural and social/domestic issues that dominates the form of the novel. In its reinforcements, there is an absence of differentiation, or of the interplay between dominant and subdominant motifs. A nocturnal order pervades *Jubilee*—like under the confines of the slave community, where movement is constantly under surveillance; secret meetings; flights from the overseer's awful authority; illegal and informal pacts and alliances between slaves; and above all, the slave's terrible vulnerability to fluctuations of fate.

The scene of Vyry's capture after an attempted escape on the eve of the Civil War will provide a final example. After their union Vyry and Randall Ware, the free black man, have two children, Jim and Minna, and Ware makes plans for their liberation. His idea is that he or Vyry will return for the children later, but Vyry refuses to desert them. Her negotiation of a painful passage across the countryside toward the point of rendezvous groans with material burden. It has rained the day of their attempted escape, and mud is dense around the slave quarters by nightfall. Vyry travels with the two children—Jim toddling and the younger child Minna in her arms. The notion of struggle, both against the elements and the powerful other, is so forceful an aspect of tone that the passage itself painfully anticipates the fatefulness of Vyry's move; here are the nodal points:

> Every step Vyry and Jim took, they could feel the mud sucking their feet down and fighting them as they withdrew their feet from its elastic hold. . . . The baby still slept fitfully while Vyry pressed her way doggedly to the

swamps. . . . At last they were in sight of the swamps. Feeling sorry for little Jim she decided to rest a few minutes before trying to wade the creek. . . . She sat down on an old log, meaning to rest only a few minutes. . . . A bad spasm clutched her stomach instinctively. She tensed her body with the sure intuition that she was not only being watched but that the watchful figures would soon surround her. Impassively she saw the patteroller and guards, together with Grimes [the overseer] emerge from the shadows and walk toward her. . . .

This grim detail concludes with Vyry's capture and brutal punishment—"seventy-five lashes on her naked back." That Vyry has been robbed of selfhood on its most fundamental level is clear enough, but the passage further suggests that her movements replicate the paralysis of nightmare. One would move, but cannot, and wakens in spasms of terror. This direct articulation of nightmare content—puzzles and haltings, impediments and frights—dictates the crucial psychological boundaries of *Jubilee* and decides, accordingly, the aesthetic rule.

The idea that emerges here is that Vyry's condition is the equivalent of nightmare, a nocturnal order of things that works its way into the resonances of the novel's structure. Her paralysis is symptomatic of a complex of fear and repression in the service of death. We could argue that the culture of slavery projected in the novel—its modalities of work and celebration, its civic functions and legal codes, its elaborate orders of brutality and mutilation—presents a spectacle of a *culture* in the service of death. Given this reality, the slave subject has no life, but only the stirrings of it. Vyry, trapped in a bad dream, cannot shake loose, and this terrible imposed impotence foreshadows the theme of liberation and a higher liberation as well in which case the stalled movement is overcome in a gesture of revolutionary consciousness. For Vyry the freeing act is sparked by war whose intricate, formal causes are remote to her, though its mandates will require the reorganization of her human resources along new lines of stress. Above all, Vyry must move now without hesitation as the old order collapses around her.

For Vyry's class the postwar years stand as the revelation of the emotional stirrings they have felt all along. "Mine Eyes Have Seen the Glory of the Coming of the Lord" (the title of one of Walker's chapters) is as much a promise as it is an exercise in common meter, but the terms of the promise that Walker imitates are neither modern nor secular. They are eternal and self-generating, authored elsewhere, beyond the reach of human inquiry. Along this axis of time, with its accent on the eternal order of things, women and men in destiny move consistent with the stars of heaven.

This blending of a material culture located in the nineteenth century with a theme which appears timeless and is decisively embedded in a Christian metaphysic reveals the biographical inspiration behind Walker's work. *Jubilee* is, in effect, the tale translated of the author's female ancestors. This is a story of the foremothers, a celebration of their stunning faith and intractable powers of endurance. In that sense, it is not so much a study of characters as it is an interrogation into the African-American character in its poignant national destiny and through its female line of spiritual descent. A long and protracted praise piece, a transformed and elaborated prayer, *Jubilee* is Walker's invocation to the guiding spirit and genius of her people. Such a novel is not "experimental." In short, it does not introduce ambiguity or irony or uncertainty or perhaps even "individualism" as potentially thematic material because it is a detailed sketch of a *collective* survival. The waywardness of a Sula Peace, or even a Janie Stark's movement toward an individualistic liberation—a separate peace—is a trait of character development engendered by a radically different [Weltanschauung].

Their Eyes Were Watching God enforces a similar notion of eternal order in the organic metaphorical structure through which Hurston manipulates her characters, but the complexities of motivation in the novel move the reacher some distance from the limited range of responses evoked by *Jubilee*. Janie Starks, the heroine of the novel, defines a conglomerate of human and social interests so contradictory in its emphasis that a study of structural ambiguity in fiction might well include Janie Starks *and* her author. Perhaps "uncertainty" is a more useful word in this case than "ambiguity," since Hurston avoids the full elaboration or display of tensions that Janie herself appears to anticipate. In short, Janie Starks is a bundle of contradictions: raised by women, chiefly her grandmother, to seek security in a male and his properties, Janie quite early in her career rejects Nanny's wisdom. In love with adventure, in love with the very idea of adventure, Janie is determined to know exactly what independence for the female means for her. This includes the critical quest of sexual self-determination. Janie's quite moving sense of integrity, however, is undercut in puzzling and peculiar ways.

Janie marries her first husband Logan Killicks because her grandmother wants her to do so, but Janie has little interest in a man who is not only not "glamorous" (as Joe Starks and Virgible "Teacake" Woods will be), but also not enlightened in his outlook on the world and the specifically amorous requirements of female/male relationship. Killicks gets the brunt of a kind of social criticism in *Their Eyes Were Watching God* which mocks the rural person—hardworking, unsophisticated, "straight-arrow," earnest—and Hurston makes her point by having Killicks violate essentially Janie's "dream of the horizon." Janie will shortly desert Killicks for a man far more in keeping with her ideas concerning the romantic, concerning male gracefulness. Jody Starks, up from Georgia and headed for an adventure in real estate and town government, takes the place of Logan Killicks with an immediacy, which, in "real" life, would be somewhat disturbing, a bit indecent; but here the "interruption" is altogether lyrical, appropriate, and unmourned. Starks's appearance and intention are even "cinematic" in their decidedly cryptic and romantic tenor—Janie literally goes off "down the road" with the man.

Their destination is Eatonville, Florida, a town which Joe Starks will bring to live with his own lovely ego, shortly to turn arrogant and insulting as he attempts to impose on Janie his old-fashioned ideas about woman's place and possibilities. The closure on this marriage is not a happy one either, troubled by Starks's chauvinistic recriminations and Janie's own disenchantment. Starks dies of a kidney ailment, leaving Janie "Mrs. Mayor" of Eatonville and not particularly concerned, we are led to believe, to be attached again.

Janie's new love affair with Teacake is untrammeled by incompatibility between the pair, though her friends express great concern that Teacake's social and financial status is not what it ought to be, let alone comparable to Jody Starks's. Janie is, however, at once traditionally romantic in her apparently male-centered yearnings and independent in her own imagination and the readiness to make her own choices. The convergence of these two emotional components is, in fact, not the diametrical opposition which contemporary feminists sometimes suppose; heterosexual love is neither inherently perverse nor necessarily dependence-engendering, except that the power equation between female and male tends to corrupt intimacies.[12] The trouble, then, with the relationship between Janie and Teacake is not its heterosexual ambience, but a curiously exaggerated submissiveness on Janie's part that certain other elements of the heroine's character contradict.

When, for instance, Janie follows Teacake to the Florida Everglades to become a migrant farm worker for several seasons, their love is solid and reliable, but the male in this instance is also perfectly capable, under Hurston's gaze, of exhibiting qualities of jealousy and possession so decisive that his occasional physical abuse of the female and his not-so-subtle manipulation of other females' sexual attraction to him seem condoned in the name of love. Hurston's pursuit of an alleged folk philosophy in this case—as in, all women enjoy an occasional violent outburst from their men because they know then that they are loved—is a concession to an obscene idea. One example will suffice. "Before the week was over he had whipped Janie. Not because her behavior justified his jealousy, but it relieved that awful fear inside him. Being able to whip her reassured him in possession. No brutal beating at all. He just slapped her around a bit to show he was boss. . . . It aroused a sort of envy in both men and women. The way he petted and pampered her as if those two or three slaps had nearly killed her made the women see visions and the helpless way she hung on him made men dream dreams. . . ."[13]

One might well wonder, and with a great deal of moral, if not poetic, justification if the scene above describes a *working posture* that Hurston herself might have adopted with various lovers. This scene is paradigmatic of the very quality of ambiguity/ambivalence that I earlier identified for this novel. The piece threatens to abandon primitive modes of consciousness and response from the beginning, but Hurston seems thwarted in bringing this incipience to fruition for reasons which might have to do with the way that the author understood certain popular demands brought to bear on her art. Hurston has detailed some of her notions of what Anglo-American audiences expected of the black writer and the black female writer of her time,[14] but it is not clear to me what African-American audiences expected of their chroniclers. The more difficult question, however, is what Hurston demanded of herself in imagining what was possible for the female, and it appears that beyond a certain point she could not, or would not plunge. *Their Eyes Were Watching God*, for all its quite impressive feminist possibilities, is an instance of "double consciousness," to employ W. E. B. Du Bois's conceptualization in quite another sense and intention.[15] Looking two ways at once, it captivates Janie Starks in an entanglement of conflicting desires.

More concentrated in dramatic focus than *Jubilee*, Hurston's novel was written during the mid thirties; finished in seven weeks during the author's visit to Haiti, the novel is not simply compact. It is hurried, intense, and above all, haunted by an uneasy measure of control. One suspects that Hurston has not said everything she means, but means everything she says. Within a persistent scheme of metaphor, she seems held back from the awful scream that she has forced Janie to repress through unrelieved tides of change. We mistrust Janie's serenity, spoken to her friend Phoeby Watson in the close of the novel; complementarily, the reconciliation is barely acceptable in either structural or dramatic terms. Janie Starks, not unlike her creator, is gifted with a dimension of worldiness and ambition that puts her in touch with broader experience. This daughter of sharecroppers is not content to be heroic under submissive conditions (except with Teacake?); for her, then, nothing in the manners of small town Florida bears repeating. Its hateful, antisocial inclinations are symbolized by Janie's grandmother, whom she hates "and [has] hidden from herself all these years under the cloak of pity." "Here Nanny had taken the biggest thing God ever made, the horizon . . . and pinched it into such a little bit of a thing that she could tie it about her granddaughter's neck tight enough to choke her. She hated the old woman who had twisted her so in the name of love. . . ."

The grandmother not only represents a personal trauma for Janie (as the grandmother does in the author's autobiography),[16] but also terror and repression, intruding a vision of impoverishment within the race. Clustered around the symbolic and living grandmother are the anonymous detractors of experience who assume no discriminating feature or motivation beyond the level of the mass. Hurston's rage is directed against this faceless brood with a moral ferociousness that verges on misogyny. This profound undercurrent is relieved, however, by a drift toward caricature. Exaggerating the fat of misshapen men and calling attention to their sexual impotence in public, gaining dimensions of comic monologue, and leaving no genuine clue for those who gaze at her, Janie has elements of a secret life which sustains her through the adventures of three husbands, a flood, justifiable homicide, trial, and vindication.

This psychological bent informing Janie's character is deflected by an anthropological strategy that all but ruins this study of a female soul. The pseudodialect of Southern patois gives Janie back to the folk ultimately, but this "return" contradicts other syntactical choices which Hurston superimposes on the structure through visions of Janie's interior life and Hurston's own narrative style. Janie implies new moral persuasions, while Hurston has her looking back, even returning, to the small town she desperately wishes to be free of. This dilemma of choices haunts the book from the very beginning and may, indeed, shed light on the "ancestral imperative."[17] That Janie does not break from her Southern past, symbolized in the "old talk," but grasps how she might do so is the central problematic feature of the novel, previously alluded to as an undercurrent of doubt running through Hurston's strategies.

Written long before *Jubilee*, *Their Eyes Were Watching God* anticipates the thematic emphases prominent in *Sula* to the extent that in both the latter novels only the adventurous, deracinated personality is heroic, and that in both, the roots of experience are poisonous. One would do well to avoid the plunge down to the roots, seeking, rather, to lose oneself in a larger world of chance and danger. That woman must break loose from the hold of biography as older generations impose it, even the broader movements of tribe, constitutes a controlling theme of Hurston's work.

Images of space and time, inaugurated in the opening pages of the novel, are sounded across it with oracular intensity, defining the dream of Janie Starks as a cosmic disembodiment that renders her experience unitary with the great fantastic ages. "Ships at a distance have every man's wish on board. For some they come in with the tide." Consonant with this history of fantasy life, Janie is something of a solitary reaper, disillusioned, stoical, in her perception of fate and death. "So the beginning of this was a woman and she had come back from burying the dead. . . . The people all saw her because it was sundown. The sun was gone, but he had left his footprints in the sky. It was time to hear things and talk. . . ."

The novel is essentially informed by these ahistorical, specifically rustic, image clusters, giving the whole a topological consistency. Hurston, however, attempts to counterpoise this timeless current with elements of psychic specificity—Janie's growth toward an understanding of mutability and change and other aspects of internal movement. The novel's power of revelation, nonetheless, is rather persistently sabotaged at those times when Hurston intrudes metaphorical symbolism as a substitute for the hard precision of thought. Janie actually promises more than the author delivers. As a result, the novel is facile at times when it ought to be moving, captivated in stereotype when it should be dynamic.

The flood that devastates the Florida Everglades and the homes of the migrant farm workers of which Janie and Teacake are a part provides an example. The storm sequence is the novel's high point, its chief dramatic fulcrum, on which rests the motivation that will spur both Janie's self-defense against a rabid Teacake and her return to Eatonville and the Starks house. Waiting in their cabins for the storm to recede, Janie, Teacake, and their fellow laborers are senseless with wonder at its power: "They seemed to be staring at the dark, but their eyes were watching God." What one wants in this sequence is a crack in the mental surface of character so acute that the flood cleaves the narrative precisely in half, pre- and postdiluvial responses so distinctly contrasting that the opening lines—"their souls asking if He meant to measure their puny might against His"—mature into the ineluctable event. The reader expects a convergence of outer scene and its inner correspondence, but Hurston appears to forego the fruition of this parallel rhythm, content on delineating the external behavior of the agents.

Nothing specific to the inner life of Janie appears again for several pages; the awe that greets the display of natural phenomena is replayed through the imagination of a third-person observer, dry feet and all, well above the action of furious winds. We miss the concentration on Janie's internal life which saves the entire first half of the narrative from the pathos of character buffeted by external circumstances. Janie never quite regains her former brilliance, and when we meet her considered judgments again, she has fled the 'Glades, after having had to shoot Teacake in self-defense [as a result of his violence, rabies-induced] and is seeking peace in the town where she has been "first lady." "Here was peace. She pulled in her horizon like a great fish-net. Pulled it from around the waist of the world and draped it over her shoulder. So much of life in its meshes! She called in her soul to come and see . . . ."

One is not certain how these images of loss and labor should be read, nor why they strike with such finality, except that the lines make a good ending, this rolling in of fish nets and cleaning of meshes, but if we take Janie as a kind of adventurer, as a woman well familiar with the rites of burial and grief, then we read this closure as a eulogy for the living; Janie has been "buried" along with Teacake.

The fault with this scene is not that Janie has loved Teacake, but, rather, that the author has broken the potential pattern of revolt by having her resigned, as if she were ready for a geriatric retirement, to the town of frustrated love. We know that all novels do end, even if they end with "the," and so it is probably fitting for Janie to have a rest after the tragic events unleashed by the flood. But her decision to go back to Eatonville after the trial strikes me as a naive fictional pose. Or, more precisely, what she thinks about her life at that point seems inappropriate to the courageous defiance that she has often embodied all along. The logic of the novel tends to abrogate neat conclusions, and their indulgence in the end essentially mitigates the complex painful knowledge that Janie has gained about herself and the other.

The promise to seize upon the central dramatic moment of a woman's self-realization fizzles out in a litany of poetic platitudes about as opposite to Janie's dream of the horizon as the grandmother's obsessive fear of experience has been. We miss the knowledge or wisdom of revelation in the perfectly resolved ending—what is it that Janie knows now that she has come back from burying the dead of the sodden and bloated? Are the words merely decorative, or do they mobilize us toward a deeper mysterious sense? In a mode of fictive assumptions similar to Margaret Walker's, Zora Neale Hurston inherits a fabric of mystery without rethreading it. That is one kind of strategic decision. There are others.

Sula, by contrast, closes with less assurance. "'All that time, all that time, I thought I was missing Jude.' And the loss pressed down on her chest and came up into her throat. 'We was girls together,' she said as though explaining something. 'O Lord, Sula,' she cried, 'girl, girl, girlgirlgirl.'"

Nel's lament not only closes *Sula*, but also reinforces the crucial dramatic questions which the novel has introduced—the very mystery of a Sula Peace and the extent to which the town of Medallion, Ohio, has been compelled by her, how they yearn for her, even to the point, oddly enough, of a collective rejection. Nel and Sula are more than girls together. They sustain the loss of innocence and its subsequent responsibilities with a degree of tormented passion seldom allowed even to lovers. More than anyone else in Medallion, they have been intimate witnesses of their mutual coming of age in a sequence of gestures that anticipates an ultimate disaffection between them, but the rhythm of its disclosure, determined early on by the reader as inexorable, is sporadic and intermittent enough in the sight of the two women that its fulfillment comes to both as a trauma of recognition. Nel Wright's "girl," repeated five times and run together in an explosion not only of the syntactical integrity of the line, but also of Nel's very heartbeat, is piercing and sudden remorse—remorse so long suspended, so elaborate in its deceptions and evasions that it come very well intimate the onset of a sickness-unto-death.

When Sula comes of age, she leaves Medallion for a decade in the wake, significantly, of Nel's marriage to Jude and her resignation to staid domestic life. Sula's return to Medallion, in a plague of robins, no less, would mark the restoration of an old friendship; Sula, instead, becomes Jude's lover for a brief time before abandoning him as she does other husbands of the town. Nel and Sula's "confrontation," on the deathbed of the latter, tells the reader and the best friend very little about what it is that makes Sula run. All that she admits is that she has "lived" and that if she and Nel had been such good friends, in fact, then her momentary "theft" of Jude might not have made any difference. Nel does not forgive Sula, but experiences, instead, a sense of emptiness and despair grounded, she later discovers after it doesn't matter anymore, in her own personal loss of Sula. She has not missed Jude, she finds out that afternoon, but her alter ego passionately embodied in the other woman. It turns out that the same degree of emotional ambivalence that haunts Nel plagues the female reader of this novel. What is it about this woman Sula that triggers such attraction and repulsion at once? We have no certain answers, just as Nel does not, but, rather, resign ourselves to a complex resonance of feeling which suggests that Sula is both necessary and frightening as a character realization.

In the relationship between Nel and Sula, Morrison demonstrates the female's rites-of-passage in their peculiar richness and impoverishment; the fabric of paradoxes—betrayals and sympathies, silences and aggressions, advances and sudden retreats—transmitted from mother to daughter, female to female, by mimetic gesture. That women learn primarily from other women strategies of survival and "homicide" is not news to anyone; indeed, this vocabulary of reference constitutes the chief revisionist, albeit implicit, feature of the women's liberation effort. Because Morrison has no political axe to grind in this novel—in other words, she is not writing according to a formula which demands that her female agents demonstrate a simple, transparent love between women—she is free, therefore, to pursue the delicate tissue of intimate patterns of response between women. In doing so, she identifies those meanings of womanhood which statements of public policy are rhetorically bound to suppress.

One of the structural marvels of *Sula* is its capacity to telescope the process of generation and its consequent network of convoluted relationships. *Sula* is a woman's text par excellence, even subscribing in its behavior to Woolf's intimations that the woman's book, given the severe demands on her time, is spare.[18] The novel is less than two hundred pages of prose, but within its imaginative economy various equations of domestic power are explored. For instance, Sula's relationships to her mother Hannah and grandmother Eva Peace are portrayed in selective moments. In other words, Sula's destiny is located only in part by Nel, while the older Peace women in their indifference to decorous social behavior provide the soil in which her moral isolation is seeded and nurtured. Hannah and Eva have quite another story to tell apart from Sula's, much of it induced by Eva's abandonment by her husband BoyBoy and her awful defiance in response. The reader is not privy to various tales of transmission between Eva and Hannah, but we decide by inference that their collective wisdom leads Hannah herself to an authenticity of person not alterable by the iron-clad duties of motherhood, nor the sweet, submissive obligations of female love. In short, Hannah Peace is self-indulgent, full of disregard for the traditional repertoire of women's vanity-related gestures, and the reader tends to love her for it—the "sweet, low and [guileless]" flirting, no patting of the hair, or rushing to change clothes, or quickly applying makeup, but barefoot in summer, "in the winter her feet in a man's leather slippers with the backs flattened under her heels. . . . Her voice trailed, dipped and bowed; she gave a chord to the simplest words. Nobody, but nobody, could say 'hey sugar' like Hannah. . . ."

Just as Hannah's temperament is "light and playful," Morrison's prose glides over the surface of events with a careful allegiance to the riffs of folk utterance—deliberte, inclusive, very often on the verge of laughter—but the profound deception of this kind of plain talk, allegedly "unsophisticated," is the vigil it keeps in killing silence about what it suspects, even knows, but never expresses. This hidden agenda has a malicious side which Sula inherits without moral revision and correction. Morrison's stylistic choice in this passage is a significant clue to a reading of Hannah's character, a freedom of movement, a liberty of responses, worked out in a local school of realism. Hannah Peace is certainly not a philosopher, not even in secret, but that she rationalizes her address to the other in an unfailing economy of nuances implies a potential for philosophical grace. Among the women of *Sula*, the light rhythms usually conceal a deeper problem.

One of the more perplexing characters of recent American fiction, Eva Peace embodies a figure of both insatiable generosity and insatiable demanding. Like Hannah, Eva is seldom frustrated by the trammels of self-criticism, the terrible indecisiveness and scrupulosity released by doubt. Because Eva goes ahead without halting, ever, we could call her fault nothing less than innocence, and its imponderable cruelty informs her character with a kind of Old Testament logic. Eva behaves as though she were herself the sole instrument of divine inscrutable will. We are not exactly certain what oracular fever decides that she must immolate her son Plum.[19] Perhaps even his heroin addiction does not entirely explain it, but she literally rises to the task in moments of decisiveness, orchestrated in pity and judgment. Like an avenging deity who must sacrifice its creation in order to purify it, Eva swings and swoops on her terrible crutches from her son's room, about to prepare his fire. She holds him in her arms, recalling moments from his childhood before dousing him with kerosene:

> He opened his eyes and saw what he imagined was the great wing of an eagle pouring a wet lightness over him. Some kind of baptism, some kind of blessing, he thought. Everything is going to be all right, it said. Knowing that it was so he closed his eyes and sank back into the bright hole of sleep.

> Eva stepped back from the bed and let the crutches rest under her arms.
> She rolled a bit of newspaper into a tight stick about six inches long, lit it and
> threw it onto the bed where the kerosene-soaked Plum lay in smug delight.
> Quickly, as the *whoosh* of flames engulfed him, she shut the door and made
> her slow and painful journey back to the top of the house. . . .

Not on any level is the reader offered easy access to this scene. Its enumerated, overworked pathos, weighed against the victim's painful ignorance not only of his imminent death, but also of the requirements of his manhood generates contradictory feelings between shock and relief. The reader resents the authorial manipulation that engenders such feelings. The act itself, so violently divergent from the normal course of maternal actions and expectations, marks a subclimax. Further, it foreshadows the network of destruction, both willful and fortuitous, that ensnares Sula and Nel in an entanglement of predecided motivations. Eva, in effect, determines her own judgment, which Sula will seal without a hint of recourse to the deceptions or allegiances of kinship. Sula, who puts Eva in old age in an asylum, does not mistake her decision as as stroke of love or duty, nor does it echo any of the ambiguities of mercy.

Like Eva's, Sula's program of action as an adult woman is spontaneous and direct, but the reader in Sula's case does not temper her or his angle on Sula's behavior with compassion or second thought, as she or he tends to do in Eva's case. It could be argued, for instance, that Eva sacrifices Plum in order to save him, and however grotesque we probably adjudge her act, inspired by a moral order excluding contingency and doubt, no such excuse can be offered in Sula's behalf. We must also remember that Sula's nubile *singleness* and refusal of the acts and rites of maternity have implicitly corrupted her in our unconscious judgment and at a level of duplicity which our present "sexual arrangements" protect and mandate.[20] We encounter the raw details of her individualism, not engaged by naturalistic piety or existential rage, as a paradigm of wanton vanity. Her moral shape, however, does not come unprecedented or autonomously derived. Merging Eva's arrogance on the one hand and Hannah's self-indulgence on the other, "with a twist that was all her own imagination, she lived out her days exploring her own thoughts and emotions, giving them full reign, feeling no obligation to please anybody unless their pleasure pleased her."

Just as Hannah and Eva have been Sula's principal models, they have also determined certain issues which she will live out in her own career. It is probably not accidental that the question which haunts Hannah— have I been loved?—devolves on Sula with redoubtable fury. If it is true that love does not exist until it is named, then the answer to the enigma of Sula Peace is not any more forthcoming than if it were not so. Yet, certainly the enormous consequences of being loved or not are relevant by implication to the agents of the novel. Morrison does not elaborate, but the instances of the question's appearance—halting, uncertain, embarrassed, or inappropriate words on a character's tongue—conceal the single most important missing element in the women's encounter with each other. A revealing conversation between Eva and Hannah suggests that even for the adult female the intricacies and entanglements of mother love (or perhaps woman love without distinction) is a dangerous inquiry to engage. Hannah cannot even formulate the sentences that would say the magic words, but angles in on the problem with a childlike timidity which she can neither fake nor conceal. "I know you fed us and all. I was talking 'bout something else. Like. Like. Playin' with us. Did you ever, you know, play with us?"

This conversation may be compared with one that Sula overhears the summer of her twelfth year, between Hannah and a couple of friends. The three women confirm for each other the agonies of childrearing, but can never quite bring themselves around to admitting that love is contingent and human and all too-often connected with notions of duty. Hannah tells one of the friends that her quality of love is sufficient. "You love [your child], like I love Sula. I just don't like her. That's the difference." And that's the "difference" that sends Sula "flying up the stairs," blankly "aware of a sting in her eye." until recalled by Nel's voice.

To pin the entire revelation of the source of Sula's later character development on this single episode would be a fallacy of overdetermination, but its strategic location in the text suggests that its function is crucial to the unfolding of events to come, to the way that Sula responds to them, and to the manner in which we interpret her responses. At least two other events unmistakably hark back to it. Chicken Little joins Sula and Nel later on the same afternoon in their play by the river. In the course of things Sula picked him up and "swung" him outward and then around and around. His knickers ballooned and his shrieks of frightened joy startled the birds and the fat grasshoppers. When he slipped from her hands and sailed out over the water they could still hear his bubbly laughter. . . ."

Frozen in a moment of terror, neither girl can do more than stare at the "closed place in the water." Morrison aptly recreates the stark helplessness of two trapped people, gaining a dimension of horror because the people are children, drawn up short in a world of chance and danger. That they do nothing in particular, except recognize that Shadrack, the town's crack-brained veteran of World War I, has seen them and will not tell, consigns them both to a territory of their own most terrible judgment and isolation. In this case the adult conscience of each springs forth in the eyes of the other, leaving childhood abruptly in its wake. The killing edge is that the act itself must remain a secret. Unlike other acts of rites-of-passage, this one must *not* be communicated. At

Chicken Little's funeral, Sula "simply cried," and from his grave site she and Nel, fingers laced, trot up the road "on a summer day wondering what happened to butterflies in the winter."

The interweave of lyricism and dramatic event is consistent with Morrison's strategies. Their juxtaposition does not appear to function ironically, but to present dual motifs in a progressive revelation that allows the reader to "swallow" dramatic occurrences whose rhetoric, on the face of it, is unacceptable. At the same time we get in right perspective Sula's *lack* of tension—a tension that distinguishes the character stunned by her own ignorance, or by malice in the order of things. Sula, by contrast, just goes along, "completely free of ambition, with no affection for money, property, or things, no greed, no desire to command attention to compliments—no ego. For that reason she felt no compulsion to verify herself—be consistent with herself." That Sula apparently wants nothing, is curiously free of mimetic desire and its consequent pull toward willfulness, keep pity in check and release unease in its absence.

Sula's lack of egoism—which appears an incorrect assessment on the narrator's part—renders her an antipassionate spectator of the human scene, even beholding her mother's death by fire in calculated coolness. Weeks after Chicken's burial Hannah is in the backyard of the Peace household, lighting a fire in which she accidentally catches herself and burns to death. Eva recalls afterward that "she had seen Sula standing on the back porch just looking." When her friends insist that she is more than likely mistaken since Sula was "probably struck dumb" by the awful spectacle, Eva remains quietly convinced "that Sula had watched Hannah burn not because she was paralyzed, but because she was interested. . . ."

This moment of Sula's interestedness, and we tend to give Eva the benefit of the doubt in this case, must be contrasted to her response to Chicken's drowning, precluding us from remaining impartial judges of her behavior, even as we understand its sources in the earlier event. Drawn into a cycle of negation, Sula at twelve is Sula at twenty, and the instruments of perception which the reader uses to decipher her character do not alter over the whole terrain of the work. From this point on, any course of action that she takes is already presumed by negating choices. Whether she steals Nel's husband or a million dollars matters less to the reader than to the other characters, since we clearly grasp the structure of her function as that of a radical amorality and consequently of a radical freedom. We would like to love Sula, or damn her, inasmuch as the myth of the black American woman allows only Manichean responses, but it is impossible to do either. We can only behold in an absolute suspension of final judgment.

Morrison induces this ambiguous reading through an economy of means, none of which relate to the classic *bête noire* of black experience—

the powerful predominance of white and the endless litany of hateful responses associated with it. That Sula is not bound by the customary alliances to naturalism or historical determinism at least tells us what imperatives she does not pursue. Still, deciding what traditions do inspire her character is not made easier.

I would suggest that Hurston's Janie Starks presents a clear precedent. Though not conforming at every point, I think the two characters lend themselves to a comparative formula. In both cases, the writer wishes to examine the particular details and propositions of liberty under constricted conditions in a low mimetic mode of realism, that is, an instance of realism in which the characters are not decisively superior in moral or social condition to the reader.[21] Both Janie and Sula are provided an arena of action within certain limits. In the former case, the character's dreams are usually too encompassing to be accommodated within the space that circumscribes her. The stuff of her dreams, then, remains disembodied, ethereal, out of time, nor are her dreams fully differentiated, inasmuch as all we know about them is their metaphorical conformity to certain natural or romantic configurations. It is probably accurate to say that the crucial absence for Janie has been an intellectual chance, or the absence of a syntax distinctive enough in its analytical requirements to realign a particular order of events to its own demands. In other words, Janie is stuck in the limitations of dialect, while her creator is free to make use of a range of linguistic resources to achieve her vision.

The principle of absence that remains inchoate for Janie is articulate for Sula in terms whose intellectual implications are unmistakable—Sula lacks the shaping vision of art, and the absence is as telling in the formation of her character as the lack of money or an appropriately ordered space might be for the heroines, for example, of Henry James's *Portrait of a Lady* or *Wings of the Dove;* in both of James's works the heroines are provided with *money,* a term that James's narrator assigns great weight in deciding what strategies enable women to do battle with the world, though the equation between gold and freedom is ironically burdened here. In Woolf's conception of personal and creative freedom for the woman, *money, space,* and *time* figure prominently.

It is notable that Janie and Sula, within the social modalities that determine them, are actually quite well off. Their suffering, therefore, transcends the visceral and concrete, moving progressively toward the domain of symbols. In sharp contrast to Walker's Vyry, the latter-day heroines approach the threshold of speaking and acting *for self,* or the organization of one's resources with preeminent reference to the highest form of self-regard, the urge to speak one's own words urgently. Hurston and Morrison after her are both in the process of abandoning the vision of the corporate good as a mode of heroic suffering. Precisely what will take its place defines the dilemma of *Sula* and its protagonist. The dilemma itself highlights problems of figuration for black female character whose future, whose terms of existence, are not entirely known at the moment.

The character of Sula impresses the reader as a problem in interpretation because, for one thing, the objective myth of the black American woman, at least from the black woman's point of view, is drawn in valorized images that intrude against the text, or compete with it like a jealous goddess. That this privileged other narrative is counterbalanced by its opposite, equally exaggerated and distorted, simply reinforces the heroics to the extent that the black woman herself imagines only one heroine—and that is herself. *Sula* attempts a correction of this uninterrupted superiority on the one hand and unrelieved pathology on the other; the reader's dilemma arises in having to choose. The duplicitous reader embraces the heroics with no intent of disproof or unbelief, while the brave one recognizes that the negating countermyth would try to establish a dialectical movement between the subperspectives, gaining a totally altered perspective in the process.[22] In other words, Sula, Vyry, and Janie need not be seen as the terms of an either/or proposition. The three characters here may be identified as subperspectives, or *angles onto* a larger seeing. The struggle that we bring with us to *Sula*, indeed, the implicit proposition upon which the text is based, is the imperative that requires our coming to terms with the very complexities that a juggling of perspectives demands.

Sula is not the "other" as one kind of reading would suggest, or perhaps as we might wish, but a figure of the rejected and vain part of the self—ourselves—who in its thorough corruption and selfishness cannot utter, believe in, nor prepare for, love. I am not entirely sure that Sula speaks for us on the lower frequencies—though she could very well. The importance of this text is that she speaks at all.

In a conversation with Robert Stepto, Toni Morrison confirms certain critical conjectures that are made here concerning the character of Sula. "[She] was hard, for me; very difficult to make up that kind of character. Not difficult to think it up, but difficult to describe a woman who could be used as a classic type of evil force. Other people could use her that way. And at the same time, I didn't want to make her freakish or repulsive or unattractive. I was interested at that time in doing a very old, worn-out idea, which was to do something with good and evil, but putting it in different terms. . . ."[23]

As Morrison goes on to discuss the idea, Sula and Nel are to her mind an alterity of agents—"two sides of the same person, or two sides of one extraordinary character."[24] Morrison does not attribute the birth of her idea to any particular cultural or historical event and certainly not to the most recent wave of American feminism, but it does seem fairly clear that a Sula Peace is for *for black American literature*, if not for the incredibly rich potential of black American female personality, a radical alternative to Vyry Ware and less so, to placid Jane Crawford Starks. "This was really part of the difficulty—I didn't know anyone like her. I never knew a woman like that at any rate. But I knew women who looked like that, who looked like they *could* be like that. And then you remember women who were a little bit different in [one's] town, you know."[25]

If we identify Sula as a kind of countermythology, we are saying that she is no longer bound by a rigid pattern of predictions, predilections, and anticipations. Even though she is a character in a novel, her strategic place as *potential being* might argue that *subversion* itself—law breaking—is an aspect of liberation that women must confront from its various angles, in its different guises. Sula's outlawry may not be the best kind, but that she has the will toward rebellion itself *is* the stunning idea. This project in liberation, paradoxically, has no particular dimension in time, yet it is for all time.

Notes

1. Mary Helen Washington, ed. *Black-Eyed Susans: Classic Stories by and about Black Women* (New York: Anchor Books, 1975). From the introduction.
2. "Intimate Things in Place: A Conversation with Toni Morrison" in *Chant of Saints: A Gathering of Afro-American Literature, Art, and Scholarship,* ed. Michael S. Harper and Robert B. Stepto (Urbana: University of Illinois Press, 1979).
3. Harold Bloom's by-now familiar revision on the Freudian oedipal myth in relationship to the theme of literary successions and fortunes is not applicable to the community of black American women writers, even as a necessary critical fable. Bloom speaks for a powerful and an *assumed* patriarchal tradition, posited by a dominative culture in the transmission of a political, as well as literary, wealth; in the case of black women's writing (and women's writing without modification) the myth of wealth as an aspect of literary "inheritance" tends to be sporadic. See Bloom, *The Anxiety of Influence: A Theory of Poetry* (New York: Oxford University Press, 1973), and *A Map of Misreading* (New York: Oxford University Press, 1975).
4. Toni Morrison, *Sula* (New York: Bantam Books, 1975), 105, emphases mine. All references are from this edition.
5. Bell Hooks [Gloria Watkins], *Ain't I a Woman: Black Women and Feminism* (Boston: South End Press, 1981). The particular role of Daniel Moynihan's *Report* is put in perspective here with what Hooks calls "the continuing devaluation of black womanhood."

   It is with crucial deliberation that the editors of a recent feminist collection of scholarship call their volume *All the Women Are White, All the Blacks Are Men, But Some of Us Are Brave* (Old Westbury, N.Y.: Feminist Press, 1982). Editors Gloria T. Hull, Patricia Bell Scott, and Barbara Smith realize that public discourse—certainly its most radical critical statements included—lapses into a cul-de-sac when it approaches this community of women and their writers.

6. Erich Auerbach, "Fortunata," in *Mimesis: The Representation of Reality in Western Literature*, trans. Willard Trask (New York: Doubleday Anchor Books, 1957). In tracing the shift in stylistic convention and emotional resonance from the literature of classical antiquity to the modern period Auerbach provides a definition of the change which I would consider crucial to any consideration of the issue of "realism," "the birth of a spiritual movement in the depths of the common people, from within the everyday occurrences of contemporary life, which thus assumes an importance it could never have assumed in antique literature."

7. Margaret Walker, *How I Wrote Jubilee* (Chicago: Third World Press, 1972). *Jubilee* was submitted as Walker's Ph.D. dissertation to the University of Iowa Creative Writers' Workshop. The source material for the novel is based on the life story of the author's great-grandmother, told to her by her grandmother in the best tradition of oral his/herstory. The specificities of this transmitted tale from one generation to another was researched by Walker over nearly two decades, and it anticipates another odyssey of search in Alex Haley's *Roots*, a detailed study of an African-American genealogy. Walker later on actually brought suit against Haley for the supposed plagiarizing of a theme that Walker considers special, if not unique, to her own work.

8. Paul Tillich, *A History of Christian Thought: From Its Judaic and Hellinistic Origins to Existentialism*, ed. Carl E. Braaten (New York: Touchstone, 1972). My own use of Tillich's "theonomy" is vastly simplified and lifted out of the context that the theologian establishes between the idea and its relationship to the Christian European eras of sacred theology. But I hope that we might summarize a complicated idea here without seriously violating the original.

9. The student of Americana will immediately recognize that "God" is manifest cause to worldly effect within a certain configuration of cultural values; Perry Miller's classic work on early New England communities renders a detailed analysis of the view; cf. "God's Controversy With New England," in *The New England Mind: The Seventeenth Century* (Boston: Beacon Press, 1961).

10. Margaret Walker, *Jubilee* (Boston: Houghton Mifflin, 1966).

11. Emile Durkheim, *The Elementary Forms of Religious Life*, trans. Joseph Ward Swain (New York: Free Press, 1965).

12. Robert Hemenway, *Zora Neale Hurston: A Literary Biography* (Urbana: University of Illinois Press, 1977). This important work on Hurston's life provides an exhaustive account of the writer's various relationships. Hurston herself was a lover of males, but never sustained the liaisons quite long enough for us to see any pattern in this chapter of her biography except as short-lived serial monogamies.

13. Zora Neale Hurston, *Their Eyes Were Watching God* (New York: Fawcett Premier Books, 1969).

14. Zora Neale Hurston, "What White Publishers Won't Print," in *I Love Myself When I Am Laughing . . . and Then Again When I Am Looking Mean and Impressive*, ed. Alice Walker (Old Westbury, N.Y.: Feminist Press, 1979). In discussing why white American publishers of her time would only publish the "morbid" about the lives of black Americans, Hurston suggests what is both frightening and familiar to contemplate. "It is assumed that all non-Anglo-Saxons are uncomplicated stereotypes. Everybody knows all about them. They are lay figures mounted in the museum where all may take them in at a glance. They are made of bent wires without insides at all. So how could anybody write a book about the non-existent?" But we might also consider whether or not the obscene didn't happen—if black people them-

selves did not come to see their lives as a very fixed, monolithic, immobile quality of human experience? Alice Walker in the dedication to this volume points out that if Hurston were a "colorist," as some of her critics have claimed, then she "was not blind and saw that black men (and black women) have been, and are, colorist to an embarrassing degree."

15. W. E. B. Du Bois, *The Souls of Black Folk: Essays and Sketches* (New York: Fawcett Publications, 1967). Du Bois's classic reading of the African-American predicament is posed in the opening chapter of this germinal piece. He writes, "one ever feels his twoness,—an American, a Negro: two souls, two thoughts, two unreconciled strivings, two warring ideals in one dark body, whose dogged strength alone keeps it from being torn asunder."

16. Zora Neale Hurston, "My Folks," *Dust Tracks on a Road*, introduction by Larry Neal (Philadelphia: J. P. Lippincott, 1971).

17. The term "ancestral imperative" does not originate in Albert Murray, but his use of it is dialectical and expansive. The best demonstration of Murray's argument is his *South to a Very Old Place* (New York: McGraw-Hill, 1971).

18. Virginia Woolf, *A Room of One's Own* (New York: Harcourt, Brace and World, 1957).

19. Professor Nellie McKay recently reminded me that African-American women during the era of slavery often killed their offspring in order to forestall their enslavement. Read against McKay's interpretation, Eva Peace's "intervention" is historically grounded at the same time that it does not lose its awful aspects. The convergence of historical motivation, individual willfulness, and the mother's violation of blood rites would create one of the profounder bases of tension across the work.

20. See, for example, the description of these arrangements in Dorothy Dinnerstein *The Mermaid and the Minotaur: Sexual Arrangements and Human Malaise* (New York: Harper Colphon Books, 1976).

21. The terms are taken from Northrop Frye, "Historical Criticism: Theory of Modes" in *Anatomy of Criticism: Four Essays* (Princeton: Princeton University Press).

22. Kenneth Burke, "The Four Master Tropes," in *A Grammar of Motives*, appendix (New York: Prentice-Hall, 1945). Burke's refinement of a notion of dialectics in art is significant both as an image and concept of radical revision. His "perceptive of perspectives"—the principle of the "modified noun"—locates an ideal against which we might try to imagine the future of Afro-American letters and our meditation concerning them.

23. Harper and Stepto.

24. Ibid.

25. Ibid.

◆◆◆◆◆◆◆◆◆◆◆◆◆◆

When Lindbergh Sleeps with Bessie Smith: The Writing of Place in *Sula*

HOUSTON A. BAKER, JR.

> If woman has always functioned "within" the discourse of man, a signifier that has always referred back to the opposite signifier which annihilates its specific energy and diminishes or stifles its very different sounds, it is time for her to dislocate this "within," to explode it, turn it around, and seize it; to make it hers, containing it, taking it in her own mouth, biting that tongue with her very own teeth to invent for herself a language to get inside of.
>
> Hélène Cixous, "The Laugh of the Medusa"

In an interview conducted by the Afro-American literary critic Robert Stepto, Toni Morrison describes her relationship to space and place as follows:

> I felt a very strong sense of place, not in terms of the country or the state, but in terms of the details, the feeling, the mood of the community. . . . I think some of it is just a woman's strong sense of being in a room, a place, or in a house. Sometimes my relationship to things in a house would be a little different from, say my brother's or my father's or my sons'. I clean them and I move them and I do very intimate things "in place." I am sort of rooted in it, so that writing about being in a room looking out, or being in a world looking out, or living in a small definite place, is probably very common among most women anyway.

Insofar as black domestic labor makes a narrow circuit from kitchenettes to white folk's kitchens, it may be considered beyond the reaches of conscious history by Wright and others.[1] But insofar as it becomes—in the inscription of Morrison's writing of "intimacy"—a production of order, it is at the ritual foundation of the black community's systematic definitions of itself. In fact, as avatars of those who were accessible and unshackled between the abovedeck worlds of white sailing machines and their suffocating holes, the domestic marks the boundaries of communal space.[2]

Interiority and the frontier of violation coalesce in the accessible body of the African woman. The question of propriety, a "normal" place query, is conflated or confused with one of "intimacy." The body's male owner and violator (the European slavetrader) is in an altogether different relationship to it from its intimate occupant. And the nature of the intimacy achieved by the occupant as domesticator is quintessential to definitions of Afro-American community. The occupant marks the "boundary case" of ownership.

In Morrison's description this marking, or systemization of interiority, is a function of *cleaning*. And it is the anthropologist Mary Douglas who most persuasively coalesces ideas of order and danger, cleaning and violation in her discussions of dirt in *Purity and Danger*. She writes:

> Dirt is the by-product of a systematic ordering and classification of matter, in so far as ordering involves rejecting inappropriate elements . . . We can recognise in our own notions of dirt that we are using a kind of omnibus compendium which includes all the rejected elements of ordered systems. It is a relative idea. Shoes are not dirty in themselves, but it is dirty to place them on the dining-table.

Douglas's definition of dirt as "matter out of place" is suggestive for the purifying negotiation of matters mandated by the abovedeck world of the slaveship. A rejection of the assumptions, if not the conditions, of violation—an obstinate insistence on a deeper intimacy, as it were, provided conditions of possibility for the very existence of Afro-American system. The unmediated, abovedeck world reduces the scope of concern from a desire for possession of the Western machine to a psychic quest for achieved and ordering intimacy. The shift is something like that between world historic forces and embedded ancestral energies of survival.

Continuing her conversation with Stepto, Morrison notes that when she wrote her novel *Sula*, she:

> was interested in making the town, the community, the neighborhood, as strong a character as I could. . . . My tendency is to focus on neighborhoods and communities. And the community, the black community . . . it had seemed to me . . . was always there, only we called it the "neighborhood."

What Morrison ultimately seeks in her coding of Afro-American PLACE is a writing of intimate, systematizing, and ordering black village values. For in "City Limits, Village Values," she suggests that black writers retain always a respect for "community values," for "village values." And chief among these values, in her view, is the "advising, benevolent, protective, wise black ancestor . . . imagined as surviving in the village but not in the city." Morrison, thus, pulls away from what has been considered the standard Afro-American story of a willed and unvarying progress of blacks from rural hamlets to passionate endorsement of modern, urban technological arrangements of life. Her notions of Afro-American making as they are told in *Sula*, therefore, seem almost to emanate from an altogether different expressive tradition. For *Sula* begins not in the manner or Richard Wright's *Native Son*, with airplanes over the city, but with the definition of an "intimate" black neighborhood at the moment of its negation: "In that place, where they tore the nightshade and blackberry patches from their roots to make room for the Medallion City Golf Course, there was once a neighborhood. . . . It is called the suburbs now, but when black people lived there it was called the Bottom." This is Morrison's "village" or "community" or "ancestral" home of the folk in their ritual confrontation with stark daily and yearly necessities occasioned by what the narrator of *Sula* calls "A joke. A nigger joke."³

The "nigger joke" in *Sula* is offered as an explanation for the name of "that place." It is called "the Bottom" because it originated in the tricky economics of Afro-American slavery. Having promised a slave both freedom and a piece of "bottom land" if he performed some very difficult chores, a white master reneges, granting freedom easily enough but constructing a ruse to convince the slave that barren hill land buffeted by wind and eroded by rain is "rich and fertile" *bottom land*. Explaining to the skeptical slave that from God's perspective, the barren hill is the very bottom of heaven, the white master succeeds in his deception.

This etiological tale of place naming inscribes the fact and fantasy of capitalism in *Sula*. It is the writing of an American betrayal that can be read as follows in the words of W. E. B. Du Bois: "But the vision of 'forty acres and a mule'—the righteous and reasonable ambition to become a landholder, which the nation had all but categorically promised the freedmen—was destined in most cases to bitter disappointment."⁷ The joke within the Bottom is the deprivation of the "means of production" that characterized America's relationship to former slaves. This betrayal, broken promise and sublation, are determinative in the world of *Sula*. For life in the Bottom is exalted neither through agricultural production nor productive industrial labor associated with construction and running of a "modern" world. Instead, the Bottom's character is a redaction of the folk's innovative survival of a "joke."

The joke, in fact, comes to stand as the signifying difference within the whole of the novel's discourse. It mocks the Bottom's rocky autonomy like the repressed content of preconscious thought.⁴ Drawn down into a collective white and black unconscious, the denial of black advantage re-emerges as an acceptable discursive form whose displacements and distortions allow its scandalous content to escape censure. Blacks and whites alike tell the joke to secure the meager comforts of self-esteem and self-justification. The "nigger joke," then, not only names "that place," but also provides the unconscious of Medallion and the Bottom with a slightly pleasurable rationale for the average person's powerlessness in the face of an exclusive, capitalistic control of the world. Working-class white men tell the joke when they are out of work. Immigrant men and boys tell it in order to bond with racist whites. Blacks tell it to achieve self-exoneration. All who tell it laugh to keep from crying at their powerlessness.

A community veritably created as the function of a "joke" requires special rituals for survival. The return of the repressed signalled by the "nigger joke" represents a general absence of control, an antecedent and exterior determination of, at least, the space in which a community can set life in motion. Since the denial represented is general, or global, as I have suggested by noting the variety of groups it subsumes, it seems fitting that capitalism's most indisputable moment of global/technological "modernism" should produce the preeminent ritualist of *Sula*.

Who can deny that the most awesome mobilization of capitalism's prowess the world had ever witnessed until 1914 was World War I? And who, after reading *Sula*, fails to apprehend Shadrack, the handsome young black man bathed in the terrifying fires of that global conflagration, as a blasted sign of capitalism's maddening control of man's fate?[5]

Upon his discharge from a veterans facility, Shadrack makes his way back to the Bottom and institutes an annual ritual—National Suicide Day, scheduled for the third of January. He is the first character we encounter in *Sula*, and the chapter in which his story is recounted is entitled "1919." The format of the narrator's tale is, thus, a chronicle.

Shadrack has seen a fellow private destroyed by war. The boy's face is blown off in the very first moment of the very first battle in which Shadrack participates. This carnage drives Shadrack insane. The picture of brains sliding down the back of the soldier's body which ". . . ran on, with energy and grace, ignoring the drip and slide of brains" is an image of dismembered humanity, of the absurd horror produced by exploitative workings of power. Upon his return to the Bottom, Shakrack says, "No," in madness and in thunder, to such terrifyingly unstable conditions of existence. His National Suicide Day is intended as a prophylaxis against such disorder. Through a manipulation of images and instruments of death it is meant affectively to reduce death to a "residual" category.[9] As the guardian of spaces of sudden and unpredictable death, Shadrack becomes a latter day Charon, an antinomian figure of matted hair, obscene language, and exposed genitals who provides reassuring grounds of "abnormality" for the Bottom's traditional rites of birth, harvest, and matrimony. Shadrack, one might say, is an unequivocal *public wrong* against which the Bottom defines its right. "Once the people understood the boundaries and nature of his madness, they could fit him, so to speak, into the scheme of things." Shadrack is scarcely a mere eccentric. He appears, in fact, as a gigantic, Blakean inscription on the landscape of *Sula*. His most distinctive signature is that of the existentialist. Reversing the Bible's characterization of Shadrack[10] as a man whose faith enabled him to escape the commands of authority and the fiery furnace of the State, Morrison's mad ritualist is a consciousness blasted and terrified into non-sense by the awesome workings of State power. God is decisively dead in Shadrack's universe; the initiative belongs to madmen alone. Like the Bottom community itself, Morrison sets this wrongman in distinctive contrast to Mrs. Helene Wright, the second character encountered as the chronicle moves to "1920."

Helene Wright (nee *Sabat*) has evolved in a way that directly counterpoints Shadrack's emergence. From the outlawed dominion of the Sundown House of prostitution in New Orleans where she was born and an association with witches marked by her surname "Sabat," she has moved to the sheltering Ohio matrimony that makes her "Wright." The Bottom unwittingly cooperates in the woman's obsessive flight from her mother's sexuality by domesticating her name; they call her, simply, Helen. Without sketching her history in great detail, one can surely read Helene as a descendant of the women described in Morrison's *The Bluest Eye*, black women who have tamed both their hair and their passions in order to be rid of "the funkiness. . . . The dreadful funkiness of passion, the funkiness of nature, the funkiness of the wide range of human emotions." Helene is, likewise, a precursor of that community of Dead women in *Song of Solomon* who spend their days inside the house, making artificial roses.[6] Her privileged project in *Sula* is the thinning of both her daughter's nose and her imagination.

She succeeds mightily in dimming Nel's imagination until it is but a faint remnant of the luminescent energy displayed on the daughter's return from her great-grandmother Cecile's funeral in New Orleans. On the night of her return, having glimpsed possibilities of life beyond the Bottom and having witnessed her mother's sad reversion to a coquette under the "male eyes" of a white train conductor, Nel declares her difference. Her mirror stage revery reads: "I'm me. I'm not their daughter. I'm not Nel. I'm me." The narrator comments: "Each time she said the word *me* there was a gathering in her like power, like joy, like fear." But the "me" dreamed by the daughter is effectively erased by her churchgoing, compulsively orderly, and communally respected mother. For Helen's house is one of oppressive neatness, providing a marked contrast to the Peace residence at number seven Carpenter Road.

Again, Morrison's subtle delight in nominalism, a delight that competes in *Sula* with an ironic essentialism, surfaces in the name "Peace." For surely a more cocophonous household than Eva Peace's would be difficult to discover outside of Morrison's own corpus or the provinces of Latin American fiction. Eva, the one-legged grandmother of Sula, lives in her house with assorted boarders, a white hillbilly whom she derisively calls "Tar Baby," her daughter Hannah who will "fuck practically anything" and requires "some touching every day," her son Ralph (called "Plum") for a brief time, and three four-foot tall grotesques collectively named by Eva "the deweys."

The very construction of her dwelling, described in a subtle rephrasing of Christian scripture as "a house of many rooms," testifies to a kind of antinomian disorder. Eva's place has:

> been built over a period of five years to the specifications of its owner, who kept on adding things: more stairways—there were three sets to the second floor—more rooms, doors and stoops. There were rooms that had three doors,

others that opened out on the porch only and were inaccessible from any other part of the house; others that you could get to only by going through somebody's bedroom.

The depiction reminds one of surreal constructs in the paintings of Escher. The house's ceaseless increase is a testimony to its owner's desire for expanded dominion. In a curious way, in fact, it attests the very "manlove" that we are told is the ruling creed of the Peaces. The endless stairways, for example, are a delight for the Freudian dream analyst.[7]

The multiplication of structure at Eva's, however, is finally closer to the antinomian increase of Shadrack's inversive inventories[8] than to conspicuous, capitalistic display. The ceaseless expansion is a compensatory gesture by a woman who has suffered dismemberment in the office of survival. When her husband BoyBoy (who is not unlike "the deweys" in either his name or his infantile and abusive behavior) deserts her in the dead of winter, Eva is hardpressed to find means of survival. After her infant son "Plum" almost dies of constipation and she is forced to, literally, extract the rock-like waste from his anus in a bitterly cold outhouse, she resolves to take action. She leaves her children with a neighbor and disappears for eighteen months, returning with her left leg severed and enough money in hand to depart her one-room cabin and build Number Seven Carpenter Road as a boardinghouse.

What one might say is that Eva, in Morrison's rewriting of the Biblical first woman Eve, is scarcely a chaste, whole, helpmeet for Patriarchy. She is a dismembered black woman who refuses to expire in the backwash of any man's history. Like Shadrack, she says "Uh uh. Nooo" to the given arrangement of things. In order to defeat the dreadful course of capitalism's "joke," she subjects herself to dismemberment, sacrificing a leg for the sake of insurance premiums, or so the myth of her loss is told.

She converts her very body into a dismembered instrument of defiance—and finance. Her act is as much an utterance of the *Non Serviam* as that of her slave precursor described by a Works Project Administration interviewee as follows: "I knew a woman who could not be conquered by her mistress, and so her master threatened to sell her to New Orleans Negro traders. She took her right hand, laid it down on a meat block and cut off three fingers, and thus made the sale impossible."[15]

Similarly, Eva refuses to become a will-less object of exchange left to die in barren, one-room arrangements of the Bottom. She becomes, instead, one in Party of Shadrack, advocating an inversive "manlove" that makes both her and her daughter "sooty" in the estimation of Helene Wright. In addition, she absolutely refuses to be bound by traditional, middle-class definitions of motherhood and responds to her daughter Hannah's query, "Mamma, did you ever love us?" with the following tirade:

No time [to play or engage in affectionate gestures]. They wasn't no time. Not none. Soon as I got one day done here come a night. With you all coughin' and me watchin' so TB wouldn't take you off and if you was sleepin' quiet I thought, O Lord, they dead and put my hand over your mouth to feel if the breath was comin' what you talkin' 'bout did I love you girl I stayed alive for you can't you get that through your thick head or what is that between your ears, heifer?"

In the bleak world of 1895 (the year of Booker T. Washington's Atlanta Compromise Speech and the one before the infamous *Plessy* v. *Ferguson* decision that made "separate but equal" the Jim Crow law of the land), there was *no* time for black women to engage in playful non-sense. There was but one incumbency: a dismembering sacrifice of the body to ensure survival and life for the children. The refusal of maternal non-sense is terrifyingly displayed, however, not in Eva's mere tirades against traditional behaviors, but in her fiery execution of her own son.

When Plum finally returns to the Bottom after his service in World War I, he is a heroin addict. Refusing to allow him to regress to infancy and, as she graphically states it, "crawl back in my womb," Eva pours kerosene over him and sets him on fire. She is pictured in her homicidal scene as a giant heron or eagle swooping down in dreadful judgment on her own child. It has been suggested that Eva in her fiery manifestation displays the protean character of the Indian goddess Shiva; her first relation to Plum is as a benevolent lifegiver. Burning him for heroin addiction, she becomes the fiery avenging face of the goddess.

Her act, whether god-like or more secularly murderous, places her on a plane with Bigger Thomas who rationalizes his murders in the name of an achievement of "personal" space. Eva tells Hannah: "He was a man, girl, a big old growed-up man. I didn't have that much room. . . . I done everything I could to make him leave me and go on and live and be a man but he wouldn't and I had to keep him out so I just thought of a way he could die like a man not all scrunched up inside my womb, but a man." One imagines a more intelligent Bigger talking of Bessie Mears' "solace in death," of his having helpfully removed her from the "scrunched up" confines of a narrow existence. Eva, in her throne-like chair in a child's wagon, is an imperious and arrogant agent of vengeful death, just as she is the willful namer of man's fate, labelling and constricting the three deweys to an unindividuated, libidinal existence and mocking the mountainboy of beautiful voice with the disagreeable name "Tar Baby."

She is, finally, a mythic character, not quite allegorical, and not fully developed as an avatar of some non-Christian pantheon. She is, nonetheless, a positer of a creed that literally defines her daughter and granddaughter. She is also, as we have seen, the absolute controller of more than one fate in the novel. Ironically, with all of her self-defining hatred of BoyBoy (". . . it was hating him that kept her alive and happy"), she is the chief advocate for monogamous marriage, telling her newly married women boarders just what they should do for their husbands and counseling her granddaughter Sula to settle down into marriage and a family. The admixture of advocacy and hatred, inversive survival energy and arrogant murder, make Eva the type of morally ambiguous character that Morrison seems so adept at creating and so astute in evaluating. Of Eva, she says:

> "[She] plays god, names people and, you know, puts her hand on a child. . . .
> . She decided that her son was living a life that was not worth his time. She
> meant it was too painful for her; you know the way you kill a dog when he
> breaks his leg because you can't stand the pain. He may very well be able to
> stand it, but you can't, so that's why you get rid of him."[16]

Aware of Eva's god-like response to the incumbencies of survival in 1895, Morrison draws us to her as Milton leads us to his darkly magestic Satan, only to show us, in time, the morally culpable will to power that has conditioned our own identification with evil. For Morrison, Eva is not, finally, an empowering model of Afro-American liberation but a self-absorbed and imperious survivor of disaster.

II

When we arrive at the year 1922, we are aware that Morrison, like her most readily identifiable male precursor Jean Toomer, has presented characters and details of a setting that is meant to suggest an ancestral village.[17] Polarities have been established, rituals described, and village origins and occurrences subjected to subtle scrutiny. The emergent world of the Bottom is not unlike the Dixie Pike village in Toomer's *Cane* (1923). For, as in *Cane* there is from the outset of *Sula* a strong sense that an era and its kinship and expressive structures are in decline. Toomer's narrator speaks of a "plaintive soul, leaving, soon gone," and Morrison's narrator opens her story with word of deracination—nightshade and blackberry bushes being torn away along with the rambling, commercial structures of an erstwhile neighborhood. Further implicating the tone and texture of *Cane* in *Sula* are the similar appearances in the two works of grotesques—symbolic characters who carry a burden of significance and who are, even when most lyrically described, bereft of wholeness. Toomer's Becky is an isolated white woman who violates traditional southern sexual taboos. His Fern is a sexually liberated hysteric who combines the landscape's beauty with the resonances of a Jewish cantor's singing. The men and women of *Cane*'s three sections share the qualities of beauty, strangeness, incompletion, hysteria. All tremble, at points, on the verge of the outrageous—whether in their passivity, their obsessive search for rootedness, or their distraught determination to make something—anything—happen.

What Toomer implies is that "village values" may produce an exceed-ingly resonant folk harmony when there are no radically competing sounds. At evening fall, after the sawmill has blown its final whistle, the supper getting ready songs of black women are perfect correlatives for a sensual landscape. But in the glaring light and blaring dissonances of southern industrial day and northern urban noon, village values and their expression may stand, with all their haunting nostalgia, merely as a promise—"a promise of a soil-soaked beauty; uprooted, thinning out. Suspended a few feet above the soil whose touch would resurrect. . . ."

In truth, Toomer's Georgia hamlet and his Washington world of the black bourgeoisie are not chosen places controlled by blacks. Rather, then are, like Sula's Bottom, functions of slavery. Their apparently tran-quil intimacy and autonomy remain romantic mystifications if they are not read as reaction formations of certain Western confinements. It is all too easy, for example, to blink the denial that is always co-implicated in definitions of "village values." The "joke" is as much a factor, finally, in *Cane* as in *Sula*.

What is compelling about comparison of the two works is that Mor-rison would, indeed, seem to emanate from a tradition different from that of Wright and Ellison. Henry Louis Gates, Jr. describes *Cane*'s as a lyrical or "speakerly" tradition in black letters, distinguishing writers such as Toomer and Zora Neale Hurston from realist writers such as Sterling Brown and Richard Wright.[9] And nowhere is *Sula*'s situation as lyrical and symbolic narrative better observed than in the chapter entitled "1922," which begins with the statement: "It was too cool for ice cream."

III

It is "too cool for ice cream" because Nel and Sula, as twelve-year-old black girls "wishbone thin and easy-assed," are not yet mature enough to participate physically in the sensual, sexual mysteries signified by ice cream. The location of Edna Finch's Mellow House (the ice cream parlor) in the community is at the end of a gauntlet of young and old black men who stare with "panther eyes" at the young girls. All of the men are thinking of images summoned by the phrase "pig meat," but one twenty-one-year-old black "pool haunt of sinister beauty" named Ajax, actually utters the phrase, stirring the budding sexuality of the two girls like confectionary ice on warm and eager tongues.

The opening scene of "1922" is, thus, rife with sexuality. And while the surname "Finch" carries connotations of a delicate flight and extends the bird imagery of *Sula* (we recall Eva's "heron" or "eagle"), "mellow" indicates "ripe," or "mature." The oxymoron marked by "sinister beauty" for Ajax is complemented by the innocent lust of adolescent girls and the almost blues innuendo of Morrison's handling of "ice cream." Surely, Edna's mellow confections appear more like the male equivalent of the blues' "jelly roll" than Baskin-Robbins' twenty-one flavors. Vanilla and lemon come together as follows:

> The cream-colored trousers marking with a mere seam the place where the mystery curled. Those smooth vanilla crotches invited them; those lemon-yellow gabardines beckoned to them. They moved toward the ice-cream parlor like tightrope walkers, as thrilled by the possibility of a slip as by the maintenance of tension and balance. The least sideways glance, the merest toe stub, could pitch them into those creamy haunches spread wide with welcome. Somewhere beneath all of that daintiness, chambered in all that neatness, lay the thing that clotted their dreams.

This mutual dream of Sula and Nel is scarcely one of real "ice cream." What brings the two girls together, in a word, is the Phallus, the Law of the Fathers whose "mystery" makes it a creamy veil for their adolescent dreams.[10] Now the Phallus in psychoanalytic terms is to be distinguished from the penis. For it is not a material object but a discursive signifier of the Father, or better, of the Father's Law. In the writing of Freud, infantile drives institute a tripartite pattern of lack-absence-differentiation. Originally "at one" with the breast of the Mother, the child experiences hunger (lack) as an absence of the breast. Eventually, he or she discovers in the Mother's absense his or her *difference* or differentiation from the Mother. A dyadic, or two-fold relationship is the result.

The child makes demands; the Mother has desires. The child wishes to become the desired of the Mother. (A simple instance is alimentary—the child demands food; the mother desires toilet training.) In order for Culture to occur, this dyad of desire must be interrupted by a third term. That term is the Father as Phallus, as the Law. Here we come to the Oedipal stage in which those children possessed of a penis come to want to be the absent Phallus *for* the Mother but find the Father always already there. Hence, they tremble before the thought of death (castration/lack) and subjugate themselves to the master, the Law of the Phallus. They know what they will accede to Fatherhood in due course. Children without a penis substitute a baby—as a sign of presence and satisfaction, and a possible fulfillment of desire—for the absent Phallus. What Jacques Lacan makes of the traditional corpus of Freud is a signifying drama in which the Phallus represents the condition of possibility of socio-sexual differentiation and cultural production by *standing for* the third term, or Father. It is the marker, as it were, of male power and familiarly patriarchal discourse. It is both pre-cultural and culture-founding.

Based on a myth of prehistoric murder of the Father (e.g., Freud's *Totem and Taboo*) who had hoarded the women of the clan and denied the sons, the Law of the Phallus is totemic. It represents the cultural necessities of incest-avoidance and submission to the dread of death (castration). The Phallus, in a word, is the signifier that institutes male-dominant cultural discourse and mandates a division of physiologically differentiated childen into two unequal sexes. To create a habitable space beyond the Law of the Phallus, a symbolic manipulation—an unveiling—is de rigueur.

In fact, what causes the discourse of "1922" to coalesce (or clot) is the triple repetition of Sula and Nel's ritual of the Phallus. It is important to say at the outset, however, that Sula and Nel, for all their apparent bonding, do not share a single perspective. While the Phallus may be an object common to their dreams, how very different their dreams are! Nel lapses easily into a "picture of herself lying on a flowered bed, tangled in her own hair, waiting for some fiery prince. He approached but never quite arrived." Sula, by contrast: "spent hours in the attic behind a roll of linoleum galloping through her own mind on a gray-and-white horse tasting sugar and smelling roses." Different fantasies, to be sure. Sula is a rider and a taster of confections; Nel awaits a fire that never quite kindles. The visions of both girls, however, include not only an implied relationship to the Phallus, but also the presence of some further person, a dream companion of the same gender.

This third party signals a traditional triangulation described by Nancy Chodorow in *The Reproduction of Mothering:*

> Girls cannot and do not "reject" their mother and women in favor of their father and men, but remain in a bisexual triangle throughout childhood and into puberty. They usually make a sexual resolution in favor of men and their father, but retain an internal emotional triangle.[11]

Discussing the work of the psychologist Helene Deutsch, Chodorow explains that when women are involved in heterosexual, erotic relationships with men relational triangles represent a reproduction of the type of mother-daughter bonding described in the foregoing quotation. There can be little doubt about both Nel's and Sula's erotic attraction to "the thing that clotted their dreams." Similarly, there can be little doubt about the "nontraditional" character of that signifier in their lives. For both girls are "daughters of distant mothers and incomprehensible fathers (Sula's because he was dead; Nel's because he wasn't)." In a sense—and as a consequence, at least in part, of a "nigger joke"—Nel and Sula are *not* members of a traditional "family," and, hence, cannot play out the usual family romance.[12]

For example, Sula cannot maintain any affectional preoedipal bonding with a mother who, pressed by the exigencies of her need for touching, admits to not liking her daughter, to seeing Sula (quite justifiably in the male-bereft economies of the Bottom) as a burden and a cross to bear. Hence, a rejected Sula watches her mother burn to death without so much as stirring a muscle. Similarly, Nel, as the diminished product of a mother bent on eradicating sexuality along with her daughter's distinguishing physical identity, is incapable of finding a maternal perch for her affections. The two girls, therefore, come to stand for each other as more Mother than their actual mothers. They enact their supportive displacement as a function of the incumbencies of a black "village" existence.

Similarly, Sula and Nel are required to construct the role of the Father from that assembly that marks the male gauntlet from the Time-and-a-Half Pool Hall to Edna Finch's Mellow House. This further displacement mystifies the Phallus even more in their mutual imaginings. And it is, ultimately, the displacements occasioned by the "nigger joke" that necessitate a three-fold enactment of Phallic rites in "1922."

First, there is a ludic enactment in which "the beautiful, beautiful boys . . . [whose] footsteps left a smell of smoke behind" are metaphorically appropriated as "thick" twigs peeled "to a smooth, creamy innocence," like ice cream. Sula's first act is an artist's response; she "traced intricate patterns . . . with her twig." But soon, both Nel and Sula are hollowing out holes in earth. Their separate holes join, and Nel's twig snaps. Both girls, then, throw their twigs into the hole and collect all the debris from the clearing around them and bury it, with the twigs, in the earth. The first rite is completed. The Phallus has been metaphorically exposed and exorcised; its mystery has been appropriated by the absorptive (earth) womb, which seems capable of serving as the whole (as opposed to the broken or fragmented twig) ground of bonding between the girls. It is as though a "creamy" pleasure can be shared by a common hold. Demystification and burial (a purgative burial and "cleaning") are engaged as common ritual acts.

In the second instance of the Phallic rites, however, the girls' responses dramatically differentiate them. Chicken Little comes into the clearing, and while Nel badgers him about his polluting behavior (i.e., picking his nose), Sula accepts him as he is. In an adolescent figuration of her mother's relationship to male lovers, Sula suggests that Chicken "didn't need fixing." And it is Sula alone who climbs the tree with the little boy, showing him a world beyond the river. Nel remains on the ground and, hence, is not party to a Freudian reading of tree climbing.

In the section of the *Interpretation of Dreams* entitled "representation by symbols," Freud observes: "I added [in explanation of one of his patient's dreams] from my own knowledge derived elsewhere that climbing down, like climbing up in other cases, described sexual intercourse in the vagina." Nel is further excluded from the scene when she takes no active part in burial. Sula alone responds in mocking revelry to Chicken's infantile boast of (sexual) achievement: "I'm a tell my brovver." She

> picked . . . [Chicken Little] up by his hands and swung him outward then around and around. His knickers ballooned and his shrieks of frightened joy startled the birds and the fat grasshoppers. When he slipped from her hands

and sailed away out over the water they could still hear his bubbly laughter. The water darkened and closed quickly over the place where Chicken Little sank.

Morrison's own mocking designation of the Phallus, in all of its mystery, as a false harbinger of apocalypse—"Chicken Little"—begins the demystification that is completed in the little boy's burial by water. Immediately after he sinks below the surface, Sula rushes across the footbridge to Shadrack's shack. Overwhelmed by the neatness of its interior, she forgets to ask the mad ritualist if he has seen her throw Chicken Little in the river. He, thinking she seeks reassurance about the permanence of human life, speaks the single word "always."

Sula has just discovered the absence of benevolent design and the limits of conscious control in the universe. Hence, Shadrack's reassurance is absurdly comic. And in the absurdity of what is (given Shadrack's fiery history) a common knowledge of disorder, the two characters are bonded. Sula becomes one in the party of Shadrackian antinomianism.

The final enactment of Phallic rites in "1922" expands the categorization of "the mystery" from false herald of apocalypse to Christian sign of the Transcendental Signifier—the Law itself. In its burial rites of Chicken Little, the community of the Bottom summons Jesus Christ as the metonym for the son—the son, who, as Eva tells Hannah in reference to Plum, is "hard to bear." "You wouldn't know that," she explains to her daughter, "but they is."

The women of Greater Saint Matthew's take Jesus "as both son and lover," and in his "downy face they could see the sugar-and-butter sandwiches and feel the oldest and most devastating pain there is: not the pain of childhood, but the remembrance of it." Phallic mystery, even in its most transcendental form as the Law, has as its woman's redaction loss, pain, absence. The actual fathers are disappeared by a "nigger joke" in Sula that emasculates them and denies them any legitimate means of production. They desert children who, thus, become reminders of dismemberment, dispossession. The joke's consequences demand a compensating ritual, and in Sula, it is a funereal exertion of religious frenzy: "they [the women of Greater Saint Matthew's] danced and screamed, not to protest God's will but to acknowledge it and confirm once more their conviction that the only way to avoid the Hand of God is to get in it."

And so "in the colored part of the cemetery, they sank Chicken Little in between his grandfather and an aunt." Butterflies mark the scene of this third burial—butterflies that signify graceful flight and sexual deilght and unite, once more, at a higher level of abstraction and joke-compensation, the dreams of Sula and Nel: "two young girlfriends trotting up the road on a summer day wondering what happened to butterflies in the winter."

The butterflies return as "lemon-yellow" delight when Ajax releases a jar of them in Sula's bedroom on one occasion when they make passionate love. And how, with his lemon yellow as sign, could we mistake Ajax as other than one of the party of New Orleans, Sundown House conjurations? Rochelle Sabat, in an early instance of *Sula*'s bird imagery, appears as "the woman in the canary-yellow dress" wafting an odor of gardenias.

IV

Morrison is such a careful artist and her prose is so richly nuanced that it begs attention to every detail. It would be a mistake, however, to obscure the importance of "1922" by pushing on immediately with further readings. For, it seems to me, the genealogical and thematic lines of the novel are practically all in place with the close of the third enactment of Phallic rites of that chapter.[13] Nel, who passively and quite conventionally by the bourgeois gender standards of her heritage awaits the fiery prince, is a natural for the role into which Helene Wright has "scrunched" her. She will be wife and mother, not an artistic tracer of innovative designs.

Sula, by contrast, will be the daring heir of her grandmother and mother's easy sexuality, an ally of Shadrack in an absurdly boring world where a little "touching every day" may provide the only relief—and release. Nel will shout cautions while Sula climbs trees.

It is important, however, in marking out the dynamics of Afro-American Place, not to reinscribe uncritically the Law of the Father, to remystify the Phallus by insisting too strenuously on the significance of "1922." There is, in fact, a reading of *Sula* that claims heterosexuality in general is under erasure in the novel. In "Toward a Black Feminist Criticism," the Afro-American lesbian critic Barbara Smith writes:

> Despite the apparent heterosexuality of the female characters I discovered in re-reading *Sula* that it works as a lesbian novel not only because of the passionate friendship between Sula and Nel, but because of Morrison's consistently critical stance toward the heterosexual institutions of male/female relationships, marriage, and the family. Consciously or not, Morrison's work poses both lesbian and feminist questions about Black women's autonomy and their impact upon each other's lives.

Smith is surely correct about *Sula*'s unflagging critique—in the strictest philosophical sense—of traditional heterosexual arrangements. If BoyBoy and Jude (Nel's whiny husband) are signs of the Father and Husband in *Sula*, then neither finds positive signification. Further, if Eva, Helene, Hannah, or Nel are taken as signs of the Mother and Wife, a similar absence results. Marriage does not work in *Sula* in the manner of, say, the implicit valorizations of that institution suggested by the Dick-and-Jane primer of the white family life that appears in *The Bluest Eye*. And it is surely true that Nel and Sula's relationship is the signal, foregrounded instance in the novel of productive and symbiotic human allegiance. The girls begin by loving each other with the uncritical acceptance and shared curiosity of adolescent adoration. They remain, as well, emotionally dependent upon one another—even when they are physically separated or distanced by seeming betrayal. As a representation of woman's bonding, then, *Sula* works toward Smith's specifications.

One question to be posed, however, is: How adequately does a lesbian reading, which foregrounds and privileges a loving and compatible relationship between Sula and Nel, explain the Place and dynamics of Morrison's village as a whole? I want to suggest that a lesbian reading, while persuasive in its description of the best aspects of the relationship between Nel and Sula, leaves too much of the novel's exquisitely detailed and richly imaged concern for the values of the Bottom out of account.

For example, though it is true that *Sula* does not contain a marriage that works like the Dick-and-Jane postulates of *The Bluest Eye*, it is also true that such postulates are subjected—in the very portrayal of black life in that novel and in the omniscient narrator's reduction of such postulates to gibberish-like epigraphs—to almost comic inversion. The mystifying ideality of such postulates becomes absurd in the face of lived black life. Moreover, if heterosexual arrangements that lead to a mindless and deserted reproduction of mothering are the only heterosexual arrangements considered by a critical reading of *Sula*, then it is fair to say that Morrison is unabashedly critical of them. However, there is a heterosexual relationship in *Sula* between the protagonist and Ajax that possesses—in Morrison's and her narrator's view—all of the skyward possibilities and potentially resonant camaraderie that would result if "Lindbergh . . . [were to sleep] with Bessie Smith." The following quotation from *Sula* can scarcely be read as a condemnation of heterosexuality:

> He [Ajax] liked for her to mount him so he could see her towering above him and call soft obscenities up into her face. . . . She looked down, down from what seemed an awful height at the head of the man whose lemon-yellow gabardines had been the first sexual excitement she'd known. . . .
>
> *If I take a chamois and rub real hard on the bone, right on the ledge of your cheek bone, some of the black will disappear. It will flake away into the chamois and underneath there will be gold leaf. I can see it shinning through the black. I know it is there.*
>
> How high she was over his wand-lean body, how slippery was his sliding smile.
>
> *And if I take a nail file or even Eva's old paring knife—that will do—and scrape away at the gold, it will fall away and there will be alabaster. The alabaster is what gives your face its planes, its curves. That is why your mouth smiling does not reach your eyes. Alabaster is giving it a gravity that resists a total smile. . . .*

> *Then I can take a chisel and small tap hammer and tap away at the alabaster. It will crack then like ice under the pick, and through the breaks I will see the loam, fertile, free of pebbles and twigs. For it is the loam that is giving you that smell.*
>
> She slipped her hands under his armpits, for it seemed as though she would not be able to dam the spread of weakness she felt under her skin without holding on to something.

"Weakness" translates in this scene as complimentarity, the protagonist's realization that she is the indispensable "water" for the man of sinister beauty's loam. The ritual of earth and twigs in "1922" rewrites itself as heterosexual pleasure and fulfillment, and woman is on top.

It is as though a woman blues singer like Bessie Smith flies, while a male pilot takes delight in sexual pleasure rather than achieving gratification from aggressively asserted power of the Phallus. Morrison's poetical and sensual writing of this heterosexuality suggests a bonding that might possibly bring a Bottom community down from its "suspension"— that might reroot it in a fertile loam. "He swallowed her mouth just as her thighs had swallowed his genitals, and the house was very, very quiet."

The swallowing of the actual penis, rather than the burial of the Phallus, might produce a resounding quiet and a genuine peace. In her engaging essay "Sorceress and Hysteric," Catherine Clément writes as follows about accommodative strategies for the anomalous (for "dirt," or "residual categories") delineated by Lévi-Strauss:

> The anthropoemic mode . . . consists in vomiting the abnormal one into protected spaces—hospitals, asylums, prisons. The other, the anthropophagic mode, examples of which are found especially in ahistorical societies, consists in finding a place for anomaly, delinquency, and deviancy—a place in the sun at the heart of cultural activity.

To "swallow" is to incorporate anomaly into the community as "place in the sun," not to confine it as burial. In Sula and Ajax's heterosexuality, we discover a model that rewrites the "joke" of a capitalism that emasculates the black male penis in the office of the Law of the Fathers.

Reclamation, thus, takes the form in *Sula* of an artistic, mystical, and inverted totemic feast that erases rather than reinscribes the Phallus. Sula, in the role of a male Pygmalion's deconstructor, rather than a female statue in passive transformation, goes through layers and layers of suppression in order to arrive at the soil of community. Her swallowing is beneficiently anthropophagic. Is, then, Ellison correct in his claim that black male genitals offer salvation for technological society?[24] Scarcely. Genital display in *Invisible Man* is a homosexual occasion; only men are present. In *Sula* woman is on top as the domestic flyer, the ritual blues purifier and cleaner of congestive layers whose excavation leads, finally, to fertile and reclaimed "dirt."

An interested reading of the Sula/Ajax relationship—one that led, say, to the assertion that the resonant combination of flight and blues signalled by their merger is a heroic writing of Afro-American Place— might well be accused of overprivileging a male principle. But such an accusation would be justified only if Ajax's real majesty was ascribed, exclusively and quite mistakenly, to some self-generating source. A right reading of Sula's lover does not cast him in the role of the romantic and autonomous streetcorner male. Ajax is properly understood, in a very cogent sense, not as "his own man," but as the offspring of his mother's magic:

> [Ajax's] kindness to . . . [black women] in general was not due to a ritual of seduction (he had no need for it) but rather to the habit he acquired in dealing with his mother, who inspired thoughtfulness and generosity in all her sons.
>
> She [Ajax's mother] was an evil conjure woman, blessed with seven ador- ing children whose joy it was to bring her the plants, hair, underclothing, fingernail parings, white hens, blood, camphor, pictures, kerosene, and foot- step dust that she needed, as well as to order Van Van, High John the Con- queror, Little John to Chew, Devil's Shoe String, Chinese Wash, Mustard Seed and the Nine Herbs from Cincinnati. She knew about weather, omens, the living, the dead, dreams and all illnesses and made a modest living with her skills. Had she any teeth or ever straightened her back, she would have been the most gorgeous thing alive, worthy of her sons' worship for her beauty alone, if not for the absolute freedom she allowed them (known in some quarters as neglect) and the weight of her hoary knowledge.
>
> This woman Ajax loved, and after her—airplanes. There was nothing in between. And when he was not sitting enchanted listening to his mother's words, he thought of airplanes, and pilots, and the deep sky that held them both.

The magical, black Conjure Woman as source of knowledge, as teacher of respect for women, as hoary sage whose attraction is *not* physical beauty, progenitor of seven sons who may yet seed the earth with possibilities of camaraderie for black women and a conjure-inspired love of flight—this is the village value, or locational pause, the Place, as it were, that provides conditions of possibility for successful heterosexual bonding in *Sula*. Of Ajax's perception of Sula, we learn:

> Her elusiveness and indifference to established habits of behavior reminded him of his mother, who was as stubborn in her pursuits of the occult as the women of Greater Saint Matthew's were in the search for redeeming grace. . . . [He suspected] that this was perhaps the only other woman he knew whose life was her own, who could deal with life efficiently, and who was not interested in nailing him.

But as pleasantly sanguine for a vernacular reading of *Sula* as Ajax's conjure associations may sound, we know that the heterosexual bliss of the novel comes only after Nel has discovered Sula naked and alone with her husband Jude. This discovery blasts Nel and creates a permanent rift in the friendship between the two women. Further, we know that the same materially possessive drive that makes Nel unable to forgive

Sula, forces Sula herself to transmute egalitarian flights of pleasure into a plan to "nail" Ajax. When the conjure woman's son senses her intention, he returns to a male-dominant position in intercourse and heads for a Dayton, Ohio, air show: "He dragged her under him and made love to her with the steadiness and the intensity of a man about to leave for Dayton."

Finally, then, both Nel and Sula are victims of village values that define a "pure" woman as an adoring and possessive holder of her man, a glad bearer of sons, even though the labor required to produce a boy-child is exceedingly difficult. Noting the number of children she has borne, a French woman says to Adrienne Rich: "*Vous travaillez pour l'armée, madame?*"

And the sons—so difficult to bear—are always leaving for wars, leaving to encounter Shadrack's and Plum's fates. In their wake lies only the "remembrance" of innocence. It seems apt with this description of the sons to note Morrison's dedication to *Sula:* "It is sheer good fortune to miss somebody long before they leave you. This book is for Ford and Slade [the author's sons], whom I miss although they have not left me." From a psychobiographical perspective, the author plays a series of dramatic maternal roles—from arch-destroyer, through dismembered single parent, to magically artistic conjure woman bequeathing a love of flight. It is not, however, the biographical that forms the crux of the novel.

What Morrison's novel ultimately writes is the failure of a potentially redemptive heterosexuality—a relationship in which flight is a function of black woman's conjure and not black male industrial initiative. When this failure becomes apparent, Sula has already been branded pariah by the Bottom and has assumed her role as a "witch" or sorceress who, in effect, defines boundaries of the domestic. Women become stolidly traditional mothers and loving wives under the threat of Sula's pollution:

Once the source [defined as Sula] of their personal misfortune was identified, they had leave to protect and love one another. They began to cherish their husbands and wives, protect their children, repair their homes and in general band together against the devil in their midst.

We return with this quotation to the concept of purity and danger advanced by Mary Douglas. Sula is a domestic; she is an ironic agent of systemization and purity. Her force lies, finally, in a heritage and allegiance that enable her to serve as a defining anomaly, a marginal check on the system of community. As heir to the manlove of the Peaces and self-possessed arrester of conjure's sinisterly beautiful offspring, she is a natural cohort for the thunderingly obscene Shadrack. Her hermeneutical richness is signified by the mark above her eye which is variously read as a rose, a serpent, a tadpole, and funeral ash from the seared Hannah. When she dies in a closed room, not unlike a suffocating hole, she assumes the fetal position of one who, like the riddled subject of

Sophocles' Sphinx, has come almost full circle. She slides back into the watery womb.

It is Shadrack, the mad ritualist, then, who carries the day. The most energetic defender against dismemberments and absurdities of a "nigger joke," he all but erases the joke by leading a rebellious group of Bottom inhabitants on a winter suicide parade. Like inversive Luddites, or kamikaze pilots of another war, they march against the very signs of their denial, attacking the construction from whose labor they have been barred, moving like banshees through the very center of Medallion. Many of them are killed when the ground shifts and the incomplete tunnel fills with water. Like Sula, they expire in the womb of their genesis—they are doomed victims of a joke-work that kept them "running."

Shadrack remains above the cacophony, ringing his bell, saddened by the death of Sula whom he believed would endure "always." And, perhaps, Sula does fully endure in Nel's vomiting forth of the bolus of mud and leaves, the terrible loneliness for a friend, that emerges as the circling cry and penultimate sound of the novel: "O Lord, Sula, . . . girl, girl, girlgirlgirl." The cry's repetitions, like other repetitions and eternal returns in the novel, is a bare human talisman against life's signal and absurd arrangements.

But this is not the end.

It is important to note that Nel's final appearance is appropriated to a narrative "present." *Sula*'s final chapter is entitled "1965," and we become aware that the very chronicle of *Sula* is the difference within a larger history. The Bottom's story is the always already remainder constructed by an interested voice from selected and residual categories, significant details, actively foregrounded heroisms.

In short, there is an inexorable history ruled by the "joke" inscribed in *Sula*. It runs from *present* (the opening pages of the book as "prologue") destruction and reversal of value to *present* (the final chapter, "1965," as epilogue) destruction and reversal of value. Just as the master has duped the black slave into accepting barren hill land by manipulating language, so the narratively present-day white citizens of Medallion reverse the acceptable scale of material values and declare the hill a desirable locale. Nigger heaven, one might say—a segregated point of conjure, community, and conspicuous ritual—becomes the imminent domain of white leisure, "room for the Medallion City Golf Course."

In a sense, one might say that *Sula* effects a resonantly adept refiguration of discursive priorities in which the narrator foregrounds not the historical "joke," but the selectively chronicled Afro-American Place that is the eternal and residual redaction of the joke. The Bottom is the difference, the objectified differentiation in productive expressive display that raises Sula's name above the very medal and commemoration of whiteness marked by the place-name "Medallion." As in Toomer's fascinating short sketch entitled "Esther," "the town [of Medallion] has completely disappeared" during most of the text in Morrison's writing of the village values of its Bottom. The Bottom's existence and signifying difference are notable because they are marked and remarked at the moment of their demise by one who appreciates their ancestral resonances and domestic codifications of "purified" black experience.

Morrison's *Sula*, in its brilliantly adept employment of language, becomes the signifying difference within Afro-American discourse. Reversing a traditional iconography of airplanes and flying in black fiction, it suggests that folk interiors may contain domestic conjurations that unite Lindbergh and Bessie Smith in resounding glory. Rather than a cadaverous remainder, Afro-American folk history carried by black woman's rituals signifies a symbolic difference within Afro-American discourse. And, finally, in the domain of the signifier and the signified, Place becomes not a matter of matter, but a question of symbolic manipulation. Rather than adopt an extant historiography, Morrison plays over and beyond and behind and below history, symbolically chronicling the domestic, ordering rituals of black life. *Sula*, as a result, bears little resemblance to a traditional black male historicizing of a standard story.

Morrison describes Sula as an artist without a medium, and hence a dangerous figure. What she seems to imply in this characterization is the problematic of, say, the French psychologist Jacques Lacan.[14] Rather than the Conjure Woman as medium, I think she means to suggest the expressivity of language. Language is always coextensive and coterminous with the emergence, and, ironically, the alienation, of the subject.

Briefly, Lacan claims that when the child (between six and eighteen months of age) sees his image in the mirror, he responds with a "flutter of jubilant activity" at the discovery of what he believes to be "myself," or "me." Ironically, the "self" captured by saying "I am *that*" is already alienated, a secondary identification in which the Subject is subjugated to language. There is only a secondary identification in which language remains the differentiating difference within. In *Heterologies*, Michel de Certeau captures this Lacanian problematic as follows: ". . . the lie [represented by literature or myth or iconography] is the element in which the truth can emerge, the truth that the Other always institutes the subject by alienating it."

In terms of the dynamics of Afro-American Place, these formulations translate as follows: language, myth, iconography constructed by Afro-American expressive traditions are locational mirrors to which we point in our intellectual and affective assertion "I am *that*." Such "secondary identification" is only alienating when it fails to accord with, at least, an Afro-American *Real* that is gender-diversified, characterized by village values as well as urban technological spaces—energetic laborers as well as living domestics. It is a terrain where the great American joke of denial has always held sway, but where more than one black woman has inversively decided, like Bessie Smith, or Rosa Parks: " "Mm: I can't move no moe/ There ain't no place: for a poor old girl to go."[15]

V

Refusing to give way to historiographical myths of an erasure of race by the mechanistic glories of technological flight, black women have settled down to business. Either they have appropriated flight to gainful ends like Willa B. Brown, whose Chicago flying school was one of the first of its kind in the United States.[16] Or, they have transformed the joke of Western capitalism in the manner of Sarah Breedlove, whose lineage includes the millionaire cosmetologist A'Lelia Walker.[17]

At the heart of *Sula*'s Bottom stood, among other businesses, Irene's Palace of Cosmetology, a woman's place where they "used to lean their heads back on sink trays and doze while Irene lathered Nu Nile into their hair." A'Lelia Walker's "business" was to remake herself, to stop her hair from falling out, and to get away from the scarred domestic knees and the reddened hands that had marked her mother as maid, as laundress. What she did was to energetically take care of business by taking the result of her dream life (an old man from Africa conveyed a formula for renewal to her in a dream) and doing something about her own, and all black women's hair. The mirror produced a "flutter of jubilant activity"—"I am *that!*"

Similarly, Morrison takes care of business by constructing the very mirror that holds us together, that offers a communal Place where we can come to see ourselves. Her work metaphorizes the energies of the persona framed by the Washington, D.C., poet, Ethelbert Miller in the words with which I want to end these reflection on the dynamics of Afro-American Place. Miller's poem "Only Language Can Hold Us Together" reads as follows:

> only language
> can hold us together
>
> i watch the women
> bead their hair
> each bead a word
> braids becoming
> sentences
>
> she would
> never comb her hair
> it was always wild
>
> like new poetry
> it was difficult

to understand

she would enter
rooms where old women
would stare & mumble
& bold ones would say

"where's her mother"

she never understood why
no one ever understood the
beauty of her hair

like free verse
so natural as conversation
so flowing like the french
or spanish she heard or
overheard she thought she knew

"'i want to go to
mozambique she said one day

combing her hair
finding the proper beads
after so long

"i want to go to
mozambique" she said

twisting her hair
into shape the way her
grandmother made quilts
each part separated &
plaited

"i want to go to
mozambique or zimbabwe
or someplace like luanda

i need to do something
about my hair

if only i could
remember

the words
to the language
that keeps
breaking in my
hands"

Morrison "remembers" and enables us to know our Place and to be cool about our hair. For, in truth, it has often seemed in black male writings of a putatively asexual Western technological world as our proper Place, that the dominant expressive impulse has been more toward an escape from "bad hair" than from "bad air." Morrison's linguistic cosmetology allows this very basic "badness" to be refigured as village value, as a mirroring language—a springy "lying" down if you will—in which we can find ourselves, and where especially black men may yet make a jubilant response saying, "We are *that!*" Or, in more vernacular terms:

> I will pack your water: from the boggy bayou
> Hey now tell me sweet baby, who may your manager be
> Before many more questions, won't you *please* make arrangements for
> me,
> Your hair so doggone curly and your eyes ain't blue.
> That's why baby, I'm making a fool about you.[18]

Morrison has enabled us to know precisely our Afro-American Place by showing us just what we need to do with words, values, language that we have too often allowed to break in our hands. She brings us to the founding Bottom of our lives by showing us precisely what to make of our hair. Her manipulations of the symbolic, thus, bring her into fine accord with her captivating protagonist of whom we are told: "Sula never competed; she simply helped others define themselves."

Notes

1. It seems important at this juncture to differentiate Morrison's "intimate" place from the spaces of confinement described in the magnificently suggestive study of women writers and the nineteenth-century literary imagination offered by Sandra M. Gilbert and Susan Gubar. Gilbert and Gubar write in *The Madwoman in the Attic* (New Haven: Yale University Press, 1979) as follows: "literally, women like Dickinson, Brontë, and Rossetti were imprisoned in their homes, their father's houses; indeed, almost all nineteenth-century women were in some sense imprisoned in men's houses. Figuratively, such women were, as we have seen, locked into male texts, texts from which they could escape only through ingenuity and indirection. It is not surprising, then, that spatial imagery of enclosure and escape, elaborate with what frequently becomes obsessive intensity, characterizes much of their writing." The thesis of Gilbert and Gubar stresses "escape" by imprisoned women authors as a writing of the "madwoman," the mad double who is id energy or the wantoness of the unlawful. Bertha of *Jane Eyre* is the *ur*-madwoman double. She, in Gilbert and Gubar's view, expresses the anxiety of authorship of Brontë and other women writers and represents, as well, the woman's escape from patriarchal houses and male texts into a

peculiarly woman's imaginary. The specifically Victorian and white Western psychosexual orientation of this thesis—for all its resonant clarity and persuasiveness—seem to remove it from the type of ancestral, folk codifications of space and place implied by Morrison's writing.

2. I am referring to the historian Deborah White's observation that African women who were victims of the European slave trade were not confined to the holes of ships but were allowed to go unshackled on the half and quarter decks. This, of course, rendered them not "free," but accessible to the European crew of traders. In *Ar'n't I a Woman? Female Slaves in the Plantation South* (New York: W. W. Norton, 1985), p. 63.

3. The discussion of the joke that follows relies heavily upon the observations of Sigmund Freud in *Jokes and Their Relation to the Unconscious,* trans. James Strachey (New York: W. W. Norton, 1960).

4. In *Purity and Danger,* Douglas writes: ". . . . our pollution behavior is the reaction which condemns any object or idea likely to confuse or contradict cherished classifications. We should now force ourselves to focus on dirt. Defined in this way it appears as a residual category, rejected from our normal scheme of classifications."

5. "Then Nebuchadnezzar came near to the mouth of the burning fiery furnace, and spake, and said, Shadrach, Meshach, and Abednego, ye servants of the most high God, come forth, and come *hither.* Then Shadrach, Meshach, and Abednego, came forth of the midst of the fire." *Dan.* 3:26. The ironic resemblance that Morrison's antihero bears to the biblical Shadrach lies in his seeming idolatry before the power of death, while the Shadrach of the book of *Daniel* is condemned by the king for his refusal to worship the golden image. Insofar as Morrison's character is a partisan of an *ordering* ritual, however, he does construct an alternative to the capitalist disorder of war.

6. The three women who work in the Dead house are Ruth (the wife) and the two daughters of Macon Dead—Magdalene called Lena and First Corinthians.

7. Otto Rank reports and interprets a dream as follows in the *Interpretation of Dreams:* "If we bear in mind that Freud's researches into sexual symbolism . . . have shown that stairs and going upstairs in dreams almost invariably stand for copulation, the dream becomes quite transparent. . . ."

8. Shadrack's followers increase yearly; the first to join his inversive parade are Tar Baby and the deweys.

9. Gates refers to the quality of Toomer and Hurston's prose as "lyrical" and goes on to designate what he calls a "speakerly" text (the Afro-American equivalent of Barthes' "writerly" text). Hurston's work, then, like Toomer's would consist of the lyrical production of talking books.

10. For valuable accounts of the phallus in the work of Freud and Lacan, see: Juliet Mitchell and Jacqueline Rose, eds., *Feminine Seuxality: Jacques Lacan and the école freudienne* (New York: W. W. Norton, 1982); Juliet Mitchell, *Psychoanalysis and Feminism: Freud, Reich, Laing and Women* (New York: Vintage Books, 1975); Jane Gallop, *The Daughter's Seduction: Feminism and Psychoanalysis* (Ithaca, N.Y.: Cornell University Press, 1982).

11. Adrienne Rich in her essay "Compulsory Heterosexuality and Lesbian Existence" also makes the mistake of speaking of *Sula* as a novel of "lesbian existence." Rich's essay appears in *The Signs Reader.* eds. Elizabeth Abel and Emily K. Abel (Chicago: University of Chicago Press, 1983).

12. *The Bluest Eye* begins as follows: "Here is the house. It is green and white. It has a red door. It is very pretty. Here is the family. Mother, Father, Dick, and Jane live in the green-and-white house. They are very happy." Quickly, however, the normal spacing and typeface are run together, and, finally,

reduced to mere strings of letters. The novel, thus, begins with a deconstruction of the representation of "traditional" (read: White Patriarchal) family structures that greeted so many of us as we were just learning to read. Morrison's artistry suggests another (a Black) reading of the family.

13. In *Invisible Man*, the final scene before the "Epilogue" is a nightmare vision of castration in which the protagonist's testes are launched into the air by his male adversaries and false guides and hang floating over a technological civilization as possible salvation (pp. 556–558).

14. Juliet Mitchell and Jacqueline Rose, eds., *Feminine Sexuality*, and Jane Gallop, *The Daughter's Seduction*, are excellent sources for a discussion of the Lacanian problematic, as is Luce Irigaray, *This Sex Which Is Not One* (Ithaca, N.Y.: Cornell University Press, 1977/1985).

15. Bessie Smith, "Back Water Blues."

16. Bernard C. Nalty, *Strength for the Fight: A History of Black Americans in the Military* (New York: The Free Press, 1986), p. 143. I must thank my extraordinary research assistant, Claire Satloff, for this reference and for her very dedicated work in securing sources necessary for the completion of this entire essay.

17. Paula Giddings, *When and Where I Enter: The Impact of Black Women on Race and Sex in America* (New York: Bantam Books, 1984). Giddings' history seems to me essential reading for anyone interested in feminist, or Afro-American, or general historical contours of the United States of America. Her account of Walker is my source for the discussion that follows.

18. Bo Chatman, "Arrangements for Me—Blues." For my blues citations, I have relied on the remarkable work of Michael Taft, *Blues Lyric Poetry* (New York: Garland, 1983).

◆◆◆◆◆◆◆◆◆◆◆◆◆◆

Maternal Narratives: "Cruel Enough to Stop the Blood"

MARIANNE HIRSCH

In 1976, Adrienne Rich wrote that the "cathexis between mother and daughter—essential, distorted, misused—is the great unwritten story."[1] Since that time, feminist writing and scholarship has explored motherhood and mother-daughter relationships from a variety of personal and disciplinary perspectives. Yet nearly all of those perspectives have belonged to daughters. In 1987, the "great unwritten story" remains the story of the mother herself, told in her own voice. Feminist writing and scholarship, continuing in large part to adopt a daughterly perspective, could be said to collude with patriarchy in placing the mother into the position of object and thereby keeping mothering outside of representation and maternal discourse a theoretical impossibility.

In this essay, I propose to illustrate the relationship between feminism and the maternal through a brief look at the tradition of contemporary black women's writing which defines itself as a daughterly tradition in relation to a complicated maternal past. In particular, I shall trace the confrontation and interaction of maternal and daughterly voices in Toni Morrison's *Sula*. Indeed, black women's writing of the 1960s, 1970s, and 1980s is one tradition among the various feminisms that have developed in these last decades where the mother is prominently featured in complex and multiple ways. As a generation of female/feminist writing just in the process of defining itself in relation to a maternal, largely oral past, it can provide a useful locus for the exploration of maternal discourse and points of resistance to it.

Unlike so many contemporary white women writers who define their artistic identity as separate from or in opposition to their mothers, black writers have recently been insisting on what Mary Helen Washington identifies as the "connection between the black woman writer's sense of herself as part of a link in generations of women, and her decision to write."[2] Alice Walker's "In Search of Our Mothers' Gardens" and "Saving a Life That Is Your Own,"[3] Paule Marshall's "Shaping the World of My Art"[4] and "From in the Kitchen"[5] are conscious and public attempts, as Mary Helen Washington puts it, to "piece together the story of a viable female culture, one in which there is generational continuity, in which one's mother serves as the female precursor who passes on the authority of authorship to her daughter and provides a model for the black woman's literary presence in this society." Marshall and Walker explain that in their families theirs is the first generation to be college-educated, the first generation engaged in writing down the stories handed down orally by their matrilineal heritage. Even though they sometimes choose middle-aged or older protagonists, I would argue that, for the most part, Marshall, Walker, Morrison, West, and Shange write as daughters, and not as mothers.[6] Much more than white women writers, they find it necessary, however, to "think back through their mothers" in order to assume what Sandra Gilbert and Susan Gubar have called the "authority of authorship" and to define themselves identifiably in their own voices as subjects. Their public celebration of maternal presence and influence and their portrayals of strong and powerful mothers, on the one hand, combined with the relative absence of fathers, on the other, makes this uniquely female tradition a particularly interesting one in which to explore issues of maternal presence and absence, speech and silence. If maternal discourse can emerge in one particular feminist tradition, it may not be surprising that it should be one that is in itself marginal— or, to borrow a term from Rachel Blau du Plessis, "(ambiguously) non-hegemonic"—and therefore more ready to bond with mothers and daughters, and to let go of paternal, fraternal or filial approval.[7]

Thus the issues of connection and separation which pervade this body of writing have political as well as psychological dimensions. We need to keep in mind the complicated feelings that shape the portraits of mothers, and the tremendously powerful need to present to the public a positive image of black womanhood. E. Frances White writes in her recent "Listening to the Voices of Black Feminism": "How dare we admit the psychological battles that need to be fought with the very women who taught us to survive in this racist and sexist world? We would feel like ungrateful traitors."[8] This pressure explains, perhaps, the disturbing disjunction between the celebration of mothers in the essays of black women writers and the much more ambivalent portrayals in their novels. Although mothers are present, even dominant, in the texts of black women writers, maternal discourse suffers from important and symptomatic limitations and constraints. The daughter-writer often has to define herself in opposition to and not in imitation of the maternal figure. Thus, even while Paule Marshall publically presents herself as the *griot* (Mary Helen Washington's term), preserving the stories she heard and absorbed in her mother's kitchen as she was growing up, she admits privately in an interview that "my mother never directly encouraged me to write. What I absorbed from her was more a reaction to her negativity . . . she disapproved of all my ambitions."[9] Both Marshall and Walker, in fact, situate themselves among three maternal traditions: the black oral invisible lineage in which their own mothers were artistic—storytellers and gardeners; the black written tradition of Phyllis Wheatley, Linda Brent, Zora Neale Hurston, among others; and the white written tradition of Virginia Woolf's *A Room of One's Own*, which does describe the contradiction of the woman writer, but must be revised to include the different story of the black writer. Alice Walker asks: "What did it mean for a black woman to be an artist in our grandmothers' time? In our great-grandmothers' day? It is a question with an answer cruel enough to stop the blood."[10]

These ambivalences and contradictions illuminate Toni Morrison's *Sula*,[11]—the complicated interaction of maternal and daughterly voices in this text, and, in particular, the mediated status of maternal discourse. The stories that the mothers in this novel tell are indeed "cruel enough to stop the blood." I would like to look closely at what happens when the mothers speak in this novel, at how the mothers' stories inform both the text that is structured around them and the lives of the protagonist daughters. I should add that this reading of *Sula*, far from attempting to be totalizing, is my own experiment with bringing a maternal perspective to bear on a text which itself puts such a perspective into play.

Set between 1919 and 1965, *Sula* is clearly located in the generation of Morrison's mother and grandmother and not in her own. Thus, the novel's very structure depends upon its ambivalent relation to the past. The text presents the lives of the two protagonists, Sula and Nel, as they move from adolescence to old age. Sula and Nel are presented as members of a new generation of black women, eager to construct new lives and new stories for themselves. Yet their development and their friendship, and the text itself, revolve around their relationships to the powerful maternal figures who come to represent a female past, and around their attitude to maternity itself. Although the novel is clearly not written from the perspective of the mother, its generational structure allows it to serve as an emblem for the relation of an emerging feminism (new generation of women) to the maternal (oral tradition of the past).[12]

The novel begins not with these powerful women, however, but with the story of a young man, Shadrack. In a process of a symbolic birth into a violent and racist culture, Shadrack, an army private at the end of World War I, gains his sense of self by facing his mirror image in a toilet bowl: "There in the toilet water he saw a grave black face. A black so definite, so unequivocal, it astonished him." Shadrack knows he is real because he is black, but, as a result of the war, and of his underprivileged social status, he has been dispossessed of everything, including his sense of bodily limits. Through the figure of Shadrack, and of the communal rituals he invents to survive his utter inadequacy, the community needs to confront the male impotence that defines it, represented later by Eva's son Plum. Shadrack's birth is motherless, just as Plum's death is caused by his mother: Mothers have ceased to be able to care for sons in the increasingly feminized, though clearly sexual, culture Morrison constructs. Even Ajax's mother, the "conjure woman," cannot keep her son from abandoning her and Sula.[13]

The dominating maternal presence in the novel is, of course, the matriarch Eva who rules over the enormous house in which Sula and Nel spend a great deal of their childhood. Ironically, Eva's powerful presence is defined by lack, her amputated leg which becomes the means of her survival and the mark of her distinction from the other poor and abandoned mothers in Medallion. Eva insists on flaunting her missing leg by wearing calf-length skirts which display and call attention to the beauty of her other leg. I would argue that Eva's missing leg is the mark of maternal discourse in the novel and the key to its (thematized) ambivalence toward it.

The absent leg functions as a gap in the center of the text, a gap around which Sula and Nel's stories begin to take shape. Following the account of Eva's abandonment by BoyBoy, of her miserable winter attempting to care for three children with no money at all, and of her night in the freezing outhouse helping baby Plum loosen his bowels, there is an ellipsis in the text, a silence surrounding Eva's 18-month absence from Medallion. This gap gives rise to numerous tales, some told by Eva herself to amuse the children ("how the leg got up by itself one day and walked off"), others invented by the townspeople in their effort to explain her return without one leg, but with a new black pocketbook full of money. The tales were clearly apocryphal: the mother's (self-)mutilation in the service of her own and her children's survival remains, to the end of the novel, unnarrated, and perhaps unnarratable, but the source of endless narration. Maternal speech is sparse in this novel: mothers and daughters never quite succeed in addressing each other directly, mothers fail to communicate the stories they wish to tell. This pattern of missed communication begins when Nel and her mother Helene undertake an exhausting journey south to attend the funeral of Nel's great-grandmother. Here, in the place of maternal origin, Nel cannot understand the Creole she hears her grandmother speak. Barely exchanging a few words with her mother, Helene later admits that she also does not know Creole. As Nel returns home and remembers the painful moments of the trip—her mother's profound humiliation by the white conductor and by the black men in the train, the disgust on her great-grandmother's dead face, and the coldness between her mother and grandmother, she looks into the mirror and begins a new life: "I'm me. I'm not their daughter. I'm not Nel. I'm me." Helene Wright, the mother, emerges as wrong in many ways, wrong in her adoption of middle-class values, wrong in her manipulative control of her daughter's life and in the foolish smile she flashes at the train conductor who has just insulted her, wrong too because she severed the connection with her own mother and failed to learn her mother tongue. Nel's image of her mother as formless custard barely contained by her heavy velvet dress, makes it imperative that she identify herself as separate, different from her maternal heritage, as a very definite "me." Filled with "power, joy and

fear" at this moment of self-creation, she cannot sustain this self-defini-
tion alone, but needs a friend to complete her, a friend who can offer
reflection and support but who will be free of the heavy suitcases and
the orderly house, of the history which encumbers Helene Wright. This
friend is the much less conventional Sula.

Sula's family, although more communicative, succeeds no better in
bridging the distance between the lives and the perspectives of the three
generations. An important exchange occurs between Sula's mother Hannah and her mother Eva: although Hannah is herself a mother, her discourse is circumscribed by her daughterly relation to Eva and by
conventional and clearly inapplicable conceptions of motherhood and maternal love. "Mama, did you ever love us? . . . No." Eva answers, "I
don't reckon I did. Not the way you thinkin'." Hannah cannot bear to
listen to what Eva has to tell: "I didn't mean that, Mamma. I know you
fed us and all. I was talkin' 'bout something else. Like. Like. Playin' with
us. . . . I know 'bout them beets, Mamma. You told us that a million
times. . . . There had to be some times when you wasn't thinkin' 'bout
. . . ." In response, Eva comes back with the same old stories about the
three remaining beets, about the sores in the children's mouths, about
their shitting worms, stories that clearly fail to fit into the mythology of
motherhood to which Hannah wants to subscribe.

This exchange clearly challenges this mythology, especially when
Hannah asks Eva why she set fire to her adult son Plum. Eva's response,
an interior monologue followed by the longest speech she makes in the
novel, contains hurt and pain, anger and love, but fails adequately to
explain her inconceivable act. Eva's relation to Plum is so obscenely
intimate, it has to be described in the third person: "The last food staple
in the house she had rammed up her baby's behind to keep from hurting
him too much when she slid her finger in to open up his bowels to pull
the stools out. He had been screaming fit to kill but when she found the
hole at last and stuck her finger up in it, the shock was so great he was
suddenly quiet." In her own voice Eva continues to articulate what she
sees as Plum's inadequacy as an adult male ruined by the war, his passivity, his efforts to "crawl back in my womb . . . I had room enough in my
heart," she insists, "but not in my womb, got no more." The mutual
penetration of bodies signals, perhaps, the limits of what any relationship
can sustain, and demonstrates the ambiguous status of the mother, whose
body has already been penetrated so that this child might be produced.
In trying to explain to Hannah an act which is so obviously beyond
comprehension, Eva dwells on an intense need for self-protection, a clear
drawing of her own boundaries, a definitive expression of the limits of
what she has to give, and she insists as well on Plum's boundaries which,
as a mother, she was forced to violate.

The double voice with which Eva delivers her painful explanation—
"like two people were talking at the same time, saying the same thing,

one a fraction of a second behind the other"—suggests her double identity, as an individual subject and as a mother, signalling perhaps the self-division that by necessity characterizes and distinguishes maternal discourse. The text acts out this double voice, as it combines third with first person narration, free indirect discourse with dialogue. The message too is of course double; love is mixed with anger, pain with pride, sadness with tenderness, as Eva adds her afterthought: "But I held him close first. Real close. Sweet Plum. My baby boy." This scene between Eva and Hannah, one of the few moments in the novel where mothers speak as mothers, enacts the difficulty of telling and of hearing her story. Later on, of course, Sula will send the grandmother away to an old-age home so as to silence her more completely: "Don't talk to me about how much you gave me, Big Mama, and how much I owe you or none of that."

In her conversation with her mother, Hannah, like everyone else, refrains from addressing the central question of the missing leg, although the questions she asks, however awkwardly, revolve around this untold tale. Like Hannah's, Sula and Nel's very development is determined by it, because the leg becomes for them a very graphic representation of sexual (and perhaps racial) difference, seen as lack.[14] Interpreters of the novel have seen Eva as a kind of phallic mother who assumes God-like powers of control over naming, creation and destruction.[15] For example, she calls three different boys by the same name, Dewey, and quickly they become indistinguishable. But the story Eva tells reveals a mixture of power and powerlessness that calls the very notion of phallic mother into question. The phallic mother can exist only as a child's projection. If Eva chooses to flaunt her castration, to assume the logic of the lack that is essential to the male posture, in order thereby to gain a semblance of male power, she can only reveal how much *that* power depends on a masquerade. With this term I refer to Lacan's definition of femininity as masquerade, as constructed in reference to male desire.[16] Eva's strategy demonstrates, I think, that the male phallic position is also a sham, resting on conventional constructions that are easily overturned. Thus Morrison challenges phallocentrism, even as she shows Eva's manipulation of and complicity with the phallic order.

Sula adopts Eva's powerful strategy; her first act in the novel repeats Eva's gesture of (self)-mutilation in the service of survival and her denial of her powerlessness.[17] Threatened by some boys on the way home from school, Sula takes a knife and slices off part of her finger, frightening the boys with "If I can do that to myself, what do you suppose I'll do to you?" This act is Sula's own moment of self-recognition, of her affiliation with Eva and the world of her maternal ancestors. Although Sula possesses her birthmark, a stemmed rose, ambiguously phallic and vaginal— a mark of plenitude which distinguishes her from other women—she is forced to recognize the vulnerability she shares with Eva, a vulnerability her act of self-injury, like Eva's, can only disguise but cannot change. It is this recognition which causes Sula's continued and determined rebellion against a traditional womanhood defined for her by maternity and enslavement to the family.

Like Hannah and Eva, Sula and Hannah also share a pivotal moment of (indirect) confrontation around the subject of maternal love. Sula overhears Hannah and her friends discussing their children: "'Well, Hester grown now and I can't say love is exactly what I feel.' 'Sure you do. You love her, like I love Sula. I just don't like her. That's the difference.' 'Guess so. Likin' them is another thing.'" This transgressive maternal speech determines the novel's structural progression: this scene is immediately followed by the drowning of Chicken Little. After overhearing what she takes as her mother's rejection, Sula runs off with Nel and, in a vaguely homoerotic moment of tenderness in the grass as well as in their symbolic acting out of heterosexual play with sticks in the ground, they begin to discover their own sexuality. The appearance at this point of Chicken Little, the little boy in whom both girls take a maternal interest ("Your mama tole you to stop eatin' snot, Chicken."), focuses for Sula the conjunction of maternal rejection with her budding sexuality. I read Chicken's death—he quietly slips into the river and girls don't try to save him—as a signal of Sula and Nel's rebellious, if as yet unconscious, refusal of adult heterosexuality and motherhood as they perceive it. In the novel's terms, however, this is but one in a series of murders, significantly parallel to Eva's murder of Plum.

Sula and Nel's reaction of *looking* or watching Chicken disappear in the water instead of attempting to save him, is later repeated when Sula watches her mother's accidental death by burning, thrilled and wanting "her to keep on jerking like that, to keep on dancing." This contrasts sharply with Eva's unsuccessful attempt to save her daughter: "Eva knew there was time for nothing in this world other than the time to get there and cover her daughter's body with her own." Ironically, of course, it is her original maternal act of self-mutilation, her missing leg, which prevents her from succeeding, but not from participating bodily in Hannah's painful death—she jumps out the window, drags herself across the lawn and finally has to be taken to the hospital together with her dying daughter. Sula's complicity in her mother's death is only suggested in the text—she acted crazy on that day, distracting Eva and Hannah from interpreting the dream that foreshadowed the accident, she did not try to save Hannah, and she clearly failed to hear her mother's dying words: "Help me y'all."

Eva's own complicity, even more disguised, complicates the oppositions Sula constructs, between watching and helping, oppositions which underlie her unconditional refusal of a maternal role. As she emphatically declares, silencing Eva's suggestion that she needs babies, "I don't want to make somebody else. I want to make myself." Here Sula conceives of herself as artist, as inventor of alternate plots and bodies for women. As she does so, however, she reinforces another irreconcilable dichotomy—that of mother and artist, a difference she equates with that between saving someone from dying and of watching her die. What looks at first like two contrasting reactions—Eva's and Sula's—however, emerges, more and more, as equal complicity and ambivalence, the mark of maternal discourse in the novel, a discourse from which Sula tries to but cannot escape.

In the economy of this text, Sula's rejection of maternity means an assumption of male freedom. In several published interviews, Morrison has admitted fascination with Sula's choice, although it represents the ultimate evil for a woman as far as the community is concerned. "I guess I'm not supposed to say that. But the fact that they [men] would split in a minute just delights me. . . . That has always been to me one of the most attractive features about black male life."[18] With characters like Sula and later with Jadine in *Tar Baby*, Morrison invents a female character who will not be maternal, but will try to get beyond an ideology which identifies woman with nurturing and caretaking. Yet, Nel's warning is prophetic: "You *can't* do it all. You a woman and a colored woman at that. You can't act like a man." Having children represents for Nel the crucial distinction between the male and the female position. Women, as Eva succeeds in demonstrating, can *act* like men, but in this novel, they cannot leave their children and get away with it. Yet when Sula contemplates the women who stay with their children, she is confronted with emptiness and desperation: "Those with men had had the sweetness sucked from their breath by ovens and steam kettles. Their children were like distant but exposed wounds whose aches were no less intimate because separate from their flesh. They had looked at the world and back at the children, back again at the world and back again at their children, and Sula knew that one clear young eye was all that kept the knife away from the throat's curve." Until her death, Sula is haunted by the fears of the destruction domesticity brings: witness her dream about the baking powder girl who disintegrates into a pile of dust. Whereas for Sula motherhood constitutes a threat of disintegration, for Nel it comes to mean an immutable, inescapable, desperate fusion: "They [her children] were all she would ever know of love. But it was a love that, like a pan of syrup kept too long on the stove, had cooked out, leaving only its odor and a hard, sweet sludge, impossible to scrape off."

The novel proposes female friendship as an alternative friendship to the maternal, but it does not do so unquestionably. Might her friendship with Nel have saved Sula from the slow erosion which kills her, and who is to be blamed for endangering and impairing this friendship when Sula sleeps with Nel's husband? Other—truly artistic—possibilities of expression are unavailable to Sula in her world and, suffering from an "idle imagination," she remains "an artist with no art form." Although she can assert at the end of her life that she has indeed created herself ["I got my mind. And what goes on in it. Which is to say, I got me."], her lack of attachments robs her of the food for her imagination and creativity. "*I have sung all the songs there are*," she repeats. Yet, even as she retreats totally into the utter aloneness of her head and slips from life to death, Sula longs to speak to Nel, to tell her about what death feels like. But Sula's repudiation of motherhood and attachment does not enable an alternate career as an artist. Whether under different economic and social conditions it could have, the text leaves unanswered.

The novel's conclusion—Nel's epiphanic recognition that it is her friend Sula she has missed all these years and not her husband Jude, her return to the fantasy of a perfect sisterhood—reasserts the perspective the text proposes as an alternate form of discourse to the maternal.[19] Nel's cry contrasts sharply with the literal stories told by Eva or Helene: "It was a fine cry—loud and long—but it had no bottom and no top, just circles and circles of sorrow." In her discussion of this cry, Margaret Homans presents it as an assertion of separatism, of a specifically female expression in language: "what finally expresses her woman-identified self is of necessity nonrepresentational."[20] It is perhaps understandable that such a moment should lead back to childhood, to a pre-oedipal, pre-separational female past, as yet uncontaminated by social institutions. The fusion of Sula and Nel, affirmed in the last scene by the ancient Eva who refuses to distinguish between them, offers a privileged if dangerous mode of relation and expression, one that in the economy of this novel could never be shared in by the mother. No such fusion or confusion exists between generations in this text; the roles and the voices of mother and daughter in the novel are forcibly separated, even within the characters of Hannah, Helene, and Nel, who are both. The novel's short circuit, its ultimate return to its own beginnings, only reinforces the two protagonists' inability to transcend the fate of their mothers, *as well as* their inability to repeat it. For women who reject unconditionally the lives and the stories of their mothers, there is nowhere to go. The novel both suggests and, in its own unfocused second part, actually acts out this lack of direction. Holding on to a pervasive belief in the danger of the maternal, and reiterating that danger not only in the deaths of Chicken Little and of Plum, but also in the death of a large part of the town in the half-built, womb-like tunnel at the end of the novel, the text demonstrates the trap that lies within the attempt to escape from the maternal.[21]

The mother's discourse, *when it can be voiced at all*, is always repetitive, literal, hopelessly representational. It is rooted in the body which shivers, hurts, bleeds, suffers, burns, rather than in the eyes, or in the voice which can utter its cries of pain. It is rooted in Eva's fierce bodily love for Hannah, as well as in her anger, her aggression, her violence, not in the unspoken hostility, eventually overcome, between Nel and Sula. The ancient Eva in the old age home, with her aggressive tone and her direct questions is still a threat to Nel, whose polite visit cannot accommodate the vehement anger that keeps Eva alive. Maternal discourse, the story Eva never tells as well as the stories she repeats obsessively, remains both absent and present in the novel, a mark of difference which does provide the novel with its momentum, but which to do so must to a degree remain unspoken. Is the novel suggesting, then, that the mother's story can provide only the point of departure for the text but not its content, that art, is *in fact*, primarily based on the child's drama in relation to the mother? Could it be that maternal discourse can exist in the text only on the condition that it remain framentary, incomplete and mediated through the perspective of the daughter-writer? Could it be that the novel to some degree depends on maternal silence? Adrienne Rich says, "For me, poetry was where I lived as no-one's mother, where I existed as myself,"[22] provoking Helen Vendler to ask: "Is there something about the relation with children, in contrast to relations with adults, which makes it unavailable to the writer?"

Sula, I believe, thematizes some of the ambivalences about maternal discourse more broadly present in today's European and American feminist writing. It suggests that an acknowledgement of the specificity of maternal experience could offer a perspective crucial to feminist discourse. Until feminists can find ways to speak as mothers, feminism as an intellectual movement will be unable to account for important experiential differences among women.

Inasmuch as the mother is simultaneously a daughter and a mother, a woman and a mother, in the house and in the world, powerful and powerless, nurturing and nurtured, dependent and depended upon, maternal discourse is necessarily plural, divided. And, as *Sula* demonstrates, maternal discourse is intimately tied to and tied up in social and political reality, as well as to psychological structures. Maternal knowledge, moreover, if it could be voiced, could enlarge a feminist analysis and reverse traditional conceptions of love and anger, of power and knowledge, of self in relation to other, of femininity and maturity, of sexuality and nurturance. Mothers who must work to raise children to be acceptable members of their society can reveal a great deal about the functioning of ideology and the processes of assimilation and interpellation. Most of all, if feminists don't want to "stop the blood" flowing from one generation to the next, we need to find ways of hearing and telling the stories of mothers—to politicize motherhood from within feminism— even if those stories are "cruel enough to stop [our] blood."

Further consistent exploration of maternal discourse—whether in theoretical, fictional or autobiographical writing—would reveal, I believe, notions of identity and subjectivity that correspond neither to the unified ego of ego-psychology, nor to the fluid boundaries of object-relations theory, nor to a subjectivity split against itself as outlined by

Lacanian psychoanalysis. What model or definition of subjectivity might be derived from a theory that begins with mothers rather than with children? Can we conceive of development as other than a process of separation from a neutral, either nurturing or hostile, but ultimately self-effacing "holding" background? I would suggest, that if we start our study of the subject with *mothers* rather than with *children*, a different conception of subjectivity might emerge. Although it might be difficult to define, we might try to envision a culturally variable form of interconnection between one body and another, one person and another, existing as social and legal as well as psychological subjects.

Toni Morrison's *Beloved* explores just such a maternal voice.[23] Although the novel reiterates that Sethe's story is "not a story to pass on," *Beloved* is the story of the mother and the novel's dominant voice and narrative is hers. Sethe's story—her life under slavery, the conception and care of her children in the most dire conditions, her escape and liberation, and her desperately violent and loving act of infanticide— provides, in a sense, the background for the story of Eva. *Beloved* explains Eva's anger, an anger handed down through generations of mothers who could have no control over their children's lives, no voice in their upbringing. And *Beloved* suggests why that anger may have to remain unspeakable, and how it might nevertheless be spoken. In fact, the mother-daughter conversations that do occur in *Beloved* are conversations from beyond the grave; if Sethe is to explain her incomprehensible act, she has to do so to a ghost.

Beloved provides some of the insights into mothers and women that *Sula* begins to adumbrate, and it does so all the more intensely for telling the story of a mother who is a slave. The economy of slavery circumscribes not only the process of individuation and subject-formation, but also heightens and intensifies the experience of motherhood—of connection and separation. It raises questions about what it means to have a self, and to give that self away. It raises questions about what *family* means. If mothers cannot "own" their children or themselves, they experience separation and loss all the more intensely.

At the end of the novel, the doubly bereaved Sethe, who has lost her daughter twice, is nursed back to life by her other daughter Denver and by her lover, Paul D. To her self-effacing, "she was my best thing," he insists, "you your best thing, Sethe. You are." Holding her fingers, he enables Sethe for the first time to see herself as subject, as mother and subject both: "Me? Me?" she says tentatively, and thus enables the mother's voice and subjectivity to emerge, allowing herself to question, at least for a moment, the hierarchy of motherhood and selfhood on which her life, until that moment, had rested. However, she can do so only in the context of another human bond; she can do so only because Paul D. is holding her hand. Is this a reversion to oedipal mediations and triangulations, or is it an affirmation of a subjectivity which, even when it is maternal, can only emerge in and through human interconnection? Sethe's story, is "not a story to pass on," yet this novel, more than Morrison's earlier works, does let the mother speak for herself. It allows her both to recognize her love for Beloved and her love for herself. With this novel, Toni Morrison has done more than to shift the direction of her own work and of feminist theorizing: along with writers like Grace Paley and Tillie Olsen, she has opened the space for maternal narrative in feminist fiction. That narrative is surely "cruel enough to stop the blood."[24]

Notes

1. *Of Woman Born: Motherhood as Experience and Institution* (New York: Norton, 1976), p. 225.
2. "I Sign My Mother's Name: Alice Walker, Dorothy West, Paule Marshall," in *Mothering the Mind*, p. 161.
3. Both in *In Search of Our Mothers' Gardens* (New York: Harcourt Brace Jovanovich, 1983).
4. *New Letters* 40 (Autumn 1973).
5. *New York Times Book Review* (January 9, 1983), 3, 34–5.
6. Alice Walker's "Everyday Use," in *In Love & Trouble: Stories of Black Women* (New York: Horcourt Brace Jovanovich, 1973) offers one counterexample, as does the story of Mattie Michael in Gloria Naylor's *The Women of Brewster Place* (New York: Penguin Books, 1983).
7. See "For the Etruscans," in *The Future of Difference*, Alice Jardine and Hester Eisenstein, eds. (Boston: G. K. Hall, 1979).
8. *Radical America* 18 (Spring 1985). Mary Helen Washington pointed out to me that contemporary black women writers are responding to a powerful tradition of maternal praise going back to the times of slavery and the celebration of the resilience of the slave mother. For recent explorations of mother-daughter relationships in Afro-American culture, see Gloria I. Joseph and Jill Lewis, *Common Differences: Conflicts in Black and White Feminist Perspectives* (New York: Doubleday, 1981) and a special issue on mothers and daughters of *Sage: A Scholarly Journal on Black Women* 1, no. 2 (Fall 1984).
9. Cited by Mary Helen Washington, p. 156.
10. "In Search of Our Mothers' Gardens," p. 233.
11. (New York: Bantam, 1973).
12. Hortense J. Spillers in "A Hateful Passion, a Lost Love," *Feminist Studies* 9 (Summer 1983), 293–323, stresses the radical departure of Sula in relation to the tradition of black female writing. In its novelty *Sula* is representative of its generation, she says: "The black woman as artist, as an intellectual spokesperson for her own cultural apprenticeship, has not existed before, for anyone."
13. For a different view of the novel's relation to heterosexual relations, see Houston A. Baker, Jr., "When Lindbergh Sleeps with Bessie Smith: The Writing of Place in Toni Morrison's *Sula*," Colloquium Paper, School of Criticism and Theory, Dartmouth College, 1987.

14. For an interesting discussion of lack as a figure for the experience of racial otherness, see Susan Willis, "Eruptions of Funk: Historicizing Toni Morrison," in *Black Literature and Literary Theory*, ed. Henry Louis Gates, Jr. (New York: Methuen, 1984).

15. Mary Helen Washington, in *Midnight Birds: Stories of Contemporary Black Women Writers* (New York: Doubleday, 1980), pp. 153–155, calls Eva the "creator and sovereign" who "gives and takes life." Hortense Spillers says that "Eva behaves as though she were herself the sole instrument of divine inscrutable will," 314.

16. See Jacques Lacan, "The Meaning of the Phallus," in *Feminine Sexuality: Jacques Lacan and the école freudienne*, Juliet Mitchell and Jacqueline Rose, eds. (New York: Norton, 1982), as well as "Introduction II" in the same volume, for a discussion of the notions of "phallic mother" and "masquerade." See also Joan Riviere, "Womanlines as Mascarade," IJPA, x (1929), 303–13 and Michele Montrelay "An Inquiry into Femininity," *Semiotext(e)* 10, vol. 4, 1(1981), 228–235.

17. See Susan Willis's discussion of self-mutilation as a literary figure of black confrontation with white domination, p. 277. Willis sees Sula's gesture as a more radical rebellion than I do.

18. Robert Stepto, "'Intimate Things in Place': A Conversation with Toni Morrison," *The Massachusetts Review* (Autumn 1977), 487.

19. For a discussion of the implications of the novel's celebration of female friendship, see Elizabeth Abel," (E)Merging Identities: The Dynamics of Female Friendship in Contemporary Fiction by Women," *Signs* 6, no. 3 (Spring 1981), 413–435, and Judith Kegan Gardiner "(The (Us)es of (I)dentity: A Response to Abel on '(E)Merging Identities,'" *Signs* 6 (Spring 1981), 436–444.

20. "'Her Very Own Howl': The Ambiguities of Representation in Recent Women's Fiction," *Signs* 9, no. 2 (Autumn 1983), 193.

21. Whereas critics like Hortense Spillers see in Sula's rejection of traditional womanhood a "radical alternative" and a "radical freedom," I find that the novel thematizes a much more ambivalent attitude toward the maternal, showing both its dangers and the dangers of rejecting it.

22. *Of Woman Born*, p. 31. See also, Mary Gordon, "On Mothership and Authorhood," *The New York Times Book Review* (February 19, 1985), 1, 34–5.

23. (New York: Knopf, 1987).

24. This essay is part of a longer study, *Speaking for Her: Mothers, Daughters and Narrative* (Bloomington: Indiana University Press, forthcoming).

◆◆◆◆◆◆◆◆◆◆◆◆◆◆

Song of Solomon: Continuities of Community

VALERIE SMITH

In her first three novels, *The Bluest Eye* (1970), *Sula* (1973), and *Song of Solomon* (1977), Toni Morrison explores the interplay between self-knowledge and social role. Her characters, like Ralph Ellison's Invisible Man, inhabit a world where inhospitable social assumptions obtain. But Morrison does not provide her people with the option of living underground, in isolation, beyond community. Those whom social relations exclude (like Pecola Breedlove of *The Bluest Eye* or Sula) lack self-knowledge and are destroyed by themselves or by others. My analysis here centers on *Song of Solomon*, the only one of Morrison's novels in which her protagonist completes successfully his/her search for psychological autonomy. Yet, no discussion of the search for identity in *Song of Solomon* would be complete without some mention of Morrison's two earlier novels. The structure and thematic concerns of these two works establish a framework in terms of which we may understand the meaning and status of Milkman's discovery.

I

The black characters in Morrison's early novels are especially vulnerable to the defeats that accompany isolation; in *The Bluest Eye* and in *Sula*, she examines the complex economic, historical, cultural and geographic factors that problematize their relations within the black community and the world beyond. Pecola Breedlove, on whom *The Bluest Eye* centers, typifies Morrison's outsiders. Her story illustrates the destructive potential of a culture that recognizes only one standard of physical beauty and equates that standard with virtue. Ostensibly, Pecola is driven mad by her inability to possess blue eyes. But her insanity really results from the fact that she serves as the communal scapegoat, bearing not only her own self-loathing, but that of her neighbors and family as well. Soaphead Church's failure to provide her with blue eyes is thus simply the proverbial back-breaking straw.

The Bluest Eye does not address the hard questions directly. The book does not undertake to explain, for example, why black Americans aspire to an unattainable standard of beauty; why they displace their self-hatred onto a communal scapegoat; how Pecola's fate might have been averted. The metaphors of Claudia MacTeer that frame and image Pecola's story, and the very structure of the novel itself, suggest that such considerations are irresolvable. "This soil is bad for certain kinds of flowers," Claudia remarks. "Certain seeds it will not nurture, certain fruit it will not bear." Claudia accepts as a given the fact that certain "soils" will reject both marigolds and plain black girls. To her, the reasons for this incompatibility are structural, too intricately woven to distinguish. She therefore believes that any attempt to explain Pecola's deterioration will be fruitless and concludes that *"There is really nothing more to say—except why. But since* why *is difficult to handle, one must take refuge in* how."

I would argue that not only Claudia, but the novel itself, avoids "why," taking refuge instead in "how." Claudia, the narrator of the primer, and the ostensibly omniscient narrator all tell stories—tell "how" fast and furiously. These stories, in general, demonstrate what it means to find inaccessible the possessions and attributes that one's culture values. Their thematic similarity reveals the representative nature of Pecola's story: self-loathing leads inevitably to some form of destruction. Perhaps more importantly, the remarkable number of stories symbolizes the complex sources and effects of this cycle of self-loathing. The form is therefore a figure for the cultural condition the novel addresses.

The structure of *The Bluest Eye* underscores the proliferation of stories and of narrative voices within the novel. The body of the text is divided into four chapters which are, in turn, subdivided. Each begins with an episode, usually involving Pecola, told from the point of view of Claudia the child but shaped by her adult reflections and rhetoric. Claudia's stories then yield place to one or two stories told by an apparently objective, omniscient narrator. This narrator usually recalls information to which Claudia would not have had access: he/she tells stories from Pecola's life that involve other characters and weaves flashbacks from the lives of these other characters (Polly or Cholly Breedlove, Geraldine, or Soaphead Church, for example) into Pecola's story. In addition, in each chapter several garbled lines from the primer separate Claudia's voice from that of the omniscient narrator.

The chapters counterpoint three moments in time: a past before the narrative present (the flashbacks), the eternal present of the primer, and the narrative present of Pecola's story as told by Claudia. The different narratives in each chapter provide variations on a specific theme. This technique demonstrates here and throughout Morrison's fiction the interconnectedness of past and present. The form implies that the meaning of Pecola's story may only be understood in relation to events that predated her birth.

The cacophony of voices in *The Bluest Eye* demonstrates that Pecola is inextricably linked to the linguistic community that forms the novel. Yet she is clearly denied a place in the world the text purports to represent; her involuntary isolation from others leads to her psychological disintegration. *Sula* as well features a scapegoat-protagonist, although Sula clearly cultivates those qualities that distinguish her from her neighbors. Here, too, Morrison's plot relies on a multiplicity of narratives to implicate Sula in the very community from which she is alienated. Although Sula, unlike Pecola, chooses her isolation, it is precisely that distance that destroys her.

Sula centers on a character who believes that she can create for herself an identity that exists beyond community and social expectations. "An artist with no art form," Sula uses her life as her medium, "exploring her own thoughts and emotions, giving them full reign, feeling no obligation to please anybody unless their pleasure pleased her." She thus defies social restraints with a vengeance. She disavows gratuitous social flattery, refusing to compliment either the food placed before her or her old friends gone to seed, and using her conversation to experiment with her neighbors' responses. As the narrator remarks: "In the midst of pleasant conversation with someone, she might say, 'Why do you chew with your mouth open?' not because the answer interested her but because she wanted to see the person's face change rapidly." Worst of all in her neighbors' judgment, she discards men, black and white, as rapidly as she sleeps with them, even the husband of her best friend, Nel.

There are moments when the text seems to validate Sula's way of life; the narrator suggests, for example, that Sula's independence has bestowed upon her a kind of immortality:

> Among the weighty evidence piling up was the fact that Sula did not look her age. She was near thirty and, unlike them, had lost no teeth, suffered no bruises, developed no ring of fat at the waist or pocket at the back of her neck. It was rumored that she had had no childhood diseases, was never known to have chicken pox, croup or even a runny nose. She had played rough as a child—where were the scars?

But by interweaving Sula's story with Shadrack's and Nel's, Morrison demonstrates structurally the collective nature of human identity.

Sula's story stands in analogous relation to Shadrack's, symbolic evidence that her situation, like Pecola's, is hardly unique. The communal response to Sula is identically Shadrack's response to the unexpected. Shadrack, the insane World War I veteran whose story opens the novel, exemplifies in the extreme this need to explain or find a place for the inexplicable. By creating National Suicide Day, he finds a way of controlling his fear: "If one day a year were devoted to [death], everybody could get it out of the way and the rest of the year would be safe and free."

The people of the Bottom of Medallion, Ohio, ridicule Shadrack's holiday, but their survival, like his, depends upon finding ways of controlling their terrors. Superstitions, which recur in the narrative and in their collective discourse, help them explain disturbing disruptions. When Hannah, Sula's mother, dies suddenly, Eva, Sula's grandmother, reflects that she would have been prepared for the tragedy if she had read properly the omens she had received. Likewise, the denizens of the Bottom remark that they should have anticipated Sula's deleterious effect on their community, because her return was accompanied by a plague of robins. Like Eva, the townspeople find a sign or a reason for their trouble after the fact. Their retrospective justifications are finally no different from Shadrack's.

And just as they must find a way of controlling the unexpected evils that beset them, so do they find a place for Sula. Since they do not understand her, they call her evil and hold her responsible for the injuries and deaths that befall their community. As the narrator notes, the townspeople actually become more generous when they shun Sula because they assign to her their own baser impulses. For all her efforts to transcend the community, then, Sula remains an integral part of it.

Morrison also undercuts Sula's aspirations to originality by characterizing her as only half a person. As several critics have argued, Sula and Nel complement each other psychologically, and neither is fully herself after geography, and Sula's relation to Jude, separate them.

Sula and Nel are products of two different styles of childrearing: their friendship grows out of their fascination with their dissimilarities. Sula's family is the source of her independence of mind and sexual nonchalance. Her mother is known especially for her sexual generosity; her grandmother, Eva, for selling her leg to support her children. Eva's home provides a figure for her family, replete with an ever-changing cast of boarders, gentleman callers, and foundlings:

> Sula Peace lived in a house of many rooms that had been built over a period of five years to the specifications of its owner, who kept on adding things: more stairways—more rooms, doors and stoops. There were rooms that had three doors, others that opened out on the porch only and were inaccessible from any other part of the house; others that you could get to only by going through somebody's bedroom.

Nel, on the other hand, is raised in a well-ordered but repressive household, and is thus prepared to choose a life of limited options such as the one she shares with Jude. Haunted by the image of her own mother, a prostitute, Nel's mother tries to launder the "funk" out of her daughter's life. During their childhood and adolescence, Nel provides Sula with restraints, and Sula offers Nel license. More importantly, they offer each other a kind of security that neither finds in her own family. Together they begin to discover the meaning of death and sexuality. As the narrator remarks:

> Because each had discovered years before that they were neither white nor male, and that all freedom and triumph were forbidden to them, they had set about creating something else to be. Their meeting was fortunate, for it let them use each other to grow on. Daughters of distant mothers and incomprehensible fathers (Sula's because he was dead; Nel's because he wasn't), they found in each other's eyes the intimacy they were looking for.

Their relationship is permanently destroyed when Sula sleeps with Jude, although Sula reflects that she never intended to cause Nel pain. Without Nel, "the closest thing to both an other and a self," Sula is cut off from the only relation that endowed her life with meaning, and she drifts to her death. Nel, too, is rendered incomplete when her friendship with Sula ends. She may think that her inescapable grief is the result of having lost her husband, but as she realizes at the end of the novel, what she had missed for so many years was not Jude, but Sula.

The descendant of a line of relatively autonomous women, Sula attempts to go them one better and create herself outside of the collective assumptions of women's behavior. Morrison denies the feasibility of such a choice most obviously by killing off her protagonist. But the narrative structures she employs in *Sula* further undercut Sula's aspirations. By characterizing her as both a scapegoat and the second self of her more conventional best friend, Morrison denies Sula the originality she seeks.

II

Song of Solomon centers on Milkman Dead's unwitting search for identity. Milkman appears to be doomed to a life of alienation from himself and from others because, like his parents, he adheres to excessively rigid, materialistic, Western values and an attendant linear conception of time. During a trip to his ancestral home, however, Milkman discovers his own capacity for emotional expansiveness and learns to perceive the passage of time as a cyclical process. When he incorporates both his familial and his personal history into his sense of the present, he repairs his feelings of fragmentation and comprehends for the first time the coherence of his own life.

Milkman's father, Macon Dead, Jr., is a quintessential self-made man. Orphaned and disinherited in his adolescence, he wheeled and dealt his way into his position as the richest black man in town. Milkman can therefore brag about his father's houses, cars, assets and speculations, to the delight of the Reverend Mr. Cooper and his Danville companions. The avid materialism and rugged individualism that made Macon financially successful have exacted their price from him in other ways, however. Macon has come to believe that money, property and keys are what is real in the world; his financial success has thus cost him his capacity for communication and emotion. As he advises his son:

"Come to my office; work a couple of hours there and learn what's real. Let me tell you right now that one important thing you'll ever need to know: Own things. And let the things you own own other things. Then you'll own yourself and other people too."

The Macon Deads exemplify the patriarchal, nuclear family that has been traditionally a stable and critical feature not only of American society, but of Western civilization in general. The primary institution for the reproduction and maintenance of children, ideally it provides the individual with the means for understanding his/her place in the world. The degeneration of the Dead family, and the destructiveness of Macon's rugged individualism, symbolize the invalidity of American, indeed Western values. Morrison's depiction of this family demonstrates the incompatibility of received assumptions and the texture and demands of life in black American communities.

Macon, Jr. believes that a successful businessman cannot afford to be compassionate. Reflecting that his first two keys to rental units would never have multiplied had he accommodated delinquent accounts, he sees his tenants as only so much property. Moreover, he objectifies his family. He brutalizes his wife Ruth both subtly and overtly because he suspects her of incestuous relations with her father and son. Despite his concern for Milkman, he only speaks to him "if his words [hold] some command or criticism." And by refusing to acknowledge Pilate as his sister, Macon denies her humanity as well. His resentment is based in part on his belief that she stole the gold that the two of them should have shared. More significantly, though, he eschews her company because he considers her deportment to be socially unacceptable. He fears that the white bankers will cease to trust him if they associate him with a woman bootlegger.

Weak and pathetic as she is, Ruth finds subtle metho... of objectifying the members of her family as well. She retaliates against her husband's cruelty by manipulating him. Since she cannot attract his attention in any other way, she demeans herself until, out of disgust, he lashes out at her. Similarly, she remarks that her son has never been "a person to her." Before he was born, Milkman was "a wished-for bond between herself and Macon, something to hold them together and reinstate their sex lives." After she realizes that her husband will never again gratify her sexually, she uses Milkman to fulfill her yearnings by breastfeeding him until he is old enough to talk, stand up and wear knickers.

Pilate Dead, Macon's younger sister, provides a marked contrast to her brother and his family. Like Macon, Pilate presides over a household which is predominantly female. But while Macon's love of property and money determines the nature of his relationships, Pilate's sheer disregard for status, occupation, hygiene and manners enables her to affirm spiritual values such as compassion, respect, loyalty and generosity.

If the Macon Deads seem barren and lifeless, Pilate's family bursts with energy and sensuality. Pilate, Reba and Hagar engage ceaselessly in collective activity, erupting spontaneously into harmonious song. On his way to his own emotionally empty house one evening, Macon, Jr. peeks through the window of his sister's home in search of spiritual nourishment. He hears the three women sing one song, Pilate stirring the contents of a pot, Reba paring her toenails and Hagar braiding her hair. Macon is comforted both by the soothing and unending motion of each character in the vignette and by the harmony and tranquility of the music they make together.

As Pilate introduces vitality into her brother's life, so does she introduce a magical presence into the otherwise spiritually lifeless world of Part I of the novel. The circumstances of her birth make her a character of larger-than-life dimensions—one who has transcended the limitations of her historical moment and milieu. Pilate delivered herself at birth and was born without a navel. Her smooth stomach isolates her from society, since those who know of her condition shun her. Moreover, her physical condition symbolizes her thorough independence of others; even as a fetus she did not need to rely on another person for sustenance. Her isolation and self-sufficiency enable her to "throw away every assumption she had learned and [begin] at zero." She is therefore neither trapped nor destroyed by decaying values as her brother's family is. Like Macon she is self-made, but her self-creation departs from, instead of coinciding with, the American myth. Pilate decides for herself what is important to her, and instead of appropriating collective assumptions, she remakes herself accordingly. After cutting her hair:

> [Pilate] tackled the problem of trying to decide how she wanted to live and what was valuable to her. When am I happy and when am I sad and what is the difference? What do I need to stay alive? What is true in the world?

Quintessential self-made man that he is, Macon predicates his behavior on a linear conception of time. To his mind, future successes determine identity and justify one's actions in the past and in the present. Macon's futuristic, linear vision of time and of identity is evidenced by his failure to consider his past as part of himself. He denies the importance of his relationship with his sister and of their shared past. Moreover, as he remarks while telling Milkman about his days in Lincoln's Heaven, he does not even allow himself to think about his past:

> He had not said any of this for years. Had not even reminisced much about it recently. . . . For years he hadn't had that kind of time, or interest.

Macon's linear vision of time is also partly responsible for his sense of family and of morality. Because he believes that the coherence and significance of his identity lie in his future, he cares only about his relationship to his son. To his patriarchal mind, it is in that connection that the most important genealogical transfer occurs. But Macon has no time whatsoever for any connection that would cause him to exercise his capacity for horizontal or (what would be to him) peripheral vision.

Macon's ability to see the world only in linear, exclusive terms, explains his lack of sympathy in yet other ways. He believes that the ends justify any means; as a result, he excuses his own corruption by considering only the financial profits it brings him. He feels no need to offer Mrs. Bains (one of his tenants) charity because charity will not increase his wealth. And he encourages Milkman and Guitar to steal what he thinks is Pilate's gold, despite the kindness she has shown them all.

In contrast to Macon's, Pilate's vision of time—indeed, of the world—is cyclical and expansive. Instead of repressing the past, she carries it with her in the form of her songs, her stories and her bag of bones. She believes that one's sense of identity is rooted in the capacity to look back to the past and synthesize it with the present; it is not enough simply to put it behind one and look forward. As she tells Macon:

"You can't take a life and walk off and leave it. Life is life. Precious. And the dead you kill is yours. They stay with you anyway, in your mind. So it's a better thing, a more better thing to have the bones right there with you wherever you go. That way it frees up your mind."

Before Milkman leaves Michigan, he perceives the world in much the same way that his father does. His steadiness of vision and lack of compassion allow him to abuse remorselessly and unself-consciously the people around him. For instance, his letter to Hagar reveals his inability to understand her feelings and psychology despite their years of intimacy. He fails to accept responsibility for ending their relationship: instead, he writes little more than a business letter suggesting that he leave her for her own best interest. Moreover, his sister Lena tells him that he has "urinated" on the women in his family. That is, he has demanded their service and shown them no consideration. He has presumed to know what is best for them without knowing them at all.

Milkman's search for gold indicates further the similarity between his father's vision of the world and his own. He thinks that leaving his hometown, his past and his responsibilities will guarantee him a sense of his own identity. As he becomes increasingly implicated in the scheme to retrieve Pilate's gold, Milkman acquires a clearer but equally false sense of what freedom means. He believes that gold will provide him with a "clean-lined definite self," the first sense of identity he has ever known.

Milkman's assumption that the key to his liberation may be found in Danville and Shalimar is correct, although it is not gold that will free him. In his ancestors' world, communal and mythical values prevail over individualism and materialism; when he adopts their assumptions in place of his own, he arrives at a more complete understanding of what his experience means. When Milkman arrives in the South he wears a "beige three-piece suit, button down light-blue shirt and black string tie, [and] beautiful Florsheim shoes." He ruins and loses various articles of clothing and jewelry as he looks first for gold and then for the story of his people. Indeed, just before his epiphanic moment in the forest, he has changed from his cosmopolitan attire to overalls and brogans. Similarly, the people he meets in Shalimar force him to throw off his pretenses before they offer him the help and information he needs. Only when he ceases to flaunt his wealth and refer to their women casually do they admit him into their community. Until he sheds the leaden trappings of materialism, Milkman is like the peacock he and Guitar see: too weighted down by his vanity to fly.

While in Michigan, Milkman believes that when he finally achieves his freedom, he will no longer need to submit to the claims of others. In the woods, away from the destructive effects of "civilization," he realizes that human connection—horizontal vision—is an inescapable part of life:

> It sounded old. Deserve. Old and tired and beaten to death. Deserve. Now it seemed to him that he was always saying or thinking that he didn't deserve some bad luck, or some bad treatment from others. He'd told Guitar that he didn't "deserve" his family's dependence, hatred, or whatever. That he didn't even "deserve" to hear all the misery and mutual accusations his parents unloaded on him. Nor did he "deserve" Hagar's vengeance. But why shouldn't his parents tell him their personal problems? If not him, then who?

While previously he had dehumanized his friends and relations, he now empathizes with his parents and feels shame for having robbed Pilate:

> . . . the skin of shame that he had rinsed away in the bathwater after having stolen from Pilate returned. But now it was as thick and as tight as a caul. How could he have broken into that house—the only one he knew that achieved comfort without one article of comfort in it. No soft worn-down chair, not a cushion or a pillow. . . . But peace was there, energy, singing, and now his own remembrances.

In keeping with this new awareness of others and of his personal past, Milkman, insensitive to Hagar and unwilling to accept responsibility for her in life, understands her posthumously and assumes the burden of her death. He acknowledges the inappropriateness of his letter to her and realizes that he has used her. Moreover, he knows without being told that she has died and he is to blame. As Pilate has carried with her the bones of the man she believes she has murdered, so too does Milkman resolve to carry with him the box of Hagar's hair: a symbol of his newly acquired cyclical vision of a past he no longer needs to escape.

Macon, Sr., Milkman's grandfather, was an American Adam, a farmer who loved the land and worked it profitably. Moving north cost Macon, Jr. some of the talent he had inherited from his father; still able to manipulate cold cash, he lost his father's organic connection to the soil. In the south, Milkman, too, seems disconnected from nature. Graceful in the "civilized" world, he is clumsy and obtuse when he enters the wilderness. However, he becomes increasingly attuned to nature's rhythms as he grows in self-awareness. During the bobcat hunt he senses through the contact between his fingertips and the ground beneath him that someone is about to make an attempt on his life. And as he returns to the town, Milkman feels as if he is part of the "rock and soil" and discovers that he no longer limps.

Finally, however, Milkman's discovery of his identity lies not so much in his connection with the earth, or in his ability to understand his own past; these accomplishments only attend his greater achievement—learning to complete, to understand and to sing his family song. Milkman comes to know fully who he is when he can supply the lyrics to the song Pilate has only partially known. Throughout his life, Milkman has had an inexplicable fascination with flight. Robert Smith's abortive attempt to fly from the hospital roof precipitated his birth. Riding backward makes him uncomfortable because it reminds him of "flying blind, and not knowing where he [is] going." And as he approaches Circe's house, he recalls his recurring childhood fantasy of being able to take flight. When Milkman knows the entire song, however, and can sing it to Pilate as she has sung it to others, he can assume his destiny. Flight is no longer a fantasy that haunts him, appearing unsummoned in his consciousness. He now understands it as a significant action from his ancestral past. Indeed, the ultimate sign of his achievement of identity is his ability to take flight in the way his grandfather did. In the process of assuming himself, Milkman discovers that his dreams have become attainable.

Milkman acquires a sense of identity when he immerses himself in his extended past. He comes full round from the individualism his father represents and advocates. Assuming identity is thus a communal gesture in this novel, as, indeed, Morrison suggests in her two earlier novels. Knowing oneself derives from learning to reach back into history and horizontally in sympathetic relationship to others. Milkman burst the bonds of the Western, individualistic conception of self, accepting in its place the richness and complexity of a collective sense of identity.

◆◆◆◆◆◆◆◆◆◆◆◆◆

Narrative Dilemma: Jadine as Cultural Orphan in *Tar Baby*

MARILYN SANDERS MOBLEY

Based on a chapter from *Roots and Wings*, by Marilyn Sanders Mobley, Case Western Reserve University, 1987. (A version of this essay was presented as a paper at the NEMLA Conference in Boston, Massachusetts, on April 3, 1987.)

> Not to know is bad; not to wish to know is worse.
> —African proverb

Of Toni Morrison's first four novels, *Tar Baby* (1981) is the most problematic. It might appear that this is so because Morrison attempts two new narrative strategies—situating the central plot within an insular setting beyond the geographical boundaries of the United States mainland and juxtaposing black and white characters to dramatize the racial complexities that determine the American cultural landscape. While dislocation and cross-cultural relationships figure strongly in the novel, the characterization of the protagonist, Jadine, draws attention to a more fundamental narrative problem than either of these strategies might suggest. On one hand, Morrison wants to affirm the self-reliance and freedom of a black woman who makes choices for her own life on her own terms. On the other hand, she also seeks, according to her statements from an interview published in *Black Women Writers (1950–1980): A Critical Evaluation*, to "point out the dangers . . . that can happen to the totally self-reliant if there is no historical connection." More specifically, Morrison's dilemma in *Tar Baby* is how to narrate the quest of the contemporary black female hero when she happens to be a cultural orphan, one whose sense of self is based upon a denial of her own cultural heritage and an identification with one that is not her own.

Nowhere are the dynamics of Morrison's narrative dilemma more clearly articulated than in the description of Jadine as she stands in the "circle of trees" where the Caribbean island swamp literally entraps her in its black sticky substance:

> . . . the women hanging in the trees looked down at her . . . and stopped murmuring. They were delighted when they first saw her, thinking a runaway child had been restored to them. But looking closer they saw differently. This girl was fighting to get away from them. The women hanging from the trees were quiet now, but arrogant—mindful as they were of their value, their

exceptional femaleness, knowing as they did that the first world of the world had been built with their sacred properties, that they alone could hold together the stones of pyramids and the rushes of Moses's crib; knowing their steady consistency . . . they wondered at the girl's desperate struggle down below to be free, to be something other than they were.

Not only does this passage express the problem Morrison attempts to address in writing the novel, but it points to the central conflict that Jadine faces in her quest to come to terms with her life. For Morrison, the women in the trees symbolize the women she seeks to affirm—the mothers, grandmothers and sisters to whom she dedicates the novel. For Jadine, the women in the trees represent all the women who make her feel "inauthentic." While on one level *Tar Baby* appears to be simply the story of a failed love affair between a man and a woman with diametrically opposed values and lifestyles, on a deeper level, the novel is about the disparity Morrison sees between the women of her remembered past and the women of the present epitomized in the character of Jadine. Consequently, the biblical epigraph to the novel—which reads: ". . . it hath been declared . . . by them . . . of the house of Chloe, that there are contentions among you"—does not simply foreshadow the conflicts that arise in the Valerian Street household. Instead, it points to the serious conflicts or "contentions" that Morrison (born Chloe Anthony Wofford) examines in the character of Jadine. Indeed, the text reveals the dilemma Morrison faced in trying to depict the potential consequences of success predicated upon disconnection from one's racial identity and cultural heritage.

Morrison attempts to solve her dilemma by transforming the well-known Afro-American folktale of the tar baby into a modern cautionary tale. As Roger Abrahams explains in his collection, *Afro-American Folktales*, the cautionary tales are *moral stories* that "illustrate how disorderly and unmannerly people act and what happens to them . . . because of their misbehavior." Thus, *Tar Baby* can be interpreted as a modern cautionary tale in which Morrison draws on the Afro-American oral narrative tradition to expose the pitfalls of white middle-class aspirations for the black woman and to illustrate the consequences of her social and cultural "misbehavior." Although the text illustrates these consequences by examining the tensions inherent in the binary oppositions of black and white, poor and rich, female and male, mother and daughter, African and European, Afro-American and American, the central reasons for Jadine's divided consciousness have to do with her rejection of the cultural constructions of race and mothering that are part of her Afro-American heritage. Jadine's quest is one for psychic wholeness, but because she does not heed the cautions that come to her in various forms, she experiences a failed initiation or an aborted quest. Indeed, her quest for wholeness is unsuccessful because she accepts values and mores of white middle-class culture without question and she rejects the very cultural constructions of race and mothering that could heal and transform her consciousness.

Ironically, while Morrison was still in the process of writing *Tar Baby*, she delivered the 1979 commencement address at Barnard College, which expresses the precise thematic concerns of the novel:

> I am suggesting that we pay as much attention to our nurturing sensibilities as to our ambition. You are moving in the direction of freedom and the function of freedom is to free somebody else. You are moving toward self-fulfillment and the consequences of that fulfillment should be to discover that there is something just as important as you are. In your rainbow journey toward the realization of personal goals, don't make choices based only on your security and your safety . . . Let your might and power emanate from the place in you that is nurturing and caring.

The double-voiced nature of this speech foreshadows the dilemma Morrison faced in writing *Tar Baby*. On one hand, she speaks as a peer or "daughter" cognizant of the lure of the present toward self-fulfillment. The first person pronouns, "I" and "we," thus signify an empathetic identification with her audience. On the other hand, the second person pronoun, "you," signifies that she then speaks as an authority or "mother" rooted in the knowledge of the past. The novel gives voice to both perspectives in varying degrees of success. But, more importantly, it deconstructs the difference that Jadine sees between these perspectives by employing mothering as a metaphor for nurturing. By so doing, Morrison affirms the recent and historical nourishment that indigenous black culture could provide. The novel serves, then, both as a remembrance of a cultural tradition of nurturing and as a cautionary tale for those like Jadine, who define themselves against themselves and their cultural past in the interest of self-fulfillment.

Tar Baby is essentially the narrative of Jadine's flight from crisis. Uncertain about whether her white boyfriend in Paris wants to marry her for *her* or wants to marry just "any black girl," and distraught over the transcendent beauty and insulting gesture of an African woman dressed in yellow, she flees to the Caribbean to the home of her adoptive parents where she hopes to "sort out things before going ahead." Jadine is actually adopted twice—first, by her aunt and uncle who raise her from the time she literally becomes an orphan at the age of twelve, and, second, by Valerian Street, the wealthy, white benefactor who pays for her Sorbonne education. Although her European education leads to a degree in art history and a career as a highly acclaimed fashion model, both adoptions take her further from her actual and metaphorical birthplace and contribute to the emotional and spiritual uncertainty that plague her. While she is in the process of sorting out the direction for her life, Son, a renegade, intrudes into the household. His presence, little by little, throws the entire house into a state of disarray which exposes the hostilities, lies, secrets and untold narratives that had been concealed under the guise of being "like a family." Yet Son is only partially to blame for the chaos that disrupts the false sense of familial calm. Instead, it is the revelation of mothering gone awry—the secret narrative that Valerian's wife, Margaret, had abused their son, Michael, when he was a small child—that creates the most serious form of rupture. In the wake of the chaos that ensues from this revelation, Jadine and Son become lovers and flee from the island. More than lovers, they attempt to become rescuers of one another. In New York City, she attempts to rescue him from a romanticized view of Afro-American life and culture. In Eloe, Florida, Son's all-black hometown, he attempts to rescue her from ignorance of and disdain for her cultural heritage. Their fundamental cross-purposes preclude the existence of their relationship. Jadine flees from this crisis, first, by returning to the island and, ultimately, by returning to Paris. In trying to find her, Son returns to the Caribbean, where the indigenous blacks try to dissuade him from his search. He ultimately yields to the maternal powers of nature and joins the blind horsemen in the tree-covered hills, who, according to the traditional black myth and folklore of the island, had once been runaway slaves.

What this synopsis of the novel cannot account for are the various forms in which Jadine is warned implicitly and explicitly about the dangers of rejecting her cultural heritage. The most striking form of this caution occurs early in the narrative when, on the happiest day of Jadine's life, an African woman with "skin like tar" makes her feel "lonely and inauthentic." Jadine views her as a "woman's woman—that mother/sister/she; that unphotographable beauty." The image of this woman haunts Jadine throughout the text as a sign of how, in rejecting her blackness, Jadine rejects her African past and her ancestral mothers.

The next significant form of caution to appear in the text comes from Michael, the son of Margaret and Valerian. Although he is conspicuously absent throughout the novel, the reader is aware of his importance, first because Christmas plans revolve around his mother's frenzied anticipation of his arrival even though he regularly does not come home for Christmas or much of anything else. His absence is made even more conspicuous when the revelations that Margaret abused him as a child ruin the Christmas dinner far more than his failure to arrive. Ironically, the novel also raises questions about the father-son relationship, for Valerian disdainfully labels Michael a "cultural orphan," someone who is a purveyor of "other cultures he could love without risk or pain." The validity of Valerian's judgment is doubtful, however, when we consider that he is described as a "man who respected industry" in the tradition, if not the spirit, of capitalism. Therefore, he has no respect for Michael's socialist political leanings, his anthropological pursuits or his insistent desire "for value in life not money." In light of his apparent estrangement from both parents, Michael is an orphan in the spiritual sense of the word. But the concern here is not with Michael, per se, but with his assessment of Jadine. All the discussion about whether he will show up for dinner prompts Valerian to ask Jadine whether she remembers him. Not only does she share her memories of him, which date back to her first year of college at the Sorbonne, but she tells of his misgivings about her identity, her education, her values.

Indeed, Michael's queries about Jadine's priorities call attention to her as the real cultural orphan. He questions, for example, why she "was studying art history at the snotty school instead of . . . organizing or something." He further admonishes her for "abandoning" her "history" and her "people." (He apparently overlooks how his anthropological excursions into minority cultures represent his own attempt to abandon or disguise his membership in the group that has exploited them.) Jadine's response to his criticism reveals that his judgment of her is essentially valid. As she reflects on her conversation with Michael, she admits,

> I knew what I was leaving . . . But he did make me want to apologize for what I was doing, for what I felt. For liking 'Ave Maria' better than gospel music . . . Picasso *is* better than an Itumba mask. The fact that he was intrigued by them is proof of his genius, not the mask-makers'.

In this statement, Jadine not only reveals her negative, stereotypical attitudes toward Afro-American and African culture, but she attempts to justify her distance from that culture. Indeed, having been raised by her aunt and uncle to mirror rather than question white Western values, she rejects what those values reject. That she values Picasso's work over the original African masks that inspire it only reiterates the extent to which her values are distorted. Ironically, although she describes Michael as "clearheaded—independent," she gives no credence to the cautionary message behind his criticism of her. Jadine's attitude toward black culture recalls historian Carter G. Woodson's dictum in the *Miseducation of the Negro* that "the education of any people should begin with the people themselves, but Negroes . . . have been dreaming about the ancients of Europe and about those who have tried to imitate them."

The third and most direct form of caution comes from Son. As the "forepresence of Michael," someone Valerian can rescue from "Margaret's hysteria" as he used to rescue Michael from lonely childhood singing "under the sink," Son attempts to rescue Jadine from her state of cultural orphanage. Indeed, his cautionary words to her echo Michael's in one sense and extend them in another. In the heat of an argument in which Jadine and Son confront each other about their inability to live in the other's world, Jadine says that while he has been on the run hiding from sheriffs and lawyers, she's been "learning how to make it in *this* world." Son replies that the "truth is that whatever you learned in those colleges that didn't include me ain't shit . . . If they didn't teach you that, then they didn't teach you nothing because until you know about me, you don't know nothing about yourself." Their differences can be summed up in the geographical and cultural places they draw on for nurturing. Son is from Eloe, an "all black town in Florida," and Jadine is from Baltimore, Philadelphia, and Paris. In Son's words, she is "not *from* anywhere." While he values the nurturing aspects of home and fraternity, she is rootless and places greater value on what she can own. Yet as the tar baby that Valerian creates, Jadine initially lures Son to her.

In New York, the place she feels most at home, they lead a fairy tale existence of "nestling" as husband and wife, and for a time, Jadine feels what she describes as an "orphan's delight." The word "delight" not only suggests a kind of childlike pleasure that borders on fantasy, but it foretells the temporary nature of her feeling. Indeed, Son's insistence that they go to Eloe, his "home," is what brings the fantasy to its inevitable conclusion. It is in Eloe, moreover, that this cautionary tale takes on its strongest implications. Jadine resents how the "nestling" she experiences in New York gives way to being "shunted off" with the women and children, "while the men grouped on the porch and . . . ignored her." In the small room she has to stay in, she feels "she might as well have been in a cave, a grave, the dark womb of the earth." The imagery clearly points to mothering and birth, but it also points to the primal source of black cultural nourishment symbolized by the mother. At the same time, the claustrophobic connotations that the text assigns to this imagery signify Jadine's resistance and aversion to the various received cultural constructions of what it means to be black and female. The aversion to her female self becomes most apparent when she and Son attempt to make love:

> Cheyenne [Son's dead wife] got in, and then the rest: Rosa and Thérèse and Son's dead mother and . . . Ondine and Soldier's wife Ellen and . . . her own dead mother and even the woman in yellow. All there crowding into the room. Some of them she did not know, recognize, but they were all there . . . They each pulled out a breast and showed her. 'I have breasts too,' she said or thought or willed . . . But they didn't believe her.

The women in Eloe represent her familial past, while the women in the trees, cited earlier, represent historical tradition in that they are the women who mate with the runaway slaves according to Caribbean folk narratives. All these women symbolize Jadine's refusal to define herself in terms of familial past, historical tradition and cultural heritage. In rejecting these women, she rejects the very sources that could teach and nourish her. By denying them, she both literally and metaphorically denies her own mother. As Adrienne Rich describes this denial, it is "matrophobia—rebellion against the imposed female image," a denial whose tragic consequences are represented in Jadine's divided consciousness and troubled psyche. The fact that these images haunt her suggests that psychic wholeness will continue to elude her until she bridges the cultural gulf between what they represent and who she is. Collectively, these images introduce the most powerful form of caution in the entire narrative.

The scene at the muck or swamp called Sein de Vieilles is where the Afro-American folktale upon which the novel is based dramatically comes alive. In the process of trying to get closer to the trees to draw them on her sketch pad, Jadine sinks deeper and deeper into the muck and literally becomes a tar baby. Clearly, the black substance signifies the blackness she so persistently rejects. Yet, its adhesive quality signifies that Jadine, in rejecting the received cultural constructions of her own racial and sexual identity, fails to recognize the dimensions of these constructions that could heal and affirm her sense of self. As Morrison explains in her 1981 interview with Thomas LeClair titled "The Language Must Not Sweat":

> I found that there is a tar baby in African mythology. I started thinking about tar. At one point, a tar pit was a holy place, at least an important place, because tar was used to build things. It came naturally out of the earth; it held things together. For me, the tar baby came to mean the black woman who can hold things together.

Hence, this statement reveals that Morrison draws on this folktale in two possibly contradictory respects. On one hand, she focuses on the connotations of entrapment that we usually associate with the Afro-American version of the narrative. On the other hand, she also focuses on the not-so-familiar positive connotations found in the African version of the tale. Both sets of connotations deepen the portrait of Jadine as the tar baby that entraps Son, and as the woman who cannot sustain a relationship because she lacks the ancestral power of being able to "hold things together."

The relationship between Son and Jadine does not hold together. Jadine believes she is rescuing him

> from the night women who wanted him for themselves, wanted him feeling superior in a cradle deferring to him; wanted to settle for wifely competence when she could be almighty, to settle for fertility rather than originality, nurturing instead of building.

Because she only sees mutually exclusive choices, she does not realize it is possible to nurture *and* to build. As Morrison says in an interview in Claudia Tate's *Black Women Writers at Work:* "Black women seem able to combine the nest and the adventure." The fact that Morrison creates a fictional black woman who cannot achieve this combination exposes the contradiction between the women Morrison affirms in her extratextual statements and the protagonist she indicts in her text. The indictment is expressed most clearly in Son's question, "Culture-bearing black woman, whose culture are you bearing?" Interpreting the novel as a cautionary tale offers the reader a means of understanding this contradiction, the disturbing portrayal of Jadine and the failure of the Jadine-Son relationship. Because Son is rooted in the past, symbolized by his romantic attachment to Eloe, and because she feels the key to personal and collective success is to forget the past, their relationship cannot hold itself together. The novel goes full circle in that once again a crisis causes Jadine to flee. Unable to resolve it any other way, she returns to Paris.

At the end of the novel, the words of Ondine, Jadine's aunt and adoptive mother, suggest that she feels responsible for the cultural orphan Jadine has become. She laments not having told her that

> a girl has got to be a daughter first . . . If she never learns how to be a daughter, she can't never learn how to be a woman; a woman good enough even for the respect of other women . . . you don't need your own natural mother to be a daughter.

Just as Son's narrative of the tar baby folktale to Jadine is of no avail, likewise, Ondine's advice to Jadine comes too late to be of use to her. In response to Ondine, Jadine argues:

> There are other ways to be a woman . . . Your way is one, I guess . . . but it's not my way. I don't want to be . . . like you . . . I don't want to learn how to be the kind of woman you're talking about because I don't want to be that kind of woman.

As in the case of her relationship with Son, Jadine and her aunt arrive at a narrative impasse. The irony of the rupture in her relationship with Ondine is that earlier, her aunt considers their relationship ideal because it lacked the "stress of a mother-daughter relationship." Clearly, however, the rupture they experience reveals that the mother-daughter tensions had been just beneath the surface all the while. Disconnected from the cultural knowledge of self and nurturing that could heal this rupture, Jadine seems fated to remain a cultural orphan, in a state of permanent "motherlessness."

Out of this complex portrayal of Jadine emerges Toni Morrison's most severe cultural statement to date. In the March 30, 1981, *Newsweek* discussion of her writing, she says her novels

> should clarify roles that have been obscured; they ought to identify those things in the past that are useful and those . . . that are not; and they ought to give nourishment.

If we assume by "roles" that Morrison refers solely to male/female roles, then *Tar Baby* surely fails to satisfy her own narrative requirements. If, however, we understand that she seeks to illustrate the consequences of rejecting one's cultural heritage and the value of both nurturing and building in the quest for freedom and self-actualization, then the novel satisfies her criteria. Ultimately, it shows that the black woman who denies her "historical connections" and "sacred properties" risks psychic chaos and alienation from the very resources that could empower her. By drawing on the Afro-American storytelling tradition, Morrison becomes the writer as cultural archivist. Yet she does not revive the tar baby folktale merely to entertain us. Instead, to use her words, she "dusts it off," transforms it and entraps us with its rich, metaphorical complexity. As a cautionary tale for our time, *Tar Baby* criticizes much, but beneath the critique and implicit in the warning is an affirmation that can heal even as it instructs.

♦♦♦♦♦♦♦♦♦♦♦♦♦♦

Images of Nurturance in
Tar Baby

PETER B. ERICKSON

The extent to which *Tar Baby* (1981) is a sharp departure from Toni Morrison's three earlier novels has been exaggerated;[1] this exaggeration has deflected attention from the ways in which the new novel continues and extends Morrison's previous concerns. Despite the more prominent role played by white characters, despite the larger social and geographical range in *Tar Baby*, Morrison's key focal point remains the identity of a black woman, Jadine. Particularly crucial are the issues of maternal sexuality and of generational continuity among black women.

The organizing force in *Sula* (1973) is black female lineage as embodied in the two sequences: Cecil Sabat, Rochelle, Helene (Wright), Nel; Eva Peach, Hannah, Sula. However painful and ironic Sula's female heritage is, it is also rich and powerful, creating strong bonds that define Sula. In spite of her antagonism toward Eva, Sula is drawn to—in effect becomes—her grandmother when she withdraws into her room with the boarded window and dies there. By contrast, in *Tar Baby* we are made more aware of the disconnections rather than the connections among the principal black women: Thérèse, Ondine, and Jadine. This absence of connection, which in large measure is responsible for the "contentions among you" to which Morrison alludes in her prefatory citation, is the subject of *Tar Baby*. Specifically, Jadine stands outside her tradition in a way that Sula does not. Because Jadine more explicitly and decisively renounces the maternal role, *Tar Baby* dramatizes a pronounced crisis in cross-generational sustenance. Jadine achieves an independence not attained by Sula, but Toni Morrison concentrates on the cost and negative aspects of Jadine's achievement. The result is that Jadine is less attractive and the novel's rendering of her more ambivalent than might have been expected.

In their final exchange, Nel criticizes the dying Sula's independence and lack of children: "You can't act like a man. You can't be walking around all independent-like, doing whatever you like, taking what you want, leaving what you don't."[2] Though Sula eloquently defends her defiance—"Girl, I got my mind. And what goes on in it. Which is to say, I got me. . . . My lonely is *mine*. Now your lonely is somebody else's. Made by somebody else and handed to you"—her efforts are mocked by her illness and immobilization. Sula's virtual defeat is replaced in *Tar Baby* by Jadine's spectacular success, yet Nel's accusatory voice comes through clearly in the new novel, making Jadine's independence appear highly problematic and suspect.

I

In building the novel's narrative momentum, Morrison draws on two separate sources of suspense. First, and more obvious, is the suspense associated with the black fugitive, Son. It is his mysterious adventure, viscerally presented in the opening segment, that carries us so swiftly into the ongoing narrative current. The sense of menace and uncertainty attaching to Son never entirely disappears. At the end of the novel, as at the beginning, our curiosity is still propelled by the elementary question, What is he going to do?

The second area of suspense involves the other son, Michael, and the relationship with his mother, Margaret. At the simplest level, the issue is whether or not he will arrive on the Caribbean island to spend the Christmas holiday with his parents. But the moment when this issue is resolved—"Nobody came"—becomes the occasion for revealing the deeper mystery of Margaret's violation of maternal responsibility. Proclaiming at Christmas dinner that Margaret is "no mother," Ondine, the black cook, explains:

> "You cut him up. You cut your baby up. Made him bleed for you. For fun you did it. Made him scream, you, you freak. You crazy white freak. She did," Ondine addressed the others, still shouting. "She stuck pins in his behind. Burned him with cigarettes."

Part of the reason that this climactic disclosure of Margaret's mistreatment of her son is so arresting is that we could not have anticipated it. The dramatic impact is increased because we are unprepared, unprotected. There has been an oblique suggestion that Margaret's defensive anxiety about her son conceals something:

> When he was an infant he seemed to want everything of her, and she didn't know what to give. She loved him even then. But no one would believe it. They would think she was one of those mothers in the *National Enquirer.*

But we understand this hint only in retrospect, on a second reading of the novel. Morrison, it turns out, has been building a suspense about which we have been unaware. Once we are abruptly informed, the mystery is deepened rather than dispersed.

The two realms of suspense are not of equal strength. Because Son's intrusion upon the Street household is a less serious threat than the disruption from within caused by the emergence of Margaret's secret maternal past, I propose that the former be viewed as ancillary, the latter as primary. Son is assimilated with astonishing ease: first welcomed by the white proprietor, Valerian Street; then, after the conflict with Valerian, adopted by Thérèse, the black woman who represents the indigenous culture of the island. But Margaret's act cannot be assimilated: it is not only unacceptable but also unfathomable. Her belated effort to share her burden with her husband becomes a caricature. She is released from preoccupation with her son only because her devastated husband becomes a baby whom she can benignly mother. The transmission of her story to Valerian is analogous to maternal feeding: "Margaret told her husband in pieces. Little by little, she spooned it out to him a sip here a drop there. . . . She told him in bite-sized pieces, small enough to swallow quickly . . ." Margaret's new maternal role is made explicit in Jadine's subsequent observation that "She talks about Valerian like he was a patient, or a baby."

It is not immediately evident why the graphic image of Margaret's damaging her baby's body should loom so large in the novel as a whole. The significance of this failed nurturance becomes clear when we cease to treat it as an isolated episode and instead see how it goes to the core of the novel's overall concern with mothering. Margaret's betrayal of maternal trust resonates with a network of minor, semi-amusing perversions of nurturance, all of which connect food with family and can be traced ultimately to the ideal of the nursing mother with "magic breasts" (as well as to the presumption that women have exclusive responsibility for infant care).

The wealth that sustains the Caribbean house derives from "a family shop" for the manufacture of candy. The maternal aspect of the business is emphasized by the origin of "their main confection," which "had been made first by their workaholic mother as a treat for Theodore, her youngest son," and by the beneficent, symbiotic environment:

> [T]he people who lived in the factory's neighborhood stayed there largely because of the marvelous candy odor that greeted them in the morning and bid them goodnight. Smelling it was almost like having it and they could have it back then, because damaged lots of Teddy Boys were regularly given to children and homeless men. . . . The childhood of the children growing up in that candy air never quite left, and may have been why they never quite grew up.

Valerian Street, "the future of the family" because he is the one male born to the four sons running the business, has a candy made of "syrup sludge" named after him. He identifies this candy with the seventeen-year-old girl whom he savors as his potential second wife, the first having been a "termagant" who bore him no children: "She was so young and so unexpectedly pretty he swallowed air and had a coughing fit. She was all red and white, like the Valerians." The overlapping (or confusion) of love with food is reinforced by the constant presence of the dedicated black servants, Sydney and Ondine, who cook and serve Valerian and who are virtually members of his family. Appropriately, this artificially prolonged, sweetened maternal paradise is shattered at a Christmas dinner intended as a festive family celebration. Family is defined in terms of food, with Margaret insisting on turkey—"We have to have turkey for Christmas. This is a family Christmas, an old-fashioned family Christmas . . ."—and Valerian requiring the confirmation of Ollieballen—"All that was needed was that holiday bread Grandmother Stadt used to make."

Having established this larger context of nurturance gone awry, we can then note that since other characters are implicated in a family system in which food is a principal medium of emotional exchange, Margaret is not solely to blame for her abuse of maternity. Her husband's complicity is suggested by his refusal to pursue the awareness that something was wrong:

> Every now and then I'd come home, he'd be under the sink. Humming to himself. When I'd pull him out, ask him what he was doing there, he'd say he liked the soft. . . . I used to try to be it for him, but I wasn't there during the day.

Inaction is justified by his role as "absent father" whose job prevents full participation in the domestic sphere. When Valerian is able to formulate an appropriate response, his son is almost thirty and it is too late: "Suddenly he knew exactly what to do: go to him. Go to Michael. Find him, touch him, rub him, hold him in his arms. Now. He tried to stand but the spastic legs defied him."

The emblem for his refusal of knowledge and of involvement is the greenhouse, the self-enclosed, sealed-off world into which Valerian withdraws after his retirement to engage in the pseudo-nurturance of plants, to correspond with "nurseries from Tokyo to Newburgh, New York." The use of the greenhouse as an alternative to contact with his son is made explicit: "When he knew for certain that Michael would always be a stranger to him, he built the greenhouse as a place of controlled ever-flowering life to greet death in." The alcohol- and music-induced haze with which Valerian surrounds himself in the greenhouse mimics a quasi-maternal symbiosis in which the illusion of benevolent purity can be maintained. After the collapse of this illusion, Valerian "began going back to his greenhouse," which he now allows to lapse into a wasteland: "Didn't sow or clip or transpose. Things grew or died where and how they pleased." He is forced to acknowledge that his putative innocence is actually a form of guilt.

> He had not known because he had not taken the trouble to know. . . . Knowing more was inconvenient and frightening. . . . Margaret knew the bottomlessness—she had looked at it, dived in it and pulled herself out—obviously tougher than he. What an awful thing she had done. And how much more awful not to have known it.

By contrast, it is knowing that makes Ondine seem complicit in Margaret's attacks on her son. Ondine has done what Valerian could not bring himself to do: "I used to hold him and pet him. He was so scared." But while she has repaired the damage inflicted by Margaret, her silence had permitted Margaret to continue:

> "There was nobody to tell. It was woman stuff. I couldn't tell your husband and I couldn't tell mine. . . . I guess I thought you would let us go. If I told Sydney he might tell Mr. Street and then we'd be out of a job—a good job. . . . But once I started keeping it—then it became my secret too."

The problematic nexus of Michael's nurturance has a narrative function that goes beyond its own story, for it provides the detailed background that makes vivid Jadine's struggle against maternity. This struggle, I would argue, is the novel's fundamental crux. We are introduced to Jadine through the powerfully rendered section in which she recalls having seen an African woman in a Parisian grocery store—a sight that Jadine had experienced as an unaccountably troubling "vision." Though the novel makes many twists and turns, it always returns to the exploration of this vision and of Jadine's relation to it.

II

Jadine is struck by the maternal appeal of the African woman whose "too much hip, too much bust" and three carefully held eggs suggest fertility and abundance next to which her own superficially successful life seems suddenly empty, "inauthentic." It no longer matters that "the items on her shopping list were always there." She has a "hunger" for "that woman's woman—that mother/sister/she," a hunger to which she is all the more vulnerable because the loss of her own mother has left Jadine with the feeling that "I'm an orphan." The connection between the African woman and Jadine's mother is enforced by the "dream of large hats," containing "the center of the fear," which precedes the recollection of the Parisian vision. These hats, we later learn, are multiples of the one she wore to her mother's funeral—"the awful hat she'd worn to the funeral. Too big and grown-up for a girl of twelve."

Jadine's sense of vulnerability is increased by the African woman's "insulting gesture" of spitting while she "looked right at Jadine," as if expressing a contemptuous rejection. Ultimately Jadine breaks the hold of this vision by learning to reciprocate this rejection. The visionary model of maternity becomes a "tar baby" from which Jadine must break free. The African woman whose skin was "like tar" metamorphoses into the island swamp:

> Now it sat in one place and became a swamp the Haitians called Sein des Veilles. And witch's tit it was: a shriveled fogbound oval seeping with a thick black substance that even mosquitoes could not live near.

The association of the swamp with the tar baby image is later confirmed: "As they passed Sein des Veilles, Jadine's legs burned with the memory of tar." She has been literally entrapped in the slime of the swamp, overseen by natural forces that are explicitly female:

> The women looked down from the rafters of the trees and stopped murmuring. They were delighted when first they saw her, thinking a runaway child had been restored to them. But upon looking closer they saw differently. This girl was fighting to get away from them. . . . [T]hey wondered at the girl's desperate struggle down below to be free, to be something other than they were.

The symbolic action of Jadine's escape from this "exceptional female-ness," of her determination "to be something other than they were," is subsequently translated into her conscious struggle against "the night women" who include "her own dead mother and even the [African] woman in yellow."

Jadine's second waking vision, which occurs in the traditional, small-town black society of Eloe, Florida, is even more upsetting and urgent than the earlier one in Paris. In her windowless bedroom, "she might as well have been in a cave, a grave, the dark womb of the earth." Son is oblivious to the women's visitation: they were against "her alone—not him." Only Jadine, Daughter, is alert to their claustrophobic pressure as they display and flaunt maternal breasts:

> "I have breasts too," she said or thought or willed, "I have breasts too." But they didn't believe her. They just held their own higher and pushed their own farther out and looked at her. And the breasts they thrust at her like weapons were soft, loose bags closed at the tip with a brunette eye. . . . [T]hey all seemed somehow in agreement with each other about her, and were all out to get her, tie her, bind her. Grab the person she had worked hard to become and choke it off with their soft loose tits.

Jadine's effort to defeat the night women is concluded when she renounces the obligation to take care of her surrogate parents, Sydney and Ondine. This negotiation is conducted exclusively with Ondine, who had appeared as one of the women in the room—"and *Nan*adine!" so that it is dramatized entirely as a mother-daughter conflict (which belies Ondine's earlier belief that she could foster her niece "without the stress of a mother-daughter relationship." Ondine, in effect representing all the maternal figures from whom Jadine has been feeling such pressure, initiates the confrontation by defining the role of daughter:

> "Jadine, a girl has got to be a daughter first. She have to learn that. And if she never learns how to be a daughter, she can't never learn to be a woman. I mean a real woman: a woman good enough for a child; good enough for a man. . . . A daughter is a woman that cares about where she come from and takes care of them that took care of her."

Jadine's answer, the answer to the night women, resists this single definition: "There are other ways to be a woman, Nanadine. . . . I don't want to be like you." Despite Ondine's disapproval—"There ain't but one kind"—Jadine resolves to live out her own view. She departs, leaving Sydney and Ondine to puzzle and accuse: "There's a whole bunch of stuff they can do that we never knew nothing about. . . . Old black people must be a worrisome thing to the young ones these days." Ondine is resigned: "I think we're going to have to bury ourselves, Sydney."

The denouement impels us to have mixed emotions and doubts about Jadine's final triumph. Her success in articulating and holding to a new definition of black female identity is made to depend heavily on an unfeeling attitude toward the "parents" who raised her. Taking care of elders is a highly charged issue for Morrison, who has given powerful testimony to her experience of the black community as a neighborhood:

> And there was this life-giving, very, very strong sustenance that people got from the neighborhood. . . . And legal responsibilities, all the responsibilities that agencies now have, were the responsibilities of the neighborhood. So that people were taken care of, or locked up or whatever. If they were sick, other people took care of them; if they needed something to eat, other people took care of them; if they were old, other people took care of them. . . .[4]

In this regard, Morrison comments on Sula's placing her grandmother in a nursing home: "Sula did the one terrible thing for black people which was to put her grandmother in an old folks' home, which was outrageous, you know. You take care of people!" *Tar Baby* goes a step further: whereas Sula's violation of communal values is a unique, idiosyncratic act, Jadine's defiance of conventional expectation has an exemplary, generalized force that implies the break-up and complete dissolution of neighborhood ideals. *Tar Baby*, in this sense, is a work of mourning for the passing of those ideals.

Sula eventually pays the price for her treatment of her grandmother, but Jadine is not punished in any similar way for her abandonment of Sydney and Ondine. The possibility exists that Jadine (unlike Margaret) will "get away scot-free," unless we attribute to her moral and psychological disabilities equivalent to the physical deterioration suffered by Sula. In *Tar Baby*, Son's is perhaps the most eloquent voice to make the case against Jadine's disregard for Sydney and Ondine: "*They* are the ones who put you through school, woman, they are the ones. Not him [Valerian]. They worked for him all their lives. . . . You should cook for *them*." The indictment is especially telling because, from Son's point of view, neglect of Sydney and Ondine signifies that Jadine is cut off from her roots, with the result that her own identity is impoverished and distorted:

> "If they [college] didn't teach you that, then they didn't teach you nothing, because until you know about me, you don't know nothing about yourself. And you don't know anything, anything at all about your children and anything at all about your mama and your papa."

We can notice that Son automatically assumes that her identity will include having children; nonetheless, the question remains whether or not we, as readers, should accept the essential validity of his critique of Jadine.

III

The central fact about the Jadine-Son relationship is its failure; hence the interest lies in the reasons for the failure.[5] Jadine's renunciation of Sydney and Ondine and her rejection of Son are parallel, related gestures; for Son has assimilated the values of the traditional black community exemplified by Eloe and, in particular, comes to represent the lure and threat of orthodox motherhood.

Jadine's definitive decision to break with Son—"I can't let you hurt me again"—is immediately preceded by her recollection of "the mother-daughter day" at college: "In April the girls met their mothers there to sing and hold hands and sway in the afternoon light. . . . Pale sulfur light sprinkled so softly with lilac it made her want to cry." Jadine simultaneously gives up Son and this suffusion with maternally tinged light. Son has pressed the claims of community and of family: "He smiled at the vigor of his own heartbeat at the thought of her having his baby." But his image of community is shaped by the standard provided by Eloe. Morrison juxtaposes Son's romanticized, dream-like version of Eloe with the more close-up, qualified view we are given when Son brings Jadine home to visit. Jadine immediately feels the constriction of the rigid lines which divide gender into separate male and female realms when she cannot "understand (or accept) her being shunted off with Ellen and the children while the men grouped on the porch. . . ." Jadine's unwillingness to adapt to this sex-role segregation and, consequently, her separation from Son are prefigured from the outset:

> He woke thinking of a short street of yellow houses with white doors which women opened wide and called out, "Come on in here, you honey you," their laughter sprawling like a quilt over the command. But nothing sprawled in this woman's voice. "I'm never lonely," it said. "Never."

The voice is of course Jadine's. Son's efforts "to insert his own dreams into her" of "the fat black ladies in white dresses minding the pie table in the basement of the church" are futile.

Jadine, rather than Son, lays the stronger claim to the status of orphan, to remaining unattached. In this respect, the relationship is a partial reworking of that in *Sula* between Sula and Ajax. The roles are to some extent reversed. Here the woman takes the initiative, ends the relationship, goes off; the man's desire for connection has made him vulnerable: "For if he loved and lost this woman, . . . he would surely lose the world." So striking is this reversal that Jadine's satisfaction about being "so expert at the leaving" is presented as masculine: "Now *she* felt lean and male, having left quickly with no peeping back just in case—no explanatory, loophole-laden note."[6] *Tar Baby* implicitly raises the question of whether or not this assertion of power by a woman can be seen as a legitimate positive development. The reply is at least as much negative as affirmative. This surprising outcome is the result of an authorial intervention which rights the imbalance between Jadine and Son in his favor and at her expense.

Morrison has been praised—correctly I think—for her capacity to conceive her characters with extraordinary fullness and generosity. The portrait of Margaret in *Tar Baby* offers brilliant testimony. Margaret ought to be merely paltry and pathetic, but with "carefully casual" art, Morrison gradually reveals enough details about her family background to make us not only understand but sympathize. Even Valerian concedes that "she wasn't ready for him [her son]." In particular, Margaret is humanized by the powerfully poignant statement about what drove her to hurt the baby:

> And she was outraged by that infant needfulness. There were times when she absolutely had to limit its *being there;* stop its implicit and explicit demand for her best and constant self. She could not describe her loathing of its prodigious appetite for security—the criminal arrogance of an infant's conviction that while he slept, someone is there; that when he wakes, someone is there; that when he is hungry, food will somehow magically be provided.

Jadine is an exception to the general rule of Morrison's infinite tolerance and sympathy. It is almost as if Margaret's angry, destructive response to an infant's total dependence on her is better than Jadine's avoidance of such dependence. Morrison's generosity appears taxed and constrained with regard to Jadine because her characterization verges at times on the implausible. For instance, the brief reference to Jadine's first exposure to sexuality when the bitch dog is punished for being in heat seems insufficient to account for her psychological state, for her attraction to modeling as a vicarious erotic mode. Equally reductive, Jadine's opposition of high art to black culture seems forced and unnecessarily uncharitable. "Picasso *is* better than an Itumba mask. The fact that he was intrigued by them is proof of *his* genius, not the maskmakers'," Jadine confides to the "patron" who paid for her education. Such dialogue is unconvincing because it lends itself to ready-made condemnation, makes her too easily a target according to the critical image: "Culture-bearing black woman, whose culture are you bearing?"

The images of fruitfulness and birth associated with Son are designed to win our approval, while the corresponding negative images for Jadine neatly undercut our sympathy for her. For example, our response to Jadine is quickly compromised by her naked lolling in the coat—a gift

from her white lover—composed of "the hides of ninety baby seals
stitched together so nicely you could not tell what part had sheltered
their cute little hearts and which had cushioned their skulls." Jadine
compounds her imperviousness to these dead babies by her use of the
coat for sexual excitement: "She pressed her thighs deep into its dark
luxury. Then she lifted herself up a little and let her nipples brush the
black hairs, back and forth." Her erotic stimulation is made to seem
meretricious, as if her work as a fashion model has led her to experience
her body as an object to be advertised as she would a fur coat. Such
cultivation of her body puts Jadine inevitably at odds with the maternal
breasts of the night women who will later haunt her.

Son, by contrast, has seen the seals in their natural state: "He had
seen them gliding like shadows in water off the coast of Greenland. . . ."
His erotic power, unlike Jadine's, is not detached from fertility. He reju-
venates Valerian's waste land when he shakes the greenhouse plants so
that they begin to blossom. The human significance of this event is made
clear by its connection with Son's body: "Valerian looked at his genitals
and the skinny black thighs." And Son's fertilization of the greenhouse
inspires even Valerian and Margaret, who normally sleep in separate
rooms, to try to make love. While Jadine is unaware that "the avocado
tree watched her go then folded its leaves tightly over its fruit," Son is
responsive and sustained:

> Moving his hand an inch or two up the tree in preparation to go his fingers
> grazed a breast, the tight-to-breaking breast of a pubescent girl three months
> pregnant. . . . Just then the wind, or perhaps it was the tree herself, lifted
> the leaves and, precisely as he had done a moment ago, parted wide the
> leaves. The avocado swung forward and touched his cheek.

To enlarge the metaphor, we can say that Morrison as author withholds
the avocado from Jadine and gives it spontaneously to Son, an action
which indicates her view of Jadine's negative, and Son's positive, relation
to reproduction.

IV

From the start, Son harmoniously collaborates with the maternal
sexuality that is the source of his fertility. The novel's prologue demonstrates Son's involvement in the connections among food, survival, and
the support of a nurturant female force. When he plunges into the "soft
and warm" sea, Son undergoes a rite of passage that consists in submission to a mother nature personified as "the water-lady."

> Like the hand of an insistent woman it pushed him. He fought hard to break
> through, but couldn't. . . . His strength was leaving him and he knew he
> should not waste it fighting the current. He decided to let it carry him for a
> while.

Once he has submitted, the "insistent woman" becomes kind, allows him to live and guides him. Son carries with him "the smell of human after-birth" and emerges with "the immediate plans of a newborn baby."

His "sweet expectation" is fulfilled by the discovery of an inexhaustible supply of chocolate, to which Thérèse has given him access. On land, she takes over the water-lady's role as benevolent maternal sponsor. At first sight, Thérèse seems to possess merely "comic book quality," to relocate one of the novel's pungent phrases. Her "magic breasts" are akin to the "Sein des Veilles," created when—as Morrison allegorizes with purposeful pathetic fallacy—masculine civilization desecrated the pristine female landscape. Like the river deformed into a swamp, Thérèse has atrophied, her maternal function displaced by Enfamil formula.

But Thérèse gains stature as the novel progresses, a stature that derives from the growing strength of Son's affiliation with her. Like Son, Thérèse excels at narrative improvisation. The first to detect Son's presence on the island, she not only feeds her "chocolate eater" but invents his identity: "She had seen him in a dream smiling at her as he rode away wet and naked on a stallion. So she knew he was in agreement with her. . . ." Ultimately, in the concluding section, the novel will grant Thérèse power to realize her vision. Prompted by her, Son acknowledges in the end his primary bond with Thérèse. In a reenactment of the prologue, she guides him through the water to the island. She offers an alternative to Son's attachment to Jadine, to whom she has all along been hostile, contemptuously alluding to her as "The chippy. The fast-ass," "the copper Venus." Thérèse presents Son with a choice when he feels he has none but pursuit of Jadine:

> "The men are waiting for you. . . . You can choose now. You can get free of her. They are waiting in the hills for you. They are naked. . . . [T]hey race those horses like angels all over the hills where the rain forest is, where the champion daisy trees still grow. Go there. Choose them."

Thérèse imagines a space where masculine civilization has not encroached and maternal nature still thrives on the heroic activities of her naked sons.

Son's loyalty to Thérèse has been manifested earlier. He is the only one at the island house concerned to know her real name; her dismissal for attempting to steal apples at Christmas arouses him to open rebellion against Valerian. When Son obeys Thérèse, he is reborn in her image of him as the term "nursing" and the metaphor of a baby's learning to walk suggest:

> First he crawled the rocks one by one, one by one, till his hands touched shore and the nursing sound of the sea was behind him. He felt around, crawled off and then stood up. Breathing heavily with his mouth open he took a few tentative steps.

This adventure transcends the previous critical image of "Mama-spoiled black man," transforms Son into a legendary male: "The mist lifted and the trees stepped back a bit as if to make the way easier for a certain kind of man."

The argument Thérèse uses to convince Son that he should give up the search for Jadine echoes Morrison's dedication page. "Forget her. There is nothing in her parts for you. She has forgotten her ancient properties" and finds a counterpart in Morrison's praise of women who "knew their true and ancient properties." The ancient properties—the "sacred properties"—are the maternal ones foregone by Jadine. In this perspective, even Thérèse's wildest fantasy begins to make sense:

> She would also have a chance to ask the American black herself whether it was really so that American women killed their babies with their fingernails.

> * * *

> About free abortions and D & C's. The scraping of the womb. But that Thérèse had her own views of understanding that had nothing to do with the world's views.

At any rate, Morrison's authorial presence stands behind Thérèse's defense of ancient maternal properties, the loss of which convicts Jadine.[7]

By contrast, Morrison appears to endorse the romantic mythology of black male flight that she describes in the *MR* Interview:

> "The big scene is the traveling Ulysses scene, for black men. They are moving. . . . Although in sociological terms that is described as a major failing of black men—they do not stay at home and take care of their children, they are not there—that has always been to me one of the most attractive features about black male life. I guess I'm not supposed to say that."

She evokes this image in *Tar Baby* when celebrating Son's participation in the "great underclass of undocumented men":

> What distinguished them from other men (aside from their terror of Social Security cards and *cédula de identidad*) was their refusal to equate work with life and an inability to stay anywhere for long. Some were Huck Finns; some Nigger Jims. Others were Calibans, Staggerlees and John Henrys.

The excessive idealization here is never checked. Jadine's attempts to criticize this way of life cannot compete with the strength Morrison allows the mythology:

> "It's not romantic. And it's not being free. It's dumb. You think you're above it, above money, the rat race and all that. But you're not above it, you're just without it. It's a prison, poverty is. Look at what its absence made you do: run, hide, steal, lie."

But Son's running at the end is marvelous. Jadine's criticism sounds feeble next to the thrill of the lyrical closure: "Then he ran. Lickety-split. Lickety-split. Looking neither to the left nor to the right. Lickety-split. Lickety-split. Lickety-lickety-lickety-split."

V

In so ending, the novel veers away from Jadine's more complex, unresolved destiny. The problem of her uncertain female identity is perhaps insoluble within the framework of gender envisaged here. Jadine is placed in an impossible bind. The novel will not allow her avoidance of motherhood to be perceived sympathetically, yet the maternal issue presents itself in the form of a conflict between mutually exclusive imperatives: the night women require Jadine "to settle for fertility rather than originality, nurturing instead of building." Within the context of the novel, there is little suggestion that Jadine could, with complete dignity, choose only "originality" and "building." There is also little suggestion that she could have both "nurturing" and "building."[8]

Morrison's depiction of gender in *Tar Baby* is triumphantly heterosexual. The love between Son and Jadine temporarily challenges New York City's "beautiful black males who had found the whole business of being black and men at the same time too difficult and so they had dumped it. They had snipped off their testicles and pasted them to their chests." And: "Betty, who had been 'into' bisexuality for six months, couldn't get back into the closet fast enough when Son was in the room. . . ." But this outright opposition to homosexuality and bisexuality extends to a tacit exclusion of "androgyny" in favor of a strong sense of male/female differentiation. Any revaluation and mixing of traditional gender categories threatens the sexual confusion that fascinates Thérèse: "[F]or a bar of gold a doctor could put you into a machine and, in a matter of minutes, would change you from a man to a woman or a woman to a man. . . . [It] was not uncommon or strange to see people with both penises and breasts." So important is gender polarization as a defense against this chaos that Son's D. H. Lawrence-like remark to Valerian— "They like women, you have to jack them up every once in a while. Make em act nice, like they're supposed to"—is never decisively repudiated. Nor is his protest against "sexual equality" clearly questioned; his view of women's superiority is comfortable because it is based on the conventional female identity of mother, as in his deference to Thérèse's authority.

Sula provides a useful perspective for two key questions. First, what happens when a woman, setting aside standard definitions of femininity, enters into traditionally masculine territory? The answer appears to be that she suffers repercussions, some form of defeat. As Morrison puts it, "she can't get away with that." This result is particularly obvious in Sula's case, but Jadine suffers a more sophisticated version of the same fate. We are left feeling that she is at loose ends, drifting, in trouble, and that her desire to "make it" may be self-destructive.

Second, what happens to a man who ventures into traditionally female territory? We cannot really answer because Morrison's imagination as expressed in these two novels does not allow men to experiment with nurturance in any substantial way. Ajax leaves at the moment Sula becomes interested in a permanent relationship. This situation permits the interpretation that Sula's character is being enlarged at this moment and Ajax's deficiencies exposed. But Morrison prefers to attribute the failure to Sula's learning the lesson of "love as possession," and to side with Ajax for not being "interested in learning" it. At the end of *Tar Baby*, Son becomes an Ajax. Insofar as Son has been involved in nurturance, his involvement has been strictly limited by his belief in the gender divisions of his hometown. He does not achieve a nurturant identity of his own, but rather fuses with the nurturance proffered by a maternal figure. Yet the development of nurturant capacity in a male character, independent of a mothering female who routinely provides it for him, is one precondition for a way out of the impasse in which the novel leaves Jadine.

Notes

1. An example of the exaggeration to which I refer can be seen in the review by Darryl Pinckney: "Every Which Way," *The New York Review of Books*, 28 (April 30, 1981), 24–25.
2. Toni Morrison, *Sula* (New York: Bantam, 1973), p. 123.
3. Toni Morrison, *Tar Baby* (New York: Random House, 1981), p. 194.
4. "'Intimate Things in Place': A Conversation with Toni Morrison," *The Massachusetts Review*, Autumn 1977, p. 474. Hereafter cited as *MR* Interview.
5. My approach to the novel here differs from that of John Irving because I do not think, as Irving does, that it is permissible to ask the question, "Will Son ever connect with Jadine again?"—"Morrison's Black Fable," *The New York Times Book Review*, March 29, 1981, p. 31. *Tar Baby* seems to me conclusive on this point: The relationship has been tried and is over. What is genuinely open-ended about the novel is, as I shall argue, the status of Jadine. More generally, Irving's stress on the Jadine-Son relationship—"This affair is the book's erotic and dramatic center"—leaves out of account Jadine's crucial relations with other black women.
6. Morrison sees Sula as masculine as well: "She will do the kinds of things that normally only men do. . . . She really behaves like a man. She picks up a man, drops a man, the same way a man picks up a woman, drops a woman. . . . She's masculine in that sense. She's adventuresome, she trusts herself, she's not scared, she really ain't scared. . . . So that quality of masculinity—and I mean this in a pure sense—in a woman at that time is outrage, total outrage. She can't get away with that. . . ." (*MR* Interview, p. 487).
   But Sula's masculine behavior comes abruptly to an end after she enters the relationship with Ajax. No such obvious circumscription is placed on Jadine's adventuresomeness; hence, her potential for "getting away with" "total outrage."

7. Writing about *Tar Baby* in *The New Yorker*, Susan Lardner comments on Morrison's use of omniscience to convey "attitudes that are not exactly her own and for which she is not responsible" ("Unastonished Eye," *The New Yorker*, 15 June 1981, p. 147). Lardner elaborates on the evasiveness she detects: Morrison is "careful not to ally herself with any one of them for too long or to stand for too long in one place. She hovers over the scene for as long as she cares to, moving in close, pulling back for a better look, and withdrawing before she has much of a stake in the outcome."

   I think Lardner properly raises the issue of authorial location and stance, but her formulation prematurely settles the issue instead of pursuing it. As I try to suggest, a more fruitful approach is to focus sharply on Morrison's attitudes toward Jadine. The ambiguity permeating Morrison's portrayal of Jadine can be clarified by saying that it reflects an authorial self-division that Morrison does not fully acknowledge. To put it schematically, insofar as Morrison takes on the role of daughter she is sympathetic to Jadine's plight; but insofar as she is the mother she is skeptical, harshly critical of Jadine. Lardner also fails to appreciate the richness of Morrison's enactment of authorial conflict with regard to Jadine, even if the enactment of this tension includes some evasiveness.

8. Outside the novel, in an interview in the July 1981 issue of *Essence*, Morrison has indicated her belief in the compatibility of "nurturing" and "building": "The problem is not paying attention to the ancient properties—which for me means the ability to be 'the ship' *and* 'the safe harbor.' Our history as black women is the history of women who could build a house *and* have some children, and there was no problem."

   The same interview confirms her critique of Jadine (and her defense of Son): "In *Tar Baby*, Son loves those pie ladies from his hometown. . . . Son loved those women, but Jadine found them 'backwards.' She perceives his relationship with them as spoiling—'They spoiled you and kept you infantile,' she says—which she is not about. She has lost the tar quality, the ability to hold something together that otherwise would fall apart—which is what I mean by the nurturing ability."

   Just as Jadine encounters the night women, so Morrison imagines meeting her foremothers. The contrast is clear-cut: where Jadine rejects, Morrison connects: "Since it was possible for my mother, my grandmother and her mother to do what they did. . . . And if they can do that, surely I can work at Random House and cook. . . . I know I can't go to those women [mothers and grandmothers] and say, 'Well, you know, my life is so hard. . . .' I don't want to meet them people nowhere—ever!—and have them look at me and say, 'What were *you* doing back there?'"

   But while Morrison's dedication to the women who preceded her is compelling in the context of the interview, Jadine's need to resist their vividly rendered claustrophobic pressure seems equally convincing and valid. The interview encourages an oversimplified view of the novel by reducing the richness and complexity of the analogous moment as we experience it in art. This discrepancy between interview and novel can be summarized in the formula "Never trust the artist. Trust the tale." For example, Morrison in the interview gives strong testimony to her own maternal commitment: "If I'm a hundred and they [her sons] are 70, I would still go to them if they break a hip." "The future for me is always my children—whether I can stay healthy long enough to be there or be available to them." Though these expressions of dedication are moving, they also seem extreme and one-sided; the novel restores the balance by raising doubts and admitting negative aspects of mothering, aspects which the interview sharply disavows.

♦♦♦♦♦♦♦♦♦♦♦♦♦♦

Eruptions of Funk: Historicizing Toni Morrison

SUSAN WILLIS

"I begin to feel those little bits of color floating up into me—deep in me. That streak of green from the june-bug light, the purple from the berries trickling along my thighs. Mama's lemonade yellow runs sweet in me. Then I feel like I'm laughing between my legs, and the laughing gets all mixed up with the colors, and I'm afraid I'll come, and afraid I won't. But I know I will. And I do. And it be rainbow all inside."

This is the way Polly Breedlove in *The Bluest Eye* remembers the experience of orgasm—*remembers* it, because in the grim and shabby reality of her present, orgasm (which we might take as a metaphor for any deeply pleasurable experience) is no longer possible.[1] Living in a storefront, her husband fluctuating between brutality and apathy, her son estranged, her daughter just plain scared, Polly has no language to describe the memory of a past pleasure, except one drawn from her distant childhood.

The power of this passage is not just related to the fact that it evokes the most intense female experience possible. Much of the impact is produced by the way it describes. Morrison defamiliarizes the portrayal of sensual experience. Adjectives become substantives, giving taste to color and making it possible for colors to trickle and flow and, finally, to be internalized like the semen of an orgasmic epiphany.

As often happens in Morrison's writing, sexuality converges with history and functions as a register for the experience of change, i.e., historical transition. Polly's remembrance of childhood sensuality coincides with her girlhood in the rural South. Both are metaphorically condensed and juxtaposed with the alienation she experiences as a black emigrant and social lumpen in a Northern industrial city. The author's metaphoric language produces an estrangement of alienation. Although her metaphors are less bold in their form and content, they still achieve an effect very similar to that of the negritude poets. Indeed, the image of an internal rainbow evokes the poetics of surrealism, but in a language less disjunctive because prose reveals the historical and artistic process through which the image is produced.[2]

When Polly Breedlove reminisces, her present collides with her past and spans her family's migration from the hills of Alabama to a small Kentucky town and her own subsequent journey as the wife of one of the many black men who, in the late thirties and early forties, sought factory jobs in the industrial North. The rural homeland is the source of the raw material of experience and praxis, which in the border-state small town is abstracted to colors, tastes, and tactile sensations. Ohio is, then, the site where images are produced out of the discontinuity between past and present.

Neither Morrison's use of metaphor, nor her general drive to return to origins is rooted in a nostalgia for the past. Rather, the metaphoric rendition of past experience represents a process for coming to grips with historical transition. Migration to the North signifies more than a confrontation with (and contamination by) the white world. It implies a transition in social class. Throughout Morrison's writing, the white world is equated with the bourgeois class—its ideology and life-style. This is true of *Song of Solomon* in which Macon Dead's attitudes toward rents and property make him more "white" than "black." This is true of *Tar Baby* in which notions of bourgeois morality and attitudes concerning the proper education and role of women have created a contemporary "tar baby," a black woman in cultural limbo. And it is made dramatically clear in *The Bluest Eye*, whose epigrammatic introduction and subsequent chapter headings are drawn from a white, middle-class "Dick-and-Jane" reader. In giving voice to the experience of growing up black in a society dominated by white, middle-class ideology, Morrison is writing against the privatized world of suburban house and nuclear family, whose social and psychological fragmentation does not need her authorial intervention, but is aptly portrayed in the language of the reader: "Here is the family. Mother, Father, Dick, and Jane live in the green-and-white house. They are very happy."

The problem at the center of Morrison's writing is how to maintain an Afro-American cultural heritage once the relationship to the black rural South has been stretched thin over distance and generations. Although a number of black Americans will criticize her problematizing of Afro-American culture, seeing in it a symptom of Morrison's own relationship to white bourgeois society as a successful writer and editor, there are a number of social and historical factors that argue in support of her position. These include the dramatic social changes produced by recent wide-scale migration of industry to the South, which has transformed much of the rural population into wage laborers; the development, particularly in the Northern cities, of a black bourgeoisie; and the coming into being, under late capitalism, of a full-blown consumer society capable of homogenizing society by recouping cultural difference. The temporal focus of each of Morrison's novels pinpoints strategic moments in black American history during which social and cultural forms underwent disruption and transformation. Both *The Bluest Eye* and *Sula* focus on the forties, a period of heavy black migration to the cities, when, particularly in the Midwest, black "neighborhoods" came into being as annexes of towns that had never before had a sizable black population. *Sula* expands the period of the forties by looking back to the First World

War, when blacks as a social group were first incorporated into a modern capitalist system as soldiers, and it looks ahead to the sixties, when cultural identity seems to flatten out, and, as Helene Sabat observes, all young people tend to look like the "Deweys," the book's nameless and indistinguishable orphans. *Song of Solomon* focuses on the sixties, when neighborhoods are perceived from the outside and called ghettos, a time of urban black political activism and general countercultural awareness. And *Tar Baby*, Morrison's most recent book, is best characterized as a novel of the eighties, in which the route back to cultural origins is very long and tenuous, making many individuals cultural exiles.

With this as an outline of modern black history in the United States, Morrison develops the social and psychological aspects that characterize the lived experience of historical transition. For the black emigrant to the North, the first of these is alienation. As Morrison defines it, alienation is not simply the result of an individual's separation from his or her cultural center, although this is a contributory factor that reinforces the alienation produced by the transition to wage labor. For the black man incorporated into the wartime labor pool (as for many white Appalachians),[3] selling one's labor for the creation of surplus value was only half of alienation, whose brutal second half was the grim reality of unemployment once war production was no longer necessary. The situation for the black woman was somewhat different. Usually employed as a maid and therefore only marginally incorporated as a wage laborer, her alienation was the result of striving to achieve the white bourgeois social model (in which she worked but did not live), which is itself produced by the system of wage labor under capitalism. As housemaid in a prosperous lakeshore home, Polly Breedlove lives a form of schizophrenia, in which her marginality is constantly confronted with a world of Hollywood movies, white sheets, and tender blond children. When at work or at the movies, she separates herself from her own kinky hair and decayed tooth. The tragedy of a woman's alienation is its effect on her role as mother. Her emotions split, Polly showers tenderness and love on her employer's child, and rains violence and disdain on her own.

Morrison's aim in writing is very often to disrupt alienation with what she calls eruptions of "funk." Dismayed by the tremendous influence of bourgeois society on young black women newly arrived from the deep South cities like "Meridian, Mobile, Aiken and Baton Rouge," Morrison describes the women's loss of spontaneity and sensuality. They learn "how to behave. The careful development of thrift, patience, high morals, and good manners. In short, how to get rid of the funkiness. The dreadful funkiness of passion, the funkiness of nature, the funkiness of the wide range of human emotions."

For Polly Breedlove, alienation is the inability to experience pleasure ever again—orgasm or otherwise—whereas for the "sugar-brown Mobile girls," whose husbands are more successful and therefore better assimilated into bourgeois society, alienation is the purposeful denial of pleasure. Once again Morrison translates the loss of history and culture into sexual terms and demonstrates the connection between bourgeois society and repression:

> He must enter her surreptitiously, lifting the hem of her nightgown only to her navel. He must rest his weight on his elbows when they make love, ostensibly to avoid hurting her breasts but actually to keep her from having to touch or feel too much of him.
>
> While he moves inside her, she will wonder why they didn't put the necessary but private parts of the body in some more convenient place—like the armpit, for example, or the palm of the hand. Someplace one could get to easily, and quickly, without undressing. She stiffens when she feels one of her paper curlers coming undone from the activity of love; imprints in her mind which one it is that is coming loose so she can quickly secure it once he is through. She hopes he will not sweat—the damp may get into her hair; and that she will remain dry between her legs—she hates the glucking sound they make when she is moist. When she senses some spasm about to grip him, she will make rapid movements with her hips, press her fingernails into his back, suck in her breath, and pretend she is having an orgasm.

At a sexual level, alienation is the denial of the body, produced when sensuality is redefined as indecent. Sounds and tactile sensations that might otherwise have precipitated or highlighted pleasure provoke annoyance or disdain. Repression manifests itself in the fastidious attention given to tomorrow's Caucasian-inspired coiffure and the decathexis of erogenous stimulation. Although repression inhibits sexual pleasure, it does not liberate a woman from sexuality. In faking an orgasm, the woman negates her pleasure for the sake of her husband's satisfaction, thus defining herself as a tool of his sexual gratification.

To break through repressed female sexuality, Morrison contrasts images of stifled womanhood with girlhood sensuality. In *The Bluest Eye*, the author's childhood alter ego, Claudia, is fascinated by all bodily functions and the physical residues of living in the world. She rebels at being washed, finding her scrubbed body obscene due to its "dreadful and humiliating absence of dirt." Even vomit is interesting for its color and consistency as it "swaddles down the pillow onto the sheet." In wondering how anything can be "so neat and nasty at the same time," Claudia shows a resistance toward the overdetermination of sensual experience, which, as Morrison sees it, is the first step toward repression. Openness to a full range of sensual experience may be equated with polymorphous sexuality, typified by the refusal of many young children to be thought of as either a boy or a girl. As my own four-year-old daughter sees it, "Little girls grow up to be big boys," and because there is no firm distinction between the sexes, her teddy bear is "both a boy and a girl." The refusal to categorize sensual experience—and likewise sex—captures the essence of unrepressed childhood, which Morrison evokes as a mode of existence prior to the individual's assimilation into bourgeois society.

The ultimate horror of bourgeois society against which Morrison writes and the end result of both alienation and repression is reification.[4] None of Morrison's black characters actually accedes to the upper reaches of bourgeois reification, but there are some who come close. They are saved only because they remain marginal to the bourgeois class and are imperfectly assimilated to bourgeois values. In *Song of Solomon*, Hagar offers a good example. Rejected by her lover, she falls into a state of near-catatonia, oblivious to all around her. However, chancing to look in a mirror, she is horrified by her appearance and marvels that anyone could love a woman with her looks. Thus roused from her withdrawal, Hagar embarks on a daylong shopping spree, driven by the desire to be the delightful image promised by her brand-name purchases:

> She bought a Playtex garter belt, I. Miller No Color hose, Fruit of the Loom panties, and two nylon slips—one white, one pink—one pair of Joyce Fancy Free and one of Con Brio ("Thank heaven for little Joyce heels"). . . .
>
> The cosmetics department enfolded her in perfume, and she read hungrily the labels and the promise. Myrurgia for primeval woman who creates for him a world of tender privacy where the only occupant is you, mixed with Nina Ricci's L'Air du Temps. Yardley's Flair with Tuvaché's Nectaroma and D'Orsay's Intoxication.

Hagar's shopping spree culminates in a drenching downpour. Her shopping bags soaked, everything—her "Sunny Glow" and "fawn-trimmed-in-sea-foam shortie nightgown"—her wished-for identity and future—falls into the wet and muddy street. Returning home, Hagar collapses with fever and dies after days of delirium.

Hagar's hysteria and death mark the limits of her assimilation into bourgeois culture. Neither through withdrawal nor through commodity consumption can Hagar transform herself into an object. Her marginality, by reason of race and lumpen background, is the basis for her inalienable human dimension. As Morrison might have put it, she is simply too black, too passionate, too human ever to become reified.

Reification, although never attained by any of Morrison's characters—not even those drawn from the white world[5]—is, instead, embodied in a number of figural images from *The Bluest Eye*. These are celluloid images of Shirley Temple or her "cuute" face on a blue-and-white china cup, and the candy-wrapper images of Mary Jane. Most of all, reification is evident in the plastic smile and moronic blue eyes of a white Christmas baby doll. When Claudia destroys these—dismembering the doll and poking its eyes out—her rebellion is not just aimed at the idea of beauty incarnated in a white model. She is also striking out against the horrifying dehumanization that acceptance of the model implies—both for the black who wears it as a mask and for the white who creates commodified images of the self.

For Morrison, everything is historical; even objects are embedded in history and are the bearers of the past. For those characters closest to the white bourgeois world, objects contain the residues of repressed and unrealized desires. For Ruth Foster in *Song of Solomon*, the daughter of the town's first black doctor and wife of the slumlord Macon Dead, a watermark on a table is the stubborn and ever-present reminder of her husband's remorseless rejection. The bowl of flowers around which their hatred crystallized is no longer present; only its sign remains, an opaque residue indelibly written into the table. If, for the bourgeois world, experience is capable of being abstracted to the level of sign, this is not the case for the world of the marginal characters. To cite another example from *Song of Solomon*, Pilate, Ruth Foster's sister-in-law and in every way her antithesis, enjoys a special relationship to all levels of natural experience—including a specific shade of blue sky. Now, color does not function as a sign in the way that the watermark on the table does. Although it bears a concrete relationship to a real object (the blue ribbons on Pilate's mother's hat), it is not an abstract relationship in the way that the watermark stands for the bowl of flowers. For Ruth Foster, the watermark is an "anchor" to the mental and sexual anguish imprisoned in the sign. In contrast, when Pilate points to a patch of sky and remarks that it is the same color as her mother's bonnet ribbons, she enables her nephew Milkman (Ruth Foster's overly sheltered son) to experience a unique moment of sensual perception. The experience is liberational because Pilate is not referring to a specific bonnet—or even to a specific mother; rather, the color blue triggers the whole range of emotions associated with maternal love, which Pilate offers to anyone who will share the experience of color with her.

In contrast to the liberational aspect of *Song of Solomon*, Morrison's most recent novel, *Tar Baby*, registers a deep sense of pessimism. Here, cultural exiles—both white and black—come together on a Caribbean island where they live out their lives in a neatly compartmentalized bourgeois fashion: the candy magnate Valerian Street[6] in his stereophonic-equipped greenhouse; his wife, cloistered in her bedroom; and the servants, Odine and Sydney, ensconced in their comfortable quarters. Daily life precludes "eruptions of funk," a lesson poignantly taught when Margaret Lenore discovers the bedraggled wild man, Son, in her closet. Although Son's appearance suggests Rastafarianism and outlawry, any shock value stirred by his discovery is canceled when he, too, proves to be just another exile. Except for one brief incident, when Odine kills a chicken and in plucking it recalls a moment from her distant past when she worked for a poultry butcher, there are no smells, tastes, or tactile experiences to summon up the past. Rather, there is a surfeit of foods whose only quality is the calories they contain.

In contrast with Morrison's earlier novels, the past in *Tar Baby* is never brought to metaphoric juxtaposition with the present. Rather, it is held separate and bracketed by dream. When Valerian Street, sipping a brandy in his greenhouse, lapses into daydream, his recollection of the past, which in essence contrasts entrepreneurial capitalism to modern corporate capitalism, does not intrude on his present retirement. The past is past, and the significant historical transition evoked is perceived as inaccessible and natural.

The past is made more remote when it informs a nighttime dream. This is the case for Sydney, who every night dreams of his boyhood in Baltimore. "It was a tiny dream he had each night that he would never recollect from morning to morning. So he never knew what it was exactly that refreshed him."[7] For the black man hanging to the coattails of the white upper bourgeoisie, who thinks of himself as a "Philadelphia Negro," the back streets of Baltimore are a social debit. His desire for assimilation to white bourgeois culture and the many years spent in service to the bourgeois class negate his ever experiencing the deep sensual and emotional pleasure that Pilate has whenever she beholds a blue sky or bites into a vine-ripened tomato.

With every dreamer dreaming a separate dream, there are no bridges to the past and no possibility of sharing an individual experience as part of a group's social history. Although a reminiscence like Pilate's recognition of the color blue can be communicated, a dream, as Son finds out, cannot be pressed into another dreamer's head. Son's dream of "yellow houses with white doors" and "fat black ladies in white dresses minding the pie table in the church" is an image of wish fulfillment, rooted in private nostalgia. It bears no resemblance to his real past as we later come to understand it out of what the novel shows us of Eloe, Florida, where tough black women with little time for pie tables have built their own rough-hewn, unpainted homes.

For the "tar baby," Jadine, fashioned out of the rich white man's indulgence and the notions of culture most appealing to bourgeois America (European education and Paris "haute couture"), the past is irretrievable and no longer perceived as desirable. As the individual whose cultural exile is the most profound, Jadine is haunted by waking visions, born out of guilt and fear. In her most terrifying vision, a mob of black women—some familiar, some only known by their names— crowds into her room. Revealing, then waving, their breasts at her, they condemn Jadine for having abandoned the traditional maternal role of black women.

Whereas Jadine lives her separation from the past and rejection of traditional cultural roles with tormented uncertainty and frenzied activity, Milkman, in Morrison's previous novel, experiences his alienation from black culture as a hollow daily monotony. Jadine, whose desire to find self and be free leads to jet hops between Paris, the Caribbean, and New York, has not had the benefit of a powerful cultural mentor like Pilate, who awakens Milkman's desire to know his past. In contrast, all of Jadine's possible cultural heroes are bracketed by her rupture with the past and her class position. Jadine rejects family—her Aunt Odine, for her homey ways and maternal nature—and culture—the black island- ers, so remote from Jadine's trajectory into the future that she never even bothers to learn their names.

Milkman, on the other hand, has been born and raised in the ghetto, albeit in the biggest house. He has never been to college, but he has had the benefit of teachers—both the street-wise Guitar and the folk-wise Pilate. If Milkman's present is a meaningless void of bourgeois alienation, the possibility of a past opens out to him like a great adventure. A quest for gold initiates Milkman's journey into the past—and into the self— but gold is not the novel's real object. Imagining that gold will free him from his father's domination and his family's emotional blackmail, Milkman comes to realize that only by knowing the past can he hope to have a future.

There is a sense of urgency in Morrison's writing, produced by the realization that a great deal is at stake. The novels may focus on individ- ual characters like Milkman and Jadine, but the salvation of individuals is not the point. Rather, these individuals, struggling to reclaim or redefine themselves, are portrayed as epiphenomenal to community and culture, and it is the strength and continuity of the black cultural heritage as a whole that is at stake and being tested.

As Morrison sees it, the most serious threat to black culture is the obliterating influence of social change. The opening line from *Sula* might well have been the novel's conclusion, so complete is the destruction it records: "In that place, where they tore the night shade and blackberry patches from their roots to make room for the Medallion City Golf Course, there was once a neighborhood."[8] This is the community Mor- rison is writing to reclaim. Its history, terminated and dramatically oblit- erated, is condensed into a single sentence whose content spans from rural South to urban redevelopment. Here, as throughout Morrison's writing, natural imagery refers to the past, the rural South, the reser- voir of culture that has been uprooted—like the blackberry bushes—to make way for modernization. In contrast, the future is perceived of as an amorphous, institutionalized power embodied in the notion of "Medallion City," which suggests neither nature nor a people. Joining the past to the future is the neighborhood, which occupies a very different temporal moment (which history has shown to be transitional), and defines a very different social mode, as distinct from its rural origins as it is from the amorphous urban future.

It is impossible to read Morrison's four novels without coming to see the neighborhood as a concept crucial to her understanding of history. The neighborhood defines a Northern social mode rather than a Southern one, for it describes the relationship of an economic satellite, contiguous to a larger metropolis rather than separate subsistence economics like

the Southern rural towns of Shalimar and Eloe. It is a Midwestern phenomenon rather than a Northeastern big-city category, because it defines
the birth of principally first-generation, Northern, working-class black
communities. It is a mode of the forties rather than the sixties or the
eighties, and it evokes the many locally specific black populations in the
North before these became assimilated to a larger, more generalized,
and less regionally specific sense of black culture that we today refer to
as the "black community."

The fact that Milkman embarks on a quest for his past is itself symptomatic of the difference between the forties neighborhood and the sixties community. In contrast with Milkman, the black youth of the forties
had no need to uncover and decipher the past simply because enough of
it was still present, born on successive waves of Southern black immigrants. For Milkman the past is a riddle, a reality locked in the verses
of a children's song (the "song of Solomon") whose meaning is no longer
explicit because time has separated the words from their historical content. Childhood and the way children perceive the world are again a
figure for a mode of existence prior to the advent of capitalism and bourgeois society. And in *Song of Solomon*, it coincides with the function of
song in all marginal cultures as the unwritten text of history and culture.

Milkman's quest is a journey through geographic space in which the
juxtaposition of the city and the countryside represents the relationship
of the present to the past. In tracing his roots from the Detroit ghetto,
where he was familiar with Pilate's version of the Solomon song; to Danville, Pennsylvania, where his father grew up; and then to Shalimar,
Virginia, where his grandfather was born and children still sing of Solomon, Milkman deciphers the twin texts of history: song and genealogy.
In so doing, he reconstructs a dialectic of historical transition, in which
the individual genealogy evokes the history of black migration and the
chain of economic expropriation from hinterland to village, and village
to metropolis. The end point of Milkman's journey is the starting point
of his race's history in this country: slavery. The confrontation with the
reality of slavery, coming at the end of Milkman's penetration into historical process, is liberational because slavery is not portrayed as the
origin of history and culture. Instead, the novel opens out to Africa, the
source, and takes flight on the wings of Milkman's great-grandfather,
the original Solomon. With the myth of the "flying Africans" Morrison
transforms the moment of coming to grips with slavery as an allegory of
liberation.

The fact that geographic space functions for history is symptomatic
of a time when a people's past no longer forms a continuity with the
present. It is one of the features that differentiates literary modernism
from realism, in which people's lives are portrayed as integral to the flow
of history. Because the past is perceived as problematical and historical
transition is represented by the relationship among countryside, village,

and city, *Song of Solomon* is very similar to the great modernist novels of the Latin American "Boom" (the literary movement born with the Cuban Revolution and brought to an end with the assassination of Allende). In Morrison's *Song of Solomon*, as in the Peruvian Mario Vargas Llosa's *La Casa Verde*, the synchronic relationship defined in geographic space stands for a diachronic relationship. The most interesting feature about these modernist texts is that, in reading them, the reader, like Milkman, restores diachrony to the text and, in so doing, realizes the historical dialectic that the text presents as inaccessible.

Milkman's journey into the past takes him out of consumer society, where he, Christmas shopping in the Rexall store, practices the translation of human emotions into commodities, and thrusts him into the preindustrial world of Shalimar, where for the first time in his life Milkman sees women with "nothing in their hands." Stunned, Milkman realizes that he "had never in his life seen a woman on the street without a purse slung over her shoulder, pressed under her arm, or dangling from her clenched fingers." The vision of women walking empty-handed produces an estrangement of Milkman's normal view of women who, conditioned by a market economy, haul around purses like grotesque bodily appendages.

The descent into the past means stepping out of reified and fetishized relationships. Milkman's sensitivities are abruptly awakened when, trudging through the woods, he is scratched by branches, bruised by rocks, and soaked in a stream. As all of his commodified possessions fall away—his watch, his Florsheim shoes, and his three-piece suit—he comes to realize a full range of sensual perceptions (along with some human social practices—like sharing) he had never before experienced. Entering Solomon's General Store, Milkman is struck by its dramatic antithesis to the big-city department store, in which money (rather than need or use) mediates the exchange of human identities for brand names.

For Macon Dead, Milkman's father, all human relationships have become fetishized by their being made equivalent to money. His wife is an acquisition; his son, an investment in the future; and his renters, dollar signs in the bank. The human sentiments he experienced as a boy have given way to the emotional blackmail he wages as an adult. Driven by the desire to own property, the basis of bourgeois class politics, Macon Dead uses property, like a true capitalist, for further accumulation through the collection of rents. When Milkman, echoing his father's words, refers to money as "legal tender," he reveals how deeply fetishized and abstracted the concept of money itself has become. In this context, the search for gold takes on new meaning as a search for the only unfetishized form of value and, in an allegorical sense, as the retrieval of unfetishized human relationships.

However, Macon Dead is not so totally integrated into the bourgeois class that he cannot sense the impoverishment of his life—"his wife's

narrow unyielding back; his daughters, boiled dry from years of
yearning; his son, to whom he could speak only if his words held some
command or criticism." A phantom in search of some vision of human
fulfillment, Macon wanders one evening into the southside ghetto, his
sister's neighborhood. There, drawn by her singing, he pauses to peer
in her window. In every way Pilate is her brother's emotional and social
antithesis. What Macon sees when he looks into Pilate's house is a totally
alternative life-style, whose dramatic opposition to the spiritual impoverishment of Macon's world gives rise to a utopian moment:

> . . . he crept up to the side window where the candlelight flickered lowest,
> and peeped in. Reba was cutting her toenails with a kitchen knife or a
> switchblade, her long neck bent almost to her knees. The girl, Hagar, was
> braiding her hair, while Pilate, whose face he could not see because her back
> was to the window, was stirring something in a pot. Wine pulp, perhaps.
> Macon knew it was not food she was stirring, for she and her daughters ate
> like children. Whatever they had a taste for. No meal was ever planned or
> balanced and served. Nor was there any gathering at the table. Pilate might
> bake hot bread and each one of them would eat it with butter whenever she
> felt like it. Or there might be grapes, left over from the winemaking, or
> peaches for days on end. If one of them bought a gallon of milk they drank it
> until it was gone. If another got a half bushel of tomatoes or a dozen ears of
> corn, they ate them until they were gone too. They ate what they had or
> came across or had a craving for. Profits from their wine-selling evaporated
> like sea water in a hot wind—going for junk jewelry for Hagar, Reba's gifts
> to men, and he didn't know what all.

In its journey back to rural origins, the novel demonstrates that
Pilate's household is not, as this passage tends to suggest, structured in
infantile desires and relationships, but that the world of childhood is
rooted in rural society, where reciprocity and the unmediated response
to desire determine social life. The utopian aspects of Pilate's household
is not contained within it, but generated out of its abrupt juxtaposition
to the bourgeois mode of her brother's household. In contrast to Macon's
world, which is based on accumulation, Pilate's household is devoted
in true potlatch fashion to nonaccumulation. With everyone working to
separate berries from thorns, winemaking is not a means for creating
surplus value, but a communal social activity whose natural raw material
suggests, in Morrison's symbolic register, another link to rural agricultural society. Reba, who wins lotteries and department-store giveaways,
enjoys a noncommodified relationship to objects, in which value is defined
not by an object's monetary equivalent but by the spontaneous way she
comes to possess it and the pleasure it renders in the giving. Finally,
Pilate's only pretense to property ownership is purely symbolic: a bag of
bones, which turn out to be her father's, and rocks, a single one gathered
from every state she has visited.

Throughout her writing Morrison defines and tests the limits of individual freedom. Unlike those characters who realize total freedom and,

as a result, are incapable of living in society and maintaining human relationships, like Cholly Breedlove[9] and Sula, Pilate lives an unencumbered life that is the basis for a social form of freedom, rich in human understanding and love, which is neither sexual nor familial. In the text, Pilate's freedom, which makes her different from everybody else, has a very curious explanation: namely, the lack of a navel.

Now, it would be wrong simply to see Pilate's lack as just one more example of the mutilated, deformed, and stigmatized characters who tend to crop up in Morrison's writing. And it would be equally wrong to dismiss these forms of physical difference as nothing more than the author's obsession with freaks of nature. Rather, as Morrison herself indicates, Pilate's lack is to be read in social terms. The lack of a navel, like the other versions of physical deformity, functions as a metaphor that allows the reader to perceive a unique personal relationship to society as a whole.

Born without a navel, Pilate is a product of an unnatural birth. In social terms, her father dead and having never known her mother, she is an orphan. Her smooth, unbroken abdominal skin causes her to be shunned by everyone who either befriends her or comes to be her lover. Consequently, she has "no people." Because no clan claims her, she is outside all the potentially limiting aspects of blood relationships and traditional forms of social behavior. Apparently without a past and a place, Pilate embodies the "mythic hero"[10] first portrayed by Faulkner's Thomas Sutpen in *Absalom! Absalom!* The difference between Faulkner and Morrison, conditioned by the intervening years, which have brought black civil rights, countercultural politics, and the feminist perspective, is that, while Morrison invests her "mythic hero" with utopian aspirations, Faulkner does not. In making Sutpen and his "design" for plantation and progeny the epitome of Southern class society, Faulkner negates the utopian potential that his mythic outsider first represents in opposition to the stifled, small-town sensibilities of Jefferson, Mississippi.

Another dimension that Pilate's lack of a navel allows the reader to experience is the child's discovery of sexual difference. The metaphor of lack articulates the relationship between the advent of adult sexuality and the way it transforms the individual's relationship to others. As a child, having seen only her brother's and father's stomachs, Pilate imagines that navels, like penises, are something men have and women lack. Later, when others point to her lack as a form of freakishness, Pilate achieves adult sexuality only to have it denied her. Deprived of sex because of her unique body and the superstitious fear it creates, Pilate's lack becomes the basis for her liberation from narrowly defined human relationships based on sexuality and the expansion of her social world to one based on human sensitivity. This is very different from the way Pilate's sister-in-law, Ruth Foster, lives her sexual deprivation. Shunned by her husband, she turns inward to necrophiliac fantasies of her father, a mildly obscene relationship with her son, and masturbation. Ruth, like many of Morrison's female characters, is dependent on a possessive and closed heterosexual relationship; she never comes to see human relationships as anything but sexual. For her, the denial of sex simply means a more narrowly defined sexuality and the closure of her social world.

The only aspect of Pilate's lack as a metaphor for social relationships that is not explicit but does, nevertheless, inform Morrison's treatment of Pilate is its function as a figure for the experience of racial otherness. This is not the case for other instances of lack, which, like Pecola's lack of blue eyes and Hagar's lack of copper-colored hair, capture the horror of seeing oneself as "other" and inferior. Although Pilate, like many of Morrison's other characters, does undergo a moment of looking at (and into) the self, during which she recognizes her lack (or difference) and, as a consequence, determines to live her life according to a very different set of values, her moment of self-recognition (unlike many of theirs) is not couched in racial terms. Because lack in every other instance is a figure for the experience of race, it would seem to be implicit—if not explicit—in the characterization of Pilate. There is just no need for Pilate to affirm herself through race as the shell-shocked Shadrack does in *Sula* when, amnesiac and terrified by his own body, he glimpses the reflection of his face and sees in it the bold reality of his "unequivocal" blackness. For Pilate, blackness is already unequivocal. And pastlessness does not endanger identity, or separate her from society, as it does for Shadrack. Rather, it liberates the self into society.

As a literary figure for examining the lived experience of social difference, and testing the human potential for liberation, lack has its opposite in a full term: bodily stigma. In contrast to Pilate, who has no mark, Sula possesses a striking birthmark above her eye. A patch of skin unlike that found on any other human, Sula's birthmark is thought to represent a tadpole, a flower, or a snake depending on the mood of the beholder. Stigma is the figural equivalent of Sula's role in the community. As a social pariah branded as different, she is the freedom against which others define themselves.

Bodily deformity is another metaphor for the experience of social difference. When Shadrack awakes in a hospital bed, he comes into a world so totally fragmented and sundered that he is unsure where his own hands might be; after all, "anything could be anywhere." When he finally does behold his hands, he imagines that they are monstrously deformed—so terrifyingly that he cannot bear to look at them. Totally disoriented, his hands hidden behind his back, Shadrack is expelled from the hospital and pushed out into the world—a lone, cringing figure in an alien landscape.

For Morrison, the psychological, like the sensual and sexual, is also historical. In a novel whose opening describes the leveling of a neighborhood and its transformation into the Medallion City Golf Course, Shadrack's experience of bodily fragmentation is the psychological equivalent of annihilating social upheaval, which he was subjected to as an army draftee (the army being the first of capitalism's modern industrial machines to incorporate black men). Shadrack's imagined physical deformity is a figure for the equally monstrous psychological and social transformations that capitalism in all its modes (slavery, the military, and wage labor) has inflicted on the minds and bodies of black people.

Shadrack's affirmation of self, arising out of the moment he sees his image reflected in a toilet bowl and beholds the solid and profound reality of his blackness, ranks as one of the most powerful literary statements of racial affirmation. Race is the wellspring of Shadrack's inalienable identity. Everything about him and within him may be subject to transformation, but his blackness is forever. This sense of continuity in the face of chaos lies at the heart of Shadrack's cryptic, one-word message to the child Sula: "'Always.'" It is the basis for both Shadrack's and Sula's reinsertion into society as representations of freedom. As both messiah and pariah, Shadrack is marginal, accepted by, but never assimilated into, the black community. He, like Sula and Morrison's other social pariah, Soaphead Church, provides a point of perspective on the community that is both inferior and exterior; he allows the community to define itself against a form of freedom, which being a social unit, it cannot attain. Morrison's characters demonstrate that the black community tolerates difference, whereas the white bourgeois world shuts difference out. She underscores the fact that for the white world, under capitalism, difference, because it articulates a form of freedom, is a threat and therefore must be institutionalized or jailed.

In *Tar Baby*, bodily deformity takes a very different form. Because this novel describes an already-sundered black community whose exiles have neither the wish nor the capacity to rediscover the source of black culture, freedom cannot be articulated (as it was in the previous novels) by an individual's moment of self-affirmation and reinsertion into society. Having no possible embodiment in the real world—not even as a pariah— freedom takes mythic form and defines the text's alternate, subterranean world, in which, in sharp contrast with the bourgeois world of manor houses and leisure, a centuries-old band of blind black horsemen rides the swamps.

Blindness is another way of giving metaphoric expression to social difference and freedom.[11] It overlaps with the function of lack in that the lack of sight, which in bourgeois society is the basis for an individual's alienation, is in the mythic world the basis for the group's cohesion and absolute alternality. This is because blindness is not portrayed as an individual's affliction, but rather a communally shared way of being in the world. Once again, the figure of deformity evokes a historical reality.

The myth of the blind horsemen has its roots in the many real maroon societies whose very existence depended on seclusion and invisibility. This is the social reality for which blindness is a metaphoric reversal.

A final metaphor for social otherness is self-mutilation.[12] Unlike lack and deformity, self-mutilation represents the individual's direct confrontation with the oppressive social forces inherent in white domination. Because it functions as a literary figure, self-mutilation is portrayed in Morrison's writing as liberational and contrasts sharply with all the other forms of violence done to the self. For instance, when Polly Breedlove lashes out at her child Pecola, berating her and beating her for spilling a berry cobbler while at the same time comforting and cuddling the white child in her charge, she internalizes her hate for white society and deflects the spontaneous eruption of violence away from its real object and toward a piece of herself. Unlike Polly Breedlove's violence toward the self, which locks her in profound self-hatred, self-mutilation is portrayed as a confrontational tactic that catapults the individual out of an oppressive situation. Because it involves severing a part of the body, self-mutilation coincides with the figure of lack and intensifies (by reason of direct articulation) the potential for expressing freedom. In Morrison's writing, self-mutilation brings about the spontaneous redefinition of the individual, not as an alienated cripple—as would be the case in bourgeois society—but as a new and whole person, occupying a radically different social space.

When, as an adolescent, Sula is confronted by a band of teenage Irish bullies, she draws a knife. Instead of threatening the boys with it or plunging it into one of them, she whacks off the tip of her own finger. Terrified, the boys run away. Sula's self-mutilation symbolizes castration and directly contests the white male sexual domination of black women that the taunting and threatening boys evoke. Her act, coupled with words of warning, "If I can do that to myself, what you suppose I'll do to you?" represents the refusal—no matter how high the cost—to accept and cower in the face of domination.

For its defiance of oppressive social norms as well as its symbolic nature, Sula's act of self-mutilation has its precedent in her grandmother's solution to a similar confrontation with bourgeois-dominated society. Abandoned by her husband, with three small children and nothing but five eggs and three beets among them, Eva Peace takes a truly radical course of action that lifts her out of the expected role of an abandoned black mother circa 1921, who could do no more than live hand-to-mouth, and gives her a very different future. Leaving her children in the care of a neighbor, she sets out. "Eighteen months later she swept down from a wagon with two crutches, a new black pocketbook, and one leg." Eva never confirms neighborhood speculation that she allowed a train to sever her leg because the way in which she lost it is not important. The real issue is what her self-mutilation enables her to achieve. As the juxtaposition between Eva's "new black pocketbook" and "one leg" suggests, monthly insurance checks make it possible for her to build a new life. The construction of a rambling, many-roomed house for family and boarders gives physical evidence of Eva's confrontation with and manipulation of the written laws of white society, whose unwritten laws would have condemned her to a life of poverty.

Yet the most radical aspect of Eva's act is not the simple and direct contestation of capitalism that her self-mutilation represents but the subsequent lack that allows a wholly new social collective to come into being around her. If the loss of a limb means that Eva practically never leaves her room, it does not signify withdrawal. Instead, Eva is "sovereign" of an entire household, which includes three generations of Peace women as its nucleus (Eva, Hannah, and Sula); their boarders (the young married couples and an alcoholic hillbilly); and their adopted outcasts (the three Deweys). For its fluid composition, openness to outsiders, and organization on a feminine principle, Eva's household represents a radical alternative to the bourgeois family model.

At one level, Morrison writes to awaken her reader's sensitivity, to shake up and disrupt the sensual numbing that accompanies social and psychological alienation. This is the function of her "eruptions of funk," which include metaphors drawn from past moments of sensual fulfillment as well as the use of lack, deformity, and self-mutilation as figures for liberation. At a deeper level, and as a consequence of these features, Morrison's writing often allows an alternative social world to come into being. When this happens, "otherness" no longer functions as an extension of domination (as it does when blackness is beheld from the point of view of racist bourgeois society, or when the crippled, blind, and deformed are compared to the terrorizing totality of a whole and therefore "perfect" body). Rather, the space created by otherness permits a reversal of domination and transforms what was once perceived from without as "other" into the explosive image of a utopian mode. Morrison's most radical "eruption of funk" is the vision of an alternative social world. It comes into view when Macon Dead peers into Pilate's window; when the child Nel, the product of her mother's stifled bourgeois morality, scratches at Sula's screen door; and when the intimidated and fearful Pecola visits her upstairs neighbors, the three prostitutes.

It is not gratuitous that in all these cases the definition of social utopia is based on a three-woman household. This does not imply a lesbian orientation, because in all cases the women are decidedly heterosexual. Rather, these are societies that do not permit heterosexuality as it articulates male domination to be the determining principle for the living and working relationships of the group, as it is in capitalist society.

Morrison's three-woman utopian households contrast dramatically with an earlier literary version that occurs, paradoxically again, in Faulkner's *Absalom! Absalom!* During the grinding culmination of the Civil War, the men all gone—siphoned off by the army, the economy reduced to bare subsistence, the novel brings together three women: Judith, Sutpen's daughter and heir; Clytie, Sutpen's black nonheir; and the young spinstress, Miss Rosa, Sutpen's nonbetrothed. Taking refuge in the shell of a once-prosperous manor house, they eke out their survival on a day-to-day basis:

> So we waited for him. We led the busy eventless lives of three nuns in a barren and poverty-stricken convent: the walls we had were safe, impervious enough, even if it did not matter to the walls whether we ate or not. And amicably, not as two white women and a negress, not as three negroes or three whites, not even as three women, but merely as three creatures who still possessed the need to eat but took no pleasure in it, the need to sleep but from it no joy in weariness or regeneration, and in whom sex was some forgotten atrophy like the rudimentary gills we call the tonsils or the still-opposable thumbs for old climbing.[13]

In considering the cataclysm of the Civil War and its destruction of traditional Southern society, Faulkner is led to imagine the basis for a potentially radical new form of social organization, based on subsistence rather than accumulation and women rather than men. However, the incipient possibility of social utopia dies stillborn, because the male principle and the system of patrimony have not been transformed or refuted, but merely displaced. Sutpen, even in his absence, is still the center of the household. Race, too, is not confronted or transcended. Rather, it, like sex, is simply dismissed. And with it go all vestiges of humanity.

The tremendous differences between Faulkner and Morrison, which include historical period, race, and sex, lie at the heart of their dramatically opposed images: the one dystopian; the other utopian. Rather than dwell on the social and historical factors that shape their fiction, I will emphasize the ways in which historical differences are manifested in the texts. Faulkner's dehumanized monads and the routinized lives they lead contrast sharply with Morrison's portrayal of Pilate's household, in which individual differences between the three women function to test the social dynamic within the group, and between it and society at large. Faulkner's retrenched espousal of the male-dominated social model and his tenacious refusal to imagine anything else condition his bleak vision of society. On the other hand, Morrison's projection of a social utopia arises from its confrontation with and reversal of the male-dominated bourgeois social model. Rather than systematically leveling social problems, Morrison foregrounds them. The utopian aspect of her vision is produced by the totality of its opposition to society at large—not by its individual members. This makes her portrayal very different from classical literary utopias, whose individuals are presented as perfect and harmonious models. None of Morrison's individual characters in any of her three utopias is perfect. Rather than supplying answers to social problems, they give rise to questions about social relationships and society as a whole. Thus, Pilate demonstrates the insufficiency of the agrarian social mode to provide for its members once they are transplanted to urban consumer society. Her strength and resourcefulness cannot be passed on to her daughter and granddaughter because each is more distant from the rural society in which Pilate worked and grew up. Their experience of insufficiency leads to hollow consumption (Reba's of sex and Hagar's of commodities) and demonstrates the way consumer society penetrates and impoverishes human relationship.

When in *Tar Baby* "funk" erupts as myth, its potential for estranging fetishized relationships is minimized because of its distance from urban and suburban settings that condition the lives of more and more Americans, both black and white. Son's quest for the mythic community of blind maroon horsemen that ends *Tar Baby* may represent a dramatic departure from his previous endeavors, but it does not bring disruption into the heart of social practice, as occurs when the image of Pilate's household bursts upon Macon Dead's alienated and numbed sensibilities. Although *Song of Solomon* also has a mythic dimension, myth is not the novel's only form of "funk." Then, too, myth is integral to Milkman's concrete past, as he discovers by following his family's route back to slavery, whereas for Son, it represents a very distant cultural source not directly linked to his present.

"Funk" is really nothing more than the intrusion of the past into the present. It is most oppositional when it juxtaposes a not-so-distant social mode to those evolved under bourgeois society. Morrison's method might be thought of as a North American variant of the magical realism that we have come to associate with Gabriel García Marquez. If in his *One Hundred Years of Solitude* pleasurable delight is synonymous with barbed political criticism, this is because the text's metaphoric incidents and characters are created out of the juxtaposition of First and Third World realities. Just as domination and dependency create separation and inequality between North and South America, so too do Marquez's metaphors represent the unresolved contradiction between two possible readings: the one mythic and pleasurable, the other historical and critical. The same holds true for Morrison, only the terms of her geographic and historical equation are bound up and framed by the history of the United States. North/South, black/white, these are the ingredients of Morrison's magical realism whose tension-fraught and unresolved juxtapositions articulate the continuation of domination in our society and the persistence of racism, and at the same time provoke Morrison's creative and critical imagination.

Notes

1. Much of the criticism of Morrison's work is done from a sociological point of view. See, for example, Joan Bischoff, "The Novels of Toni Morrison: Studies in Thwarted Sensitivity," Studies in Black Literature 6, 3: 21–23; Phyllis Klotman, "Dick-and-Jane and the Shirley Temple Sensibility in *The Bluest Eye*," Black American Literature Forum 13: 123–25; Barbara Lounsberry and Grace Anne Hovet, "Principles of Perception in Toni Morrison's *Sula*," Black American Literature Forum 13: 126–29. These studies focus on the erosion of the individual's sensitivity by white cultural domination, on the one hand, and ordering mechanisms within the black neighborhood on the other. The critics tend to agree that, although Morrison regrets the loss of sensitivity, she favors a practical and pragmatic point of view.

   Without denying the objective social fact or the importance of literary studies that document the social in literature, I am more interested in how texts subvert the limitations within which they are written. The focus of this study is, thus, on those instances in Morrison's writing in which the literature does something more than simply monitor and confirm social fact.

2. The surrealist metaphors of the negritude poets resist being read in the way we can read through Morrison's metaphors, progressively constructing their referents and meaning. An example from Aimé Césaire's *Cahier d'un Retour au Pays Natal* in *Aimé Césaire*, trans. Clayton Eshleman and Annette Smith (Berkeley: Univ. of California Press, 1983) exemplifies the difference between the poetics of negritude and Morrison's use of metaphor.

   Conjuring up the Congo, Césaire depicts a rich natural setting:

   > où l'eau fait
   > likouala—likouala

   "Where the water goes likouala—likouala." This is followed by one of the most complex and condensed examples of surrealist metaphor:

   > où l'éclair de la colère lance sa hache verdâtre
   > et force les sangliers de la putréfaction dans
   > la belle orée violente des narines

   Reading the metaphor produces something like this: "Where the lightning bolt of anger hurls its green ax and forces the wild boars of putrefaction over the beautiful and violent edge of the nostrils."

   Overall, the image evokes the powerful and driving force of nature and the hunt. Individual words are themselves metaphors, linked together to form a total metaphoric image whose meaning does not reside in a particular referent, but in the myriad cross-references pulled into the whole.

   The "lightning bolt of anger" captures the essence of the poem as a whole, for it voices the enraged outcry of black people and reverses the image of the meek, long-suffering "comical and ugly nigger" ("un nègre comique et laid") produced by colonialism. The image of "wild boars pouring over the nostrils" (like snot) extends the notion of putrefaction, which is itself a code word for the effects of colonialism. This is developed at length in the poem's opening pages where the Antilles are portrayed not as a tropical island paradise but as a degraded, diseased, and decayed speck of land:

   > Ici la parade des risibles et scrofuleux bubons, les poutures des microbes très étranges, les poisons sans alexitère connu, les sanies de plaies bien antiques, les fermentations imprévisibles d'éspèces putrescibles.

> Right here the parade of laughable and scrofulous buboes, the forced feedings of very strange microbes, the poisons without known alexins, the sanies of really ancient sores, the unforeseeable fermentations of putrescible species.

Bodily orifices, too, are in more than one instance related to the visage of colonialism. But these observations do not translate what the metaphor says; rather, they are embraced by it. There is no single, comprehensive way to decipher Césaire's metaphor as there is for Morrison's. This is because, although history infuses the image, the metaphor resists being tied to any specific referent or set of referents. The effect is finally an explosion of meanings, created out of the convergence of many possible interpretations, as opposed to Morrison's revelation of meaning, made possible by linking images to referents.

3. Harriette Arnow's *The Dollmaker* (New York: Avon, 1973), an account of an Appalachian family's migration to Detroit during World War II, is very similar to Morrison's portrayal of black Southern migration. Notably, it documents the initial experience and assimilation to wage labor, the erosion of folk culture, and the fragmentation of the family unit. In Arnow as in Morrison, the individual's experience of alienation is portrayed in relation to fetishization under the commodity form. For a brief discussion of *The Dollmaker*, see Susan Willis, "A Literary Lesson in Historical Thinking," *Social Text:* 136ff.

4. See Georg Lukács, "Reification and the Consciousness of the Proletariat," in *History and Class Consciousness* (London: Merlin Press, 1971). According to Lukács, reification occurs when the "commodity structure penetrates society in all its aspects and remoulds it in its own image." This differentiates bourgeois society from previous social modes, in which the commodity form may have pertained to certain endeavors or may have been only partially developed. Reification means the transformation of all human functions and qualities into commodities "and reveals in all its starkness the dehumanized and dehumanizing function of the commodity relation."

5. Referred to as "The Principal Beauty of Maine," Margaret Lenore from *Tar Baby* (New York: Knopf, 1981), comes closest to embodying bourgeois reification. Her characterization may well be a literary allusion to another great beauty and bourgeois stereotype in contemporary fiction: "The Most Beautiful Woman in the World," in Gabriel García Marquez's *One Hundred Years of Solitude* (New York: Avon, 1971). Both Margaret Lenore and Marquez's "Most Beautiful Woman" are first beheld by their future husbands as beauty-contest winners in a parade and draped in ermine. However, neither Margaret Lenore nor Marquez's Fernanda define total reification. First of all, neither is originally of the bourgeois class: Fernanda is the sole survivor of a transplanted and bankrupt Spanish aristocracy and Margaret Lenore is the daughter of struggling Italian immigrants. Both develop forms of hysteria as a result of the discontinuity between their pasts and presents and their imperfect assimilation into bourgeois culture. Margaret Lenore abuses her infant son and Fernanda develops a relationship with imaginary doctors she hopes will cure her bodily ailments through telepathic surgery (a situation not unlike Margaret Lenore's long-distance telephone conversations with her son, which, because no one witnesses or overhears them, appear to be imaginary).

6. In Morrison's writing, candy is often associated with capitalism. In *Song of Solomon*, candy is the symbolic payoff given by the boss's wife when Guitar's father is crushed in a mill accident. In *The Bluest Eye*, candy is a penny's

worth of sweetness in the life of a little girl who will never find satisfaction in human terms. And in *Tar Baby*, candy is a metaphor for all of capitalist production. The association is not gratuitous, for the connection between candy and capitalism extends far beyond the current glut of sugary breakfast cereals and junk foods. As Immanuel Wallerstein explains in *The Modern World System*, (New York: Academic Press, 1974) sugar production in the New World was essential to the rise of capitalism. Rather than simply satisfying luxury consumption, a lot of the sugar produced under slavery in the Caribbean found its way into the daily diet of the growing European proletariat. With many peasants leaving the countryside to seek jobs in the cities, there was an increased need for food production and a shrinking rural labor force. The need for more food was met neither by increased cereal production (which would have required substantial transformations in production techniques) nor by increasing meat production (which was basically intended for the bourgeoisie). Rather, sugar became—and remains today—a substitute for real food. Capable of providing increased energy output at the expense of long-term health, sugar is the opiate of the working class under capitalism. See also Sidney Mintz, *Sweetness and Power* (New York: Viking, 1985).

7. Toni Morrison, *Tar Baby* (New York: Knopf, 1981).

8. Toni Morrison, *Sula* (New York: Knopf, 1974).

9. Abandoned at birth by his mother, rejected by his father for the sake of a poker game, and having experienced the ultimate moment of objectification when two white hunters catch him in his first sex act, Cholly Breedlove finds absolute freedom in the realization that he has nothing to lose. In many ways he is Pilate's antithesis, his freedom being a barrier rather than a bridge to others. Unlike Pilate, who similarly did not know her mother's name, who lost her father, and also experienced the freezing "look" of others for her lack of a navel, Cholly can neither communicate nor share his freedom.

10. Many modernist novels from the Third World include "mythic heroes" very similar to Faulkner's Thomas Sutpen. In Mario Vargas Llosa's *The Green House* (New York: Avon, 1973), Don Anselmo bursts upon a stodgy, backwater town, shrouded in mystery, apparently without a past or a name. Like Sutpen, he embarks on an enterprise that the townspeople marvel at and at first do not comprehend. What Don Anselmo builds symbolizes exploitation in the Third World: a brothel. The "mythic hero" creates a distance from society, which produces an estrangement effect and reveals that what was first perceived as very different and foreign is nothing more than that society's ultimate representation.

11. The otherness of blindness and the fear it instills in a repressive bourgeois society are developed in *Sobre Héroes y Tumbas*, (Buenos Aires: Editorial Losada, 1966), the great historical novel by the Argentinian Ernesto Sábato. Similar to Morrison's portrayal, Sábato conjures up an underground society of the blind whose otherness, perceived as grotesque from the point of view of the Peronist social model, is the basis for the group's solidarity and resistance to assimilation by the forces of domination.

12. The relationship between forms of mutilation and freedom is not unique to Morrison, but recurs in the history of slavery and its literature. In his mythic account of the Haitian Revolution, *The Kingdom of This World* (New York: Collier, 1970), Alejo Carpentier portrays the mutilation of Mackandal, an early slave leader, in terms that coincide with Morrison's treatment. His arm crushed in a cane mill and amputated, Mackandal is unfit for most forms of plantation labor. Freed from the most grueling forms of toil, he wanders the countryside watching over his master's livestock. There he discovers and

studies plant and animal life, learning the secrets of science and voodoo. Mutilation is thus the means for Mackandal's liberation from labor and access to learning. Furthermore, because Mackandal, as voodoo priest, is capable of undergoing various metamorphoses, his human body and its mutilation are not perceived as permanently disabled, but rather, as one more manifestation of transitory and transitional matter. Mackandal's spiritual liberation—made possible by his mutilation—finally transcends his earthy form.

13. William Faulkner, *Absalom! Absalom!* (1936; rpt. New York: Random House, 1972).

◆◆◆◆◆◆◆◆◆◆◆◆◆

Escaping Slavery but Not Its Images[1]

TRUDIER HARRIS

Ownership and possession are characteristic of slavery. They reflect the monetary exchange involved in that system of dehumanization as well as the psychological control usually attendant upon the physical imprisonment. I am using "ownership" here to refer to the practice of masters having legal rights to the bodies and labor of their slaves. I am using "possession" to refer to the psychological dimension of the relationship, in which masters were able to convince some slaves to *believe* in the institution of slavery and to concede that their situation was hopeless. These mind-controlling tactics took a variety of forms, beginning with the destruction of family and linguistic groups in the assigning of slaves to plantations in the New World. The psychological damage attendant upon realizing that one was separated from blood relatives and kinspeople, essentially alone in the world, worked to the benefit of the slaveholder and was designed to teach dependency in the slave. At the least sign of uppityness, slaveholders could further "break" slaves with a series of barbaric punishments, including whipping, branding a letter on the face or back, cropping an ear or a finger, confining them in bits, or selling them "down the river," which had connotations of horror that far outstripped any actual physical punishment. All of these tactics were everyday reminders to slaves that the masters possessed their very minds and memories—had indeed erased if not destroyed their histories—even as they owned their bodies.

In *Beloved* (New York: Knopf, 1987), Toni Morrison makes clear where ownership leaves off and possession begins in the psychologically warping system called slavery. Stamp Paid, one of the most engaging characters in the book, is certainly owned during slavery, but he is not possessed. In the classic sense of the creation of an alternative reality that Ralph Ellison identified with the ingenuity that shaped black folk tradition, Stamp Paid learns to separate his vision of himself from those of the slaveholders who would define his essence for him. Like Frederick Douglass, Stamp Paid's body may be enslaved, but his mind is elsewhere. When he actually frees his body, he turns to collecting what slaveholders owe black people by ferrying recently escaped slaves into the free territory of Ohio and other points North. His activities are also a recognition of what he articulates as his debt to his fellow blacks.

Formerly called by the slave name Joshua, Stamp Paid is a man who has earned his freedom by acquiescing in the repeated rape of his young wife Vashti by the youthful heir to the plantation where he grew up; he had without violence or verbal objection "handed over his wife to his master's son." "With that gift, he decided that he didn't owe anybody anything. Whatever his obligations were, that act paid them off. . . . So he extended this debtlessness to other people by helping them pay out and off whatever they owed in misery. Beaten runaways? He ferried them and rendered them paid for; gave them their own bill of sale, so to speak. 'You paid it; now life owes you.'"

Joshua had remained quiet, at his wife's insistence, during the period of her degradation. His silence has been an additional burden on his soul, for what man, he probably reasoned, if truly a man, would allow his wife to be so degraded? And manhood *is* the focus of the issue. The master's son uses Vashti to assert/declare his manhood; that act simultaneously signals to Joshua that he, a slave, can never be a man. Joshua can neither claim nor protect hearth or wife, for the ownership of the wife's most private parts are the privilege of the slaveholder. Unlike the Sweet Home men, who have a definition of manhood, no matter how distorted, Joshua must go begging, through the white woman, for her white husband to return Joshua's black wife to him. While on the surface Joshua may accept Vashti's request that he not risk his life defending her so that she can have someone to turn to when the white man tires of her, it is also probable that her request was a relief because it absolved him of trying to assume the actions of a man when that status was by definition of the system denied to him. The courage and fortitude necessary to defend his wife are antithetical to his very existence. Vashti therefore becomes a triple pawn in the dynamics of black male/white male interaction during slavery; everyone—her husband, her master, and her mistress—can decide her fate except her.

Joshua's reaction to Vashti is like that of many victims who recognize the powerlessness of their situations. He has at one point tried unsuccessfully to turn his anger toward Vashti and kill her for a set of circumstances over which she had no control. But his fleeting desire to kill her is really his longing for suicide, a desire to destroy himself when he recognizes the same powerlessness in himself. Instead of snapping her neck, however, he changed his name, thereby sparing her life and his own. At the end of nearly a year, the master's son dismissed Vashti from his bed. Any number of motivations may have caused the termination of the affair: his wife's displeasure finally registered with him, he found a more appealing substitute, or his father insisted that he assume his public duties as a *white* man and therefore become more circumspect and intermittent in his private indiscretions. Upon Vashti's return, Stamp settles into a dissipation from which he eventually arises into a new awareness of what his "gift" to his master has meant. He recognizes that powerlessness is not equivalent to hopelessness, that being owned is not equivalent to being possessed. He can thereby be free in the way that some other Morrison characters, such as Cholly Breedlove (*The Bluest*

Eye, 1970), Sula Peace (*Sula*, 1973), and Guitar Bains (*Song of Solomon*, 1977), are free. Unlike these other characters, whose freedom is described as being "dangerous," Stamp manages to direct his anger into more constructive channels. He has reached a level of maturity or self-control in his freedom that other Morrison characters outside the law or community mores have apparently been unable to attain.

The telling of his story becomes a ritual of affirmation for Stamp Paid and a rite of passage for Paul D, to whom Stamp relates the incident as they sit on the steps of the church where Paul D is living once he leaves Sethe's house. Perhaps the tale is intended to suggest that Paul D, like Sethe, should lay his burdens down, that while he may have been hurt by learning that Sethe killed Beloved, that is not the worst horror he can experience in life. At some point Paul D will have to realize what Joshua had realized and what Sixo proved: slavery could not ultimately dehumanize anyone who did not grant his or her definition of self to the potential dehumanizer; Sethe may have killed Beloved, but she, like Stamp, had paid the dues for that action.[2]

"Stamp Paid," then, is not only Joshua's public acknowledgment of what he has suffered under slavery and how he has responded to it, but is also a phrase that complements the thematic structure of the novel. All of the characters who have escaped or been freed from slavery have given more than their weight in gold to that system; they have offered up "gifts," like Stamp, that far outweigh the designations of value assigned to them. In exchange for her share of human misery, Sethe has given up her back to be marked with a tree and suffered the death of her daughter, the loss of her sons, and the insanity of her husband. Baby Suggs has given up her eight children, seven of whom were dispersed before her very eyes; well does she know the value system underlying slavery, with its images of bartering human flesh: ". . . men and women were moved around like checkers. Anybody Baby Suggs knew, let alone loved, who hadn't run off or been hanged, got rented out, loaned out, bought up, brought back, stored up, mortgaged, won, stolen or seized. . . . What she called the nastiness of life was the shock she received upon learning that nobody stopped playing checkers just because the pieces included her children." Paul D has offered up his share to misery in the sale of one brother, the death of another, the bit in his mouth, and a stint in prison. Ella has given up maternal and sexual instincts as a result of being victimized unspeakably by "the lowest yet"; and the community collectively has given its sons, daughters, husbands, and wives in exchange for shattered lives, broken spirits, and the general dissolution of families that has accompanied slavery.

With all of this offering up of sacrifices to human misery, with all these "gifts" having been extracted from the former slaves, it is somewhat surprising that one of the recurring images in the novel is debt-based, as if these characters, who were existentially if not nominally free during slavery, still have external claims upon their personhood, as if they still, inexplicably, have debts to pay. At striking jolts in the narrative, Morrison reverts our attention to the buying and selling of human beings by inserting images of monetary units to describe physical features and to convey states such as frustration and remorse. She suggests thereby that the characters are not as free as they now profess to be, that they have inadvertently inculcated concepts of value from their slave masters, frequently to their own detriment. She also uses the imagery ironically to comment on current practices or incidents in the black community that bring to mind those bartering notions of ownership from slavery, which suggest that *some* black people may have modeled their behavior too closely on that of their masters. And she textures the language with images of finance to remind readers constantly of the overall outline and subject of the novel: the unrelenting psychological and physical damage from a system where human beings were equated to poker chips.

Monetary images also become the language of desire in the novel, as characters express their greatest wants in financial terms. Denver recognizes Beloved long before Sethe does and believes that she is the long-lost Presence (like Pauline waiting for Cholly Breedlove) who will make a difference in her life. Denver does not want to question Beloved overly much for fear that she will leave. She therefore resigns herself to be content to gaze upon Beloved, to stare at her in a hunger-fulfilling strategy that savors Beloved's presence and stifles the urge to ask questions about how she came to be in 124 Bluestone Road: ". . . she was careful to appear uninquisitive about the things she was dying to ask Beloved, for if she pressed too hard, she might lose the penny that the held-out palm wanted, and lose, therefore, the place beyond appetite." Denver's desire to keep Beloved is perhaps as great as Beloved's desire to stay and possess Sethe. The expression of both desires in a single, shiny penny points to the childishness in both girls, to the intensity with which they hope to achieve their objectives. The simplicity of the penny crystallizes desire as a part of the ownership-possession theme. The penny is basic, elemental, first on the scale of value; it therefore connotes that basic, unbridled desire is not to be denied.

While desire might seem simple, easily met, its depth is masked—by the use of the coin imagery as well as by the demeanor that Beloved initially presents. This simple country girl who seems to have lost her way and just stumbled into 124 Bluestone Road is really a sinister presence intent upon having her way at all costs. The value of the coin is inversely proportional to the intensity of Beloved's desire, just as value assigned to human beings during slavery was similarly mismatched, sometimes dangerously so—as in the case of the gap between Sixo's assumed value and his violent actions.

Morrison shows how the past continues to impinge upon the future by tying its possibilities to her monetary imagery. She refers to the "coin of life" when Paul D is trying to forge a future with Sethe after his indiscretion with Beloved. Paul D meets Sethe at the restaurant to tell her of his brief affair with Beloved, but he ends up asking her to have a baby with him. The request is a stalling action at a crucial moment in their relationship; it could have dire consequences for their future, yet Paul D is willing to take the chance. "Still, he'd gotten a little more time, bought it, in fact, and hoped the price wouldn't wreck him. Like paying for an afternoon in the coin of life to come."[3] Since so much misery for these two in the past has depended upon the monetary value placed on them or their relatives, it is ironic that the same images, reinforced by repetition ("bought," "price," "paying," "coin"), would be used to describe their potential for post-slavery happiness. The threat to that potential makes their future just as precarious as the lives of Paul A, Paul F, and Sixo during slavery.

Paul D is gambling on his future in the way that Southern slaveholders used human ante in their games on the riverboats of the Mississippi, or the way that Baby Suggs's seducers/rapists/owners played checkers with her children and relatives. Is there too much of a tendency to possession in the relationship to put it on any other than a monetary footing? Have the very psyches of these former slaves been so saturated with the prices placed on them (Schoolteacher taught Paul D "the dollar value of his weight, his strength, his heart, his brain, his penis, and his future") that they cannot conceive of worth in any other way?

At another key juncture in the novel, Morrison also selects her comparative images from finance. Stamp feels that the memory of Baby Suggs is "scorching his soul like a silver dollar in a fool's pocket" when he contemplates the damage he may have done to the memory of their friendship by telling Paul D about Sethe killing Beloved. What Stamp has done could potentially destroy Sethe and ruin her chances for happiness with Paul D. It is appropriate that such an act weighs on his soul, especially since he has spent his life lifting burdens from black people's souls. Like the fool who is overeager to spend his fortune, Stamp becomes overly anxious to make up for his indiscretion in telling Paul D about Sethe. But the imagery also works in another way: the gap between the silver dollar and the fool's ability to estimate value is symbolically the gap between Stamp's intent and the outcome of his showing Paul D that destructive newspaper clipping about Sethe. It is also the gap between true human worth and the monetary value slaveholders would have assigned to such worth. Stamp has thus violated his own philosophy and erroneously assumed that there was yet another price Sethe had to pay for her place in the world, a price that may mean the end of her happiness. In that brief slip in his philosophy, Stamp also shares kinship with those slaveholders who would continue to extract pay, further "gifts," from people whose accounts should all be stamped "paid."

Stamp tries to mitigate this violation by approaching Sethe's house with a talisman of his debt-free philosophy. He carries a faded red ribbon from the head of a lynched (possibly raped) young black girl ("He clutched the red ribbon in his pocket for strength,"); it reminds him of his gift of his wife to his master because Vashti had worn a black ribbon to all of her meetings with her seducer/owner (he had given it to her). Stamp "fingers" and "worries" the ribbon like a worn dollar bill; the debt he owns to Baby Suggs's memory gets wrapped up with the victimization of his wife and the young girl and the knowledge that their debtors did not pay, and with the debt he now owes Sethe for having threatened her future. The only account-balancing option he has is to pay off his debt to Sethe.

Although slavery is over, black people are still judging each other through the eyes and with the units of measure of those who enslaved them. For the brief moment when Stamp has told Paul D about Sethe, he has abandoned his usual generosity and has joined in sentiment with the black townspeople who have punished Baby Suggs for what they perceive as her uppityness by not warning her about the approaching schoolteacher (as the people in the Bottom avoid Sula for not adhering to their mores). They have concluded that she should pay for her pride in the same way that a slaveholder might conclude that an uppity slave should be punished. Judgment tied to value and expressed in coins ironically shows the human faults in black people that align them with their enslavers. The higher goal of freedom has not yet been complemented with a *consistent* higher goal of morality.

The coin imagery surfaces again when Denver finally gets enough nerve to leave 124 and ask neighbors for help. She encounters an image at the Bodwin house not unlike the Sambo doll that haunts the Invisible Man:

> . . . she had seen, sitting on a shelf by the back door, a blackboy's mouth full of money. His head was thrown back farther than a head could go, his hands were shoved in his pockets. Bulging like moons, two eyes were all the face he had above the gaping red mouth. His hair was a cluster of raised, widely spaced dots made of nail heads. And he was on his knees. His mouth, wide as a cup, held the coins needed to pay for a delivery or some other small service, but could just as well have held buttons, pins or crab-apple jelly. Painted across the pedestal he knelt on were the words "At Yo Service."

This object is quickly recognizable as one of the many images of Sambo, as Joseph Boskin makes clear in *Sambo: The Rise and Demise of an American Jester* (New York: Oxford, 1986) and as the film, *Ethnic Notions*, traces through an extensive period of American history. Sambo is the image of black people controlled by white people, usually signalled by its distorted facial features, especially eyes and mouth, and its exuding of a palpable willingness to please. In history as in literature, Sambo is ever self-effacing, ever obsequious and subservient, ever willing "to grin and bear it," ever willing to be trampled on by whites because its irrepressible spirit will rise up and beg to be degraded again. This popular stereotype of black people saturated the white American mind for centuries; not only was it complimentary to whites, whose money could evoke such distorted grins, but it was comforting to them, for it was infinitely more pleasant to imagine grinning darkies than knife-wielding ones.

It is ironic that this stereotypical image is in the home of the Bodwins, who were formerly abolitionists, yet it makes clear how pervasive the Sambo stereotype was, how even so-called liberals could not resist its "charm." This minstrel Sambo alludes as well to the gift-giving nature that has been identified with blacks throughout the novel. Slaves by their nature are presumed to exist for the service of their masters. In addition to his regular services as a slave, Halle has served Garner with five years of Sundays in exchange for Baby Suggs (who has paused in the Bodwin kitchen with Janey), and Sethe and the Sweet Home men could document a volume of services they have rendered without remuneration. As a female slave, Baby Suggs has had the additional responsibility of servicing her masters sexually, just as Nan has been forced to nurture their offspring at her breasts. Whether as mammies or sluts, or sometimes sexual partners, or cooks, or nursemaids, black women were especially in the service of their masters during slavery. One dominant image Sethe has retained of herself from that period is that of someone who has "enough for all," whether it is milk for Beloved and Denver, meat for the dogs at Sawyer's Restaurant, or food and milk for Paul D, Denver, and Beloved; she has always been at somebody's service, whether voluntarily or not.

It is noteworthy that this Sambo caricature *could* have had other functions, just as black people could have been defined (and some did define themselves) in healthier ways during slavery. But it is Denver who observes and imprints the image on her mind. What is its significance to her? While it would be questionable to say that she is astute enough to understand the complex psychological warping and role confinement that slavery produced, she has nonetheless heard and seen some of the consequences in her own family. She had expected to escape such degradation of the human spirit by going to the Bodwins to ask for work. If they have such an image in their home, perhaps it serves as a forewarning to her of what she can become and must guard against. Service need not mean distortion of the human spirit. With this image before her, perhaps Denver is being offered a choice for how to shape her own destiny: give good work in exchange for pay but remember that even *good* white folks may create situations that could be benignly destructive to black people not on guard against such a possibility (former abolitionists need not necessarily support social equality). Without a modicum of that level of analysis, however, Denver can simply note that the Sambo object is black and distorted, but that it is grotesquely happy to be giving. If she merely concludes that it is not what she wants to be, her pausing to observe the Sambo would have served its purpose, would have suggested an alternative pattern of behavior in interacting with whites.

Though the repulsive object is not immediately tied to Sethe and Beloved, it is nonetheless against the backdrop of their interactions that Denver has a chance to observe it. It therefore keeps the notion of value before us and prompts, at this position in the story, our consideration of whether or not Sethe has become the wide-eyed, gaping servant willing to suffer any humiliation at Beloved's hands. Are her actions with Beloved mirrored in the subservience of the object Denver sees? Has Sethe, in spite of fighting so valiantly to escape from slavery, allowed her own value to slip until she becomes the "nigger-slave" to Beloved's "masterful," authoritative presence? The coinage of exchange, the dynamics of value have now come to undermine the mother/daughter relationship that Sethe sought so desperately to release from the system of bartering with human lives.

Like an insatiable, exacting slave master who feels *entitled* to service, Beloved never gets enough of anything; all of Sethe's efforts must be exerted for her pleasure.

> Anything she wanted she got, and when Sethe ran out of things to give her, Beloved invented desire. . . . She took the best of everything—first. The best chair, the biggest piece, the prettiest plate, the brightest ribbon for her hair . . . When once or twice Sethe tried to assert herself—be the unquestioned mother whose word was law and who knew what was best—Beloved slammed things, wiped the table clean of plates, threw salt on the floor, broke a windowpane.

Beloved's power resides in Sethe's willingness to please; though it is based in guilt, its surface manifestation is no different from that of the acquiescent slave who believes that, other possibilities notwithstanding, his destiny resides with his master, and he is just as willing to serve as the stereotypical Sambo suggests. Sethe, too, has learned this relationship in slavery even if she has not previously been called upon to display that knowledge.

This objectification of the relationship between Sethe and Beloved clarifies for Denver toward whom her sympathies should be directed. Though she may have wished fervently for Beloved's presence, any power strong enough to reduce her mother to such obsequiousness does not need further assistance from her. For as certainly as the object is cast in its kneeling and serving position, just as certainly something or someone has conceptualized it as such and reduced it to that status. Indeed, it is appropriate in this analysis that the creator of the object is not visible, for it ties in nicely with Beloved's questionable origins and make-up. The Sambo, then, further serves to strengthen Denver's realization that she is the only member of the trio detached enough from the situation to do anything about it.

The theme of payment connected to the Sambo harks back to an earlier observation Denver has made of what she owes for the difficulty of her birth. She especially savors the story when she is relating it to Beloved.

> Denver stopped and sighed. This was the part of the story she loved. She was coming to it now, and she loved it because it was all about herself; but she hated it too because it made her feel like a bill was owing somewhere and she, Denver, had to pay it. But who she owed or what to pay it with eluded her.

Unconsciously, Denver has adopted the measures she has heard her mother use to define relationships during slavery; even as Sethe holds the crying Denver in her arms shortly after Paul D's arrival, she asserts: "No more running—from nothing. I will never run from another thing on this earth. I took one journey and I paid for the ticket, but let me tell you something, Paul D Garner: it cost too much! Do you hear me? It cost too much." Certainly we can tie references to the cost of human bodies to the usual colloquial expressions of benefit received to energy exerted, but the images nonetheless, in this context, also connect the value relationships directly to those from which the characters have recently escaped. By venturing out to ask help from the neighbors, Denver is "buying her mother's freedom," releasing her from slavery, in ways comparable to those in which Halle "paid for" Baby Suggs; Denver is offering up her labor, her "gift" to misery, just as her father has done earlier.

In describing physical features, Morrison uses the nickel as her monetary frame of reference. At Lady Jones's house on her first solo outing in many years, Denver reveals such innocence that Lady Jones perceives her eyes as "nickel-round," reflective of the child-like state in which the sheltered Denver has remained. Connotations of the wide-eyed, frightened slave and the buck-eyed minstrel also come to mind, for eyes have been one of the central focal points of stereotyping black people throughout their history in America (as they—and the mouth—are in the image in the Bodwin kitchen). Denver has attended Lady Jones' school briefly with "a beautiful boy as smart as she was with a birthmark like a nickel on his cheek." The latter image almost literally evokes the notion of branding slaves; the suggestion of a coin undermines these symbolic acts of value and ownership and goes directly to the foundation of the system: economics.

Ultimately, these monetary images succeed in sending mixed messages about how well the characters in *Beloved* have succeeded in transcending slavery. If black people are indeed free of slavery, then why burden them with evocations of that condition?[4] If they indeed have a superior morality (as Stamp Paid implies when he observes about white people—"What *are* these people?" and as Baby Suggs implies when she asserts "There is no bad luck in the world but whitefolks"), then why is it so confused? But perhaps that is precisely the point. Perhaps Morrison once again makes clear the futility of trying to find any absolutes in such a distorted, complex world. I would maintain, however, that it is necessary to have some stable point of reference—even when values are not absolute. There must be something to balance the horror of slavery; otherwise, why would slaves risk so much to be free? If the coinage imagery sends mixed messages, then perhaps Morrison's overall message about slavery and black people's transcendence of it is itself ambivalent.

Or perhaps she is redirecting the imagery to comment on the distorted relationships that exist in the novel. The possession theme usually associated with slavery is certainly relevant in a discussion of the interactions of Sethe, Beloved, and Denver. All of the women emphasize possession-ownership over love. Denver asserts her claim to Beloved after Beloved almost chokes Sethe to death in Baby Suggs's Clearing: "Whatever her power and however she used it, Beloved was *hers*. Sethe asserts her claim to her children by gathering them all together in an effort to save them from Schoolteacher. Beloved asserts her claim to Sethe by virtue of having been killed. And they all assert their claims to each other in the litany of passages that reverberate with ownership.

Is ownership, ostensibly with love as its basis, any different from ownership by designation as chattel? Or are these women locked in a duel that is potentially more destructive than slavery? Sethe has exhibited almost superhuman qualities in escaping from slavery in her pregnant condition. She has also shown uncommon self-possession during slavery, when she witnessed the lynching of her mother, the lynching of Paul F, and numerous other atrocities. None of these incidents has brought on insanity. Yet she borders on that state under Beloved's demands. She has remained a functional human being through all her trials and tribulations, yet she becomes dysfunctional upon Beloved's arrival. Is her love, as Paul D asserts, "too thick"? Can Sethe's and Beloved's perceptions of mother love or sister love, as they are manifested here, be put on the same par of anathema with slavery? In carving out a definition of motherhood in a world where she had no models for that status, in shaping a concept of love from a void, Sethe has erred on the side of excess, a destructive excess that inadvertently gives primacy to the past and death rather than to life and the future.

How can these women so locked in the past find a road to the future? The ownership-subservience tied to the coinage imagery occurs at important decision-making points in the novel, where characters have the option of moving forward to the future or returning to the past. All of these points presumably occur where human interaction is voluntary rather than forced, yet the characters frequently continue the forced interactions of previous conditions. Thus the question becomes one of how to confront the past, make one's peace with it, and move on into the future.

From this perspective, then, the coinage image is less about slavery than about the *price* of living. "How much is a nigger supposed to take?" Paul D asks Stamp Paid, who replies, "All he can. . . . All he can." Taking all one can becomes almost biblical, because the assumption is that there is a *manageable* limit, no matter how painful, to the atrocities of life ("Take your burdens to the Lord and leave them there." "Jesus knows just how much we can bear."). Baby Suggs reached hers and was broken, but the new generation of younger, freed slaves dares not give up. Somehow, one finds the strength to continue. Insanity is not a viable option because it is finally an escape, just as Paul D giving up on Sethe would be, or as Sethe giving up on herself and "doing a Baby Suggs" would be.

The philosophy Morrison develops here is that the price of human existence cannot be placated through escapism—not that of Sethe killing her child, or of Baby Suggs willing herself to death, or any other form. Unquestionably slavery was horrible, but no horror can outweigh the gift of life. Morrison's assertion that killing Beloved was the right thing to do, but that Sethe didn't have the right to do it seems to support this idea; given the moment in slavery and the moment in Sethe's anxious existence, only that solution seemed possible for her, yet if she does not have the right to kill Beloved, then some other option must have been available (a return to slavery for a later escape attempt? Killing School-teacher instead of her child and suffering that consequence?). Even with Beloved's death, Sethe's safety and that of her children is not guaranteed. It is only what Schoolteacher perceives as the sheer atrocity of her act that makes him turn and go (and perhaps shatters his theories of the human and animal divisions he has made); he could still remand the other children to slavery, take them back to Kentucky, find a nanny for them, and either raise them to work on Sweet Home or sell them for a profit.

Making another human being one's own "best thing," then, is ultimately to devolve into a condition worse than slavery and into a transference of devotion from the source of life to its image. Such a transference can only lead to warping distortions, not to freedom. Human freedom, finally, is not about ownership or possession; it is about responsibility, caretaking, and the grace beyond imagining that Baby Suggs eliminated from her vision.

Notes

1. I am grateful to Michelle Cliff for her insightful reading of an earlier version of this paper. Her incisive comments helped me to sharpen and clarify several key points in the discussion.
2. Of course the difficulty here is that Stamp Paid has caused Paul D's distress by telling him about Sethe. His motivation is unclear, but perhaps he had concluded that knowledge, no matter the pain it caused, was preferable to ignorance. Perhaps Stamp believes that Paul D must transcend pain just as he and Sethe have done, and keep on loving the object of the pain.
3. Later in this scene, Sethe and Paul D walk through a snowstorm where the flakes are "fat enough and heavy enough to crash like nickels on stone."
4. Certainly the novel is about reconciling oneself to the past, but the haunting in these sometimes seemingly innocuous ways raises more issues than it resolves.

◆◆◆◆◆◆◆◆◆◆◆◆◆◆

"Circling the Subject": History and Narrative in *Beloved*[1]

VALERIE SMITH

These undecipherable markings on the captive body render a kind of hieroglyphics of the flesh whose severe disjunctures come to be hidden to the cultural seeing by skin color. We might well ask if this phenomenon of marking and branding actually "transfers" from one generation to another, finding its various *symbolic substitutions* in an efficacy of meanings that repeat the initiating moments?[2]

Physical pain has no voice, but when it at last finds a voice, it begins to tell a story.[3]

In a very real sense, a full century or so "after the fact," "slavery" is *primarily* discursive, as we search vainly for a point of absolute and indisputable origin, for a moment of plenitude that would restore us to the real, rich "thing" itself before discourse touched it.[4]

I

Charles B. Dew remarks upon the popularity of slavery as a topic of historical research when he writes: "Slavery is an area of southern historical scholarship that seems to be in a perpetual state of reinterpretation and renewal."[5] This observation holds true as well for black fiction writers and Afro-Americanist literary critics in the late twentieth century, as Deborah McDowell, Arnold Rampersad, and Hazel Carby, among others, have noted. During the past twenty years or so a significant number of Afro-American fiction writers have written novels that go back to and revise the story of slavery. Critics of Afro-American literature, almost without exception, begin accounts of the Afro-American literary tradition with the slave narratives. In her essay entitled "Ideologies of Black Folk: The Historical Novel of Slavery," Carby suggests that the writers' and critics' preoccupation with slavery reflects an impulse to romanticize the folk presence in Afro-American culture.[6] Her point is, however, more an observation about historiography—the uses to which the texts of slavery have been put—than it is about the texts themselves.

I would suggest that slavery as a subject continues to hold a particular fascination at least in part because it provides the ground upon which writers of critical and imaginative literature alike may investigate an array of issues that are pressing in contemporary culture. For instance, retelling the story of slavery has allowed contemporary fiction writers such as David Bradley and Charles Johnson to explore the relationship between the commodification of black physical labor in the antebellum period and the commodification of black creative and intellectual labor in the late twentieth century. In their retellings of slavery, Bradley and Johnson, as well as Octavia Butler, Sherley Anne Williams, Gayl Jones and Toni Morrison, all consider the construction of black male and female gender roles and sexuality, and the relationship between literature and history. In addition, these authors' investigations of slavery engage questions about the nature of representation.

It is a truism of structuralist and post-structuralist discourse that experience is an effect of representation, not its unproblematic referent—that representation, in other words, is inescapable. We are never more fully aware of this fact than when issues of slavery or other experiences of suffering are raised. For if we acknowledge the inaccessibility of experience except through representation, then we must admit that our best-intended attempts to understand another's (indeed our own) experience of suffering are always finally about language or other signifying systems. To recognize this then prompts its own series of questions and considerations. We begin to ask how to articulate the relationship between "experience" and representations of that "experience." If experience cannot help but be mediated by narrative, then we begin to ask about the politics of narrative interventions. And perhaps most insistently, we ask about the status of actual bodies in the discourse around human suffering.

Although at one level the texts and the institution of slavery seem especially compatible with the activity and concerns of contemporary critical discourse—raising issues of gender, commodification, sexuality and representation—at another level they seem to *challenge* some of the fundamental assumptions of post-structuralism. To take but one example, the philosophical denial of slave subjectivity may seem properly deconstructive, but the political and economic denial of the identities of slaves as a group led to disenfranchised and broken black bodies. Likewise, to acknowledge the discursive quality of slavery, as I do here, may seem to lead inevitably to the denial of the existence of "real" slaves. However, politically and culturally I cannot renounce the existence of these real bodies even if they are knowable only through the medium of signifying systems. So I admit up front that in this paper I have been unable to resolve the apparent contradiction between my belief in the inescapability of representation and my belief in the existence of real slaves. So long as real people continue to suffer, it seems to me that we need to find ways of talking about that suffering that acknowledge this paradox.

Recent scholarship on the texts of slavery—for example, McDowell's "Negotiating between Tenses: Witnessing Slavery after Freedom— *Dessa Rose*"; Spillers's "Changing the Letter: The Yokes, The Jokes of Discourse, or Mrs. Stowe, Mr. Reed"; David Van Leer's "Reading Slavery: The Anxiety of Ethnicity in Douglass's *Narrative*"; and Karen Sanchez-Eppler's "Writing Slavery, Righting Sex"—elaborates upon the implications of the assumption that although "real-life human beings" existed who were slaves, we only know their experiences, and we only know the institution of slavery, through the mediation of socially constructed signifying systems. Their work thus differs from earlier studies, such as the chapters on slave narratives in Robert Stepto's *From Behind the Veil,* and my own *Self-Discovery and Authority,* and James Olney's article "'I Was Born': Slave Narratives, Their Status as Autobiography and as Literature," that examine the strategies of the narratives but take the reality of the system of slavery as a given.

Contemporary *novels* that revise the story of slavery draw on and participate in the debate around representation and social constructionism in critical discourse, examining self-consciously what it means to write about slavery. I think here, to mention only two examples, of *The Chaneysville Incident,* in which David Bradley explores the ability of a variety of narrative forms to express the complexity of slavery. And I think also of *Dessa Rose,* in which Sherley Anne Williams displays the ways the central character is construed first by others, then by herself. As McDowell forcefully argues, *Dessa Rose* "engages not only details from inherited texts of slavery but also implicitly questions, comments on, agrees with, and challenges many issues at the forefront of the hydra-headed enterprise . . . that we loosely term contemporary critical discourse."[7]

McDowell's assertion implies that contemporary revisions of slavery by Afro-American writers are informed by developments in literary criticism and theory—that critics and fiction writers participate in a joint enterprise. The inseparability of issues of representation from the very conception of slavery itself is emphasized all the more dramatically in the work of Van Leer and Sanchez-Eppler, who consider ways in which the antebellum narrators themselves inscribe the complexity of representation. Van Leer examines Douglass's positioning of himself and his white readership within the 1845 *Narrative* in order to reveal his own (that is, Douglass's) subtle understanding of the political, and finally epistemological, problems of the slave narrative as a mode of communication. And by exploring Harriet Jacobs's considerations of the problems associated with the telling of the female slave's sexual experience, Sanchez-Eppler argues that *Incidents in the Life of a Slave Girl* is "as much about the act of writing as it is about the 'incidents' themselves."[8]

Toni Morrison's much-acclaimed, much-debated novel *Beloved,* published in 1987, participates in the ongoing discourse among historians,

critics, and other fiction writers that revises and reassesses th
of slavery both to the past and in the present. As is the case with
other contemporary novels and in a range of recent critical discu
Morrison's novel explores the implications of representing slavery
for the former slaves themselves as well as for their cultural descend﹍us.
In my remarks today, I want to consider some of the ways in which at
the level of plot Morrison addresses the status of narrative in relation
to the former slaves' own memories of their enslavement. In addition, I
will argue that the strategies of the novel problematize the project of
writing the story of slavery as fully as the plot complicates the characters' own relation to their past.

II

'Here,' [Baby Suggs] said, 'in this here place, we flesh; flesh that weeps,
laughs; flesh that dances on bare feet in grass. Love it. Love it hard. Yonder
they do not love your flesh. They despise it. They don't love your eyes; they'd
just as soon pick em out. No more do they love the skin on your back. Yonder
they flay it. And O my people they do not love your hands. Those they only
use, tie, bind, chop off and leave empty. Love your hands! Love them. Raise
them up and kiss them. Touch others with them, pat them together, stroke
them on your face 'cause they don't love that either. *You* got to love it, *you!*
And no, they ain't in love with your mouth. Yonder, out there, they will see
it broken and break it again. What you say out of it they will not heed. What
you scream from it they do not hear. What you put into it to nourish your
body they will snatch away and give you leavins instead. No, they don't love
your mouth. *You* got to love it. This is flesh I'm talking about here. Flesh that
needs to be loved. Feet that need to rest and to dance; backs that need
support; shoulders that need arms, strong arms I'm telling you. And O my
people, out yonder, hear me, they do not love your neck unnoosed and
straight. So love your neck; put a hand on it, grace it, stroke it and hold it
up. And all your inside parts that they'd just as soon slop for hogs, you got
to love them. The dark, dark liver—love it, love it, and the beat and beating
heart, love that too. More than eyes or feet. More than lungs that have yet
to draw free air. More than your life-holding womb and your life-giving private
parts, hear me now, love your heart. For this is the prize.[9]

Set in Cincinnati in 1873, eight years after the end of the Civil War,
Beloved is nevertheless a novel about slavery. The characters have been
so profoundly affected by the experience of slavery that time cannot
separate them from its horrors or undo its effects. Indeed, by setting
the novel during Reconstruction Morrison invokes the inescapability of
slavery, for the very name of the period calls to mind the havoc and
destruction wrought during the antebellum and war years.

Sethe, the central character of the novel, and Paul D, her friend from
the Sweet Home plantation who comes to live with her and her daughter
Denver shortly after the novel opens, are both haunted by memories of
slavery that they seek to avoid. Sethe tries to block out the experience
of having her breast milk stolen and being beaten by Schoolteacher's

nephew, of killing her daughter to prevent her from being taken back into slavery, and of exchanging sex for the engraving on that same daughter's tombstone. Paul D wants desperately to forget having seen the physical and psychological destruction of his fellow Sweet Home men; having been forced to wear a bit; and having endured the hardships of the chain gang.

The former slaves' desire for forgetfulness notwithstanding, the past will not be kept at bay. The slightest sensation triggers memories that overwhelm. The novel problematizes the characters' adversarial relationship to their past, explores what it means for them to confront the history of their suffering, and considers, additionally, what it means to move beyond that past. Perhaps most importantly, it considers the place of black bodies in the construction of narratives of slavery.

Increasingly, as I reread the novel, I am compelled by the centrality to the text of the passage spoken by Baby Suggs that serves as the epigraph to this section. Baby Suggs, Sethe's mother-in-law, early in her life in freedom, becomes a preacher—unchurched, uncalled, unrobed, and unanointed—one who brings a message of salvation to the black fugitive and former slaves outside Cincinnati. Her message, which transforms the Christian message of self-abnegation and deliverance after death, is meant to heal the broken and suffering bodies of those who endured slavery. As she herself, with legs, back, head, eyes, hands, kidneys, womb and tongue busted by slavery has resolved to use her heart in the service of her vast congregation, she preaches the word to restore the bodies of those battered by their enslavement.

Readers may be inclined to read her use of "heart" metaphorically, to assume that by "heart" she means compassion, generosity of spirit. But in the context of this litany of broken body parts, one is reminded that the word "heart" points to an organ as well as to an emotional capacity. In this context it becomes more difficult to make the familiar move from the corporeal referent to the metaphysical: for this erasure of the corporeal might be read as analogous to the expendability of black bodies under slavery.

The instability of meanings that attaches to the word "heart" interrogates the distinction between body and spirit. It typifies the suspicion of dichotomies that Deborah McDowell identifies in *Sula* in her essay entitled "'The Self and the Other': Reading Toni Morrison's *Sula* and the Black Female Text."[10] Moreover, this play with referentiality points to a strategy employed throughout the novel, a strategy about which I will say more shortly. The point I wish to emphasize here, however, is that the reclamation, indeed sanctification of the body displayed in Baby Suggs's speech is especially important within a text that revises slavery. These gestures respond to a hierarchical system of racial differentiation in which blacks are associated with bodily labor, whites with spiritual and intellectual gifts. By questioning the dichotomy between spirit and flesh, the novel interrogates as well the very basis of the system of slavery.

The focus on bodies in the novel is certainly clear in the predominance of scenes of physical suffering and scarred bodies. The focus on bodies is evident also in the fact that the characters experience the past sensorily. Although Sethe tries to forget her enslavement, sensory perceptions set flashbacks in motion: when washing stinging chamomile sap off her legs, something,

> The plash of water, the sight of her shoes and stockings awry on the path where she had flung them; or Here Boy lapping in the puddle near her feet, and suddenly there was Sweet Home rolling, rolling, rolling out before her eyes, and although there was not a leaf on that farm that did not want her to scream, it rolled itself out before her in shameless beauty.

Here the sensations of the present trigger visions of the past.

Slaves in the novel are shown to withstand oppression at a number of levels. Paul D feels a kind of existential humiliation when he realizes that he was only a Sweet Home man because of the whims of his master and that the barnyard rooster possessed greater autonomy than he himself did. Sethe felt profoundly insulted by Schoolteacher's research on her own and her fellow slaves' racial characteristics. Sethe and Baby Suggs are acutely sensitive to the power that slavery has over the bonds between kin. Yet despite the recognition of these sorts of philosophical and political and emotional deprivations, *Beloved* seems especially engaged with the havoc wrought upon black bodies under slavery: the circular scar under Sethe's mother's breast and the bit in her mouth; the bit in Paul D's mouth; Sethe's stolen breast milk and flowering back; Sixo's roasting body, to name but a few.

Not only do Sethe's memories of slavery come to her sensorily, through her body, but perhaps more obviously, she wears on her body the signs of her greatest ordeal at the Sweet Home plantation. The story of the brutal handling she endured under slavery—the stealing of her breast milk and the beating that ensued—is encoded in the scars on her back. Their symbolic power is evident in the number of times that others attempt to read them. Amy Denver names the scars a chokecherry tree in bloom. For Baby Suggs, the imprint from Sethe's back on the sheets looks like roses of blood. And Paul D, who cannot read the words of the newspaper story about Sethe's act of infanticide, reads her back as a piece of sculpture: "the decorative work of an ironsmith too passionate for display." Paul D further reads the suffering on her body with his own: "He rubbed his cheek on her back and learned that way her sorrow, the roots of it; its wide trunk and intricate branches. . . . [He] would tolerate no peace until he had touched every ridge and leaf of it with his mouth, none of which Sethe could feel because her back skin had been dead for years."

Moreover, Paul D registers, in an incessant trembling, the humiliation he felt before Brother, the rooster, and the indignity of being forced to wear leg irons and handcuffs. No one knew he was trembling, the narrator tells us, "because it began inside":

> A flutter of a kind, in the chest, then the shoulder blades. It felt like rippling— gentle at first and then wild. As though the further south they led him the more his blood, frozen like an ice pond for twenty years, began thawing, breaking into pieces that, once melted, had no choice but to swirl and eddy. Sometimes it was in his leg. Then again it moved to the base of his spine. By the time they unhitched him from the wagon and he saw nothing but dogs and two shacks in a world of sizzling grass, the roiling blood was shaking him to and fro.

To the extent that characters feel suffering through their bodies they are healed, physically and psychically, through the body as well. As Marianne Hirsch has noted, Sethe is three times cured by healing hands: first Amy Denver's, then Baby Suggs's, and finally Paul D's. When Baby Suggs is finally free, the change in her status is recorded in terms of physical sensations; she claims ownership of her hands and heart.

Indeed, one might read Beloved's sexual relations with Paul D as a bodily cure. Paul D refuses to speak too fully the pain of his suffering in slavery. This refusal reflects his sense that his secrets are located in what remains of his heart: "in that tobacco tin buried in his chest where a red heart used to be. Its lid rusted shut." However, when Beloved, ghost made flesh, compels him to have sexual relations with her—in other words, to encounter her physically—she tells him, in language that recalls Baby Suggs' earlier speech, 'to touch her on the inside part." The description of this scene suggests that the act of intercourse with Beloved restores Paul D to himself, restores his heart to him:

> She moved closer with a footfall he didn't hear and he didn't hear the whisper that the flakes of rust made either as they fell away from the seams of his tobacco tin. So when the lid gave he didn't know it. What he knew was that when he reached the inside part he was saying, 'Red heart. Red heart,' over and over again.

In a variety of ways, then, Morrison calls attention to the suffering that bodies endured under slavery. The project of the novel, much like Baby Suggs's project, seems to be to reclaim those bodies, to find a way to tell the story of the slave body in pain.

III

Of the opening of *Beloved*, Toni Morrison has written:

The reader is snatched, yanked, thrown into an environment completely foreign, and I want it as the first stroke of the shared experience that might be
possible between the reader and the novel's population. Snatched just as the
slaves were from one place to another, from any place to another, without
preparation and without defense. No lobby, no door, no entrance—a gang-
plank, perhaps (but a very short one). And the house into which this
snatching—this kidnapping—propels one, changes from spiteful to loud to
quiet, as the sounds in the body of the ship itself may have changed.[11]

In this passage Morrison indicates a desire to make readers of *Beloved* self-conscious about the process of reading the novel, so that our
experience of the text becomes an analogy for the slaves' sense of dislocation. I would suggest that the novel turns on an additional analogy as
well. Just as the characters seek out ways of telling the experience of
their suffering, so too is the novel involved in the project of reclaiming
or recovering those bodies in narrative for posterity.

Of course, however evocatively Morrison renders human suffering in
Beloved, finally the reader experiences only narrative representations of
human suffering and pain. To speak what is necessarily and essentially
and inescapably unspoken is not to speak the unspoken; it is rather only
to speak a narrative or speakable version of that event or thing. As
David Van Leer argues in his analysis of Frederick Douglass's *Narrative*,
the act of telling the story of suffering, even one's own, requires one to
position oneself outside that experience of suffering. Douglass and his
fellow slaves endure enslavement at one register. In order to narrate
that suffering, however, Douglass has to locate himself as a voyeur of
that experience.

Beloved, like any account of suffering and pain, thus occupies a paradoxical position—in the very process of calling attention to the absence
of human bodies from the discourse of slavery, it too necessarily circles
the subject. In at least two places, the novel marks the gap between
representation and the actual slaves' suffering. Early in the novel, for
instance, in a state of willed forgetfulness, Sethe is described running
across a field. What she is trying to forget possesses for her the status
of the unspeakable—it is clearly prelinguistic. Yet the narrator inter-
venes here and names what Sethe cannot:

She might be hurrying across a field, running practically, to get to the pump
quickly and rinse the chamomile sap from her legs. Nothing else would be on
her mind. The picture of the men coming to nurse her was as lifeless as the
nerves in her back where the skin buckled like a washboard. Nor was there
the faintest scent of ink or the cherry gum and oak bark from which it was
made. Nothing.

en the "Nothing" in Sethe's mind and the picture and
rrator names identifies the space between "experience"
tervention.

f narrative as intervention is evident also when Sethe
y of the acts of infanticide her own mother performed.
Here, too, the body is implicated in the process of memory: the smell of
burning hair is partly responsible for setting this recollection in motion;
the rapid, repeated motion of folding laundry eases and accompanies the
reflection.

What she recalls, what the narrator calls "Something privately
shameful that had seeped into a slit in her mind right behind the slap on
her face and the circled cross," is an explanation told to her in a language
she had long forgotten. What she recalls, the narrator remarks, is meaning picked out of a code she no longer understood. The narrator conveys
that message to the reader in language we can understand. That very
accomplishment, however, again emphasizes the inability of the text to
convey Sethe's experience of what can no longer be spoken.

These points in the novel display a striking self-reflexivity, calling
attention as they do to the inexpressibility of what the narrative can only
"circle." To the extent that the novel undertakes a project so elusive—
representing the body, speaking the unspoken—I would suggest that its
dominant mode of articulation is analogical. Unable to resolve the paradox of narrating the body, uttering the unutterable, it's as if the novel
replicates that paradox. For it sets up and explodes an array of dichotomies: those between life and afterlife, living and dead, oral and written,
self and other, and so on.

The figure of Beloved herself most obviously calls into question the
relationship between narrative and the body. As a ghost made flesh, she
is literally the story of the past embodied. Sethe and Denver and Paul
D therefore encounter not only the story of her sorrow and theirs; indeed, they encounter its incarnation. Beloved's presence allows the generally reticent Sethe to tell stories from her past. Once Sethe realizes
that the stranger called Beloved and her baby Beloved are one and the
same, she gives herself over fully to the past, and to Beloved's demand
for comfort and curing. Indeed, so complete are her attempts to make
things right with Beloved that she is almost consumed by her. Without
Denver's and her neighbors' and Paul D's interventions pulling her back
into the present, she would have been doomed to annihilation.

The very name "Beloved" functions as a site where a number of oppositions are interrogated. Simultaneously adjective and noun, the world
problematizes the distinction between the characteristics of a thing and
the thing itself. As Gwen Bergner has noted, the word "beloved" "is an
adjective before it is a noun. As the title of this book its sense as modifier
calls attention, before the first sentence, to an absence—the absence of
the thing it modifies."

Bergner further remarks that the word "beloved" names not only the girl baby returned; in the funeral service the word addresses the mourners of the dead. She writes, "the address 'Beloved,' in effect, shifts back again away from the child and the memory of events past to the present, people and time."

To Bergner's comments I would add that the word "Beloved" calls attention to the space between written and oral, for until we as readers know the context from which her name comes, we do not know even how to speak that name: Beloved or Belovéd. In the terms the novel offers, Beloved might be understood to exemplify what Sethe calls rememory—something that is gone yet remains. Recalling both remember and memory, "rememory" is both verb and noun; it names simultaneously the process of remembering and the thing remembered.

The reader confronts the instability, indeed the inadequacy, of language perhaps most powerfully in the passages of interior monologue told from Sethe's, Denver's, and Beloved's points of view. After telling Paul D about Sethe's murder of her daughter, Stamp Paid, the man who conveyed the family to freedom, is turned away from Sethe's house, 124 Bluestone Road, by the "undecipherable language . . . of the black and angry dead." The narrator tells us that mixed in with those voices were the thoughts of the women of 124—"unspeakable thoughts, unspoken." In the four sections that follow, we read the unspeakable and unspoken thoughts of Sethe, Denver, and Beloved, first separately, then interwoven. Here from Sethe's perspective are her memories of killing her daughter, of being beaten, of being abandoned by her mother. Largely addressed to Beloved, Sethe's words convey recollections she could never utter to another. Likewise, in her section, Denver expresses her fear of her mother and her yearning to be rescued by her father, anxieties that, for the most part, had been hidden previously in the novel.

Beloved's is, however, the most riveting and most obscure of the monologues. For here is represented the preconscious subjectivity of a victim of infanticide. The words that convey the recollections and desires of someone who is at once in time and out of time, alive and dead, are richly allusive and defy interpretation.

The linguistic units in this section, be they sentences, phrases, or single words, are separated by spaces, not by marks of punctuation. Only the first person pronoun and the first letter in each paragraph are capitalized. The effect of this arrangement is, I think, to place all the moments of Beloved's sensation and recollection in a continuous and eternal present.

From the grave, Beloved yearns to be reunited with her mother: "her face is my own and I want to be there in the place where her face is and to be looking at it too." But in addition to her feelings and desires from the grave, Beloved seems also to have become one, in death, with the black and angry dead who suffered through the Middle Passage: "In the beginning the women are away from the men and the men are away from the women   storms rock us and mix the men into the women and the women into the men." In the body of Beloved, then, individual and collective pasts and memories seem to have become united and inseparable. Indeed, as Marilyn Mobley has written in her forthcoming essay, "A Different Remembering: Memory, History and Meaning in Toni Morrison's *Beloved*," the language of the passage suggests "not only the seamlessness of time, but also the inextricability of the past and present, of ancestors and their progeny."

One is tempted in reading her monologue to try to seek out referents, to figure out what, for example, "the hot thing" is that recurs throughout the section, why white men are called "the men without skin," what are "the sweet rocks" the men without skin bring to the black and angry dead. However, this section of the novel resists explication. It prompts, rather, the recognition that what is essentially and effectively unspoken can never be conveyed and comprehended linguistically.

The final portion of the novel similarly calls attention to the inexpressibility of its subject. One might try to figure out the difference between the loneliness that rocks and the loneliness that roams, but what seems even more striking are the ways in which the passage comes unwritten even as it is being written. For instance, in the second paragraph, the narrator sets up a series of oppositions between Beloved and her neighbors and relatives:

> Everybody knew what she was called, but nobody anywhere knew her name. Disremembered and unaccounted for, she cannot be lost because no one is looking for her, and even if they were, how can they call her if they don't know her name? Although she has claim, she is not claimed. In the place where long grass opens, the girl who waited to be loved and cry shame erupts into her separate parts, to make it easy for the chewing laughter to swallow her all away.

When, in this passage, Morrison distinguishes between knowing what someone was called and knowing his or her name, she underscores the inadequacy of the available language. Naming is not necessarily either apostrophic or evocative.

The neologism "disremembered," which combines "dismember" and "remember," recalls the earlier consideration of the relationship between the process or act of memory and the thing remembered. Beloved's existence is predicated upon a communal memory of her; she dissolves when they forget and swallow her all away. And yet in her very dissolution and absence, in the communal denial of her existence, she remains present. The narrator here again locates her in a prelinguistic moment. Dependent upon the recognition of others, Beloved exists nevertheless and as well in the spaces prior to their acknowledgment of her. To paraphrase the narrator, although they have forgotten her, she may be found in the rustle of a skirt that hushes when they wake, in the knuckle that brushes against a sleeper's cheek that seems to belong to the sleeper, in the subtle shifts of a photographic image.

IV

Beloved is a novel of such extraordinary plenitude that new meanings and ways of reading emerge whenever one repositions oneself as critic. One might say of the text what the narrator says of the photograph of a close friend or relative: looked at too long, it shifts, and something else moves there. The novel sustains a broad range of interpretations. I have clearly been compelled by the gestures it makes toward the unspeakable. Much might also be said of its relation to mythic subtexts. It supports discussions of its revisions of slave narratives and relation to historical discourse, as Marilyn Mobley eloquently argues. Or it might be read as a text that examines the construction and expression of maternal subjectivity, as Marianne Hirsch persuasively shows.

And yet my sense is that the novel's reliance on paradox and indeterminacy finally undermines the authority of any single reading or interpretive posture. I want to conclude with a brief assessment of the implications of this assumption.

I began with the rather cynical assertion that critics and novelists return to the story of slavery at the present time because it provides a context within which we may consider issues that resonate in contemporary critical discourse. That is, of course, only partly the reason for our need to reassess and revise. The story of slavery compels as well because it is seen by many as an originary moment for Afro-American culture in the twentieth century. As Hortense Spillers suggests, the markings on the slave body may well transfer symbolically from one generation to the next, in ways that repeat the initiating moments. To the extent that these hieroglyphic scars remain written on black bodies and black consciousness even to the present day, our racial and national survival may depend ultimately on our learning to read that scarring.

In the final section of *Beloved*, the sentence "It was not a story to pass on" is repeated twice, once with the substitution of "This" for "It." This refrain refers at least in part to the complicated, interwoven narratives of suffering contained within the text, re-emphasizing the unspeakability of the subject. It might point also to the novel itself, naming the difficulties that attend the project of writing a novel about slavery. As the "this" and "it" remain ambiguous, so too does the meaning of the phrase "to pass on." "To pass on" might mean either to transmit or to overlook. This is not a story either to retell or to fail to retell.

The multiple meanings of the phrase "to pass on," suggesting that this is a story that cannot be told yet must be told, encapsulate the dilemma posed by this kind of reading. I appear to have argued that the novel is about both the inaccessibility of the suffering body to narrative and about the inescapability of representation. Nevertheless, I do not want to conclude with the implication that since we can never know slavery, all efforts to represent it will remain fruitless. For to return to my opening formulation, the system of slavery may have been culturally constructed, and we may only know the experiences of slaves through signifying systems, but real human beings did suffer the whipping and chaining, and torture, and rape and murder. Moreover, the same people, like Schoolmaster, who controlled the representations of slaves—the marks on the page—were implicated in marking their bodies. The dichotomization of culture and experience that led to the split between narrative and the body undergird as well systems of oppression that render some bodies more expendable than others.

My sense is that by representing the inaccessibility of the suffering of former slaves, Morrison reveals the limits of hegemonic, authoritarian systems of knowledge. The novel challenges us to use our interpretive skills, but finally turns them back upon themselves. By representing the inexpressibility of its subject, the novel asserts and reasserts the subjectivity of the former slaves and the depth of their suffering. The novel reminds us that our critical acumen and narrative capacities notwithstanding, we can never know what they endured. We can never enjoy a complacent understanding of lives lived under slavery. To the extent that *Beloved* returns the slaves to themselves, the novel humbles contemporary readers before the unknown and finally unknowable horrors the slaves endured.

Notes

1. I am grateful to many people for sharing their ideas and writing with me during the time that I have been working on this essay. The students in my graduate and undergraduate seminars on "Slavery and Recent Afro-American Literature" at Princeton University displayed an extraordinary commitment to the project of interpreting the novel. I especially thank Gwen Bergner for permission to quote from her unpublished essay: "." I wish to thank those who attended my seminars on *Beloved* at the Summer Institute sponsored by the Oxford Center for African Studies for a rich and lively set of exchanges about the novel; from that group I am particularly grateful to Jennifer Brodie, Nahum Chandler, Amy Robinson, Jeri Johnson, Gargi Bhattacharyya, and Kate Ward-Perkins. I thank Marilyn Mobley and Karen Sanchez-Eppler for graciously allowing me to read their work. And as always I am grateful to Marianne Hirsch, Gail Reimer, and David Van Leer for letting me read their essays-in-progress and for their willingness to exchange and worry ideas with me.
2. Hortense J. Spillers, "Mama's Baby, Papa's Maybe: An American Grammar Book," *Diacritics* (Summer 1987), 67.

3. Elaine Scarry, *The Body in Pain: The Making and Unmaking of the World* (New York: Oxford University Press), 3.
4. Hortense J. Spillers, "Changing the Letter: The Yokes, the Jokes of Discourse, Or Mrs. Stowe, Mr. Reed," in ed. Deborah E. McDowell and Arnold Rampersad, *Slavery and the Literary Imagination* (Baltimore: The Johns Hopkins University Press, 1989), 29.
5. Charles B. Dew, "The Slavery Experience," in ed. John B. Boles and Evelyn T. Nolen, *Interpreting Southern History: Historiographical Essays in Honor of Sanford W. Higginbotham* (Baton Rouge: Louisiana State Press, 1987), 120.
6. Hazel V. Carby, "Ideologies of Black Folk: The Historical Novel of Slavery," in McDowell and Rampersad, *Slavery and the Literary Imagination*, pp. 125–43.
7. McDowell, "Negotiating Between Tenses," in McDowell and Rampersad, *Slavery and the Literary Imagination*, p. 147.
8. Sanchez-Eppler, p. 17.
9. Toni Morrison, *Beloved* (New York: Alfred A. Knopf, 1987), pp. 88–89.
10. Deborah E. McDowell, "'The Self and the Other': Reading Toni Morrison's *Sula* and the Black Female Text," in ed. Nellie Y. McKay, *Critical Essays on Toni Morrison* (Boston: G. K. Hall & Co., 1988), pp. 77–90.
11. Toni Morrison, "Unspeakable Things Unspoken: The Afro-American Presence in American Literature," *Michigan Quarterly Review* 28 (Winter 1989): 32.

◆◆◆◆◆◆◆◆◆◆◆◆◆◆

A Different Remembering: Memory, History, and Meaning in *Beloved*

MARILYN SANDERS MOBLEY

The slave woman ought not to be judged by the same standards as others.
—Harriet Jacobs, *Incidents in the Life of a Slave Girl*

. . . when we get a little farther away from the conflict, some brave and truth-loving man, with all the facts before him . . . will gather . . . the scattered fragments . . . and give to those who shall come after us an impartial history of this the grandest moral conflict of the century. [For] Truth is patient and time is just.
—Frederick Douglass[1]

Every age re-accentuates in its own way the works of its most immediate past.
—Mikhail Bakhtin, "Discourse in the Novel"

In 1974 Toni Morrison edited an often overlooked publication called *The Black Book*.[2] This collection of memorabilia represents 300 years of black history, and not only records the material conditions of black life from slavery to freedom, but also exhibits the black cultural production that grew out of and in spite of these conditions. Compiled in scrapbook fashion, it contains everything from bills of sale for slaves to jazz and poetry. Through diverse images of black life presented in such items as photos of lynchings, sharecropping families and slave-made quilts, and encoded in excerpts from such sources as slave narratives, folk sayings and black newspapers, *The Black Book* tells a complex story of oppression, resistance and survival. More importantly, it was published at a moment in American history when many feared that the black power movement of the 1960s and early 1970s would be reduced to faddish rhetoric and mere image rather than understood for its cultural and political implications. Morrison herself feared the movement propounded a kind of historical erasure or denial of those aspects of the past which could not be easily assimilated into its rhetorical discourse or into the collective consciousness of black people as a group. She feared, for example, that the rhetoric of the movement, in its desire to create a new version of history that would affirm the African past and the heroic deeds of a few great men, had inadvertently bypassed the equally heroic deeds of ordinary African Americans who had resisted and survived the painful traumas of slavery. In other words, she questioned what she perceived to be a romanticization of both the African past and the American past that threatened to devalue 300 years of black life on American soil before it was fully recorded, examined or understood for its complexity and significance. Thus, *The Black Book* was a literary intervention in the historical dialogue of the period to attest to "black life as lived" experience.[3]

What is particularly pertinent, however, is that in the process of editing *The Black Book*, Morrison discovered the story that would become the basis of her fifth novel, *Beloved*.[4] Indeed, on the tenth page of *The Black Book* is a copy of a news article, "A Visit to the Slave Mother Who Killed Her Child," that documents the historical basis for what would later become Morrison's most challenging fictional project.[5] Although the relevance of history informs all of her novels from *The Bluest Eye* to *Tar Baby*, it is in *Beloved* that history simultaneously becomes both theme and narrative process.[6] In other words, *Beloved* dramatizes the complex relationship between history and memory by shifting from lived experience as documented in *The Black Book* to remembered experience as represented in the novel.

Yet, the intertextual relationship between *The Black Book* and *Beloved* is not the only one that can illuminate the compelling intricacies of this novel. Several reviewers place it in the American literary tradition with intertextual connections to Harriet Beecher Stowe's *Uncle Tom's Cabin* (1852). Others compare Morrison's narrative strategies to those of William Faulkner, who incidentally, along with Virginia Woolf, was the subject of her master's thesis. Certainly, the thematics of guilt and the complex fragmentation of time that shape Morrison's fiction are inherent in Faulkner's writing, as well as in the work of many other white authors of the American literary tradition. Yet, Morrison's own expressed suspicions of critical efforts to place her in a white literary tradition are instructive. She explains:

> Most criticism . . . justifies itself by identifying black writers with some already accepted white writer . . . I find such criticism dishonest because it never goes into the work on its own terms. It comes from some other place and finds content outside of the work and wholly irrelevant to it to support the work . . . It's merely trying to place the book into an already established literary tradition.[7]

With Morrison's own comments in mind, I would like to suggest that the intertextual relationship between *Beloved* and the slave narratives—the genre that began the African-American literary tradition in prose—offers significant interpretive possibilities for entering the hermeneutic circle of this novel. More specifically, I would like to argue that Morrison uses the trope of memory to revise the genre of the slave narrative and to thereby make the slave experience it inscribes more accessible to contemporary readers. In other words, she uses memory as the metaphorical sign of the interior life to explore and represent dimensions of slave life that the classic slave narrative omitted. By so doing, she seeks to make slavery accessible to readers for whom slavery is not a memory, but a remote historical fact to be ignored, repressed or forgotten. Thus, just as the slave narratives were a form of narrative intervention designed to disrupt the system of slavery, *Beloved* can be read as a narrative intervention that disrupts the cultural notion that the untold story of the black slave mother is, in the words of the novel, "the past something to leave behind."[8]

One of the first observations often made about the slave narratives is the striking similarities that exist among the hundreds of them that were written. In the "Introduction" to *The Classic Slave Narratives*, Henry Louis Gates, Jr. accounts for this phenomenon by reminding us that "when the ex-slave author decided to write his or her story, he or she did so only after reading and rereading, the telling stories of other slave authors who preceded them."[9] While we cannot know exactly which narratives Morrison read, it is certain that she read widely in the genre and that she is familiar with the two most popular classics—Frederick Douglass's *Narrative* (1845) and Harriet Jacobs's *Incidents in the Life of a Slave Girl* (1861).[10] As prototypal examples of the genre, they adhere to the narrative conventions carefully delineated and described by James Olney. According to him, the vast majority of narratives begin with the three words "I was born" and proceed to provide information about parents, sibling, the cruelty of masters, mistresses and overseers, barriers to literacy, slave auctions, attempts, failures and successes at escaping, name changes, and general reflections on the peculiar institution of slavery.[11] As Valerie Smith points out, however, the important distinction between the narratives of Douglass and Jacobs is that while his narrative not only concerns "the journey from slavery to freedom but also the journey from slavery to manhood," her narrative describes the sexual exploitation that challenged the womanhood of slave women and tells the story of their resistance to that exploitation.[12]

Beloved contains all of these characteristics with several signifying differences. While the classic slave narrative draws on memory as though it is a monologic, mechanical conduit for facts and incidents, Morrison's text foregrounds the dialogic characteristics of memory along with its imaginative capacity to construct and reconstruct the significance of the past. Thus, while the slave narrative characteristically moves in a chronological, linear narrative fashion, *Beloved* meanders through time, sometimes circling back, other times moving vertically, spirally out of time and down in space. Indeed, Morrison's text challenges the Western notion of linear time that informs American history and the slave narratives. It engages the reader not just with the physical, material consequences of slavery, but with the psychological consequences as well. Through the trope of memory, Morrison moves into the psychic consequences of slavery for women, who, by their very existence, were both the means and the source of production. In the words of the text, the slave woman was "property that reproduced itself without cost." Moreover, by exploring this dimension of slavery, Morrison produces a text that is at once very different from and similar to its literary antecedent with its intervention in the cultural, political and social order of black people, in general, and of black women, in particular. What the reader encounters in this text is Morrison as both writer and reader, for inscribed in her writing of the novel is her own "reading"—a revisionary rereading—of the slave's narrative plot of the journey from bondage to freedom. In the process of entering the old text of slavery from a "new critical direction," Morrison discovers what Adrienne Rich refers to as a "whole new psychic geography to be explored," and what Morrison herself identifies as the "interior life of black people under those circumstances."[13] Ultimately, *Beloved* responds to Fredric Jameson's dictum to "always historicize" by illustrating the dynamics of the act of interpretation that memory performs on a regular basis at any given historical moment.[14]

Unlike the slave narratives which sought to be all-inclusive eye-witness accounts of the material conditions of slavery, Morrison's novel exposes the unsaid of the narratives, the psychic subtexts that lie within and beneath the historical facts. In the author's words, she attempts to leave "spaces so the reader can come into it."[15] Critic Steven Mallioux refers to such hermeneutic gaps as places where the text must be "supplemented by its readers before its meaning can be discovered."[16] By examining the use of memory in *Beloved*, we not only can discover to what extent she revises the slave narrative, but we can also explore how her narrative poetics operate through memory and history to create meaning.

The actual story upon which the novel is based is an 1855 newspaper account of a runaway slave from Kentucky named Margaret Garner. When she realizes she is about to be recaptured in accordance with the Fugitive Slave Law, she kills her child rather than allow it to return to a "future of servitude."[17] Indeed, the story itself involves a conflation of past, present and future in a single act. In the novel, Margaret Garner becomes Sethe, a fugitive slave whose killing of her two-year-old daughter, Beloved, haunts her first as a ghost and later as a physical reincarnation. But time is not so much conflated as fragmented in the fictional rendering of the tale. Moreover, the text contains not only Sethe's story or version of the past, but those of her friend and eventual lover, Paul D, her mother-in-law, Baby Suggs, her remaining child, a daughter named Denver, and later, Beloved herself. Each of their fragments amplifies or modifies Sethe's narrative for the reader. In that the fragments constitute voices which speak to and comment on one another, the text illustrates the call and response pattern of the African-American oral tradition.[18]

The setting of the novel is 1873 in Cincinnati, Ohio, where Sethe resides in a small house with her daughter, Denver. Her mother-in-law, Baby Suggs, has recently died and her two sons, Howard and Buglar, have left home, unable to live any longer in a ghost-haunted house with a mother who seems oblivious or indifferent to the disturbing, disruptive presence. Sethe seems locked in memories of her escape from slavery, the failure of her husband, Halle, to show up at the planned time of escape, her murder of her child, and the Kentucky plantation referred to by its benevolent white slave owner as Sweet Home. One of the Sweet Home men, Paul D, inadvertently arrives on her porch after years of wandering locked in his own guilt, alienation and shame from the psychic scars of slavery. They become lovers, but more importantly, his arrival initiates the painful plunge into the past through the sharing of their individual stories, memories and experiences. Unable to tolerate the presence of the ghost, however, he drives it away, only to be driven away himself by his inability to cope with Sethe's obsession with Denver, whom he calls a "room-and-board witch." A bond of affection unites Sethe, Denver and Beloved until Denver realizes that her mother has become oblivious to her and has begun to devote her attention exclusively to Beloved. As she watches her mother deteriorate physically and mentally in the grips of overwhelming guilt and consuming love, Denver realizes she must abandon the security of home to get help for her mother and to rid their lives of Beloved once and for all. With the help of the black community, she eventually rescues her mother and Beloved vanishes.

What this cursory synopsis of the plot cannot account for is the ways in which Sethe modifies, amplifies and subverts her own memory of the murder that serves as the locus of the narrative. In fact, even in freedom, she lives in a kind of psychic bondage to the task of "keeping the past at bay." While she had murdered Beloved to save her from the future, she raises Denver by "keeping her from the past." The two different manifestations of maternal love are just one source of the novel's narrative tension that evolve from Sethe's response to slavery. The more compelling source of tension lies in the complexity Morrison brings to the normal property of literature Frank Kermode refers to as the "secrecy of narrative."[19] While all texts develop to a certain extent by secrecy or by what information they withhold and gradually release to the reader, the text of *Beloved* moves through a series of narrative starts and stops that are complicated by Sethe's desire to forget or "disremember" the past. Thus, at the same time that the reader seeks to know "the how and why" of Sethe's infanticide, Sethe seeks to withhold that information not only from everyone else, but even from herself. Thus, the early sections of the novel reveal the complex ways in which memories of the past disrupt Sethe's concerted attempt to forget.

The first sign of this tension between remembering and forgetting occurs on the second page of the text in a scene where Denver and Sethe attempt to call the ghost forth. When Denver grows impatient with the seeming reluctance of the ghost to make its presence felt, Sethe cautions her by saying "you forgetting how little it is . . . She wasn't even two years old when she died." Denver's expression of surprise that a baby can throw such a "powerful spell" is countered in the following passage:

> "No more powerful than the way I loved her," Sethe answered and there it was again. The welcoming cool of unchiseled headstones; the one she selected to lean against tiptoe, her knees wide open as any grave. Pink as a fingernail it was, and sprinkled with glittering chips . . . Counting on the stillness of her own soul, she had forgotten the other one: the soul of her baby girl.

In this passage we have several things occurring at once. First, Sethe's verbalization of love triggers her memory of selecting a tombstone for the baby she murdered. The phrase "there it was again" signals that this is a memory that recurs and that brings the ambivalent emotions of consolation and anguish. Second, the memory of the tombstone triggers her memory of the shameful circumstances of getting it engraved. In this memory, the reality of gender and oppression converge, for the engraver offers to place seven letters—the name "Beloved"—on the headstone in exchange for sex. She also remembers that for ten more minutes, she could have gotten the word "dearly" added. Thirdly, this memory raises the issue around which the entire novel is constructed and that is the consequences and/or responsibility that she must carry for her actions.

Throughout the novel there are similar passages that signal the narrative tension between remembering and forgetting. At various points in the text, a single phrase, a look or the most trivial incident rivets Sethe's attention to the very details of the past she is least ready to confront. In the words of the text, "she worked hard to remember as close to nothing as was safe." In another place the text refers to the "serious work of beating back the past." Moreover, a mindless task such as folding clothes takes on grave significance, as the following passage suggests: "She had to do something with her hands because she was remembering something she had forgotten she knew. Something privately shameful that had seeped into a slit in her mind." Morrison even includes vernacular versions of words to suggest the slaves' own preoccupation with mnemonic processes. For example, at one point "rememory" is used as a noun, when Sethe refers to what Paul D stirs up with his romantic attention to her. Later, the same word is used as a verb, when Sethe begins to come to terms with the past through her relationship with Beloved. She allows her mind to be "busy with the things she could forget" and thinks to herself: "Thank God I don't have to rememory or say a thing."

vernacular word for forgetting—"disremember"—calls our at-
its binary opposite of remembering.

... Paul D arrives at Sethe's home on 124 Bluestone, Denver seeks
to frighten this unwanted guest away by telling him they have a "lonely
and rebuked" ghost on the premises. The obsolete meaning of rebuked—
repressed—not only suggests that the ghost represents repressed memory, but that, as with anything that is repressed, it eventually resurfaces
or returns in one form or another. Paul D's arrival is a return of sorts
in that he is reunited with Sethe, his friend from Mr. Garner's Sweet
Home plantation. His presence signals an opportunity to share both the
positive and negative memories of life there. On one hand, he and Sethe
talk fondly of the "headless bride back behind Sweet Home" and thus
share a harmless ghost story of a haunted house. On the other hand,
when they remember Sweet Home as a place, they regard it with ambivalence and admit that "it wasn't sweet and it sure wasn't home."
Sethe warns against a total dismissal of it, however, by saying: "But it's
where we were [and it] comes back whether we want it to or not."

What also comes back through the stories Paul D shares are fragments of history Sethe is unprepared for, such as the fact that years ago
her husband had witnessed the white boys forcibly take milk from her
breasts, but had been powerless to come to her rescue or stop them.
Furthermore, his personal stories of enduring a "bit" in his mouth—the
barbaric symbol of silence and oppression that Morrison says created a
perfect "labor force"—along with numerous other atrocities such as
working on the chain gang, introduce elements of the classic slave narrative into the text. Perhaps more importantly, these elements comprise
the signs of history that punctuate the text and that disrupt the text of
the mind which is both historical and ahistorical at the same time.

I believe the meaning of Morrison's complex use of trope of memory
becomes most clear in what many readers regard as the most poetic
passages in the text. These passages appear in sections two through five
of Part Two, where we have a series of interior monologues that become
a dialogue among the three central female characters. The first is Sethe's,
the second is Denver's, the third is Beloved's, and the last one is a
merging of all three. Beloved's is the most intriguing, for the text of
her monologue contains no punctuation. Instead, there are literal spaces
between groups of words that signal the timelessness of her presence as
well as the unlived spaces of her life. Earlier in the novel, Sethe even
refers to Beloved as "her daughter [who had] . . . come back home from
the timeless place." Samples of phrases from Beloved's monologue reveal
the meaning of her presence: "[H]ow can I say things that are pictures   I am not separate from her   there is no place where I
stop   her face is my own . . . all of it is now   it is always now."
These words suggest not only the seamlessness of time, but the inextrica-

bility of the past and present, of ancestors and their progeny. In the last interior "dialogue," the voices of Sethe, Denver and Beloved blend to suggest not only that it is always now, but to suggest that the past, present and future are all one and the same.

In an article entitled "Rediscovering Black History," an article written on the occasion of the publication of *The Black Book*, Toni Morrison speaks of the "complicated psychic power one had to exercise to resist devastation."[20] She was speaking, of course, not just of slavery, but of the black existence in America after slavery as well. *Beloved* and all of her novels, to a certain extent, bear witness to this psychic power. It must be stated as I conclude, however, that my intertextual reading of this novel as a revision of the slave narrative should not be construed as an attempt to diminish the form and content of the slave narratives themselves in any way. It is, instead, a recognition of the truth that Gates offers in the introduction to *The Slave's Narrative:*

> Once slavery was abolished, no need existed for the slave to write himself [or herself] into the human community through the action of first-person narration. As Frederick Douglass in 1855 succinctly put the matter, the free human being "cannot see things in the same light with the slave, because he does not and cannot look from the same point from which the slave does." . . . The nature of the narratives, and their rhetorical strategies and import, changed once slavery no longer existed.[21]

Beloved is a complex, contemporary manifestation of this shift. In a larger sense, however, it is what Mikhail Bakhtin calls a "reaccentuation" of the past (in this case, the past of slavery) to discover newer aspects of meaning embedded in the classic slave narrative.[22] Morrison's purpose is not to convince white readers of the slave's humanity, but to address black readers by inviting us to return to the very part of our past that many have repressed, forgotten or ignored. At the end of the novel, after the community has helped Denver rescue her mother from Beloved's ferocious spell by driving her out of town, Paul D returns to Sethe "to put his story next to hers." Despite the psychic healing that Sethe undergoes, however, the community's response to her healing is encoded in the chorus-like declaration on the last two pages of the text, that this was "not a story to pass on." Yet, as readers, if we understand Toni Morrison's ironic and subversive vision at all, we know that our response to the text's apparent final call for silence and forgetting is not that at all. Instead, it is an ironic reminder that the process of consciously remembering not only empowers us to tell the difficult stories that must be passed on, but it also empowers us to make meaning of our individual and collective lives as well.

Notes

1. Quoted in the opening epigraph of Charles T. Davis and Henry Louis Gates, Jr., eds., *The Slave's Narrative* (New York: Oxford University Press, 1985).
2. Middleton A. Harris, comp., *The Black Book* (New York: Random House, 1974). A shorter version of the text of this essay was presented at the annual convention of the Modern Language of America on December 29, 1988, in New Orleans, Louisiana. I am grateful to my colleagues of the First Draft Club—Carolyn Brown, Evelyn Hawthorne, Ann Kelly and especially, Claudia Tate—for their generous response to this essay.
3. Toni Morrison, "Behind the Making of *The Black Book*," *Black World*, 23 (February 1974): 86–90. Compiled by Middleton A. Harris, *The Black Book* does not identify Morrison as its editor. In this article, however, she not only discusses her role as editor, but describes the project of producing the book as an act of professional service and personal mission: "I was scared that the world would fall away before somebody put together a thing that got close to the way we really were." Ironically, although *The Black Book* omits any mention of Morrison as its author, it names her parents, Ramah Wofford and George Carl Wofford, in the acknowledgments, as two of the people who contributed to the text "with stories, pictures, recollections and general aid."
4. See Amanda Smith, "Toni Morrison," *Publishers Weekly* 21 August 1987, 51. This article is a report on an interview with Morrison a month before the publication of *Beloved*.
5. See Harris, *The Black Book*, 10.
6. Toni Morrison, *The Bluest Eye* (New York: Holt Rinehart and Winston, 1970); *Sula* (New York: Knopf, 1973); *Song of Solomon* (New York: Knopf, 1977) and *Tar Baby* (New York: Knopf, 1981). Of the first four novels, *Song of Solomon* is most clearly engaged with the subject of history. Specifically, it connects the African past with the lived life of African Americans from slavery to the recent past of the 1960s.
7. Claudia Tate, ed., *Black Women Writers at Work* (New York: Continuum, 1984), 122.
8. Toni Morrison, *Beloved* (New York: Knopf, 1988), 256. All subsequent references to this novel are cited in the text parenthetically. The term "narrative intervention" is one I borrow from Hazel Carby's analysis of the uses of fiction in moments of historical crisis. See Hazel Carby, *Reconstructing Womanhood: The Emergence of the Afro-American Woman Novelist* (New York: Oxford University Press, 1987), 121–144.
9. Henry Louis Gates, Jr., ed., *The Classic Slave Narratives* (New York: New American Library, 1987), x.
10. Frederick Douglass, *The Narrative of the Life of Frederick Douglass* (New York: Signet, 1968); Harriet Jacobs, *Incidents in the Life of a Slave Girl*, ed. Jean Fagan Yellin (Cambridge: Harvard University Press, 1987).
11. See James Olney, "'I Was Born': Slave Narratives, Their Status as Autobiography and as Literature," *Callaloo*, 7 (Winter 1984): 46–73. Reprinted in Davis and Gates, *The Slave's Narrative*, 148–175.
12. Valerie Smith, *Self-Discovery and Authority in Afro-American Narrative* (Cambridge: Harvard University Press, 1987), 34. See also Mary Helen Washington, ed., *Invented Lives: Narratives of Black Women 1860–1960* (Garden City: Anchor Press, 1987), 3–15.

13. Adrienne Rich, "When We Dead Awaken: Writing as Re-Vision," *College English*, 34 (October 1972): 18–26; Morrison's words are quoted in Smith, *Publishers Weekly*, 51.
14. Fredric Jameson, *The Political Unconscious: Narrative as a Socially Symbolic Act* (Ithaca: Cornell University Press, 1981), 9.
15. Tate, *Black Women Writers*, 125.
16. Steven Mallioux, *Interpretive Conventions: The Reader in the Study of American Fiction* (Ithaca: Cornell University Press, 1982), 170.
17. See Helen Dudar, "Toni Morrison: Finally Just a Writer," *The Wall Street Journal* 30 September 1987, 34. This is one of several newspaper articles to appear around the time of *Beloved's* publication in which Morrison discussed the actual story upon which the novel is based.
18. See Sherley Anne Williams, "The Blues Roots of Contemporary Afro-American Poetry" in Dexter Fisher and Robert Stepto, eds., *Afro-American Literature: The Reconstruction of Instruction* (New York: Modern Language Association of America), 73. In the novel, the statements of individual characters shape the "call" to which other characters offer a "response" by sharing their versions of the past. This pattern of call and response then shapes the collective story of slavery that binds the members of the community together. This pattern resonates with similar patterns found in the blues and other forms of African-American oral expression.
19. Frank Kermode, *The Genesis of Secrecy: On the Interpretation of Narrative* (Cambridge: Harvard University Press, 1979), 144.
20. Toni Morrison, "Rediscovering Black History," *New York Times Magazine* 11 August 1974, 18.
21. Davis and Gates, *The Slave's Narrative*, xiii.
22. Mikhail Bakhtin, "Discourse in the Novel," *The Dialogic Imagination*, Michael Holquist, ed., Caryl Emerson and Michael Holquist, trs. (Austin: University of Texas Press, 1981), 421.

INTERVIEWS

◆◆◆◆◆◆◆◆◆◆◆◆◆

"The Language Must Not Sweat": A Conversation with Toni Morrison

THOMAS LECLAIR

Toni Morrison's *Song of Solomon* was published in 1977 to unreserved praise; American readers had found a new voice. The plot of the novel, a young man's search for a nourishing folk tradition, was familiar from other Afro-American books, but Morrison's fireside manner—composed yet simple, commanding yet intimate—gives the novel a Latin American enchantment. Reading backward through *Sula* (1973) to Morrison's first novel, *The Bluest Eye* (1970), one sees her trying out different versions of what she calls her "address," rehearsing on more modest subjects the tone and timbre that give original expression to the large cultural materials in *Song of Solomon*.

How and why she arrived at that special voice were the questions that brought me to Toni Morrison's busy office at Random House (where she is an editor) just after she finished *Tar Baby*. Although our interview was interrupted several times, when Toni Morrison started talking about writing she achieved remarkable concentration and intensity. This—not editorial business or author small talk—was clearly where she lived. No matter what she discussed—her loyalty to the common reader, her eccentric characters, her interest in folklore—her love of language was the subtext and constant lesson of her manner. She *performs* words. Gertrude Stein said poetry was "caressing nouns." Toni Morrison doesn't like to be called a poetic writer, but it is her almost physical relation to language that allows her to tell the old stories she feels are best.

* * *

Thomas LeClair: You have said you would write even if there were no publishers. Would you explain what the process of writing means to you?

Toni Morrison: After my first novel, *The Bluest Eye*, writing became a way to be coherent in the world. It became necessary and possible for me to sort out the past, and the selection process, being disciplined and guided, was genuine thinking as opposed to simple response or problem-solving. Writing was the only work I did that was for myself and by myself. In the process, one exercises sovereignty in a special way. All sensibilities are engaged, sometimes simultaneously, sometimes sequentially. While I'm writing, all of my experience is vital and useful and possibly important. It may not appear in the work, but it is valuable.

Writing gives me what I think dancers have on stage in their relation to gravity and space and time. It is energetic and balanced, fluid and in repose. And there is always the possibility of growth; I could never hit the highest note so I'd never have to stop. Writing has for me everything that good work ought to have, all the criteria. I love even the drudgery, the revision, the proofreading. So even if publishing did grind to a halt, I would continue to write.

LeClair: Do you understand the process more and more with each novel that you write?

Morrison: At first I wrote out of a very special place in me, although I did not understand what that place was or how to get to it deliberately. I didn't trust the writing that came from there. It did not seem writerly enough. Sometimes what I wrote from that place remained sound, even after enormous revision, but I would regard it as a fluke. Then I learned to trust that part, learned to rely on that part, and I learned how to get there faster than I had before. That is, now I don't have to write 35 pages of throat-clearing in order to be where I wish to be. I don't mean that I'm an inspired writer. I don't wait to be struck by lightning and don't need certain slants of light in order to write, but now after my fourth book I can recognize the presence of a real idea and I can recognize the proper mode of its expression. I must confess, though, that I sometimes lose interest in the characters and get much more interested in the trees and animals. I think I exercise tremendous restraint in this, but my editor says "Would you stop this *beauty* business." And I say "Wait, wait until I tell about these ants."

LeClair: How do you conceive of your function as a writer?

Morrison: I write what I have recently begun to call village literature, fiction that is really for the village, for the tribe. Peasant literature for *my* people, which is necessary and legitimate but which also allows me to get in touch with all sorts of people. I think long and carefully about what my novels ought to do. They should clarify the roles that have become obscured; they ought to identify those things in the past that are useful and those things that are not; and they ought to give nourishment. I agree with John Berger that peasants don't write novels because they don't need them. They have a portrait of themselves from gossip, tales, music, and some celebrations. That is enough. The middle class at the beginning of the industrial revolution needed a portrait of itself because the old portrait didn't work for this new class. Their roles were different; their lives in the city were new. The novel served this function then, and it still does. It tells about the city values, the urban values. Now my people, we "peasants," have come to the city, that is to say, we live with its values. There is a confrontation between old values of the tribes and new urban values. It's confusing. There has to be a mode to do what the music did for blacks, what we used to be able to do with each other in private and in that civilization that existed underneath the white civilization. I think this accounts for the address of my books. I am not explaining anything to anybody. My work bears witness and suggests who the outlaws were, who survived under what circumstances and why, what was legal in the community as opposed to what was legal outside it. All that is in the fabric of the story in order to do what the music used to do. The music kept us alive, but it's not enough anymore. My people are being devoured. Whenever I feel uneasy about my writing, I think: what would be the response of the people in the book if they read the book? That's my way of staying on track. Those are the people for whom I write.

As a reader I'm fascinated by literary books, but the books I wanted to write could not be only, even merely, literary or I would defeat my purposes, defeat my audience. That's why I don't like to have someone call my books "poetic," because it has the connotation of luxuriating richness. I wanted to restore the language that black people spoke to its original power. That calls for a language that is rich but not ornate.

LeClair: What do you mean by "address"?

Morrison: I stand with the reader, hold his hand, and tell him a very simple story about complicated people. I like to work with, to fret, the cliché, which is a cliché because the experience expressed in it is important: a young man seeks his fortune; a pair of friends, one good, one bad; the perfectly innocent victim. We know thousands of these in literature. I like to dust off these clichés, dust off the language, make them mean whatever they may have meant originally. My genuine criticism of most contemporary books is that they're not *about* anything. Most of the books that are about something—the books that mean something—treat old ideas, old situations.

LeClair: Does this mean working with folklore and myth?

Morrison: I think the myths are misunderstood now because we are not talking to each other the way I was spoken to when I was growing up in a very small town. You knew everything in that little microcosm. But we don't live where we were born. I had to leave my town to do my work here; it was a sacrifice. There is a certain sense of family I don't have. So the myths get forgotten. Or they may not have been looked at carefully. Let me give you an example: the flying myth in *Song of Solo-*

mon. If it means Icarus to some readers, fine; I want to take credit for that. But my meaning is specific: it is about black people who could fly. That was always part of the folklore of my life; flying was one of our gifts. I don't care how silly it may seem. It is everywhere—people used to talk about it, it's in the spirituals and gospels. Perhaps it was wishful thinking—escape, death, and all that. But suppose it wasn't. What might it mean? I tried to find out in *Song of Solomon.*

In the book I've just completed, *Tar Baby,* I use that old story because, despite its funny, happy ending, it used to frighten me. The story has a tar baby in it which is used by a white man to catch a rabbit. "Tar baby" is also a name, like nigger, that white people call black children, black girls, as I recall. Tar seemed to me to be an odd thing to be in a Western story, and I found that there is a tar lady in African mythology. I started thinking about tar. At one time, a tar pit was a holy place, at least an important place, because tar was used to build things. It came naturally out of the earth; it held together things like Moses's little boat and the pyramids. For me, the tar baby came to mean the black woman who can hold things together. The story was a point of departure to history and prophecy. That's what I mean by dusting off the myth, looking closely at it to see what it might conceal. . . .

LeClair: Do you think it's risky to do this kind of writing?

Morrison: Yes. I think I can do all sorts of writing, including virtuoso performances. But what is hard for me is to be simple, to have uncomplex stories with complex people in them, to clean the language, really clean it. One attempts to slay a real dragon. You don't ever kill it, but you have to choose a job worth the doing. I think I choose hard jobs for myself, and the opportunity to fail is always there. I want a residue of emotion in my fiction, and this means verging upon sentimentality, or being willing to let it happen and then draw back from it. Also, stories seem so old-fashioned now. But narrative remains the best way to learn anything, whether history or theology, so I continue with narrative form.

LeClair: In the kind of fiction you have described, isn't there a danger that it will be liked for something it is not? Are you ever worried about that?

Morrison: No. The people who are not fastidious about reading may find my fiction "wonderful." They are valuable to me because I am never sure that what they find "wonderful" in it isn't really what is valuable about it. I do hope to interest people who are very fastidious about reading. What I'd really like to do is appeal to both at the same time. Sometimes I feel that I do play to the gallery in *Song of Solomon,* for example, because I have to make the reader look at people he may not wish to look at. You don't look at Pilate. You don't really look at a person like Cholly in *The Bluest Eye*. They are always backdrops, stage props, not the main characters in their own stories. In order to look at them in fiction, you have to hook the reader, strike a certain posture as narrator, achieve some intimacy.

LeClair: As an editor, you look for quality in others' work. What do you think is distinctive about your fiction? What makes it good?

Morrison: The language, only the language. The language must be careful and must appear effortless. It must not sweat. It must suggest and be provocative at the same time. It is the thing that black people love so much—the saying of words, holding them on the tongue, experimenting with them, playing with them. It's a love, a passion. Its function is like a preacher's: to make you stand up out of your seat, make you lose yourself and hear yourself. The worst of all possible things that could happen would be to lose that language. There are certain things I cannot say without recourse to my language. It's terrible to think that a child with five different present tenses comes to school to be faced with those books that are less than his own language. And then to be told things about his language, which is him, that are sometimes permanently damaging. He may never know the etymology of Africanisms in his language, not even know that "hip" is a real word or that "the dozens" meant something. This is a really cruel fallout of racism. I know the standard English. I want to use it to help restore the other language, the lingua franca.

The part of the writing process that I fret is getting the sound without some mechanics that would direct the reader's attention to the sound. One way is not to use adverbs to describe how someone says something. I try to work the dialogue down so the reader has to hear it. When Eva in *Sula* sets her son on fire, her daughter runs upstairs to tell her, and Eva says "Is?" you can hear every grandmother say "Is?" and you know: a) she knows what she's been told; b) she is not going to do anything about it; and c) she will not have any more conversation. That sound is important to me.

LeClair: Not all readers are going to catch that.

Morrison: If I say "Quiet is as kept," that is a piece of information which means exactly what it says, but to black people it means a big lie is about to be told. Or someone is going to tell some graveyard information, who's sleeping with whom. Black readers will chuckle. There is a level of appreciation that might be available only to people who understand the context of the language. The analogy that occurs to me is jazz: it is open on the one hand and both complicated and inaccessible on the other. I never asked Tolstoy to write for me, a little colored girl in Lorain, Ohio. I never asked Joyce not to mention Catholicism or the world of Dublin. Never. And I don't know why I should be asked to explain your life to you. We have splendid writers to do that, but I am not one of them. It is that business of being universal, a word hopelessly stripped of meaning for me. Faulkner wrote what I suppose could be called regional literature and had it published all over the world. It is good—and universal—because it is specifically about a particular world. That's what I wish to do. If I tried to write a universal novel, it would be water. Behind this question is the suggestion that to write for black people is somehow to diminish the writing. From my perspective, there are only black people. When I say "people," that's what I mean. Lots of books written by black people about black people have had this "universality" as a burden. They were writing for some readers other than me.

LeClair: One of the complaints about your fiction in both the black and white press is that you write about eccentrics, people who aren't representative.

Morrison: This kind of sociological judgment is pervasive and pernicious. "Novel A is better than B or C because A is more like most black people really are." Unforgivable. I am enchanted, personally, with people who are extraordinary because in them I can find what is applicable to the ordinary. There are books by black writers about ordinary black life. I don't write them. Black readers often ask me, "Why are your books so melancholy, so sad? Why don't you ever write about something that works, about relationships that are healthy?" There is a comic mode, meaning the union of the sexes, that I don't write. I write what I suppose could be called the tragic mode in which there is some catharsis and revelation. There's a whole lot of space in between, but my inclination is in the tragic direction. Maybe it's a consequence of my being a classics minor.

Related, I think, is the question of nostalgia. The danger of writing about the past, as I have done, is romanticizing it. I don't think I do that, but I do feel that people were more interesting then than they are now. It seems to me there were more excesses in women and men, and people accepted them as they don't now. In the black commuity where I grew up, there were eccentricity and freedom, less conformity in individual habits—but close conformity in terms of the survival of the village, of the tribe. Before sociological microscopes were placed on us, people did anything and nobody was run out of town. I mean, the community in *Sula* let her stay. They wouldn't wash or bury her. They protected themselves from her, but she was part of the community. The detritus of white people, the rejects from the respectable white world, which appears in *Sula* was in our neighborhood. In my family, there were some really interesting people who were willing to be whatever they were. People permitted it, perhaps because in the outer world the eccentrics had to be a little servant person or low-level factory worker. They had an enormous span of emotions and activities, and they are the people I remember when I go to write. When I go to colleges, the students say "Who are these people?" Maybe it's because now everybody seems to be trying to be "right."

LeClair: Naming is an important theme in *Song of Solomon*. Would you discuss its significance?

Morrison: I never knew the real names of my father's friends. Still don't. They used other names. A part of that had to do with cultural orphanage, part of it with the rejection of the name given to them under circumstances not of their choosing. If you come from Africa, your name is gone. It is particularly problematic because it is not just *your* name but your family, your tribe. When you die, how can you connect with your ancestors if you have lost your name? That's a huge psychological scar. The best thing you can do is take another name which is yours because it reflects something about you or your own choice. Most of the names in *Song of Solomon* are real, the names of musicians for example. I used the biblical names to show the impact of the Bible on the lives of black people, their awe of and respect for it coupled with their ability to distort it for their own purposes. I also used some pre-Christian names to give the sense of a mixture of cosmologies. Milkman Dead has to learn the meaning of his own name and the names of things. In African languages there is no word for yam, but there is a word for every variety of yam. Each thing is separate and different; once you have named it, you have power. Milkman has to experience the elements. He goes into the earth and later walks its surface. He twice enters water. And he flies in the air. When he walks the earth, he feels a part of it, and that is his coming of age, the beginning of his ability to connect with the past and perceive the world as alive.

LeClair: You mentioned the importance of sound before. Your work also seems to me to be strongly visual and concerned with vision, with seeing.

Morrison: There are times in my writing when I cannot move ahead even though I know exactly what will happen in the plot and what the dialogue is because I don't have the scene, the metaphor to begin with. Once I can see the scene, it all happens. In *Sula*, Eva is waiting for her long lost husband to come back. She's not sure how she's going to feel, but when he leaves he toots the horn on his pear-green Model-T Ford. It goes "ooogah, ooogah," and Eva knows she hates him. My editor said the car didn't exist at the time, and I had a lot of trouble rewriting the scene because I had to have the color and the sound. Finally, I had a woman in a green dress laughing a big-city laugh, an alien sound in that small-town street, that stood for the "ooogah" I couldn't use. In larger terms, I thought of *Sula* as a cracked mirror, fragments and pieces we have to see independently and put together. In *Bluest Eye* I used the primer story, with its picture of a happy family, as a frame acknowledging the outer civilization. The primer with white children was the way life was presented to the black people. As the novel proceeded I wanted that primer version broken up and confused, which explains the typographical running together of the words.

LeClair: Did your using the primer come out of the work you were doing on textbooks?

Morrison: No. I was thinking that nobody treated these people seriously in literature and that "these people" who were not treated seriously were me. The interest in vision, in seeing, is a fact of black life. As slaves and ex-slaves, black people were manageable and findable, as no other slave society would be, because they were black. So there is an enormous impact from the simple division of color—more than sex, age, or anything else. The complaint is not being seen for what one is. That is the reason why my hatred of white people is justified and their hatred for me is not. There is a fascinating book called *Drylongso* which collects the talk of black people. They say almost to a man that you never tell a white person the truth. He doesn't want to hear it. Their conviction is they are neither seen nor listened to. They also perceive themselves as morally superior people because they do *see*. This helps explain why the theme of the mask is so important in black literature and why I worked so heavily with it in *Tar Baby*.

LeClair: Who is doing work now that you respect?

Morrison: I don't like to make lists because someone always gets left out, but in general I think the South American novelists have the best of it now. My complaint about letters now would be the state of criticism. It's following post-modern fiction into self-consciousness, talking about itself as though it were the work of art. Fine for the critic, but not helpful for the writer. There was a time when the great poets were the great critics, when the artist was the critic. Now it seems that there are no encompassing minds, no great critical audience for the writer. I have yet to read criticism that understands my work or is prepared to understand it. I don't care if the critic likes or dislikes it. I would just like to feel less isolated. It's like having a linguist who doesn't understand your language tell you what you're saying. Stanley Elkin says you need great literature to have great criticism. I think it works the other way around. If there were better criticism, there would be better books.

◆◆◆◆◆◆◆◆◆◆◆◆◆◆

"Intimate Things in Place":
A Conversation with Toni Morrison
ROBERT B. STEPTO

This interview was conducted in Ms. Morrison's office at Random House
Publishers in New York City on May 19, 1976.

[STEPTO]: I want to start with something we've talked about before, and
that is this extraordinary sense of place in your novels. By that I mean
you create communities, the community that Pecola, Claudia and the
rest live in, in *The Bluest Eye,* and of course, in *Sula,* the Bottom. The
places are set in time; there are addresses—we know Sula's address,
right down to the house number. Years are mentioned, seasons are mentioned, details are given, and I was struck by these features in two ways.
First, by the extent to which you seem to be trying to create specific
geographical landscapes, and second, by how landscape seems to perform
different functions in the two novels.

[MORRISON]: I can't account for all aspects of it. I know that I never felt
like an American or an Ohioan or even a Lorainite. I never felt like a
citizen. But I felt very strongly—not much with the first book; more
with the second; and very much with the one I'm working on now—I felt
a very strong sense of place, not in terms of the country or the state,
but in terms of the details, the feeling, the mood of the community, of
the town. In the first book, I was clearly pulling straight out of what
autobiographical information I had. I didn't create that town. It's clearer
to me now in my memory of it than when I lived there and I haven't
really lived there since I was seventeen years old. Also, I think some of
it is just a woman's strong sense of being in a room, a place, or in a
house. Sometimes my relationship to things in a house would be a little
different from, say my brother's or my father's or my sons'. I clean them
and I move them and I do very intimate things "in place": I am sort of
rooted in it, so that writing about being in a room looking out, or being
in a world looking out, or living in a small definite place, is probably very
common among most women anyway.
 The other thing was that when I wrote *Sula* I was interested in
making the town, the community, the neighborhood, as strong as a character as I could, without actually making it "The Town, they," because
the most extraordinary thing about any group, and particularly our
group, is the fantastic variety of people and things and behavior and so

on. But nevertheless there was a cohesiveness there in my mind and it was true in my life. And though I live in New York, I don't relate easily to very, very large cities, because I have never lived in a huge city except this one. My tendency is to focus on neighborhoods and communities. And the community, the black community—I don't like to use that term because it came to mean something much different in the sixties and seventies, as though we had to forge one—but it had seemed to me that it was always there, only we called it the "neighborhood." And there was this life-giving, very, very strong sustenance that people got from the neighborhood. One lives, really, not so much in your house as you do outside of it, within the "compounds," within the village, or whatever it is. And legal responsibilities, all the responsibilities that agencies now have, were the responsibilities of the neighborhood. So that people were taken care of, or locked up or whatever. If they were sick, other people took care of them; if they needed something to eat, other people took care of them; if they were old, other people took care of them; if they were mad, other people provided a small space for them, or related to their madness or tried to find out the limits of their madness.

They also meddled in your lives a lot. They felt that you belonged to them. And every woman on the street could raise everybody's child, and tell you exactly what to do and you felt that connection with those people and they felt it with you. And when they punished us or hollered at us, it was, at the time, we thought, so inhibiting and so cruel, and it's only much later that you realize that they were interested in you. Interested in you—they cared about your behavior. And then I knew my mother as a Church woman, and a Club woman—and there was something special about when she said "Sister," and when all those other women said "Sister." They meant that in a very, very fundamental way. There were some interesting things going on inside people and they seemed to me the most extraordinary people in the world. But at the same time, there was this kind of circle around them—we lived within 23 blocks—which they could not break.

[S]: From what you're telling me, it would seem that creating Medallion in *Sula* might have been a more difficult task than creating the neighborhood in *The Bluest Eye*.

[M]: Oh, yes, Medallion was more difficult because it was wholly fabricated; but it was based on something my mother had said some time ago. When she first got married, she and my father went to live in Pittsburgh. And I remember her telling me that in those days all the black people lived in the hills of Pittsburgh, but now they lived amid the smoke and dirt in the heart of that city. It's clear up in those hills, and so I used that idea, but in a small river town in Ohio. Ohio is right on the Kentucky border, so there's not much difference between it and the "South." It's an interesting state from the point of view of black people because it is right there by the Ohio River, in the south, and at its northern tip is Canada. And there were these fantastic abolitionists there, and also the Ku Klux Klan lived there. And there is really one large city. There are hundreds of small towns and that's where most black people live. You know, in most books, they're always in New York or some exotic place, but most of our lives are spent in little towns, little towns all throughout this country. And that's where, you know, we live. And that's where the juices came from and that's where we *made it*, not made it in terms of success but made who we are. So I loved writing about that because it was so wide open.

Sula was hard, for me; very difficult to make up that kind of character. Not difficult to think it up, but difficult to describe a woman who could be used as a classic type of evil force. Other people could use her that way. And at the same time, I didn't want to make her freakish or repulsive or unattractive. I was interested at that time in doing a very old, worn-out idea, which was to do something with good and evil, but putting it in different terms. And I wanted Nel to be a warm, conventional woman, one of those people you know are going to pay the gas bill and take care of the children. You don't have to ask about them. And they are magnificent, because they take these small tasks and they do them. And they do them without the fire and without the drama and without all of that. They get the world's work done somehow.

[s]: How did Nel get to that point, given the background you provided her with? Why does her grandmother have those "questionable roots"? How does that lead to Nel?

[m]: It has to do with Nel's attraction for Sula. To go back, a black woman at that time who didn't want to do the conventional thing, had only one other kind of thing to do. If she had talent she went into the theater. And if she had a little voice, she could sing, or she could go to a big town and she could pretend she was dancing or whatever. That was the only outlet if you chose not to get married and have children. That was it. Or you could walk the streets; although you might get there sort of accidentally; you might not choose to do that. So that Nel's grandmother just means that there's that kind of life from which Nel comes; that's another woman who was a hustler; that part is already in Nel and accounts for her attraction to Sula. And also those are the kinds of women there were. Here is this woman, Nel, whose mother is just busy, busy, busy, reacting against her own mother, and goes to the far extreme of having this rather neat, rather organized, rather pompous life, forcing all of the creativity out of Nel. But Nel wants it anyway, which is what makes it possible for

her to have a very close friend who is so different from her, in the way she looks at life. And I wanted to make all of that sort of reasonable. Because what was the attraction of Nel for Sula? Sula for Nel? Why would they become friends in the first place? You see? And so I wanted to say, as much as I could say it without being overbearing, that there was a little bit of both in each of those two women, and that if they had been one person, I suppose they would have been a rather marvelous person. But each one lacked something that the other one had.

[S]: It's interesting you should mention this, because my students wanted to pursue the question of Sula and Nel being perhaps two sides of the same person, or two sides of one extraordinary character. But this character is nevertheless fractured into Sula and Nel.

[M]: Precisely. They're right on target because that was really in my mind. It didn't come to me quite that way. I started out by thinking that one can never really define good and evil. Sometimes good looks like evil; sometimes evil looks like good—you never really know what it is. It depends on what uses you put it to. Evil is as useful as good is, although good is generally more interesting; it's more complicated. I mean, living a good life is more complicated than living an evil life, I think. And also, it wasn't hard to talk about that because everyone has something in mind when they think about what a good life is. So I put that in conventional terms, for a woman: someone who takes care of children and so on and is responsible and goes to church and so on. For the opposite kind of character, which is a woman who's an adventurer, who breaks rules, she can either be a criminal—which I wasn't interested in—or lead a kind of cabaret life—which I also wasn't interested in. But what about the woman who doesn't do any of that but is nevertheless a rule-breaker, a kind of law-breaker, a lawless woman? Not a law-abiding woman. Nel knows and believes in all the laws of that community. She *is* the community. She believes in its values. Sula does not. She does not believe in any of those laws and breaks them all. Or ignores them. So that she becomes more interesting—I think, particularly to younger girls—because of that quality of abandon.

But there's a fatal flaw in all of that, you know, in both of those things. Nel does not make that "leap"—she doesn't know about herself. Even at the end, she doesn't know. She's just beginning. She just barely grabs on at the end in those last lines. So that living totally by the law and surrendering completely to it without questioning anything sometimes makes it impossible to know anything about yourself. Nel doesn't even know what questions she's asking. When they come to touch one another in the bedroom, when Sula's sick, Nel doesn't even know why she's there. Sula, on the other hand, knows all there is to know about herself because she examines herself, she is experimental with herself, she's perfectly willing to think the unthinkable thing and so on. But she has trouble making a connection with other people and just feeling that lovely sense of accomplishment of being close in a very strong way. She felt that in a way, of course, with Nel, but then obviously they lost one another in friendship. She was able to retrieve it rather nicely with a man, which is lovely, except that in so many instances, with men, the very thing that would attract a man to a woman in the first place might be the one thing she would give over once she learned Nel's lesson, which is love as possession. You own somebody and then you begin to want them there all the time, which is a community law. Marriage, faithfulness, fidelity; the beloved belongs to one person and can't be shared with other people—that's a community value which Sula learned when she fell in love with Ajax, which he wasn't interested in learning.

[s]: Richard Wright said in "How Bigger Was Born" that there were many Biggers that went into creating Bigger Thomas. Are there many Pecolas in Pecola. Or many Sulas in Sula?

[m]: Oh, yes! Well, I think what I did is what every writer does—once you have an idea, then you try to find a character who can manifest the idea for you. And then you have to spend a long time trying to get to know who those people are, who that character is. So you take what there is from whomever you know. Sula—I think this was really part of the difficulty—I didn't know anyone like her. I never knew a woman like that at any rate. But I knew women who looked like that, who looked like they *could be* like that. And then you remember women who were a little different in the town, you know; there's always a little bit of gossip and there's always a little bit of something. There's a woman in our town now who is an absolute riot. She can do anything she wants to do. And it occurred to me about twenty years ago how depleted that town would be if she ever left. Everybody wanted her out, and she was a crook and she was mean and she had about twenty husbands—and she was just, you know, a huge embarrassment. Nevertheless, she really and truly was one of the reasons that they called each other on the telephone. They sort of used her excitement, her flavor, her carelessness, her restlessness, and so on. And that quality is what I used in Sula.

[s]: What about Sula's mother and grandmother?

[m]: Oh, Hannah, the mother—I tell you, I think I feel more affection for her than for anybody else in that book. I just loved her. What I was trying to do was to be very provocative without using all of the traditional devices of provocation. And I think—that's why I wrote so

slowly—I think I know how to do it by simply relying an awful lot on what I believe the reader already knows. I wanted Sula to be missed by the reader. That's why she dies early. There's a lot of book after she dies, you know. I wanted them to miss her presence in that book as that town missed her presence. I also wanted them to dislike her a lot, and to be fascinated, perhaps, but also to feel that thing that the town might feel—that this is something askew. And I wanted for them to realize at some point—and I don't know if anybody ever realizes it—that she never does anything as bad as her grandmother or her mother did. However, they're alike; her grandmother kills her son, plays god, names people and, you know, puts her hand on a child. You know, she's god-like, she manipulates—all in the best interest. And she is very, very possessive about other people, that is, as a king is. She decided that her son was living a life that was not worth his time. She meant it was too painful for her; you know, the way you kill a dog when he breaks his leg because he can't stand the pain. He may very well be able to stand it, but you can't, so that's why you get rid of him. The mother, of course, was slack. She had no concept of love and possession. She liked to be laid, she liked to be touched but she didn't want any confusion of relationships and so on. She's very free and open about that. Her relationship to her daughter is almost one of uninterest. She would do things for her, but she's not particularly interested in her.

[S]: That conversation in the kitchen . . .

[M]: That's right: "I love her, but I don't like her," which is an honest statement at any rate. And she'd sleep with anybody, you know, husbands. She just does it. But interestingly enough, the point was that the women in the town who knew that—they didn't like the fact—but at the same time *that* was something they could understand. Lust, sexual lust, and so on. So that when she dies, they will come to her aid. Now Sula might take their husbands, but she was making judgments. You see what it was—it wasn't about love. It wasn't about even lust. Nobody knows what that was about. And also, Sula did the one terrible thing for black people which was to put her grandmother in an old folks' home, which was outrageous, you know. You take care of people! So *that* would be her terrible thing. But at the same time, she is more strange, more formidable than either of those other two women because they were first of all within the confines of the community and their sensibilities were informed by it. Essentially, they were pacific in the sense of what they did do. They wanted to make things come together; you know, bring it together. Hannah didn't want to disturb anything. She did her work and she took care of people and so on; and Eva was generous, wide-spirited, and made some great sacrifices.

[S]: I'm fascinated by all of the women in the two novels: your portraits are so rich. It's not just the main characters—you get that woman from Meridian, Geraldine, in *The Bluest Eye*, and of course Mrs. McTeer, who isn't always talked about, but she certainly is the kind of figure you were describing earlier as a mother to anybody and everybody who will take you in and knows how to raise everybody. With all of these various characters that you've created, certainly you must have some response to the feeling in certain literary circles that black women should be portrayed a certain way. I'm thinking now of the kinds of criticism that have been lodged against Gayl Jones.

[M]: Do you mean black woman as victims, that they should not be portrayed as victims?

[S]: Either that or even—and I'm thinking more of Sula here—as emasculating.

[M]: Oh yes. Well, in *The Bluest Eye*, I try to show a little girl as a total and complete victim of whatever was around her. But black women have held, have been given, you know, the cross. They don't walk near it. They're often on it. And they've borne that, I think, extremely well. I think everybody knows, deep down, that black men were emasculated by white men, period. And that black women didn't take any part in that. However, black women have had some enormous responsibilities, which in these days people call freedoms—in those days, they were called responsibilities—they lived, you know, working in other people's, white people's, houses and taking care of that and working in their own houses and so on and they have been on the labor market. And nobody paid them that much attention in terms of threats, and so on, so they had a certain amount of "freedom." But they did a very extraordinary job of just taking on that kind of responsibility and in so doing, they tell people what to do. Now I have to admit, however, that it's a new idea to me— the emasculating black woman. It really is new—that is, in the last few years. I can only go by my own experience, my own family, the black men I knew—the men I knew called the shots, whether they were employed or unemployed. And even in our classic set of stereotypes—Sapphire and Kingfish?—he did anything he was big enough to do! Anything! Talk 'bout free! And she bitched—that she was going to work and so on. But there is an incredible amount of magic and feistiness in black men that nobody has been able to wipe out. But everybody has tried.

Now, Sula—I don't regard her as a typical black woman at all. And the fact that the community responds to her that way means that she's unusual. So she's not the run-of-the-mill average black woman.

[S]: If she weren't unusual, they'd know how to deal with her.

[M]: That's right. There wouldn't have been that confusion about her. They did not know how to deal with her. So she's very atypical and perhaps she would be, you know, a kind of ball-breaker, in that sense. However, the one man who talked to her, and thought she was worthy of conversation, and who let her be, was the one man she could relate to on that level that would make her want something she had never been interested in before, which was a permanent relationship. He was a man who was not intimidated by her; he was interested in her. He treated her as a whole person, not as an extension of himself, not as a vessel, not as a symbol. Their sex was not one person killing the other—that's why I pictured her on top of him, you know, like a tree. He was secure enough and free enough and bright enough—he wasn't terrorized by her because she was odd. He was interested. I think there was a line in the book—he hadn't met an interesting woman since his mother, who was sitting out in the woods "making roots." When a man is whole himself, when he's touched the borders of his own life, and he's not proving something to somebody else—white men or other men and so on—then the threats of emasculation, the threats of castration, the threats of somebody taking over disappear. Ajax is strong enough. He's a terribly unemployed dude, who has interests of his own, whose mother neglected him, but nevertheless assumed all sorts of things about him that he lived up to like he knew he was doing. So he had a different kind of upbringing. Now that, I think, is interesting; that part of it interested me a lot, so that when he would see a woman like Sula, who had been somewhere and had some rather different views about life and so on, he was not intimidated at all. Whereas a man like Jude, who was doing a rather routine, macho thing, would split—you know, he was too threatened by all of that. Just the requirements of staying in the house and having to apologize to his wife were too much for him.

[S]: Now you mention Jude, and that balance between Jude and Ajax is clear in the book. What about Ajax and Cholly Breedlove in *The Bluest Eye?*

[M]: Exactly alike, in that sense. I don't mean that their backgrounds were alike. But in a way, they sort of—through neglect of the fact that someone was not there—made up themselves. They allowed themselves to be whomever they were. Cholly, of course, lives a very tragic life, tragic in the sense that there was no reward, but he is the thing I keep calling a "free man," not free in the legal sense, but free in his head. You see, this was a free man who could do a lot of things; and I think it's a way of talking about what some people call the "bad nigger." Not in the sense of one who is so carousing, but that adjective "bad" meaning, you know, bad and good. This is a man who is stretching, you know, he's stretching, he's going all the way within his own mind and within whatever his outline might be. Now that's the tremendous possibility for masculinity among black men. And you see it a lot. Sometimes you see it when they do art things, sometimes just in personality and so on. And it's very, very deep and very, very complex and such men as that are not very busy. They may end up in sort of twentieth-century, contemporary terms being also unemployed. They may be in prison. They may be doing all sorts of things. But they are adventuresome in that regard.

And then when you draw a woman who is like that, which is unusual and uncivilized, within our context, then a man like that is interested in her. No, he doesn't want to get married, he doesn't want to do all those things, for all sorts of reasons, some of which are purely sociological. The other kind of man who is more like the Nel syndrome would be very, very preoccupied with it, and his masculinity is threatened all the time. But then you see a man who has had certain achievements—and I don't mean social achievements—but he's been able to manipulate crap games or, you know, just do things—because Cholly has done *everything*—in his life. So that by the time he met Pauline, he was able to do whatever his whims suggested and it's that kind of absence of control that I wanted—you know, obviously, that I'm interested in characters who are lawless in that regard. They make up their lives, or they find out who they are. So in that regard Cholly Breedlove is very much like Ajax.

[S]: Is the progression from girlhood in *The Bluest Eye* to womanhood in *Sula* an intentional progression? Might we view the two novels in these terms?

[M]: Yes. I think I was certainly interested in talking about black girlhood in *The Bluest Eye* and not so interested in it in *Sula*. I wanted to move it into the other part of their life. That is, what do the Claudias and Friedas, those feisty little girls, grow up to be? Precisely. No question about that.

The book that I'm writing now is about a man, and a lot of the things that I learned by writing about Cholly and Ajax and Jude are at least points of departure, leaping-off places, for the work that I'm doing now. The focus is on two men. One is very much like Ajax and Cholly in his youth, so stylish and adventuresome and, I don't know, I think he's truly masculine in the sense of going out too far where you're not supposed to go and running toward confrontations rather than away from them. And risks—taking risks. That quality. One of the men is very much like that. The other will learn to be a complete person, or at least have a notion of it, if I ever get him to the end of the book. When I wrote that section on Cholly in *The Bluest Eye*, I thought it would be very hard for me because I didn't know that as intimately as I knew Pauline. And I thought, well, let me get started on this 'cause I'm going to have a tough time trying to really feel that kind of thing. But it's the only time I've ever written anything in my life when it all came at once. I wrote it straight through. And it took me a long time, maybe eight or nine hours the first time, not stopping at all.

When I got to Pauline, whom I knew so well, I could not do it. I could not make it. I didn't know what to write or how. And I sort of copped out anyway in the book because I used two voices, hers and the author's. There were certain things she couldn't know and I had to come in. And then there were certain things the author would say that I wanted in her language—so that there were the two things, two voices, which I had regarded, at any rate, as a way in which to do something second-best. I couldn't do it straight out the way I did every other section. That was such a fascinating experience for me to perceive Cholly that way.

[S]: Will these two men in the new book balance as Nel and Sula do?

[M]: No. That is, they're friends and they're different from each other, but they're not incomplete the way and Nel and Sula are. They are completely whoever they are and they don't need another man to give them that. They love each other—I mean, men love the company of other men—they're like that. And they enjoy the barber shop and the pool room and so on, and there's a lot of that because they aren't just interested in themselves. But their relationship is based on something quite different. And I think in the friendship between men there is, you know, something else operating. So the metaphors changed. I couldn't use the same kind of language at all. And it took a long time for the whole thing to fall together because men are different and they are thinking about different things. The language had to be different.

[S]: Will neighborhood or a sense of neighborhood be just as important in this book?

[M]: Yes. Well, I have one man who is a sort of middle-class black dude, whose mother was the daughter of the only black doctor. His father, who is a kind of self-taught man, owns a lot of shacks in the black part of the town and he loves things, you know, he's accumulating property and money and so on. And his son is the main character who makes friends with people in the kind of community that is described in *Sula*. You know, it's a different social class, there is a leap, but I don't think the class problems among black people are as great as the class problems among white people. I mean, there's just no real problems with that in terms of language and how men relate to one another—black men relate to one another whatever class they come from.

[S]: Sort of like people living on the same block, going to the same barber shop . . .

[M]: Yes, because whatever it is, you know, the little community is by itself. You go to the same barber shop and there you are. So this one has a little bit of money and that one doesn't but it doesn't make any difference because you're thrown into the same and you get your "stuff" from one another.

[S]: Will there also be a character somewhat like Soaphead Church or Shadrack in this book? Tell me something about your two crazies.

[M]: Well, in the first place, with Shadrack, I just needed, wanted, a form of madness that was clear and compact to bounce off of Sula's strangeness. And you know, he likes her and she goes to his house and he remembers her and so on. So there's a connection between the two of them. And I wanted the town to respond to him in one way and to her in another. They're both eccentrics, outside the law, except that Shadrack's madness is very organized. He has organized the world. He just wants all this to be done on one day. It's orderly, as madness is— isolation, total isolation and order. You know, it's trying to get order in what is perceived by the madman as a disordered world. So the town understands his own way of organizing chaos, once they find out what he's doing—you know, National Suicide Day.

With Soaphead, I wanted, needed someone to give the child her blue eyes. Now she was asking for something that was just awful—she wanted to have blue eyes and she wanted to be Shirley Temple, I mean, she wanted to do that white trip because of the society in which she lived and, very importantly, because of the black people who helped her want to be that. (The responsibilities are ours. It's our responsibility for helping her believe, helping her come to the point where she wanted that.) I had to have someone—her mother, of course, made her want it in the first place—who would give her the blue eyes. And there had to be somebody who *could*, who had the means; that kind of figure who dealt with fortune-telling, dream-telling and so on, who would also believe that she was right, that it was preferable for her to have blue eyes. And that would be a person like Soaphead. In other words, he would be wholly convinced that if black people were more like white people they would be better off. And I tried to explain that in terms of his own West Indian background—a kind of English, colonial, Victorian thing drilled into his head which he could not escape. I needed someone to distill all of that, to say, "Yeah, you're right, you need them. Here, I'll give them to you," and really believe that he had done her a favor. Someone who would never question the request in the first place. That kind of black. It was very important in the story that the miracle happen, and she does get them, although I had to make it fairly logical in that only she can see them and that she's really flipped by that time.

[S]: Does your job as an editor get in the way of your writing? I ask this partly because I remember so well having a creative writing teacher who told me once how his being an English major in college got in the way of his writing, so he became an anthropology major . . .

[M]: In order to free himself?

[S]: Yes. A number of things can get in the way of writing; lots of teachers of literature would like to write, but perhaps their teaching gets in the way of the writing. Now, you are a writer, and an editor, and a teacher—how do you do it?

[M]: Well, I suspect that full-time teaching would get in the way of writing for me because you have to think a certain way about the literature you're teaching, and I think that would spill over into the way in which one has to think when writing. The critical stance—which is what teaching is—sometimes makes me feel, if I move right into my writing, too self-conscious. You're so aware of the theory and the effort and so on, that you become very self-conscious and maybe a little too tight about it. For me, it has to be very private and very unrelated. When I write, I can't read other people that I like. I have to read detective stories or things like that. I have to feel as if it's being done almost in a very separate womb of my own construction. Wholly free. And because it's the only activity at all that I engage in wholly for myself, it's the one place that I can't have any other interference of that sort.

The editing is no problem, because that is such a different way of thinking about things. I don't have to exercise the same skills or talent. I don't create as an editor, I simply do more of what one does in teaching, but in terms of someone who is creating—you see, that is my work, so I don't feel anything strong or deeply personal about it at all. What I want to do with an author is to get him into the position to do the best work he can, and then to try to publish it so it will receive the widest amount of attention, and look elegant, and be well-received. That's quite different. It's sort of like fishing—you catch fish, which is different from cooking them. You don't have to know one in order to do the other, and you can do one well and not do the other well. So that I don't find a conflict there. The problem, of course, is time, trying to find enough time for all of those things. And I like it all, you know, but probably the only one that I couldn't live without is the writing. I think that if all the publishers disappeared, I would write anyway, because that is a compulsion with me. To write, to think that way.

[s]: How did the teaching go this term?

[M]: Oh, I enjoyed it. I really did. I had a good time in both classes and in the "Black Women and Their Fiction" class, it was nice because I was able to discuss contemporary women and maybe introduce students to some women that they had never read before. And also, it was nice going into almost untrammeled territory with them. There isn't a lot of first-rate criticism about black women writers, so that in their papers I insisted that they make reference to the text that we had read in class. And I had given them outlines and general questions which we dealt with in class to get around to a decent topic for term papers. But they knew that they were very free to introduce ideas—in other words, there were not a lot of secondary sources to which they could go. I told them to feel free to draw their own conclusions. A couple of them did really first-rate work.

[s]: You're quite right—there isn't very much good criticism of black literature and particularly of the literature of black women. What kinds of things do you feel, as a writer, a teacher, and as an editor, need to be pursued in this regard? Should criticism take a particular direction—do certain questions need to be asked more than others?

[M]: Certain questions occur to me when I try to think of the body of black literature that there is in general and the body of black literature that women have produced. In the course, for example, I was very interested in how contemporary black women looked at the stereotype of black women. Did they accept that role? Did the writers believe, in the works we studied, that that was pretty much the way we were? Were there characters representative of the mammy, whore, whatever? show-girl, whatever? And emasculation and so on? How political were they? Were the writings very, very directed by new political awarenesses or were they distant from that, were they outside the so-called realm of politics? What were their perceptions about their role? How did they really see themselves? And even—if we could get a little bit deeper, if you could think in terms of not just characters but plot and tone and the attitude of the woman writer toward the world in which she lives— does she really feel burdened and harassed? Frequently, what I found so lacking in most black writing by men that seems to be present in a lot of black women's writing is a sense of joy, in addition to oppression and being women or black or whatever. With some exceptions. Gayl Jones is an exception to that. She never writes about joy. I think that's because she's young. But with others, there is a sense of comfort in being who one is, there's an expression of good times, not in the sense of "going out somewhere." There's a scene in *Sula* where the women are just having some fun, talking to one another. They enjoy that. That kind of woman. In Lucille Clifton's *Generations*, there's that sense of fun and joy. In Toni Cade, there's that sense of high-spiritedness. I don't mean comedy, and I don't mean jokes or anything. But part of this business of living in the world and triumphing over it has to do with a sense that there's some pleasure. And where do they get that pleasure from: How do they look at what we would call beauty in the world? What do they think it is? What pleases them? Just to see what the black woman's sensibilities are when she writes. What is she preoccupied with? What does she think are the crucial sorts of questions about existence, life, man-woman relationships? Are they seen the same way as the way in which the men have seen them?

[S]: Most of the major male characters in black literature are in motion. They're frequently much more like Ajax—maybe not always as grand and high-spirited as Ajax—but mobile. I think of such books as *Invisible Man* and *Autobiography of an Ex-Colored Man*, where there's this movement and quite often, there's no name, in contrast to how women are named, how they are lovingly named. An exception to this might be Leon Forrest.

[M]: But even there, he has that marvelous man, James Fishbond, you know, who is just a traveling man. Both of these things are very interesting to me. The name thing is a very, very strong theme in the book that I'm writing, the absence of a name given at all, the odd names and the slave names, the whole business, the feeling of anonymity, the feeling of orphanage. That's very important and became immediately clear to me in this new book. But the first thing you said about being in motion is also true, because I think that one of the major differences between black men's work—the major black characters—and black women's work is precisely that. The big scene is the traveling Ulysses scene, for black men. They are moving. Trains—you hear those men talk about trains like they were their first lover—the names of the trains, the times of the trains! And, boy, you know, they spread their seed all over the world. They are really moving! Perhaps it's because they don't have a land, they don't have dominion. You can trace that historically, and one never knows what would have been the case if we'd never been tampered with at all. But that going from town to town or place to place or looking out and over and beyond and changing and so on—that, it seems to me, is one of the monumental themes in black literature about men. That's what they do. It is the Ulysses theme, the leaving home. And then there's no one place that one settles. I mean, one travels. And I don't mean this in the sense of the Joycean character or even in the sense of just going off to find one's fortune in the classic sort of fairy tale, going off to see where the money is. But something else. Curiosity, what's around the corner, what's across the hill, what's in the valley, what's down the track. Go find out what that is, you know! And in the process of finding, they are also making themselves. Although in sociological terms that is described as a major failing of black men—they do not stay home and take care of their children, they are not there—that has always been to me one of the most attractive features about black male life. I guess I'm not suppose to say that. But the fact that they would split in a minute just delights me. It's part of that whole business of breaking ground, doing the other thing. They would leave, go someplace else. There was always that possibility. They were never—I don't say they were never, obviously there were exceptions to all of this—but they didn't just let it happen, just let it happen. That's part of that interesting magic I was talking about. And you know, the traveling musician, the theater group, those people who just stayed on the road, lived a different life. It's very beautiful, it's very interesting, and in that way, you know, they lived in the country, they lived here, they went all over it.

[s]: It's interesting to compare that motif to what you did to Sula, in that she is in motion in a sense . . .

[m]: Very much.

[s]: . . . at the same time that she is most stationary and in those enclosures, like that bedroom where she dies.

[m]: She is a masculine character in that sense. She will do the kinds of things that normally only men do, which is why she's so strange. She really behaves like a man. She picks up a man, drops a man, the same way a man picks up a woman, drops a woman. And that's her thing. She's masculine in that sense. She's adventuresome, she trusts herself, she's not scared, she really ain't scared. And she is curious and will leave and try anything. So that quality of masculinity—and I mean this in the pure sense—in a woman at that time is outrage, total outrage. She can't get away with that—unless she were in this sort of strange environment, this alien environment—for the normal—which would be the theater world, in which you realize, the people are living, even there, by laws. You know, somebody should do something interesting on that kind of

show business woman—Billie Holiday, Bessie Smith—not just their art form, but their lives. It's incredible, that sense of adventure that those women had. And I think that's why they were there in the first place. They were outside of that little community value thing. It's more normal among men, but it's attractive, and with men, it seems to me to be one of the very interesting things to talk about when one is doing any criticism of black writing, rather than doing those books in which you do five hundred people and you say a little bit about this one, a little bit about that one. If somebody could get one or two of the really major themes that are part and parcel of this canon. And there are some traceable, identifiable themes, and that's the kind of criticism that I would love to see. There may be some things that you could do with both men and women. But certainly this seems to me one of the major themes. And then there's the black woman as parent, not as a mother or father, but as a parent, as a sort of umbrella figure, culture-bearer, in that community with not just her children but all children, her relationship in that sense, how that is handled and treated and understood by writers, what that particular role is. We talk about all these things in terms of what her huge responsibilities have been, but a really penetrating analysis might be very helpful.

[S]: You've just described, very well, some new directions for criticism. Can you say something about new directions in fiction?

[M]: What I think is happening?

[S]: Well, what you think is happening, what may happen in fiction by some of the writers we've been discussing, in this decade.

[M]: Oh, I went to some meeting recently and there was a great deal of despair, it seemed to me, about what was happening in publishing and black fiction, the suggestion being that there was not much being published but that now it's not so popular anymore and that white publishers have decided that our age is over and that we are no longer fashionable as we were in the late sixties and early seventies. I think part of that's right—that is, we're no longer fashionable in that sense—all of which I am so grateful for, absolutely relieved to find, because some brilliant writers, I think, can surface now. Once you get off of the television screen, you can go home and do your work, because your responsibilities are different. Now I don't mean that there's any lessening of political awareness or political work, but I do think that one can be more fastidious, more discriminating. And it's open, it's just freer, that's all, and there's room, there's lots of room. People tend to think that the whole literary thing is a kind of pyramid, that somebody is on top, which is total anathema to me. There is enormous space! I think of it in terms of the one other art form in which black people have always excelled and that is music, an art form that opens doors, rather than closes them, where there are more possibilities, not fewer. But to continue to write the way somebody believes is the prescribed way is death. And if I know anything about black artists, I know they don't pay any attention to any prescriptions that anybody gives them at all!

It's harder perhaps in literature, because it has to be purchased by somebody in a publishing house, so that you're always under the eye of some other person. Nevertheless, it's exciting and it's new and it's marvelous and it's as though somebody pulled out the plug and we were left again to our own devices, not somebody else's, not the television's devices, not the *New York Times'* version of what we were supposed to do, but our own devices, which are the ones which we have to be left to. White writers, you know, write about us all the time. There are major black characters in Updike, in *Ragtime*, in all of them. That's where all the life is. That's where the life is. And the future of American literature is in that direction. I don't mean that's the only group, but that certainly is one of the major groups. Obviously, lots of people are interested in it, not just for research purposes as you know, but in terms of the gem, the theme, the juice, of fiction. And we are certainly, obviously, interested; we have all sorts of philosophical attitudes about "the predicament." There's that incredible kind of movement which yields an artistic representation of something that one takes for granted in history. I think that accounts for the success of Gayl Jones's first book, where you have the weight of history working itself out in the life of one, two, three people; I mean a large idea, brought down small, and at home, which gives it a universality and a particularity which makes it extraordinary.

But there's so much that nobody ever, ever does. You know, I go sometimes and, just for sustenance, I read those slave narratives—there are sometimes three or four sentences or half a page, each one of which could be developed in an art form, marvelous. Just to figure out how to—you mean to tell me she beat the dogs and the man and pulled a stump out of the ground? Who is she, you know? Who is she? It's just incredible. And all of that will surface, it *will surface*, and my *huge* joy is thinking that I am in some way part of that when I sit here in this office and that somehow there must be those of us in white established publishers where a black author can feel that he's going to go and get some respect—he doesn't have to explain everything—somebody is going to understand what he's trying do do, in his terms, not in somebody else's, but in his. I'm not saying that only black editors can do it, but I'm certainly saying that it's important that we are here to participate, to contribute to "the shelf"—as Forrest likes to call it.

[S]: I have one last question. What's the name of the new novel?

[M]: At the moment, it's called *Milkman Dead*. [The novel was published as *Song of Solomon* in the fall of 1977.]

◆◆◆◆◆◆◆◆◆◆◆◆◆◆

An Interview with Toni Morrison

NELLIE MCKAY

In life and in art, the outstanding achievements of writer Toni Morrison extend and enlarge the tradition of the strength, persistence, and accomplishments of black women in America. In life, her immediate models are first, her grandmother who, in the early part of this century, left her home in the South with seven children and thirty dollars because she feared white sexual violence against her maturing daughters; and second, her mother who took "humiliating jobs" in order to send Morrison money regularly while she was in college and graduate school. Her artistic precursors are equally impressive. The first black person in America to publish a book was a woman—Phillis Wheatley—a slave, whose *Poems on Various Subjects, Religious and Moral* appeared in 1773. The single most substantial fictional output of the much celebrated Harlem Renaissance of the 1920s was the work of a woman, Jessie Fauset, who published four novels between 1924 and 1933. In 1937, Zora Neale Hurston's Janie, in *Their Eyes Were Watching God*, heralded the coming of the contemporary black feminist heroine to American literature. Morrison is aware of both the burdens and the blessings of the past. "In all of the history of black women," she told me during our interview, "we have been both the ship and the harbor. . . . We can do things one at a time, or four things at a time if we have to."

Toni Morrison was born in Lorain, Ohio, in the 1930s. Southern roots extend up and out from both branches of her family background. Her mother's parents traveled North from Greenville and Birmingham, Alabama, by way of Kentucky, in a flight from poverty and racism. There her grandfather worked in the coal mines. The search for a better education for their children provided the incentive that propelled them to Ohio. Morrison's father came from Georgia, and the racial violence with which he grew up in that state had a lasting impact on his vision of white America. The most valuable legacy he left his daughter was a strong sense of her own value on her own terms.

Black lore, black music, black language, and all the myths and rituals of black culture were the most prominent elements in the early life of Toni Morrison. Her grandfather played the violin, her parents told thrilling and terrifying ghost stories, and her mother sang and played the numbers by decoding dream symbols as they were manifest in a dream book that she kept. She tells of a childhood world filled with signs, visitations, and ways of knowing that encompassed more than concrete reality.

Then in adolescence she read the great Russian, French, and English novels and was impressed by the quality of their specificity. In her writing she strives to capture the richness of black culture through its specificity.

Morrison's first novel, *The Bluest Eye*, was published in 1970. The book examines the experiences of a young black girl as she copes with the ideal of beauty and the reality of violence within the black community. Within the novel Morrison demonstrates that even with the best intentions, people hurt each other when they are chained to circumstances of poverty and low social status. "Violence," says Morrison, "is a distortion of what, perhaps, we want to do." The pain in this book is the consequence of the distortion that comes from the inability to express love in a positive way.

In *Sula*, her second novel (1974), the main theme is friendship between women, the meaning of which becomes illuminated when the friendship falls apart. The indomitable Peace women, especially Eva and Sula Peace, grandmother and granddaughter, are two of the most powerful black women characters in literature. Sula, counterpart to the Biblical Ishmael, her hand against everyone, and everyone's hands against her, is an unforgettable and anomalous heroine.

In *Song of Solomon*, the fictive world shifts from that of black women in their peculiar oppression to that of a young black man in search of his identity. But Milkman Dead lives in a world in which women are the main sources of the knowledge he must gain, and Pilate Dead, his aunt, a larger-than-life character, is his guide to that understanding. *Song of Solomon* won Toni Morrison the prestigious National Book Critics Circle Award in 1977.

Tar Baby, her fourth novel, was published in 1981. The action moves from the Caribbean to New York, to a small town in Florida. A Sorbonne-educated, successful black model and a young black male who rejects middle-class American values are at center stage in a work that examines the relationships between men and women, as well as between blacks and whites, that are possible in the conditions of contemporary society.

Toni Morrison is a major twentieth-century black woman writer. She is a member of the American Academy and Institute of Arts and Letters, and an active member of the National Council on the Arts. In addition to her position as Senior Editor at Random House, she teaches, lectures nationally and internationally, and is a single mother with two sons. "How do you do all of these things?" I asked her. "Well, I really only do two things," she said. "It only looks like many things. All of my work has to do with books. I teach books, write books, edit books, or talk about books. It is all one thing. And the other thing that I do is to raise my children which, as you know, I can only do one minute at a time."

Q. In exploring black women's writings, I have a strong sense that in the time which predates contemporary literature, black women found ways to express their creativity in a society that did everything to repress it and them. Alice Walker's tribute to her mother's artistry in her flower garden is a good example of this. Paule Marshall talks about the stories that her mother and her mother's friends told around the kitchen table after work. Both Walker and Marshall explain these phenomena as the sources of their own "authority" to create. The mothers of these women could not express themselves in the printed word, but they did in other ways, and in so doing used their imaginative powers to confirm their identities. Are there ways in which you feel joined to these early black women who, deliberately denied a public voice in American society, managed anyhow to express themselves inventively, creatively, imaginatively, and artistically?

A. Yes, I do feel a strong connection to "ancestors," so to speak. What is uppermost in my mind as I think about this is that my life seems to be dominated by information about black women. They were the culture bearers, and they told us [children] what to do. But in terms of story-telling, I remember it more as a shared activity between the men and the women in my family. There was a comradeship between men and women in the marriages of my grandparents, and of my mother and my father. The business of story-telling was a shared activity between them, and people of both genders participated in it. We, the children, were encouraged to participate in it at a very early age. This was true with my grandfather and grandmother, as well as with my father and mother, and with my uncles and aunts. There were no conflicts of gender in that area, at the level at which such are in vogue these days. My mother and my father did not fight about who was supposed to do what. Each confronted whatever crisis there was.

Q. So, within your family, women's creativity was a natural part of family life as a whole.

A. Yes. That is why the word "comrade" comes to mind in regard to the marriages I knew. I didn't find imbalance or unevenness in these relationships. I don't think that my mother's talents were hidden from males or white society, actually—they were very much on display. So I don't feel a tension there, or the struggle for dominance. The same was true for my grandparents—my mother's parents—whom I knew. I remember my great-grandmother, too. Her husband died before I was born, but I remember that when my great-grandmother walked into a room her grandsons and her nephews stood up. The women in my family were very articulate. Of course my great-grandmother could not read, but she was a midwife, and people from all over the state came to her for advice and for her to deliver babies. They came for other kinds of medical care too. Yes, I feel the authority of those women more than I do my own.

Q. If it is generally true that contemporary black women writers consistently look back to their mothers and grandmothers for the substance and authority in their voices, I suspect that this is an important and distinguishing element of black women's approach to their art. In contrast, many white women writers say that they are *inventing* the authority for their voices pretty much from scratch in an effort to break the silence of Shakespeare's sisters. Black women writers—having the example of authoritative mothers, aunts, grandmothers, great-grandmothers—have something special to contribute to the world. They have a distinctive and powerful artistic heritage. It is not white, and it is not male.

There is something else I would like to ask you. I have been wondering if there is a deliberate line of development in your work. How do you see your own growth and development as a successful writer?

A. Sometimes I see connections, but that is in hindsight. I am unaware of them at the time of writing. Still, it seems to me that from a book that focused on a pair of very young black girls, to move to a pair of adult black women, and then to a black man, and finally to a black man and a black woman is evolutionary. One comes out of the other. The writing gets better, too. The reading experience may not, but the writing gets better. I am giving myself permission to write books that do not depend on anyone's liking them, because what I want to do is write better. A writer does not always write in the ways others wish. The writer has to solve certain kinds of problems in writing. The way in which I handle elements within a story frame is important to me. Now I can get where I want to go faster and with more courage than I was able to do when I began to write.

Q. Your canvasses have gotten larger. You began with a closed community, the community of Lorain, Ohio. Then you sent Sula out into the world from Medallion. Milkman goes from North to South, and Jadine and Son have the United States, Paris, and the West Indies in which to find themselves. They participate in a very large world.

A. I found that I had to leave the town in *Song of Solomon* because the book was driven by men. The rhythm of their lives is outward, adventuresome. Milkman needs to go somewhere, although he hangs around that town for a long time—not listening to what he hears, not paying any attention to what it is. In *Tar Baby*, I wanted to be in a place where the characters had no access to any of the escape routes that people have in a large city. There were no police to call. There was no close neighbor to interfere. I wanted the characters all together in a pressure cooker, and that had to be outside of the United States. Of course it could have been on a remote farm, too. But it seemed easier to isolate them in a kind of Eden within distance of some civilization, but really outside of it. So when they find a "nigger in the woodpile," there's nothing they can do about it. And when they are upset because they think that he is going to rape them, there is no place to go. Then they, the lovers, can look for a place to live out their fantasies, in one of two places: in New York and/or in Eloe. They alone manage to get to the United States. Everyone else is confined to the island by Valerian who has dominion over everything there. I wanted to examine that kind of fiefdom. And I wanted them to be in an ideal place. What makes such vacation spots ideal is the absence of automobiles, police, airplanes, and the like. When a crisis occurs, people do not have access to such things. The crisis becomes a dilemma and forces the characters to do things that otherwise would not be required of them. All the books I have written deal with characters placed deliberately under enormous duress in order to see of what they are made.

Q. Can you tell us something about how you handle the process of writing? What is it like to have characters whose actions you cannot always predict?

A. I start with an idea, and then I find characters who can manifest aspects of the idea—children, adults, men or women.

Q. Do you tell them what to do?

A. I give them a circumstance that I like and try to realize them fully. I always know the endings. It seems clear to me that if I begin a book with a man flying off the roof of a hospital, then somebody's going to fly at the end, especially since the book comes out of a black myth about a flying man. What I don't know when I begin is how the character is going to get there. I don't know the middle.

Q. You work that through with the character?

A. Yes. I imagine the character, and if he or she is not fully imagined, there is awkwardness. Obviously, I can force characters to do what I want them to do, but knowing the difference between my forcing them and things coming out of the givenness of the situation I have imagined is part of knowing what writing is about. I feel a kind of fretfulness when a writer has thought up a character, and then for some reason made the character execute certain activities that are satisfying for the author but do not seem right for the character. That happens sometimes. Sometimes a writer imagines characters who threaten, who are able to take the book over. To prevent that, the writer has to exercise some kind of control. Pilate in *Song of Solomon* was that kind of character. She was a very large character and loomed very large in the book. So I wouldn't let her say too much.

Q. In spite of keeping her from saying much, she is still very large.

A. That's because she is like something we wish existed. She represents some hope in all of us.

Q. I've wondered if Pilate is the step beyond Sula. Sula had limitations, in her inability to make the human connection. She was not able to love anyone. Pilate realizes the fullness of love in a positive way.

A. Not Sula, but Eva. Pilate is a less despotic Eva. Eva is managerial. She tells everybody what to do, and she will dispute everybody. Pilate can tell everybody what to do, but she's wide-spirited. She does not run anybody's course. She is very fierce about her children, but when she is told by her brother to leave, she leaves, and does not return. She is wider scaled and less demanding about certain things. She trusts certain things. She does behave in a protective way with her children, but that's purely maternal. That strong maternal instinct is part of her otherworldliness. Eva was this-worldly. She wanted to arrange everybody's life and did so—and was generally liked. That is the connection I see between the two women in those books.

Q. There are some issues surrounding Pilate's granddaughter, Hagar, that have been disquieting for readers. Hagar dies because Milkman rejects her, and she is unable to cope with that. Milkman goes on to fulfill the role of the transcendent character in the novel. Aren't there disturbing implications in this type of plot—the young woman dying so that the young man can learn and rise?

A. There is something here which people miss. Milkman is willing to die at the end, and the person he is willing to die for is a woman.

Q. But what of Hagar?

A. Hagar does not have what Pilate had, which was a dozen years of a nurturing, good relationship with men. Pilate had a father, and she had a brother, who loved her very much, and she could use the knowledge of that love for her life. Her daughter Reba had less of that, but she certainly has at least a perfunctory adoration or love of men which she does not put to very good use. Hagar has even less because of the absence of any relationships with men in her life. She is weaker. Her grandmother senses it. That is why Pilate gives up the wandering life.

Strength of character is not something one can give another. It is not genetically transferred. Pilate can't give Hagar her genes in that sense, can't give her that strength; and Hagar does not take what she has available to her anyway. The first rejection she ever has destroys her, because she is a spoiled child.

I could write a book in which all the women were brave and wonderful, but it would bore me to death, and I think it would bore everybody else to death. Some women are weak and frail and hopeless, and some women are not. I write about both kinds, so one should not be more disturbing than the other. In the development of characters, there is value in the different effects.

Q.   The men in your novels are always in motion. They are not "steady" men. Where are the stable black men?

A.   But it is not true that all those men are "unsteady." Claudia's father is stable, Sidney is stable, and there are lots of stable black men in my books. On the other hand, I'm not obliged to write books about stable black men. Who is more stable than Milkman's father?

Q. But we don't admire Milkman's father.

A. Why not? The people in these novels are complex. Some are good and some are bad, but most of them are bits of both. I try to burrow as deeply as I can into characters. I don't come up with all good or all bad. I do not find men who leave their families necessarily villainous. I did not find Ajax villainous because he did not want Sula. Milkman was ignorant. That was his problem. He wanted to be comfortable, and he didn't want to go anywhere, except to chase something that was elusive, until he found out that there was something valuable to chase. It seems to me that one of the most fetching qualities of black people is the variety in which they come, and the enormous layers of lives that they live. It is a compelling time for me because no single layer is "it." If I examine those layers, I don't come up with simple statements about fathers and husbands, such as some people want to see in the books.

There is always something more interesting at stake than a clear resolution in a novel. I'm interested in survival—who survives and who does not, and why—and I would like to chart a course that suggests where the dangers are and where the safety might be. I do not want to bow out with easy answers to complex questions. It's the complexity of how people behave under duress that is of interest to me—the qualities they show at the end of an event when their backs are up against the wall. The important thing about Hagar's death is the response to it— how Pilate deals with the fact of it—how Milkman in his journey caused real grief. One can't do what he did and not cause enormous amounts of pain. It was carelessness that caused that girl pain. He has taken her life. He will always regret that, and there is nothing he can do about it. That generally is the way it is—there is nothing that you can do about it except do better, and don't do *that* again. He was not in a position to do anything about it because he was stupid. When he learns something about love, it is from a strange woman in another part of the country. And he does not repeat the first mistake. When he goes South with Pilate he is ready to do something else. That is the thrust of it all. A woman once got very angry with me because Pilate died. She was very incensed about it. I told her that first, it was of no value to have Guitar kill someone nobody cared anything about. If that had been the case it would not show us how violent violence is. Some character that we care about had to be killed to demonstrate that. And second, Pilate is larger than life and never really dies in that sense. She was not born, anyway—she gave birth to herself. So the question of her birth and death is irrelevant.

Q. Can you say something about Milkman's relationship to Pilate?

A. Milkman's hope, almost a conviction, has to be that he can be like her.

Q. One of the things that I observe about your novels is that no one who reads them ever seems to forget them. When the reading is done, one is not through with the book. The themes are haunting; they do not go away.

A. I am very happy to hear that my books haunt. That is what I work very hard for, and for me it is an achievement when they haunt readers, as you say. That is important because I think it is a corollary, or a parallel, or an outgrowth of what the oral tradition was, which is what we were talking about earlier in relationship to the people around the table. The point was to tell the same story again and again. I can change it if I contribute to it when I tell it. I can emphasize special things. People who are listening comment on it and make it up, too, as it goes along. In the same way when a preacher delivers a sermon he really expects his congregation to listen, participate, approve, disapprove, and interject almost as much as he does. Eventually, I think, if the life of the novels is long, then the readers who wish to read my books will know that it is not I who do it, it is they who do.

Q. Do what?

A. Who kill off, or feel the laughs, or feel the satisfactions or the triumphs. I manipulate. When I'm good at it, it is not heavy-handed. But I want a very strong visceral and emotional response as well as a very clear intellectual response, and the haunting that you describe is testimony to that.

Q. Your concern is to touch the sensibilities of your readers.

A. I don't want to give my readers something to swallow. I want to give them something to feel and think about, and I hope that I set it up in such a way that it is a legitimate thing, and a valuable thing.

I think there is a serious question about black male and black female relationships in the twentieth century. I just think that the argument has always turned on something it should not turn on: gender. I think that the conflict of genders is a cultural illness. Many of the problems modern couples have are caused not so much by conflicting gender roles as by the other "differences" the culture offers. That is what the conflicts in *Tar Baby* are all about. Jadine and Son had no problems as far as men and women are concerned. They knew exactly what to do. But they had a problem about what work to do, when and where to do it, and where to live. Those things hinged on what they felt about who they were, and what their responsibilities were in being black. The question for each was whether he or she was really a member of the tribe. It was not because he was a man and she was a woman that conflict arose between them. Her problems as a woman were easily solved. She solved them in Paris.

Q. But in Paris she was not happy either?

A. Because of her *blackness*! It is when she sees the woman in yellow that she begins to feel inauthentic. That is what she runs away from.

Q. Is that woman the roots—the past?

A. The time is not important. It is that she is a real, a complete individual who owns herself—another kind of Pilate. There is always someone who has no peer, who does not have to become anybody. Someone who already "is."

Q. She walks in and out of the novel without saying a word, yet she leaves such a powerful impact behind her!

A. Such people do. The genuine article only has to appear for a moment to become memorable. It would be anticlimactic to have a conversation with her, because that person is invested with all the hopes and views of the person who observes her. She is the original self—the self that we betray when we lie, the one that is always there. And whatever that self looks like—if one ever sees that thing, or that image—one measures one's other self against it. So that with all of the good luck, and the good fortune, and the skill that Jadine has—the other is the authentic self. And as for Son, he has a similar loss. He loved Eloe, and he loved all those people, but he wasn't there. Eloe is the kind of thing that one takes when one leaves, and harbors it in the heart.

Q. Later, when he looks at the pictures, Jadine destroys it for him.

A. Maybe it wasn't real anyway. If it were, she could not destroy it with a camera. He did not live in that world either. Maybe there was just a little bit of fraud in his thinking as he did since he was away. So you can't really trust all that he says.

Q. One of the things that this conversation with you seems to emphasize is that it is wrong to see your characters in any kind of limited symbolic way. But even so, I've been wondering if Son represents black culture, the black community that seems lost to our modern way of life.

A. He represents some aspects of it. But it is the combinations in characters that are the best part of writing novels—the combinations of virtue and flaw, of good intentions gone awry, of wickedness cleansed and people made whole again. If you judge them all by the best that they have done, they are wonderful. If you judge them all by the worst that they have done, they are terrible. I like the relationship between Sidney and Ondine. He is, in the jargon of the seventies, a good old Uncle Tom. But I feel enormous respect for him. He is a man who loved work well done. He is not befuddled and confused about who he is. And when all the world seems as though it is horrible, he takes over. He does not want to do so, but if Valerian is not going to run things, he will. There is the touching and tenderness between him and his wife. They have an abiding trust in one another. There is Ondine's sorrow for having sacrificed her whole life for this child, Jadine, and still she has not given her the one thing she needed most: the knowledge of how to be a daughter. I liked Sidney's willingness to blow Son's head off if he behaved badly. These people do not respect bad behavior, no matter where it comes from. And they are different from Son. The fact that he does not like them does not mean that I do not.

Q. Sidney is a "Philadelphia Negro." Do you love all of your characters?

A. Always!

Q. Do you identify with any one of them?

A. No, that would not be a good position to take.

Q. Would such a position create a problem for you in writing?

A. Yes. I love them and I cherish them, and I love their company as long as I am with them. The point is to try to see the world from their eyes, and I think that is probably what causes readers some dismay. I like to do what I think actors do on stage. My work is to become those characters in a limited way, to see what they see, not what I see. I need to see how they see the world. Each one speaks his or her own language, has an individual set of metaphors, and notices certain things differently from other people. If I have a scene such as the one in which Nel and Sula are talking [when Nel visits the sick Sula], I let them talk, but they may not be talking to each other. Each has something else on her mind. That is part of the excitement of being incarnate, as it were, in the flesh. We have to learn more about the other person. Sometimes we have perfect conversations, as with Sidney and Ondine. They don't have to feed each other whole sentences. But sometimes people need whole paragraphs of arguments, as Son and Jadine do, in order to explain themselves, except when they are doing something specific. They don't need to talk about lust. There are differences in the way people talk to each other when they are hanging on some sort of hook, and they are trying to touch and to reach. But what prevents them from achieving that is all the baggage that they bring with them through life. We have to understand that. And there are revelations that take place. The characters have revelations, large or small, which might not have happened but for the preceding information in the book.

Q. What happens to your characters under such circumstances?

A. They learn something. Nel pursues something at the end that she did not know before. So does Milkman. So does Jadine. So does the narrator of *The Bluest Eye*. And in most of these circumstances there is a press towards knowledge, at the expense of happiness perhaps.

Q. Is Jadine ever going to know who she is?

A. I hope so. She has a good shot at it, a good chance. Now she knows something that she did not know before. She may know why she was running away. And maybe, the biggest thing that she can learn, even if she never gets back to Son, is that dreams of safety are childish.

Q. Can you tell me why you ended *Tar Baby* with "lickety-split"?

A. I wanted it to have the sound of the Tar Baby story, which is lickety-split towards or away from or around the briar patch. But I also wanted to suggest that this journey is Son's choice—although he did not think it up, Thérèse did. He said he had no choice, so she manipulated his trip so that he had a choice. On his way back to Valerian's house in order to get the address so he can find Jadine, there is a strong possibility that he joins or is captured by the horsemen—captured by the past, by the wish, by the prehistoric times. The suggestion in the end, when the trees step back to make way for a certain kind of man, is that Nature is urging him to join them. First he crawls, then he stands up, he stumbles, then he walks, and last, he runs, and his run is lickety-split, lickety-split, has a movement of some confidence, and also suggests the beat of a rabbit running.

Q. And he is surrounded by water and darkness.

A. There is a birth in the beginning of the book. Close to the opening of the book, Son is going towards the island through the water. In the last part of the book he is doing the same thing, going towards the island through the water. Neither of these sections has a chapter head—they are parentheses around the book. In the first one, the suggestion was birth because the water pushes and urges him away from the shore, and there is the ammonia-scented air. He comes out of it as from a womb. In the last part there is a similar kind of birth, except that this time he is being urged by the water to go ashore. This time he stands up and runs, and there is cooperation with the land and the fog.

Q. Is there anything that you would like especially to add to the things that you have already said today?

A. Everything I really have to say is in my books. I can clarify and illuminate some small things. Critics of my work have often left something to be desired, in my mind, because they don't always evolve out of the culture, the world, the given quality out of which I write. Other kinds of structures are imposed on my works, and therefore they are either praised or dismissed on the basis of something that I have no interest in whatever, which is writing a novel according to some structure that comes out of a different culture. I am trying very hard to use the characteristics of the art form that I know best, and to succeed or fail on those criteria rather than on some other criteria. I tend not to explain things very much, but I long for a critic who will know what I mean when I say "church," or "community," or when I say "ancestor," or "chorus." Because my books come out of those things and represent how they function in the black cosmology. Sula's return to Medallion can be seen as a defeat for her in the eyes of some critics, because they assume that the individual, alone and isolated, making his or her way, is a triumphant thing. With black people, her return may be seen as a triumph and not a defeat, because she comes back to where she was at the beginning. As much of a pariah as she is in that village, she is nevertheless protected there as she would not be elsewhere. I am yearning for someone to see such things—to see what the structures are, what the moorings are, where the anchors are that support my writings.

Q. I think I understand what you mean. Black writers and black critics share similar frustrations in this area. There is a tension between what comes from inside of the critic (that which is a function of black culture) and what comes from outside of him or her (that which has been imposed on the individual by the larger world). At the beginning of this conversation I noted that black writers ply their trade out of a multiplicity of intersecting traditions. All of black life in Western culture shares in this, and sometimes I like to believe that it is the richness that derives from this conglomeration that makes black people special. There is joy and there is pain; there are successes and failures; but always there is tension, a tension that is the struggle for integrity.

A. I am always aware of those tensions. It is as easy to explain as saying that if I am going to do the work that I do, I can't do it on my home street. I live in and among people who may misunderstand me completely. Also, one's grades are given on other people's scales. So it is always a balancing act. My plea is for some pioneering work to be done in literary criticism, not just for my work, but for all sorts of people's work, and now that the literature exists, there can be that kind of criticism. Our—black women's—job is a particularly complex one in that regard. But if we can't do it, then nobody can do it. We have no systematic mode of criticism that has yet evolved from us, but it will. I am not *like* James Joyce; I am not *like* Thomas Hardy; I am not *like* Faulkner. I am not *like* in that sense. I do not have objections to being compared to such extraordinarily gifted and facile writers, but it does leave me sort of hanging there when I know that my effort is to be *like* something that has probably only been fully expressed perhaps in music, or in some other culture-gen that survives almost in isolation because the community manages to hold on to it. Sometimes I can reflect something of this kind in my novels. Writing novels is a way to encompass this—this something.

Q. You are looking for a special relationship between the literature and the criticism of black writers—a relationship that will enable the literature to be heard as it really is—a criticism that will illuminate whatever story black people have to tell from its inside.

A. Black people have a story, and that story has to be heard. There was an articulate literature before there was print. There were griots. They memorized it. People heard it. It is important that there is sound in my books—that you can hear it, that I can hear it. So I am inclined not to use adverbs, not because I am trying to write a play, but because I want to try to give the dialogue a certain sound.

Q. It is not difficult to detect that sound.

A. Yes, you hear that. What you hear is what you remember. That oral quality is deliberate. It is not unique to my writing, but it is a deliberate sound that I try to catch. The way black people talk is not so much the use of non-standard grammar as it is the manipulation of metaphor. The fact is that the stories look as though they come from people who are not even authors. No author tells these stories. They are just told—meanderingly—as though they are going in several directions at the same time. I had to divide my books into chapters because I had to do something in order for people to recognize and understand what I was doing. But they don't necessarily have to have that form. I am not experimental, I am simply trying to recreate something out of an old art form in my books—the something that defines what makes a book "black." And that has nothing to do with whether the people in the books are black or not. The open-ended quality that is sometimes a problematic in the novel form reminds me of the uses to which stories are put in the black community. The stories are constantly being retold, constantly being imagined within a framework. And I hook into this like a life-support system, which for me, is the thing out of which I come. It is an easy job to write stories with black people in them. I look beyond the people to see what makes black literature different. And in doing this my own style has evolved. It is not the only style, but it is a style by which I recognize my own work. Another writer, another black writer, such as Toni Cade Bambara, has another style. She has a very clear style, and there is no question that it is black. She could write about anything—birds, stamps—it would still sound that way. Gayl Jones has another style. So it is not a question of *a* black style, but it is a question of recognizing the variety of styles, and hanging on to whatever that ineffable quality is that is curiously black. The only analogy that I have for it is in music. John Coltrane does not sound like Louis Armstrong, and no one ever confuses one for the other, and no one questions if they are black. That is what I am trying to get at, but I don't have the vocabulary to explain it better. It can be copied, just like the music can be copied. But once one has it, it is distinguishable and therefore recognizable for itself. If it is written, it can be learned—but to be learned, it has to be in print.

I also want my work to capture the vast imagination of black people. That is, I want my books to reflect the imaginative combination of the real world, the very practical, shrewd, day to day functioning that black people must do, while at the same time they encompass some great supernatural element. We know that it does not bother them one bit to do something practical and have visions at the same time. So all the parts of living are on an equal footing. Birds talk and butterflies cry, and it is not surprising or upsetting to them. These things make the world larger for them. Some young people don't want to acknowledge this as a way of life. They don't want to hark back to those embarrassing days when we were associated with "haints" and superstitions. They want to get as far as possible into the scientific world. It makes me wonder, in such cases, if the knowledge we ignore is discredited because we have discredited it.

Q. Speaking of knowledge, what do you think about the special kind of knowledge that black women have always had, and how do you think that is seen in the world?

A. Much of that knowledge is also discredited, and I think it is because people say it is no more than what women say to each other. It is called old wives' tales, or gossip, or anything but information. In the same way, friendship between women is not a suitable topic for a book. Hamlet can have a friend, and Achilles can have one, but women don't, because the world knows that women don't choose each other's acquaintanceship. They choose men first, then women as second choice. But I have made women the focal point of books in order to find out what women's friendships are really all about. And the same thing is true about why I wrote *Song of Solomon* the way I did. I chose the man to make that journey because I thought he had more to learn than a woman would have. I started with a man, and I was amazed at how little men taught one another in the book. I assumed that all men ever learn about being men they get from other men. So that the presence of Pilate, and the impact that all the other women had on Milkman's life, came as a bit of a surprise to me. But it made it work out right, because there were two sets of information he needed to learn in order to become a complete human being.

Q. He learns one set of information from Guitar, and he learns another set of information from Pilate, so there is a balance between what he learns from a man and what he learns from a woman.

A. And that kind of harmony is what makes it possible for him to do what he does toward the end of the book, and to do something important instead of figuring how he can live better and more comfortably, and easier.

Q. You have been very open with your feelings about your writings. This is a rare opportunity for me.

A. I'm a bit more open about it now than I was before, because when I first began writing I assumed a lot of things that were not true. Then I began to see odd things in odd places—like people having to talk about Northrup Frye or somebody like that in order to get through. I don't mean to say that Frye is inapplicable, just to point out that at some point one has to move with some authority into one's own structure. But the new structure must be well constructed, and it could not be constructed until there was a library out of which to build something.

Q. We have that now.

A. We can tell it the way it is. We have come through the worst, and we are still here. I think about what black writers do as having a quality of hunger and disturbance that never ends. Classical music satisfies and closes. Black music does not do that. Jazz always keeps you on the edge. There is no final chord. There may be a long chord, but no final chord. And it agitates you. Spirituals agitate you, no matter what they are saying about how it is all going to be. There is something underneath them that is incomplete. There is always something else that you want from the music. I want my books to be like that—because I want that feeling of something held in reserve and the sense that there is more— that you can't have it all right now.

Q. They have an idiom of their own?

A. That's right. Take Lena [Horne] or Aretha [Franklin]—they don't give you all, they only give you enough for now. Or the musicians. One always has the feeling, whether it is true or not, they may be absolutely parched, but one has the feeling that there's some more. They have the ability to make you want it, and remember the want. That is a part of what I want to put into my books. They will never fully satisfy—never fully.

◆◆◆◆◆◆◆◆◆◆◆◆◆

Interview With Toni Morrison
BY CHRISTINA DAVIS

From *Présence Afrikaine*, First Quarterly, 1988

In 1986, Christina Davis met with Toni Morrison in Albany, New York. The interview that follows was carried out with the 30th Anniversary of the First International Conference of Black Writers and Artists (held at the Sorbonne in September 1956) in mind.

Toni Morrison was born in Lorain, Ohio, and studied at Howard University and Cornell University. She taught at Howard and other Universities before becoming the first black woman to hold the position of Senior Editor at Random House Publishing Company in New York. While there, she edited the work of Toni Cade Bambara, Angela Davis, Gayl Jones and Muhammad Ali, among others. She is currently Schweitzer Professor of the Humanities at the State University of New York at Albany.

While teaching at Howard, Toni Morrison began to write. Her first novel, *The Bluest Eye*, was published in 1970. It was followed by *Sula* (1973), *Song of Solomon* (1977), *Tar Baby* (1981) and *Beloved* (1987). In early 1986, the Capital Repertory Company in Albany performed *Dreaming Emmett*, Toni Morrison's first play, based on the lynching of 14-year-old Emmett Till in 1955. The author has received numerous awards for her work and was named Distinguished Writer of 1978 by the American Academy of Arts and Letters. Her novels have been translated into many foreign languages, including French.

She is an active member of organizations such as the National Council on the Arts, the Helsinki Watch Committee and the Board of Trustees of the New York Public Library. She is Chairperson of the New York State Education Department's Committee on Adult Illiteracy.

Christina Davis: September 1986 marks the 30th Anniversary of the First International Conference of Black Writers and Artists at the Sorbonne. Among the themes of the Conference was the need for *Africans* to discover and explore the historical truth about Africa. How has the discovery and affirmation of the truth about the black experience in the United States been a preoccupation of Black American writers?

Toni Morrison: I think it's the *only* preoccupation of Black American writers. The way in which they see that experience of course varies from time to time. Some energy was spent trying to persuade mainstream white America that the experience that most black people had was insuf-

ferable and changeable and that black people were worthy of their compassion (. . .) Some of the interest has been to find whatever cultural
connections there were between Afro-Americans and Africans, but it's
always been interesting to me that Africans are not interested in it at
all.

My own preoccupations are quite different—or maybe they're not
quite different, but what has interested me is the fact that those two
descriptions I just gave you were geared toward educating or clarifying
or stimulating something, some response in the white community—which
is a legitimate pursuit on the face of it—and perhaps very little attention
was given to addressing certain kinds of problems among the members
of the black community in a way that was not pedagogical. There was a
long period of pedagogy going on in fiction among black people. It seems
to me that black people patronizing black people is as unfortunate as
being patronized by white people . . .

I respect the emotional and intellectual intelligence of black people
because I respect my own emotional intelligence, therefore I did not
want to write books that had simple-minded points. I wanted to explore
the imagination as well as the problems of black people and it seems to
me that this is a more contemporary and perhaps more recent pursuit
among black writers.

Christina Davis: When you talk about *"names that bore witness"* in
Song of Solomon, would they be part of the historical experience of
Blacks in the United States?

Toni Morrison: Yes, the reclamation of the history of black people in
this country is paramount in its importance because while you can't really
blame the conqueror for writing history his own way, you can certainly
debate it. There's a great deal of obfuscation and distortion and erasure,
so that the presence and the heartbeat of black people has been systematically annihilated in many, many ways and the job of recovery is ours.
It's a serious responsibility and one single human being can only do a
very very tiny part of that, but it seems to me to be both secular and
non-secular work for a writer. You have to stake it out and identify those
who have preceded you—resummoning them, acknowledging them is just
one step in that process of reclamation—so that they are always there
as the *confirmation* and the affirmation of the life that I personally have
not lived but is the life of that organism to which I belong which is black
people in this country.

Christina Davis: What do you feel are links between African and
Afro-American literatures?

Toni Morrison: I'm only discovering those links in a large sense—
that is, as a reader and as a scholar—and I'm not sure which ones are
genuine and which ones are not. I know the impact that African authors
have had on me as a reader, the doors that were opened for me by that

414 • TONI MORRISON

contact through literature, because that's the only contact I had. I'm also aware of the vocabulary used to describe what we say as black people in this country—the scholarly vocabulary used in traditional texts to describe *how* we say and how we are is a code designed for destruction, so that one's job is to clear away the code and see what really is in the language and what are the connections.

When I first began to write, I would do no research in that area because I distrusted the sources of research, that is, the books that were available, whether they were religion or philosophy and so on. I would rely heavily and almost totally on my own recollections and, more important, on my own insight about those recollections, and in so doing was able to imagine and to recreate cultural linkages that were identified for me by Africans who had a more familiar, an overt recognition (of them). So much of what is true about Afro-Americans is not only the African but the American—we are very much that and trying to separate those things out can be very difficult, if you *want* to separate them out. We are a brand new human being in this country.

Christina Davis: I understand you dislike having your work described as "magic realism." Why is that?

Toni Morrison: I was once under the impression that that label "magical realism" was another one of those words that covered up what was going on. I don't know when it began to be used but my first awareness of it was when certain kinds of novels were being described that had been written by Latin American men. It was a way of *not* talking about the politics. It was a way of *not* talking about what was in the books. If you could apply the word "magical" then that *dilutes* the realism but it seemed legitimate because there were these supernatural and unrealistic things, surreal things, going on in the text. But for literary historians and literary critics it just seemed to be a convenient way to skip again what was the truth in the art of certain writers.

My own use of enchantment simply comes because that's the way the world was for me and for the black people that I knew. In addition to the very shrewd, down-to-earth, efficient way in which they did things and survived things, there was this other knowledge or perception, always discredited but nevertheless there, which informed their sensibilities and clarified their activities. It formed a kind of cosmology that was perceptive as well as enchanting, and so it seemed impossible for *me* to write about black people and eliminate that simply because it was "unbelievable." It functioned as a raiment—the body that was in the middle was something quite different—and also it was part and parcel of this extraordinary language. The metaphors and the perceptions came out of that world. So I have become indifferent, I suppose, to the phrase "magical realism" but I was very alert at the beginning when I heard it because when I would read the articles about it, it always seemed to me that it was just another evasive label.

Christina Davis: All the forces, spiritual forces and so on, are very *real* in their own way, although they're different from what's usually called realism, and they're promptly dismissed as magical.

Toni Morrison: Of course, that *is* the reality. I mean, it's not as though it's a thing you do on Sunday morning in church, it's not a tiny, entertaining aspect of one's life—it's what *informs* your sensibility. I grew up in a house in which people talked about their dreams with the same authority that they talked about what "really" happened. They had visitations and did not find that fact shocking and they had some sweet, intimate connection with things that were not empirically verifiable. It not only made them for me the most interesting people in the world—it was an enormous resource for the solution of certain kinds of problems. Without that, I think I would have been quite bereft because I would have been dependent on so-called scientific data to explain hopelessly unscientific things and also I would have relied on information that even subsequent objectivity has proved to be fraudulent, you see. But for my mother to decide that myself and my sister, when we were infants, would not go into a tuberculosis hospital as this doctor said we should because we had been exposed to tuberculosis was not based on scientific evidence. She simply saw that no one ever came out of those sanitoriums in the '30s and also she had visitations. It was interesting to me that they were treating tubercular patients at that time in a way that would kill them because they didn't *have* all of the right information.

Christina Davis: This of course is very similar to the African relationship with the ancestors and the passing from one state to another rather than death as the Western world knows it.

Toni Morrison: It's interesting—the concept of an ancestor not necessarily as a parent but as an abiding, interested, benevolent, guiding presence that is yours and is concerned about you, not quite like saints but having the same sort of access, none of which is new information. It's just that when it comes from discredited people it somehow has some other exotic attachment: thus the word "magic." I remember many people were very upset when some major journalistic work was done on my work and the heading was "Black Magic": that is to say, my work was black magic. It was a favorable heading to them but the implication was that there was no intelligence there, it was all sort of, you know, "the panther does not know he is graceful because it is his nature to leap that way."

Christina Davis: Another theme of the Sorbonne Conference was defining the unity of black people scattered all over the world. To what extent do you feel contemporary literature reflects that unity or disunity?

Toni Morrison: Well, certain questions have surfaced. There was a time when the literature that was being written, non-fiction as well as fiction, hammered away at the connections and it got very romantic, which I suppose was inevitable but was unfortunate. Then it took another turn in which it just got very interesting. Recent books seem to take either that connection for granted or to explore it in some way that is a little bit different from the sort of wonderful, illusory connection that they thought existed. You know, it was easy for Black Americans, Afro-Americans—some of them—to think about Africa almost the way the conquistadors thought about it, or as one big continent full of everybody in their neighborhood, instead of very distinct, very different, very specific, widely divergent people and what connected them *perhaps* was their skin, but not really that. So that the *enormous* differences are more interesting to me than the similarities because it's too easy to get into the trap of the monolithic black person, you know, the classic, "uni" person.

Christina Davis: Would you like to mention a few of the differences that you find interesting among Africans or among Africans and Afro-Americans, as far as literature is concerned?

Toni Morrison: Well, I think there are certain things that have come through, rained down on us in America, that don't seem to have happened in Africa. Color—skin color, the privileges of skin in this country are different. I don't mean they don't exist in Africa, they must. Concept of beauty. License, sexual license in this country versus sexual license in African literature. *Enormous* differences in gender, you know: the expectations of one gender of another, what black women in America expect of black men and what black men in America expect of black women, and differences there. And then just the impact of the white world on an African country—the difference between Kenya and South Africa. I mean it's *huge* differences, you see. And what the similarities are between the impact of the white world on a black human being in Boston versus that same impact in South Carolina and Mississippi. Those things leaped up at me. Reading Camara Laye, for example—*The Radiance of the King*—was an important thing for me. Just being in that position and watching that man stripped as it were, going farther and farther and farther back and the complex array of people that he met, Africans that he met or who came into his purview, was for me an extraordinary thing: a very narcotic kind of experience, a journey for me that was overwhelming, quite.

Christina Davis: I wanted to ask if there's an African writer or African writers that you feel particularly akin to or whose work you feel especially close to?

Toni Morrison: Well, neither akin nor close but certainly a real education for me. Chinua Achebe was a *real* education for me, a real education. And certainly the plays of Soyinka and *The Beautyful Ones Are Not Yet Born* of Ayi Kwei Armah—those things were at that time real, and they're the kinds of books that one can re-read with enormous discoveries subsequently.

Christina Davis: We've been talking about literature but I'd like to ask what you feel that Afro-American and African *writers* have in common *as writers*? Or, on the contrary, what separates them in their respective positions?

Toni Morrison: The major thing that binds us—there may be others because I don't dwell on it quite that much—is the clear identification of what the enemy forces are, not this person or that person and so on, but the acknowledgment of a way of life dreamed up for us by some other people who are at the moment in power, and knowing the ways in which it can be subverted. That *is* a connection: we know who he is. What separates us are the things that separate all people, one of which is the way you identify what the problems are and the disguises in which they appear.

This country is so full of material things. There's a great deal of freedom in terms of movement in one sense or in terms of ability to acquire *things*. It can hide misery and pain enormously and also can imprison you in a way, you know, because you have your things but you have to take care of them. And that's a real problem for Black Americans, it's a real problem for all Americans, but it's a serious problem for Black Americans who envision success in certain ways and have difficulty manipulating power once it's in their hands. Because the definitions of success and the ways in which one acquires and therefore *holds* power are quite different in a *totally* capitalistic country. And it can be a dead weight, you know: it can be just heavy shoes that you're walking around in so that certain spiritual things get lost or defrauded in a way. Sometimes people from other countries come here and are quite overwhelmed by the variety of things that are easily found, a wide variety, and its size, and they think how marvelous it all is and I suppose in relative terms it is.

I was fascinated to hear some South Africans on the radio once who were measuring the freedom of black people here against their own and being very curious about what black people were complaining about. They didn't understand it and why should they understand it, because they are relative things. They were sitting in New York in the U.N. so maybe . . . I mean the conversation was there.

Interesting things have happened since that time—the awareness of just the basic hell, the outlines of a basic hell are much more obvious among Black Americans now. There are organizations that are quite serious and there's a movement afoot now that at the moment is concentrated on relief, but it will not stop there.

Christina Davis: Is there anything of all this similarity or difference among the writers that's particular to women writers, African women writers and Afro-American women writers?

Toni Morrison: I think there's something very special about women writers, black women writers in America and those that I know of in any real sense in Africa—Bessie Head, for example, in Africa or Gloria Naylor here. There's a gaze that women writers seem to have that is quite fascinating to me because they tend not to be interested in confrontations with white men—the confrontation between black women and white men is not very important, it doesn't center the text. There are more important ones for them and their look, their gaze of the text is unblinking and wide and very steady. It's not narrow, it's very probing and it does not flinch. And it doesn't have these funny little axes to grind. There's something really marvelous about that.

Christina Davis: I'm sure I'm not the first person who has remarked on the similarity between your speaking or reading voice and your written voice. How did you find your voice as a writer?

Toni Morrison: Tell me what you mean: my speaking voice and my written voice?

Christina Davis: The only way I can describe it to you is to tell you that I've heard other writers read and found a cleavage between the voice that comes off the page and the voice that comes into the ear.

Toni Morrison: Ah well, that may mean that my efforts to make aural literature—A-U-R-A-L—work because I do hear it. It has to read in silence and that's just one phase of the work but it also has to *sound* and if it doesn't *sound* right . . . Even though I don't speak it when I'm writing it, I have this interior piece, I guess, in my head that reads, so that the way I hear it is the way I write it and I guess that's the way I would read it aloud. The point is not to need the adverbs to say how it sounds but to have the sound of it in the sentence, and if it needs a lot of footnotes or editorial remarks or description in order to say how it sounded, then there's something wrong with it.

So I do a lot of revision when I write in order to clean away the parts of the book that can *only* work as print, but it also must work as a total story because that is one of the major characteristics of black literature as far as I'm concerned—it's not just having black people *in* it or having it be written by a black person, but it has to have certain kinds of fundamental characteristics (one of) which is the participation of the *other*, that is, the audience, the reader, and that you can do with a spoken story.

You have to learn how much information to give and how much to keep out and when you need color and when you need a metaphor and when you don't, so that two people are busy making the story. One is me and one is you and together we do that, we invent it together and I just hold your hand while you're in the process of going there and hearing it and sharing it, and being appalled by this and amused by that and happy about this and chagrined about that and scared of this and grateful for that. An artist, for me, a black artist for me, is not a solitary person who has no responsibility to the community. It's a totally communal experience where I would feel unhappy if there was no controversy or no debate or no anything—no *passion* that accompanied the experience of the work. I want somebody to say amen!

Christina Davis: Ruth and Pilate in *Song of Solomon* are very different women, yet each has her particular strengths and, on occasion, they join forces. In both *Song of Solomon* and *Sula*, three generations of women live together. Do your women characters have a special rôle to play in your work?

Toni Morrison: Well, in the beginning I was just interested in *finally* placing black women center stage in the text, and not as the all-knowing, infallible black matriarch but as a flawed here, triumphant there, mean, nice, complicated woman, and some of them win and some of them lose. I'm very interested in why and how that happens, but here was this vacancy in the literature that I had any familiarity with and the vacancy was me, or the women that I knew. So that preoccupied me a great deal in the beginning. It still does, except now I'm interested also in the relationships of black men and black women and the axes on which those relationships frequently turn, and how they complement each other, fulfill one another or hurt one another and are made whole or prevented from wholeness by things that they have incorporated into their psyche.

Christina Davis: At the end of *Song of Solomon* we leave Milkman flying through the air. And we don't know what ultimately happens to Son in *Tar Baby* either. Why do you end your novels ambiguously?

Toni Morrison (laughs): Well, I can't shut the door at a moment when the piont of the book was the availability of choices and Milkman in *Song of Solomon:* the quality of his life has improved so much and he is so complete and capable that the length of it is irrelevant really. It's not about dying or not dying, it's just that this marvelous epiphany has taken place and, if I close the door, then it would be misleading to say one thing or the other.

For Son, his lament was that he had no choice in this matter, he really was stuck, and he was then provided with one by a woman, but I couldn't make the choice *for* him. I just had to show what the two possibilities were: you join the twentieth century with all of its terror or you abandon the twentieth century and live in some mythological world in private, and which is the briar patch? The reader had to figure that out for him- or herself and that is also part of ending stories. You don't end a story in the oral tradition—you can have the little message at the end, your little moral, but the ambiguity is deliberate because it doesn't end, it's an ongoing thing and the reader or the listener is in it and you have to THINK *(laughs)*. That's what I mean by participating—you have to think what do you want it to be: you want him to live, you want him to die, you want him to go with Jadine, you want him to join the men, you want him to kill Guitar, you want Guitar to kill him or what? You're there, you really are, and I just cannot pass out these little pieces of paper with these messages on them telling people who I respect "this is the way it is" and close the door, because I don't want anybody to do that to me (laughs).

Christina Davis: That really disturbs people—to be made to think.

Toni Morrison: Well, I know. We do read books quite differently. I mean we're taught to read them like you open a medicine cabinet and get out an aspirin and your headache is gone. Or people are looking for the "how-to" book—you know, thirty days and you'll have a flat stomach, or three days as the case may be. So that they are looking for easy, passive, uninvolved and disengaged experiences—television experiences, and I won't, I won't do that.

Christina Davis: I've been impressed by the seriousness with which you prepare your participation in round-tables and panels—the fact that when you come to participate you have something to say that you've obviously thought about, and you're not waiting for somebody to ask you some kind of leading question. This is not true of every writer, unfortunately. Would you have a comment on that?

Toni Morrison: I don't go anywhere because I'm asked, just as I don't write anything just because I can. I have to have something to say, if for no other reason than to stay awake! So that if I do agree to lecture or discuss any topic with somebody else it's something that I'm interested in—what I think about it or what other people think about it—and want to articulate it. So I don't take any of that casually and, also, I think I have something to say or some questions to ask anyway. If I don't have the right answers, sometimes I just have the right questions.

Christina Davis: In your opinion, have these past thirty years been important for the renaissance and growth of black culture?

Toni Morrison: I think so, in a very special way, because I'm not sure that the other Renaissance, the Harlem one, was really ours. I think in some ways it was but in some ways it was somebody else's interest in it that made it exist. This one is interesting because it may have started out as a fashionable thing to do because of the Civil Rights Movement and so on, but it ended up as . . . we snatched it! (laughs). So maybe this is really *our* Renaissance for the moment, rather than entertaining or being interesting to the Other.

Christina Davis: I'd like to end the formal interview here and thank you.

Essayists

MICHAEL AWKWARD is an associate professor of English and Afro-American and African Studies at the University of Michigan, Ann Arbor. He is the author of *Inspiring Influences: Tradition, Revision, and Afro-American Women's Novels* and the editor of *New Essays on* Their Eyes Were Watching God.

HOUSTON A. BAKER, JR. is the Albert M. Greenfield Professor of Human Relations at the University of Pennsylvania. His many books include *Afro-American Poetics: Revisions of Harlem and the Black Aesthetic; Blues, Ideology, and Afro-American Literature; The Journey Back;* and *Workings of the Spirit: The Poetics of Afro-American Women's Writing.*

KEITH E. BYERMAN is a professor of English at Indiana State University, Terra Houte. He is the author of *Fingering the Jagged Grain: Tradition and Form in Recent Black Fiction* and *Alice Walker: An Annotated Bibliography 1968–86.*

BARBARA CHRISTIAN is a professor of African-American Studies at the University of California, Berkeley. She is the author of *Black Feminist Criticism: Perspectives on Black Women Writers* and *Black Women Novelists: The Development of a Tradition 1892–1976.*

PETER B. ERICKSON is the author of *Patriarchal Structures in Shakespeare's Drama* and *Rewriting Shakespeare, Rewriting Ourselves*, and co-editor of *Shakespeare's "Rough Magic": Rennaisance Essays in Honor of C. L. Barber.*

DONALD B. GIBSON is a professor of English at Rutgers University, New Brunswick. His books include *The Politics of Literary Expression: A Study of Major Black Writers* and *The Red Badge of Courage: Redefining the Hero.*

TRUDIER HARRIS is a professor of English at the University of North Carolina, Chapel Hill. Her many books include *Fiction and Folklore: The Novels of Toni Morrison* and *Exorcising Blackness: Historical and Literary Lynching and Burning Rituals.*

MARIANNE HIRSCH is an assistant professor of French and comparative literature at Dartmouth University. She is the editor, with Evelyn Fox Keller, of *Conflicts in Feminism*, and the author of *The Mother/Daughter Plot: Narrative, Psychoanalysis, Feminism* and *The Voyage In: Fictions of Female Development.*

MARILYN SANDERS MOBLEY is an assistant professor of English at George Mason University in Fairfax. She is the author of *Folk Roots and Mythic Wings in Sarah Orne Jewett and Toni Morrison.*

ROBERTA RUBENSTEIN is a professor of literature at American University. She is the author of *Boundaries of the Self: Gender, Culture, Fiction* and *The Novelistic Vision of Doris Lessing: Breaking the Forms of Consciousness.*

VALERIE SMITH is a professor of English at the University of California, Los Angeles. She is the author of *Self-Discovery and Authority in Afro-American Narrative* and the editor of *African American Writing.*

HORTENSE J. SPILLERS is a professor of English and women's studies at Emory University. She is the editor of *Comparative American Identities: Race, Sex, and Nationality in the Modern Text* and, with Marjorie Pryse, *Conjuring: Black Women, Fiction, and Literary Tradition.* She is presently at work on *In the Flesh: A Situation for Feminist Inquiry.*

SUSAN WILLIS is an associate professor of English at Duke University. She is the author of *Specifying: Black Women Writing the American Experience* and *A Primer for Everyday Life.*

Chronology

1931	February 18: Born Chloe Anthony Wofford in Lorain, Ohio, to George and Ramah (Willis) Wofford.
1953	Receives BA from Howard University in Washington, D.C.
1955	Receives MA from Cornell University. Works as instructor in English at Texas Southern University in Houston 1955–57.
1957	Instructor in English at Howard University 1957–64.
1958	Marries Harold Morrison.
1964	Divorces Harold Morrison. Has two children, Harold Ford and Slade Kevin.
1965	Senior Editor, Random House in New York City, 1965–
1969	Publishes *The Bluest Eye*
1971	Associate professor of English at State University of New York at Purchase, 1971–72.
1973	Publishes *Sula*.
1974	Edits *The Black Book* (anthology).
1975	Receives National Book Award nomination and Ohoana Book Award for *Sula*.
1977	Publishes *Song of Solomon* (Book-of-the-Month Club Selection). Receives National Book Critics Circle Award and the American Academy and Institute of Arts and Letters Award for *Song of Solomon*. Serves as visiting lecturer at Yale University 1976–77.
1980	Appointed to the National Council on the Arts by then-President Carter.
1981	Publishes *Tar Baby*. Elected to the American Academy and Institute of Arts and Letters.
1984	Schweitzer Professor of the Humanities at State University of New York at Albany 1984–89.
1986	Her play "Dreaming Emmett" is first produced in Albany, N.Y., on January 4, 1986. Receives New York State Governor's Art Award. Visiting lecturer at Bard College 1986–88.
1987	Publishes *Beloved*. Regent's Lecturer at University of California, Berkeley.
1988	Wins Pulitzer Prize for fiction and Robert F. Kennedy Award for *Beloved*. Receives Melcher Award and Before Columbus Foundation Award. Receives Elizabeth Cady Stanton Award from National Organization for Women.

1989   Robert F. Goheen Professor of Humanities at Princeton University.
            Wins the Modern Language Association of America's Common-
            wealth Award in Literature.

1990   Awarded Chianti Ruffino Antico Fattore International Literary
            Prize.

1992   Publishes *Jazz*, a novel, and *Playing in the Dark: Whiteness and
            the Literary Imagination*, a book of literary criticism. Edits *Race-
            ing Justice, En-Gendering Power: Essays on Anita Hill, Clarence
            Thomas, and the Construction of Social Reality*.

Bibliography

"Person to Person." Interview with Morrison. *Black Seeds* (1980): 28–29.

"Toni Morrison: A Special Section." *Callaloo* (Summer 1990): 471–525.

"Toni Morrison's Narrative Strategies." *Texas Studies in Literature and Language* (Spring 1991): 89–123.

Alexander, Harriet S. "Toni Morrison: An Annotated Bibliography of Critical Articles and Essays, 1975–1984." *CLA Journal* (September 1989): 81–93.

Alwes, Karla. "'The Evil of Fulfillment': Women and Violence in *The Bluest Eye*." In *Women and Violence in Literature: An Essay Collection*, edited by Katherine Anne Ackley (Garland, New York, 1990): 89–104.

Amgelo, Bonnie. "The Pain of Being Black." *Time* (May 22, 1989): 120–23.

Atlas, Marilyn Judith. "A Woman Both Shiny and Brown: Feminine Strength in Toni Morrison's *Song of Solomon*." *Society for the Study of Midwestern Literature Newsletter* (1979): 8–12.

———. "The Darker Side of Toni Morrison's *Song of Solomon*." *Society for the Study of Midwestern Literature Newsletter* 10 (1980): 1–13.

———. "Toni Morrison's *Beloved* and the Reviewers." *Midwestern Miscellany* (1990): 45–57.

Awkward, Michael. "Roadblocks and Relatives: Critical Revision in Toni Morrison's *The Bluest Eye*." In *Critical Essays on Toni Morrison*, edited by Nellie Y. McKay (Boston: Hall, 1988): 57–68.

———. "'Unruly and Let Loose': Myth, Ideology, and Gender in *Song of Solomon*." *Callaloo* (Summer 1990): 482–98.

———. *Inspiring Influences: Tradition, Revision, and Afro-American Women's Novels*. New York: Columbia University Press, 1991.

Bakerman, Jane S. "Failures of Love: Female Initiation in the Novels of Toni Morrison." *American Literature* 52 (January 1981): 541–63.

Banyiwa-Horne, Naana. "The Scary Face of the Self: An Analysis of the Character of Sula in Toni Morrison's *Sula*." *Sage* 2 (Spring 1985): 28–31.

Barksdale, Richard. "Castration Symbolism in Recent Black American Fiction." *CLA Journal* 29 (June 1986): 400–13.

Baum, Rosalie Murphy. "Alcoholism and Family Abuse in *Maggie* and *The Bluest Eye*." *Mosaic* 19 (Summer 1986): 91–105.

Bayles, Martha, "Special Effects, Special Pleading." *The New Criterion* (January 1988): 34–40.

Bell, Pearl K. "Self-Seekers." *Commentary* 72 (August 1981): 56–60.

Berret, Anthony J. "Toni Morrison's Literary Jazz." *College Language Association Journal* (March 1989): 267–83.

Bischoff, Joan. "The Novels of Toni Morrison: Studies in Thwarted Sensitivity." *Studies in Black Literature* 6 (1975): 21–23.

Blake, Susan L. "Folklore and Community in *Song of Solomon*." *Melus* 7 (1980): 77–82.

Bloom, Harold ed. *Toni Morrison*. New York: Chelsea House, 1990.

Bogus, S. Diane. "An Authorial Tie-Up: The Wedding of Symbol and Point of View in Toni Morrison's *Sula*." *CLA Journal* (September 1989): 73–80.

Bowers, Susan. "*Beloved* and the New Apocalypse." *The Journal of Ethnic Studies* (Spring 1990): 59–77.

Bowman, Diane Kim. "Flying High: The American Icarus in Morrison, Roth, and Updike." *Perspectives on Contemporary Literature* 8 (1982): 10–17.

Brenner, Gerry. "*Song of Solomon:* Morrison's Rejection of Rank's Monomyth and Feminism." *Studies in American Fiction* 15 (Spring 1987): 13–24.

Bruck, Peter, and Wolfgang Karrer, eds. *The Afro-American Novel Since 1960.* Amsterdam: Gruner, 1982.

Bryant, C. G. "The Orderliness of Disorder: Madness and Evil in Toni Morrison's *Sula.*" *Black American Literature Forum* (Winter 1990): 731–45.

Bulsterman, Allison A. "'Sugarman Gone Home': Folksong in Toni Morrison's *Song of Solomon.*" *Publication of the Arkansas Philological Association* 10 (Spring 1984): 15–28.

Butler, Robert James. "Open Movement and Selfhood in Toni Morrison's *Song of Solomon.*" *Centennial Review* 28–29 (Fall–Winter 1984/85): 58–75.

Butler-Evans, Elliott. *Race, Gender, and Desire: Narrative Strategies in the Fiction of Toni Cade Bambara, Toni Morrison, and Alice Walker.* Philadelphia: Temple University Press, 1989.

Byerman, Keith E. "Intense Behaviors: The Use of the Grotesque in *The Bluest Eye* and *Eva's Man.*" *CLA Journal* 25 (June 1984): 447–57.

Campbell, Josie P. "To Sing the Song, to Tell the Tale: A Study of Toni Morrison and Simone Schwarz-Bart." *Comparative Literature Studies* 22 (Fall 1985): 394–412.

Caputi, Jane. "'Specifying' Fannie Hurst: Lanston Hughes's *Limitations of Life*, Zora Neale Hurston's *Their Eyes Were Watching God*, and Toni Morrison's *The Bluest Eye* as 'answers' to Hurst's *Imitiation of Life.*" *Black American Literature Forum* (Winter 1990): 697–719.

Carby, Hazel. "The Canon: Civil War and Reconstruction." *Michigan Quarterly Review* (Winter 1990): 35–43.

Christian, Barbara. "Community and Nature: The Novels of Toni Morrison." *The Journal of Ethnic Studies* 7 (Winter 1980): 65–78.

Clark, Norris. "Flying Black: Toni Morrison's *The Bluest Eye*, *Sula* and *Song of Solomon.*" *Minority Voices* 4 (Fall 1980): 51–63.

Coleman, James W. "The Quest for Wholeness in Toni Morrison's *Tar Baby.*" *Black American Literature Forum* 20 (Spring/Summer 1986): 63–73.

———. "Beyond the Reach of Love and Caring: Black Life in Toni Morrison's *Song of Solomon.*" *Obsidian II* 1 (Winter 1986): 151–61.

Cooper, B. E. "Milkman's Search for Family in Toni Morrison's *Song of Solomon.*" *CLA Journal* (December 1989): 145–47.

Cowart, David. "Faulkner and Joyce in Morrison's *Song of Solomon.*" *American Literature and Bibliography* (March 1990): 87–100.

Davis, Cynthia A. "Self, Society, and Myth in Toni Morrison's Fiction." *Contemporary Literature* 23 (Summer 1982): 323–42.

De Arman, Charles. "Milkman as the Archetypal Hero: 'Thursday's Child has Far to Go.'" *Obsidian* 6 (Winter 1980): 56–59.

Denard, Carolyn. "The Convergence of Feminism and Ethnicity in the Fiction of Toni Morrison." In *Critical Essays on Toni Morrison*, edited by Nellie Y. McKay (Boston: Hall, 1988): 171–179.

Dickerson, Vanessa D. "The Naked Father in Toni Morrison's *The Bluest Eye.*" In *Refiguring the Father: New Feminist Readings of Patriarchy*, Patricia Yaeger and Beth Kowaleski-Wallace, eds., and Nancy Miller (afterword), Carbondale: University of Illinois Press, 1989, 108–27.

Dittmar, Linda. "'Will the Circle Be Unbroken?' The Politics of Form in *The Bluest Eye.*" *Novel: A Forum on Fiction* (Winter 1990): 137–55.

Domini, John. "Toni Morrison's *Sula:* An Inverted Inferno." *High Plains Literary Review* (Spring 1988): 75–90.

Dowling, Colette. "The Song of Toni Morrison." *Topic* 125 (1980): 62–65.

Duvall, John N. "Authentic Ghost Stories: *Uncle Tom's Cabin, Absalom, Absalom!* and *Beloved.*" *The Faulkner Journal* (Fall 1988–Spring 1989): 83–97.

———. "Doe Hunting and Masculinity: *Song of Solomon* and *Go Down, Moses.*" *Arizona Quarterly* (Spring 1991): 95–115.

Edelbrg, Cynthia Dubin. "Morrison's Voices: Formal Education, the Work Ethic, and the Bible." *American Literature* 58 (May 1986): 217–37.

Erickson, Darlene E. "Toni Morrison: The Black Search for Place in America." *The Dolphin: Publications of the English Department, University of Aarhus* (Spring 1991): 45–54. 32.

Everson, S. C. "Toni Morrison's *Tar Baby:* A Resource for Feminist Theology." *Journal of Feminist Studies in Religion* (Fall 1989): 65–78.

Fabre, Genevieve. "Genealogical Archeology of the Quest for Legacy in Toni Morrison's *Song of Solomon.*" In *Critical Essays on Toni Morrison,* edited by Nellie Y. McKay (Boston: Hall, 1988): 105–114.

Ferguson, Rebecca. "History, Memory and Language in Toni Morrison's *Beloved.*" In *Feminist Criticism: Theory and Practice,* Susan Selers, ed. and introd.; Linda Hutcheon and Paul Perron, eds. (Toronto: University of Toronto Press, 1991): 109–27.

Fick, Thomas H. "Toni Morrison's 'Allegory of the Cave': Movies, Consumption, and Platonic Realism in *The Bluest Eye.*" *The Journal of the Midwest Modern Language Association* (Spring 1989): 110–22.

Fields, Karen E. "To Embrace Dead Strangers: Toni Morrison's *Beloved.*" In *Mother Puzzles: Daughters and Mothers in Contemporary American Literature,* Mickey Pearlman, ed. (Westport, CT: Greenwood, 1989): 159–69.

Fikes, Robert, Jr. "Echoes from Small Town Ohio: A Toni Morrison Bibliography." *Obsidian* 5 (1979): 142–48.

Finney, Brian. "Temporal Defamiliarization in Toni Morrison's *Beloved.*" *Obsidian II* (Spring 1990): 20–36.

Fishman, Charles. "Naming Names: Three Recent Novels by Women Writers." *Names* 32 (March 1984): 33–44.

Foner, Eric. "The Canon and American History." *Michigan Quarterly Review* (Winter 1989): 44–50.

Gillespie, Diane, and Missy Dehn Kubitschek. "Who Cares? Women-Centered Psychology in *Sula.*" *Black American Literature Forum* (Spring 1990): 21–48.

Gobel, Walter. "Canonizing Toni Morrison." *Arbeiten aus Anglistik und Amerikanistik,* 1990, 127–37.

Goldman, Anne E. "'I Made the Ink': (Literary) Production and Reproduction in *Dessa Rose* and *Beloved.*" *Feminist Studies* (Summer 1990): 313–30.

Grant, Robert. "Absence into Presence: The Thematics of Memory and 'Missing' Subjects in Toni Morrison's *Sula.*" In *Critical Essays on Toni Morrison,* edited by Nellie Y. McKay (Boston: Hall, 1988): 90–103.

Guerrero, E. "Tracking "the Look" in the Novels of Toni Morrison." *Black American Literature Forum* (Winter 1990): 747–60.

Harris, A. Leslie. "Myth and Structure in Toni Morrison's *Song of Solomon.*" *Melus* 7 (1980): 69–76.

Harris, Trudier. "Reconnecting Fragments: Afro-American Folk Tradition in *The Bluest Eye.*" In *Critical Essays on Toni Morrison,* edited by Nellie Y. McKay, 68–76.

————. *Fiction and Folklore: The Novels of Toni Morrison*. Knoxville: University of Tennessee Press, 1991.

Hawthorne, Evelyn. "On Gaining the Double-Vision: *Tar Baby* as Diasporan Novel." *Black American Literature Forum* 22 (Spring 1988): 97–107.

Henderson, Mae Gwendolyn. "Speaking in Tongues: Dialogics, Dialectics, and the Black Woman Writer's Literary Tradition." In *Changing Our Own Words: Essays on Criticism, Theory, and Writing by Black Women*, Cheryl A. Wall, ed. (New Brunswick: Rutgers University Press, 1989): 16–37.

Henderson, Stephen E., introduction. *Black Women Writers (1950–1980): A Critical Evaluation*. Garden City: Anchor-Doubleday, 1984.

Hilfer, Anthony C. "Critical Indeterminacies in Toni Morrison's Fiction: An Introduction." *Texas Studies in Literature and Language* (Spring 1991): 91–95.

Holloway, Karla F. C. "*Beloved:* A Spiritual." *Callaloo* (Summer 1990): 516–25.

Homans, Margaret. "'Her Very Own Howl': The Ambiguities of Representation in Recent Women's Fiction." *Signs* 9 (Winter 1983): 186–205.

Horvitz, Deborah. "Nameless Ghosts: Possession and Dispossession in *Beloved*." *Studies in American Fiction* (Fall 1989): 157–67.

House, Elizabeth B. "The 'Sweet Life' in Toni Morrison's Fiction." *American Literature* 56 (May 1984): 181–202.

————. "Artists and the Art of Living: Order and Disorder in Toni Morrison's Fiction." *Modern Fiction Studies* 34 (Spring 1988): 27–44.

————. "Toni Morrison's Ghost: The Beloved Who Is Not Beloved." *Studies in American Fiction* (Spring 1990): 17–26.

Hovet, Grace Ann and Barbara Lounsberry. "Flying as Symbol and Legend in Toni Morrison's *The Bluest Eye, Sula,* and *Song of Solomon*." *CLA Journal* 27 (December 1983): 119–40.

Hulbert, Ann. "Poor Conception: The Farfetched Case for Teenage Motherhood." *New Republic* (12 November 1990): 21–24.

Inoue, Kazuko. "A Study on Toni Morrison: The Quest for a Real Woman." *Language and Culture* 10 (1986): 133–44.

————. "'I Got a Tree on My Back': A Study on Toni Morrison's Latest Novel, *Beloved*." *Language and Culture*, 1988: 69–82.

Irving, John. "Morrison's Black Fable." *The New York Times Book Review* (29 March 1981): 1, 30–31.

Jones, Bessie W. and Audrey L. Winson. *The World of Toni Morrison: Explorations in Literary Criticism*. Dubuque, IA: Kendall/Hunt, 1985.

Joyce, Joyce Ann. "Structural and Thematic Unity in Toni Morrison's *Song of Solomon. CEA Critic* 49 (Winter/Summer 1986–1987): 185–98.

Klotman, Phyllis R. "Dick-and-Jane and the Shirley Temple Sensibility in *The Bluest Eye*." *Black American Literature Forum* 13 (September 1979): 123–25.

Lange, Bonnie Shipman. "Toni Morrison's Rainbow Code." *Critique* 24 (Spring 1983): 173–81.

Lawrence, David. "Fleshly Ghosts and Ghostly Flesh: The Word and the Body in *Beloved*." *Studies in American Fiction* (Fall 1991): 189–201.

Lee, Dorothy H. "Song of Solomon: To Ride the Air." *Black American Literature Forum* 16 (Summer 1982): 64–70.

————. "The Quest for Self: Triumph and Failure in the Works of Toni Morrison." In *Black Women Writers (1950–1980): A Critical Evaluation*, Mari Evans, ed. and preface; Stephen E. Henderson, introduction. (Garden City: Anchor-Doubleday, 1984): 346–60.

Lepow, Lauren. "Paradise Lost and Found: Dualism and Edenic Myth in Toni Morrison's *Tar Baby*." *Contemporary Literature* 28 (Fall 1987): 363–77.

Levy, Andrew. "Telling *Beloved*." *Texas Studies in Literature and Language* (Spring 1991): 1124–33.

Lewis, Vaschti Crutcher. "African Tradition in Toni Morrison's *Sula*." *Phylon* 48 (March 1987): 91–97.

Lounsberry, Barbara and Grace Anne Hovet. "Principles of Perception in Toni Morrison's *Sula*." *Black American Literature Forum* 13 (1979): 126–29.

Lupton, M. J. "Clothes and Closure in Three Novels by Black Women." *Black American Literature Forum* 20 (Winter 1986): 409–21.

MacKethan, Lucinda H. "Names to Bear Witness: The Theme and Tradition of Naming in Toni Morrison's *Song of Solomon*." *CEA Critic* 49 (Winter/Summer 1986–1987): 199–207.

Magness, Patricia. "The Knight and the Princess: The Structure of Courtly Love in Toni Morrison's *Tar Baby*." *South Atlantic Review* (November 1989): 85–99.

Marshall, Brenda. "The Gospel According to Pilate." *American Literature* 57 (October 1985): 486–49.

Martin, Curtis. "A Bibliography of Writings by Toni Morrison." In *Contemporary American Women Writers: Narrative Strategies*, Catherine Rainwater and William J. Scheick, eds. (Lexington, KY: University Press of Kentucky, 1985): 205–207.

Martin, Jacky. "From Division to Sacrificial Reconciliation in Toni Morrison's Novels." *Obsidian II* (Summer 1990): 80–99.

Mathieson, Barbara Offutt. "Memory and Mother Love in Morrison's *Beloved*." *American Imago* (Spring 1990): 1–20.

Mbalis, Doreatha D. *Toni Morrison's Developing Class Consciousness*. Susquehanna University Press, Selinsgrove; and Associated University Presses, London: 1991.

McDowell, Deborah E. "'The Self and the Other': Reading Toni Morrison's *Sula* and the Black Female Text." In *Critical Essays on Toni Morrison*, edited by Nellie Y. McKay (Boston: Hall, 1988): 77–90.

McDowell, Margaret B. "The Black Woman as Artist and Critic: Four Versions." *The Kentucky Review* 7 (Spring 1987): 19–41.

McKay, Nellie. "An Interview with Toni Morrison." *Contemporary Literature* 24 (Winter 1983): 413–29.

———., ed. *Critical Essays on Toni Morrison*. Boston: G. K. Hall, 1988.

Middleton, Victoria. "*Sula:* An Experimental Life." *CLA Journal* 28 (June 1985): 367–81.

Minakawa, Harue. "The Motif of Sweetness in Toni Morrison's *Song of Solomon*." *Kyushu American Literature* 26 (October 1985): 47–56.

Miner, Madonne M. "Lady No Longer Sings the Blues: Rape, Madness, and Silence in *The Bluest Eye*." In *Conjuring: Black Women, Fiction, and Literary Tradition*, Marjorie Pryse ed. and introduction; Hortense Spillers, ed. and afterword (Bloomington: Indiana University Press, 1985): 176–91.

Mitchell, Leatha S. "Toni Morrison, My Mother, and Me." In *In the Memory and Spirit of Frances, Zora, and Lorraine: Essays and Interviews on Black Women and Writing*, Juliette Bowles, ed. (Washington, D.C.: Institute for the Arts and the Humanities, Howard University, 1979): 58–60.

Mobley, Marilyn Sanders. *Folk Roots and Mythic Wings in Sarah Orne Jewett and Toni Morrison: The Cultural Function of Narrative*. Baton Rouge: Louisiana State University Press, 1991.

Montgomery, Maxine Lavon. "A Pilgrimage to the Origins: The Apocalypse as Structure and Theme in Toni Morrison's *Sula.*" *Black American Literature Forum* (Spring 1989): 127–37.

Moody, Joycelyn K. "Ripping Away the Veil of Slavery: Literacy, Communal Love, and Self Esteem in Three Slave Women's Narratives." *Black American Literature Forum* (Winter 1990): 633–49.

Morey, Ann-Janine. "Toni Morrison and the Color of Life." *The Christian Century* (16 November 1988) 1039–43.

Morrison, Toni. "Memory, Creation, and Writing." *Thought* 59 (December 1984): 385–90.

———. "Unspeakable Things Unspoken: The Afro-American Presence in American Literature." *Michigan Quarterly Review* (Winter 1989): 1–34.

Munro, C. Lynn. "The Tattooed Heart and the Serpentine Eye: Morrison's Choice of an Epigraph for *Sula.*" *Black American Literature Forum* 18 (Winter 1984): 150–54.

Myers, Linda Buck. Neil Nakadate, response; Marco A. Portales, response; Richard L. Herrnstadt, response. "Perception and Power through Naming: Characters in Search of a Self in the Fiction of Toni Morrison." *Explorations in Ethnic Studies* 7 (January 1984): 39–55.

Naylor, Gloria. "Gloria Naylor and Toni Morrison: A Conversation." *Southern Review* 21 (July 1985): 567–93.

Nodelman, Perry. "The Limits of Structures: A Shorter Version of a Comparison Between Toni Morrison's *Song of Solomon* and Virginia Hamilton's *M.C. The Great.*" *Children's Literature Association Quarterly* 7 (Fall 1982): 45–48.

O'Shaughnessy, Kathleen. "'Life life life life': The Community Chorus in *Song of Solomon.*" In *Critical Essays on Toni Morrison*, edited by Nellie Y. McKay (Boston: Hall, 1988): 125–33.

Ogunyemi, Chikwenye Okonjo. "Order and Disorder in Toni Morrison's *The Bluest Eye.*" *Critique* 19 (1977): 112–20.

———. "*Sula:* 'A Nigger Joke.'" *Black American Literature Forum* 13 (1979): 130–33.

Ordonez, Elizabeth J. "Narrative Texts by Ethnic Women: Rereading the Past, Reshaping the Future." *Melus* 9 (Winter 1982): 19–28.

Osundare, Niyi. "Toni Morrison in Madison." *African Literature Association Bulletin* (1991): 18–19.

Otten, Terry. *The Crime of Innocence in the Fiction of Toni Morrison.* Columbia, MO: University of Missouri Press, 1989.

Paquet, Sandra Pouchet. "The Ancestor as Foundation in *Their Eyes Were Watching God* and *Tar Baby.*" *Callaloo Arts and Letters* (Summer 1990): 499–515.

Park, Sue. "One Reader's Response to Toni Morrison's *Beloved.*" *Conference of College Teachers of English Studies* (September 1991): 39–46.

Parker, Bettye J. "Complexity: Toni Morrison's Women: An Interview Essay." In *Sturdy Black Bridges: Visions of Black Women in Literature*, Roseann P. Bell, Bettye J. Parker, and Beverly Guy-Sheftall, eds. (Garden City, New York: Anchor-Doubleday, 1979): 251–57.

Pinkser, Sanford. "Magic, Realism, Historical Truth, and the Quest for a Liberating Identity: Reflections on Alex Haley's *Roots* and Toni Morrison's *Song of Solomon.*" In *Studies in Black American Literature Vol. I: Black American Prose Theory*, edited by Joe Weixlmann and Chester J. Fontenot. (Greenwood, FL: Penkevill Press, 1984): 183–97.

Portales, Marco. "Toni Morrison's *The Bluest Eye:* Shirley Temple and Cholly. *The Centennial Review* 30 (Fall 1986): 496–506.

Powell, T. B. "Toni Morrison: The Struggle to Depict the Black Figure on the White Page." *Black American Literature Forum* (Winter 1990): 747–60.

Rabinowitz, Paula. "Naming, Magic and Documentary: The Subversion of the Narrative in *Song of Solomon, Ceremony,* and *China Men.*" 26–42 In *Feminist Re-Visions: What Has Been and Might Be,* Vivian Patraka, ed. and introduction; Louise A. Tilly, ed. and preface. Ann Arbor: Women's Studies Program, University of Michigan, 1983.

Rainwater, Catherine. "Worthy Messengers: Narrative Voices in Toni Morrison's Novels." *Texas Studies in Literature and Language* (Spring 1991): 96–113.

Reckley, Ralph. "On Looking into Morrison's *Tar Baby.*" In *Amid Visions and Revisions: Poetry and Criticism on Literature and the Arts,* edited by Burney J. Hollis (Baltimore: Morgan State University Press, 1985): 132–38.

———. *Twentieth Century Black American Women in Print.* Acton, MA: Copley Publishing Group, 1991.

Reddy, Maureen T. "The Tripled Plot and Center of *Sula.*" *Black American Literature Forum* 22 (Spring 1988): 29–45.

Reed, Harry. "Toni Morrison: *Song of Solomon* and Black Cultural Nationalism." *The Centennial Review* (Winter 1988): 64.

Reyes, Angelita. "Ancient Properties in the New World: The Paradox of the 'Other' in Toni Morrison's *Tar Baby.*" *Black Scholar* 17 (March–April 1986): 19–25.

———. "Politics and Metaphors of Materialism in Paule Marshall's *Praisesong for the Widow* and Toni Morrison's *Tar Baby.*" In *Politics and the Muse: Studies in the Politics of Recent American Literature,* Adam J. Sorkin, ed. (Bowling Green: Popular, 1989): 179–205.

Rhodes, Jewell Parker. "Toni Morrison's *Beloved:* Ironies of a 'Sweet Home' Utopia in a Dystopian Slave Society." *Utopian Studies* (1990) 77–92.

Rigney, Barbara Hill. *The Voices of Toni Morrison.* Columbus: Ohio State University Press, 1991.

Rodrigues, Eusebio L. "The Telling of *Beloved.*" *Journal of Narrative Technique* (Spring 1991): 153–69.

Rosenberg, Ruth. "'And the Children May Know Their Names': Toni Morrison's *Song of Solomon.*" *Literary Onomastic Studies* 8 (1981): 195–219.

———. "Seeds in Hard Ground: Black Girlhood in *The Bluest Eye.*" *Black American Literature Forum* 21 (Winter 1987): 435–45.

Royster, Philip M. "A Priest and a Witch Against the Spiders and the Snakes: Scapegoating in Toni Morrison's *Sula.*" *Umoja* 2 (1978): 149–68.

———. "Milkman's Flying: The Scapegoat Transcended in Toni Morrison's *Song of Solomon.*" *CLA Journal* 24 (June 1981): 419–40.

Rushdy, Ashraf H. A. "'Rememory': Primal Scenes and Constructions in Toni Morrison's Novels." *Contemporary Literature* (Fall 1990): 300–23.

Samuels, Wilfrid D. "Liminality and the Search for Self in Toni Morrison's *Song of Solomon.*" *Minority Voices* 5 (Spring–Fall 1981): 59–68.

———., and Clenora Hudson-Weems. *Toni Morrison.* Boston: Twayne Publishers, 1990.

Sargent, Robert. "A Way of Ordering Experience: A Study of Toni Morrison's *The Bluest Eye* and *Sula.*" In *Faith of a (Woman) Writer,* edited by Alice Kessler-Harris and William McBrien (Westport, CT: Greenwood Press, 1988): 229–36.

Schroeder, Aribert. "An Afro-American Woman Writer and Her Reviewers/Critics: Some Ideological Aspects in Current Criticism of Toni Morrison's Fiction." *Arbeiten aus Anglistik und Amerikanistik* (1990): 109–25.

Scruggs, Charles. "The Nature of Desire in Toni Morrison's *Song of Solomon.*" *Arizona Quarterly* 38 (Winter 1982): 311–35.

Shannon, Anna. "'We Was Girls Together': A Study of Toni Morrison's *Sula*." *Midwestern Miscellany* 10 (1982): 9–22.

Shapiro, B. "The Bonds of Love and the Boundaries of Self in Toni Morrison's *Beloved*." *Contemporary Literature* (Summer 91): 194–210.

Smith, Barbara. "Toward a Black Feminist Criticism." In *In The Memory and Spirit of Frances, Zora and Lorraine: Essays and Interviews on Black Women and Writing*, Juliette Bowles, ed. (Washington, D.C.: Institute for the Arts and the Humanities, Howard University, 1979): 32–40.

Smith, Valerie. "The Quest for and Discovery of Identity in Toni Morrison's *Song of Solomon*." *Southern Review* 21 (Summer 1985): 721–32.

Somerville, Jane. "Idealized Beauty and the Denial of Love in Toni Morrison's *The Bluest Eye*." *The Bulletin of the West Virginia Association of College English Teachers* 9 (Spring 1986): 18–23.

Spallino, Chiara. "*Song of Solomon:* An Adventure in Structure." *Callaloo* 8 (Fall 1985): 510–24.

Stein, Kara F. "Toni Morrison's *Sula:* A Black Woman's Epic." *Black American Literature Forum* 18 (Winter 1984): 146–50.

Stein, Karen. "'I Didn't Even Know His Name': Name and Naming in Toni Morrison's *Sula*." *Names* 28 (September 1980): 226–29.

Story, Ralph. "An Excursion into the Black World: The 'Seven Days' in Toni Morrison's *Song of Solomon*." *Black American Literature Forum* (Spring 1989), 149–58.

Stryz, Jan. "Inscribing an Origin in *Song of Solomon*." *Studies in American Fiction* (Spring 1991): 31–40.

Tate, Claudia. "Toni Morrison." In *Black Women Writings at Work*, Claudia Tate, ed.; Tillie Olsen, foreword (New York: Continuum, 1983): 117–131.

Terrell, Lyne. "Storytelling and Moral Agency." *Journal of Aesthetics and Art Criticism* (Spring 1990): 115–26.

Tignor, Eleanor Q. "Toni Morrison's Pecola: A Portrait in Pathos." *MAWA Review* 1 (Spring 1982): 24–27.

Turner, Darwin T. "Theme, Characterization, and Style in the Works of Toni Morrison." In *Black Women Writers (1950–1980): A Critical Evaluation*, Mari Evans, ed. and preface; Stephen E. Henderson, introduction (Garden City: Anchor-Doubleday, 1984): 361–69.

Umeh, Marie A. "A Comparative Study of the Idea of Motherhood in Two Third World Novels." *CLA Journal* 31 (September 1987): 31–43.

Vrettos, Athena. "Curative Domains: Women, Healing and History in Black Women's Narratives." *Women's Studies* (October 1989): 455–74.

Wade-Gayles, Gloria. "The Truths of Our Mothers' Lives: Mother-Daughter Relationships in Black Women's Fiction." *Sage* 1 (Fall 1984): 8–12.

Wagner, Linda W. "Toni Morrison: Mastery of Narrative." In *Contemporary American Women Writers: Narrative Strategies*, Catherine Rainwater and William J. Scheick, eds. (Lexington, KY: University Press of Kentucky, 1985): 191–207.

Walker, Melissa. *Down from the Mountaintop: Black Women's Novels in the Wake of the Civil Rights Movement 1966–89*. Neven: Yale University Press, 1991.

Wang, Jiaxiang. "The Works of Toni Morrison: A Survey." *Foreign Literatures* (1988): 76–86.

Warner, Anne Bradford. "New Myths and Ancient Properties: The Fiction of Toni Morrison." *The Hollins Critic* (June 1988): 1–11.

Weever, Jacqueline de. "The Inverted World of Toni Morrison's *The Bluest Eye* and *Sula*." *CLA Journal* 22 (1979): 402–14.

———. "Toni Morrison's Use of Fairy Tale, Folk Tale and Myth in *The Song of Solomon*." *Southern Folklore Quarterly* 44 (1980): 131–44.

Wegs, Joyce. "Toni Morrison's *Song of Solomon:* A Blues Song." *Essays in Literature* 9 (Fall 1982): 211–223.

Weixlmann, Joe. "Culture Clash, Survival, and Trans-Formation: A Study of Some Innovative Afro-American Novels of Detection." *Mississippi Quarterly* 38 (Winter 1984–85): 21–32.

Werner, Craig H. "The Briar Patch as Modernist Myth: Morrison, Barthes and *Tar Baby* As-Is." In *Critical Essays on Toni Morrison*, edited by Nellie Y. McKay (Boston: Hall, 1988): 150–67.

Wilkerson, Margaret B. "The Dramatic Voice in Toni Morrison's Novels." In *Critical Essays on Toni Morrison*, edited by Nellie Y. Mckay (Boston: Hall, 1988): 179–90.

Willis, Susan. "I Shop Therefore I Am: Is There a Place for Afro-American Culture in Commodity Culture?" In *Changing Our Own Words: Essays on Criticism, Theory, and Writing by Black Women*, Cheryl A. Wall, ed. (New Brunswick: Rutgers University Press, 1989): 173–95.

Wolff, Cynthia Griffen. "'Margaret Garner': a Cincinnati Story." *The Massachusetts Review* (Fall 1991): 417–41.

Wong, Shelley. "Transgression as Poesis in *The Bluest Eye*." *Callaloo* (Summer 1990): 471–81.

Acknowledgments

Untitled review of *The Bluest Eye* by Haskel Frankel from *The New York Times Book Review* (1 November 1970), © 1970 by The New York Times Co. Reprinted with permission.

"Beginner's Luck." Review of *The Bluest Eye* by L. E. Sissman from *The New Yorker* (23 January 1971), © 1971 by The New Yorker Magazine, Inc. Reprinted with permission.

Untitled review of *Sula* by Sarah Blackburn from *The New York Times Book Review* (30 December 1973), © 1973 by The New York Times Co. Reprinted with permission.

"Something Ominous Here." Review of *Sula* by Jerry H. Bryant from *The Nation* (6 July 1974), © 1974 by Nation Associates, Inc. Reprinted with permission.

"The Black Family Chronicle." Review of *Song of Solomon* by Reynolds Price from *The New York Times Book Review* (11 September 1977), © 1977 by The New York Times Co. Reprinted with permission.

"Word of Mouth." Review of *Song of Solomon* by Susan Lardner from *The New Yorker* (7 November 1977), © 1977 by The New Yorker Magazine, Inc. Reprinted with permission.

"A Novel of Exile and Home." Review of *Tar Baby* by Maureen Howard from *The New Republic* (21 March 1981), © 1981 by The New Republic, Inc. Reprinted with permission.

"Morrison's Black Fable." Review of *Tar Baby* by John Irving from *The New York Times Book Review* (29 March 1981), © 1981 by The New York Times Co. Reprinted with permission.

"Death Duties: Toni Morrison Looks Back in Sorrow." Review of *Beloved* by Ann Snitow from *The Village Voice Literary Supplement* (September 1987), © 1987 by The Village Voice. Reprinted with permission.

"Haunted by Their Nightmares." Review of *Beloved* by Margaret Atwood from *The New York Times Book Review* (13 September 1987), © 1987 by The New York Times Co. Reprinted with permission.

"Her Soul's High Song." Review of *Jazz* by John Leonard from *The Nation* 254 (25 May 1992), © 1992 by Nation Associates, Inc. Reprinted with permission.

"The Clearest Eye." Review of *Jazz* by Edna O'Brien from *The New York Times Book Review* (5 April 1992), © 1992 by The New York Times Co. Reprinted with permission.

"The Contemporary Fables of Toni Morrison" by Barbara Christian from *Black Women Novelists: The Development of a Tradition, 1892–1976* by Barbara Christian, © 1980 by Barbara Christian. Reprinted with permission.

"Beyond Realism" (originally entitled "Beyond Realism: The Fictions of Gayl Jones and Toni Morrison") by Keith E. Byerman from *Fingering the Jagged Grain: Tradition and Form in Recent Black Fiction* by Keith E. Byerman, © 1985 by the University of Georgia Press. Reprinted with permission.

"Pariahs and Community" (originally entitled "Pariahs and Community: Toni Morrison") by Roberta Rubenstein from *Boundaries of the Self: Gender, Culture, Fiction* by Roberta Rubenstein, © 1987 by the Board of Trustees of the University of Illinois. Reprinted with permission.

"Text and Countertext in *The Bluest Eye*" (originally entitled "Text and Countertext in Toni Morrison's *The Bluest Eye*") by Donald B. Gibson, © 1990 by Donald B. Gibson. Printed with permission.

"'The Evil of Fulfillment': Scapegoating and Narration in *The Bluest Eye*" by Michael Awkward from *Inspiriting Influence: Tradition, Revision, and Afro-American Women's Novels* by Michael Awkward, © 1989 by Michael Awkward. Reprinted with permission.

"A Hateful Passion, a Lost Love" by Hortense J. Spillers from *Feminist Studies* 9 (Summer 1983), © 1983 by Feminist Studies. Reprinted by permission.

"When Lindbergh Sleeps with Bessie Smith: The Writing of Place in *Sula*" (originally entitled "When Lindbergh Sleeps with Bessie Smith: The Writing of Place in Toni Morrison's *Sula*") by Houston A. Baker, Jr., © 1990 by Houston A. Baker, Jr. Printed with permission.

"'Cruel Enough to Stop the Blood': *Sula* and Maternal Narrative" (originally entitled "Maternal Narratives: Cruel Enough to Stop the Blood")

"An Interview with Toni Morrison" by Nellie McKay from *Contemporary Literature* 24 (Winter 1983), © 1983 by the Board of Regents of the University of Wisconsin System. Reprinted with permission.

"Interview with Toni Morrison" by Christina Davis from *Présence Africaine: Revue Culturelle du Monde Noir/Cultural Review of the Negro World* (1st Quarterly, 1988), © 1988 by Revue Présence Africaine. Reprinted with permission.

Index

Faulkner, William, ix, 37, 41,
    45, 54–55, 116, 181, 319,
    324, 328n, 329n, 357, 408
Fauset, Jessie, 37, 396
Felice (character), 48, 50, 54
Fern (character), 243
Fernanda (character), 327n
Fetterley, Judith, 196–97, 209n
Finch, Edna, 244, 247
First Corinthians (character),
    42, 113, 259n
Fishbond, James (character),
    391
Fisher, Dexter, 365n
Fitzgerald, F. Scott, 196
Forbes, Thomas Rogers, 156n
Forrest, Leon, 391, 394
Foster, Ruth (character), 313,
    319–20
Frankel, Haskel, 3–4
Franklin, Aretha, 411
Freud, Sigmund, 46, 198, 199,
    245, 247, 259n
Frost, Robert, 175
Frye, Northrop, 235n, 410
Fuller, Samson (character), 68

Gaines (character), 9, 105, 125
Gallop, Jane, 259n
Gardiner, Judith Kegan, 273n
Garner, Margaret, 359
Garner, Mr. (character), 33
Garner, Mrs. (character), 33
Garner, Paul D. (character),
    26–28, 30–31, 33–34, 44,
    271, 332, 334–36, 338, 340,
    341n, 345–48, 350–51, 359–
    63
Garrison, William Lloyd, 180
Gates, Henry Louis, Jr., 52–55,
    201, 208n, 209n, 244, 259n,
    358, 364n, 363, 365n
Geertz, Clifford, 198, 199, 209n
Geraldine (character), 61, 64–

65, 71–73, 104, 173n, 192–
    94, 206, 275, 384
Gibson, Donald, xi, 159–72, 421
Giddings, Paula, 260n
Gideon (character), 42
Gilbert, Sandra, 175, 258n, 262
Gilligan, Carol, 151, 157n
Giovanni, Nikki, 182–83, 208n
Gobineau, Joseph Arthur de,
    159, 172n
Golden Gray (character), 48
Gordon, Mary, 273n
Gradgrind (character), 21
Graie sisters (characters), 131
Grandma Baby (character), 29
Green, Paul, 53
Green, Son (character), 18–20,
    23–25, 42–43, 118, 119–24,
    127, 132–33, 139–40, 152–
    53, 286–91, 294, 300, 302–
    6, 307n, 314–15, 399, 404–
    7, 419
Greene, Jude (character), 82–
    83, 88–89, 95, 109–12, 134,
    137, 225–26, 249, 252, 277–
    78, 385, 386
Greene, Nel (character), 75
Gubar, Susan, 175, 258n, 262

Hagar (character), 42, 117,
    135–36, 279, 281–82, 312,
    320, 325, 401–2
Haley, Alex, 234n
Hamer, Fannie Lou, 37
Hardy, Thomas, 21, 25, 408
Harper, Michael S., 233n, 235n
Harris, Middleton A., 364n
Harris, Trudier, xii, 330–40,
    421
Hawthorne, Evelyn, 364n
Head, Bessie, 418
Heddy (character), 117
Hedin, Raymond, 178–79, 208n
Hemenway, Robert, 234n

This is one of six volumes of literary
criticism launching the
AMISTAD LITERARY SERIES
which is devoted to literary fiction
and criticism by and about African Americans.

◆

The typeface "AMISTAD" is based
on wood and stone symbols
and geometric patterns seen throughout
sixteenth-century Africa. These hand-carved
motifs were used to convey the diverse
cultural aspects evident among
the many African peoples.

◆

Amistad typeface was designed
by Maryam "Marne" Zafar.

◆

This book was published with the
assistance of March Tenth, Inc.
Printed and bound by Haddon Craftsmen, Inc.

◆

The paper is acid-free
55-pound Cross Pointe Odyssey Book.